Countries, Peoples & Cultures

East Asia & The Pacific

Countries, Peoples & Cultures

East Asia & The Pacific

First Edition

Volume 9

Editor

Michael Shally-Jensen, PhD

SALEM PRESS
A Division of EBSCO Information Services, Inc.
Ipswich, Massachusetts

Publisher's Cataloging-In-Publication Data
(Prepared by The Donohue Group, Inc.)

East Asia & the Pacific / editor, Michael Shally-Jensen, PhD. – First edition.

    pages : illustrations, maps ; cm. – (Countries, peoples & cultures ; volume 9)

    Includes bibliographical references and index.
    ISBN: 978-1-61925-790-0 (v. 9)
    ISBN: 978-1-61925-800-6 (set)

    1. East Asia – History. 2. Pacific Area – History. 3. East Asia – Economic conditions. 4. Pacific Area – Economic conditions. 5. East Asia – Social life and customs. 6. Pacific Area – Social life and customs. I. Shally-Jensen, Michael. II. Title: East Asia and the Pacific III. Series: Countries, peoples & cultures ; v. 9.

DS504.5 .E27 2015
950

First Printing
PRINTED IN CANADA

Contents

Publisher's Note..vii

Introduction...ix

East Asia...1
China...3
Japan...27
Mongolia...51
North Korea...71
South Korea...91
Taiwan...113

Pacific..135
Australia...137
Fiji..159
Kiribati...177
Marshall Islands..197
Micronesia, Federated States of...217
Nauru...237
New Zealand..255
Palau..279
Papua New Guinea..297
Samoa..317
Solomon Islands..337
Tonga...357
Tuvalu..375
Vanuatu..391

Appendix One: World Governments...409
Commonwealth..410
Communist...412
Confederation/Confederacy..414
Constitutional Monarchy...416
Constitutional Republic...418
Democracy...420
Dictatorship/Military Dictatorship..422
Ecclesiastical...424
Failed State..426
Federal Republic..428
Federation..430
Monarchy...432

Parliamentary Monarchy..434
Parliamentary Republic..436
Presidential..438
Republic 440
Socialist...442
Sultanate/Emirate..444
Theocratic Republic 446
Totalitarian 448
Treaty System 450

Appendix Two: World Religions..453
African Religious Traditions...454
Bahá'í Faith...460
Buddhism 466
Christianity..473
East Asian Religions 480
Hinduism...487
Islam..494
Jainism 501
Judaism 507
Sikhism 514

Index 521

Publisher's Note

Countries, Peoples & Cultures: East Asia & The Pacific is the ninth volume of a new 9-volume series from Salem Press. *Countries, Peoples & Cultures* offers valuable insight into the social, cultural, economic, historical and religious practices and beliefs of nearly every country around the globe.

Following the extensive introduction that summarizes this politically and physically complex part of the world, this volume provides 20-page profiles of the 20 countries that make up East Asia and the Pacific. Each includes colorful maps—one highlighting the country's location in the world, and one with its major cities and natural landmarks—and a country flag, plus 10 categories of information: General Information; Environment & Geography; Customs & Courtesies; Lifestyle; Cultural History; Culture; Society; Social Development; Government; and Economy. Each profile also includes full color photographs, valuable tables of information including fun "Do You Know?" facts, and a comprehensive Bibliography.

Each country profile combines must-have statistics, such as population, language, size, climate, and currency, with the flavor and feel of the land. You'll read about favorite foods, arts & entertainment, youth culture, women's rights, health care, and tourism, for a comprehensive picture of the country, its people, and their culture.

Appendix One: World Governments, focuses on 21 types of governments found around the world today, from Commonwealth and Communism to Treaty System and Failed State. Each government profile includes its Guiding Premise, Structure, Citizen's Role, and modern-day examples.

Appendix Two: World Religions, focuses on 10 of the world's major religions from African religious traditions to Sikhism. Each religion profile includes number of adherents, basic tenets, major figures and holy sites, and major rites and celebrations.

The nine volumes of *Countries, Peoples & Cultures* are: *Central & South America; Central, South & Southeast Asia; Western Europe; Eastern Europe, Middle East & North Africa; East & Southern Africa; West & Central Africa; North America & The Caribbean;* and *East Asia & The Pacific.*

Introduction

East Asia

East Asia encompasses the area formerly known as the Far East. The countries usually included in this region are China (both mainland China and Taiwan), Japan, and the Koreas. Mongolia is sometimes also included, as it is in the present volume. East Asia as a whole is a region where Confucianism underlies the major civilizations that arose there.

Vast segments of this region, such as Mongolia in the north and Tibet in the southwest, are partly or entirely encircled by giant mountain ranges. From the Tarim Basin, in the far western section, eastward, there are some 5 million square miles (13 million sq km) of high plateau and interior drainage, where no river reaches the sea and some rivers simply expire in the desert. Foremost among deserts in the region is the Gobi Desert, lying at the border of China and Mongolia and occupying about 500,000 square miles (1.3 million sq km). Below these highland areas stand the floodplains of eastern China. This region is made up of three great river valleys: the Yellow (Huang) in the north, the Yangtze (Chang) in the middle, and the Xi in the south. This is where the majority of China's nearly 1.4 billion inhabitants live. To the extreme northeast, across the Yellow Sea, lie North and South Korea, occupying a peninsula of eroded mountains rimmed by coastal strips. North and South Korea together are home to some 75 million people. To the west of the Koreas are the Japanese Islands, even more mountainous than the Korean Peninsula and situated along one of the world's major fault zones. Honshu is the largest island and is referred to as the Japanese mainland. Japan's population is about 127 million. Finally, Taiwan, off mainland China, is one of the most densely populated countries of the world, with over 23 million people living on an island of just under 14,000 square miles (36,000 sq km).

Traditional Chinese society, which influenced much of the rest of the region, was based on the concept of *guo-jia,* a nearly untranslatable term that suggests "nation," "people," or "national community." Equally important was the Confucian doctrine that a perfect society was one in which each person lived in accordance with his given status and role. Social hierarchy was key: below the imperial family and nobility were four distinct classes made up of scholars, farmers, artisans or craftspeople, and merchants. Social mobility was possible only through a nationwide exam system; by and large, people remained put, in part because they were also tied to a clan and a village. The entire social system depended on loyalty to the emperor as possessor of the mandate of heaven, and rootedness in one's place. A ruler could be overthrown if he failed to carry out the will of heaven, and this occurred frequently enough in the long and storied history of China and the other nations of the region.

China

From about 1760 Canton (now Guangzhou) was open to European trade. Further incursions into China by foreign interests led to the Opium Wars (1839–42; 1856–60), fought over trade and Chinese sovereignty; the Taiping Rebellion (1851–64), a civil war between the ruling Manchus and a Christian sect; and the Sino-Japanese War (1894–95), between the Qing dynasty and Japan over control of Korea. The Boxer Rebellion (1899–1901) was, similarly, a reaction to foreign imperialism. The Qing dynasty fell in 1912 and a republic was proclaimed by Sun Yat-sen. The republic, however, failed to form owing to the actions of warlords. Sun's successor, Chiang Kai-shek, achieved partial unification in the 1920s, but Chiang and his Kuomintang, or Nationalist Party, then broke with the Communists, who formed their own armies. Manchuria was invaded by

Japan in 1931; its occupation lasted until 1945. The Communists gained support after the Long March across China (1934–35) and Mao Zedong emerged as their leader. With Japan's surrender at the end of World War II, a civil war erupted in China. By 1949 the Nationalists had fled to Taiwan and the Communists proclaimed the People's Republic of China. They undertook radical reforms, including massive communalization of agriculture and industry under the Great Leap Forward (1958–60), resulting in a major famine. A Tibetan uprising was suppressed in 1959, and various minor clashes with the Soviet Union occurred in the 1960s. The Cultural Revolution (1966–76) sought to revitalize leftist values, at the expense of ordinary citizens. That calamity and the death of Mao (1976) caused a return to moderation under Deng Xiaoping, who undertook economic reforms and renewed China's ties to the West. The regime suppressed the Tiananmen Square student demonstration in 1989, incurring international disapproval. Under Deng and his successors the economy transitioned from central planning and state-run enterprises to a mix of state-owned and private enterprises. The size of the Chinese economy surpassed that of the United States in 2015, yet on a per-capita basis it still remains below the world average, and the speed and scale of economic growth in China has caused major environmental problems. The first meeting in over 50 years between leaders of China and Taiwan (which China continues to claim) occurred in November 2015.

Japan

For centuries Japan borrowed from Chinese culture, but by 1000 C.E. it had developed a unique culture of its own. Feuding families ruled various parts of the country until the late 1500s, when unification was achieved. During the Tokugawa period, starting in 1603, the government pursued a policy of isolation. In 1854 an American, Commodore Matthew Perry, obtained the first commercial treaty. Japan adopted a constitution during the Meiji period (1868–1912), along with programs aimed at modernization and Westernization. The nation fought a war

with China over Korea in 1894–95, and with Russia over Korea and Manchuria in 1904–05. It annexed Korea in 1910 and occupied Manchuria and Shanghai in 1931–32, rattling the Chinese. Allied with Germany and Italy during World War II, Japan attacked US forces in Hawaii and the Philippines (December 1941) and occupied European colonial possessions in Southeast Asia. Numerous engagements in the Pacific with the United States and its allies followed. In 1945 the United States dropped atomic bombs on Hiroshima and Nagasaki, and Japan surrendered to the Allied powers. In the postwar period, the United States occupied Japan to help it transition to a constitutional democracy. In rebuilding Japan's ruined economy, new technology was used in every major industry. A great economic recovery resulted, and Japan became one of the world's wealthiest nations. It has remained so despite various ups and downs of its financial fortunes in the global economy. A devastating earthquake and tsunami hit the country in 2011, causing not only massive destruction and loss of life but a nuclear disaster involving the Fukushima Daiichi power plant.

Korea

Korea, or rather the Kingdom of Choson, was ruled by the Yi dynasty from 1392 to 1910. It long sought to keep out foreigners but was forced, in 1876, to open ports to Japan. Indeed, it became a Japanese protectorate following the Russo-Japanese War (1904–05), and was annexed to Japan in 1910. Freed from Japanese control at the end of World War II, the country was divided into two zones of occupation, Russian in the north and American in the south. The nations of North and South Korea were established in 1948, the North as a communist state and the South as a democratic republic. Seeking to unify the peninsula, North Korea invaded South Korea in 1950, launching the Korean War. UN forces intervened on the side of South Korea and Chinese soldiers backed the North Korean army; the war ended with an armistice in 1953. South Korea was rebuilt with US aid and prospered in the postwar era. North Korea, led by Kim Il-sung, became one of the most closed and regimented societies in the world, its state-run economy failing to produce needed levels of food and supplies for its citizens. The country continued to endure periodic shortages under Kim's son and successor, Kim Jong-Il, and has done likewise under the latter's son and successor, Kim Jong-Un. A summit in 2000 between the leaders of North and South Korea, and reunions between families from both countries, lifted hopes for reunification, but today tensions remain over the North's nuclear weapons program and other concerns.

Taiwan

After Taiwan became the home of the Nationalists in 1949, the Taiwanese government received strong US backing and financial support, leading to the development of a powerful economy there. Travel restrictions between Taiwan and mainland China were removed in 1988, but political tensions continue to this day.

Mongolia

A Eurasian power in medieval times, the Mongols became part of the Chinese Qing dynasty in the 1600s. With the fall of the Qing in 1912, Mongol leaders drew on Russian support to proclaim independence in 1921. A communist state was established in 1924. With the fall of the Soviet Union, a new constitution was written (1992). Since then the country has liberalized.

The Pacific

Oceania is the collective name for the groups of islands in the Pacific Ocean lying between the southeastern shores of Asia and the western shores of the Americas, together with the continent of Australia and the island nations of New Zealand and Papua New Guinea (these last three are sometimes referred to as Australasia). The lands of Oceania are generally grouped according to their inhabitants and settlement histories into Melanesia (e.g., Papua New Guinea, Solomon Islands, Vanuatu, New Caledonia, Fiji), Micronesia (e.g., Marshall Islands, Mariana Islands, Caroline Islands, Kiribati), and Polynesia (e.g., Samoa, Hawaii, Tonga, Tuvalu,

Easter Island). New Zealand is usually considered part of Polynesia; while Australia stands apart in having its own rather unique settlement history.

Australia

Identified on early European maps as "Terra Australis" ("unknown southern land"), Australia was first settled by humans some 40,000 years ago. The first inhabitants likely used watercraft to make the relatively short crossing from Southeast Asia (specifically, the Indonesian island chain), but at times during this period they could have used land bridges linking the Australian continent to New Guinea and other islands. Successive generations drifted from the northeast corner of Australia south into the unoccupied territories, eventually spreading over the entire land. For the most part the indigenous Australians, or Aboriginals, were nomadic peoples, subsisting on roots, seeds, and game rather than crops. The Aboriginals never exceeded 300,000 individuals; yet they remained in possession of all Australian territory until the arrival of the Europeans. At the time of contact, about 250 languages were spoken on the continent.

Melanesia

Melanesians are ethnically distinct from peoples of adjoining areas in the western Pacific, but at the same time they comprise diverse racial and cultural groups. Anthropologists are not in complete agreement on the ancestral origins of Melanesian peoples. Most believe that, like the Australian Aboriginals, Melanesians are descendants of Asian migrants who arrived in the area at least 20,000 years ago, when land bridges between the island chains were present. Few generalizations can made about the entire range of indigenous cultures in Melanesia, given that art forms, cultural practices, and even languages differ significantly over short distances. More than 800 languages are present in New Guinea alone. Most of the people pursued an agricultural economy or one based on fishing, hunting, and gathering, supplemented by trade. Coastal areas developed more advanced technologies and trading systems before the arrival of the Europeans.

Micronesia

The evidence from prehistory suggests that the first Micronesians migrated from Malaysia or the Philippines some 3,500 years ago. Settlement likely occurred over a long period of time. As with Melanesia, Micronesia's cultural diversity is apparent in the number of mutually unintelligible languages—around 17—that are spoken in a region that is quite sparsely populated. Culturally, one can divide Micronesian cultures into "high-island" and "low-island" forms. The division is rather tentative, however, marking only the difference between living on islands with internal landforms and living on low-lying atolls with relatively little land area. In any case, Micronesians are a maritime people who have highly developed skills in navigation and use of ocean resources.

Polynesia

Likewise, the Polynesians were consummate mariners. No single theory has been accepted as a definitive explanation of the origin and spread of Polynesians, but many researchers believe that the early Polynesians occupied parts of Malaysia, Indonesia, and/or Melanesia before migrating eastward on oceangoing outrigger canoes between 2,000 and 3,000 years ago. Rather than settling the various Polynesian islands at once, or over a short period of time, it is thought that landing was made on a single island or island chain, whence subsequent migrations to outlying locations were made at later dates. Settlement of New Zealand, home of the Maori people, occurred late in this sequence, around 1280 CE. Whatever their origins and circumstances of dispersal, Polynesians clearly had exceptional skills in long-distance oceanic navigation, and culturally they retained a marked degree of similarity throughout the scattered Polynesian lands.

Historical Development

The history of contact between the Pacific islanders and Europeans is long and complex. It begins with the voyage of Ferdinand Magellan in 1521, when he found the Ladrone Islands, later named the Marianas. It includes, among various other luminaries, Captain James Cook and his landings at the Cook Islands in 1773, New Caledonia in 1774, and, most famously, the Hawaiian Islands in 1788. The 16th century of Pacific exploration belongs to the Spaniards; the 17th to the Dutch; and the 18th to the English (and French). By the start of the 19th century, Europeans were living on most of the large islands of Oceania, some of them deserters from passing ships who settled there, and others whalers or collectors of sandalwood (the oil of which is used in perfumes). Parts of Australia were established as penal colonies for British convicts. Missionaries also made inroads in the region, and by the mid-19th century most Polynesians and many Micronesians and Melanesians had accepted Christianity. At the same time, more European traders, planters, and colonial officials arrived on the scene, spawning budding conflicts in some cases. With the development of air travel in the 20th century, Oceania acquired strategic military value as well as value within the tourism industry. During World War II, many of its lesser known islands and atolls became scenes of combat between Japan and the United States. After the war, the United States conducted nuclear tests in the Pacific, wreaking havoc on local populations and the environment. Independence movements beginning in the 1960s led to the emergence of a number of new states or new statuses vis-à-vis former colonial powers. At the same time, Australia and New Zealand continued to grow into major industrial powers. Today, the twin spirits of independence and belonging, of separateness and connection to the community of nations, motivate the many and varied peoples of Oceania.

Michael Shally-Jensen, PhD

Bibliography

Borthwick, Mark. *Pacific Century: The Emergence of Modern Pacific Asia.* Boulder, CO: Westview Press, 2014.

Ebrey, Patricia and Anne Walthall. *Modern East Asia, from 1600: A Cultural, Social, and Political History,* 3rd ed. Boston: Wadsworth, 2014.

Hau'ofa, Epeli. *We Are the Ocean: Selected Works.* Honolulu: University of Hawaii Press, 2008.

Holcombe, Charles. *A History of East Asia: From the Origins of Civilization to the Twenty-First Century.* New York: Cambridge University Press, 2011.

Rapaport, Moshe, ed. *The Pacific Islands: Environment and Society.* Honolulu: University of Hawaii Press, 2013.

Vltchek, André. *Oceania: Neocolonialism, Nukes, and Bones.* Waikato, NZ: Atuanui Press, 2013.

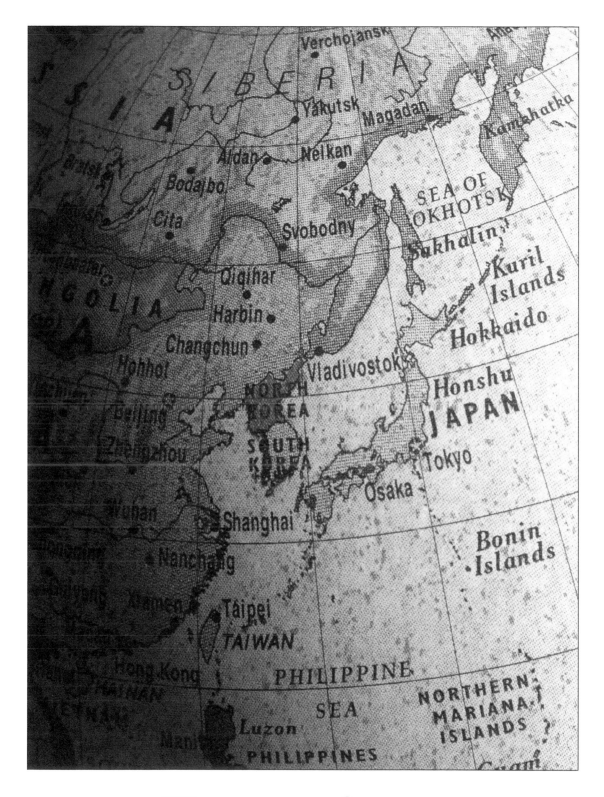

EAST ASIA

The Great Wall of China. iStopck/NI QIN

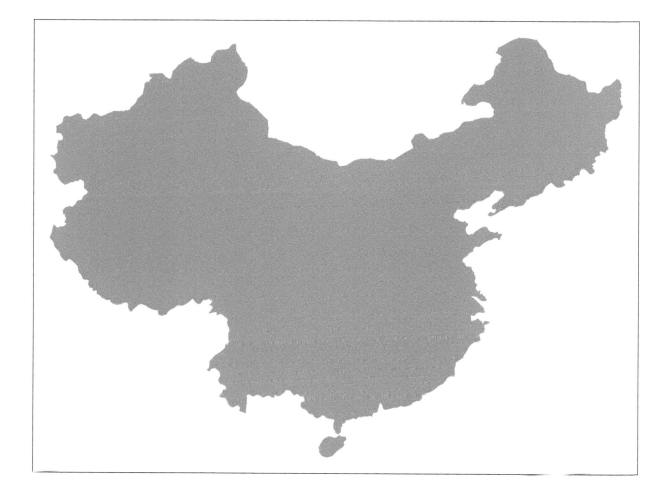

CHINA

Introduction

The People's Republic of China (PRC), known informally as China, is a nation in East Asia. It borders the Pacific Ocean and twelve countries, including Russia and Kazakhstan, the Koreas, Laos, India and Afghanistan.

Ancient China was one of the most advanced and powerful cultures in world history, leaving to future generations a legacy of the arts, language, medicine, and society unrivalled in the West. Today, contemporary China is re-emerging as a world power, possessing a huge population, economic strength, and rapid modernization.

Beijing is the capital of the People's Republic of China. Called the "Northern Capital," Beijing is one of the oldest cities in the world, having been occupied by the Chinese people for over 4,000 years and serving as the capital of multiple Chinese dynasties.

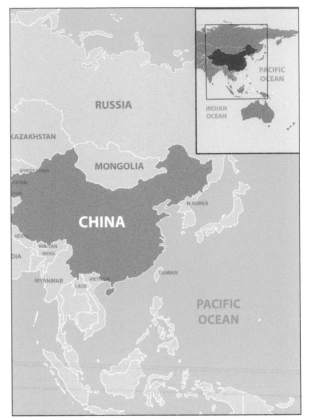

GENERAL INFORMATION

Official Language: Standard Mandarin Chinese; in Hong Kong, both English and Chinese are recognized as official languages.
Population: 1,401,586,609 (2015)
Currency: Renminbi
Coins: The renminbi exists in denominations of 1, 2, and 5 fen coins. 1 Yuan coins are also available.
Land Area: 9,596,960 square kilometers (3,705,386 square miles)
National Anthem: "Yiyongjun Jinxingqu" ("March of the Volunteers")
Capital: Beijing

Time Zone: China Standard Time (GMT +8), which is observed year-round, despite the country spanning several time zones.
Flag Description: The flag of China is red. In the upper left corner, a large golden star sits with four smaller stars to its right. The red color represents China's communist revolution, the large star represents the Communist Party of China, and the four smaller stars represent China's four social classes: the peasants, the working class, the urban bourgeoisie, and the national bourgeoisie.

Population

China is the most populous country in the world, officially home to over 1.4 billion people. Unofficial counts add another 100 million. One-fifth of the planet's human inhabitants live in China, more than the combined populations of the European Union (510 million), United States (321 million), Brazil (203 million), Russia (142 million), Mexico (125 million), and Canada (35 million).

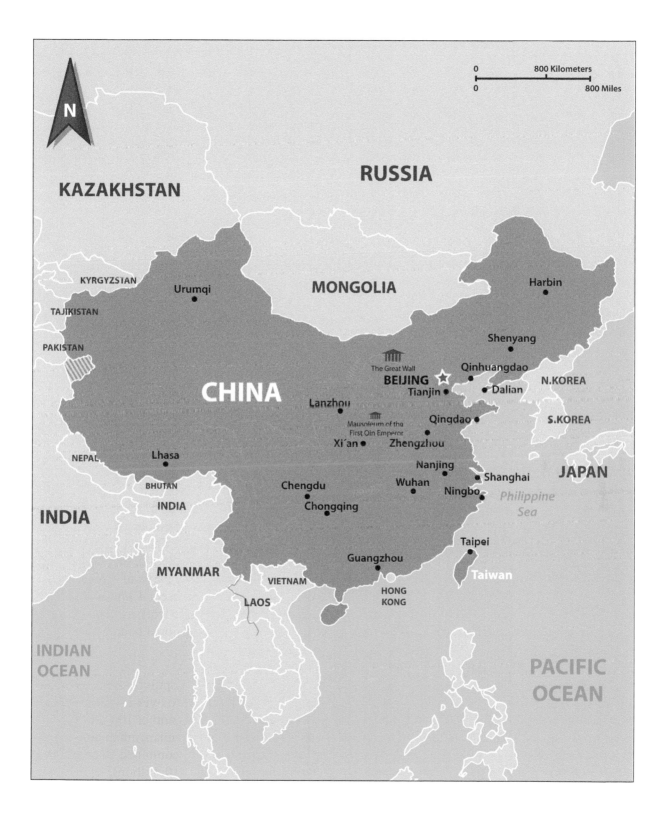

Principal Cities by Population (2015):

- Shanghai (23,741,000)
- Beijing (11,716,620)
- Tianjin (11,090,314)
- Guangzhou (11,071,424)
- Shenzhen (10,358,381)
- Wuhan (9,785,388)
- Dongguan (8,000,000)
- Chongqing (7,457,600)
- Nanjing (7,165,292)
- Xi'an (6,501,190)

In 2015, there were about sixty cities with populations of over 1 million, compared to only thirteen in the US. One report stated that in 2015, China also had fifteen megacities--cities with more than 10 million people. Shanghai is the largest city, followed by the capital, Beijing. Other large cities include Hong Kong, Tianjin, Wuhan, and Shenyang.

In recent decades, there has been a massive migration from China's rural areas to its cities. More than half the country's population now lives in urban areas. Most migration has been to China's bustling southeastern coastline.

Languages

The Han, Manchu, and Hui speak Mandarin Chinese. Other dialects include Yue (Cantonese), Wu (Shanghaiese), Minbei (Fuzhou), and Minnan (Hokkien-Taiwanese).

Native People & Ethnic Groups

The Han ethnic group makes up 92 percent of the population and dominates Chinese culture. The Zhuang are the largest minority group, with over 15 million people. Smaller ethnic groups of between 5 and 10 million include the Manchu, Hui, Miao, Uigur, Yi, and Tujia. Notable minorities of between 1 and 5 million include Mongol, Tibetan, and Korean.

China is part of one of the world's oldest civilizations. The country claims the first fossil record of Homo erectus, the 1.7 million-year-old Yuanmou Man. It is believed that Homo sapiens arrived in China from Africa around 65,000 years ago. Recorded evidence of various tribal civilizations in China dates from 5,000 to 8,000 years ago.

Religions

Because of the government's official support of atheism, accurate statistics on religious affiliation in China are unavailable. Buddhism, Islam, Christianity, and Taoism are practiced in at least 85,000 worship venues throughout the country.

Climate

Most of China's weather is influenced by two trends: cold, dry winter winds blowing south and east, and wet, warm westerly summer monsoon winds off the Pacific Ocean.

The southeastern part of the country is subtropical. Hong Kong's average winter temperature is 16° Celsius (61° Fahrenheit); its summer average is 28° Celsius (82° Fahrenheit). Approximately 80 percent of the region's annual rainfall arrives between May and September.

Along the coast, roughly fifteen tropical cyclones per year strengthen to become typhoons (hurricanes), half of which push torrential rains into southeast China. Southwest China's higher elevation promotes cooler summers, but winters remain mild, creating an extended growing season.

Central China's continental climate features cold, dry winters and warm, humid summers, much like the central United States. Beijing's average winter temperature is –4° Celsius (25° Fahrenheit); its average summer temperature is 26° Celsius (79° Fahrenheit). About 90 percent of annual rainfall occurs between April and August. The autumn months (September and October) are generally the most hospitable.

There are desert and arctic climates to the north and west. The average January temperature atop Mount Qomolangma is –36° Celsius (–33° Fahrenheit) with an average wind chill of –70° Celsius (–94° Fahrenheit).

ENVIRONMENT & GEOGRAPHY

Topography

China's land area is more than 9,500,000 square kilometers (3,668,000 square miles), nearly the same as the United States. Much of this vast terrain is mountainous, including the Himalaya, Kunlun, and Tian mountain ranges.

Mount Qomolangma on China's border with Nepal in the Himalayas, better known in the West as Mount Everest, is the highest peak in the World at 8,848 meters (29,029 feet) above sea level. Below it, the Tibetan Plateau, the "rooftop of the World," stretches out at an average elevation of 4,510 meters (14,800 feet).

China generally slopes downward from west to east. Only about 12 percent of the country's area settles into flat plains regions. Its coastline stretches for 14,500 kilometers (9,010 miles) along thousands of islands in territorial waters. China's length and width are both over 5,200 kilometers (3,200 miles).

There are more than 1,500 significant rivers, 2,800 large natural lakes, and 2,000 man-made reservoirs throughout China. Its rivers typically drain eastward to the Pacific Ocean. The longest, the Yangtze River at 6,300 kilometers (3,915 miles), connects Shanghai with inland cities. The second largest Huang He (Yellow) River, in the northern part of the country, fills China's largest reservoir, the Long Men, at 35.4 billion cubic meters (1,250 billion cubic feet) capacity.

Poyang in Jiangxi Province is China's largest freshwater lake. Other large lakes include Dongting Tai, Hongze, and Gaoyou. Qinghai Lake is the country's largest inland saltwater lake.

Plants & Animals

Forests accounted for about 22 percent of China's land area in 2011. China's wide variety of forests, including tropical, subtropical, temperate, and boreal, are estimated to hold approximately 30,000 native plant species, twice as many as are found in the US. Subtropical southern ranges contain numerous tree species, including ginko, oak, bamboo, pine, magnolia, and azalea.

Thousands of plants native to China are grown around the world, including food crops such as soybeans, oranges, peaches and apricots; and flowers including forsythias, gardenias, magnolias, peonies, primroses, and rhododendrons.

Common animals in China's tropical areas include primates such as rhesus macaques. Temperate areas are home to dogs, cats, foxes, and wolves. Less abundant are bears and large cats. Wild horses roam upland western steeps. Camels, yaks, and water buffalo are used as work animals.

Rare animals include the endangered giant panda, found only in a few places in western central China, and the white-flag dolphin, a freshwater whale discovered in the Yangtze River in 1980 and last seen in 2002.

CUSTOMS & COURTESIES

Greetings

Generally, the Chinese greet one another informally. A typical greeting may involve a polite nod or a slight bow, often accompanied by the saying, "Chi le ma?" ("Have you eaten?"). The accepted response is typically "Chi le" ("Yes"). It is common to reply with this response even if the individual has not eaten, out of politeness. A more formal greeting is "Ni hao" ("Hello, I'm pleased to meet you").

Introductions are typically formal, with the oldest person greeted first, and then often addressed with his or her honorific title and surname. Chinese family names usually consist of one syllable; the given name, which consists of one or two syllables, follows the family name. In general, the Chinese address each other with their full name—family and given—and title rather than their given names, unless invited to do otherwise. Handshakes are commonly used for first time greetings and may be held for a long time. Many Chinese look at the ground during greetings as a sign of humility. A bow is usually made to show respect to the elderly or to officials.

Children are typically greeted with a gentle pat on the cheek or shoulder, but never touched on the head. In fact, adults refrain from touching another person on the head as well, because the head is considered a sacred part of the body. Generally, the Chinese are careful not to touch people they do not know at all, except when in crowded places.

Gestures & Etiquette

Honorable intentions are of great significance in Chinese culture. Typically, the Chinese do not offer criticism and are not direct in their opinions. It is considered polite to be reserved, quiet, and gentle, and the Chinese are careful to avoid hurting the feelings of others. For example, it is common for the Chinese to agree outwardly with someone, even if they disagree inwardly. Additionally, during a conversation it is considered impolite to frown or stare into the other person's eyes, as these are considered disrespectful actions. The use of the feet to move something, such as a door, is also considered disrespectful.

Gestures commonly used in Western cultures, such as pointing or waving, are basically meaningless in China. In fact, some can be construed as rude, such as pointing with the index finger or snapping one's fingers. Instead, the whole hand, palm up, should be used when pointing at something. Members of the opposite sex do not generally touch each other in public but will stand close to each other. Friends of the same sex, however, will sometimes hold hands or walk arm-in-arm.

Eating/Meals

The social habits and customs of dining do not vary much between rural and urban areas, nor across cultures. Meals are typically eaten with chopsticks and spoons. Food is often served communally and taken from bowls placed in the center of the table. Often, food is served to the guests by the host. Because of the communal nature of meals, it is generally not considered impolite to reach for food. However, the last bit of food is never taken from the bowl, and each person eating should leave some food on

his plate. In addition, bones and seeds are never placed in the rice bowl or on a plate from which food is being eaten, but are placed on the table or in a bowl provided for that purpose. Chopsticks should never be left in the rice bowl, as this is considered bad manners and bad luck.

At restaurants, the host is expected to pay, although the guest may politely offer. Eating is generally for pleasure, and business is not usually discussed. Napkins are not commonly found at tables in restaurants. Banquets, in which food is plentiful, are common in China, and usually last for two or three hours. It is polite for a guest to try a little bit of everything at banquets, complimenting each dish. Although there are many street vendors in urban China, it is considered to be somewhat impolite to eat food while walking down the street (children are generally exempt from this rule).

Visiting

It is common in China for guests to drop in unannounced. Invitations are issued when the gathering is to be a more formal one. When guests arrive, it is considered polite to be punctual and to conduct oneself with restraint and dignity. Loud talking and boisterous laughter is avoided, and shoes should be removed upon entering the house. The guest should not complement items inside the home, such as artwork, as this may make the host feel obligated to give the object to the guest as a gift.

When visiting, it is appropriate for guests to bring a small gift for the host, but not anything too extravagant. Fruit, tea, wine, or candy are considered good gifts and should be given and received with both hands. Gifts are not typically opened immediately nor in the presence of the guests.

Refreshments are usually offered, and it is not impolite to refuse them, although the host will offer several times. If dinner is being served, guests will wait for the host to direct them where to sit. Conversation will usually center on the food. It is not uncommon for guests to be asked to participate in the entertainment at a party, such as singing. In these situations, it is considered rude to refuse the host. Since evenings usually end early in China—most Chinese arise very early to begin work—it is not uncommon for the host, in an effort to thank the guest for coming, to politely escort the guest out the door and even down the street.

LIFESTYLE

Family

In the 21st century, China is rapidly emerging as a world power. This economic and political transition has affected every aspect of Chinese life, including the family unit. In the past, couples traditionally lived with the husband's parents. Marriages were arranged by parents or by the "work unit" boss, and divorce was almost unheard of. In addition, public security bureaus checked communist credentials before marriage licenses were issued.

Today, China no longer subsidizes apartments or guarantees jobs, and young adults are expected to find their own spouses, as marriages are no longer arranged. Western-style weddings are considered a status symbol. Once married, many Chinese forgo living at home, as earlier generations did. However, most choose to settle only a few blocks away from their parents. Divorce is more common in the early 21st century than it ever was and continues to increase as women become more economically marketable and independent.

For decades, China maintained a one-child policy. This law stated that married couples must have only one child for the good of the country. However, couples could pay a fee in order to have more than one child, and rural couples could have a second child if the first child was a girl or was disabled. Critics of this policy point out that this hurts the elderly, as one adult child will eventually be taking care of two parents and four grandparents. In order to solve this problem, some provinces allowed couples where each parent was an only child to have two children rather than just one. In 2014 this policy started to ease, and in 2015 was abandoned.

Housing

Housing in China varies widely from simple farmhouses in rural areas to luxury high-rise apartments in the cities. Prior to the mid-1980s, it was highly uncommon for the Chinese to own their homes. Before the reform policy, housing was mostly provided by work unions, and the size and quality of the housing provided depended on the person's position in the company. Today, it is common for the Chinese to purchase their own homes. As such, investing in real estate has become popular.

Most people who live in urban areas make their homes in high-rise apartment communities. Typically, luxury high-rise apartments have electricity, central heating, and air-conditioning, with hot water and plumbing for kitchens and bathrooms. In contrast, homes in rural areas are usually detached and modest in design, with no running water or electricity. In addition, the average living space in urban apartments is 10.6 square meters (114 square feet), compared to 20.7 square meters (222 square feet) for homes in rural areas.

It is not easy for low-income families to buy an apartment. To help, the government has used public funds to design low-income housing projects, such as the "Warm Home Project" in Beijing. The residents pay a small percentage of the price and are given a low-interest loan for the rest. It is still common in most Chinese cities to see neighborhoods composed of older, traditional housing, typically consisting of cement-built one-room homes squeezed in between high-rise apartments.

Food

Chinese cuisine is largely defined by region. While there are eight important regional styles—Anhui, Cantonese, Fujian, Hunan, Jiangsu, Shandong, Sichuan, and Zhejiang (called the Eight Great Traditions)—four major and influential regions or styles categorize Chinese cuisine. These are Beijing, Shanghai, Sichuan/Szechuan, and Cantonese (called the Four Great Traditions). Cantonese is most familiar to Americans, as it is the most popular style served in Chinese restaurants overseas.

However, the regional cuisines of China share many similarities. For example, foods common to all regions include staples such as potatoes, noodles, rice, meal, and other grains. In addition, fruits and vegetables are commonly eaten according to season, with the mixing of vegetables with sauce a common regional characteristic. Meat is usually mixed with rice, and includes pork, beef, chicken, or fish. Dairy is rare in rural areas. A dish common to all areas of China are jiaozi, or dumplings. Jiaozi are typically fried, boiled, or steamed, and can be filled with almost any food. They are popular with street vendors as a snack food and are common in fine restaurants. Jiaozi tang, or dumpling soup, is also very popular.

Beijing's most famous dish is the Peking roast duck. An unnamed palace chef first created Peking duck for the emperor during the Ming Dynasty. Later, the recipe was smuggled out of the palace kitchens and onto the streets of Beijing. To create the dish, the duck is first air-dried, then coated with a special mixture of syrup and soy sauce before being roasted. This creates a delicate, crispy skin. It is then presented to the patrons and carved into pieces, which are wrapped in pancakes with onions, cucumber, turnips, and plum sauces.

Shanghai's food is usually seafood-based and often features heavy and spicy sauces. Typically, this regional style is prepared with lots of oil. A favorite dish in Shanghai is the da zha xie (hairy crab). Normally eaten in the winter, it is a crab only found in rivers. They are steamed in bamboo containers and served with vinegar.

Sichuan/Szechuan food is typically very spicy and is often prepared with the Sichuan peppercorn, a strong, fragrant, plant that produces numbing, citrus-y flavor. This flavor can be found in the one of the more popular Sichuan dishes, kung pao chicken. To make the original Sichuan version of this dish, the wok (a traditional round-bottomed cooking vessel) is first seasoned. Red chilies and Sichuan peppercorns are flash-fried to add their essence to the oil. Then, chicken that has been previously diced and left soaking in a Saoxing wine marinade is stir-fried, along with vegetables and peanuts.

Cantonese food is the most popular style of Chinese food found outside of China. It comes from the Guangzhou region in southern China and consists of a huge variety of dishes made from all kinds of foods. Soup, consisting of a clear broth prepared by simmering meats and spices for hours, is important in Cantonese meals and is usually served first.

Fresh seafood is a Cantonese specialty. Dishes made with prawns and shrimp are especially popular. Another popular Cantonese food is char siu, or barbecued pork. This dish consists of long strips of boneless pork coated with a seasoning made from sugar, soy sauce, red food coloring, sherry, and five-spice powder. This sauce turns the meat dark red during cooking. The pork is cooked on a long fork held over a fire and served with rice or in a bun.

Hong Kong bills itself as the "culinary capital of Asia," a title that refers to the incredible amount and variety of food available in the region. According to Hong Kong's board of tourism, the territory boasts more than 12,000 licensed restaurants. Most, though not all, of the territory's residents enjoy a Cantonese-style diet of rice, meat, fish, and vegetables that are usually stir fried in oil or water and served in soy or ginger-based sauces.

For purposes of tourism, the territory is broken up into food "districts," including Causeway Bay, Kowloon City, Lan Kwai Fong and Soho, Sai Kung, Lamma Island, and Lei Yue Mun, Stanley, Tsim Sha Tsui, and Hung Hom. Each district has a mixture of culinary styles, but tends toward a particular regional cuisine. Aberdeen Harbor is famous for its floating restaurants.

Hong Kong is famous for its dim sum, a ceremonial meal served in the morning and made of a wide variety of bite-sized finger foods. Meat or seafood-filled dumplings, buns, and seafood balls all appear on the dim sum trolleys from which diners choose their selections.

Hong Kong's cosmopolitan style also includes foods from other parts of Asia and China, as well as from Europe, South America, and North America.

Life's Milestones

Bloodlines are extremely important in Chinese culture, and producing children to maintain those bloodlines has long been an important part of Chinese tradition. As such, the birth of a child is greeted with great joy, and rituals continue throughout the child's first year of life. After giving birth, the mother rests in her bed for one month, during which time family and friends wait upon her. At the end of the month, the family typically has a "one-month" celebration for the baby, including offering sacrifices for the baby's protection if that family is Buddhist or Taoist. Prayers to the ancestors are offered as well, informing them of the baby's birth. This celebration is very similar to parties thrown in Western cultures for a baby's first birthday (first birthdays are typically not celebrated in Chinese culture).

As part of the celebration, the parents of the baby give gifts to relatives and friends. Red eggs are usually part of the gift, as they are a symbol of the beginning of life. (Red is also considered the color of happiness). Other gifts may include cakes and even chickens. Then, it is the family's turn to give gifts to the baby. The presents include things that the baby may need or like, such as food or toys. However, the baby is more commonly given money wrapped in red paper. In addition, grandparents usually give the baby something made of gold or silver. The celebration usually concludes with a rich feast given by the parents, at either their home or a restaurant. Babies in China are considered "one" the moment they are born.

CULTURAL HISTORY

Art & Architecture

The earliest patrons of the arts were China's emperors. They would issue royal decrees concerning the creation of art, and how art was to be applied. Thus, a long tradition of artists being largely employed and controlled by the royal court or the government was established. Often, early Chinese artists were encouraged to continue the artistic styles and traditions of previous dynasties. Amateur artists, on the other hand, were free to create art that reflected their individual tastes. This division led to the creation of two groups of art that lasted for centuries: imperial art, which was often similar in design and theme, and independent art, which varied widely from imperialistic trends.

The Bronze Age in China (roughly 2000–700 BCE), which encompassed the Shang Dynasty (c. 176–1122 BCE) to the Six Dynasties (222–589 CE), featured art that focused on the dead. During this era, members of the royal court were intent on securing immortality and commissioned artists to construct and decorate lavish tombs. Artists also created beautiful bronze vessels and weapons to be placed near the coffins for the deceased to take with them into the next world. Other items often placed in tombs include carved jades and ceramics.

Buddhism arose following the collapse of the Han Dynasty (202 BCE–220 CE), and brought with it a new style of art from India. During this period, the subject matter of art became worldlier, with less focus on death. Landscape and portrait painting flourished, and sculpture gained popularity. Sculpture was particularly created on a grand scale. Massive stone carvings of Buddha, such as those created in the mountains of Henan and Shensi, were common. Gu Kaizhi (Ku K'ai-chih), considered the father of landscape painting, was a preeminent artist during this period. Wooden pagodas also became popular during this time.

The Tang period (618–907 CE), often referred to as China's "golden age," was a time when all art began to flourish. The stable government and strong economy of this period led to strong interests in painting, ceramics—particularly porcelain—metalwork, music and poetry. The dynasties following the Tang Dynasty did not introduce new art, but rather refined and expanded on the Tang Dynasty's achievements.

During the Song Dynasty (1960–1279 CE), landscape painting became more popular, especially among amateur artists. Within the royal court, portrait painting rose to prominence, and paintings depicting royal families were often produced in great quantities. Birds and flowers were also favorite subjects of the royalty. Calligraphy was elevated to an art form during this time. The Yuan Dynasty (1279–1368), also known as the Mongol Dynasty, was a quieter time in the history of Chinese art, since the Mongol invasion caused many court artists to retire.

The Ming Dynasty (1368–1644 CE) marked the end of Mongol rule in Chinese history. The Ming court was known for its lavish and highly detailed decorative arts and for establishing the royal painting academy. This academy was renowned for producing famed Chinese artists such as Wen Zhengming (1470–1559), a leading painter of the Ming era. Because he chose simple subjects, Wen Zhengming's paintings are known for evoking a sense of strength arising from humble origins.

In 1644, the Manchu nation (a group of people originating in what is now northeastern China) seized control of China. The rulers embraced the art of the Ming Dynasty, often improving on the ornate styles associated with that period. During the Qing Dynasty (1644–1912), the last ruling dynasty of China, Chinese art increased in popularity abroad.

The post-imperial period began in 1911 with the formation of the Republic of China under Sun Yat-sen (1866–1925). Under this new republic, the people of China, including artists, began to feel pressure to accept Western ideas in the name of modernization. Many artists studied overseas and brought back new ideas such as the use of bold colors, abstraction, and European brushwork in painting. Most decorative arts, however, remained traditional in style. In 1949, the socialist People's Republic of China (PRC) was founded, and painting and decorative arts were infused with political content, largely under the direction of Mao Zedong (1893–1976). Most themes deliberately praised socialism, a political philosophy which property and the distribution of wealth are community or state-controlled. However, since Mao's death in 1976, Chinese art has become less political.

The structural principals of Chinese architecture were established as early as the Neolithic period, or the New Stone Age, in China (c. 10,000–2,000 BCE). They remained largely unchanged until the 20th century, when Western influences introduced a fusion of traditional Chinese designs with modern needs. Throughout its history, there have been many different styles of Chinese architecture, including Buddhist architecture, Taoist architecture, garden architecture, and Imperial architecture, all with their own unique and ornate styles.

Chinese architecture is based on several principles that emphasize balance and symmetry. One of the most important principles is the emphasis on the horizontal axis. Quite simply, traditional Chinese architecture is constructed in a vertical manner, and the width is emphasized over depth or height. As such, a building was typically supported by columns or pillars, with walls merely serving as screens within. Large roofs and low ceilings heights are also common.

Another principle found in Chinese architecture is the emphasis on bilateral symmetry and articulation. This principle is found in all types of buildings, from modest farmhouses to palaces. Enclosing space within the building is also common and can be seen in the use of open courtyards and the "sky yard." The latter is created when closely spaced buildings form intersections. In addition, the sky can be typically seen through small openings in the roof.

A final principle in Chinese architecture involves the placement of buildings on a property. For example, secondary structures considered less important are built alongside the main building, typically positioned as wings on either side. In this way, Chinese architecture is also hierarchical. In addition, the most important buildings have doors that face the front of the property, while buildings that face away from the front are the least important. The more private parts of property are reserved for buildings that house elder members of the family.

While these structural principles of Chinese architecture have transcended time and socioeconomic boundaries, certain architectural styles and traditions were based on the projected use of the building. For example, houses for commoners such as farmers or merchants were generally built in a "U" shape, with the center being a shrine for ancestors. Next to the shrine were bedrooms for the elders, and wings or additions were built for extended family members. Certain architectural features were reserved strictly for the Imperial family. Yellow (the Imperial color) roof tiles and red (favored by the ancient Chinese) walls signify royalty and can still be seen in the Forbidden City. In addition, the Chinese dragon was used on roofs, doors, and pillars of Imperial buildings.

One of the most important elements of traditional Chinese architecture is the use of timber framework. A traditional residence is typically constructed with a timber frame, with pillars supporting a roof and earthen walls on three sides. Typically, the fourth side is the front side and contains the door and windows. Decorative art and carvings were then added. The use of wood, representing life, is important to the Chinese. Although colorful lacquer, or varnish, is applied to the wood to preserve it, most traditional buildings did not survive very long, and very few buildings now predate the Ming Dynasty (1368–1644 CE). This basic structural form, however, lasted into the modern age. Chinese architecture was also largely influential in developing the styles of Korean, Vietnamese, and Japanese architecture.

Music, Dance & Theater

Music and dance represent two of the oldest art forms in Chinese culture. In fact, Chinese dancing figures are depicted on ceramic artifacts dating back to the fourth millennium BCE. Music was often used in early Chinese rituals and official ceremonies. As music evolved in ancient China, it was gradually used for almost any activity and added structure and routine to daily life.

The earliest forms of dance were divided into two groups: military and civilian dancing. Civilian dances generally depicted everyday events such as hunting. Often, dances were created to simply express joy or to be incorporated into religious worship. In fact, from these early religious dances came the first forms of Chinese theater. (Theater continued to evolve over the years, and by the Han Dynasty, it had become the most important art form in China.) Although musicians were of lower status than painters, music was seen as central to the harmony of the state. Early Chinese folk music and dance was typically maintained and developed by each subsequent emperor. Traditional Chinese music was also heavily influenced by foreign music, especially folk music from East Asia.

A state-controlled music bureau was established during the Han Dynasty, and efforts were made to collect and preserve folk songs and dances. However, as other people of Asia invaded China, their forms of dancing merged with the Chinese. During the Tang Dynasty, culture and dance flourished and many dance and music academies were formed. The lavish and extraordinary "Ten Movement Dance," which featured elements from several different Asian countries, was performed during this time. This art form later evolved into the earliest form of Chinese opera.

The development of Chinese theater reached its pinnacle during the Yuan Dynasty. During this period, Chinese theater first began to be known as operas. These operas were organized around plots both historical and contemporary, and were typically performed with lavishly decorated costumes and stages. Later forms of the opera included the famous Peking Opera, which features song, dance, elaborate props, and displays of martial arts and acrobatics.

Western music became influential during the New Culture Movement, a period spanning 1917 to 1923 during which China's cultural heritage was criticized. Chinese musicians returning from abroad began to include the Western style of music in their work (Western music is based on an eight-note scale rather than the traditional five-note scale found in Chinese music). Many Chinese philosophers criticized the new sound. Regardless, symphony orchestras arose in major cities, and jazz was blended with traditional sounds.

Beginning the 1940s, the government launched a campaign to change folk music, adding revolutionary songs to further the goals of communism. Any folk songs considered superstitious or rebellious were repressed. Soon, the government denounced Chinese popular music as harmful and began to heavily promote revolutionary songs. The Cultural Revolution (roughly 1966–1976), a period marked by political and cultural tension in which certain aspects of life were forbidden, made these songs popular and they became the predominant form of music in China.

During the rebellions of the early 1990s, a new fast-tempo style of Chinese music arose as a way to counter the government. This style gave way to rock music, which remains popular in contemporary China. Music and dance, however, are still very much state-owned in China. In fact, the government owns the media as well as all major concert halls. Today, folk dances are protected and still performed at state ceremonies. Western forms of dance are also popular, and many dance academies throughout China cater to young people wishing to learn ballet, modern dance, and others non-traditional forms.

Literature

Chinese literature has its beginnings in the earliest recorded court archives of thousand-year old dynasties. Woodblock printing was invented during the Tang Dynasty and movable type printing during the Song Dynasty. The Ming Dynasty saw the rise of the fictional novel. In more modern times, author Lu Xun (1881–1936), the pen name of Zhou Shuren, founded baihau literature, or literature written in standard Mandarin. This style of literature was typically easier to read than earlier literature, which was often written in ancient forms of the Chinese language.

Generally, the history of Chinese literature can be divided into four periods: classical, contemporary, modern, and present day. Classical literature refers to the earliest recorded written words from over 3,000 years ago, as well as literary works written prior to the end of the Qing Dynasty in 1911. Most famously, the

first thousand years of writing are attributed to Confucius (551–479 BCE) and are based on the famous Chinese philosopher's conversations with students and other social thinkers. Written in ancient languages, most ancient Chinese literature is extremely difficult to understand and is focused entirely around the Chinese feudal society.

Contemporary literature covers the period from the late Qing Dynasty to the spring of 1919, when the rise of patriotic movements against imperialism and feudalism arose. During this period, literary reformers such as Hu Shi (1891–1962) and Chen Duxiu (1879–1942) proclaimed the classical language "dead." Chinese authors began to absorb and reflect Western thoughts and ideas. Novels and poetry often embraced themes of patriotism and reviled social ills. Baihau literature, as popularized by Lu Xun, is included in this period.

Modern literature spans the time from 1919 to the founding of the PRC in 1949. Literature during this time featured strong political views, and an eye toward the future. To appeal and communicate with readers, literature during this period often featured the ordinary lives of the Chinese people. In addition, women authors became quite popular, such as Ding Ling (1904–1986). Her story "Diary of Miss Sophie" is largely credited with giving the public direct access to female thought and feelings.

Present day literature refers to literature created from 1949 to the present. During the years 1949 to 1976, the Communist Party slowly nationalized the publishing industry in China. The government thus controlled book distribution, forcing writers to join the Writers Union. In this way, they were able to censor their work. However, following the Cultural Revolution there was an explosion of writing. Writers were free to write about sensitive subject matter in unconventional styles, and literature turned commercial and escapist. Wang Shuo (b.1958–) is one such writer known for commercialism in his writing. Not all modern Chinese literature is commercial, however. Women authors, most notably Chen Ran (b.1962–), began focusing on societal issues such as the rapidly changing role of women in Chinese modern society.

CULTURE

Arts & Entertainment

The place of the arts in contemporary China is very different from only a few decades ago. The Cultural Revolution saw the destruction of a large number of cultural treasures, and the practice of most arts and crafts was severely curtailed or forbidden. In the 1980s, the Chinese government repudiated those policies and began efforts to renew China's artistic heritage. With restrictions loosened, artists are now free to explore subjects other than propaganda and often adopt Western techniques and themes in the process.

China has a long, rich literary tradition, due in part to the development of printing in the 11th century. Chinese ink-brush calligraphy has been used for thousands of years and is an art in itself. The country's dramatic landscape has inspired painters for centuries and the art of penjing ("tray scenery") gardening is an ancient forerunner of the Japanese art of bonsai.

Chinese culture suffered under the communist government's Cultural Revolution. Popular Beijing (Peking) opera groups could only perform government-sanctioned propaganda works. However, a pervasive interest in Western culture accompanied later economic reforms.

Still, government censorship remains an issue in contemporary China. The role of the government in promoting the arts is combined with its ability to control them. Recently, a painting entitled *Birds Nest, in the Style of Cubism* by Zhang Hongtu (1943–) was banned from display in China because it featured pro-Tibetan language. The government has also outlawed performance art in China, although Chinese performance artists continue to work outside of the country.

Cinemas are popular, often showing Western or Japanese films, as are traditional acrobatic shows by groups such as the Shanghai Acrobatic Troupe.

Cultural Sites & Landmarks

Perhaps China's most significant and iconic landmark is one that took successive dynasties to build and over one million men to fortify: the Great Wall of China. Considered one of the New Seven Wonders of the World, the Great Wall is historically and architecturally significant. It stretches across plains, mountains, desserts, and valleys, running east to west across China for approximately 6,700 kilometers (4,163 miles). The wall was built and rebuilt in sections over several centuries (fifth century BCE to the 16th century CE), and was successfully joined during the Qin Dynasty. In addition to being named one of the wonders of the world, in both medieval and modern times, the Great Wall was listed as a World Heritage Site in 1987.

In fact, China is home to forty-eight United Nations Educational, Scientific, and Cultural Organization (UNESCO) World Heritage Sites, boasting one of the largest collections of such sites in the world. Many of these sites are areas of historic or natural interest, and include mountains and valleys, national parks, ancient cities and villages, and traditional burial grounds and temples. One particularly unique World Heritage Site is the Peking Man Site at Zhoukoudian, where human remains dating back 500,000 years were unearthed.

The Summer Palace, a beautiful and popular tourist attraction located in the capital of Beijing, is another World Heritage Site. Built in 1750 and restored in 1886, it is a stunning example of Chinese garden landscaping, which represents the Chinese philosophy of combining the works of humans and nature into a pleasing design. In this case, the works of humans consist of halls with intricately carved designs, temples, bridges, and palaces. The natural landscape is made up of hills, open water, indigenous plants, and ponds.

Mount Emei, inscribed as a World Heritage Site in 1996 and located in Sichuan Province, is the location of the first Buddhist temple ever built in China. Built in the first century CE, this temple was followed by many others, including the Giant Buddha of Leshan. Carved directly into a hillside during the Tang Dynasty, it took over ninety years to build. It is the largest Buddha in the world and stands at approximately 71 meters (233 feet) high. Each finger is 3 meters (9 feet) long, and each shoulder is wide enough to serve as a basketball court.

Xian, one of the oldest cities in Chinese history, also contains one of the most significant archaeological finds of the 20th century, the Terra Cotta Warriors and Horses. At the age of thirteen, the first Emperor of China, Qin Shi Huang (259–210 BCE), began to build his mausoleum immediately upon taking the throne. Discovered in 1974 by peasants digging for a well, the mausoleum site was immediately protected and excavated. The museum that stands there today is made up of three pits covering an area of 16,300 square meters (175,451 square feet), all featuring several thousand life-sized terracotta figures of warriors (including weapons), horses and chariots arranged in battle formations. In total, over 7,000 of these pottery figures have been unearthed and restored.

Libraries & Museums

Beijing is China's cultural center, home to museums such as the Forbidden City (built 1420 and made into a museum in 1925) and the National Art Museum of China (1958 at its current location; preparation for a new venue has begun). The China Art Museum (formerly Shanghai Art Museum) (original site 1952; current site 1996) houses ancient Chinese art. Five science museums opened in Shanghai between 1999 and 2001, including the Science and Technology Museum. Classical gardens such as Shanghai's Yuyuan Garden, once the province of the country's elite, are now public.

Holidays

Spring Festival is the most important holiday in the People's Republic of China, coinciding with the traditional Chinese lunar New Year in late January or early February. Spring Festival celebrations may last for ten days or more.

Other major state holidays are International Labor Day, beginning May 1, and often running for a full week, and National Day (October 1), which usually runs for ten days from Friday to Sunday. Minor holidays include Buddha's Birthday (May 16), and recognition of Western holidays such as New Year's Day and Christmas.

Youth Culture

Generally, the youth of China are characterized as a generation struggling to find their identity. Parental obsession with academic achievement has typically driven young urban Chinese to overachieve and focus singularly on their education. Often, colleges undervalue volunteer work or other extracurricular activities, which results in low participation in these activities. In addition, urban youth, in particular, do not usually hold jobs. The importance of religion has declined among younger generations, and personal identity is more commonly defined by consumer brands and technology.

Cell phones and the Internet have become very important to Chinese youth, and form the basis of their connections to one another. In fact, Chinese youth have been generally quick to adopt text messaging and instant messaging as common forms of communication. Often, the understanding of or access to technology serves as a social status indicator among youth. This dependence upon technology has been largely criticized by older generations for the country's rising levels of early teen sex and recent cases of teen homicides and suicides among Chinese youth.

SOCIETY

Transportation

Bicycles and motorbikes are extremely popular and are the predominant mode of transportation in urban China, second only to walking. In 2013, it was estimated that approximately 200 million electric bicycles were being used in China. The average Chinese citizen uses a bicycle to get to work, shopping, and other activities. The country's economic growth has increased the number of Chinese citizens who are able to afford automobiles and sales have increased greatly in recent years. China's Ministry of Commerce has estimated that China is now home to the world's largest car market.

Transportation Infrastructure

Rail is a widely used mode of transportation in China, and the country has the world's third largest rail network. Railways connect every part of the country and extend into Tibet and bordering countries. The total amount of track as of 2014 was 191,270 kilometers (118,849 miles).

China also has around 500 airports and more than 2,000 ports. Most major cities in China either have operating subway systems or are in the process of building them. In 2015, Beijing alone had plans for three new subway projects with a price tag of $7 billion each.

The paved road and expressway system in China covers more than 84,946 kilometers (52,782 miles), making China's system of highways second only to the United States (U.S.) in size. This has led to a rapid increase in automobile use.

Media & Communications

State agencies own and control all media in China, including the Internet. There are over 2,000 newspapers in China and over 2,000 television stations. Although state-run and bound by restrictions—for example, criticism of the communist party is forbidden—media content is becoming more and more diverse. This diversity arose because the government is no longer paying subsidies to these media outlets. Instead, they are expected to pay most of the costs from advertising revenue, which necessitates competition for viewers and produces more interesting and diverse programming.

China has more Internet users than any other country in the world: over 600 million. China's censorship of the Internet is extremely sophisticated, and one estimate puts the number of blocked websites at 3,000. These blocked sites include the BBC, Facebook, Twitter, and Google (replaced with Google China). However, absolute control over Internet content has proven difficult, and controversial domestic and international stories sometimes slip through censors.

China also has the highest number of mobile phone users: over 1.3 billion. Even migrant workers carry cell phones, which are usually obtained from South Korea. Cell phone users tend to be very serious about their phones and are sharply divided by generation. In China, as in most Asian countries, users buy cards with minutes to add to their phones, rather than committing to a long-term cell phone usage plan.

Films in China must be deemed suitable for viewing by all ages in order to be screened. Oftentimes, scenes are removed from foreign films before they are shown and the government limits the amount of time foreign films are shown in theaters.

SOCIAL DEVELOPMENT

Standard of Living

In 2014, China was ranked 91 out of 187 countries on the United Nations Human Development Index. It was one of the most dramatically improved of ranked countries, although the rural population often lives at near-subsistence levels.

Water Consumption

Water pollution is severe due to erosion and industrialization. Approximately 200 million Chinese drink water that is below safe bacteria levels and, approximately 980 million drink water that is partially polluted. Water shortages are frequent; due to dams, irrigation, silt, and reservoirs, the Yellow River runs dry for more than 1,000 kilometers (600 miles) from its former mouth on the northeastern coast.

The government announced 172 major water conservation projects by 2020. Issues related to water supply and consumption are overseen by the Water Resources Ministry. Drought has also been a continuing problem in parts of China.

Education

During the 1960s, China's communist government closed most schools. In the 1980s, new leader Deng Xiaoping made education a much greater priority. The 1986 "Compulsory Education Law of the PRC" mandates primary education (generally six years) for all children. Three years of junior secondary schooling is also standard in urban areas. Today, an estimated 90 percent of all children complete primary school, and 73 percent complete junior secondary education.

In 2004, China had 17 million students enrolled in more than 2,000 colleges and advanced vocational schools, triple the number from 1999. Students receive strong encouragement to study science and engineering. In contrast to shrinking enrollments in the United States, China graduated 325,000 engineering students in 2004, as opposed to 65,000 in the U.S. The average literacy rate in China is high, at 96 percent (98 percent among men and 94.5 percent among women) as of 2015.

Hong Kong's educational system earns attention apart from the rest of China because it is loosely based on the English model inherited from 19th-century colonizers. Most children attend kindergarten for up to three years. Most primary schools teach in Chinese and teach English as a second language. The many international schools in Hong Kong teach in other languages with different curricula. Primary and secondary education in the public schools is free.

Under the Secondary Schools Allocation System, each finishing primary school student is directed to a particular "band" for secondary school, based on the student's performance in primary school and the primary school's performance within the Hong Kong system.

Students must attend five years of secondary school: three years of general education and two years of specialized studies. Secondary school grade levels are called "forms." After completing form five, students take the Hong Kong Certificate of Education Examination in order to be promoted to form six (lower six). Those who score satisfactorily on the Hong Kong Advanced Level Examinations the following year attend upper six (form seven).

Those students who have completed upper six in secondary schools are rated by examina-

tion performances and other factors for admission to one of Hong Kong's numerous colleges and universities. The most prominent of these are the University of Hong Kong, the Chinese University of Hong Kong, and the Hong Kong University of Science and Technology.

Women's Rights

The promise of equality and equal rights for women first surfaced in China in 1949. That is when Mao's revolution put an end to the ancient practice of foot binding and created marriage laws that made men and women equal. These changes represented a drastic shift from the traditions of ancient China, where women were largely perceived as property owned by men. While the status of women has risen steadily, most of the effects are felt only in the more educated and urban areas of the country.

In urban China, women are claiming new status and power, especially in the workplace. For example, women in cities earn an average of over 40 percent of their household's income. Girls in China are earning higher grades than their male counterparts do, and more women are now attending college. In rural China, however, poor families are more apt to maintain old traditions, such as choosing husbands and arranging marriages for their daughters. Women in rural China do not work outside of the home, nor do they initiate divorce, although Chinese law gives them that right. Furthermore, higher education among women in rural China is alarmingly low.

Unfortunately, discrimination and violence against women remain common problems in China. Public awareness of domestic violence is low, and there are many rural areas that have no access to women's services. Sons are still preferred over daughters, and this has led to selective-sex abortions and higher rates of female infant mortality. More importantly, China's one-child policy has caused a gender imbalance in the country. Abusive enforcement measures such as forced abortions and sterilizations have been documented for years.

To combat the gender imbalance, the Chinese government has recently launched a campaign entitled "Care for Girls." The campaign focuses on raising awareness of the societal stereotypes surrounding girls and women, educating the public on their equal value. This advocacy program was created mainly for parents in rural areas in order to change cultural attitudes toward having girls. In 2004, economic support was offered to girl-only families who live in these rural areas.

Health Care

Health care in China is administered through village, township, and county hospitals. Village doctors must finish junior secondary school and complete three to six months of training. Township doctors must complete primary and secondary education and three years of medical school. County hospital physicians are the most capable, typically completing four to five years of medical school.

Insurance and state-assisted health care financing has evolved rapidly as the state struggles to provide care for all citizens. In 2004, it was estimated that 38 percent of the population ignored illness or injury due to the cost of professional medical treatment. In 2008, the government made a commitment to provide affordable health care for all its citizens by 2020 and in 2015, the government said it had reached 95 percent of its goal.

China's birth rate declined dramatically after 1980 due to government intervention that encouraged contraception, late marriage, and a "one couple, one child" policy. Due to a number of factors, such as an aging population and a growing gender ratio imbalance, it is reported that this policy changed in late 2015 to allow for two children per couple. In 2015, the birth rate was roughly 2.5 births per 1,000 people. The infant mortality rate was 12 deaths per 1,000 live births in 2015. The average life expectancy was seventy-five years; seventy-seven years among women and seventy-three years among men (2015 estimate).

GOVERNMENT

Structure

China's Chinese Communist Party (CCP) came to power in 1949 under Mao Zedong. It emphasized centralized power, state-owned industry, and communal farms. Modern leadership has moved toward Western-style business practices, but China's constitution, last updated in 2004, is largely ceremonial in light of continued tight control over freedom of speech, political protest, and interpretation of law.

The Premier leads the powerful State Council, and the General Secretary heads the Communist Party. Elected members of the National People's Congress appoint State Council members. All 2,987 elected members of the 2033 congress were first approved by the CCP.

Protest over political restrictions flared in 1989, led by students in Beijing's Tiananmen Square. After about two months, government tanks and troops put a forceful end to the demonstrations. China's government has also used violence to silence ethnic unrest, the cases of Tibetan and Uighur independence and autonomy being the most recent.

Regional government is divided into twenty-two provinces, five autonomous regions, the municipalities of Beijing, Shanghai, Tianjin, and Chongqing, and the special administrative regions of Hong Kong and Macau.

Political Parties

The Communist Party of China (CPC) is the dominant political force throughout China, and the country is essentially a single-party state. All other minority parties that exist in the country do so at the approval and direction of the CPC. Among these are the Revolutionary Committee of the Kuomintang, the China Democratic League, and the China Zhi Gong.

Although parties opposing the communist system of government are not publicly banned, their message is censored and their activists are repressed—sometimes by imprisonment. These parties include the Chinese Democracy and

Justice Party, the China Democracy Party, the Party for Freedom and Democracy in China, and the Human Rights Party.

Local Government

China's twenty-two provinces (Taiwan is considered a 23rd province by China) are subdivided into districts, counties, and cities. At the local level, authority resides with local people's councils. Often, in areas far from urban centers, local government operates via more traditional and cultural systems of organization. Nonetheless, the central party retains dominant control. China's urban centers hold elections, but they are strictly supervised by the government.

Judicial System

China's judicial system is divided into local courts, special courts, and supreme courts. The Supreme People's Court in Beijing overseas all decisions made by subordinate courts. Additionally, Courts of Special Jurisdiction include the Military Court of China, the Railway Transport Court of China, and the Maritime Court of China.

Local courts have jurisdiction over criminal and civil matters. Local courts are divided into three levels: High People's Courts, the Intermediate People's Courts, and the Primary People's Courts.

Critics of China's judicial system claim that the country's courts have to work in a political environment that demands allegiance to the communist government. However, academics who specialize in Chinese law also state that the courts are becoming more responsive to the people. An outline for reform of the court system was released in 2014 with the government vowing to make it more independent and professional.

Taxation

The Ministry of Finance establishes tax policies. The State Administration of Taxation oversees tax collection in China. Taxes make up the largest source of revenue for the Chinese government, and a wide variety of corporate and individual taxes exist in the country. Among these are the following: individual income tax, business tax,

city maintenance and construction tax, and house property tax. Vehicle taxes and agricultural taxes are also collected.

Taxes are collected for both local and central government use. In addition, shared taxes are collected. In 2012, the Chinese government collected an estimated $1.9 trillion (USD) in tax revenue.

Armed Forces

Chinese's armed forces operate under a single moniker, that of the People's Liberation Army (PLA). The army consists of the PLA Ground Force, the PLA Navy, and the PLA Air Force, as well as the Second Artillery Corps. The chair of the Central Military Commission of the Communist Party commands the PLA. Since 1990, individuals who held this post have held the post of general secretary of the Communist Party of China, who also serves as president of the People's Republic of China.

Military service in China is compulsory. The PLA represents the world's largest military force, consisting of some 2.3 million active members. In 2009, China's military reserves were estimated at 429 million.

Foreign Policy

As a founding member of the United Nations (UN), China works actively to maintain diplomatic relationships with most of the major countries in the world (the PRC government in Beijing assumed China's UN seat in 1971 after the Republic of China was expelled). In addition, China has a permanent seat on the United Nations Security Council (UNSC). However, in order to establish diplomatic relationships with a country, China has a requirement: the country must acknowledge China's claim to Taiwan and sever official ties with Taiwan's government. This particular foreign policy has been the source of frequent tension between China and other countries.

In recent history, China has had some conflicts with foreign countries, including the United States during the U.S.-China spy plane incident in 2001 and Japan over the country's refusal to acknowledge atrocities committed during World War II. In addition, the European Union (UN) has maintained an arms embargo on China following the Chinese government's response to the Tiananmen Square protests of 1989, in which many civilians were killed or injured.

In 2004, China proposed a new East Asian Summit (EAS) framework that pointedly excludes the U.S.. This forum was created to deal with regional security issues, and includes the Association of Southeast Asian Nations (ASEAN), as well as India, Australia and New Zealand. In 2011, the sixth EAS expanded to include the U.S. and Russia. China also maintains membership in numerous international organizations, many of which are regional and economic in nature, such as the Asian Development Bank (ADB) and the Asia-Pacific Economic Cooperation (APEC). China is also a member of the World Health Organization (WHO) and the World Trade Organization (WTO). China's trade influence has also increased in recent years; for example, as of 2011, it is the second largest trading partner to Africa behind the U.S. Though African leaders have praised China for investing in the continent's infrastructure, human rights and pro-democracy advocates have remained skeptical about the country's increasing influence, and its impact on ordinary African citizens.

China, along with Russia, has the distinction of bordering the most countries in the world. In the past, the PRC has had a number of international territorial disputes, including over islands in the East and South China Seas, and disputed borders with India, North Korea, and Tajikistan. A long-standing dispute with Russia ended when Russia transferred Yinlong Island and one-half of Heixiazi to China. Since the 1990s, however, it is believed that the PRC has maintained a policy of quiet diplomacy with its neighbors in order to ease concerns over China's growing military numbers and nuclear capabilities.

Tibet and Taiwan are the most immediate foreign issues confronting China. Tibet is under the administration of the PRC and is identified as an autonomous province. However, unlike other autonomous regions such as Hong Kong, Tibet

has a vast majority of inhabitants who are of one ethnicity. Because of this, there is disagreement as to how autonomous Tibet actually is. Human rights organizations regularly accuse China of oppressing and persecuting the local population. The Tibetan Government in Exile, headed by the Dalai Lama, considers Tibet to be a distinct sovereign nation, and accuses China of illegitimate military occupation. However, that the Dalai Lama has stated that he would accept an autonomous status similar to Hong Kong.

Taiwan, or the Republic of China (ROP), is an island in East Asia currently claimed by the PRC. China has never actually controlled Taiwan or any of its territories. However, the PRC argues that it ruled Taiwan for four years, from 1945 to 1949, and claims it to be an illegitimate government. The political environment between the two countries is tense due to the possibility of military conflict in the event of actions taken by either country towards reunification or independence. (The PRC has established military outposts on the Fujian coast to use force to ensure reunification.) The U.S. has intervened by providing the ROP with military arms and supporting a quid pro quo basis between both Chinese states, further heightening tensions in an already uneasy relationship between China and the U.S.

Hong Kong is a Special Administrative Region (SAR) of the People's Republic of China. Composed of peninsular territories and islands on the South China seacoast of China, Hong Kong is a vibrant metropolis in its own right. Though relatively small, Hong Kong boasts one of the world's most important business centers, and plays a pivotal role in business relations between Asia and the West.

In 1997, Britain returned sovereignty of Hong Kong to the Chinese government. Under an innovative "one country, two systems" approach, China has permitted Hong Kong to keep its capitalist economic system and local autonomy while taking control of its international affairs and national defense.

Like Hong Kong, Macau is not an independent nation, but a Special Administrative Region of China. Once a Portuguese territory, Macau is a tiny set of two islands (Taipa and Coloane), and one peninsula (Macau), all interconnected by bridges. Lying on the coast of China's Canton Province, Macau is about 60 kilometers (37 miles) west of Hong Kong. In 1999, Portugal transferred possession of the tiny islands to the Chinese government after more than 400 years of Portuguese rule.

Dependencies

The political status of the island of Taiwan as the Republic of China (ROC) remains a topic of heated political and cultural debate in China. The Kuomintang of China (KMT), which yields significant political influence in Taiwan, is a national party that supports continued unification of the island with China; they assumed office in Taiwan in 2009. However, the Democratic Progressive Party, which is proponent of an independent Taiwan, also has a significant presence on the island.

Human Rights Profile

The 2015 report for China by Human Rights Watch stated that while the country had undertaken positive steps in certain areas, such as abolishing the arbitrary detention system known as Re-education through Labor (RTL), and making social reforms for migrants and persons with disabilities, open hostility towards human rights activists still is rampant.

International human rights law insists that states respect civil and political rights, and promote an individual's economic, social, and cultural rights. The United Nations Universal Declaration on Human Rights is recognized as the standard for international human rights. Its authors sought the counsel of the world's great thinkers, philosophers, and religious leaders, and were careful to create a document that reflects the core values shared by every world culture. (To read this document or view the articles relating to cultural human rights, visit http://www.un.org/en/documents/udhr/.)

China's constitution is written in language that declares that all citizens are declared equal before the law regardless of race, religion, or gender, as stated in Article 2 of the UDHR. The constitution, as it is written, also supports the basic human rights of freedom of speech and press. However, China's constitution also contains broad language that states citizens must defend the "security, honor, and interests of the motherland." This single statement allows the Chinese government to limit or restrict these human rights if they deem the activities of Chinese citizens as endangering or threatening the country.

For these reasons, China is ranked 175th out of 180 countries in the Reporters Without Borders 2014 index of press freedom. The rights to freedom of speech and expression in China, as outlined in Article 19 of the UDHR, are subject to autocratic, unwarranted restrictions, censorship, and are bound by laws regarding media regulations that are full of vague language. These laws allow authorities to harass and imprison journalists by claiming their stories endanger the country by revealing classified state information.

The two main censoring agencies that review and enforce these laws are the General Administration of Press and Publication (GAPP) and the State Administration of Radio, Film, and Television (SARFT). These agencies oversee information coming into, out of, and within China. The GAPP, which issues licenses, has the authority to shut down publishers and publications. SARFT has authority over television, film, radio and the Internet. The Communist Party's Central Propaganda Department (CPD), whose job it is to make sure that information agrees with and promotes the communist party doctrine, oversees both the GAPP and SARFT. The CPD instructs media outlets as to what content they are allowed to cover, and what content they are restricted from broadcasting—most notably, protests over issues surrounding Tibet and Taiwan.

Corruption and abuse of power by local officials within the legal system is common. In general, it is very difficult for Chinese commoners to obtain justice over issues involving the government, including forced evictions, corruption, wages, or illegal land seizures. Often, lawyers defending human rights cases have found themselves disbarred or unable to get their yearly licenses renewed. In addition, the rights of defendants are almost non-existent. For example, it is legal in China to detain "minor offenders" for up to four years without trial. There is also evidence that pretrial torture remains prevalent.

Article 18 of the UDHR outlines freedom of religion. The Chinese constitution recognizes the right to this freedom. However, it limits worship to churches, temples, mosques, and monasteries that are controlled by the government. These religious institutions must also be registered, the process of which typically takes an enormous amount of time and effort. Once registered, the religious organization must endure ongoing scrutiny of publications, personnel, financial records and membership lists. In addition, the government must first approve any group activities or outings of the religious organization.

The right to assemble, outlined in Article 20, is linked to freedom of speech in the Chinese constitution. However, like freedom of speech, the right is not supported in reality. Social activists, critics and protestors often have their movements restricted, or are detained under unofficial house arrest. Large-scale protests were reported in almost all of China's provinces in 2007, and several of these demonstrations involved tens of thousands of people. These protests were not disclosed to the general public or shown in Chinese media.

China's human rights record was brought to the forefront when Beijing served as the host for the 2008 Summer Olympics. Although China received international praise for its organization of the Olympic Games, the country was also routinely criticized for its handling of dissidents and human rights activists before, during, and after the Olympics. In particular, many protestors and activists were simply rounded up and detained in labor camps or deported. In addition, freedom of the press during Olympic coverage was often curtailed in China, most notably access to the Internet by foreign journalists. In addition, the Olympics also brought into question the rigorous training and expectations imposed upon China's athletes. In 2014, Beijing won the bid to host the 2022 Winter Olympics.

Migration

A significant number of Chinese people are moving from the country's rural regions to urban centers in search of employment, education, and an improved standard of living. By 2014, 274 million migrant workers arrived in China's cities. Migrant workers have helped fuel the engine of China's economy, which has seen unprecedented growth in recent years.

ECONOMY

Overview of the Economy

China's is an economy on the move. In late 1978, the Chinese government began embracing a more market-oriented economic system. Since that time, the country's gross domestic product (GDP) has quadrupled.

In 2004, China overtook the U.S. as the world's largest consumer, besting the U.S. in consumption related to energy, food, industrial commodities such as steel, and consumer products such as cell phones and televisions. In 2010 China became the world's largest exporter and in 2014 surpassed the U.S. as the having the largest economy in the world, even though in per capita terms it remains below the world average.

In 2014, China's GDP was estimated at just over $10 trillion (USD). The per capita GDP was $12,900 (USD).

Industry

China's GDP is led by industry and services. Services account for more than 48 percent of China's GDP, followed by industry at 42 percent and agriculture at 9 percent. China is a manufacturing giant, accomplished not only in traditional skills such as textiles and metalworking, but also in complex engineering and assembly work supporting the automotive and aviation industries. Development of industry has been concentrated along the coast, from Hong Kong up to Shanghai.

China joined the World Trade Organization (WTO) in late 2001, helping to increase its exports by 15 percent. Most exports go to the U.S. (17 percent) and Japan (6 percent). In 2010, China became the world's largest exporter, and in 2014, it shipped goods valued at $2.3 trillion (USD). Top exports include heavy equipment, apparel, iron and steel, furniture, medical equipment, footwear and toys.

Labor

China's greatest resource lies in its people. Whereas countries that are more modern can easily outspend China in high technology, Chinese manufacturers can rely on labor rates that are one-fifth to one-tenth that of developed nations, thanks to the country's enormous population.

Energy/Power/Natural Resources

China is the world's leading coal producer. Most of the country's electric plants are coal-fired. Uranium is mined for use in China's nuclear power plants. The country's petroleum reserves kept up with demand until 1993, when industrial growth required imported oil.

Other important mineral deposits include graphite, iron ore, bauxite, manganese, molybdenum, mercury, and phosphates.

According to (World Health Organization) WHO standards, China has seven out of the ten most polluted cities in the world. The use of coal is slowing down in China as a broader use of hydroelectric power, solar and wind is being encouraged. Beijing plans to close all major coal power plants in the city in order to cut pollution. Cities in northern coal mining areas including Linfen, Yangquan, and Datong were the most polluted.

Fishing

Fish farms are common, often stocked with carp, and shellfish are an important catch along the coast.

Forestry

China's forests and grasslands have been dramatically reduced by farming and a voracious appetite for building materials. However, many remote, nearly inaccessible forested areas have helped protect a wide range of plant and animal diversity.

Mining/Metals

Important mineral deposits include graphite, iron ore, bauxite, manganese, molybdenum, mercury, and phosphates.

Agriculture

Roughly one-third of the country's labor force is engaged in agriculture. Rice is China's major crop, grown mainly in the south, followed by wheat in the northern plain regions. Other major crops include corn, soybeans, cotton, barley, potatoes, peanuts, apples, oranges, and tangerines. The country remains the world's top producer of green teas.

Animal Husbandry

The raising of livestock and poultry in China remains the smallest part of an otherwise massive agricultural economy. The country is the leading producer of swine, which is the largest livestock segment of the economy. Pork is a major Chinese export; the country produced over 720 million in 2014. Approximately 185 million sheep were raised in China in 2013. They are used as livestock and for milk and dairy production. China also leads the world in honey and silk production.

Tourism

The estimated number of visitors to China topped 100 million for the first time in 2004, accounting for more than $25 billion (USD) in revenue. The total represented a 20 percent increase over 2003, when tourism was dampened by fears over the SARS virus. The number of international tourists declined slightly overall from 2007 through 2014 due to a number of factors. Most tourists come from China's major trade partners, along with Russia and surrounding countries such the Philippines, Malaysia, and Singapore. Domestic tourism has gained momentum due to the improvement in Chinese living standards.

Beijing is the top destination due to the Forbidden City, Summer Palace, Beijing Zoo, and its many hotels and restaurants. Just over 70 kilometers (40 miles) to the northwest, at Badaling, stands the Great Wall of China. Often referred to as one of the Seven Wonders of the World, it measures 6,000 kilometers (4,000 miles) long and is an average 8 meters (25 feet) high. Also near Beijing are the Ming Tombs, holding the remains of thirteen Chinese emperors.

Another major tourist attraction, only discovered in 1974, is the 2,200–year-old Tomb of the Terracotta Warriors in Xi'an. These 7,000 life-size clay soldiers, complete with chariots, horses and weapons, were built to protect the burial site of Emperor Qin Shi Huang, a task assumed to be the life's work of approximately 700,000 laborers.

April Sanders, John Pearson, Micah L. Issit, Amy Witherbee

DO YOU KNOW?

- The word "China" in English is believed to derive from the name "Qin." In the late third century BCE, the Qin Dynasty united many of China's ancient regional powers under the first Chinese empire and built the Great Wall of China.

- In Mandarin Chinese, China is called Zhongguo, which means "Middle Kingdom."

- Great Chinese inventions include the compass, gunpowder, movable type printing, and paper-making.

- Hong Kong's Central-Mid-Levels Escalator and Walkway System is the world's longest covered escalator system, with three moving walkways and twenty elevated walkways that stretch 800 meters (2,625feet) long.

- The name Macau is said to be short for Amagoa or A-Ma-Gao ("Bay of A-Ma" in Cantonese.) A-Ma or Ling-Ma is the name of a Chinese goddess popular with fishers and sailors.

- The Chinese writing system is roughly 4,000 years old. China is one of the World's only civilizations to develop a written language independent of a spoken language.

- Wushu, one of China's indigenous sports, is often known as kung fu in the United States and Europe. Beijing holds an international competition for wushu athletes from around the world, and the Beijing Wushu Association has petitioned the International Olympic Committee to designate wushu as an official sport in the Olympic Games.

Bibliography

Davis, Edward. *Encyclopedia of Contemporary Chinese Culture*. New York: Routledge, 2008.

Flower, Kathy. *China - Culture Smart: a quick guide to customs and etiquette* (Culture Smart). London: Kuperard, 2006.

Hollihan, Sheila. *Art and Architecture of China: The History and Culture of China*. Broomall PA: Mason Crest Publishers, 2005.

Keay, John. *China: A History*. New York: Basic Books, 2011.

Morton, Scott and Charlton Lewis. *China: Its History and Culture* (4th Edition). New York: McGraw-Hill, 2004.

Sang, Ye. *China Candid: The People on the People's Republic*. Berkeley: University of California Press, 2006.

Starr, John Bryan. *Understanding China: A Guide to China's Economy, History, and Political Culture*. New York: Hill & Wang, 2010.

Wenzhong, Hu and Cornelius Lee. *China A to Z: Everything You Need to Know to Understand Chinese Customs and Culture*. New York: Penguin Group, 2007.

Yamashita, Michael and William Lindesay. *The Great Wall: From Beginning to End*. New York: Sterling, 2007.

Works Cited

Basulto, Dominic. "China's Big Bet on Infrastructure Shows a Commitment to Innovation." *Washington Post*. The Washington Post, 28 May 2015. Web. 10 Nov. 2015.

"The Best Ways To Go To China and Travel Around." *ChinaHighlights*. Web. 10 Nov. 2015. http://www.chinahighlights.com/travelguide/transportation.

Brink, Susan. "What China Can Teach The World About Successful Health Care." *NPR*. NPR, 3 Apr. 2015. Web. 10 Nov. 2015. http://www.npr.org/sections/goatsandsoda/2015/04/03/397158218/what-china-can-teach-the-world-about-successful-health-care.

"China Cuisine." *ChinaTour*. Web. www.chinatour.com/cuisine/cuisine.htm.

"China Tourism." *: Statistics and Data*. Web. 10 Nov. 2015. http://www.travelchinaguide.com/tourism/.

"Chinese Etiquette." *, Manners, Proprieties and Customs Tips*. Web. 10 Nov. 2015. http://www.travelchinaguide.com/essential/etiquette.htm.

Fox, Travis. "Redefining China's Family." *Washington Post*. The Washington Post, 12 June 2015. Web. 10 Nov. 2015.

"Housing in China." *-ABC Central West NSW*. Web. 10 Nov. 2015. http://www.abc.net.au/local/stories/2008/07/18/2287784.htm.

Krause-Jackson, Flavia20. "China Has Even More Megacities Than You Thought." *Bloomberg.com*. Bloomberg, 20 Apr. 2015. Web. 10 Nov. 2015.

Marquand, Robert. "Love and Money Reshape Family in China." *The Christian Science Monitor*. The Christian Science Monitor. Web. 10 Nov. 2015.

#NotTrending Stashing Packages, Paying Indonesia's Poor. "China." *PBS*. PBS. Web. 10 Nov. 2015. http://www.pbs.org/newshour/bb/asia/china/.

"Supporting Women's Rights in China." *Supporting Women's Rights in China*. Web. 10 Nov. 2015. http://www.hrichina.org/en/supporting-womens-rights-china.

"UNESCO World Heritage Centre." *UNESCO World Heritage Centre*. United Nations. Web. 10 Nov. 2015.

"World Report 2015: China." *Human Rights Watch*. 09 Jan. 2015. Web. 10 Nov. 2015.

Xu, Beina. "Media Censorship in China." *Council on Foreign Relations*. Council on Foreign Relations, 7 Apr. 2015. Web. 10 Nov. 2015.

Zimmermann, By Kim Ann. "Chinese Culture: Customs & Traditions of China." *LiveScience*. TechMedia Network, 20 Jan. 2015. Web. 10 Nov. 2015.

JAPAN

Introduction

Japan is a mountainous island nation in East Asia. It is an archipelago made up of thousands of islands, although the Home Islands (or main islands) of Hokkaido, Honshu (mainland Japan), Shikoku, and Kyushu comprise nearly all of the country's total land area.

Japan's closest neighbors are South Korea and North Korea to the west and a strip of Russia to the northwest, north of which sits China. The major bodies of water surrounding Japan are the Sea of Japan, which separates it from the Korean Peninsula, the North Pacific Ocean to the east, and the Philippine Sea and the East China Sea to the west.

Since its recovery following the Second World War, a conflict that ended with the atom bombing of Hiroshima and Nagasaki, Japan remains one of the world's leading economic and cultural powers, setting a global standard for technology and the arts. From the earliest Buddhist sculptures and temples to traditional paper arts, 21st-century robotics, and the modern visual era of anime and manga popular culture, Japanese arts have remained among the world's most unique examples in their respective styles.

The Fukushima Daiichi nuclear disaster, precipitated by Tōhoku earthquake and tsunami on March 11, 2011, had a significant deleterious impact on the country's economy (and on the international perception of nuclear generation as a viable power source). Classified as a Level 7, or a "major accident," on the International Nuclear Event Scale used by the Atomic Energy Agency, Fukushima is one of the most devastating nuclear-reactor disasters in history, second only to Chernobyl in 1986. The disaster—that is, both the tsunami and the nuclear meltdown—had a profound effect on the national consciousness in Japan.

GENERAL INFORMATION

Official Language: Japanese
Population: 126,919,659 (2015 estimate)
Currency: Japanese yen

Coins: One hundred sen equal one yen. Coins are issued in denominations of 1, 5, 10, 50, 100, and 500 yen. Sen and rin coins were taken out of circulation in 1953.
Land Area: 364,485 square kilometers (140,728 square miles)
Water Area: 13,430 square kilometers (5,185 square miles)
National Anthem: "Kimigayo" ("His Imperial Majesty's Reign")
Capital: Tokyo

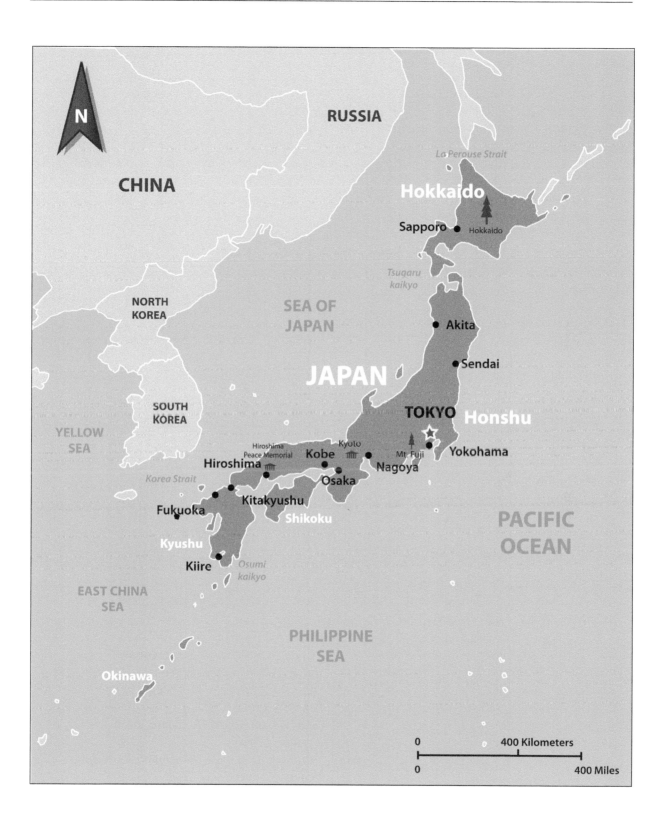

Principal Metropolitan Areas by Population (2015):

- Tokyo (also, Tōkyō) (38,001,000)
- Ōsaka-Kōbe (20,238,000)
- Nagoya (9,406,000)
- Kitakyushu-Fukuoka (5,510,000)
- Yokohama (3,710,008)
- Sapporo (2,571,000)
- Kyōto (1,474,000)
- Kawasaki (1,437,266)
- Saitama (1,251,549)

Time Zone: GMT +9

Flag Description: The Japanese flag features a red disk (symbolizing the sun) centered on a white flag. The flag is officially called Nisshōki ("sun-mark flag"), but is more commonly referred to as the Hinomaru, or the ("circle of the sun").

Population

The population of Japan is overwhelmingly (98.5 percent) of Japanese ethnicity. The minority populations of Japan consist of Koreans (0.5 percent); Chinese (0.4 percent); and others (0.6 percent), including Western Europeans, Canadians, Americans, and Filipinos. Many Japanese are considered Yamato, the dominant ethnic group in Japan. The Yamato, who hail from the mainland, distinguish themselves from island ethnic groups, such as the Ryukyuan from the Okinawa Prefecture; the Ainu and Oroks from the island of Hokkaido; and the Nivkh, who inhabit the island of Sakhalin, once jointly ruled by Japan and Russia through the 1855 Treaty of Shimoda. In the 1990s, an estimated 230,000 Brazilians of Japanese descent migrated to Japan for work opportunities. By 2004, some of these Brazilian nationals returned; however, many still remain in Japan and have raised families there.

The urban areas (which comprised 93.5 percent of Japan's population in 2015) can be very dense and overpopulated. In 2015, Japan population growth rate is in the negative, at –0.16 percent. Estimates show a continuing decline in the Japanese population through 2050; in 2010, the government forecasted a 25 percent decline, to 95.2 million, by 2050.

The greater Tokyo metropolitan area has over 38 million residents, 8.5 million of which live in the twenty-three special wards. Immigrants make up approximately 1.5 percent of Japan's population. Of these, about 32 percent are from North or South Korea, and another 24 percent are ethnic Chinese. Taken as a whole, Japan is one of the world's most ethnically homogenous countries. Tokyo contains the majority of the country's foreign residents.

Languages

The vast majority of Japanese speak standard Japanese or one of its dialects. Japan's other indigenous languages include Ainu and Ryukyuan languages. Ainu is nearly extinct, although many Ainu people in Hokkaido are either fluent or partial speakers. The Ryukyua languages include Okinawan and other varieties that are unique to the Southwest Islands. Common second languages spoken among Japanese are English and Korean.

Native People & Ethnic Groups

The Ainu of Hokkaido are Japan's indigenous people. Their population may be as high as 25,000, and as many as 1 million Japanese may have some Ainu heritage. Many Ainu have been assimilated into Japanese culture.

Historically, the Japanese have dominated Ainu, but some efforts have been underway to publicize their struggles, particularly by the Ainu-controlled Hokkaido Utari Association. Since their official recognition by the Japanese government in the 1990s, the Ainu have been granted some land rights and cultural protection.

In the southwestern islands, the Ryukyuans populate Okinawa and other surrounding islands. Ryukyuan culture contains strong influences from its neighbors, Taiwan, Korea, and China, even though the Japanese government enacted a number of efforts to subvert Ryukyuan culture in the early and mid-20th century. Okinawans or Ryukyuans have sought recognition of their status as an indigenous or minority people from the Japanese government, but have met with resistance. The Ryukyuans have also fought for removal of the American air base on Okinawa, the largest American air base in Asia, to no avail.

Religions

Unlike in many Western nations, religion is not a central focus of most people's lives in Japan. Commonly, Japanese are believers in either (or both) Shintoism (79.2 percent) and Buddhism (66.8 percent). A small minority, approximately 1.5 percent, practice Christianity.

Climate

Japan is rainy and humid, with pronounced seasonal changes throughout the year. From north to south, Japan is climatically diverse, with four distinct regions. Hokkaido is subarctic, while the region along the Pacific Ocean is hot with seasonal winds from the Pacific. The western side, which faces the Sea of Japan, is rainy and snowy, while the southwestern region around Okinawa is subtropical. There are three rainy seasons, the first in winter, with large snowfall, another between May and July, and still another between August and October. Additionally, late summer brings typhoon season.

Because of its topographical diversity, the average temperatures and precipitation across Japan vary greatly from region to region. In Sapporo, on Hokkaido (in the north), the average annual temperature is 8.9° Celsius (48° Fahrenheit), with around 300 days of precipitation per year. In Tokyo, in the Kanto region of Honshu, the average temperature is 16.3° Celsius (61.34° Fahrenheit).

In Fukuoka, on Kyushu, the average temperature is 7° Celsius (46° Fahrenheit) with 286 days of precipitation per year. At Naha, a city on the island of Okinawa, the average temperature is 22° Celsius (72° Fahrenheit), and the rainy season may last from May through November.

ENVIRONMENT & GEOGRAPHY

Topography

Japan's location off the Asian mainland has served its political and social interests for centuries and contributed greatly to its relative isolation until its historic opening to the West in 1868. Japan's closest neighbors are South Korea and North Korea to the west and a strip of Russia to the northwest, north of which sits China.

Its de-facto capital, Tokyo, is located in the Kanto Plain on Honshu, the largest of Japan's islands. The city is situated in the geographic center of the Japanese archipelago. The central area of the city consists of twenty-three special wards.

Aside from the four main islands of Hokkaido, Honshu, Shikoku, and Kyushu, there are over 6,000 smaller Japanese islands, including the Ryukyu Islands, the Kuril Islands (disputed first with the Soviet Union and then modern-day Russia), and the Izu Islands. The main islands themselves are divided into east and west by a central mountainous portion that runs the length of the islands. (Mountains cover 75 percent of the country.)

Most of Japan's major cities are situated in the flatter areas, which make up only a small percentage of the country. The highest point in Japan is at Mount Fuji, in the Tokai district of Honshu; its peak rises to a height of 3,776 meters (12,387 feet).

Because of its position at the intersection of four tectonic plates, Japan is vulnerable to disastrous earthquakes and volcanoes. The country contains 108 active volcanoes, and experiences 1,500 seismic occurrences per year. The most recent devastating seismic incident, considered an undersea megathrust earthquake, was the March 2011 Tōhoku earthquake and tsunami, which initiated the Fukushima Daiichi nuclear disaster. An estimated 15,893 people died from the earthquake/tsunami alone, while the seismic activity is reported to have moved the main island of Japan 2.4 meters (8 feet) east and shifted the earth's axis between 10 and 25 centimeters (4 inches and 10 inches).

Plants & Animals

Approximately 67 percent of Japan is forested. Common plants found in Japan include the sakura with its cherry blossoms (a national symbol), bonsai, cedar, maple and pine trees, and bamboo. Lotus, lilies, hydrangeas, azaleas, peonies, and wisteria are also common.

Japan boasts a diverse animal population, with 153 species of mammals. Three species—the iriomote cat, tshushima leopard cat, and the gloomy tube-nosed bat—are critically endangered. Twenty-two are endangered, including the Japanese macaque, the Bonin fruit bat, the fin whale, the Asiatic black bear, the steller sea lion, the sea otter, and the Japanese dormouse. Other species vital to the overall ecosystem are tanuki (raccoon dogs), shika deer, foxes, badgers, bears, giant spider crabs, sparrows, thrushes, and the giant salamander.

CUSTOMS & COURTESIES

Greetings

The most commonly used form of greeting in Japan is the bow, an action that takes a range of forms, depending upon the status of the person to whom the bow is directed relative to the person doing the bowing. The deeper and longer the bow, the more respect is conveyed, whereas a more casual greeting to a friend would involve a simple nod of the head. Bowing is also used to express gratitude, apologize and to make a request. It is not unusual to see someone bowing while engaged in a telephone conversation.

When meeting someone for the first time, particularly in a business environment, it is also customary to exchange meishi (business cards). It is also customary for the recipient to receive the card with both hands and to read it to show interest. It is also considered impolite if the card is crumpled or placed in one's pocket. Treating the card with respect demonstrates respect for the person.

Verbal greetings vary by the time of day. "Ohayo Gozaimasu" means "Good morning" and is sometimes shortened to the more casual "Ohayo." "Konnichiwa" is a greeting used from late morning through early evening, and "Konbanwa" means "Good evening."

The suffix "-san" is attached to a person's name as an all-purpose title and to show respect. It can be used for men or women. Usually the family name is used to address a person, especially when directed to Japanese people (e.g. Suzuki-san), but for foreigners sometimes the first name is used (e.g., John-san).

Gestures & Etiquette

Hand gestures are much less common in Japan than in many other countries. As such, large gestures or odd facial expressions are typically not used. Furthermore, personal space is highly valued; the Japanese rarely consider it appropriate to touch one another, more so if the person is of the opposite sex. When pointing to oneself—as if to say, "Me?", for example—it is customary to point to one's nose rather than the chest. When beckoning someone, it is not appropriate to use the Western style palm up motion, as this is used only for animals. Instead, the palm should face down. Additionally, Japanese women will usually cover the mouth with their hand when laughing or smiling.

The Japanese are often uncomfortable using the word "no," since it implies a certain degree of directness that may be considered rude. The use of "yes, but…" may sometimes be an attempt to indicate "no" in a polite fashion.

Gift giving is an important part of Japanese society. For example, it is customary to give a small gift to work colleagues when returning from a trip. When accepting a gift, it is usual for the recipient to refuse a couple of times before accepting it, or at least apologize for the trouble that it may have caused. At the same time, the person offering the gift will be very self-deprecating, insisting that it is nothing. In addition, it is customary to receive a gift with both hands. More importantly, gifts are not usually opened in the presence of the giver, as the emphasis is on the act of giving and the presentation (the wrapping, for example) rather than the contents of the package. The number four and odd numbers should not be used in gifts as they are considered unlucky.

Eating/Meals

Japanese typically eat three meals a day. Typically, rice is a feature of each meal (the word for "meal" also means "rice"), and chopsticks are commonly used. Meals often consist of rice, soup, and pickled vegetables. Fish, meat, or tofu may also be served.

It is important to begin and end a meal with the correct phrases in Japan. Before eating, one should say "Itadakimasu," which means, "I am grateful to receive." After finishing the meal, the correct phrase is "Gochisosama deshita," meaning "Thank you for the meal, it was a delicious feast." During the meal, one should wait until everyone has been served before eating. It is traditionally considered polite to pour drinks for others and for them to reciprocate this show of respect. Leaving a glass full often indicates that a person would not like to receive more. Additionally, it is considered rude to point chopsticks at another person while eating. However, slurping noises are considered acceptable. When retrieving food from a shared plate, it is expected that the chopsticks will be inverted so that the portion that touches the mouth does not enter the communal dish.

Many Japanese consider it impolite to eat while walking in public. Although this is no longer a universally held belief, especially among young people, eating in public may attract stares. As such, many roadside food stands provide a seating area.

Visiting

To be invited into a Japanese home is considered a great honor, and it is important to follow correct etiquette procedures so that the host is not offended. It is customary to remove one's shoes when entering a Japanese house (shoes are typically placed in a small entryway). In addition, slippers may be provided for guests for wearing inside the house on hardwood floor or tiled areas. If entering a tatami (straw mat) room, slippers must be removed. Slippers should also

be changed when going to the bathroom. In this situation, special bathroom slippers may be provided so that those used in the rest of the house do not touch the bathroom floor.

The host will typically provide refreshments, usually green tea. It is considered impolite to refuse this, and although the guest does not have to drink all of it, it is polite to take a sip. In many Japanese homes, guests will often sit on the floor. Men may cross their legs in front of them while women may tuck their legs to the side. Sitting seiza (literally, "proper sitting," or kneeling) is formal and perfectly acceptable, but may prove uncomfortable for long periods. Sitting with legs stretched out in front is considered rude, and should be avoided.

LIFESTYLE

Family

The traditional Japanese family unit will typically follow the extended model, with several generations ranging from children to great-grandparents all living under the same roof. This remains true in rural areas. However, it is increasingly common to find the nuclear model (typically, a mother, father, and two children) in urban areas. It is expected that Japanese will care for their parents in old age, and nursing or residential homes for the elderly are less common than in Western societies.

Women will typically leave the workforce after having children. While their husbands spend long hours at work, the mother will become the driving force of the household, taking full responsibility for managing the finances, raising the children, and caring for elderly relatives. Additionally, the divorce rate remains lower in Japan than most other countries, but has increased in recent decades.

Housing

Housing styles in Japan vary a great deal, depending upon climate and location. Cities are densely populated, with many people living in high-rise apartments and condominiums, whereas traditional wooden houses are still common in areas that are more rural. Houses are typically heated by kerosene or electric space heaters, and central heating or air conditioning is rare due to the frequency of earthquakes and the necessity of reconstruction.

Generally, both houses and apartments tend to be much smaller than those in Western countries are, partly because of the large number of people in such a small geographical area. Rooms will typically serve many functions, and are used as a communal living space during the day and as a sleeping area at night. Sliding doors and partitions between rooms also make it easy to change the use of each room. Often, rooms are measured in terms of how many tatami mats will fit in them (the mats come in a standard size of 180 centimeters by 90 centimeters).

Food

Unlike most other Asian cuisines, Japanese food is remarkably simple and makes little use of spice. Emphasis is placed upon purity of flavor, rather than rich blends. In fact, the Japanese diet is believed to be among the healthiest in the world. Generally, the staples of Japanese cuisine are rice, vegetables, fish, and soy. Since food is typically prepared from scratch, it is not uncommon for Japanese consumers to shop each day to ensure the freshest of ingredients. A typical meal will involve steamed rice, boiled or steamed vegetables, a little meat or fish, and miso soup. Miso is a soy-based paste, mixed into a clear broth, often with seaweed and tofu.

Sashimi and sushi are the best-known Japanese dishes, and both include raw fish. Thin slices of skillfully cut raw fish are dipped in soy sauce and wasabi (a green horseradish paste) and often served with shavings of pickled ginger root, called gari. The dipping sauce is designed to add flavor without hiding the taste of the fish. Seaweed is also an important and highly nutritious part of the Japanese diet. Different forms are used in salads, soups, sushi, and even as gelling agents.

Aside from seaweed, soy is another widely used ingredient in Japanese cooking. Soy can take a number of forms. The beans (edamame) are eaten by themselves as a snack, and soy sauce is used as a dipping sauce or flavoring. Tofu (soybean curd), traditionally made by hand and sold door to door, is now readily available in every supermarket. Miso, a salty paste made by fermenting rice and soybeans, is used for soup. Another dish, often less pleasant to Western palates, is nattō. Often praised as the ultimate health food, nattō is a pungent smelling dish of fermented soybeans and is slimy in consistency. It has been a popular breakfast dish in Japan since feudal times and is very high in protein.

Green tea is widely drunk. Beer and sake are the most popular alcoholic drinks.

Life's Milestones

Many Japanese consider themselves both Shinto and Buddhist, and many special occasions and ceremonies reflect this combination. Japanese weddings are often elaborate affairs, beginning with a Shinto ceremony that only the immediate family attends. This is typically followed by a large reception. Although traditional wedding kimonos are worn to the Shinto temple, the bride may wear a number of dresses at the reception, including a Western-style white wedding dress. Traditionally, marriages were arranged by family members ("miai," or "omiai"). A large number are still arranged, and many believe that this is a better arrangement than Western-style marriages.

Whereas weddings follow Shinto tradition, funerals in Japan are strictly Buddhist ceremonies. The body is cremated and the ashes buried in a family grave. Although in the past, white was the color of funerals, black is now worn by guests and Buddhist prayer beads are often carried. In addition, gifts of money are given by guests at both weddings and funerals, traditionally to help pay for the expense.

CULTURAL HISTORY

Art

Japan's contributions to the world of art and design have been substantial, and range from delicate lacquerware (objects decorated with varnish) and ceramics, to paintings and woodblocks. In fact, various discovered examples of Japanese lacquer work are estimated to be 9,000 years old. Additionally, yakimono (literally, "fired thing"), or Japanese pottery, is one of the country's oldest traditional arts.

Various techniques have been used over the years to create lacquerware. Techniques may also vary according to the region in which the work is produced. The style known as maki-e (literally, "sprinkle picture") developed during the Heian Period (794–1185), when it was used to decorate a number of items, from screens to boxes. To make maki-e, gold or silver powder is sprinkled or brushed onto wet lacquer, using a makizutsu (a sprinkling canister) or an extremely fine kebo brush. A great deal of skill is needed to create the fine designs. Red and black lacquers are most commonly used.

Probably the best-known examples of Japanese art are the paintings and woodblock prints known as ukiyo-e, which means "art of the floating world." These prints were produced between the 17th and 20th centuries. This art is particularly highly regarded for its portraits of Japanese life when the nation was still isolated from the West (before 1867). Typical subject matter included geisha (professional female entertainers), teahouses, and the pleasure quarters of Tokyo. However, the genre also encompasses scenes of nature, such as those made famous by Hokusai (1760–1849), including the *Thirty-six Views of Mount Fuji* series and the individual painting *The Great Wave off Kanagawa*, and Hiroshige (1797–1858). Many ukiyo-e images of landscapes, samurai, and geisha remain very popular today, and are often reproduced in Western popular culture. Such works were a direct influence on impressionist and postimpressionist painters, such as Claude Monet, James Tissot, Edgar Degas, Édouard Vuillard, and Pierre Bonnard, among many others.

There are many styles of yakimono, often connected to specific geographical areas. The pottery from each region varies widely according to composition of the clay, firing methods and the use of additional minerals, as well as visual differences. Early pottery was often influenced by Chinese or Korean styles, but, as has typically happened throughout Japanese history, the country evolved its own distinct artistic character. Traditional styles continue to be passed down through families of artists today, often as closely guarded secrets.

Architecture

Historically, traditional Japanese architecture was influenced by Chinese architectural styles. Gradually, Japanese architecture adopted various other elements, notably Buddhist and Zen principles, and developed a distinct and unique style of its own. Today, Japanese architecture offers a blend of traditional and modern. For example, traditional wooden houses can be found next to towering office blocks and avant-garde or experimental and modernist designs in Japan's densely populated cities.

Two of the world's oldest wooden buildings are the Buddhist temples of Hōryū-ji and Tōdai-ji, still standing in Nara, Japan. Hōryū-ji (also Hōryū Gakumonji, "Learning Temple of the Flourishing Law") was built during the Asuka Period (592–710 CE), and Tōdai-ji (Eastern Great Temple) was built during the Nara Period (710–794 CE). Both temple complexes reflect the Chinese Buddhist style of pagodas and ceramic tiled roofs. During the Heian Period (794–1185), Buddhist temples displayed their increasing wealth with more pagodas and mandalas, or geometric designs, often depicting the universe. The materials changed to meet the demands of building in mountainous areas. For example, wood replaced earthen floors and ceramic tile gave way to bark roofing. Buildings reflected the cultural focus on aestheticism (devotion to, or acceptance of, art and beauty as fundamental) with elaborate, yet delicate, detailing.

With the advent of Japan's militaristic age, characterized by the prevalence of shoguns and samurai, architecture began to focus on the sturdy and practical. Buddhism moved away from the decorative and adopted Zen principles of simplicity. The tea ceremony grew as an art form and teahouses were a popular gathering spot. The use of wood and straw illustrated the Zen interest in nature. In addition, a number of fortresses were also built during this time, indicative of encroaching European influences in architecture.

In fact, the next major influence upon Japanese architecture was the influx of Western culture during the Meiji Period (1868–1912). Japanese architecture began to embrace European styles. The National Diet Building in Tokyo, for instance, was constructed in the modernist architectural style popular in Europe during the early 20th century. The post-World War II years brought further change to the landscape of Japan, as much of the country needed to be rebuilt. Steel and concrete were the favored construction materials during this period, particularly since they offered greater resistance to earthquakes.

Drama

Historically, Japanese theater was influenced by Chinese theater and culture. Three of the major traditional forms of Japanese theater that developed are kabuki, noh, and bunraku (also, Ningyō jōruri). During the 20th century, Japanese theater began to incorporate more Western-style elements of modern drama and acting. Generally, Japanese theater is highly stylized, and performances often last an entire day. Often, the audience can become quite involved in the theatrics.

Bunraku, the traditional puppet theater, should not be confused with Western style puppetry, which is often thought of as a form of children's entertainment. Bunraku is highly elaborate and stylized, with each puppet typically requiring three people to operate it. Furthermore, the puppeteers (Ningyōzukai) do not remain hidden from view as they manipulate the puppets (ningyō) with strings, but instead appear on stage.

The traditional theater form of Noh originated in folk theater and appears to have developed as a form in its own right during the 14th century. Little has changed in Noh as it is performed in modern-day Japan. One of the key features of Noh drama is that the lead actors often wear a variety of often-grotesque masks throughout the performance. Additionally, the masks themselves are considered an art form.

The theatrical tradition of kabuki began as a female-only form of theater in 1603. Women played both male and female roles in this genre, which instantly became popular. Since many of the performers were believed to be engaged in prostitution, it was decided that women degraded the art, and in 1629, women were banned from performing in kabuki. Until very recently, it remained a male-only theatrical style. As with many forms of Japanese art, the skills are typically passed down through families. Often, lines can be traced back through as many as seventeen generations.

Music

Music in Japan falls into several categories: art, folk, and pop music. Art music finds its roots in the Japanese upper classes and nobility, beginning with Gagaku (Heian Period, 794–1185). Gagaku was common in Korea and China, particularly in the court, and features purely instrumental or vocal music with an instrumental accompaniment (flutes, zither, drums, and other wind instruments). Shomyo, a vocal style common during the Heian Period, was performed at Buddhist ceremonies. Later, during the Kamakura Period (1185–1333), Nohgaku music developed, as an accompaniment to Noh dramas, and has two elements: a vocal component that includes chanting and singing by actors and an instrumental element performed on various wind instruments and drums to enhance the drama.

The 16th century saw the development or evolution of musical instruments such as the shakuhachi (bamboo flute), koto (string instrument consisting of thirteen strings strung across a shaped wooden bridge), and shamisen (three-stringed guitar-type instrument). The shakuhachi was often played by priests and often with the koto and shamisen. The koto was played in Sokyoku style music, for which different schools—the Ikuta and Yamada schools—developed, and which placed different emphasis on either instrumental or vocal elements. The shamisen was often played as an accompaniment to narrative or singing, sometimes with dance, as well as purely instrumental performances.

Folk music, or min'yō, often accompanied daily tasks or occupations and formal ceremonies, or was religious in nature. Children's music also developed as a folk music form. Most folk music was local in nature; its preservation suffered much from assimilation policies and abandonment to popular culture. Folk music fell into two styles, one characterized by a free rhythm often accompanied by a shakuhachi, and another with a metric rhythm accompanied by drums. Ethnic Ainu and Ryukyuan music are both distinct from Japanese folk music and very much alive in Japan.

Western classical music, introduced in the 19th century, has taken hold in Japan. Today, Japanese children are often exposed to classical music instruction at a young age, as is evidenced in the Suzuki style of music instruction, which emphasizes immersion and a child's self-propelled progression, as opposed to more aggressive instruction.

Popular music in Japan is thriving, consisting of Western rock, jazz, and country music imports, as well as Japanese musical groups. Often, Japanese performers will sing Western tunes in translation. The Japanese have successfully adopted these Western-style musical genres, and alternative, heavy metal, club, country, hip-hop, and other musical forms are now ingrained in Japanese culture.

Literature

Japan gained its first writing system in the eighth century, when kanji (Chinese characters) were introduced from China. Over time, these characters were adapted to become the distinctly Japanese writing system used today.

Some of the earliest works were anthologies of poetry, history, and mythology, written during the Nara Period (710–794). However, the most famous example of classical Japanese literature comes from the Heian Period (794–1185). *The Tale of Genji* by Lady Murasaki Shikibu (c. 973/978–c. 1014/1031), written in the early

11th century, is still considered a masterpiece of fiction. It is also indicative of how women in the royal court were instrumental in developing Japanese literature as an art form, as Lady Murasaki was a maid of the imperial court. The book, which tells of the romances and adventures of the emperor's son, is fifty-four chapters long and is believed to be the world's first novel.

Historically, poetry was a widely practiced art within the royal court. Even in contemporary Japan, important dates are often marked by the publication of a poem written by the emperor or empress. Kanshi, or "Han poetry," was written in Chinese, influenced by Chinese poetry and culture, and popular during the Heian Period (794–1185). Tanka, shi, and haiku are the other primary forms of Japanese poetry. Each follows strict stylistic and thematic rules, with nature remaining a common theme. Matsuo Bashō (1644–1694) perfected the popular haiku format of three lines and seventeen syllables.

The rapid industrialization and Westernization that accompanied the Meiji Period (1868–1912) were catalysts for a great deal of literary development in the late 19th and early 20th centuries. Fukuzawa Yukichi (1835–1901), the prominent writer of philosophical Enlightenment literature, produced seventeen volumes between 1872 and 1876, all focusing on national identity, principles of equality and the importance of study as progress.

Periods of literary realism, classicism, naturalism, and modernism all followed each other in quick succession, and by the 1920s, literature was a means of expressing political radicalism. The Second World War saw a continuation of political themes, as featured in the war fiction of former soldier Ashihei Hino (1907–1960), and the writing of poet Mitsuharu Kaneko (1895–1975) and author Jun Ishikawa (1899–1987). In 1968, Yasunari Kawabata (1899–1972) became the first Japanese writer to be awarded the Nobel Prize in Literature in recognition of his works, which included *Snow Country* and *Thousand Cranes*. Kenzaburō Ōe (b. 1935–) was also awarded the prize in 1994.

CULTURE

Arts & Entertainment

The arts remain an integral part of Japanese society. Delicate brush calligraphy (traditional highly stylized writing) continues to be taught in schools. Ikebana (flower arranging) and tea ceremony classes are popular among adults. The contemporary arts in Japan have also received immense support from the government. The Agency for Cultural Affairs, a branch of the Ministry of Education, was established in 1968 to promote Japanese arts and culture both at home and overseas. The National Museums of Art, the Japan Art Academy, and the National Institute for Japanese Language, as well as a multitude of other arts facilities, all fall under the care of the agency. Festivals, filmmaking, exhibitions, exchange programs, and the preservation of monuments are also supported, and the agency provides grants to promising young artists.

In order to support the continuation of traditional Japanese arts, one role of the cultural affairs agencies is to recognize those who have achieved exceptional skill in a particular area. Certain artists and groups are given the title of mukei bunkazai (intangible cultural assets), while major figures in the traditional arts are designated ningen kokuhō (living national treasures), as provided for under the 1950 Law for Protection of Cultural Properties. There are typically seventy ningen kokuhō at any one time and are certified by the country's Minister of Education, Culture, Sports, Science and Technology. As of 2010, living treasures included nine porcelain and pottery specialists, eighteen textile and kimono makers, ten metalsmiths, ten masters of Maki-e and Kyūshitsu lacquerware, seven woodworkers, three papermakers, and two doll makers. In addition, Japan also hosts an annual National Arts Festival, which features a number of major nationwide performances of kabuki, noh, ballet, opera, and film.

To ensure that traditional arts are continued, a number of programs are also in place that are geared toward children. Groups tour schools and regions offering educational workshops and performances of kabuki and traditional Japanese dance. Regions are also encouraged to hold culture festivals with members of the community participating.

Cultural festivals and celebrations remain an important part of the Japanese calendar. Typically, every shrine had its own celebration and countless festivals are held each year, often within a small geographic area. Each festival typically features a procession where the Shinto shrine's kami (spirit or deity) is paraded through town in a portable shrine called a mikoshi. The processions are often lively events, accompanied by music and street vendors. Some of the best-known festivals include the week long Sapporo Snow Festival in Hokkaido, Kyoto's Gion Festival, the Chichibu Night Festival, and the Awa Odori (dance festival) in Tokushima.

In the 1990s and beyond, Japanese cinema has spread to an international audience. This is largely due to the rise in popularity of Japanese anime (a style of animation) and horror films. The animated film *Spirited Away* achieved success overseas, winning the Academy Award for best animated feature in 2002. Meanwhile, a number of so-called J-horror films—an umbrella term for Japanese horror films that have influenced popular culture—have been remade in English with much success. Often, their success drew fans to the original Japanese versions upon which they were based.

Japanese pop music (J-pop, jeipoppu) has not had the same level of success outside of Asia, with the exception of when it is featured in video games. Nevertheless, it remains a vital part of Japanese culture and songs are featured everywhere, from television theme music to ring tones. Many of the songs can also be heard in karaoke venues nationwide.

Popular sports in Japan include baseball, sumo wrestling, martial arts (such as kendo, karate, and judo), golf, and soccer. Japanese teams have proven to be formidable opponents in such international tournaments as the Football World Cup and the Asia Cup (which they won in 1992, 2000, 2004, and 2011), Olympic sports, and baseball tournaments.

Sumo wrestling is considered Japan's national sport, and professional sumo tournaments have a long history, dating back to the first professional event held at the Tomioka Hachiman Shrine in 1684. The event was likely organized by rōnin—samauri warriors without masters or benefactors—seeking substitute income. It is a highly ritualized sport whose participants belong to training stables that control most aspects of their life, including their diet, training, daily schedule, and clothing. The higher rank a wrestler (rikishi) achieves, the easier his life within the stable. Lower-ranking rikishis have a challenging training period, as they often are responsible for completing tasks for the higher-ranked sekitori. A sumo event begins with several rituals to drive away bad spirits (such as stomping) and purify the ring (throwing salt). These matches last only a few minutes, until a wrestler steps out of the ring or some part of his body (other than the soles of his feet) touches the ground.

Cultural Sites & Landmarks

The culture of ancient Japan is well preserved in a wealth of shrines, temples, castles and national treasures, many of which have been designated as World Heritage Sites by the United Nations Educational, Scientific and Cultural Organization (UNESCO). Japan is also unique in that the sobering reminder of the destruction wrought by the atomic bombs of World War II is memorialized in the Hiroshima Peace Memorial, formerly the Genbaku Dōmu (also, Atomic Bomb Dome), which was designated as a UNESCO World Heritage Site in 1996. The dome's battered shell is now a protected symbol of world peace and nuclear disarmament, and paper cranes—Japanese symbols of peace—hang everywhere. However, perhaps the greatest landmark in Japan is Mount Fuji.

While Mount Fuji may be the highest mountain in Japan at 3,776 meters (12,388 feet) tall, its significance is much greater than its height. Perhaps the country's most recognized symbol, the mountain is also considered a sort of spiritual home to the Japanese, many of whom try to climb it at least once during their lifetime. Visible from the capital of Tokyo on a clear day, it is also popular with tourists during the summer climbing season. In addition, the forest at the base of Mount Fuji, called Aokigahara, or "Sea of Trees," remains a haunting site in Japanese myth and legend. The forest is also considered one of the world's most popular suicide sites, which is why it is also dubbed "Suicide Forest."

The capital of Tokyo is home to a vast number of cultural attractions, both old and new. The Imperial Palace Gardens are open to visitors and are particularly popular during the spring for cherry blossom viewing. Akihabara is the city's famed electronics district and is popularly known as "Electronic Town." Harajuku and neighboring Yoyogi Park present opportunities for both shopping and immersing oneself in the local culture.

The city of Kyoto offers a marked contrast to the bustling corporate environment prevalent in Tokyo. The city creates a sense of traditional Japan with its multitude of temples and shrines. Sanjūsangen-dō was built in 1266, a reconstruction of the earlier one which had burned in 1249. Within the temple are housed 1,001 statues of the Buddhist Thousand-armed Kannon. Kinkaku-ji is another popular destination where crowds flock to see the famous golden pavilion. The Gion District of Kyoto is still home to several geisha teahouses and restaurants, though many of these are not open to foreigners. Additionally, just a short trip from Kyoto is Nara, which was the capital of Japan from 710–794 CE. It is home to the Buddhist temple of Tōdai-ji (Eastern Great Temple) is, which was the largest wooden building in the world until 1998, when it was surpassed by northern Japan's wooden stadium, Odate Jukai Dome. Tōdai-ji also houses one of the largest bronze Buddhas to be found anywhere.

Japan has many castles, of which Himeji-jo is the most famous. Built in the 14th century, the castle has been listed as a World Heritage Site since 1993. It is one of the few Japanese castles to have survived the years, undamaged by earthquakes, war, or fire. With its white plaster walls and its towering site, Himeji is considered the most magnificent and prototypical Japanese castle.

Another famous site is Hokkaido, Japan's northernmost island, which is a favored spot for hiking in the summer and skiing in the winter. The island is also home to an ice sculpture festival and several museums honoring the history of the Ainu, the native people of Hokkaido. At the opposite end of the Japanese archipelago lie the islands that make up Okinawa Prefecture, which held distinct military importance during World War II. The castle remains and ruins of the independent Kingdom of Ryukyu (1429–1879), located on the Ryukyu Islands, were listed as a World Heritage Site in 2000.

Libraries & Museums

Japan has many museums, one of which is the Tokyo National Museum, which houses the largest collection of Japanese art in the world. The museum is made up of five buildings featuring Japanese art and artifacts as well as regional Asian works. The Edo-Tokyo Museum focuses on preserving Tokyo's history and culture and is built to resemble an elevated warehouse. The Hakone Open-Air Museum (Chokoku-no-Mori, Hakone) is a 20th-century sculptural museum featuring artists such as Picasso and Rodin. The Museum Meiji Mura in Nagoya is an architectural museum in an open setting that displays over sixty structures on 250 acres. The museum system in Japan is both broad and valued.

The National Diet Library serves as Japan's only national library, and has two facilities in Tokyo and Kyoto. Originally intended to serve as the library for the National Diet (legislative body), the library boasts an extensive catalog and enjoys significant public use.

Holidays

Holidays in Japan include New Years Day (January 1), Coming-of-Age Day (2nd Monday of January), National Foundation Day (February 11), the Vernal Equinox and Autumnal Equinox, Constitution Memorial Day (May 3), Greenery Day (May 4). Also celebrated are Children's Day (May 5), Marine Day (3rd Monday of July), Respect for the Aged Day (3rd Monday of September), Health-Sports Day (2nd Monday of October), Culture Day (November 3), Labor Thanksgiving Day (November 23), and the Emperor's Birthday (December 23).

Youth Culture

Japanese youth are very much focused on academics, and many attend juku (literally, "cram schools"), or after-school tutoring centers, to ensure success in examinations. Ninety percent of students graduate from high school, and entrance exams for university are extremely competitive. However, some pundits have recently pointed to what they perceive as a trending decrease in motivation among Japanese youth.

Young people in Japan have wielded a significant amount of consumer spending power in the early 21st century. Anime, manga (comics), music, and fashion, particularly denim and footwear, are multimillion-dollar industries. The popularity of characters such as Hello Kitty—an example of the popular kawaii (cute) concept which originated in Japan—have become widespread in other parts of Asia, as well as in the US and Europe. Additionally, certain popular fashion and music styles, particularly hip-hop, are largely influenced by American culture. Typically, worldwide technology trends—particularly in gaming and mobile media—often start in Japan.

SOCIETY

Transportation

Since cars are subject to expensive taxation and high tolls, most people prefer to use public transportation, and it is common for people to travel long distances by train or bus. In urban areas, despite the high cost of car ownership, it is still common for people to drive or to travel by subways and buses. This has led to high levels of congestion and pollution in cities such as Tokyo, which has one of the world's largest commuter populations, especially in the central districts, where the number of residents can more than double between day and night. To service such a large business population, Tokyo has developed the world's most extensive public transportation systems. Subways, buses, and a commuter monorail have all set global records for ridership. Many Japanese auto manufacturers have also developed hybrid vehicles as a means of combating the pollution. Traffic moves on the left-hand side of the road.

Transportation Infrastructure

Japan has a highly extensive and efficient public transportation system that is widely used. The railway system, in particular, is considered both punctual and safe. Approximately 250 Shinkansen (bullet trains) connect Tokyo with most of the major cities on Honshu, and with Fukuoka on the island of Kyushu. It typically runs at speeds of up to 320 kilometers (200 miles) per hour.

Japan also has an extensive system of highways, 1.2 million kilometers (745,645 miles) of paved roads. Constructing highways is both difficult and expensive because of Japan's natural geography and the risk of earthquakes. The high cost is offset by tolls which are payable on all highways.

Japan has 176 airports; with Tokyo's Narita International Airport, the country's largest. In 2014 alone, it handled 35,594,965 passenger and 2,043,372 metric tons (2,252,432 tons) of cargo. Other important international air gateways include Kansai International Airport, which serves the Osaka, Kobe, and Kyoto metro regions, and the Chūbu Centrair International Airport, near Nagoya.

Media & Communications

Japan has one of the world's highest literacy rates (99 percent) and a high level of newspaper readership. *The Asahi Shimbun* (*Morning Sun Newspaper*) and *The Daily Yomiuri* are available in both Japanese and English. *The Mainichi Shimbun* (*Daily News*), the nation's oldest newspaper, has been in circulation since 1872 and has an online presence in English. There are also numerous local and regional newspapers. Freedom House ranks Japan's media and internet

as "free" and has done so since their rankings began in 1998.

There are six national television networks, each with varying political viewpoints. Nippon Hoso Kyokai (NHK) is the country's only public network, supported by a license fee system similar to that used in the United Kingdom. NHK has a reputation for taking an impartial stance and avoiding political statements because it is not privately owned. Satellite and cable subscriptions are available and provide access to international channels.

In 2014, an estimated 109.3 million, or 86 percent of Japanese were regular users of the Internet. Broadband service in Japan is widely available, inexpensive, and much more technologically advanced than the services available elsewhere in the world. Many people use their cell phones to access the Internet. Often, cell phones are commonly available with features that have not yet reached Western countries.

SOCIAL DEVELOPMENT

Standard of Living

Japan ranked seventeenth on the 2014 United Nations Human Development Index of 187 countries. The 2014 index measures standard of living indicators, using data from 2012. The average life expectancy in Japan is nearly eighty-four years—eighty-one for men and eighty-eight for women (2015 estimate).

Water Consumption

As an industrialized nation, Japan has an advanced drinking water and sanitation infrastructure, with improved water sources and sanitation systems in 100 percent of urban and rural areas. Not only is the nation advancing its own water resource plan that involves development in the Tone, Arakawa, Toyokawa, Kiso, Yodogawa, Yoshino and Chikugo river systems, it is also participating in water resource development projects in developing nations. Moreover, since the devastating 2011 earthquake, the country is seeking to reinforce its water distribution systems and dams.

Especially important to the city of Osaka is Lake Biwa, which feeds the Yodo River and ultimately supplies the city with drinking water.

Education

The Japanese educational system is very similar to most Western systems, but with some small differences. Education is compulsory through junior high school, but many students continue on to college. Most elementary schools are public, with only 1 percent attending private school. That number increases to about 55 percent at the lower-secondary and higher-secondary levels. School is in session year-round, with short breaks. Up until 2002, Japanese students attended school on Saturdays.

Japanese students are given extensive preparation in both Japanese and English language skills, as well as mathematics and science courses. One aspect of Japanese schooling that many in the West are familiar with are the private jukus, or "cram schools," which help students to prepare rigorously for placement examinations at prestigious high schools and universities. Juku attendance may take up a considerable portion of a Japanese youth's school life and lead to considerable anxiety over their future education and career.

Japan maintains a very prestigious Imperial University system. There are hundreds of colleges and universities throughout the country. The University of Tokyo and Waseda University (the country's second-oldest university) in Tokyo are among the country's most prestigious, as well as Kyoto University and Keio University (the oldest university). Eikaiwa gakkō schools offer private education in English conversation, an important skill between the Japanese.

Women's Rights

In the 2014 World Economic Forum's report on the global gender gap, Japanese women rank 104th out of 142 countries. And while the report also shows that Japanese women rank well when it comes to health and survival concerns—coming in 37th out of 142 in this specific category—they face discrimination and significant challenges within the workforce, the political sphere, and in the educational system.

Although many Japanese women continue to work after marriage, gender inequality is a serious issue in the workplace. Furthermore, once a woman has had children, she faces societal pressure to remain home and focus on raising a family, thus removing her economic opportunities and independence. The positions that do remain for mothers within the workforce are largely part-time, with little opportunity for career advancement. Sexual harassment of women in the workplace is widespread, but rarely reported to avoid bringing shame upon the victim. However, it is not uncommon for Japanese women to manage both the household and its finances.

Women's educational opportunities are limited by societal expectations that they will marry and become mothers. Of the women who pursue postsecondary education, many choose two-year junior colleges; however, the rate at which women enroll and matriculate from four-year universities has been increasing. The number of women majoring in engineering, sciences, and medicine is small, but is also slowly increasing.

Women in Japan were permitted to attend political meetings as early as 1921, but did not gain voting rights until April 1946. Today, women still are still underrepresented among elected officials and Japan ranks 129th out of 142 countries in women's political empowerment in the World Economic Forum's gender gap report of 2014. As of 2015, women made up just 13.4 percent of the bicameral National Diet. According to the United Nations (UN), statistics at the local level were no better. The UN issued a statement in 2009 encouraging the Japanese government to increase efforts towards female participation in local and national government.

The concept of feminism is typically seen as a Western concept, and Japanese culture has historically viewed the separation of male and female worlds (business and home) as positive. The role of mother is regarded with great reverence in Japanese society, and so most movements for political change have centered on providing better protection and rights for mothers. The concern for mothers and health has in turn led to a significant level of women's involvement in environmental issues.

Health Care

Japan provides universal health care to its citizens through National Health Insurance (NHI) or Employee Health Insurance (EHI). Enrollment in either system is compulsory and is based on the sector in which one works. NHI covers agriculture, forestry and fisheries workers, as well as the self-employed, unemployed, students, and the elderly, while all others are covered by EHI. Under either plan, patients will pay a certain portion of costs up to a ceiling, at which point they enjoy full coverage. In 2013, health care expenditures represented 10.5 percent of the GDP. The average life expectancy in Japan is nearly eighty-five years: eighty-one for men and eighty-eight for women (2015 estimate).

GOVERNMENT

Structure

Japan is a constitutional monarchy. Its current constitution dates from May 3, 1947, two years after Japan surrendered to the Allied powers at the end of the Second World War. Japan's parliamentary government is divided into executive, legislative, and judicial branches. The executive branch consists of the prime minister (also the head of government), deputy prime minister, an appointed cabinet, and the emperor, who is the chief of state, a largely symbolic role.

The Diet (Kokkai), the most powerful of the three branches of government, is the bicameral legislature of Japan, consisting of the House of Councillors (Sangi-in) and the House of Representatives (Shugi-in). The House of Councillors is comprised of 242 seats, with members elected to 6-year terms during elections held every three years. The House of Representatives boasts 475 members, elected to four-year terms during elections held every two years. The Diet appoints the prime minister (via the emperor), who is usually the leader of the

majority party or majority coalition in the House of Representatives. The judicial branch consists of the Supreme Court, members of which are also designated by the Diet and appointed by the emperor.

At the end of World War II, with defeats in several major military outposts, the Japanese Empire had begun to recede. In August 1945, the United States dropped atomic weapons on the cities of Hiroshima (Honshu) and Nagasaki (Kyushu), putting a decisive end to Japan's advance. The ensuing post-war period brought changes not only to the structure of Japanese society, but also to its economic and political aspirations. Its aggressive, expansionist tendencies gave way to pacifist, protectionist ideals, contributing to one of the 20th century's most surprising political and economic turnarounds.

Political Parties

Japan's legislature is characterized by a large number of political parties, but is dominated by two: the Liberal Democratic Party (LDP) and the Democratic Party (DPJ). In these parliamentary systems, parties develop coalitions with other parties sharing the same legislative goals. These coalitions have a tendency to shift between election years in terms of political platform and their alliance with other parties sharing common interests. Coalitions of two or more parties that unite to form a majority coalition are not unusual. These coalitions differ in nature, with some coalitions having a lasting strength and others failing to govern at all. Additionally, it is not unusual for parties to dissolve because of personality conflicts within the organization.

Of the two major parties in Japan, the most powerful in 2015 is The Liberal Democratic Party (LDP), a conservative, pro-business, and pro-American party, which dominated Japanese politics from 1955 through 2009 (with the exception of brief periods between 1993 and 1994 and 2009 and 2012). In the July 2013 election, the LDP took 292 Representatives and 115 Councillors. The center-left Democratic Party of Japan (DPJ), which formed a coalition with several other anti-LDP parties in the late 1990s, is the second most powerful party, with seventy-three Representatives and fifty-nine Councillors. Other important parties include the nationalist, neoconservative Innovation Party (JIP); the center-left, Buddhist-supported Kōmeitō Party; and the Communist Party (JCP), which was formed in 1922, making it the country's oldest political party.

Because of repeated conflict with the Ministry of Finance, Prime Minister Shinzō Abe dissolved the House of Representatives and held a snap parliamentary election in December 2014, two years earlier than scheduled. Voters gave the LDP 291 seats, the DPJ 73 seats, and the Innovation Party 41 seats. Kōmeitō took 35 seats, while the Communist Party achieved 21 seats. Japanese-nationalist and neoconservative Future Generations Party took two seats.

Suffrage in Japan begins at age twenty.

Local Government

Japan is divided into forty-seven prefectures (todōfuken), or administrative districts, part of a governance system first assigned by the Meiji government in July 1871. These prefectures take different forms, including the metropolitan district of Tokyo, two urban districts of Kyoto and Osaka, and the territory of Hokkaido; the remaining prefectures are rural in nature. Prefectures are administered by directly elected governors (chiji), while each has an assembly (gikai), to which members are elected for four-year terms. Cities, many of which fall within a prefecture, are separately administered and are governed by mayors and assemblies, except in towns or villages that choose to administer only through an assembly.

Local governments in Japan are responsible for healthcare and social insurance, public safety, planning and development, and education.

Judicial System

The Japanese judicial system is based in part on the American system and partially on the German civil law system. The Supreme Court (Saiko saibansho) is the country's highest court. Comprised of fourteen justices and a chief jus-

tice, it reviews legislative acts and rules on constitutional issues. Subordinate judicial tiers include eight high courts (Koto-saiban-sho); fifty district courts (chihō saibansho), each of which has an associated family court and under whose purview 203 branches also operate; and 438 summary courts in which 806 judges ad hoc hear cases.

Instead of a jury system, judges make rulings based on legal statutes.

Taxation

Japan levies a progressive personal income tax that ranges from 5 percent to 45 percent, depending on income level. There is also a local habitation tax, capital gains (10 percent on shares sold), real estate (39 percent), and a consumption tax (5 percent). Corporate taxes stand at 23.9 percent of earnings in 2015, down from 25.5 percent in 2013. Deductions and credits apply in certain circumstances.

Armed Forces

Under Article 9 of Japan's constitution forbids the existence of a standing army. The country does have the Japan Self-Defense Force, consisting of ground, maritime, and air divisions. These forces have participated in United Nations peacekeeping operations and are considered both technologically sophisticated and well trained. Reconsideration of Article 9 is underway. Additionally, concerns have been raised as to Japan's security situation relative to the buildup of militaries in North Korea and China.

The US maintains military bases in Okinawa, but no formal agreement exists for the US to defend Japan's national interests.

Foreign Policy

The prime minister and the cabinet establish and exercise foreign policy. The National Diet of Japan, the country's legislative body, must ratify any treaties. The Ministry of Foreign Affairs oversees international diplomacy.

Since the end of the Second World War, Japan and the US have shared a close military and economic relationship. The ties have evolved over the years and have not been without strain. After the end of the Allied occupation in 1952, the Japanese economy progressed with a sense of dependence as the country rebuilt. By the 1980s, Japan's increasing economic power served to place it on an equal footing with the U.S. In the 1990s, there were growing levels of unease in response to the high levels of Japanese investment in American industry.

In addition, the U.S. military maintains a number of bases in Japan, particularly in Okinawa, where 10 percent of the land is used for U.S. military installations, and where there have been repeated calls for the U.S. military to leave the area. Tensions ran particularly high in 1995, when three U.S. servicemen were arrested for the rape of a twelve-year-old girl, and again in 2008, when a U.S. Marine was arrested for the abduction and rape of a fourteen-year-old girl.

Japan may be seeking to redefine its historically tense relationship with China. Much of Japanese culture, architecture, religion, and law originated in China, and for centuries, China was the more advanced of the two. Following the opening up of Japan to Western trade in the Meiji era, Japan's increasing adoption of Western culture led to the nation's view of China as antiquated, or outmoded. Japanese imperialist actions in Manchuria during the 1930s were followed by a cordial relationship between the two nations in the 1950s. Since then, the relations between the countries have been somewhat tenuous, with alternating periods of suspicion and friendship. In particular, Japan's government—specifically under the LDP—has expressed concern over the rapid growth of the Chinese economy and military, while China still voices occasional fears of a potential military growth in Japan. The two countries, along with Taiwan, are also involved in a territorial dispute over the uninhabited Senkaku Islands, located west of Okinawa.

Tensions exist between Russia and Japan, as the two nations have yet to sign a peace treaty to end officially World War II. This is fueled in part by the disputed ownership of the Kuril Islands—specifically, Etorofu, Kunashiri, Shikotan, and the Habomai group, all located in the northern Pacific Ocean. The Soviets invaded and occupied these islands in 1945 and expelled the native Japanese population—some 17,000 people—by 1946. Tensions surround the issue, and in 2006, a Japanese angler was shot and killed by Russian authorities after he entered disputed waters. In July 2008, new Japanese school textbooks stated Japanese sovereignty over the Kuril Islands, again leading to criticism from Russia. The islands have a population of nearly 19,434 people, consisting of mostly Russian, Ainu, and other ethnicities.

Japanese and South Korean relations have improved in recent years, although there is still significant negative sentiment demonstrated by Japanese nationalists who organize anti-Korean protests in the Little Korea neighborhoods of major cities, like Tokyo. Still, the 1988 Olympic Games and 2002 Soccer World Cup were cohosted by both nations as a demonstration of their friendship, and the two countries now share trade and cultural exchanges. In early November 2015, Japan, China, and South Korea held their first trilateral meeting in three years, during which they discussed joining forces to increase trade, halt North Korea's nuclear development, and pursue joint research in robotics.

Human Rights Profile

International human rights law insists that states respect civil and political rights and promote an individual's economic, social, and cultural rights. The United Nations Universal Declaration on Human Rights (UDHR) is recognized as the standard for international human rights. Its authors sought the counsel of the world's great thinkers, philosophers, and religious leaders and were careful to create a document that reflects the core values shared by every world culture. (To read this document or view the articles relating to cultural human rights, visit http://www.ohchr.org/EN/UDHR/Pages/Introduction.aspx.)

Overall, Japan has a good human rights record, with some exceptions. The Japanese constitution provides citizens with a series of protected rights that closely follow Article 2 of the Universal Declaration of Human Rights.

According to the constitution, all citizens are entitled to equal legal rights, regardless of gender or race. In practice, this equality is often lacking. Discrimination against women and minorities such as the burakumin and the Ainu, as well as non-Japanese, remains a societal problem. In addition, immigrant populations from China, Korea, the Philippines, and other nations often face discrimination in finding housing and employment. Human Right Watch reports that ethnic Koreans in Tokyo's Shin-Okubo district regularly experience threats and racist treatment and endure weekly anti-Korean rallies led by ultranationalists groups.

Article 18 of the UDHR protects freedom of religion. Religious discrimination in Japan is rare. Freedom of speech and expression is constitutionally protected, in accordance with Article 19. There are no restrictions on Internet use. Freedom to assemble is also generally respected, as outlined in Article 20.

A significant emerging human rights issue is the institutionalization of orphaned and abused children. Human Rights Watch estimates that some 40,000 children in the nation live in alternative care institutions rather than with foster families, and at many of these institutions, children are subject to bullying, hazing, and maltreatment by staff. Some of these children were already removed from abusive home lives, were relinquished by parents unable to care for them, or were orphaned. Many have not been taught necessary life skills that would allow them to function independently when released on their eighteenth birthday, and those without such skills frequently become homeless.

One of Japan's most highly contested human rights issues is that of "comfort women" during World War II. Thousands of women who were forced into sexual slavery during the war continue to demand apologies and compensation from the Japanese government. The women, mostly from Korea and the Philippines, report that they were coerced into prostitution, and were beaten and raped. Despite formal resolutions from other world governments and organizations requiring Japan to apologize and provide adequate compensation to the women, the government has refused to do so. In 1995, the Asian Women's Fund was established, following an official acknowledgment of what happened, and atonement money was distributed to several hundred women. Many have refused the money, demanding that the government take legal responsibility and pay direct compensation. The fund was dissolved in 2007.

Japan's treatment of prisoners also comes under regular scrutiny. The death penalty is used in Japan and executions are usually carried out without notifying the prisoner's family. (The prisoner, too, is usually given little notice of his or her execution, usually only hours before it is scheduled to take place). This practice contradicts the International Covenant on Civil and Political Rights (ICCPR).

Migration

In the 1990s, Japan relaxed its immigration laws, which resulted in an influx of foreign workers, particularly from Brazil, immigrating to the nation in search of manufacturing work. In the wake of the global financial crisis that began in 2008, Japan has had to confront the issue of unemployment among these immigrant populations. In 2009, the Japanese government began to offer foreign workers $3,000 USD to return to their home countries (and $2,000 to family members), under the condition that they would not return until employment and economic conditions improve. As Japan's population ages and its manufacturing sector recovers, some believe that the issue of immigration policy reform begs attention. As of 2015, the migratory population has stabilized, with an estimated zero migrants per 1,000 people.

ECONOMY

Overview of the Economy

Japan has the world's second (or third, depending on how one chooses to measure it) largest economy and, as a result, is one of the most powerful countries on earth. Its ability to not only rebuild itself after its defeat by the Allied powers in the Second World War, but to accelerate to such an important place in the world economy over the subsequent sixty years, is one of the more remarkable economic achievements of the modern era. Despite periods of economic slowdown since the 1940s, Japan is on track to remain an economic power for many years to come.

Tokyo, Yokohama, and Kawasaki are Japan's three main economic centers. Each district accounts for nearly one-third of the country's economy. Tokyo's industries include electronics, steel, and automobile production. In 2014, Japan's GDP was $4.751 trillion USD, and its estimated per capita GDP was $ $37,400 USD.

Industry

Among the most important Japanese industries are automobiles (Toyota, Nissan, Subaru, Honda, to name just a few of its brand names); electronics (including Sony, Toshiba, and Panasonic [formerly Matsushita Electric], among others); machine tools; steel and nonferrous minerals; and steel ships. In addition, manufacturing and related industry contributes to 24.5 percent of the GDP and employing 26.2 percent of the labor force.

Japan's main exports include motor vehicles (14.9 percent), iron and steel products (5.4 percent), electronics (5 percent), auto parts (4 percent), electric generators (3.5 percent), and plastics (3.3 percent). In 2014, the country's main trading partners were the United States (18.9 percent), China (18.3 percent), South Korea (7.5 percent), Hong Kong (5.5 percent), and Thailand (4.5 percent).

Despite the importance of its manufacturers, however, Japan's service sector is its most important, employing nearly 71 percent of the labor force and contributing 74.3 percent to the GDP (2014 estimate).

Labor

Japan's labor force numbered 65.48 million people in early 2015. The unemployment rate was estimated at 3.6 percent in 2014. The primary employer of Japanese workers is the service sector, which accounts for 70.9 percent of workforce jobs. Slightly more than 26 percent of the workforce is employed in manufacturing activities, and 2.9 percent labor in the agricultural sector.

Energy/Power/Natural Resources

Japan's natural resources include some mineral deposits, which are considered "negligible" by most measures, meaning that they have little importance to the nation's economy. Japan is rich in lumber, hydroelectric power and fish, however. Japan does have some oil reserves, which, in 2015, were proven to equal 541.6 million barrels. In 2014, the country also produced 4,666 barrels of crude oil per day, but also imported 3.441 million barrels per day to meet total consumption. In 2014 alone, Japan produced 4.728 billion cubic meters of natural gas; their proven reserves amount to 20.9 billion cubic meters.

Areas of environmental concern include air pollution, acidification of water resources, overuse of fisheries and lumber resources, and landfill shortages.

Fishing

Commercial fishing and aquaculture is a $14 billion-dollar industry in Japan, and economically crucial wild-catches include sardine, crab, shrimp, marlin, swordfish, salmon, and tuna. Eel populations are also important but declining, and domestically, octopus and squid are important cuisine staples. Both freshwater and marine aquaculture is practiced in all forty-seven prefectures, with Japanese- and greater amberjack species representing a quarter of aquaculture production. Japan is also one of the world's leading whaling nations, which draws criticism from environmentalists worldwide, as does the country's passion for shark fin. Kesennuma, 250 miles north of Tokyo, conducts 90 percent of the shark fin trade and kills approximately 73 million sharks each year, removing fins and dumping bodies. The practice has raised concerns about the upset to ecosystems and extirpation of shark species, especially the blue shark, which represents 80 percent of catches. Concerns about radiation levels in fish and marine life caught in and around Fukushima has negatively affected the local fishing industry since the disaster in 2011.

Forestry

Approximately 67 percent of Japan is forested, with 58 percent privately owned, 31 percent government owned, and 11 percent municipally owned. Although 45 percent of the forested land consists of plantations and reforestation efforts following WWII have resulted in trees that are, in the second decade of the 21st century, sixty years old, the logging industry is not well developed. In fact, Japan is one of the world's leading nations in the import of wood, pulp, and paper products. Some attribute the lack of industry development to the cheap cost of imports, and the devaluation of domestic stock, with one fifty-year old cedar tree netting, on average, just $20 (USD). Others believe that it is because of changing building codes following the 1995 Great Hanshin Earthquake, which made much of Japan's native species unsuitable for construction use. The majority of imported lumber comes from the U.S. (32 percent) and Russian (30 percent), with New Zealand (14 percent) and Canada (12 percent) not far behind.

Japanese cedar, cypress, and red pine are among the most sought after woods in the nation.

Mining/Metals

Japan's mining industry is small, and the country's mineral needs are largely supplied through the import of nonferrous metal, including copper and zinc. While coal operations are in place in the extreme north and south, the extracted coal is not of good quality, but is used to generate electricity. As of 2015, Japan is the largest importer of coal and liquefied natural gas. It is the second largest importer of petroleum products after China.

Agriculture

Agriculture accounted for 1.2 percent of the country's GDP in 2013. Japanese agricultural products include rice, wheat, barley, flowers, sugar beets, sugar cane, potatoes, yams, taro, legumes, and cabbage. Although the agricultural sector is relatively small, Japanese farmers supply most of the rice consumed in Japan. The country must import most of its other food products.

Animal Husbandry

In 2009, the dairy and beef industry in Japan was valued at $10 billion (USD). In addition, in 2009, it was reported that Japan imported 75 percent of its feed for livestock and was the world's largest corn importer. However, the U.S. and several other countries banned the importation of Japanese beef beginning in 2004 due to fears of spreading hoof and mouth disease and dispersing meat bearing bovine spongiform encephalopathy (commonly known as mad-cow disease), which were both confirmed to exist in some Japanese herds. Moreover, for this reason and because domestic production could not keep pace with demand, beginning in 2010, Japan began importing beef from the US, Australia, and New Zealand with increasing frequency, enhancing the price of cattle for these countries.

Tourism

In 2014, an estimated 13,413,600 foreign visitors came to Japan, the majority hailing from Taiwan (2,829,800), South Korea (2,755,300), China (2,409,200), and Hong Kong (925,900). Four years before, in 2010, the government raised the tourism agency's budget and announced plans to increase visitation from China, which has come to fruition in 2014 with a more than 1.4 million increase in Chinese tourists over the country's 2009 numbers. Following the Fukushima Daiichi nuclear disaster in March 2011, tourism numbers dropped by 25 percent but has been on the rebound since 2013.

Popular tourist destinations include the gardens, temples, and shrines found in most major cities and regions, including Kyoto, Japan's cultural capital, and Tokyo, one of the ancient cities of Japan and currently one of the cultural capitals of the world. Other important tourist sites include the Imperial Palace, Himeji Castle in Hyōgo Prefecture (near Kyoto), Mount Fuji, and Japan's many national parks and world heritage sites.

Fiona Young-Brown, Craig Belanger, Micah L. Issitt, & Savannah Schroll Guz

DO YOU KNOW?

- "Japan" (or "Japon") and "Nippon" are synonyms; both words mean "origin of the sun."
- The Yunessun Spa Resort in Hakone-machi offers coffee, green tea, or red wine baths to patrons.
- Though Tokyo is generally regarded as the capital of Japan, the city was never officially declared the capital. Some historians argue that Kyoto should still be considered the official capital, despite the fact that the government and administrative offices are now located in Tokyo.

Bibliography

Berger, Thomas U., Mike M. Mochizuki, & Jitsuo Tsuchiyama, eds. *Japan in International Politics: The Foreign Policies of an Adaptive State.* Boulder, CO: Lynne Rienner Publishers, 2007.

Booth, Shirley. *Food of Japan.* Northampton, MA: Interlink Publishing, 2002.

Bornoff, Nicholas & Perrin Lindelauf. *National Geographic Traveler: Japan.* 4th ed. Washington, DC: National Geographic Books, 2013.

De Mente, Boye Lafayette. *Etiquette Guide to Japan: Know the Rules that Make the Difference.* Ed. Geoff Botting. 3rd ed. North Clarendon, VT: Tuttle, 2015.

Inoura, Yoshinobu. *The Traditional Theater of Japan.* Warren, CT: Floating World Editions, 2006.

Iwao, Sumiko. *The Japanese Woman: Traditional Image and Changing Reality.* Reprint. New York: Free Press, 1998.

Leiter, Samuel L. *Historical Dictionary of Japanese Traditional Theatre.* 2nd ed. Lanham, MD: Rowman & Littlefield Publishers, 2014. Historical Dictionaries of Literature and the Arts Ser.

Paine, Robert Treat & Alexander Soper. *The Art and Architecture of Japan.* 3rd ed. New Haven, CT: Yale University Press, 1992. Pelican History of Art Ser.

Rowthorn, Chris, Ray Bartlett, et al. *Lonely Planet Japan.* 14th ed. London: Lonely Planet, 2015.

Sadao, Tsuneko S. & Stephanie Wada. *Discovering the Arts of Japan: A Historical Overview.* New York: Abbeville Press, 2010.

Sugimoto, Yoshio. *The Cambridge Companion to Modern Japanese Culture.* Cambridge, UK: Cambridge University Press, 2009. Cambridge Companions to Culture Ser.

Tsuji, Shizuo. *Japanese Cooking: A Simple Art.* 25th Anniversary Edition. Tokyo/London: Kodansha International, 2012.

Vogel, Stephen, ed. *U.S.–Japan Relations in a Changing World.* Washington, DC: Brookings Institution Press, 2002.

Works Cited

BBC. "Japan, China and South Korea 'restore' fraught ties." *BBC News.* BBC, 1 Nov. 2015. Web. http://www.bbc.com/news/world-asia-34691596.

Bestor, Theordore and Helen Hardacre. "The Japanese Family." *Contemporary Japan: Culture & Society.* Columbia University, 2004. http://afe.easia.columbia.edu/at_japan_soc/common/all.htm#family.

Bureau of East Asian and Pacific Affairs. "U.S. Relations with Japan." *US Department of State.* US Department of State, 1 Feb. 2015. Web. http://www.state.gov/r/pa/ei/bgn/4142.htm.

Central Intelligence Agency. "Japan." *The World Factbook.* CIA, 2015. Web. https://www.cia.gov/library/publications/the-world-factbook/geos/ja.html.

Freedom House. "Japan." *Freedom in the World 2015.* Freedom House, 2015. Web. https://freedomhouse.org/report/freedom-world/2015/japan.

Gender Equality Bureau Cabinet Office. "APEC Women in the Economy 2015 Fora." *Gender Equality Bureau Home.* Gender Equality Bureau Cabinet Office, 2015. Web. http://www.gender.go.jp/english_contents/index.html.

Human Rights Watch. "Japan." *Human Rights Watch.* HRW, 21 Oct. 2015. Web. https://www.hrw.org/asia/japan.

Irvine, Dean. "Japan's hidden people: Ainu try to keep ancient traditions alive." *CNN.* Cable News Network/Turner Broadcasting System, Inc., 9 Feb. 2015. Web. http://www.cnn.com/2015/02/09/travel/cnngo-travel-hokkaido-ainu/.

Japan Arts Council. *An Introduction to Bunraku: A Guide to Watching Japan's Puppet Theatre.* Japan Arts Council, 2004. http://www2.ntj.jac.go.jp/unesco/bunraku/en/.

Johansson, Hans Olof. *Ukiyo-e: The Pictures of the Floating World.* Hans Olof Johansson. http://www.ukiyo-e.se/.

McCurry, Justin. "Japan Calls Snap Election." *The Guardian.* Guardian News and Media Ltd, 18 Nov. 2014.

Web. http://www.theguardian.com/world/2014/nov/18/japan-calls-snap-election-shinzo-abe.

———. "Shark fishing in Japan—a messy, blood-spattered business." *The Guardian*. Guardian News and Media Limited, 11 Feb. 2011. Web. http://www.theguardian.com/environment/2011/feb/11/shark-fishing-in-japan.

Nishide, Mariko. "Urushi." *Urishi-Kobo.com*. Mariko Nishide, 2015. Web. http://www.urushi-kobo.com/urushi.html.

Obara, Kakuyu, Michael J. McConnell, & John Dyck. *Japan's Beef Market: Report from the Economic Research Service*. USDA & Economic Research Service, August 2010. Web. http://www.ers.usda.gov/publications/ldpm-livestock,-dairy,-and-poultry-outlook/ldpm194–01.aspx

Osaki, Tomohiro. "Human rights champ Doi battles social injustice in Japan." *Japan Times*. The Japan Times, Ltd., 6 Apr. 2014. Web. http://www.japantimes.co.jp/news/2014/04/06/national/human-rights-champ-doi-battles-social-injustice-in-japan/#.VjYU-WBdFMt.

Rabouin, Dion. "Japanese Election Results 2014: Officially A Huge Win For Shinzo Abe's Liberal Democratic Party." *International Business Times*. IBT Media, Inc, 14 Dec. 2014. Web. http://www.ibtimes.com/japanese-election-results-2014-officially-huge-win-shinzo-abes-liberal-democratic-1755570.

Tabucki, Hiroko. "Fears Accompany Fishermen in Japanese Disaster Region." *New York Times*. The New York Times Company, 25 Jun. 2012. Web. http://www.nytimes.com/2012/06/26/world/asia/fears-accompany-fishermen-in-japanese-disaster-region.html?_r=0.

Tajima, Daisuke. *Forestry in Japan: Solutions for the Future*. Portland, OR: World Forest Institute, 2010. PDF.

UN Development Programme. "Table 1: Human Development Index and its components." *Human Development Reports*. UNDP, 2015. Web. http://hdr.undp.org/en/content/table-1-human-development-index-and-its-components.

UNESCO. "World Heritage List." *UNESCO World Heritage Centre*. United Nations, 2015. Web. http://whc.unesco.org/en/list.

World Economic Forum. "Economies: Japan." *The Global Gender Gap Report 2014*. World Economic Forum, 2015. Web. http://reports.weforum.org/global-gender-gap-report-2014/economies/#economy=JPN.

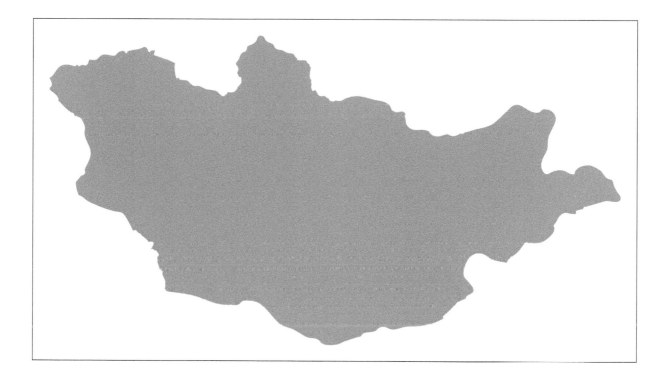

MONGOLIA

Introduction

Mongolia is a landlocked country in Central and East Asia bordering China and Russia. Vast, uninhabited countryside dominates much of Mongolia, and great distances stretch between cities, towns, and communities; hotels outside of Ulaanbaatar, the capital, are extremely rare. As such, nomadic Mongolians are typically very welcoming and hospitable to passing travelers.

Once the seat of the great Mongol Empire governed by Genghis Khan, the area now known as Mongolia was incorporated into China, and gained its independence in 1911. Between 1924 and 1992, it was a communist country closely aligned with the Soviet Union. Mongolia has made a peaceful transition to democracy and is steadily restructuring its economy and social welfare system, in recent years aligning itself more and more with China.

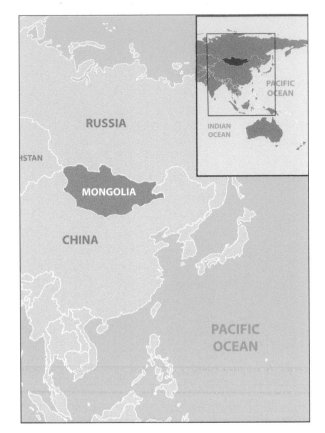

GENERAL INFORMATION

Official Language: Khalkha Mongol
Population: 2,992,908 (2015 estimate)
Currency: Mongolian tögrög (or tugrik)
Coins: Coins are available in denominations of 20, 50, 100, 200, and 500 tögrög.
Land Area: 1,553,556 square kilometers (599,831 square miles)
Water Area: 10,560 square kilometers (4,077 square miles)
National Anthem: "Mongol ulsyn töriin duulal" ("National Anthem of Mongolia")

Capital: Ulaanbaatar
Time Zone: GMT +8
Flag Description: The flag of Mongolia features a bicolor design composed of three equal and vertical stripes of red, blue, and then red. Centered in the left (or hoist-side) band is the national emblem, the Soyombo symbol, in yellow. The Soyombo symbol is a character from the Soyombo script, used to transcribe the Mongolian language, and features representations of elements such as water and fire, as well as the moon, sun, and earth, along with a yin-yang symbol.

Population

Mongolia's young, growing population—roughly 40 percent of Mongolia's population is between the ages of sixteen and thirty-five, ranking it as one of the world's most youthful—is sparsely distributed. It is most heavily concentrated in the north and west. Today, nearly three quarters of the population lives in urban centers which is an estimated 72 percent in 2015. Ulaanbaatar is the

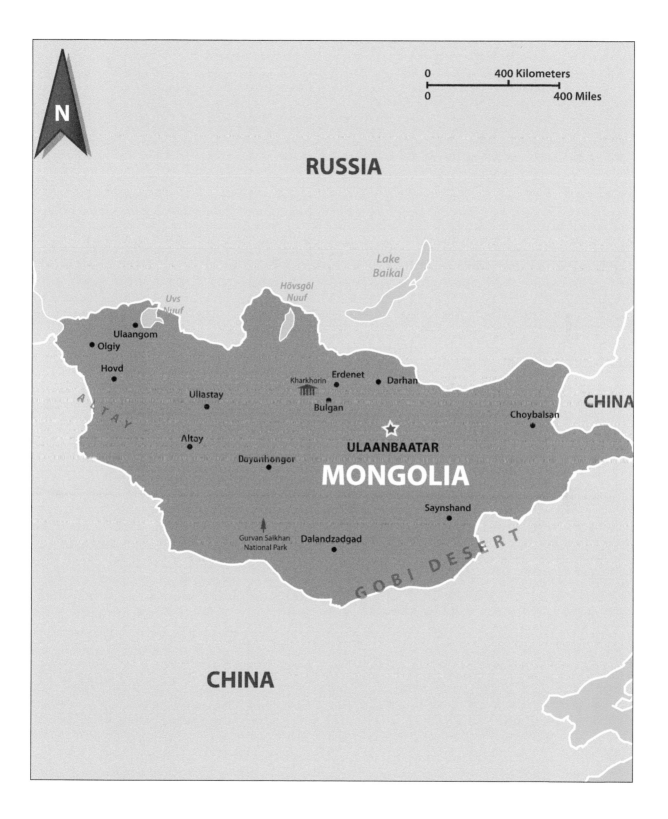

Principal Cities by Population (2012):

- Ulaanbaatar (or Ulan Bator, 885,140)
- Erdenet (79,550)
- Darkhan (76,616)
- Choibalsan (48,578)
- Mörön (35,500) (2008 estimate)
- Ölgii (32,677)
- Zuunharaa (31,699)
- Khovd (30,500) (2008 estimate)

largest city, with a population of 885,140 (2012). Other cities include Erdenet and Darhan. Even in urban areas, many Mongolians choose to live in traditional round tents called gers. The population growth rate was estimated at 1.3 percent in 2015.

The ethnic make-up of the population is quite homogenous, 90 percent being Mongolian. Of this ethnic group, Khalkha Mongols comprise the vast majority (an estimated 75 percent of the populace). Kazakhs, who reside in the far west, are the largest minority (5 percent). Other ethnic groups include Buryat Mongols (the northernmost major Mongol group, the largest of which is concentrated in Siberia), and Chinese and Russian minorities are present in small numbers in the capital.

Ulaanbaatar is the capital of Mongolia. Also called Ulan Bator, it is the largest city in Mongolia. The population of Ulaanbaatar has increased rapidly in the last several years because of immigration from rural areas. Such migrants often live in ger (yurt) communities, which are settlements composed of temporary housing. People in Ulaanbaatar are influenced by many cultures and nations; for example, the streets are full of Japanese cars, English-language ads, and red-robed Lamaist monks (those who follow Tibetan Buddhism).

Languages

Mongolian, spoken by 90 percent of the population, is an Altaic language and related to Turkish, Kazakh, and Uzbek. The dialects spoken within the country are mutually comprehensible, and

the Khalkh (or Khalkha) dialect is considered standard Mongolian. A modified Cyrillic alphabet was adopted during the communist era and is still prevalent. However, the process of returning to the traditional Mongolian alphabet, written vertically and from left to right, is underway. The government has also instituted a drive to make English the country's second language.

Native People & Ethnic Groups

Ethnic Mongolians and Kazakhs have ancient histories in the region. Within the country, inter-ethnic and intertribal relations have generally been peaceful. Conflict has instead come from Mongolia's dominating neighbors.

Independence from China brought some degree of subjugation by Russia. The most brutal period occurred in the 1920s and 1930s, when communist revolutionaries suppressed religious practices, killed many shamans and lamas or deported them to prison camps, and destroyed or closed temples and monasteries in an effort to eradicate any challenge to communist ascendancy.

Religions

An estimated 50 percent of the population subscribes to Tibetan Buddhism, which largely supplanted Shamanism in the 16th century. At the beginning of the 20th century, Buddhist practices were widespread, and there were over 3,000 monasteries and temples. Religion was repressed during the communist era, but the country has shown a resurgence in the interest and practice of the Buddhist faith, as well as the building and restoration of religious buildings, since democratic reforms took hold. Other religions include Sunni Islam, practiced by the Kazakhs, and Shamanism, practiced by a small percentage of rural Mongolians. As of 2004, an estimated 40 percent of the population professed no adherence to any particular religion.

Climate

Mongolia has a continental climate. The country averages 257 clear days a year because of the mountain ranges that block weather patterns from the Atlantic and Pacific Oceans. Winters are long, cold, and dry with temperatures ranging between −21° and −30° Celsius (−5° and −22° Fahrenheit). At night, the temperature can drop as low as −40° Celsius in January and February, the coldest months.

Blizzards occasionally occur in winter. It is more common for these storms to leave frost and ice than snow on the steppe. Snow is heavy in mountain regions, and permafrost covers more than half of the terrain.

Summers are short, warm, and unpredictable. A brief rainy season occurs during summer, and torrential storms can erupt suddenly and cause flooding. The north receives the most rain, between 20 and 35 centimeters (8 and 14 inches) annually. The south averages roughly half this amount, though in the deep south of the Gobi Desert, there might be several years without any precipitation at all. Daily temperatures average between 10° and 27° Celsius (50° and 80° Fahrenheit) and drop significantly at night. Strong winds and sandstorms are common in the spring and fall. Frequent seismic activity occurs in the northern and western portions of the country.

ENVIRONMENT & GEOGRAPHY

Topography

Mongolia's elevation averages 1,580 meters (5,180 feet), and most of it is a high plateau. In general, the elevation decreases from the western and northern mountains to the lower southern and eastern regions.

The land is predominantly semiarid steppe, but has five climatic zones: mountain, steppe, and desert, and the transitional zones between each, which run in west-east belts. Forests, or taiga, covering approximately 7 percent of the land, occur in the north. In the far south, the area known as the Gobi transitions from arid steppe to barren desert.

The Altai, the Hangayn, and the Hentiyn are Mongolia's three major mountain ranges. The Altai Mountains are the highest. They occupy the west and southwest in two spurs and contain the country's highest point, the snow-capped Tavan Bogd Uul, rising 4,374 meters (14,350 feet) in the far west. The fertile Selenge River basin lies between the other two ranges.

The Selenge, with its tributary the Orhon, is Mongolia's major river system. It flows north into Russia's Lake Baikal. Portions of this system are navigable. Other rivers of lesser importance flow east to the Pacific or south into the desert, where they collect in salt lakes or disappear.

There are numerous lakes in the Altai Mountains. The saltwater Lake Uvs is the largest by surface area, while the largest by volume is the freshwater Hövsgöl Lake. Rivers and freshwater lakes are covered with ice during the winter.

Mongolia's capital, Ulaanbaatar, sits 1,350 meters (4,430 feet) above sea level on the Tuul River, in the northeast part of the great Mongolian plateau that forms much of the nation. To the northeast rise the Hentyn Mountains. The Altai Mountains dominate the landscape to the southwest.

Plants & Animals

Plant and animal life in Mongolia is diverse, widespread, and less endangered than in other parts of Asia. The northern taiga zone supports larch, cedar, birch, spruce, and pine; the steppe and the northern desert support grass and shrubs. Except in oases, only scattered shrubs and grasses are found in the southern desert.

Wolf, reindeer, wild boar, brown bear, and lynx inhabit the taiga. Near its edge and into the northern steppe live muskrat, fox, sable, and marmot. Gazelle and migratory birds abound on the steppe. Further south, in the drier steppe regions and the desert, there are wild ass, antelope, bears, sheep, gazelles, and ibex as well as the critically endangered Bactrian camel. Wild horses, called takhi, have been successfully reintroduced to this region.

Reptiles found in the desert include sand boas and geckos. Bird life is particularly rich around the eastern lakes, which also support a variety of fish species. In the western Altai Mountains live the Argali sheep, Siberian ibex, lynx, and the endangered snow leopard.

CUSTOMS & COURTESIES

Greetings

As in many cultures, elders in Mongolia are highly respected and are usually greeted before anyone else in a group. Urban Mongolians will typically maintain eye contact with the person they are greeting and shake hands with their right hands. Removing gloves before shaking hands is considered an important show of respect. Many rural Mongolians, however, do not shake hands in greeting, but rather outstretch their arms. Mongolians will also typically say "Sain baina uu" ("Hello").

Greetings are also often dictated by specific situations. For example, Mongolians living in Ulaanbaatar and other cities and urban areas will often greet with the equivalent of "How are you?" The appropriate response, regardless of actual circumstance, would be "Fine." On the other hand, countryside greetings often involve questions about animals or family, or how one is faring in the current season. Additionally, most men, particularly in the countryside, will offer a snuffbox to male visitors or friends as a form of greeting and welcoming. It would be rude to refuse, so it is customary to accept and carry out the motions of taking some of the snuff, before returning the snuffbox.

Mongolian nomadic culture is intimately associated with horses and horse riding, and young children learn to ride almost as soon as they can walk. Therefore, related idioms and forms of address have crept into the vernacular. Examples of greetings and farewells that many rural Mongolians use with each other include, "Have you ridden well?", and "Ride in peace."

Gestures & Etiquette

Mongolian culture is dominated by Buddhist philosophy, which recognizes a distinct symbolic hierarchy in the human body. As such, the head—and all objects associated with the head—is far more personal than the feet. Therefore, it is considered extremely rude to handle another person's hat. Though hats are common, and nearly all men wear them, they must be taken off indoors. This same belief is also the principle behind the taboo of pointing one's feet at other people or important places and objects, such as a fire or religious altar. Additionally, as in many cultures, certain hand or finger signals can be very expressive. In Mongolia, an outstretched little finger is universally understood to represent something bad.

Vast, uninhabited countryside dominates much of Mongolia. Great distances stretch between cities, towns and communities, and hotels (outside of Ulaanbaatar) are extremely rare. As such, nomadic Mongolians are typically very welcoming and hospitable to passing travelers. Strangers are often offered food and rest for the night in the host's ger. The following day, passing travelers may also be accompanied for a small distance to ensure that they find their way.

Mongolians will often use terms of respect for people older than themselves, even if they are strangers. Addressing an older individual as "akh-aa" (roughly equivalent to older brother or uncle) is common. Superstitions also play a role in certain subjects that are considered taboo. Any talk of death, tragedies, accidents, or sickness is not received well by Mongolians, even if only in jest. Lastly, when eating, or even exchanging items with another person, Mongolians will exclusively use their right hands, palm up when possible. The left hand is typically used to support the elbow of the right arm.

Eating/Meals

For nomadic Mongolian families, mealtime is an opportunity for the family to come together and sit around the cooking fire. Rural families are self-supporting by necessity, and meals tend to include copious amounts of meat and dairy products from the family's herd. As in many Asian cultures, cooking and meal preparation is traditionally the responsibility of women. Mongolians also typically eat with their fingers, and almost exclusively use their right hands.

The largest meals in Mongolian culture are typically breakfast and lunch. In fact, there is a traditional saying that goes, "Breakfast, keep for yourself; lunch, share with your friends; dinner, give to your enemies." As dinner is not a popular meal, many restaurants and guanz (small cafeterias or food stalls) close early in the evening. In addition, Mongolians living in Ulaanbaatar have more options for domestic and international dining. Although many families still buy fresh ingredients at markets to cook at home, young Mongolians increasingly choose to dine out at restaurants.

Visiting

More so than in many other countries, appropriate behavior and etiquette in Mongolia is dominated by a complex series of traditional rules, rituals, and superstitions. Visitors traditionally announce their arrival with a shout of "Nokhoi khor!" outside the entrance. Though this greeting literally means, "Hold the dogs," it is commonly understood to mean, "Can I come in?" It is also considered rude to knock on the door of a ger, the traditional Mongolian home also known as a yurt (sounds like "yert").

Once invited in, visitors should enter and move to the left, as the western side of the central stove is reserved for men and special guests. The host family will often offer food, which traditionally consisted of snacks of dried cheese, hardened milk curds (aaruul), vodka, or tea. To avoid offense, good manners dictate that visitors sample at least a small amount of anything that is offered.

Among the many rules of behavior enforced when visiting a ger, one should never lean against a support column, whistle, touch anyone's hat, eat (or take food) with the left hand, point a knife blade first, or point one's feet at the central stove, altar, or another person. The two central bagana, or support columns, have special significance in a ger. Together, they support and hold up the home, much as a husband and wife support the family. Therefore, it is traditionally considered impolite to walk between or lean against the columns. Fire is also considered sacred to Mongolians. Trash is never thrown on a fire and fires should never be extinguished by stamping it with one's feet. Mongolians will simply let a fire die out of its own accord, when it is no longer needed for light, warmth, or cooking.

LIFESTYLE

Family

Mongolian society has traditionally been, and continues to be, nomadic in nature. Families tend to live in close proximity with each other in single-room gers, even in urban areas. Urban apartments also tend to be only one or two rooms in size. Though families tend to be physically and emotionally close, strong hierarchical relationships exist between generations. As in most Asian countries, respect for the elderly and for one's parents is strong, and younger generations are expected to value and follow the examples set forth by their elders. Many Mongolians continue to adhere to the traditional Mongolian proverb, "Regardless of how good a son is born, he can never be wise without a father's instructions."

Similar to Chinese culture, the Spring Festival (Lunar New Year) is a major holiday and occasion for families to come together. On New Year's Eve, the entire family will gather for singing, dancing, storytelling, and feasting, while offering thanks to the elder generations. Celebrations will often last through the night. For many families that inhabit the generally isolated countryside, this is a rare opportunity for togetherness, festivities, and thanksgiving.

Traditionally, Mongolians viewed the family as their primary obligation. Therefore, the family, rather than the individual, is usually seen as the most basic unit of social organization. Since many Mongolians lead nomadic lifestyles and/or live in very remote locations, parents were historically responsible for disciplining and educating their children, as access to formal education was nonexistent. Many urban families now have the option to send children to public school or private boarding schools. Rural families, however, still have very limited options, and many children in the countryside continue to spend most of their childhoods herding livestock.

Housing

The most iconic image of Mongolian housing is the ger, commonly known as the yurt, which is a round, wooden-framed structure that is the preferred, if not exclusive, home design in rural areas. The interior wooden frame, or khana, easily collapses, making the design incredibly convenient for the historically nomadic people who populated the Mongolian countryside. The khana is typically covered with a layer of felt or animal hides for warmth and insulation, and then an outer layer of white canvas for aesthetics and weatherproofing. Two central columns, known as bagana, support the entire structure and lead to the toono, a smoke hole at the top of the ger.

Traditionally, the ger is always positioned so that the door faces south, toward Mecca. Buddhist Mongolians might place a religious altar against the wall opposite the door and sleep with their heads toward this altar. The stove occupies a central location inside the ger. Male family members and guests sit on the western side of the stove, while women and children sit on the eastern side.

Most people in Ulaanbaatar live in large, Soviet-style apartment blocks. Many of these buildings are old and the exteriors are often stale and characterless. Apartments are centrally heated and cooled by government energy supplies. Many families live in gers in smaller urban areas as well.

Food

True Mongolian cuisine is vastly different from the artificial Western concept of "Mongolian barbeque," which is really just a variation of Chinese cuisine. The staple ingredient (and often only menu choice) in Mongolia is mutton, or sheep's meat. It is prepared and served in a variety of ways: grilled, fried, boiled, and stewed. Many Mongolians will eat simple boiled mutton, but they will also prepare mutton with noodles, with rice, or as dumplings. Since much of the Mongolian lifestyle surrounds livestock and the herding of cows, goats, camels and sheep, dairy products such as milk, cheese, cream, and yogurt are popular. Known as white foods, these products are traditionally made with the milk of any particular livestock.

Two uniquely Mongolian dishes, prepared on special occasions, are khorkhog and boodog. For khorkhog, an entire sheep is cut up and placed inside a sealed container, along with vegetables and hot stones. Water fills the container, and the resulting steam created by the hot stones cooks the meat. To prepare boodog, the internal organs are removed from a goat or marmot (ground squirrel) and replaced with hot stones. The animal is then exposed to a strong flame, which heats the stones and cooks the meat from the inside out.

As in many Asian cultures, tea is a very popular drink. Mongolians tend to prefer a variation known as salty tea (süütei tsai). Russian influence is most notable in the widespread Mongolian taste for vodka. Herders in the countryside also distill their own alcoholic drink known as airag, made from fermented mare's milk.

Life's Milestones

In Mongolia, couples will often marry when they are between eighteen and twenty-five years of age. Traditionally, married couples occupy their own ger, or yurt, where they will live. The ger is a traditional wedding present from the groom's family. Many local customs and traditions are involved in the process of courtship and marriage. Rites include, among others, the common practice of repeated proposals by the bridegroom before his offer is accepted. He must show determination and persistence in winning the woman's hand by repeatedly bringing gifts and offerings to her family.

If all the gifts are accepted, the engagement is official. Some communities continue the "refusal" process by slamming the door in the face of the soon-to-be in-laws. Again, after several attempts, the door will finally open and the two families will welcome the couple as betrothed. Traditionally, a local lama, or Buddhist priest, will choose an auspicious day for the wedding ceremony. The official joining of husband and wife is often a private affair, only witnessed by immediate family and enforced as legitimate by both fathers. In general, wedding celebrations are often elaborate and attended by entire communities.

Local customs relating to the end of life often dictate exact burial practices, but Mongolians are known to practice cremation, burial in the ground, and natural burial (also called wilderness burial). Today, the most common practice is to bury the deceased in community cemeteries. Mongolians living in China cremate their dead. The wilderness burial has its roots in Lamaist Buddhism and is nearly identical to the Tibetan "sky burial." The body of the deceased is left unprotected on the uninhabited steppe, and belief holds that as wild animals and birds eat the remains, the deceased's soul rises to heaven. Though still practiced in certain parts of the country, the wilderness burial is becoming less common.

CULTURAL HISTORY

Art

Much of Mongolia's artistic culture is closely tied to Buddhism (particularly Tibetan Buddhism) and religious expression. Though severely repressed and nearly extinguished by the communist regime that came to power in the early 20th century, many stellar examples of Mongol art and sculpture have survived. Mongolia's most famous artist was Zanabazar (1635–1723), who was designated by the Dalai Lama as a "Living Buddha." A type of Renaissance man, Zanabazar composed music, sculpted, painted, and was considered an exceptional religious scholar. He is particularly known for his bronze sculptures of Buddhist deities, with feature exquisite detail and expressive characteristics.

Another form of Buddhist art that proved popular and enduring in Mongolia was scroll painting. Though Buddhist scroll paintings are generally associated with Tibet, Mongolia also had a thriving history of developing highly detailed and superb examples of the form. Many historical paintings did not survive the communist regime and religious purges of the 20th century, but scroll paintings are once again beginning to find their way into Mongolian temples and households.

Mongolian folk art has typically been limited to jewelry and clothing. The predominantly nomadic lifestyle often precluded development of ornate, overly ornamental folk art. Unique patterns, designs, and colors often distinguish ethnic groups. They are found on a wide variety of utilitarian objects, such as horse saddles and paraphernalia, traveling bags, and the del, a one-piece garment that is traditionally worn by most Mongolians. Costumes and masks made for tsam dances are among the few forms of exceptionally vibrant and elaborate folk art.

Architecture

Mongolian architecture is largely characterized by the moveable, framed, rope-girdled, and felt-covered dwellings known as gers, or yurts. Historians contend that these traditional and portable dwellings are the foundation of Mongolian architectural heritage, and centric construction has also been a prominent feature of Mongolian architecture. Early on, as settlement took hold, enlarged gers were used as temples (the use of stone, beams, and brick added to the permanence of these structures). Religion continued to play a prominent part in the country's architectural heritage through the medieval centuries; Buddhist temples adorned with frescoes and palaces illuminated with large windows (as if to evoke the great steppe) and decorated with rooftop sculptures are still extant. The architecture of the 16th through the 19th centuries is largely influenced by the Tibetan and Chinese traditions, evident in the monastic construction of temples or the prevalence of stupas. The Soviet influence ushered in a period of classicism as defined by the socialist (or Stalinist) architecture of the Soviet Union, a style that exudes a sense of utilitarianism and "mass production."

Drama

Mongolia has a history of dramatic productions dating back to at least the Mongol-ruled Yuan

Dynasty in China during the 13th and 14th centuries. Like many other forms of artistic expression, drama suffered during the communist regime, and has only relatively recently begun to show a resurgence. Ulaanbaatar is today home to several theaters, and some of them stage traditional cultural performances, typically for tourists. Others, such as the State Opera and Ballet Theatre and the National Academic Drama Theatre, stage performances of original Mongolian plays, ballets, and operas.

Music

Traditional Mongolian music uses a range of instruments. Many of these are unique variations of instruments familiar to other cultures, such as the horse head fiddle, lute, trumpet, flute, zither (string instrument), and drums. The most unique and well-known components of traditional Mongolian music, however, are the solo singing styles known as khuumii and urtiin duu.

Khuumii, or throat singing, is performed without instrumental accompaniment. The sound comes from deep in the larynx and throat, and produces the effect of two distinct notes at the same time. Khuumii developed in western Mongolia and the present-day Russian republic of Tuva. This style of singing is thought to have developed because of animistic religious beliefs surrounding the inherent spirituality in nature, and people's attempts to mimic these sounds. The open expanse of the Eurasian Steppe was also favorable for this type of singing, which allowed voices to travel long distances with minimal effort.

Urtiin duu, or long songs, date back to the 13th century, when the style was practiced as a professional art. Urtiin duu relate intricate stories about the natural beauty of the land and the rituals of daily life. The vocal style is similar to khuumii in that it takes a talented, practiced singer in order to perform well. The sounds are drawn-out and require extreme control of the singer's breath and guttural techniques. Some examples of this style have been recorded to have as many as 20,000 verses, thus earning the name "long songs." One of the most famous

singers of urtiin duu was Namjilyn Norovbanzad (1931–2002), who was celebrated for her crystal-clear voice and excellent command of the style.

The United Nations Educational, Scientific and Cultural Organization (UNESCO) has recognized two traditional forms of music associated with Mongolia as an intangible cultural heritage (ICH). These are culturally significant traditions that are passed orally, and recognized for their importance to world culture and humanity. In 2003, UNESCO recognized the traditional music of the morin khuur, a traditional two-stringed fiddle, and in 2005, the Urtiin Duu, or "long song," was recognized.

Dance

Another aspect of Mongolian culture that is heavily influenced by Buddhist doctrine and belief is traditional dance. The most significant dance is the tsam dance. Like Buddhism itself, tsam dances originally came to Mongolia from India through Tibet. Tsam dances are tantric rituals designed to exorcise evil spirits, purify unclean environments, prevent suffering, and encourage good fortune. Only highly trained, specialized lamas can perform tsam dances. In addition, tsam dances are meant to cleanse the spirits of those involved and lead them on the true Buddhist path. The masks worn during the dances are vibrantly colored, elaborate masks that represent various Buddhist deities or mythological figures.

In 1940, the National Circus of Mongolia was founded. Since then, it has grown and prospered. Today, it has become one of the leading exporters of Mongolian culture to the world. More a cultural variety show than a Western-style circus, the Mongolian Circus incorporates traditional music, dance, clothing, and contortion acts into its repertoire.

Literature

Mongolia has a rich cultural heritage of literature and storytelling that dates back many centuries. In ancient times, many stories and legends were passed on in the form of oral epics, which were often sung. Today, this oral tradition survives in the form of long songs. The three classic stories are *Jangar*, *King Gesar*, and *Manas*. These epic poems concern the battle of good against evil, the origin myth, and development and proliferation of Buddhism, and the archetypal hero's journey. These epics remain part of the living heritage of many Mongolians and other Central Asian cultures. They are also unique in their length—by some accounts totaling nearly a million lines each.

Mongolian literature also developed because of the culture's intimate association with Buddhism. Countless sutras, treatises, and other religious texts have been discovered that date back centuries. The pages of the sacred sutra, Sanduin jud, are famously made of thin silver plates, with letters engraved in gold. (In Buddhism, sutras are canonical scriptures that derive from the oral teachings of the Buddha). It is claimed that this sutra contains almost 115 pounds of gold and more than 880 pounds of silver.

The Secret History of the Mongols is perhaps the single most important work of classical Mongolian literature. It is the oldest known work, dating to the 13th century, and includes the most comprehensive native account of Chinggis (Genghis) Khan (c. 1162–1227) and his family. The only version currently known to exist is a Chinese translation, though the original Mongolian masterpiece skillfully combined poetry and narrative text.

CULTURE

Arts & Entertainment

From the early 20th century to the early 21st century, Mongolia has progressed from a very pastoral, nomadic society to a suppressive communist regime, to one that is opening up to the world with great enthusiasm for democracy and capitalism. In recent years, Mongolia is developing its identity in a wider international context. Consequently, Mongolia's contemporary arts scene is influenced and informed by this unique historical worldview.

During the communist rule of the 20th century, many fields of art were state controlled. They focused almost exclusively on the glories of the communist regime, the ideal working class individual, and the perceived perfection of a communist system. Since democratization in the 1990s, contemporary arts have been allowed to develop free of censorship and restraint. Artists creating music, paintings, and literature have managed to identify and nurture a unique Mongolian "voice." Today, contemporary arts are, compared to the situation as recent as the 1980s and 1990s, flourishing.

Mongolia's capital, Ulaanbaatar, is the center for virtually all expansion in the contemporary art scene. (Outside of the capital, there are very few influential contemporary art communities.) Ironically, the organization that was originally founded by the communist government to suppress alleged radical forms of art, the Union of Mongolian Artists, has developed into one of the most influential and relevant sources of support for a wide variety of artistic expression. Several museums, art galleries, and performance spaces are now open in Ulaanbaatar. Though the modern art scene may not be thriving, all indications suggest that it is healthy and continuing to grow.

Today, khuumii, or throat singing, has become internationally known. However, many Mongolians still enjoy listening to and singing traditional music such as khuumii and long songs, young people, as in most countries, tend to prefer modern pop music. There are many local groups that perform in the Mongolian language, but much of the music is influenced by Western and Russian musical styles, such as rock, funk, hip-hop, and heavy metal.

The formation of the state philharmonic in 1957 was also a source of national pride. Successful Mongolian composers include Luvsanyamts Murdorj (1915–1996) and Bilegiin Damdinsüren (1919–1991), both credited with composing the national anthem of Mongolia.

Another form of artistic expression that is relatively new for the country is narrative film. Mongolia is not renowned for its cinema, but there have been several significant advances in film in recent years. *The Story of the Weeping Camel* was a 2003 documentary by Mongolian filmmaker Byambasuren Davaa (1971–). The film was nominated for a 2004 Academy Award in the documentary category. Focusing on the trials of everyday life for a nomadic family in rural Mongolia, the film blended its true subjects with an element of drama.

In 2007, an international co-production (including Mongolia) produced *Mongol*, a film about the early years in the life of Chinggis (Genghis) Khan. Though directed by a Russian and filmed primarily in Mongolian regions of China, the film's central subject is essentially Mongolian. *Mongol* was nominated for a 2007 Academy Award in the best foreign language film category. The film is the first in a planned trilogy about the life of the Mongolian ruler.

The most popular Mongolian sports are incorporated into the Naadam festival, the country's prime sporting event, which takes place over several days each summer. The festival includes archery, horseracing, and wrestling. Each of these sports have long been integral to the Mongolian identity, and the popularity and respect reserved for them indicate that they will continue to be so, even as a sedentary lifestyle gradually overtakes the traditional nomadic lifestyle.

Cultural Sites & Landmarks

Though Mongolia does have many cultural sites, museums, and tourist attractions, the real destination is Mongolia itself. The abundant natural beauty, astonishing expanse of countryside, diversity of environments, and vibrant cultural events and festivals are the major lures for travelers and visitors. The country, its landscape, and the rich cultural heritage of its people are also the pride and joy of the Mongolians themselves.

Compared to other world capitals, Ulaanbaatar has a laid-back, small town feel. Sükhbaatar Square is centrally located within the capital, and was the location of several defining moments in Mongolian history. In 1921, it was the place where Mongolian military leader Damdin Sükhbaatar (1893–1923) proclaimed that Mongolia was

The traditional clothing in Mongolia includes the del (or deel), made in a distinct style for each ethnic group, and boots with upturned toes.

finally an independent country, free of Chinese rule. A large statue of his likeness dominates the square. Sükhbaatar Square was also the site where the first rallies against the communist regime were held in 1989. Surrounding the square are imposing government office buildings, and it was also the site, until 2005, of Damdin Sükhbaatar's massive mausoleum.

Also in Ulaanbaatar is Gandantegchinlen Khiid (Gandan Khiid), the largest and most important Buddhist monastery in all of Mongolia. Construction began in 1835, and the monastery luckily survived the destructive communist regime, spared in order to remain a cultural centerpiece of tourism. As of 2008, more than 400 monks were in residence at the monastery, which is also home to Zanabazar Buddhist University and several other schools devoted to religion and traditional medicine.

Founded in 1220 by Chinggis (Genghis) Khan, Kharkhorin served as the capital of the Mongolian empire before Kublai Khan moved the capital to what is now Beijing in the People's Republic of China. It was later destroyed and eventually replaced with the modern industrial town of the same name. The archaeological remains and historical significance of Kharkhorin have been inscribed on the UNESCO World Heritage List as part of the Orkhon Valley Cultural Landscape.

While central and eastern Mongolia are characterized by rolling grasslands and prairies known as steppes, the north is predominantly taiga (subarctic coniferous forest). The far west is home to the towering Mongol Altai Nuruu mountain range. However, dominating nearly one-third of the country, including the entire south, is the Gobi Desert. Only small portions of it claim the iconic sand dunes that have become the stereotyped image, with the most famous being Khongoryn Els. These remarkable, 800 meter-high (2,624 feet) dunes are located in Gurvan Saikhan National Park, one of the most visited national parks in the country. This park is also famous for the discovery of dinosaur fossils and bones, and a small glacier that remains frozen year round.

The most famous cultural attraction, and the biggest festival of the year in Mongolia, is the Naadam Festival. Held in the capital in early July and in the countryside as well, this festival is the rough equivalent of a Mongolian Olympics. Naadam focuses on the three masculine sports of wrestling, archery, and horseracing, all popular since ancient times. Spread over three days, competition in the three events draws Mongolians from across the country and tourists from around the world.

Libraries & Museums

After the collapse of the Soviet Union, Ulaanbaatar underwent a cultural transformation, and numerous museums and other cultural sites opened. The Museum of Natural History, just north of Sukhbaatar Square, features the com-

plete fossilized remains of two dinosaurs. The University of Mongolia, established in 1942, is the only institution of higher education in the country. The university's library contains ancient Mongolian, Chinese, and Tibetan manuscripts. In addition, the city has more than seventy private cultural institutions, six cinemas, three state-sponsored cultural centers, eight libraries, seven museums and ten professional art and entertainment organizations.

The National Library of Mongolia, home to approximately three million volumes of books, is located near Sukhbaatar Square in the capital of Ulaanbaatar.

Holidays

National holidays in Mongolia include Mother and Child Day (June 1); Independence Day (July 11), marking the country's independence from China; and Constitution Day (November 26).

The largest and most important holiday is Tsagaan Sar (White Month), celebrated in late February as the beginning of the new lunar year and the end of winter. The holiday entails three days of feasting, the first of which occurs on the eve of the holiday. Families and friends gather to eat and give gifts. They also don new clothes and visit monasteries.

Youth Culture

Roughly, 40 percent of Mongolia's population is between the ages of sixteen and thirty-five. This ranks the country as one of the most youthful, and with statistics pointing toward a downward trend in average age, Mongolia promises to become more youthful with the coming generation. However, Mongolia remains a developing country with a noticeable lack of infrastructure outside of the capital, Ulaanbaatar. Western-style entertainment options are few and, outside of the capital, virtually nonexistent. Furthermore, Mongolian youth generally have very little, if any, disposable income, meaning luxuries such as technology or personal accessories, or the latest designer clothing trends, have minimal impact on youth culture.

Ulaanbaatar has a number of bars and discos (clubs) that primarily cater to more affluent tourists, but which also attract many young Mongolians. Shopping malls, cinemas, and other places typically associated with youth hangouts in Western cultures simply do not exist in Mongolia. In the countryside, most youth are engaged with domestic or rural responsibilities, such as tending to the family livestock. As they come of age, many choose to marry early (in the early twenties) and begin their own family, and continue working and living a nomadic lifestyle.

SOCIETY

Transportation

The Trans-Mongolian Railway passes straight through the center of Mongolia with several major stops, including Ulaanbaatar. The capital also has a public bus system. The one-track subway, Ulaanbaatar Metroo, carries 120,000 passengers daily over eight kilometers (about five miles). The Metroo was built in 1994. All the country's major roads and caravan routes meet in Ulaanbaatar.

While the main roadways radiating out from Ulaanbaatar are paved, most of the country is connected with basic, unpaved overland tracks. Because of this, trucks and four-wheel drive vehicles are popular. Long-distance bus service does not exist, and most people travel overland by shared vans and jeeps. Traffic moves on the right-hand side of the road.

Transportation Infrastructure

Mongolia has more than 1,770 kilometers (1,100 miles) of railway track. A vast majority of this track forms the Trans-Mongolian Railway that connects Mongolia with Russia to the north, and China to the south. While Mongolia and Russia both use the same broad gauge rail system, China uses a standard gauge system. Consequently, when trains cross the Mongolia-China border, each car must be lifted and its wheels changed.

Air transport is heavily used in order to travel conveniently the long distances between cities. There are forty-four airports in Mongolia, and thirteen have paved runways. Chinggis Khan International Airport is located in Ulaanbaatar.

Media & Communications

Prior to 1990, the communist regime exercised tight control over the media and very few freedoms were granted to the press. Adoption of the democratic constitution in 1992 created a new landscape for Mongolian journalism and media. Print, radio, and television media outlets prospered throughout the country due to the freedoms guaranteed in the constitution. Today, the most widely read newspapers include *Zuunii Medee* (*Century News*), *Unuudur* (*Today*) and *Udriin Sonin* (*Daily News*). Among 175 recognized newspapers, a vast majority are published in Mongolian, while fifteen are available in foreign languages.

The growth of the Internet has also played a role in the development of a free press. Due to a lack of infrastructure, dial-up Internet access is still the most widely used system in Mongolia. Faster services such as wireless and broadband access are beginning to have an impact, and in 2014, Internet users made up an estimated 17.9 percent of the population. Television, though still an emerging medium in Mongolia, is also an incredibly influential and popular form of media. Popular channels include the state-controlled National Central TV and UBTV.

Mobile phones are not only very popular in Mongolia; they are also the preferred form of communication. A full telephone communications network was never implemented throughout much of the country, and cell phone stations and towers are effectively connecting the country for the first time.

SOCIAL DEVELOPMENT

Standard of Living

Mongolia ranked 103rd on the 2014 United Nations Human Development Index, which measures quality of life and standard of living indicators.

Water Consumption
In a country where 70 percent of the land is dry surface area, water is a precious commodity. Groundwater provides an estimated 80 percent of water consumption, while 20 percent is sourced from surface water. Water consumption, per capita, is extremely low. According to 2015 statistics from the World Health Organization, approximately 64 percent of the population has access to sources of improved drinking water, while 60 percent of the population has access to improved sanitation (though these numbers have been reported as low as 40 percent and 25 percent, respectively).

Education
Since the early 1990s, Mongolia has struggled to reform its educational system, and has made significant progress towards its modernization. Education is free and compulsory until the age of fifteen. Primary school enrollment is nearly perfect, but enrollment in secondary school drops to 70 percent. At this level, girls outnumber boys nearly two-to-one, since boys traditionally take on the responsibility for their family's livestock. The disparity between rural and urban education is partially alleviated by a system of boarding schools that allows the children of nomads to attend school. The literacy rate in Mongolia is 98 percent.

Higher education is centered in Ulaanbaatar. The National University of Mongolia is the country's oldest. It specializes in the natural and social sciences and the humanities for both undergraduates and post-graduates. Other institutes include the Mongolian Technical University and the Mongolian University of Arts and Culture.

The Gender Gap Index 2014, published by the World Economic Forum, analyzes the role of gender on issues such as health care, educational attainment, and political representation. Overall, Mongolia ranked 42nd among the 142 countries analyzed in 2014. According to the 2014 Index, the gender gap in education has largely closed in Mongolia, particularly concerning enrollment in primary education; however, women's enrollment in secondary and tertiary education is slightly higher than that of men's. The even literacy rates for men and women (98 percent and 98 percent, respectively, in 2014) demonstrate the country's success in equalizing access to education.

Women's Rights
The Mongolian constitution directly provides equal rights for men and women and prohibits gender discrimination. However, Mongolian culture, though changing, continues to devalue the traditional roles and responsibilities of women. For example, women have yet to make major headway in national politics (though a woman has twice held the position of minister of foreign affairs) and domestic violence against women has become a serious issue in Mongolia, and is showing signs of worsening. Though laws exist prohibiting domestic abuse and rape, some observers believe that nearly some form of domestic abuse has affected one-third of all Mongolian women.

Alcohol abuse has also been on the rise in Mongolia, and many see the two trends as closely related. Traditionally, issues such as domestic violence, child abuse, and alcohol abuse were seen as private family matters, not broader social concerns. This perception is changing as these issues and their destructive effects have been brought into the public consciousness through media coverage and public discussion. High alcohol abuse rates have directly led to an increase in reported physical abuse cases, joblessness, and single-parent families (typically headed by the mother). Mongolian law provides equal rights for men and women, equality of pay, and universal suffrage. However, a comprehensive women's rights agenda suffers in several respects.

There is no law prohibiting spousal rape, prostitution is legal (though public solicitation is illegal), there are no laws against sexual harassment, and there is no government office responsible for the oversight of women's rights. In

2004, the Mongolian Parliament passed the Law against Domestic Violence, which highlighted prevention activities, duties of the police, rights of the victims, and liabilities and responsibilities of perpetrators. The United Nations Development Fund for Women (UNIFEM) claims, "The laws are inadequate or discriminatory, resources are short, law enforcement officials need more sensitization, and a dearth of statistics means the issue of violence is never clearly defined."

According to a 2003 human rights report by the U.S. Department of State, there was only a single shelter in the country for victims of domestic abuse, which was largely financed by international organizations. Domestic Mongolian institutions dedicated to women's rights and social advancement include the National Center against Violence, Mongolian Women Lawyer's Association, Mongolian Women Farmers' Association, and the National Human Rights Commission (Mongolia).

Regionally, UNIFEM and other organizations are involved in a number of initiatives to reverse the negative trend currently seen in women's rights and domestic violence. One such project is the 2006 UN Trust Fund in Support of Actions to Eliminate Violence against Women. These projects aim to empower women, provide them with a voice, and offer constructive and viable opportunities to improve their situations.

Health Care

The Mongolian government has pledged to bring basic health care to every citizen. Over the last decade, the system has undergone positive changes in its structure and reach, with special attention being paid to pre-natal and post-natal care, including a successful immunization program. The infant mortality rate has thus decreased significantly.

Overall, there are adequate numbers of nurses and physicians. However, the rural population receives less care than the urban population because of the remoteness of some settlements and the extreme climatic conditions that prevail across the country. Public awareness campaigns regarding good hygiene practices, reproductive health, and nutrition are making headway.

GOVERNMENT

Structure

Mongolia has had a parliamentary system of government since the new constitution was implemented in 1992. A president is chief of state, and a prime minister heads the government. Presidents are elected by direct vote to a four-year term, with a two-term limit, after being nominated by the legislature's political parties. The prime minister is the leader of the political party, which wins the majority in legislative elections.

The unicameral legislature is called the Great Hural (Assembly). It is composed of seventy-six members who are directly elected to four-year terms. The president and the legislature are together responsible for building the cabinet.

Political Parties

Since the end of one-party Communist rule, several political parties have come into being. They include the Citizens' Will Republican Party, the Democratic Party, the Motherland-Mongolian New Social Democratic Party, and the Mongolian People's Revolutionary Party. As of the 2012 parliamentary elections, the Democratic Party is the ruling party, holding thirty-one seats. The opposition party is the Mongolian's People's Party, with twenty-five seats, and there are two parties with fewer than twelve seats.

Local Government

Mongolia is divided into twenty-one provinces and one municipality (Ulaanbaatar). The provinces are further divided into districts. Assemblies, headed by directly elected representatives, make up the local governments.

Judicial System

The judicial branch is presided over by the Supreme Court, below which are administrative and appellate courts in the capital, and provincial courts and district courts. A General Council of Courts installs the judges, pending presidential approval. The judiciary mixes both German and Soviet legal systems.

Taxation

Mongolia has a top competitive corporate tax rate of 25 percent, while the income tax rate is a flat rate levied at 10 percent. Other taxes include a dividend tax, excise tax, and a value-added tax (or VAT, similar to a consumption tax).

Armed Forces

The Mongolian armed forces consist of three branches: a general-purpose force, border defense force, and an internal security force. Conscription is practiced and consists of a twelve-month service obligation between the ages of eighteen and twenty-five (though conscripts can opt to serve in an alternative service such as the police). As of 2006, women were not deployed overseas. The armed forces have participated in global peacekeeping missions and other international activities, including Iraq (post-war) and areas of conflict on the African continent.

Foreign Policy

Prior to the democratic reforms begun in 1990, Mongolia was a one-party, communist nation with very close political ties to the former Soviet Union. Since 1990, and the ratification of Mongolia's democratic constitution in 1992, the government and nation of Mongolia have opened up to the world and foreign affairs considerably.

Geographically, Mongolia is landlocked between Russia and China and, therefore, has a high level of interest in friendly, productive relationships with both countries. Historically, and as recently as the 1980s, Mongolia and China have had periods of tense relations. Mongolia did not join the UN until 1961 because of repeated threats by China to veto its acceptance. Until 1921, Mongolia was a Chinese province, and China did not recognize the legitimacy of an independent Mongolia.

Since the deterioration of Mongolia's one-party communist rule, the two nations have sought to improve relations. Several high-level diplomatic visits between heads of state have taken place in recent years. Since the 1990s, and in the interest of both domestic growth and regional security, Mongolia has also developed productive relationships with Russia and the former Soviet republics. Diplomatic relations and trade agreements with both Russia and China continue to develop and are arguably the healthiest they have ever been.

Mongolia's leaders have also focused foreign policy efforts on constructing and maintaining their place within a stable Asia, particularly with respect to Northeast and Central Asia. In 1998, Mongolia became a full participant in the Association of Southeast Asian Nations (ASEAN) and joined the Pacific Economic Cooperation Council (PECC) two years later. Mongolia also has, and continues to develop, international relationships with regional neighbors in Asia, particularly South Korea, and Japan, both of which contribute a significant amount of aid. In recent years, Mongolia has grown increasingly closer to China.

Diplomatic relations with the United States were established in 1987. Since that time, the U.S. has demonstrated, through trade and investment agreements and development assistance, considerable interest in a democratic Mongolia with a viable, effective economy and government. In 2007, the Millennium Challenge Compact for Mongolia was signed between both countries. Administered by the Millennium Challenge Corporation (MCC), a U.S. government entity that assists poor and developing countries, its specific aims in Mongolia are to promote rail modernization, individual property rights, technical training and education, and health.

Human Rights Profile

International human rights law insists that states respect civil and political rights, and promote an individual's economic, social, and cultural rights. The United Nations Universal Declaration on

Human Rights (UDHR) is recognized as the standard for international human rights. Its authors sought the counsel of the world's great thinkers, philosophers, and religious leaders, and were careful to create a document that reflects the core values shared by every world culture. (To read this document or view the articles relating to cultural human rights, visit http://www.udhr.org/UDHR/default.htm.)

The relatively young democratic Mongolia has, overall, broad respect for human rights and the individual freedoms of its citizens. Cases of politically motivated killings or disappearances are rare, as are reports of political prisoners or detainees. However, several issues attract criticism and the concern of international human rights organizations. These include poor prison conditions and abuse of prisoners, corruption within the police and judicial system, a lack of governmental transparency, and widespread domestic violence against women.

Mongolian prisons are often cited for their lack of basic amenities such as food, heat, and medical care. In many instances, the lack of such essentials unduly threatens the lives of prisoners. Overcrowding is a perennial problem and, outside of Ulaanbaatar, juveniles younger than eighteen are often housed in the same population as adults. Though the government does not inhibit the work and monitoring of international non-governmental organizations (NGOs), there has been little improvement in conditions.

Article 19 of the UDHR outlines freedom of expression and the press. Mongolian law prohibits censorship or government manipulation of the free press and, in general, these rights are respected. There are no restrictions on Internet access and there have been no reports of government monitoring or censorship of expression via the Internet. However, a lack of basic infrastructure throughout the country prevents equal access in the countryside to all available news publications and perspectives. Members of the press have also reported unofficial harassment by government officials in the form of libel and slander lawsuits, physical confrontations, and threats.

Religious freedoms, as set forth in Article 18, are generally widespread and established in Mongolia. Mongolians are predominantly Buddhist, and there is no endemic suppression of Muslim or Christian beliefs. Institutionalized tolerance and citizens' attitudes are usually accepting of all religious differences, with few exceptions. Western Mongolia is home to a Kazakh Muslim minority, and this community is closely monitored by authorities for ties to extremism, terrorism, or political separatism. Tov aimag (province), in central Mongolia, has also been criticized for repeated and routine denials of Christian church registration. As of 2006, no churches were registered in the province.

ECONOMY

Overview of the Economy

The reformed Mongolian economy has had to cope with decades of central economic planning based on a communist model, then a severe crisis precipitated by the loss of all funding from the Soviet Union in 1991. It now has a developing market economy, with only a few major industries and public works still owned by the state.

The per capita gross domestic product (GDP) was an estimated $11,900 in 2014. One-third of the population lives below the poverty line.

Industry

The industrial sector, based primarily in Ulaanbaatar and Darkhan, accounts for 35 percent of the GDP, and 21 percent of the work force. Animal husbandry is central to Mongolia's industrial sector, which processes the animal products for domestic and export markets. Meat and goods made of wool and leather are processed within the country. Other products include construction materials, beverages, and canned fish.

Labor

The labor force numbered approximately 1.128 million in 2014, with a reported unemployment rate of 7.7 percent. The majority of the work force—an estimated 50 percent—was employed in the services sector.

Energy/Power/Natural Resources

Mongolia has a wide range of natural resources, though they have not been exploited extensively. Deposits of oil, copper, tungsten, tin, nickel, coal, zinc, gold, silver, iron and wolfram are present, while the northern forests are a significant source of timber and fur-bearing animals.

Industry and urbanization have caused environmental problems in Mongolia, most acutely in Ulaanbaatar. The air pollution is worst in winter, when coal is burned as a source of heat. Other problems include soil erosion and a wider pattern of desertification from overgrazing and deforestation.

Fishing

Fishing is not a significant economic sector in Mongolia and fish are not widely consumed domestically. Though the country is home to more than 4,000 lakes, most are shallow. Structured fishing is mostly concentrated on the eastern side of Buir Lake (eastern Mongolia) and throughout the western lakes.

Forestry

It is estimated that since that last decade of the 20th century, illegal cutting and fires have significantly reduced forest cover in Mongolia. Approximately 7 percent of the country's forested land is commercial forests.

Mining/Metals

Though large deposits of minerals exist, they have not yet been fully exploited. Mining activities are expanding and are concentrated on copper, molybdenum, fluorspar, iron ore, coal, gold, and oil.

Agriculture

Agriculture accounts for 21 percent of the GDP and occupies 46 percent of the labor force, mostly in the form of animal herding, which has a long history in Mongolia. Sheep are by far the most important type of livestock, but goats, cattle, horses, camels, pigs, chickens, and bees are raised. The richest grazing areas are in the northwest and northeast, but the livestock populations are vulnerable to decimation when sudden blizzards make it impossible for them to graze.

Crop growing is not a central economic activity, given that only a tiny portion of the land is arable. Nevertheless, some farming does take place in the well-watered north and in the south, where irrigated. Wheat, barely, potatoes, fodder for livestock as well as some fruits and vegetables are grown.

Animal Husbandry

Animal products include meat, fat, hides, and wool. Furs are another important product. Fur-bearing animals such as marmots and foxes are hunted while deer and ermine are raised on farms. Cows, goats, yaks, camels, and horses are the most common herded livestock, and account for some 30 million head of livestock together.

Tourism

Mongolia's tourism industry is developing along with its infrastructure. Approximately 250,000 tourists now visit each year, most of them from China, and generate $150 million (USD) annually. August is the busiest month.

The country boasts important cultural institutions, such as the National Museum of Mongolian History, the Natural History Museum, and the Museum of Fine Arts, as well as monasteries and temples. Mongolia's unspoiled scenic beauty and wildlife attract the most visitors. The Guryansaikhan Nature Reserve, which protects portions of the Gobi, and the Khustain Nuruu Nature Reserve are both popular with adventure travelers. Camel treks are promoted as the best way to experience the country's vast steppe and desert.

Jamie Green, Michael Aliprandi, Ellen Bailey

DO YOU KNOW?

- The city of Ulaanbaatar has its own banner, coat of arms, and emblem. It has established relations with many other world cities, including Seoul, Korea; Florence, Italy; Moscow, Russia; and Denver, Colorado.

- Mongolia is known as the "Land of Blue Sky" because of its numerous sunny days.

- The name "Genghis Khan" means "universal king." His real name was Temujin.

- An estimated 25 million domestic animals live in Mongolia.

- The Gobi is the world's coldest and most northerly desert.

- More dinosaur eggs have been found in Mongolia than in any other place on earth.

Bibliography

Avery, Martha. *Women of Mongolia.* Asian Art & Archaeology, 1996.

Becker, Jasper. *Mongolia: Travels in the Untamed Land.* New York: Tauris Parke, 2008.

Embassy of Mongolia, Washington, D.C. Home Page. http://www.mongolianembassy.us/.

Kahn, Paul. *Secret History of the Mongols.* Boston: Cheng & Tsui Company, 1998.

Kohn, Michael, et al. *Mongolia.* Oakland, CA: Lonely Planet, 2014.

Polo, Marco. *The Travels.* London: Penguin Books, 1958.

Rossabi, Morris. *Modern Mongolia: From Khans to Commissars to Capitalists.* Berkeley: University of California Press, 2005.

Sabloff, Paula L., ed. *Modern Mongolia: Reclaiming Genghis Khan.* Philadelphia: University of Pennsylvania Museum of Archaeology and Anthropology, 2001.

Severin, Tim. *In Search of Genghis Khan: An Exhilarating Journey on Horseback across the Steppes of Mongolia.* Cooper Square Press, 2003.

Tsog, Sh. and Simon Wickham-Smith, eds. *A Very Big White Elephant: New Voices in Mongolian Poetry.* Paul Kegan Press, 2008.

Weatherford, Jack. *Genghis Khan and the Making of the Modern World.* Three Rivers Press, 2005.

Works Cited

Lonely Planet: Mongolia 3rd ed. http://www.asia-planet.net
http://www.beyondintractability.org/reflections/personal_ reflections/peace_and_family_traditions.jsp?nid=6813
http://www.mongolfood.info/
http://www.ub-mongolia.mn
http://www.state.gov/r/pa/ei/bgn/2779.htm
http://www.mongolianembassy.us/
http://www.mongoluls.net/
http://whc.unesco.org/en/list/769
http://www.silk-road.com/folklore/manas/manasintro.html
http://www.mongolianculture.com/
http://www.mcc.gov/about/index.php
http://www.amnesty.org/en/region/mongolia/report-2008
http://www.state.gov/g/drl/rls/hrrpt/2006/78783.htm
http://www.unifem.org/gender_issues/violence_against_ women/trust_fund_grantees.php?TFCycleID=13
http://unifem-eseasia.org/projects/evaw/evawindex.htm
http://www.apwld.org/pdf/mongolia_NGO.pdf
http://travel.nytimes.com/2005/07/17/travel/17surface.html

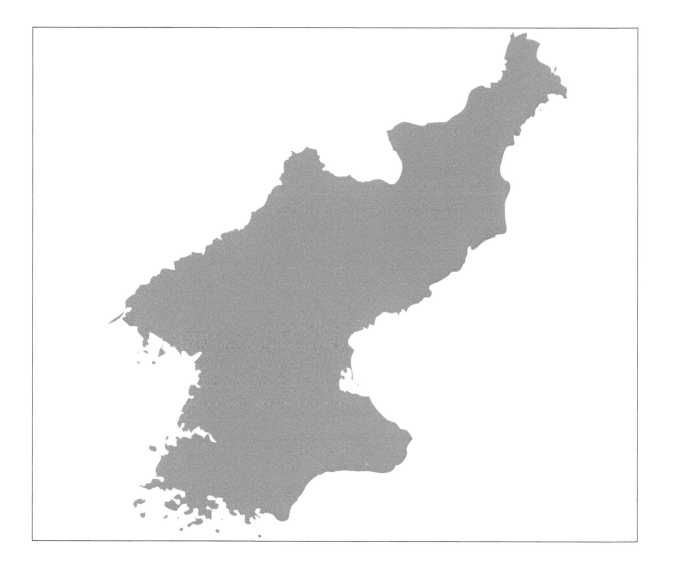

NORTH KOREA

Introduction

The Democratic People's Republic of Korea, generally referred to as North Korea, is a communist country occupying the northern half of the Korean Peninsula in East Asia. The entire Korean peninsula was once an independent kingdom under China, but split into two distinct countries after World War II, one in the north, the other in the south. With this split, North Korea's government and economy became communist.

North Korea is a culture greatly isolated from much of the world. It is governed by a powerful communist dictatorship that exerts extreme control over its citizens. Juche (or Chuch'e) is the ruling ideal or philosophy in North Korea adopted by the government and imposed upon all aspects of life. The term roughly translates to "self-reliance." This has become the official state ideology, and is a variation of communist ideologies. Its hallmarks arc leader worship, loyalty, and patriotism. The arts—their creation, content, presentation, and public distribution—are controlled by the state, and consequently reflect these ideals.

In the Korean language, the country is known as Choson Minjujuui In'min Konghwaguk.

GENERAL INFORMATION

Official Language: Korean
Population: 24,983,205 (2015 estimate)
Currency: Won
Coins: The won is subdivided into 100 chon. Coins come in denominations of 1 won, as well as 1, 5, 10, and 50 chon.

Land Area: 120,408 square kilometers (46,489 square miles)
Water Area: 130 square kilometers (50 square miles)
National Motto: "One is sure to win if one believes in and depends upon the people"
National Anthem: "Aegukka" (also known as "Ach'imun pinnara")
Capital: Pyongyang
Time Zone: GMT +9
Flag Description: The flag of North Korea features three horizontal bands of blue (top), red (middle), and blue (bottom). The red band is edged in white. On the hoist (left) side of the red band is a white circle in the center of which rests a red, five-pointed star.

Population

Aside from a very small number of Chinese residents, North Korea's population is almost completely homogenous, because of the political and cultural isolation that has affected North Korea

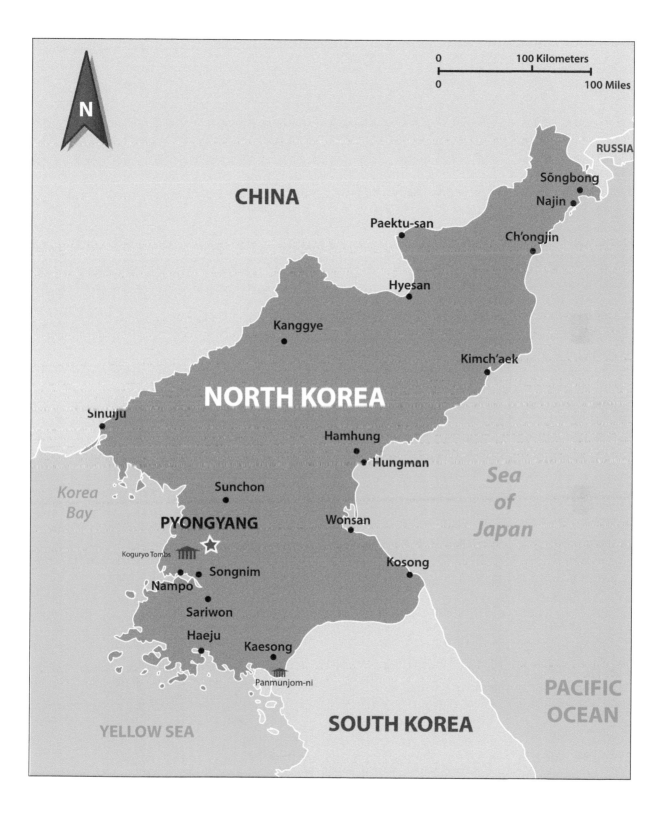

Principal Cities by Population (2012):

- Pyongyang (3,400,000)
- Hamhung (597,037)
- Namp'o (478,999)
- Hungnam (369,594)
- Koesong (361,338)
- Wonsan (348,092)
- Sinuiju (334,031) (2008 estimate)
- Ch'ongjin (331,552)

since 1945. This isolation, an outgrowth of the communist regime led by the Korean Workers' Party (KWP), deeply influences North Korea's religion, language, and population.

The government's postwar emphasis on industrialization left many of the country's farms understaffed. The majority of the population now lives in the coastal urban centers, with few people remaining in the peninsula's mountainous interiors. Most North Koreans live in government-run housing projects, many of which lack basic amenities like water and heat. Most of the rural population lives in the river valley plains or in the coastal lowlands. Some provinces, such as the Chagang and the Yanggang, have nearly been abandoned because of the land's infertility.

Between 1953 and 1980, North Korea's population doubled, to nearly twice the size of neighboring South Korea. The population growth rate was 0.4 percent in 2010. That same year, its population density was approximately 188 people per square kilometer (483 per square mile).

Languages

Korean is the official language in the country. Linguistically, North Korea has attempted to purge its language from any "loanwords" from other languages, particularly Chinese and English. The Korean script, Choson Muntcha, is rigorously censored to avoid these loanwords. North Korea has also worked to rid the country of any reminders of the Japanese colonial period, which lasted from 1910 until 1945.

Native People & Ethnic Groups

There is archaeological evidence of human habitation on the Korean Peninsula as early as 70,000 years ago. The region's first civilization, the Go-Joseon, was established around 2000 BCE.

What is now North Korea occupies the land of three provinces (Pyongyang, Hwanghae, and Hamgyong) of the Chosun Dynasty, which lasted from 1392 to 1910. These provinces were culturally and linguistically distinct, and these distinctions are reflected in the modern population. Today, the country is divided geographically by the Nangnim Mountains into east (Kwanbuk) and west (Kwanso). Like the ancient provinces, the two regions are also culturally distinct.

The vast majority of the population is ethnically Korean. There are, however, small minority groups of Chinese and Japanese.

Religions

Although the government has an official policy of religious freedom, it uses the sole North Korean religion, Ch'ondogyo, as a propaganda tool. Ch'ondogyo ("teaching of the heavenly way") was formerly known as Tonghak ("eastern learning"), and is a combination of Confucian teachings with elements of Buddhism and Christianity. Confucian teacher Ch'oe Chew founded it in 1860.

Climate

Winter lasts for four months, from December to March, with average temperatures of 6° Celsius (43° Fahrenheit). The average summer temperature is 20° Celsius (68° Fahrenheit). It tends to be several degrees warmer on the east coast than on the west coast, mainly due to the dividing mountain ranges and ocean currents.

North Korea's annual average precipitation is 1,000 millimeters (40 inches). The majority of the rain comes during the summer months (June to September), corresponding with the typhoon season. There is also a good amount of snowfall during winter.

ENVIRONMENT & GEOGRAPHY

Topography

North Korea shares borders with China and Russia on the Asian mainland. To the south is the Republic of Korea, commonly referred to as South Korea. It is bordered by the Sea of Japan on the east and by the Yellow Sea on the west. Pyongyang is the capital, located in the southwest portion of the country, about 48 kilometers (roughly 30 miles) east of Korea Bay.

The Nangnim Mountains split North Korea down the middle, dividing the country into distinct east and west regions. The highest mountain on the entire peninsula is Mount Paektu, at 2,750 meters (9,022 feet) above sea level. In between the Myohyang and Kangnam mountain ranges are river valley plains.

In general, North Korea's soil is infertile, comprised mostly of granitic or crystalline rock with little organic content. The best soil in the country can be found in the alluvial soils of the valleys and coastal plains.

Most rivers in North Korea run into the Yellow Sea. One exception is the Tumen River, which runs north for 521 kilometers (324 miles) to the Sea of Japan. The country's longest river is the Yalu River, also a source of hydroelectric power, which runs 800 kilometers (497 miles) into the Korean Bay from Mount Paektu.

Plants & Animals

Most of the forests along the coastal slopes of North Korea were cut down during the Japanese occupation in the first half of the 20th century. Now, most remaining forests of pine, spruce, and larch are located in the northern interior of the country.

Though not completely wiped out, the country's populations of deer, antelope, goats, tigers, and leopards have retreated to the most remote forests. Herons, cranes, and waterfowl are found in the rice fields in North Korea's plains. Eel and carp are commonly found in the country's rivers.

CUSTOMS & COURTESIES

Greetings

Greetings and introductions are usually formal in North Korea, and Kim Il-Sung's name is often invoked. If one is asked, "Annyong haseyo?" ("How do you do?"), the other might answer, "Thanks to the Great Leader, I am well." Bowing is the usual form of greeting, although handshakes are also used. People of younger or lower status will always bow until the other person of higher status offers a handshake or returns the bow. In addition, North Koreans typically greet their superiors with questions concerning their health and parents, while subordinates are greeted with questions concerning their spouses and children.

When North Korean men shake hands, they usually extend the right hand with the head slightly bowed. If the handshake is between professionals who are meeting for the first time, they will exchange business cards. Women rarely shake hands, but rather greet each other by extending both arms and grasping each other's hands. North Korean children always bow to adults, but usually wave to other children.

Gestures & Etiquette

North Koreans highly respect their leader, and will invoke his name when showing gratitude, greeting, or welcoming someone. Additionally, when a North Korean encounters a statue or portrait of Kim Jong Il or Kim Il Sung, he or she will bow to show love and respect. Pilgrimages are also frequently made to the place of Kim Il Sung's upbringing, and it is expected that flowers be laid by the nearest statue or mural of either leader on holidays.

It is common for North Korean men to express friendship by holding hands or simply slinging an arm around another's shoulder. However, touching a stranger or a casual acquaintance is considered highly inappropriate, especially if between two members of the opposite sex. Posture is important in North Korea and standing or sitting in a relaxed manner is considered an insult to the host or elder in attendance. In addition, a citizen of North Korea will never look his superior directly in the eye. North Koreans who live in the cities dress quite formally, with most citizens of Pyongyang wearing dark-colored suits. All citizens are expected to wear a lapel pin, which features a photo of Kim Il Sung.

Eating/Meals

In North Korean culture, both parents are expected to work, meaning families rarely eat meals together. Additionally, because the standard workdays are long—both parents usually leave early in the morning and return late at night—meals are commonly eaten at the workplace. Most Korean citizens never have the opportunity to eat in restaurants, as they are difficult to get into and very expensive.

Generally, North Koreans consider it very rude to eat while walking on the street, although children are allowed to do so. In addition, North Koreans consider eating with the fingers to be offensive, although slurping soup and noodles is commonly accepted. Meals are usually taken without much conversation, except during formal dinner parties, which are usually conducted for business reasons.

Visiting

Generally, social visits in North Korea are uncommon, and it is highly unusual for North Koreans to visit one another unannounced. There are certain exceptions—mostly holidays—such as the lunar New Year or Parent's Day. In addition, a superior never visits someone who is subordinate to them, and vice versa.

If a social visit occurs, the guest will typically bring a gift as a sign or respect. The majority of such gifts consist of a fruit or beverage. In addition, the guest should remove his or her shoes and cap upon entering the house. In a traditional North Korean home, guests will be seated on cushions on the floor. The floors in Korean homes are traditionally ondol, a feature of Korean architecture in which the floor is heated underneath by wood stove in ancient times, and now refers to basic underfloor heating. Typically, visitors are given the best the host has to offer, including the best seat or cut of meat. If there are many guests, status or age will determine this hospitable hierarchy.

LIFESTYLE

Family

Marriages in North Korea are often arranged by parents, and cannot occur without parental consent. More importantly, marriages between people of different sociopolitical and economic status are not approved by society. Therefore, classes tend to marry within themselves. North Korean women are expected to marry, although it is acceptable for a man to remain single. Marriages are often arranged for political reasons, although marrying for love is becoming increasingly common.

The minimum age for marriage has been set by the North Korean government at age twenty-seven for men, and age twenty-five for women. This allows for the completion of military service and other obligations to the state. After a marriage, couples must apply for a residence. Once approved, they will be given a house or an apartment by the North Korean government. Typically, couples from high-ranking families will receive housing much quicker.

The domestic unit in North Korea is a nuclear family (traditionally, a mother, father and their children), with elderly parents often living with their children. Typically, the father and eldest son receive great respect as the heads of the family. The eldest members of the family are also shown the greatest respect, and sons are expected to care for their aging parents. (It is considered lucky for women to have many sons.) Additionally, unlike South Korea, both parents usually work, and childcare is usually provided free of charge at the work place.

Housing

Housing in North Korea is state-controlled, and granted from the government upon application.

Families in rural areas typically live in simple huts, while those in the cities live in block apartments or metal shanties. The size of the apartment granted to an individual or newly married couple is directly related to their sociopolitical status. There are five types of standardized housing provided, the most common of which is relegated to ordinary farmers and workers. This is typically an apartment consisting of one or two rooms, which includes the kitchen. Detached housing is reserved for high-ranking members of the government. In addition, services such as water and electricity are non-existent in the countryside, and rationed in urban areas.

Food

All food in North Korea is regulated by the state, and most families try to supplement the thin government food rations with foods purchased from small local markets or stores. However, food is often supplied in abundance for state-sponsored banquets and tourists are also given abundant food. Since North Korea is a highly secretive country, not much is known about current food trends, although food shortages have been ongoing since the 1990s.

Generally, rice, noodles, and simple dishes such as meat soup were the staples of traditional cuisine in North Korea. However, the majority of North Korean citizens now subsist on soybeans, millet, and wheat. One favorite food in North Korea is naengmyon, which is a cold noodle dish. Other traditional dishes include pansang, which is the usual meal of steamed rice, soup, and side dishes, and changkuksang, which is the main dish. It is typically arranged with kimchi (seasoned and fermented vegetables), cold greens, mixed vegetables, pan-fried dishes, fruit and fruit punch. This simple meal can be served as lunch as well. In Pyongyang, street kiosks sell popular drinks such as omija, a milky drink made from beans, and Taedonggang beer.

Although prevalent in South Korea, North Koreans do not eat spicy foods such as garlic and chili peppers. In addition, basic foods are typically rationed, and preserved items such as canned meat is typically available for purchase

Traditional garb known as hanbok is worn by the bride and groom at a North Korean wedding.

from stores and farmers markets, with vegetables sometimes available. Despite international aid, food shortages have continued to worsen in North Korea and malnutrition and starvation is widespread, especially among children. In fact, an entire generation of North Korean children is several inches shorter than their South Korean counterparts are due to malnutrition.

Life's Milestones

The majority of milestones celebrated in North Korea are related to national holidays. There is very little money or time to celebrate events or observances such as birthdays or anniversaries, and traveling is often quite difficult. North Korean citizens must apply through the proper authorities before taking a weekend trip, a family vacation, or if they are going to travel on a national holiday. They are also given a vacation quota—usually four or five days annually—and cannot ask for more time if the quota has been used. Additionally, weddings are small, simple, and brief affairs, with only close friends and family members attending. There is no wedding reception, and food is not served.

CULTURAL HISTORY

Art

Korean art has its origins in prehistoric times, as evidenced by the discovery of crude statuettes and petroglyphs (drawings carved into rock), typically made by prehistoric people. Religions shaped subsequent artistic trends, beginning with the shaman art of Korea's Bronze Age (800 to 400 BCE). Intricately decorated swords and rattles, predominately used in rituals, characterized this art.

The Three Kingdoms period (c. 57 BCE to 668 CE) was marked by a rise in Buddhism, and artistic pieces were commissioned as a dedication to the Buddha. As a result, they were typically created in such a design as to reflect the Buddhist characteristics of warm, natural, and harmonious proportions. The rise of Korean celadon pottery occurred during the Goryeo Dynasty (918 to 1392 CE). This popular and beautiful pottery, distinguished by the green-blue glaze used during the coating process, was first produced in China. It was then modified by the Koreans, who created designs never seen before by the Chinese, featuring stylized birds, fishes and other forms found in nature. During this time, celadon pottery became highly valued by collectors in China and other countries, and is still popular today.

Some consider the Joseon Dynasty to be the "golden age" of Korean painting. Confucianism increased during this period, and Korean art became more distinctive and desirable, specifically the "true view" form of painting. This style of painting featured subject matter that consisted mostly of landscapes painted in a realistic manner.

During Japanese occupation (1910–1945), many old and valuable Korean art pieces vanished from private collections and museums. It is largely believed that these works of Korean art were taken to Japan. (In fact, it is said that 80 percent of all Korean Buddhist paintings are currently held in Japan, a large majority of them by private collectors.) Some original works of Korean art, however, are displayed to the public in museums, such as the Tokyo National Museum, which holds 4,800 Korean art items.

After the Korean War, North Korean artists developed a distinct form of graphic art, created from a mixture of western watercolor techniques and traditional Korean drawing methods. During the rebuilding of Pyongyang, North Korean artists were directly commissioned by the government to create works of art for the new capital. These commissioned works consisted predominantly of large murals, but also included statues, sculptures, and smaller paintings. Mainly, these works of art depict heroic figures accomplishing historic and patriotic feats, and usually consisted of Kim Il-Sung and his family, although Korean War heroes and anti-Japanese guerrilla fighters were also portrayed.

Endorsement of these works of art was never given to any individual artist. Today, all art is commissioned in the same way, strictly by the North Korean government. Ordinary North Korean citizens cannot purchase art, although there are some oil paintings done in the traditional Korean manner for sale in some of the international hotel shops in Pyongyang.

Architecture

Traditional Korean architecture is designed and created with a graceful, open floor plan, and embellished with details that reflect the conventional Korean values of humility, balance, and respect for nature. Additionally, three key aspects—simplicity, elegance and an airy design—are apparent in all Korean architecture, regardless of period.

The religious traditions of Taoism and Confucianism, both influential during the Han Dynasty (206 BCE to 220 CE), heavily influenced the traditional Korean wood-framed structure, which is open to nature on all sides and humble in design. However, with the rise of Buddhism in the fourth century CE, Korean architecture began to feature more ornate designs and greater use of color. This style is particularly seen in the architecture of Buddhist temples.

The Silla Dynasty (57 BCE to 935 CE) represented a turning point in Korean architecture, especially during the Unified Silla era (668 to 935 CE). During this period, also known as Later Silla, the kingdom of Silla occupied most of the Korean peninsula. Koreans blended foreign culture with their own to create a unique cultural heritage. This included the ideal of "contemplative beauty," or art that is in harmony with nature. This resulted in art and architecture fully identifiable as Korean. Contemplative beauty was the driving force behind all manner of Korean architectural design, and remains so today in South Korea.

Upon the establishment of North Korea's communist government in 1948, all architecture remaining after the war became the property of the state. However, due to the ravages of war, many historical buildings were destroyed, and the entire capital of Pyongyang had to be rebuilt. Although the ideal of contemplative beauty was a guiding philosophy during the rebuilding of the city, it became equally important to honor Kim Il-Sung with elaborate murals, statues, and monuments. In contemporary North Korean society, the themes of leader worship, loyalty, and patriotism dominate the decorative details of modern architecture.

Music & Dance

Traditional Korean music and dance can be traced back to the early 15th century. In its earliest forms, music, combined with dancing, was used as a form of worship. This is largely derived from the influence of Buddhism and, to a lesser degree, shamanistic beliefs. However, what is commonly identified today as traditional Korean music arose during the Joseon Dynasty (1392–1897). During this period, music and dance became extremely important because they were main components of all rituals and ceremonies. They could be divided into three formal categories: court music, Chinese music and ceremonial music. Informal folk music and dancing

became very popular during this time, including the farmer's and mask dances.

Korean music and dance changed dramatically during the Japanese occupation of Korea during the first half of the 20th century. Korean music was outlawed, and a large number of traditional dances were lost. With the formation of the Democratic People's Republic of Korea (North Korea) in 1948 came a new approach to music and drama. Ethnographers—academics who were held responsible for preserving the culture of North Korea—were instructed to restore and reintroduce traditional Korean forms of dance and music that had the proper cultural expression. This often meant discarding anything that did not promote the Juche philosophy, or further the development of a collective consciousness.

Literature

The literature of North Korea has been greatly impacted by the area's political and economic climate. Between the first and second centuries CE, Koreans began to use the Chinese writing system, as they had no native written language. The idu system, which used Chinese characters to represent the spoken Korean language, was developed between the 10th and 14th centuries. During the 16th and 17th centuries, two important forms of Korean poetry developed: the changaa, a longer, narrative form of poetry, and sijo, which were shorter emotional poems. Poets Hwang Chini (1506–1544) and Yun Sondo (1587–1671) were two of the most well-known sijo poets.

During the Japanese occupation of Korea from 1910 through 1945, Korean culture was suppressed and writers such as Ch'ae Mansik (1902–1950) and Yi Kwangsu (b. 1892) attempted to preserve it through their writing. After the Korean War, and the subsequent division of North and South Korea, writers in North Korea generated content that would support the country's socialist culture. Literature and art in North Korea began to be closely monitored by the government and the Korean Workers' Party through the Propaganda and Agitation Department, as well as the Culture and Arts Department and the

General Federation of Korean Literature and Arts Unions. This government suppression of the arts has continued into the 21st century.

Since the 1960s, state-salaried official writers have produced all literature in North Korea. Short stories, poems, and novels all reconfirm that every relationship in North Korea exists to support its leader. Romantic relationships are simple and uncomplicated, with the focus being on the good of the country and leader. The Juche philosophy is prevalent, and there are no unexpected or complicated plot lines.

Kim Il Sung has been described by the North Korean press as a writer of "classical masterpieces" such as *The Flower Girl* and *The Song of Korea*. Both these and other novels written under his direction have been described by North Korean publications as models of Juche art and are considered "heroic epics."

CULTURE

Arts & Entertainment

The arts in North Korea could be described as monochromatic, as all artists are employed by the government and are assigned to corresponding national institutes (the National Theatre for Arts, National Orchestra, National Dancing Institute, etc.). Art essentially functions as propaganda, and all work produced by individual artists must conform to the standards of the Korean Workers' Party (KWP) standards.

Cultural freedom and artistic expression in contemporary North Korea is limited to mostly didactic, or instructional, art forms, and is controlled by state-run agencies. It typically emphasizes national independence and uniqueness. The promotion of the Juche ideology is the underlying motivation. In fact, so-called "Art propaganda squads" travel between cities and provinces, performing a narrow selection of poetry, plays, and music. The performances, while polished and skilled, are meant to increase worker production.

Common themes include the martyrdom for the good of the country, the happiness of present society, and the brilliant genius of the "Great Leader." Additionally, foreigners, especially Americans and the Japanese, are presented in an unflattering way. Cultural growth is further stunted by policies that deeply curtail leisure time and privacy. As a result, most entertainment for North Koreans tends to consist of group activities, including rallies, films, and visits to museums.

Films are widely available to ordinary citizens, mainly because leader Kim Jong Il is an avid fan of cinema. The city of Pyongyang has eight movie theaters, although they often shut down early in the evening due to a lack of electricity. Starting in the late 20th century, a new form of film gained popularity in the country. Kim Jong Il ordered the kidnapping of South Koreans Shin Sang-ok and Choi Eun-hee—a director and actress, respectively, who were formerly married—in 1978 to produce realistic films. Two of the most popular of their productions were *The Blanket*, which depicted family life in a vivid style, and *Pulgusari* (1985), a propaganda monster film. In fact, the couple was forced to remarry while in North Korean captivity; they were finally able to escape in 1986 while attending a business meeting in Vienna, Austria.

Since 1987, North Korea has hosted the Pyongyang International Film Festival every two years. While the festival highlights foreign films, they are limited in scope. In 2008, the festival featured 110 films from forty-six countries, including Great Britain, Germany, Sweden, Russia, Iran, and China. Additionally, while films are inexpensive and plentiful to the public, circuses or song and dance performances have typically been reserved for national celebrations or foreign guests, and only citizens high in social status may attend.

Cultural Sites & Landmarks

Despite North Korea's isolation and state-imposed regulation of art and culture, there are numerous sites within the country linked to the region's cultural, religious, and military history, as well as natural beauty. In fact, North Korea boasts one World Heritage Site—the Complex of Koguryo Tombs. The site was recognized in 2004 by the United Nations Educational, Scientific, and Cultural Organization (UNESCO) for its cultural importance to humanity.

Koguryo (or Goguryeo) refers to an ancient kingdom that flourished in present-day North Korea during the fifth and seventh centuries CE. The tombs are believed to be the burial site for the kingdom's royalty, and are renowned for their beautiful mural paintings. While there have been over 10,000 Koguryo tombs discovered in East Asia, only ninety of them have been found to have paintings, and half of those are located at this site. The paintings offer a glimpse into daily life of the period, and depict the stories of Korean mythology. The site was also recognized for the wealth of knowledge obtained concerning ancient burial customs.

In 2004, the history of the Koguryo Kingdom became a diplomatic issue between North Korea and the People's Republic of China; both registered the site and its relics following its inscription as a World Heritage Site. The Chinese government had claimed that the kingdom was an extension of ancient China, and thus part of the regional history of China. Though a verbal agreement between China and North Korea helped settle the controversy, many critics allege that North Korea has distorted its national history so that the Koguryo Kingdom is sentimentalized as part of the Juche ideology.

Panmunjeom, a small, now deserted village located 215 kilometers (133 miles) south of Pyongyang, is a particularly important site in that it sits on the border between North and South Korea. It is located exactly in the middle of the Korean Demilitarized Zone (DMZ), the buffer zone between North and South Korea. In 1953, the truce that ended the Korean conflict was signed in the village. It is still home to several notable landmarks, namely the Joint Security Area (JSA), a heavily guarded strip of land, and the "Bridge of No Return."

The JSA is the only site where military negotiations between North and South Korea occur. It is policed by both North and South Korean guards, and joined to the capital of North Korea by the paved, six-lane Reunification Highway.

The "Bridge of No Return" became famous as the location of prisoner exchanges between both countries. The name derives from the fact that if prisoners refused to cross, they would be given no further choice to return to their respective countries. Though the bridge is no longer used, the Military Demarcation Line (MDL), the defined border between North and South Korea, continues to divide it.

Additionally, visitors coming to Panmunjeom from North Korea can see the Panmun-guk, which is the building that houses the administration of the North Korean Security force. Visitors will also be able to see, but not enter, the North Korean village of Kijong-dong, which boasts the world's tallest flagpole. The village features tall blocks of apartments, wide streets, and is believed to have virtually no inhabitants, other than a custodial crew of soldiers. South Koreans have given the village the nickname "Propaganda village," due to the amount of propaganda broadcast from the city's loudspeakers. North Koreans refer to it as "Peace Village."

North Korea has offered tours to scenic Diamond Mountain (also called Kŭmgangsan or Mount Kŭmgang). However, tours were suspended in July 2008 when a South Korean woman was shot and killed after allegedly wandering into a North Korean military restricted area. Before the suspension of the program, thousands of South Koreans flocked to the mountain each week to view the famed Nine Dragons Waterfall, autumn foliage, and to get a rare glimpse of their North Korean counterparts. The mountain area is also home to several ancient temples.

Libraries & Museums

Archaeological finds are displayed in the country's well-funded museums, but even these artifacts are used to promote a North Korean national identity. In Pyongyang, there are two major museums, the Korean Revolutionary Museum and the Korean Fine Arts Museum. In 1946, the Pyongyang Public Library was designated as the National Central Library; as of the 1970s, the library housed over two million volumes. The largest library in North Korea is the People's

Great Leader Center. Established in 1982, the center functions as a library as well as a center for Communist theory.

Holidays

National holidays such as Kim Il Sung's birthday (April 15), Foundation of the People's Army (February 8) and National Foundation Day (September 9) are celebrated with a military parade, an art festival or official congregations in governmental units.

Youth Culture

The youth of North Korea do not have a unique culture. Rather, they hold the same values and beliefs as their parents and elders. This is reflected in fashion, music tastes, and even their behavior. More importantly, every aspect of their culture, along with the national culture at large, is decided upon and controlled by the government.

Between the ages of nine and eleven, North Koreans join the Young Pioneer Corps; this membership is a celebrated occasion, with the new members receiving red scarves and gifts from their families. The Young Pioneers march through cities, singing, and spend around two hours each day receiving ideological training. They spend Saturdays performing volunteer labor. As of 2009, there were approximately three million Young Pioneers.

Between the ages of fourteen and sixteen, young people join the Kim Il Sung Socialist Youth League after passing an examination. Once in the league, young people spend more time completing volunteer labor for the state, including planting, harvesting, construction, and supplying aid during droughts and floods. It is estimated by some that members of the Youth League spend as many as 150 hours per year doing "volunteer" labor. This includes performing such feats as building power plants, despite a complete lack of experience and food. In fact, up to 40 percent of North Korean youth are said to be severely malnourished, and North Korean youth as a whole are much shorter in stature than their South Korean counterparts.

League members also participate in political study sessions, which occur three or four times a week. During these sessions, the ideology and life of Kim Il Sung are taught and discussed. Weekly self-criticism meetings also begin with membership in the league and continue for the rest of the citizen's life. Citizens are encouraged to keep a journal in which to record criticisms of others and criticisms of themselves; these points are then discussed during the meetings. These self-criticism sessions reinforce the idea that North Korean citizens are under constant surveillance.

In dress, most North Korean youth are conservative. Boys wear simple dark pants and white shirts, while girls wear long, dark skirts and plain, white blouses. In Pyongyang, however, it is not uncommon to see some of the better-educated and higher-ranking youth sporting clothing and hairstyles modeled after those found in popular South Korean TV shows. Although watching these shows is strictly forbidden, bootleg copies are often available.

Recreation for North Korean youths is largely centered on sports, predominantly soccer. There are many well-designed sports facilities in the cities, and parks are used for informal sporting events in the country. North Korea's young people often gather to visit and play in these parks on Sunday, which is the only day off from work. Card games, singing and choreographed dances—usually performed at government functions or holidays—are also popular activities among youth.

SOCIETY

Transportation

Railways are the most important form of transportation in North Korea. The country has an electrified railroad system with 8,530 kilometers (5,300 miles) of track, running north and south along the coastline and linking to South Korea, China, and Russia. Branches of the railway lead to inland areas and to Pyongyang. However, railways are mostly used for official state business and not as a general form of transportation. However, in 2007 two passenger trains traveled between South and North Korea for the first time since the start of the Korean War. This event was seen as a symbol of improving relations between the countries.

North Koreans usually get around by walking or by boating on rivers and streams, which are also used for freight transportation. The most important of these is the Taedong River, which stretches inland about 2,250 kilometers (1,400 miles). Citizens who live in Pyongyang are offered bus service, and bicycling is popular as well. In addition, the North Korean air force controls all air travel. The country offers international air services between Pyongyang and Beijing, as well as Pyongyang and Moscow.

Transportation Infrastructure

While North Korea has a substantial network of highways despite the mountainous terrain—roughly 31,000 kilometers (19,262 miles) by the turn of the 21st century—many are unpaved. Traffic in the country is believed to be generally nonexistent (motor vehicles are not readily available in North Korea). Additionally, the paved highways are considered oversized, and used only infrequent by military vehicles or the automobiles of government officials. (There is also no public lighting in the country, thus roads are always unlit at night.)

Media & Communications

The state-controlled Korean Central News Agency (KCNA) distributes all news in North Korea. Several daily newspapers are published in the country. There is one radio station, the Korean Central Broadcasting Station. In fact, radios are made with a volume knob only, as there is no need for a channel knob. Television broadcasts are state-run and controlled as well. Radio and television programs begin and end with songs in praise of Kim Il Sung and Kim Jong Il.

Television programs are limited to those that feature Kim Il Sung or Kim Jong Il, with an occasional program about farmers or miners. South Koreans are shown as longing to be under Kim Jong Il's rule. Normal human relationships are not explored, and the programs glorify the North Korean government and those that run it. Radio and television waves from neighboring countries are blocked from entering North Korea by noise-emitting towers, owned, and maintained by the government. There is no Internet service available to the public, and cell phones and wireless devices are banned.

However, the state's information blockade is weakening. Smuggled DVDs and videotapes are common on the black market. Additionally, more of the general population is being exposed to popular South Korean dramas, and the North Korean government has been forced to admit that South Koreans have more material possessions than North Koreans do. To balance that out, the North Korean government has stated that South Koreans are morally compromised by allowing themselves to be ruled by Americans, or Western culture. In fact, watching South Korean media could be punishable with arrest, the viewer accused as an enemy of the state.)

SOCIAL DEVELOPMENT

Standard of Living

The standard of living in North Korea is quite low; however, as the country has isolated itself from the vast majority of the international community, it is difficult to get accurate information on quality of life indicators, such as life expectancies, infant mortality rates, malnutrition, and human rights abuses.

Water Consumption

Information on access to water and sanitation in North Korea is difficult to attain. In 2010, however, UNICEF pledged $13.9 million (USD) to improve access to water and sanitation, particularly in rural areas of the country.

Education

Education is required for all North Korean children between the ages of five and sixteen. Schooling includes one year of preschool, four years of primary education and six years of secondary education. There is one university in the country, the Kim Il Sung University in Pyongyang, named after the country's former leader and father of its current leader, Kim Jong Il.

Education in North Korea has a strong emphasis on technology and science, and students are expected to work a job during their studies. The aims of the country's educational system are to promote the nation's communist ideology and to provide adequately trained workers for its industry.

According to the North Korean government, the literacy rate is 100 percent among both men and women (2014); however, this information is quite difficult to verify.

Women's Rights

On paper, North Korea strongly supports gender equality and the rights of women. An amendment was added to the constitution in 1972 that stated that women hold equal social status and rights with men. In 1990, the government passed laws requiring that conditions be implemented to help advance women in society. In practice, however, women's rights in North Korea, like all human rights in the country, are severely lacking.

North Korean women who live along the Chinese border are constantly in danger of being kidnapped and sold as wives or slaves to Chinese men. Sometimes North Korean women willingly marry Chinese men in order to be provided with food, shelter and clothing. Often these women are as young as thirteen or fourteen years of age.

Women and children also make up a large portion of refugees crossing the river into China. If Chinese traffickers catch the refugees, they are often sold into prostitution. If a woman protests, she will be exposed as a refugee, and sent back to North Korea to be arrested. If she is pregnant upon returning to North Korea, an abortion will be forced upon her, or her infant killed in order to keep "foreign blood" out of the country.

Women in North Korea are expected to work outside of the home, for the same amount of time and salary as men, although in actuality they earn much less and are usually placed in lower-echelon jobs than men are. The country has a labor shortage, and as such, fully expects women to help increase production with an eight-hour workday. Women are also the primary caregivers of the home and the children, though women who devote themselves to work and the government are also frequently highlighted in the media as role models.

Health Care

Although health care in North Korea is free, and there is at least one health clinic in each village, the country suffers from a shortage of doctors and medicine, and care is often inadequate. The centralized government does offer a number of assistance programs, including disability insurance, pensions, and care for the elderly.

Average life expectancy in North Korea is seventy years—seventy-four years for women and sixty-six years for men (2015 estimate). The infant mortality remains high, at 23 deaths per 1,000 live births (2015 estimate).

GOVERNMENT

Structure

North Korea is a communist dictatorship. Kim Il Sung became premiere in 1948 with the formation of the Democratic People's Republic of Korea (DPRK). His cult of personality was so strong that he was referred to only as "Great Leader," and the constitution was amended in 1998 to name him "Eternal President of the Republic."

True political power rests with the General Secretary of the Korean Workers' Party (KWP), who also holds the titles of Chairman of the National Defense Commission and Supreme Commander of the Korean People's Army.

The various branches of government are controlled by the Korean Workers' Party (KWP), which grew out of prewar communist parties. It directs the government through its various bodies. Kim Jong Il succeeded his father as General Secretary of the KWP in 1994, and he in turn was succeeded by his son Kim Jong Un in 2011.

One of these branches is the Central Procurator's Office, which prosecutes and conducts surveillance of the North Korean citizenry. Its control leaves very little privacy or room for political or personal expression in the lives of North Koreans. Coordinating the surveillance efforts are two separate surveillance offices, the Ministry of Public Security and the State Security Department.

Military service is compulsory for all North Korean men and for some women. Service usually lasts for three or four years. There is a heavy emphasis place on military security in North Korea, at the expense of other government services.

Political Parties

The Korean Workers' Party (KWP) is the de facto political party in the country and controls the two minor political parties: the Chondoist Chongu Party and the Social Democratic Party. (All political parties must be approved by the KWP.) The KWP controls all aspects of elections, which typically involve only one candidate.

Local Government

North Korea is divided into nine provinces and two municipalities that are governed by local people's assemblies, but their movements are overseen by the national government.

Judicial System

The judicial system of North Korea comprises a Central Court, provincial courts, and country courts. Individual rights are not recognized, and trials are often refused for political prisoners.

Taxation

By the end of the 20th century, North Korea had established several taxes, such as an enterprise income tax, personal income tax, inheritance tax, and property tax.

Foreign Policy

According to North Korea's 1998 Socialist Constitution, the state shall "establish diplomatic as well as political, economic and cultural relations with all friendly countries, on princi-ples of complete equality, independence, mutual respect, noninterference in each other's affairs, and mutual benefit." This, however, is negated by the Korean Worker's Party (KWP) bylaws, which outline how foreign policies should be implemented. They call for solidarity against "international imperialism," often translated into anti-United States sentiments. Kim Jong Il is the general-secretary of the KWP, and as such, he has firm control of all aspects of North Korean's foreign policy, including any initiatives that deal with the U.S.

North Korea has been a member of the United Nations since 1991. North Korea also began participating in the Association of Southeast Asian Nations (ASEAN) regional forum in July 2000. North Korea is also a member of the World Health Organization (WHO), the International Committee of the Red Cross (ICRC) and others. The country also maintains formal diplomatic ties with Canada, Germany, Italy, Australia, the United Kingdom (UK) and others. (It has no formal diplomatic ties with the France, any South American nations, or the U.S.) Recently, the country has made efforts to establish free trade agreements (FTA) with major economies, particularly New Zealand and Australia. North Korea has a tumultuous relationship with the U.S., and has been historically frustrated by the U.S.'s continually hostile stance.

North Korea has continued to test its weapons technology and foreign diplomats have continued to criticize the country's unwillingness to negotiate. In February 2005, North Korea declared that it had nuclear capabilities. In March 2005, North Korean diplomats told international delegates that it would agree to shut down its nuclear weapons facilities in exchange for aid. International Atomic Energy Agency (IAEA) inspectors were allowed to observe the shutdown. In October 2006, the country declared that it had successfully detonated a nuclear bomb. Talks began as a way to find a peaceful resolution to the security concerns posed by North Korea's interest in non-civilian nuclear power. After several rounds of talks over two years with five other countries (China, South Korea, theUnited

States, Russia and Japan), North Korea agreed to close its Yongbyon Nuclear Complex. In return, the country would receive fuel aid, and steps would be taken to normalize relationships with Japan and the U.S. In the years following this agreement, however, North Korean officials have continued to wrangle with international officials over the nuclear issues.

Nonetheless, the U.S. plays an integral role in Pyongyang's economic goals and its continual build-up of military force. The country realizes that, in order to achieve its economic reforms, U.S. cooperation is necessary (the U.S. imposed economic sanctions against North Korea). However, the likelihood of that happening is very slim as long as Pyongyang continues to seek greater military power. Further complicating the foreign relations of each country was North Korea's placement on the list of state sponsors of terrorism in 1988. However, though North Korea has frequently threatened to restart its nuclear program—and maintains the need for military might as a deterrent against an attack from the U.S.—it was removed from the terror list in October 2008, with the stipulation that it would end its nuclear programs.

Influenced by their government, North Koreans perceive South Koreans to be their kin, although socially and morally inferior due to American influence. Pyongyang officially claims the entire peninsula, although this fact is rarely discussed, and both countries see the border created after the Korean War cease-fire as temporary. The Sunshine Policy, established in 1998 by former South Korean President Kim Dae-jung, encouraged interaction between the countries and provided economic assistance to North Korea. As a direct result of this policy, North Korea grew to rely heavily on aid from South Korea, as well as funds from inter-Korean business contracts. However, political relations between the countries did not improve. South Korean President Lee Myung-bak discontinued the Sunshine Policy, and has since taken a tougher approach to North Korea. Because of this, North Korea has cut off many of its business relationships with South Korea and has even refused some commu-

nications with the country. In the last few years, under Kim Jong Un, tensions between North and South Korea have risen to new highs.

North Korea has also made efforts to normalize relations with Japan. Ongoing issues with Japan have included the fact that North Korean media portrays Japan as evil imperialists. Japan's ongoing economic sanctions have led to shortages of food and energy in North Korea, and Japan claims that North Korea owes over $50 million (USD) in unpaid debt.

Human Rights Profile

International human rights law insists that states respect civil and political rights, and promote an individual's economic, social, and cultural rights. The United Nations Universal Declaration on Human Rights (UDHR) is recognized as the standard for international human rights. Its authors sought the counsel of the world's great thinkers, philosophers, and religious leaders, and were careful to create a document that reflects the core values shared by every world culture. (To read this document or view the articles relating to cultural human rights, visit http//www.udhr.org/ UDHR/default.htm.).

North Korea is an extremely secluded country. Gaining entry is almost impossible, and the government strictly controls the domestic media. Reports of North Korea's human rights violations have come from refugees who have related information about torture, executions, inhumane prison conditions, kidnapping and the trafficking of women. Although the North Korean constitution grants equal rights to all citizens, the government has in practice never granted its citizens even the most basic of human rights. Discrimination based on social status continues to be widespread.

In North Korea, citizens are without many basic freedoms. For example, they do not have the right to vote for a change in government, are not granted a fair trial (and in some cases are not tried at all), nor do they have freedom of speech or assembly. Additionally, the government controls all forms of culture and media. The North Korean government has maintained during meetings with the European Union (EU) and the UN that most of the international human rights guidelines are subversive to the goals of the North Korean state, and therefore are considered illegitimate.

Articles 6 through 11 of the UDHR outline the rights of a person pertaining to arrest, trial, and presumption of innocence. Although the North Korean constitution agrees with this portion of the UDHR in statement, this agreement is not carried out in practice. Interviews with North Korean refugees reveal that the government routinely detains and imprisons people at will. Citizens who are suspected of crimes against the state are arrested and quickly sent to prison camps without trial. In addition, families of the arrested find it almost impossible to get information regarding the charges being made, or how long they will be imprisoned. In some cases, entire families—including children—are imprisoned if just one member of the family is accused of criminal activity.

The DPRK's constitution states that all judicial proceedings are to be carried out in accordance with the law, which covers the rights to a fair trial as listed in the UDHR. This is difficult to carry out, however, since the court is accountable to the Supreme People's Assembly, which does not acknowledge individual rights. In addition, judges for the Supreme People's Assembly who hand down "unjust judgments" are subject to criminal liability.

Religious freedom, as outlined in Article 18 of the UDHR, is guaranteed by the North Korean constitution. However, in practice religious activity is heavily discouraged. In fact, the government will not allow religious gatherings unless supervised by officially recognized groups, which are linked to the government. True religious freedom, as defined by the ability to worship freely in whatever manner one chooses, is not found in North Korea, however, an interest in Buddhism has increased due to its important role in Korean history and culture. Pyongyang is restoring several Buddhist temples, with plans to revive Buddhist ceremonies.

Human rights and religious groups outside of the country continuously report that members of underground churches in North Korea, usually Christian, are being beaten, arrested, tortured in prison camps, and even killed. Worship of Kim Il Sung and Kim Jong Il is compulsory. Refusal to accept the "Great Leader" as the supreme authority over all aspects of life is regarded as treason.

The rights to freedom of speech and the press in North Korea, as outlined in Article 19 of the UDHR, are provided for in the North Korean constitution, but forbidden in practice. All forms of media are under strict control of the government. There are no independent newspapers, television or radio stations in North Korea. Most foreign journalists are not allowed to enter the country, and those who do get to enter are kept under strict surveillance, including being restricted from traveling without a "guide."

The right to assemble, outlined in Article 20, is linked to freedom of speech in the North Korean constitution. Like freedom of speech, it is not supported in reality. Public meetings cannot be carried out without prior authorization from the government, and such permission is rarely given. Anyone suspected of attempting to gather with a purpose that may be contrary to the goals of the government will quickly be found and arrested.

Migration

It was estimated in 2008 that as many as 300,000 North Koreans have fled to China for political, social, and economic reasons, despite the country's ban on migration. If found attempting to illegally migrate from North Korea, citizens are charged with treason and sentenced to jail time.

ECONOMY

Overview of the Economy

It is difficult to attain accurate, current information about the state of the North Korean economy as all information comes from the government, which the CIA describes as a "Communist state one-man dictatorship." As the government of the politically and economically isolated country controls all information about its economic state, what data does reach the international community is unverifiable. The CIA World Factbook provides an estimate of the country's economic situation based on estimates made by British economist Angus Maddison. Overall, the economy of North Korea is considered weak and suffering from mismanagement, corruption, and unbalanced budgeting.

Overall, the economy of Pyongyang is weak, and it appears to be getting worse each year. Much of the city's resources are devoted to North Korea's military—the government has a "military first" policy—and there has been a shortage of food each year since the late 20th century.

The government controls every aspect of the North Korean economy. In 1966, faced with declining aid from the Soviet Union, the government developed a policy of self-reliance (called "Juche"). As a result, there has been very little interaction between North Korea and other countries. Moreover, frequent food and electricity shortages and massive military spending have left the country in desperate need of foreign aid. In 2013, North Korea's gross domestic product (GDP) was estimated at $28 billion (USD), with a per capita GDP of $1,800 (USD).

Industry

North Korean industry ranges from small cooperative operations, mainly in fish processing, to large state-run enterprises. Iron and steel manufacturing are the largest industries. Chemical processing is also important, as a large amount of fertilizer is necessary to farm the peninsula's generally infertile soil.

Most of the country's electric power is generated by its rivers, especially the Yalu. Though the amount of hydropower has been increasing steadily over the years, there is still not enough to keep up with national industry, and power availability fluctuates according to the country's dry season.

Labor

In 2013, it was estimated that the workforce of North Korea comprised 15.21 million workers.

Energy/Power/Natural Resources

Minerals are North Korea's most important natural resource. The country has deposits of approximately 200 different valuable minerals and metals, including iron, coal, and gold, as well as lead, zinc, tungsten, and graphite.

North Korea often experiences electrical shortages. As such, the country's streets are typically unlit at night.

Fishing

North Korea has 2,495 square kilometers (963 miles) of coastline, and its major fishing areas are the Sea of Japan and the Yellow Sea. Common fish species include Pollack, sardines, herring, mackerel, and pike.

Forestry

Common tree species include oak, larch, poplar, spruce, pine, and fir. In 1987, the country produced 3.2 million cubic meters of timber. The North Korean government has revealed little about its forestry industry in the early 21st century.

Mining/Metals

Iron is mined in the south Pyongan, the North and south Hwanghae, and the southern Hamgyong provinces. The country has significant deposits of iron ore, anthracite coal, and magnesite, which is found in the southern Hamgyong province.

Agriculture

North Korea's agricultural production is also completely state-run. All of the country's farms were centralized into about 3,000 cooperatives by 1958. They are run by management committees which determine what and how much to grow. Crops are delivered to the government and distributed via state-owned stores. Agricultural production contributes nearly one-third of GDP.

North Korean farmers grow mostly rice, wheat, corn, potatoes, and soybeans. The country has been self-sufficient in rice production since the 1950s. Other important crops include tobacco and cotton.

Contrary to its policy of self-reliance, North Korea imports grain, as well as fuel and machinery. During the 1990s, the country began to depend increasingly on foreign aid to feed its malnourished population. Only an estimated 18 to 20 percent of the land is arable. It was estimated that in 2004, the agricultural industry accounted for 37 percent of employment in the country.

Animal Husbandry

It is difficult to attain current, accurate information on that state of many of North Korea's industries, as the country is so isolated. It was estimated that in 1996, the country had over 2,800 head of cattle.

Tourism

Tourism is very limited in North Korea, and few Western tourists visit the country. Most of the country's tourists hail from Japan, Russia, and China; however, in January 2010, North Korea lifted its restrictions on U.S. tourists, who can now visit the country throughout the year. While visiting the country, tourists are under the constant supervision of North Korean guides. Tourists are limited in when they can take pictures, and of what they can take pictures.

April Sanders, Barrett Hathcock, Alex K. Rich

DO YOU KNOW?

- Though the culture of North Korea is rigorously guarded by the government from foreign influence, its leader, Kim Jong-Il, is said to be a devoted film fan, with a library of at least 20,000 films.

Bibliography

Breen, Michael. *The Koreans: Who They Are, What They Want, Where Their Future Lies*. New York: St. Martin's, 2014.

Cha, Victor. *North Korea: The Impossible State*. New York: Ecco, 2014.

Demick, Barbara. *Nothing to Envy: Ordinary Lives in North Korea*. New York: Spiegel & Grau, 2010.

French, Paul. *North Korea: State of Paranoia*. London: Zed Books, 2014.

Harden, Blain. *Escape from Camp 14: One Man's Remarkable Odyssey from North Korea to Freedom in the West*. New York: Penguin Books, 2013.

Nahm, Andrew C. *Introduction to Korean History and Culture*. Seoul: Hollym: 1993.

Oberdorfer, Don. *The Two Koreas: A Contemporary History*. New York: Basic Books, 2013.

Oh, Kongdan, and Ralph C. Hassig. *North Korea Through the Looking Glass*. Washington DC: Brookings Institution Press, 2000.

Portal, Jane. *Korea: Art and Archaeology*. New York: Thames & Hudson, 2000.

Sun-Kyung, Yi. *Inside the Hermit Kingdom*. Toronto: Key PorterBooks, 1997.

Works Cited

"2005 Population Estimates for Cities in North Korea." Mongabay.com. http://www.mongabay.com/igapo/2005_world_city_populations/North_Korea.html.

"A Brief History of Korean Architecture." Atelier Professor KOH. http://nongae.gsnu.ac.kr/~mirkoh/korb01.html.

Conway-Smith, Erin. "Young and West-Less." Maclean's 120.37 (24 Sep. 2007): 36–37. *Academic Search Complete*. EBSCO. Medford, OR. 21 Oct. 2008 http://search.ebscohost.com/login.aspx?direct=true&db=a9h&AN=26698307&site=ehost-live&scope=site.

"Human Rights Overview: North Korea." *Human Rights Watch*. http://www.hrw.org/english/docs/2006/01/18/nkorea12255.htm.

Hoare, James. "The Korean Peninsula: Fifty Years of Uncertainty." *Asian Affairs* 33.2 (May 2002): 232.

"Korea Central Broadcasting Station." John's Home Page about Korea. http://www.geocities.com/Tokyo/Market/2978/radio/index-e.html.

"Korea, North." Infoplease.com. http://www.infoplease.com/ipa/A0107686.html.

Lankov, Andrei. "Cracks in North Korean 'Stalinism'." *Asian Times*. http://atimes.com/atimes/Korea/FL07Dg01.html.

"North Korea: Border City Draws 100,000 Tourists." *New Zealand Herald*. http://www.nzherald.co.nz/travel/news/article.cfm?c_id=7&objectid=10537825&ref=rss.

"Report Faults North Korean Human Rights." *International Herald Tribune.* http://www.iht.com/articles/ap/2008/09/22/america/US-NKorea.php

Seok, Kay. "Speak Out Against Human Rights in North Korea." *Human Rights Watch.* http://www.hrw.org/english/docs/2004/04/16/nkorea8445.htm.

Strother, Jason. "South Korean Pop Culture Reaches Into North Korea." *VOA News*. http://www.voanews.com/english/archive/2008–09/2008–09–04–voa18.cfm?CFID=53603874&CFTOKEN=44185582.

"World Heritage List." UNESCO.org. http://whc.unesco.org/en/list.

SOUTH KOREA,
Republic of Korea

Introduction

The Republic of Korea, commonly known as South Korea, is an East Asian nation located on the southern half of the Korean Peninsula. Having been conquered and occupied by Japan in 1910, South Korea regained independence after the end of World War II. South Korea borders the Democratic People's Republic of Korea, known as North Korea. Following the Korean War (1950–1953), the two nations divided along the 38th parallel. Culturally and historically, the nations are still linked, and many families are split by the border. There is still a desire among many South Koreans for unification, a process that some believe has begun with the June 15th North-South Joint Declaration in 2000.

A popular tourist destination in South Korea is the DMZ, or Demilitarized Zone. This military demarcation line separates North and South Korea. It remains the most heavily guarded border in the world.

As one of the most populous cities in the world, the capital of Seoul is home to many of the world's tallest residential and commercial buildings and has a modern public transportation and freeway system. Since emerging from a turbulent past, Seoul has exhibited a rapid pace of economic and cultural growth, and is now one of the most prosperous cities in the world.

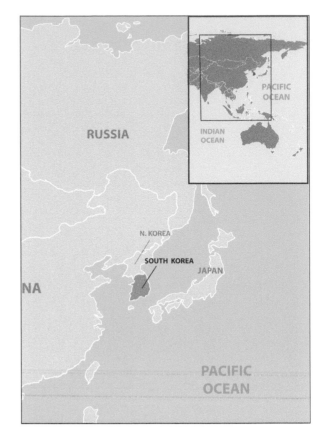

GENERAL INFORMATION

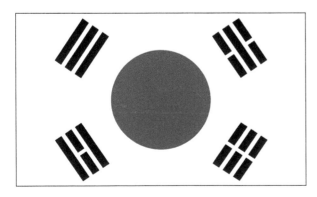

Official Language: Korean
Population: 49,115,196 (2015 estimate)

Currency: South Korean won
Coins: One hundred jeon equal one South Korean won, although the jeon is no longer used. Coins are issued in denominations of 1, 5, 10, 50, 100, and 500 won.
Land Area: 96,920 square kilometers (37,421 square miles)
Water Area: 2,800 square kilometers (1,081 square miles)
National Motto: "Gangseong Daeguk" (Korean, "Good will to all mankind")
National Anthem: "Aegukga" (Korean, "The Patriotic Song")
Capital: Seoul
Time Zone: GMT +9
Flag Description: South Korea's flag, Tegukke, is white with a centered red and blue Yin-Yang symbol. In the four corners of the flag, four different black bar formations, called kwae trigrams from the *I Ching* or the Book of Changes, are featured, each with its own meaning. The trigram in the upper left symbolizes heaven; the trigram directly

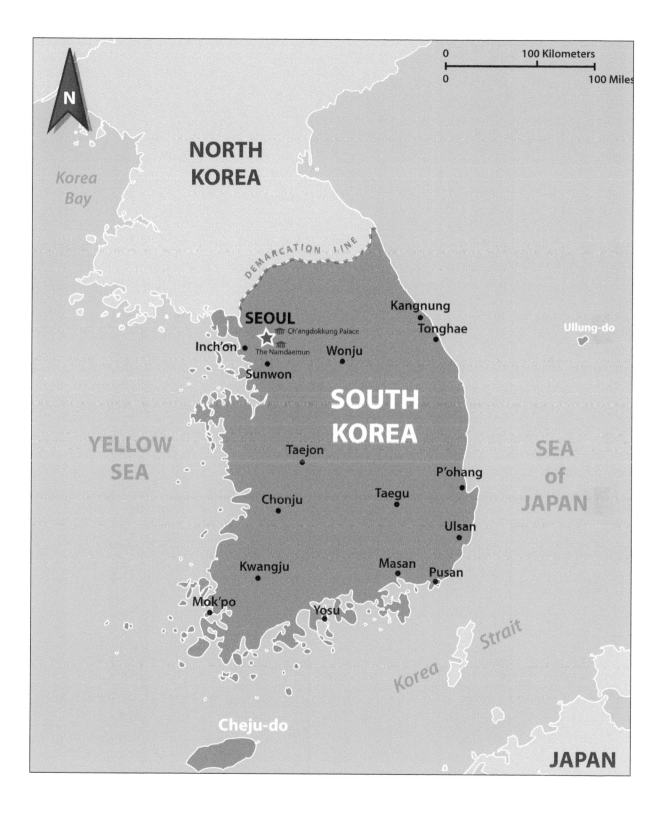

Principal Cities by Population (2014):

- Seoul (10,369,593)
- Busan (3,557,716)
- Incheon (2,957,931)
- Daegu (2,518,467)
- Daejeon (1,547,467)
- Gwangju (1,492,948)
- Ulsan (1,192,262)
- Suweon (1,209,169)
- Changwon (1,091,513)
- Goyang (1,018,013)

opposite, in the lower right, symbolizes earth; the trigram in the upper right signifies water; and the lower left stands for fire. The white in the flag stands for purity and peace.

Population

Most South Koreans live in cities, while between 15 and 20 percent live in rural areas (the 2015 urban population percentage was 82.5%). South Korea's population numbers remain somewhat steady because of low birth rate and continuing emigration to the United States and other Western nations. The most populous city in South Korea is the capital of Seoul, near the border with North Korea.

The country's growth rate is 0.14 percent. The median age of the population is forty years, with the bulk of the population (73 percent) between the ages of fifteen and sixty four. According to the CIA World Factbook, the Total Fertility Rate (TFR) in South Korea stands at 1.25 in 2015, meaning that parents are not replacing themselves and the population is declining and becoming older. The result will be a larger population of aging Koreans, needing increasing services and medical care, will be supported by a smaller population of working people. Government efforts to increase the TFR have not succeeded thus far.

Languages

The majority of South Koreans speak Korean. English is a popular second language among many South Koreans.

Native People & Ethnic Groups

Modern-day Koreans are descended from the first ethnic groups to populate the Korean Peninsula approximately 7,000 years ago, and are the indigenous people of their region. There is evidence of human habitation in the peninsula as far back as the end of the Paleolithic period of prehistory.

Ethnically and linguistically, there is no difference between North and South Koreans. Except for a very small percentage of Chinese living in South Korea, the country is made up almost entirely of people of Korean descent. Notable minority groups besides ethnic Chinese include several thousand U.S. citizens, as well as foreign workers from South Asia and Russia (many of whom are unregistered aliens).

Religions

Just over half of South Koreans are religious. The two most common religions are Christianity (31.6 percent of the population) and Buddhism (24.2 percent of the population), but other faiths, including Cheondogyo and Wonbulgyo, maintain large numbers of followers. Christianity held only a minor foothold on Korean life until an explosion of popular interest and missionary zeal in the late 20th century rapidly added to the ranks of various denominations. Additionally, it is not uncommon for Koreans to mix elements of several faiths, including Buddhism, Confucianism and shamanism, into their daily lives.

Climate

South Korea has a seasonally diverse climate. Rain, humidity and heat characterize summers, cold winds and snow arrive in winter, and moderate weather dominates autumn and spring. The rainy seasons last from late spring/early summer to fall.

ENVIRONMENT & GEOGRAPHY

Topography

The Republic of Korea, commonly known as South Korea, is an East Asian nation located on the southern half of the Korean Peninsula. South

Korea borders the Democratic People's Republic of Korea, known as North Korea; until 1948, these two nations comprised one country, Korea. The Yellow Sea lies off the western shore of South Korea, while to the east is the Sea of Japan. South Korea is separated from the island nation of Japan by the Korea Strait.

Hills and mountains, with some coastal plains in the western and southern regions, characterize South Korea's topography. The eastern region is mostly mountainous with some coastal plains, while the western region is hilly with plains and river basins. The southern region is mountainous with some valleys. Only about one-third of the country is comprised of lowlands. Its highest point is at Halla-san, or Mount Halla (1,950 meters/6,398 feet above sea level), a volcanic island to the southwest of the mainland.

There are around 3,000 islands that, along with the peninsular mainland, make up South Korea; in contrast, only a few hundred islands lie off the coast of North Korea, which comprises the upper half of the peninsula.

The longest river in South Korea is the Naktong River (521 kilometers/324 miles); it originates in the Taebaek Mountains and flows to the Sea of Japan. Its basin is in the southeast portion of the country. The Han River, the nation's second largest river, flows through the city of Seoul.

South Korea has a coastline that stretches 2,413 kilometers (1,499 miles). The country is separated from North Korea by the Demilitarized Zone, or DMZ, a line of demarcation which sits at the 38th parallel north.

Plants & Animals

South Korea has a rich variety of plant life, with more than 4,500 species found throughout the country. Pine, elm, larch, maple and acacia trees are common, as are oak, bamboo and fruit trees (especially apples and persimmons). Old-growth forests are protected throughout the country.

Common animals include deer, wild boar, black bears, voles, the Manchurian weasel, pheasant and grouse, owls, and woodpeckers.

Endangered species in South Korea include several species of whale (blue, fin and northern right), the Ussuri tube-nosed bat, the Asiatic black bear and the Siberian musk deer. Some animals (such as tigers, rhinoceros, pangolin and bear) are used to make traditional medicines.

The region between North and South Korea known as the Demilitarized Zone, because of the absence of any human activity in that area, serves as a de facto refuge for many once-endangered plants and animals.

CUSTOMS & COURTESIES

Greetings

When greeting someone in South Korea, a gentle nod of the head is customary. If one is greeting someone of higher rank or an elderly person, a bow is sometimes given (arms stiff at the waist and feet together). However, such a bow should not be exaggerated, as that would signify disrespect. In addition, children always nod their heads or give a slight bow when greeting adults. If one is meeting someone for the first time, it is customary to give a detailed introduction. When meeting another professional for the first time, business is often not initially discussed, as it is more important to get to know each other first.

There are two common verbal greetings. "Annyong haseyo?" which means "How do you do?" is a formal greeting. It is used to show respect and politeness. In situations where special respect is needed, a person might greet someone with "Annyong hashimnikka." The casual way of greeting someone is "Annyong," which is used by schoolchildren or close friends when addressing each other. Adults address children with "Annyong" as well.

It is not uncommon for urban South Korean men to shake hands, with the left hand supporting or resting under the right forearm to show respect. If the handshake is between professionals who are meeting for the first time, they will exchange business cards. Business cards are presented face up, and accepted with both hands. Women rarely shake hands.

Gestures & Etiquette

Among South Korean youth, friendship is highly valued, and it is not uncommon to see close friends of the same sex holding hands, walking down the street with arms around each other, or one hand on another's shoulder. This is much less common among older men and women as embracing older people in this manner, or even members of the opposite sex, is not considered appropriate. Furthermore, it is never considered appropriate to touch a Korean if he or she is not related to you, or is not a close friend.

Hand gestures are also important in South Korea. To hail a cab, or when beckoning to someone, the arm should be extended with the palm down, and the fingers should be moved in a quick scratching motion. One should never point with the index finger. Also, when passing something from hand to hand, the right hand should always be used, with the left hand supporting the wrist.

Courtesy is extremely important to South Koreans. South Koreans feel it is highly impolite to say "No" to someone, because that would imply a lack of effort. Therefore, the word "No" is rarely spoken. In fact, sometimes a "Yes" will be spoken in an effort to be polite, even if the "Yes" is not meant to signify agreement.

Gift giving is an important part of being courteous, and small gifts are given in almost every situation. When accepting a gift, it is customary to refuse it a couple of times before then agreeing to accept it. Refusing a gift entirely is considered to be very insulting. The polite way to take a gift is to use both hands to receive it. Gifts are usually small and not too expensive, and gifts are expected to be reciprocated. It is considered bad luck to give scissors or knives as a gift, or to wrap a gift in red paper.

Eating/Meals

South Koreans typically eat three meals a day. Rice is a staple at all three meals, and is usually eaten with chopsticks and a spoon, as are other foods. Meals are very important and are served first at a party or event, before socializing begins. Food is typically served from large communal platters, and items are passed with the right hand.

Drinks are also poured with the right hand, and one should offer to pour for the person next to them.

Oftentimes, a guest will continue to be served until food is deliberately left on the plate. It is also common for extended families to dine together. In addition, eating while walking on the street is considered impolite for adults, although it is acceptable for children. For this reason, there are usually stools set up in the streets alongside or in front of food vendors.

South Koreans in urban areas dine in restaurants quite frequently. Tipping is not practiced and is in fact considered so impolite that many restaurants will post a "No Tipping" sign for tourists. When dining with a group, the host is expected to pay for everyone, although it is considered polite to offer to pay. If two people are dining together, it is customary for the younger person to pay for the older person. After dinner, the host will usually invite his guests to go out for a drink. It is considered to be very rude to turn down such an invitation.

Visiting

In South Korea, hosting a guest is considered a great responsibility and honor. When invited to a South Korean household, the guest should remove his or her shoes upon entering. Typically, there will be an obvious place where shoes are kept near the door. Guests are usually given the best seat, and refreshments are commonly served. It is considered impolite for the guest to refuse refreshments.

In a traditional Korean home, guests will be seated on cushions on the floor. The floors in Korean homes are ondol, or heated floors, so this is considered quite comfortable. Men typically sit with their legs crossed in front of them, while women are expected to tuck their legs to the side. In urban areas, it is more common to see European-style furniture, and the guest will be offered the best seat facing the front door. It is considered polite for a guest to refuse this seat, and then accept it. Furthermore, guests invited to a South Korean home for a meal or party, are often expected to bring a gift in appreciation.

This is customarily a small gift, and usually an item that can be served at the party.

LIFESTYLE

Family

Historically in South Korea, the father arranged marriages. Although the father is still considered to be the head of the family today, most South Koreans now choose their own spouses. Formal weddings performed in hanboks, or traditional Korean attire, are still common. However, many Koreans residing in urban centers forgo these elaborate wedding ceremonies, opting instead to wear modern wedding dresses and marry in public wedding halls.

Typically, the father and eldest son receive great respect as the heads of the family. The eldest members of the family are also shown the greatest respect, and sons are expected to care for their aging parents. The nuclear family is common, and it is not unusual for elderly parents to live with the married couple and their children. It is also considered lucky for women to have many sons.

Due to Confucian influence, detailed genealogies of family histories are commonly kept. Many families have written histories that date back several centuries, and include not only birth dates, but achievements as well. South Koreans have a one-syllable family name, the most common being Kim and Yi. This is followed by a one or two-syllable given name.

Housing

Housing in South Korea varies widely from simple huts in the rural areas to metal shanties in the cities to deluxe high-rises along the river. Urban areas in Korea have expanded rapidly in the last decades. As such, it is not unusual to find a Buddhist temple surrounded by a neighborhood of old, traditional homes, which are themselves bordered by new, towering apartment buildings. Prior to 1960, few buildings were larger than ten stories high, even in Seoul. Today, high-rise buildings dominate Seoul, including blocks of apartments.

Living space in South Korea is smaller than in Western countries. Even luxury apartments are rarely larger than 111.5 square meters (1,200 square feet). Conditions within the city are typically crowded, and most residences do not have ground level gardens, although many have rooftop gardens. City services, such as water and sanitation, have generally not been able to keep up with the rapid urban growth. Even so, there is a shortage of housing in the major cities, including Seoul.

Food

Korean cuisine is largely based on vegetables, meat, noodles and rice. Traditional Korean dishes are also typically served with numerous side dishes. Kimchi is the signature Korean food. It is distinctive first and foremost by its smell, followed closely by its uniquely spicy-sour, salty-sweet taste. Many families have their own kimchi recipes that are handed down through the generations, but the basic recipe is the same. Five or more cabbages are washed, cut into two to four pieces, and soaked in salted water for eight hours. Afterwards, the cabbage leaves are covered with a mixture of the herb dropwort, green onions, radishes, fish paste, rice paste, chili pepper paste (some families make their own paste) and oysters. It is then placed into a kimchi pot and left to ferment for anywhere from a few days to weeks at a time.

Extremely nutritional, kimchi can be consumed at every meal, and often is. In addition, there are almost as many ways to serve it—including scrambled in eggs, as part of a beef stew or as a pizza topping—as there are types of kimchi. In fact, there are over 100 types of kimchi, as categorized by the Korean Food Academy. The city of Gwangju has a huge kimchi festival every year and there is a kimchi museum located in Seoul.

Barley tea is served with most meals, and Soju and beer are common alcoholic drinks. South Koreans do not usually eat sweets for dessert, but prefer fruit instead, such as the popular mango. Mango can be also found mixed with rice, as a drink or frozen on a stick. The latter is especially popular among Korean children.

Life's Milestones

Historically, the mortality rate for Korean children was very high (although it dropped to less than four in 1000 live births by 2015). This was due to a number of reasons, foremost a lack of healthcare and childhood related diseases. However, once a child reached the age of one year, their chances of survival increased dramatically. For that reason, a child's first birthday, or Tol, (pronounced with a soft "T" as in "Dol") was celebrated with great excitement and ritual. A child's Chut-tol (first birthday) is still celebrated in much the same way today.

Most Koreans live in small houses or apartments, so the Chut-tol celebration is usually held in a banquet hall in order to allow for the many friends and family who will come to celebrate. Lavish invitations are typically sent out, the hall is decorated and a huge buffet is presented to the guests, including many kinds of ddoek (rice cakes), fruit, and soups. The baby and parents wear traditional hanboks, as do some of the guests.

The highlight of the Chut-tol is the Toljabee event. The child is placed at a table facing the guests, upon which several items have been laid out. These usually include a bow and arrow, needle and thread, a bowl of rice, a book, money, and sometimes other items as chosen by the parents. The child's future is then predicted by what he or she reaches for first. For example, if the baby grabs the bow and arrow first, it is predicted that he will become a great warrior; the book means she will be a scholar; the money predicts wealth. In modern times, this is done more as a game than any ritualistic prediction of the future. In addition, the parents will usually place the items they wish the child to grab nearest to the edge of the table.

CULTURAL HISTORY

Art

Western culture has still not really developed a formal appreciation or study of Korean art. This is primarily because Korean culture has his-torically been regarded by some as nothing more than the merger of Chinese and Japanese culture. For that reason, Korean art has most often been regarded as mostly Chinese-inspired, rather than uniquely Korean. Only recently have experts began to acknowledge the way Korea adapted and transformed Chinese artistic methods to create something unique to Korea. In fact, Korean art is becoming noted for its use of natural forms, bold color and elaborate surface decorations, both in pottery and painting.

Korean art can be categorized by the country's main religions and their dominant times: Shamanist art, followed by Korean Buddhist and Confucian art, and concluding with art shaped by Western influence. As in many countries, the earliest examples of Korean art consist of Stone Age works, mainly votive sculptures, or statuettes, and petroglyphs. Petroglyphs are drawings carved into rock, typically made by prehistoric peoples. This was followed by the Shamanistic art of Korea's Bronze Age (800 to 400 BCE), characterized by lavishly decorated items such as bronze mirrors, swords, and rattles. These items were mainly used in rituals, and many were built in a design that has never been found in China.

Buddhism arose during the period of the Three Kingdoms (circa 57 BCE to 668 CE). During this period art began to be commissioned as a dedication to the Buddha. These art pieces included pins, statues and swords, and were characterized by warm, natural and harmonious proportions. Tomb murals, typically depicting scenes from everyday life, also arose during this time, and foreshadowed the arrival of Korean landscapes and portraitures.

The Goryeo Dynasty (918 to 1392 CE) saw the rise of Korean celadon pottery, still popular today. Celadon refers to the green-blue glaze used to coat the pottery and display designs. Although this type of pottery was first produced in China, Korean artists created a unique style highly valued by the Chinese. This style included the unique jadelike glaze and designs such as birds and fish. The Joseon Dynasty (1392 to 1897), considered by some to be the "golden age" of Korean painting, saw Korean art becoming more distinctive as Buddhism diminished and Confucianism increased. Landscape painting (in a realistic manner called "true view") became quite popular and reflected nationalistic sentiments.

Many old and valuable Korean art pieces are held in Japan. This is most likely a result of Japanese rule and occupation from 1910 to 1945. It is believed that 80 percent of all Korean Buddhist paintings are in Japan. In fact, the Tokyo National Museum is known to hold 4,800 Korean art items. Many more significant Korean art pieces are thought to be held by Japanese private collectors.

Prior to the Japanese annexation of the Korea peninsula in 1910, Korean arts, heavily influenced by the Chinese, were primarily a reflection of religious beliefs. During the Japanese occupation, the Korean language and all forms of Korean art were banned. As a result, many were lost forever. In 1945, Koreans recovered their national sovereignty and their language. However, they also witnessed the division of their country in 1950, with South Korea becoming heavily dependent on the United States. Nonetheless, nationalism became very important to South Koreans as their country's economy strengthened and progressed. This fierce pride in their country is reflected in their art, literature and music during the last half of the 20th and early part of the 21st centuries.

Visual arts in South Korea during the last fifty years have largely been influenced by American culture and anti-Japanese sentiment. Korean painters would even go so far as to reject the use of colors that were popular in Japanese art. The tragedy of the Korean War also influenced many artists, most notably Lee Joong-seop (1916–1956). His anguished paintings embody the heartbreak of Korea's national division. The end of the Korean War and subsequent rise of South Korea's economy also inspired Korean artists to finally search for their own identity. Artists such as Park Seo-Bo (1931–) and Kim Tschang-yeul (1929–) began to look for ways to modernize the Korean artistic tradition, often making it a point to study overseas, especially in Paris. France.

Architecture

Traditional Korean architecture has always reflected the values most important to South Koreans. These include humility, closeness to and respect for nature, and creating a sense of balance. These key aspects have contributed to Korean architecture's uniquely elegant and open design.

The basic Korean wooden frame structure was prevalent during the Han Dynasty (206 BCE to 220 CE), a period heavily influenced by ancient Chinese culture. Religions such as Taoism and Confucianism also reinforced the commitment to small, humble designs, prominent in Korean architecture. With the rise of Buddhism in the fourth century, Korean architecture began to feature more ornate designs and greater use of color. This style is evident in the building of Buddhist temples.

The Silla Dynasty (57 BCE to 935 CE) represented a turning point in Korean architecture, especially during the Unified Silla era (668 to 935 CE), when most of the Korean peninsula was occupied by the Silla Kingdom. During this era, Koreans assimilated, or blended, foreign culture with their own to create a unique cultural heritage. This included the ideal of "contemplative beauty," which resulted in art and architecture fully identifiable as Korean. This ideal was, and remains to this day, the driving force behind all manner of Korean design. Contemplative beauty is identified as being in harmony with nature. To achieve this, natural elements are left alone in both design and engineering. As a result, traditional Korean architecture is considered airy, simple, and elegant.

Drama

South Korean drama has its origins in the folk theater tradition, which some date back almost 2,000 years ago, as early Koreans sought to please their ancestors and fulfill religious obligations through various rituals that evolved into early theater. Dancing, singing and wearing masks characterized the early theatrical kiak, a form of performance that is thought to have migrated from China and would eventually make its way to Japan. In the Silla era, different dances became popular, including kommu (masked sword dance), cheoyngmu (masked dance) and muaemu (a Buddhist dance).

During the Goryeo period, acrobatic displays were popular and dominated performance art, but masked dances continued to develop. The Sande evolved into a type of morality play consisting of a religious service that ended with a play that criticized corrupt priests and the nobility. The audience for these productions tended to be from the general public, and it is said that both Buddhists and non-Buddhists enjoyed this type of play.

Puppet plays, which probably originated in India and made their way to Korea through China, also became popular. Two styles evolved, the Ggogdu-Gasi and the Mansog-Zung. Ggogdu-Gasi is a largely Buddhist play that serves as a means of cultural and political criticism (with a domestic storyline). The Mansog-Zung is a silent play with five characters performed on the Buddha's birthday.

The advent of modern Korean theater is attributed to Sin Che-Ho (1812–1884), who developed the classic musical drama. His efforts eventually led to the creation of the national theater in 1908, led by political activist and playwright Yi In-Jig, who staged his own productions, including *The Silver World* and *The Plum in the Snow*. Thus began a wave of rise theatrical productions in the country and the beginning of the "new wave" of Korean drama, characterized by more romantic and light dramas, many with Western roots. In reaction to the new wave, a more realistic school of drama also emerged.

The Society for the Study of Dramatic Arts was established in 1931, but only survived a short time before its nationalistic tendencies were quelled by the government. World War II and the subsequent division of Korea into North and South saw the theater community preoccupied with more pressing matters. Following the division of the country, South Korea regained its dramatic footing, staging some Western plays and again propagating its own dramatic identity.

Three styles of theater dominate cotemporary Korean drama: traditional (including classical Western theatrical productions), Daehakro or experimental, and popular theater, which features Broadway hits.

Music & Dance

Documented evidence of traditional Korean music has been found from as early as the 15th century. Based on Buddhist and, to a lesser degree, shamanistic beliefs, music was first used as a form of worship, and was often combined with dancing. More than thirty musical instruments were commonly used during this time period, including the twelve string gayageum, which is still played in modern Korea.

The best examples of Korean music arose during the Joseon Dynasty. During this period, music and dance became extremely important because they were main components of all rituals and ceremonies. Music was classified into three formal categories: Chinese music, ceremonial music, and court music, along with an informal secular or folk music category. Folk dancing also became very popular during this time. This included the farmer's dance and mask dances, which are still performed during ceremonies in modern day South Korea.

Historically, Koreans have always had a great love for music and dance, and music has always been a reflection of their pride in and love for their country. However, during the Japanese invasion of Korea in the early-to-mid 20th century, Korean music was outlawed, and a large number of traditional dances were lost. The onset of the Korean War in 1950 further changed the face of Korean music. South Korea accepted the influence of Western music during the war, often translating American tunes into Korean. Ultimately, two very different approaches to music emerged after the country was split into the Democratic People's Republic of Korea (North Korea) and the Republic of Korea (South Korea).

At the time of the split, composers were developing a sense of national identity, which was lost with the Korean War. Many prominent composers, such as Kim Sun-nam, went to North Korea. With the loss of composers and their compositions, however, came a rise in individual performers. These classical performers came to symbolize South Korea's new nationalism. Violinists especially enjoyed tremendous success, both in South Korea and overseas. This trend continues today, along with a rise in new composers who are creating internationally recognized compositions based on Korea's traditional twelve-tone music.

In the 1980s, a movement began to revive traditional Korean dances. However, out of the original fifty-six court dances, only few are well known today. These include the cheoyngmu (the Mask Dance) of Silla, hakchum (the Crane Dance) of Goryeo, and chunaengjeon (Nightingale-Singing-in-the-Spring Dance) of Joseon. To support their continued performance and prevent these dances from being forgotten, the government has classified them as "Intangible Cultural Properties." As such, they are maintained by the Cultural Heritage Administration (CHA).

In the 1990s, Korean music was redefined, folk music was revived, and more original tunes were created. Contemporary music in South Korea now features many world music elements as well as traditional Korean instruments. South Korean music and dance continues to be influential on the international world stage. In fact, popular classical singers such as sopranos Jo Su-mi, Shin Young-ok and Hong Hye-gyong have performed leading roles in productions at New York's Metropolitan Opera. In addition, the musical *The Last Empress*, an epic Korean tale of Empress Myeongseong (1851–1895), was performed in New York to great acclaim. It was seen by South Koreans as a chance to promote and share Korean culture with the rest of the world.

Literature

Classical Korean literature finds its roots in China. Early Korean-language literature was written using Chinese characters or was translated into Chinese. The dependence on the Chinese writing system ended, though, in the 19th century, when the focus became the Korean language and writing system.

During the Silla era (668 to 935 CE), folk songs called hyangga extolled the feats of knights and served as devotional hymns. Hyangga continued through the Goryeo period (918–1392), which also featured a rise in poetry, especially Chinese genres, and the development of Korean tales such as the *Sui chon* (Tales of the Extraordinary), a collection of folk tales. In addition, collections of Korean legends and stories also arose, such as Iryon's *Samguk yusa* (Remnants of the Three Kingdoms).

In the Joseon period (1392–1598), King Sejong introduced the han'gul alphabet for the Korean language, which prompted a flurry of works in the Korean language. "Yongbi och'on ka" (Song of the Dragons Flying to Heaven) is written in verse (akchang) and praises the founders of the dynasty, written at Sejong's request. Sejong went on to also write *Worin ch'on'gang chi kok* (The Moonlight on Ten Thousand Waters), about Queen Sohon.

In the 18th century, sijo or verse accompanied by music sprang up. Prominent author Chong Ch'ol wrote many sijo with political or philosophical themes. Kasa was another distinctly Korean longer verse form characterized by couplets. Themes in kasa might be the contemplation of nature, or a celebration of virtues or love.

Fiction writing began in the 17th century, and wide readership was fueled by commercial publishing and book rentals. *Kumo shinhwa* (New Stories from Golden Turtle Mountain), written by Kim Shi-sup, is an example of some of the fiction of the time, and is a collection of short stories featuring a "talented young man and beautiful woman," ghosts, and other worlds. It is believed to be the first attempt at a Korean novel. Other fictional efforts tackled social concerns and everyday life of Koreans.

Following the Joseon period, Korean literature felt the influence of the West and the rise of imperial Japan in the mid-19th and early 20th centuries. This period came to be known as the kaehwa kyemong (Enlightenment). Ch'angga (song), shinch'eshi (new verse) and chayushi (free verse poem) became popular and indicated a new poetic freedom in structure and meter, and was accompanied by a sometimes political edge to some works. Biographies also spoke to a nationalistic feeling in the country.

In the early 20th century, the Korean new novel, the shinsosol, emerged. Leaving behind the other worldliness of earlier novel forms, the shinsosol dealt with common realities and was written in the vernacular. Literary independence ended following the Japanese invasion of the peninsula in 1910, as the Japanese controlled the media under military rule.

With the independence movement that began in 1919, literary life in Korea reawakened, and literature reflected the rising consciousness of the people. Authors such as Yi Kwang-su wrote *Mujong* (Heartlessness, 1917), which captured the more modern feelings of colonialism, isolation, and angst. Literature in the early and mid-20th century reflected the political turmoil that Koreans felt as they struggled with democratic and socialist movements.

Modern South Korean literature has responded to the rapid changes South Korean society endured during the last fifty years. The examination of Korea's division and tragedy of war revived interest in nationalism, giving rise to such novels as Hwang Sok-yong's *Chang Kil-san*. Many of the best Korean works of literature during the late part of the 20th century are noteworthy for their reflections of Korea's culture, and for their rich use of the Korean language.

CULTURE

Arts & Entertainment

Although traditional Korean arts and culture are still a popular part of South Korean life, it is the influence of Western and Japanese culture that has helped shape modern South Korean culture. It is considered a mark of South Korea's own cultural power that much of its popular arts and entertainment, in particular motion pictures and popular music, have, in return, been successfully exported to the West and throughout Asia.

Korean modern pop culture has recently become extremely popular in Asia. It even has a nickname: Hallyu, or "Korean wave." The most popular Korean boy band, *TVXQ*, has earned wide success in Japan, as has the Korean television drama *Winter Sonata*.

In music, South Korea's own native brand of popular music, known sometimes as K-pop, is enormously popular among younger listeners; popular singers and musicians include Seo Taiji (who until the late 1990s was part of Seo Taiji and Boys) and Lee Jung-hyun (an actress). In 2012, K-pop was made internationally famous with the song "Gangnam Style," sung by Park Jae-sang, better known as PSY. Noraebang (known as karaoke in the U.S.) is a very popular pastime.

Among the more notable film directors who have made a mark in Korean film are Jae-young Kwak (*My Sassy Girl*, 2001), Je-gyu Kang (*Swiri*, 1999) and Jang Sun-Woo (*Gojitmal*, 1999). "Oldboy" (2003), directed by South Korean Chan-wook Park, was awarded the Grand Prix at the 2004 Cannes Film Festival.

Important modern South Korean authors include Park Kyong-ni (the epic novel *T'oji*, or "The Land" written between 1969 and 1994), Hwang Suk-Young (*The Shadow of Arms*), Pak Wan-so (*The Naked Tree*) and Cho Chong-Rae (*Playing with Fire*). Korean-American writer Chang-Rae Lee has received critical attention for his novels *A Gesture Life* (1999) and *Native Speaker* (1995).

Cultural Sites & Landmarks

One of Korea's most famous landmarks is the Namdaemun, or literally the "Great Southern Gate." It is considered the first of the country's national treasures and holds a special place in the hearts of South Koreans. Originally the southern gate of the ancient walls surrounding Seoul, the capital of South Korea, during the Joseon Dynasty, it has remained standing since 1398. It has been rebuilt once and renovated several times since then, and required further rebuilding after an arsonist set fire to the wooden structure in February 2008. Nearby is the popular Namdaemun market, a predominantly outdoor market that has operated for centuries.

A popular tourist destination in South Korea is the DMZ, or De-Militarized Zone. Located along the 38th parallel between North and South Korea, this military demarcation line (MDL) is 4 kilometers (2.5 miles) wide and separates North and South Korea. Created at the close of the Korean War, it has remained almost untouched for fifty-one years. Both countries declare it a temporary line and not a permanent border. Although there is a push by some groups in South Korea to preserve the DMZ as an ecotourism site, it remains the most heavily guarded border in the world.

Because the site is so heavily guarded, visitors are required to follow strict rules. This includes a formal dress code that forbids the wearing of blue jeans. The site itself contains the infamous "Bridge of No Return," where prisoners of war from both sides were allowed to choose whether to return to their home countries. Visitors are also allowed to tour the various spy tunnels dug by the North Koreans, which were discovered in the 1970s. The site also includes the United Nations (UN) room where negotiators for both North and South Korea meet. Located in the Panmunjom truce village, the room features a long table that extends into North Korea. On top of the table are microphones still used by the North Koreans to listen to tourists.

Another popular landmark is the Ch'angdokkung Palace Compound in Seoul. Built in the early 15th century, it is considered to be an exceptional example of Far Eastern palace architecture and design. Its lavish gardens and open areas are noted for how they blend into the surrounding natural landscape. These designs are also reflective of traditional Korean architecture.

Libraries & Museums

Korea's National Museum is one of the world's largest museums and contains a collection of about 150,000 objects, of which only 11,000 are on display. Featured at the museum are archeological, historical, fine art, and Asian art galleries. The National Folk Museum of Korea houses a collection of artifacts numbering more than 90,000 items classified as "national cultural

assets." The largest private art museum in Korea is the Ho-Am Art Museum south of Seoul. It has a collection of more than 1,200 Korean works of art from the collection of former chairman of the Samsug Group, Lee Byung-Chull. It also features a sculpture garden with works from French artist Antoine Bourdelle and a classical Korean garden. South Korea features many other national, private, and regional museums.

The National Library of Korea features over 7 million volumes of national and cultural significance.

Holidays

Official holidays celebrated by South Koreans include Children's Day (May 5), Foundation Day (October 3), and Constitution Day (July 17). Liberation Day, a celebration of the liberation from Japanese rule in 1945, is observed on August 15.

South Koreans also have holidays celebrating farming, the creation of Hangul (the Korean alphabet) and the birthday of Buddha, an important religious figure in South Korea.

Youth Culture

Overall, the youth in South Korea are considered technologically savvy, and it is not uncommon for a youth to consistently travel with a cell phone, portable gaming system and an iPod. Many Korean youth treat their cell phones as a piece of jewelry, decorating them lavishly and even hanging them around their necks. In addition, Korean youths typically spend a large amount of their free time online. As such, popular places for youth to socialize include Internet cafes, or "PC baangs," which are typically open twenty-four hours a day. Furthermore, 90 percent of Korean homes have affordable and fast broadband Internet access, and most Korean youth use their computers to watch current television programs or films. However, because technology has become extremely important and influential to Korean teenagers, some Korean adults feel that the youth culture in the early 21st century is, to a degree, spoiled, as they have not had to experience economic hardships.

Korean youth are also highly focused on academics. Many attend for-profit afterschool tutoring centers, or "hagwons," which leaves little time for sports or other physical activities. Children typically begin attending these private tutoring centers at the elementary level. It is also common for students to be enrolled in several centers at the same time, with each teaching a different subject.

SOCIETY

Transportation

Most South Koreans use the country's extensive railway system to travel long distances. The Korean Train Express (KTX) is a high-speed train that travels between the cities of Seoul, Busan and Makpo. In fact, the KTX transports travelers from Seoul to Busan faster than an airplane does. Air travel, although more expensive, is also becoming more popular, especially among business professionals.

South Koreans who live in urban areas usually travel via subways, buses, and taxis. All three modes of transportation are very inexpensive. The subways in particular are especially known for their clean conditions. Furthermore, many subway stations feature works of art on display, along with giant television monitors for commuters to view. Subways also represent the fastest mode of transportation between city neighborhoods. While taxis and busses are less expensive options, they often take longer than using the subway due to the high volumes of traffic on the streets. In addition, owning a car is a status symbol in the cities, especially in Seoul. Many wealthy South Koreans also hire a driver to navigate the traffic for them.

Transportation Infrastructure

The South Korean transportation system is both well developed and well funded. According to CNN, the government has allocated about $230 million per year through 2020 to an infrastructure that includes an intelligent transport system that ties information about upcoming delays on roads, bus schedules, and toll and train/bus fare payment through fiber optic networks along roadways. Their next challenge is to incorporate green technology into their long-range plans. Moves towards this effort are evident in the South Korean's testing of the Online Electric Vehicle System, a system that is powered by magnetic electrical charging stripes installed under the road.

Media & Communications

South Korea has a large number of nationally distributed newspapers. Many are printed in English, such as the *Korea Herald*. The Yonhap News Agency, South Korea's official news agency, owns several of them. Freedom of the press is guaranteed by the constitution, although this freedom was not protected in many cases prior to 1987. The Korean Broadcasting System (KBS) is publicly owned and is the largest communications company.

Internet use is widespread and nearly 92 percent of Korean homes have broadband access, which is typically inexpensive and fast. While it is illegal to download copyrighted content, copyright laws are usually not enforced. As such, downloading such content is common, especially among Korean youth. In addition, many South Korean youth use their computers to watch television shows and movies. It is also considered important for most South Koreans to have the latest technology in cell phones, or "hand phones" as Koreans call them. Due to Korea's close proximity to Japan, South Koreans often are able to obtain the latest designs and features available in cell phones months ahead of Western countries.

SOCIAL DEVELOPMENT

Standard of Living

South Korea ranked 15 out of 187 countries on the 2014 United Nations Human Development Index.

Water Consumption

South Korea is fortunate to have a central mountainous region and a number of rivers, but the steep slopes and small river basins result in large and intense floods of water in short periods of time. River systems in Korea have seasonal variations that result in summer floods and winter droughts. Challenges to water resources have to do with population density, which puts stress on water resources. The Korea Water Resources Association notes that precipitation per capita is about 10 percent of the world average.

South Korea's water and sanitation infrastructure is well developed. In 2012, 97.8 percent of the total population had access to improved drinking water (99.7 percent of urban populations).

Education

Education is highly valued in South Korea. The country's educational system is similar to that of the United States: students attend primary school (citizen's school) from the ages of six to eleven, and then attend junior high or middle school for three years, followed by three years of high school.

Education is compulsory through the age of fourteen for all students. At the age of seventeen or eighteen, many students continue on to South Korea's many universities and colleges. The capital contains nearly half of the country's colleges and universities, including Seoul National University, Korea University and Yonsei University. Many South Korean students attend private auxiliary schools (similar in nature to Japanese cram schools) to help them prepare for entrance to the nation's many competitive top-tier colleges and universities.

Aside from their regular studies, South Korean students begin learning English grammar and language skills as early as primary school.

The literacy rate in South Korea is high, at nearly 98 percent, which is comparable to the rates in the United States (97 percent) and Japan (99 percent). According to the Organisation for Economic Co-operation and Development (OECD), young people in South Korea are more likely to have a secondary education (97 percent of the population) than any other developed country in the world (2013). South Korea trails only two countries in terms of university attendance, Canada and Japan. Further, the statistics show that South Korea spends about half of what is spent per pupil in the United States and achieved much higher math test results.

Women's Rights

According to a recent World Economic Forum and UN report, South Korean women rank among the lowest in the developed world concerning gender empowerment. The majority of South Korean women are well educated, enjoy high quality health care, and are protected by anti-discrimination laws, Korean society still tends to marginalize women. Much of this marginalization stems from Confucian beliefs about the nature of women and their virtues (more obedient and soft, while men are leaders and more typically masculine).

Women often suffer from low wages, sexual harassment, and lack of reliable childcare. Laws that are meant to protect women in these matters often only apply to major corporations, or are not enforced. Only a small percentage of South Korea's gross national product (GNP) goes toward programs intended for women and children. Groups such as the United Women's Association of South Korea (KWAU) work to increase awareness of the issue. Another issue is the fact that women workers make about 60 percent of what men make when performing the same job functions.

Although more South Korean women now work outside of the home, the general concept of the woman's role is that she is responsible for the maintenance of the household and the management of the children's education. The husband is therefore considered the main source of income, while the woman is typically charged with managing that income. In fact, South Korean husbands usually defer to their wives' judgment when it comes handling the finances. Interestingly, this attitude is most prevalent among the college-educated middle class.

These attitudes, although still predominant, have subsided somewhat in recent years. This is especially true in the political realm as the first woman president of South Korea, Park Geun-hye, was elected in the beginning of 2013. This has been called a turning point in Korean politics and women's rights; yet even before then, in 1997, Kim Dae-jung's election to the role of chief executive was an outstanding achievement for Korean women. The process of change is an on-going one, but one that holds promise for women.

Although Korea is a male-dominated society, women run the families. South Korean women tend to go to college, earn a degree, enter the workforce, and then leave their jobs when they get married to concentrate on being a wife and mother. Once married, South Korean women work to appear submissive and deferential to the wishes of their husbands and in-laws. This is because, in South Korea, public assertion of a women's power is socially disapproved, even though women are typically in charge of the household. Usually, the eldest woman, or "ajuma," controls all aspects of the family's life, especially the social aspects.

As in many developed countries, a heavy value is also placed on a woman's appearance in South Korea. Most Korean women belong to gyms, and do not eat sweets. In fact, it is not uncommon to see a gym or Jim Jil Bang (spa) on almost every block in Seoul. In addition, surgeons in South Korea estimate that at least one in ten women have had some form of plastic surgery performed, with surgery to widen the eyes being the most popular operation. Apkujong is an area in Seoul that has over 400 surgery clinics, with one street nicknamed "Plastic Surgery Street." Many tourists from China and Thailand also come to Seoul to have plastic surgery. Although the KWAU and other organizations are fighting to pass laws to monitor such plastic surgery clinics, there are no safety regulations in place yet, and tragic stories of surgeries gone wrong are common.

Health Care

Since the late 1980s, South Koreans have enjoyed universal health care coverage through either National Health Insurance or the Medical Aid Program. As in many modernized countries, wealthy South Koreans may also pay for private (and more expensive) treatment.

The universal health care system is paid for by taxation, and contributions by employers and the government. Public health awareness campaigns are frequent in South Korea.

The average life expectancy among South Koreans is approximately seventy-eight years; seventy-five years for men and eighty-two years for women (2009 estimate).

GOVERNMENT

Structure

The Republic of Korea is divided into a special city (Seoul), six metropolitan cities (including Pusan and Incheon) and nine provinces. The South Korean president is the chief of state, while the prime minister is the head of government. The president is elected for a single five-year term, and the prime minister and the presidential cabinet are appointed by the president. Members of the legislature, the National Assembly (with 299 members), are elected to four-year terms. The judiciary is comprised of the Supreme Court and the Constitutional Court.

Political Parties

In recent years, there have been some changes to the major political parties in South Korea. Such parties include the Justice Party; the Liberty Forward Party, which merged with the New Frontier Party in 2012; and, the New Politics Alliance for Democracy Party, the result of a 2014 merger between the Democratic Party and the New Political Vision Party. Many other parties, such as the Unified Progressive Party, have disbanded. Several parties over the years have advocated for national unity with North Korea, peace, environmentalism, and reform. Minor parties include the Independent Party, the Creative Korea Party, the Democratic Labor Party, the Centrist Reformists Democratic Party, the Economic Republican Party, and the Korea Socialist Party.

Local Government

Local government in South Korea is complex, with the country divided into nine provinces (including Seoul, a Special City), which are then divided into counties. Six metropolitan cities and ordinary cities (which are counties with more than 150,000 people) have been distinguished from the county government structure and cities with populations in excess of 500,000 are divided into wards. Those counties that do not qualify as cities are divided into towns and districts.

Seoul is designated as a Special City, which means that it is administered by the central South Korean government, in the same manner as a province. It is divided into twenty-five wards and 522 neighborhoods. Each ward has a mayor; the mayor of the city of Seoul has three assistant mayors and a series of assistant mayors to handle administrative matters. The Metropolitan Council numbers 104 people elected to four-year terms.

Judicial System

The Supreme Court of South Korea is the country's highest court. There are six High Courts, thirteen District Courts, and Family, Administrative, and Municipal Courts. Most decisions are made by a judge, but some courts have introduced a jury system. A Constitutional Court decides matters related to the country's constitution.

Taxation

The South Korean government levies an income tax (topping off at 38.5 percent) and value-added tax (VAT) at 10 percent, as well as an inheritance, gift, property acquisition, property, and wealth taxes. Corporate taxes can be as high as 27.5 percent. Taxes and other revenues account for 24.9 percent of the annual GDP.

Armed Forces

South Korea has an Army, Navy (which includes Marines), Air Force, and Reserves Force and is one of the largest armed forces in the world. Because of tensions with North Korea, the South Korean military is at a high state of readiness.

Foreign Policy

The most important historical events in South Korean history were the 1948 division of Korea into North and South Korea, and the Korean War, which lasted between 1950 and 1953. Because the South was supported by the United States and the north by the Soviet Union and China, the Korean War has long been interpreted as a Cold War battleground between the democratic West and the communist East. Both North and South Korea, particularly the civilian populations of both nations, suffered horrendous losses before the war ended in a stalemate in 1953. The possibility that the Koreas may someday be reunited is still a major geopolitical concern.

The president of South Korea, assisted by the National Security Council, establishes major foreign policies. The State Council, whose major foreign policies advisors are the prime minister and the minister of foreign affairs, then deliberates over these policies. The Agency for National Security Planning (ANSP), which is similar to the Central Intelligence Agency, or CIA, has direct contact with the president and will conduct foreign policy at the president's personal discretion. South Korea maintains diplomatic relations with 170 countries and has been a member of the UN since 1991

South Korea's relations with the United States have been complicated and sometimes intense since the 1953 Korean War cease-fire. Since then, South Korea has become less economically or militarily dependent on the U.S. Beginning in the late 20th century, Seoul has been seeking to establish a partnership with the U.S., rather than being dominated by U.S. military policy.

However, some South Korean policymakers feel that U.S. troops should gradually withdraw from South Korea. They argue that South Korea is more than capable of dealing with North Korea. In 1990, U.S. Secretary of Defense Dick Cheney held a consultation to restructure the U.S.-South Korea security relationship, transitioning the status of the U.S. in South Korea from a leading role to a supporting role.

South Korea's relationship with North Korea is best described as tempestuous. Public opinion on how South Korea should deal with its northern neighbor varies in view, but is always emotional. While the majority of the world perceives North Korea as an international threat, most South Koreans consider the people of North Korea to be kinsmen. Many South Koreans can still name relatives lost to North Korea during the split. In fact, it is estimated that there are 10 million separated family members on the Korea peninsula.

However, Pyongyang, the capital of North Korea, has been difficult to reach. The Sunshine Policy, established in 1998 by South Korean president Kim Dae Jung, had three basic principles: no armed provocation by the North will be tolerated; the South will not attempt to absorb the North in any way; and the South will always actively seek cooperation. The main aim of the policy was to soften North Korea's attitudes toward South Korea by encouraging interaction and economic assistance. However, the Sunshine Policy did not improve political relations between the two countries, and President Lee Myung-bak (elected in 2008) discontinued it. The best progress toward a positive relationship with North Korea has been made in the area of business, as inter-Korean business contracts are growing across the Demilitarized Zone.

South Korea has always had a close relationship with China. However, when the People's Republic of China provided North Korea with supplies and forces during the Korean War, that relationship almost completely ceased. Since the end of military action during the Korean War, South Korea and China slowly began to reform a diplomatic relationship, and the two countries re-established formal diplomatic relations in 1992.

Japan and South Korea still maintain a strained diplomatic relationship, largely held over from Japanese occupation of South Korea in 1910. Recently, however, relations have been gradually improving between the two nations at the urging of the United States. In fact, Korea and Japan worked together to host the Olympics in 1988 and the Soccer World Cup in 2002. In addition, Seoul and Tokyo hold a foreign ministerial conference each year where issues such as trade, the status of Koreans residing in Japan, and Tokyo's policy toward Pyongyang are discussed. While relations are improving, they continue to be troubled.

Human Rights Profile

International human rights law insists that states respect civil and political rights, and promote an individual's economic, social, and cultural rights. The United Nations Universal Declaration on Human Rights (UDHR) is recognized as the standard for international human rights. Its authors sought the counsel of the world's great thinkers, philosophers, and religious leaders, and were careful to create a document that reflects the core values shared by every world culture. (To read this document or view the articles relating to cultural human rights, visit http://www.udhr.org/UDHR/dcfault.htm.)

Overall, the South Korean government generally respects the rights of its citizens. However, there are a few exceptions. South Korean citizens have constitutionally protected rights that are for the most part in line with Article 2 of the Universal Declaration of Human Rights. South Korea's constitution declares all citizens as equals before the law regardless of race religion or gender.

For minorities, however, this equality does not come without difficulty. Discrimination among minorities and immigrants such as Mongolians, Nigerians and Chinese is widespread. It is also very difficult for outsiders to become fully accepted in South Korea. This is partially due to the fact that South Korea is one of the most ethnically homogeneous countries in the world, and partially due to the fact that protections for the rights of minority populations are often vague, or poorly enforced. Other groups that face discrimination are children of bi-racial parents (in which one parent is not ethnically a Korean) and gay and lesbians. The latter group in particular has almost no legal protection in South Korea. In addition, gay men are not allowed to serve in South Korea's military.

Article 18 of the declaration outlines freedom of religion. South Koreans have freedom of religion, and these religious freedoms are highly respected by the general population. Religions in South Korea range from Buddhism to evangelical Christian religions, and religious discrimination is rare.

The right to freedom of speech and expression, as outlined in Article 19, is also protected for the most part. The National Security Law does, however, criminalize speech in support of North Korea or communism, but this law is unevenly enforced and easily evaded. Still, there are over 100 such cases brought each year. Censorship is more prevalent in the media. Prohibited items generally include songs and dramatic performances related to anything Japanese, or which are inordinately violent or sexual. For example, film festivals are prescreened for extreme sexual content. In addition, the government blocks websites that are North Korean and sometimes blocks major overseas blog hosting sites. Although currently allowed, the ability to make anonymous comments online has been debated in South Korea.

The right to assemble, outlined in Article 20, is also supported in a rather unusual way. Peaceful protests by university students in Seoul are common and oftentimes advertised on television and radio broadcasts before they begin. However, these protests must be registered in advance with the city, so that streets and traffic can be blocked and accommodated to make room for the students.

ECONOMY

Overview of the Economy

Prior to the 1960s, the Korean economy was highly dependent on agriculture, but after the division of Korea into northern and southern entities, the industrialization of South Korea surpassed North Korea at a rapid pace.

The divide between North and South Korea is very broad in terms of modernization, indus-trial output and economic potential, not to mention the general economic well-being of its citizenry. At the beginning of the 21st century, South Korea's is one of the most important of all Asian economies, despite some moderate economic setbacks in recent decades.

In 2014, the per capita gross domestic product (GDP) was estimated at $35,300, a significant increase from the 2009 estimate of $28,000 (USD).

Industry

The most important industries in South Korea are electronics and telecommunications (radio, television and communication equipment), automobile production, chemicals, shipbuilding, and steel. Its major exports include semiconductors, wireless telecommunication equipment, automobiles and computers. Among its most important trading partners are China (including Hong Kong), the United States, and Japan.

Labor

The most important employers in South Korea by economic sector are services (70.4 percent), industry (24 percent) and agriculture (5.7 percent). As of 2014, the unemployment rate was 3.5 percent, well below many industrialized nations. Nearly half of South Korean workers are women.

Energy/Power/Natural Resources

South Korea is the world's fourth largest net importer of oil, relying on imports to satisfy the country's energy needs, and even overtaking India in the last decade. It also leads in the import of liquefied natural gas. Coal (which is a major resource in South Korea) and natural gas are taking the place of oil in meeting the country's energy needs. Renewable resources supply only a fraction of the country's energy needs.

South Korea's most important natural resources are mostly minerals, including coal, iron ore, tungsten, graphite, molybdenum, gold, and lead. The country's hydroelectric capacity is also important.

Fishing

South Korea has the seventh largest fishing industry in the world and is a major exporter of seafood, including squid, mollusks, anchovies and tuna. However, illegal deep-sea fishing could cause a ban on Korean maritime exports to the EU, unless the industry can be more effectively regulated.

Forestry

South Korea's forests cover 6,382 hectares (15,770 acres) of land. About 42 percent of forest is covered by conifers and major species include red pine, Korean white pine, larch and oak. The South Korean government has brought back all of its forests, which in the 1950s, were severely damaged. Because most of the growth is less than thirty years old though, much of the stock is not available for harvest.

Mining/Metals

South Korea has only 10 percent of the Korean peninsula's ore deposits. Mining is not a major contributor to the economy.

Agriculture

The major agricultural industries of South Korea are rice (which is grown on more than half of the country's farmland), potatoes and sweet potatoes, barley, vegetables, and fruit (including apples, oranges, and pears).

Animal Husbandry

Pigs, cattle, goats, and other livestock are raised.

Tourism

It was expected that the South Korean tourism industry would boom after successfully co-hosting the 2002 World Cup soccer tournament with Japan, but instead South Korea suffered severe tourism losses due to an outbreak of Severe Acute Respiratory Syndrome (SARS) that spread throughout China and the region. A further outbreak, this time of Middle East Respiratory Syndrome (MERS), hindered tourism significantly in June 2015. Such outbreaks could severely damage the tourism economy, especially as approximately six million tourists visit South Korea annually, bringing over $55 million (USD) to hotels and restaurants alone. Roughly half of all visitors come from Japan. Travelers to South Korea are expected to increase in coming years; this figure may be even higher if North Korea allows travel to South Korea during this period, a reflection of the very common hope among all Koreans that there will be a form of reunification between North and South.

Popular tourist destinations are numerous and include the volcanic island of Cheju-do, Changdokkung Palace and its Secret Gardens in Seoul, ancient temple sites in Gyeongju, the resort at Hwajinpo, a multitude of national parks (including Seoraksan and Songnisan), and the seaport city of Pusan.

April Sanders, Craig Belanger, Micah L. Issitt

DO YOU KNOW?

- The Korean alphabet (known as han'gul) was invented by scholars serving under King Sejong (1418–1450). The Korean script, which contains forty symbols, is considered to be one of the most scientific languages ever invented, with a remarkable ability to reflect the phonemes of the country's spoken language.

- South Korean youth and young adults are avid video gamers, rivaling American and Japanese youth in the number of games purchased each year.

Bibliography

De Mente, Boye Lafayette. *The Korean Mind: Understanding Contemporary Korean Culture.* North Clarendon, VT: Tuttle Publishing, 2012.

Glosserman, Brad and Scott A. Snyder. *The Japan-South Korea Identity Clash: East Asian Security and the United States.* Columbia: Columbia University Press, 2015.

Hoare, James. *Korea—Culture Smart! The Essential Guide to Culture and Customs.* London: Kuperard, 2012.

Matray, James Irving. *Korea Divided: The 38th Parallel and the Demilitarized Zone.* New York: Chelsea House, 2005.

Oberdorfer, Don. *The Two Koreas: A Contemporary History.* rev. ed. New York: Basic Books, 2013.

Official Website of the Republic of Korea. Korean Culture and Information Service. http://www.korea.net/.

Tudor, Daniel. *Korea: The Impossible Country.* North Clarendon, VT: Tuttle Publishing, 2012.

Works Cited

"A Brief History of Korean Architecture." Atelier Professor KOH. http://nongae.gsnu.ac.kr/~mirkoh/korb01.html.

"Boot Camp Tackles Spoiled Korean Youth." ABCnews. go.com. http://abcnews.go.com/International/Story?id=4171647&page=1.

"Deep Sea Fishery: EU Likely to Classify Korea as IUU Fishing Country in June." *Business Korea.* 8 May 2014. http://www.businesskorea.co.kr/article/4435/deep-sea-fishery-eu-likely-classify-korea-iuu-fishing-country-june.

"Korean Demilitarized Zone." GlobalSecurity.org. http://www.globalsecurity.org/military/facility/dmz.htm.

Ledyard, Gari. "Korea, South." Funk & Wagnalls New World Encyclopedia. New York: World Almanac Education Group, 2002.

Pollman, Mina. "The Troubled Japan-South Korea Relationship." *The Diplomat.* 27 July 2015. Accessed September 23, 2015. http://thediplomat.com/2015/07/the-troubled-japan-south-korea-relationship/

"Music and Dance." Korea.net. Korean Culture and Information Service. http://www.korea.net/korea/kor_loca.asp?code=T05.

Resos, Archie. "The Empowerment of Women in South Korea." *Journal of International Affairs.* 10 March 2014. http://jia.sipa.columbia.edu/online-articles/empowerment-women-south-korea/.

"South Korea." Britannica.com. http://www.britannica.com/EBchecked/topic/322280/South-Korea.

"South Korean Youth Dump TV Programming for Piracy." Afterdawn.com. http://www.afterdawn.com/news/archive/11852.cfm.

Taylor, Adam. "South Korea to offer tourists free 'MERS insurance.'" *The Washington Post.* 16 June 2015. https://www.washingtonpost.com/news/worldviews/wp/2015/06/16/south-korea-to-offer-tourists-free-mers-insurance/.

"What countries are the top net importers of oil?" *U.S. Energy Information Administration.* Accessed September 23, 2015. http://www.eia.gov/tools/faqs/faq.cfm?id=709&t=6.

"Where They Stand: The Status of Women in South Korea." WilsonCenter.org. Michael Kugelman. http://www.wilsoncenter.org/index.cfm?event_id=166060&fuseaction=events.event_summary.

"World Heritage List." UNESCO.org. http://whc.unesco.org/en/list.

City of Taipei by night. iStock/GoranQ

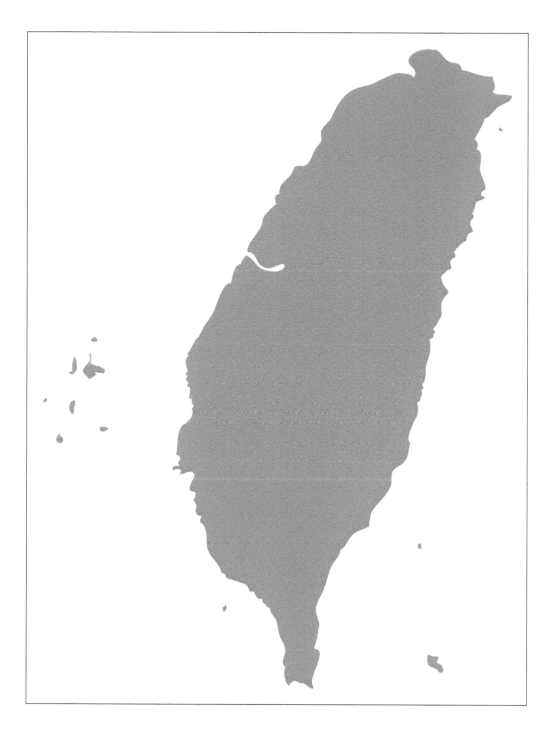

TAIWAN,
Republic of China

Introduction

Taiwan is a large East Asian island in the Pacific Ocean, off the coast of mainland China. Several smaller islands (the Pescadores, Quemoy, and Matsu) are included with the island of Taiwan as a political entity called the Republic of China (ROC). The nation's capital is Taipei, and the city is the center of political, administrative, educational, and cultural society in Taiwan. It is one of the most populous cities in the world and a popular destination for tourists from Asia, Europe, and the United States.

Taiwan maintains a contentious relationship with Mainland China, which regards the island entity as a renegade province of the People's Republic of China (PRC). In seeking to unify Taiwan, which maintains it is a separate country, China implemented the One-China policy, which establishes that Beijing is the ruling government of Taiwan. This is reinforced by the fact that, diplomatically, countries must recognize the government of the PRC. As of 2015, China had become somewhat more temperate in its views toward Taiwan and its political choices.

Taiwan, which has pushed for international recognition, recently introduced a "flexible diplomacy" strategy—a "one China, one Taiwan" approach to carve out space in the international community for both nations—in its quest to establish Taiwan as a separate cultural and political identity. A confrontational move, it has helped Taiwan to strengthen international ties in regions such as the South Pacific. However, the state must weigh such international moves against its strong economic ties with China.

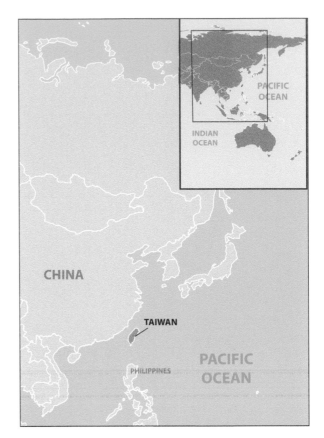

GENERAL INFORMATION

Official Language: Mandarin Chinese
Population: 23,415,126 (2015 estimate)
Currency: New Taiwan dollar
Coins: New Taiwan coins circulate in denominations of NT$1, 5, 10, 50, and 20. A NT$0.5 coin is also available, but said to be rare because of its value.

Land Area: 32,260 square kilometers (12,455 square miles)
Water Area: 3,720 square kilometers (1,436 square miles)
National Anthem: "Zhonghua Minguo gouge" ("National Anthem of the Republic of China"); "San Min Chu I" ("The Rights of the People")
Capital: Taipei
Time Zone: GMT +8

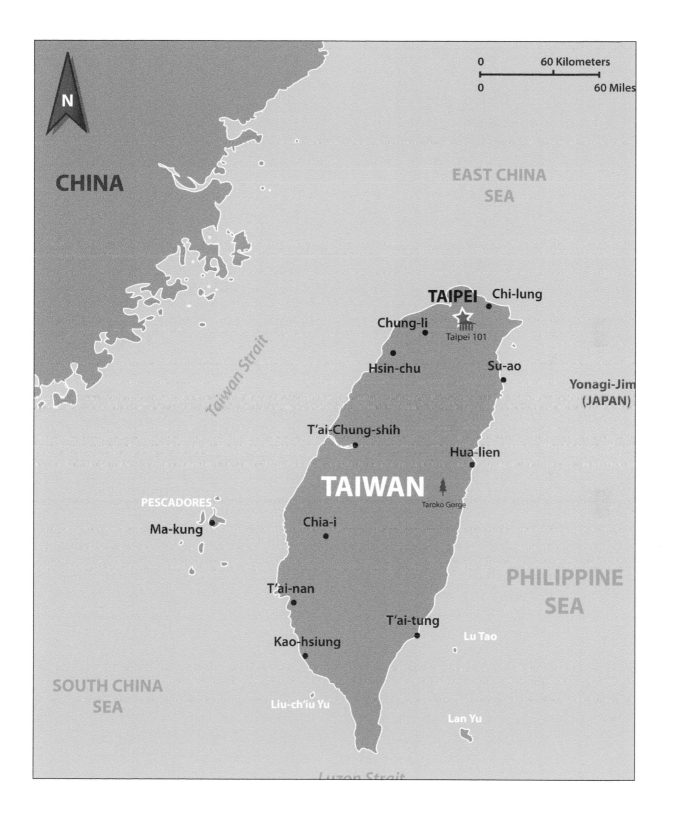

Principal Cities by Population (2014, except where noted):

- Taipei (2,702,315)
- Kaohsiung/Gaoxiong (2,778,992)
- Taichung/Taizhong (2,719,835)
- Tainan (1,884,284)
- Banciao (552,884; 2009)
- Zhonghe (414,535; 2009
- Hsinchu (411,587; 2009)
- Taoyuan (417,366)
- Xinzhuang (400,848; 2009)
- Keelung (388,321; 2009)

Flag Description: The flag of the Taiwan, officially the Republic of China, consists of a red background and a blue canton (upper hoist, or left, quarter). Within the blue canton is a white sun with twelve triangular points around its circumference. The flag bears the common name of Clear Sky, White Sun, and the Entire Earth Red.

Population

Approximately 84 percent of Taiwan's population is considered native Taiwanese, including Han Chinese and Hakka peoples. Most of these Taiwanese are descended from 19th-century immigrants from mainland China. Twentieth-century refugees or their children account for 14 percent of the population, while 2 percent of the population belongs to the twelve aboriginal tribes native to Taiwan and its islands.

Taiwan's population density is high, nearly 700 persons per square kilometer (1,838 persons per square mile), with the northern part of the island containing the most densely populated communities. According to the CIA World Factbook, in 2015, Taiwan had a population growth rate of approximately .23 percent.

Farmland is scarce because of the mountains, and an urban population predominates, living in multi-story apartments in cities. Though the capital, Taipei, is one of the world's most crowded cities, the local government has set aside a large area of land for green spaces and parks. There are nearly 800 parks in Taipei.

Languages

Mandarin Chinese is the official language of Taiwan, although many other Chinese dialects are also spoken. These include Minnan, introduced from the mainland in the 17th century, and several Hakkan dialects dating from the same migration period.

Native People & Ethnic Groups

Taiwan's government recognizes twelve aboriginal tribes in Taiwan, each with a distinctive history and culture. Few of the groups seem closely connected to other groups. They are identifiable, however, as members of the Austronesian language group scattered from Madagascar to Easter Island and New Zealand. Some scholars believe that this language group originated in Taiwan.

In recent years, there has been a cultural and linguistic revival among Hakkans, a minority group that migrated from mainland China to Taiwan centuries ago. There are five Hakka dialects spoken in Taiwan; two are nearing extinction.

On Lanyu, 62 kilometers (38 miles) off Taiwan's southeast coast, the Yami aborigines live in underground houses to avoid typhoons, speak their own language, grow taro and sweet potatoes, and catch fish.

In Taipei, the population is composed of four distinct ethnic groups: indigenous Taiwanese people, Southern Fujianese, Hakkas, and mainland Chinese. The Taiwanese census only officially recognizes people of indigenous ancestry as a separate ethnic group. The Amis and Atayal are the two largest indigenous populations in the city.

Religions

The religion of 93 percent of Taiwan's people is an amalgam of Buddhism, Confucianism, and Taoism. Less than 5 percent of the population adheres to Christianity. The remaining 2.5 percent follow other religions.

Climate

The warm ocean currents surrounding Taiwan, as well as its proximity to the Tropic of Cancer, give the island a subtropical climate moderated by seasonal winds. The average winter temperature is 15° Celsius (59° Fahrenheit), and the average summer temperature is 30° Celsius (86° Fahrenheit).

Taiwan's mountains shelter the western plain, creating an essentially tropical climate with an average annual rainfall of approximately 2,500 millimeters (100 inches), most of which falls during monsoon season, from June to August. In the mountains themselves, it snows in winter and can be cold even in summer; the mountains also receive more rainfall.

Cloudy skies are normal all year. Taiwan is vulnerable to landslides, typhoons and earthquakes. In 1999, the worst earthquake in its history killed 2,000 people and caused extensive damage.

ENVIRONMENT & GEOGRAPHY

Topography

Taiwan lies approximately 320 kilometers (200 miles) north of the Philippine island of Luzon. It is separated from the southeastern coast of China by the Taiwan Strait, which varies in width from 145 to 355 kilometers (90 to 220 miles). Taiwan is also bordered by the East China, Philippine, and South China Seas.

Tapei is the nation's capital, and it is located on the northern edge of Taiwan. The city occupies 272 square kilometers (105 square miles) and is divided into twelve districts: Songshan, Xinyi, Daan, Zhongshan, Zhongzheng, Datong, Wenshan, Wanhua, Nangang, Neihu, Shilin and Beitou. The city is surrounded by Taipei County, the largest municipality in Taiwan.

Taiwan is dominated by volcanic mountains, small hills, plateaus, and coastal plains. Two-thirds of the island is mountainous. The rugged Central Mountain Range (Chungyang or Chungyang Range) follows the length of the eastern coastline, sometimes ending in steep cliffs at the shore. The highest mountain in the range, Yu Shan, reaches 3,952 meters (14,000 feet) above sea level.

West of the mountains, land slopes gradually through rolling plains to sea level and fertile mud flats along the western shore. Taiwan also contains extensive wetlands, including swamps, lakes, ponds, tidal marshes, and estuaries.

Plants & Animals

More than half of Taiwan is covered by thick forests, predominantly of cypress trees. In addition to abundant freshwater fish and bird species, the island is home to roughly 50,000 species of insects, fifty of which are unique to Taiwan.

The tropical interior is a jungle, and at one time, the camphor forest found there was the largest in the world. Other trees and plants found growing naturally in the jungle include palms, teak, pines, tree ferns, bamboo, bananas, soap trees, azaleas and rhododendrons. Commercially cultivated plants include coffee, tobacco, indigo and cassava.

Although a surprising amount of Taiwan remains ecologically pristine, many species and environments are endangered, and some have been destroyed. The Asian spotted leopard is now presumed extinct in Taiwan. Formosan rock monkeys, Formosan Sika deer, green tree frogs, landlocked salmon, and Formosan black bears were once common, but are now rare. Waterfowl remain plentiful, but some species, like the Black-faced spoonbill, are nearing extinction.

CUSTOMS & COURTESIES

Greetings

The standard way to say hello in Taiwan is "Nĭhǎo," or "Zǎo," for "Good morning." Generally, when addressing friends or neighbors, these greetings are substituted for comments or questions about what that person is doing. These questions are asked in passing and do not merit a lengthy response. However, the most common greeting is typically "Chībǎole ma" ("Have you eaten yet?").

When business acquaintances meet for the first time, business cards are typically given and received with both hands. Upon receiving an acquaintance's card, it is considered polite to glance at it, and then put it carefully in a safe place, such as a card holder. Not looking at it, scrutinizing it too intently, or carelessly stuffing it in one's pocket is considered rude. In business scenarios, Western greetings such as handshakes are increasingly common, though bowing one's head respectfully is also standard.

Gestures & Etiquette

Etiquette during meals is both subtle and complicated. For example, it is considered polite to refill the teacups of the other diners at the table before refilling one's own. When one's tea cup is refilled, one should reply "Xièxie" ("Thank you") or tap the table three times with one's middle finger so as not to disrupt the conversation. This tradition is said to have come from the time of Japanese occupation, when subordinates bowed three times to their superiors to show respect. If the teapot needs to be refilled at a restaurant, turning the lid of the teapot upside-down and placing it in a conspicuous spot on the table will send a signal to the waiter.

It is increasingly popular, for both sanitary and environmental reasons, for diners in restaurants to bring their own chopstick set. Since many meat dishes in Taiwan have the bones intact (such as steamed whole fish or pork ribs), it is not unusual for diners to pick the bones out of their mouth with their chopsticks and set them by the side of their rice bowl on the tablecloth.

Gestures in Taiwan are primarily concerned with expressing respect for other people. For example, using the whole hand instead of one figure to point to something is considered more polite. When beckoning someone, it is polite to have the palm facing down and the fingers gesturing inward; the Western way of gesturing with the palm up and one finger is used to call animals. Additionally, using one's feet to point or move objects is not polite, as feet are considered unclean.

When in public, sitting or standing straight with one's feet close together is considered polite. In contrast, slouching, sitting with the legs apart or standing with hands placed on the hips is seen as disrespectful, or an indication of loose morals. Similarly, loud or rowdy behavior in public places is considered rude. When laughing, it is also common to hold one's hand over one's mouth, especially among young women. Unlike in Western cultures, people of the same sex (especially young women) often walk hand-in-hand if they are friends. Additionally, it is not uncommon for the Taiwanese to be very direct or frank in their conversations.

Eating/Meals

Meals are central to Taiwanese culture. In fact, the standard greeting in Taiwan is "Chībǎole ma" ("Have you eaten yet?"). Meals are usually communal, with chopsticks being the most commonly used utensil. During a meal, each person generally has a small bowl of white rice, often mixed with yams or taro (a leaf vegetable). On top of this, they place a pinch or two of various dishes from the plates on the table (by the end of the meal, the rice has absorbed the juices of the other dishes). Unlike in Western cultures, beverages are not usually consumed during the meal. Instead, at the end of the meal the rice bowl is filled with a clear soup—such as chicken broth—and consumed.

In addition, Taiwan is a major producer of oolong and other specialty teas. The tea ceremony, a complicated, ritualized way of preparing and pouring tea, is often performed when receiving guests. Business is regularly conducted over meals, with dining playing a significant part in attracting customers and thanking clients.

Visiting

Visitors to Taiwanese homes typically must take their shoes off before entering the house. The host will usually provide slippers for the guest to wear. It is considered polite for a guest to bring a nicely wrapped gift when visiting. However, it should be noted that some gifts have symbolic meaning. For example, a clock is considered an unlucky gift since it implies that the host does not have long to live. A good gift would be a specialty food or handicraft from the guest's hometown. The gift is typically offered with two hands, which indicates that the gift is an extension of oneself. The host will similarly receive the gift with two hands, and will usually not open it in the guest's presence.

Small snacks and tea are often served to make guests feel welcome. It is polite for the guest to decline several times when the host offers tea or food. However, the host will most likely give the guest tea or food anyway, and continue to refill the guest's cup or plate throughout the visit. During meals, the host will likewise put food on the guest's plate, even if the guest declines.

LIFESTYLE

Family
Family ties in Taiwan are extremely strong, and typically based on the Confucian conception of filial piety. (Confucianism is an ancient Chinese system of ethics and philosophy based on the teachings of the Chinese philosopher Confucius.) Filial piety is a Confucian virtue which emphasizes love and respect for parents and ancestors. Ancestor worship, also a Confucian conception, is also an important and traditional aspect of Taiwanese culture. For example, Tomb-Sweeping Day is a holiday where Taiwanese people honor their ancestors by tending their graves. Traditional Taiwanese families were organized in a patriarchal hierarchy, with the grandfather as the head. Women were expected to be subordinate to their mothers-in-law, and to relinquish most ties with their own family. Historically, it was common for entire extended families to live together. This practice may still be seen is some rural areas of Taiwan.

In contemporary Taiwan it is common for the father's parents to live with the family.

Grandparents often serve an important role as caretakers for the children, since it has become increasingly common for both parents to often work long hours in recent years. The Mid-Autumn Festival and the Chinese New Year serve as major occasions for families to come together to eat and celebrate.

Housing
Traditionally, houses in the countryside were built of bamboo, wood or clay bricks, whereas houses of wealthier families had brick walls and tiled roofs. Many old farmhouses are built with three sides in a shape that is meant to reflect the human body. The central room represents the head, and the two rooms on either side represent the ears and shoulders. At right angles to this central building are two additional structures which represent arms, and together the three sides enclose a courtyard, the stomach. Traditionally, the ancestors' shrine is put in the "head" part of the house, and the sons of the family live in either arm with their wives and children.

More recently, many Taiwanese families live in apartment buildings in cities or towns. In smaller towns, apartments on the ground floor often have a front wall that can slide away, letting the front room of the house serve as a porch or possibly a garage. Additionally, tile of all sizes and colors is a popular covering for houses and apartment buildings. In larger cities, it is common (though usually illegal) for residents of the top floors of apartment buildings to build rooftop shacks out of aluminum siding or concrete blocks, and rent these mini-dwellings out for additional income.

Food
Taiwan cuisine has largely been influenced by Chinese food traditions, and is often associated with certain Chinese regional cuisines, most notably from the Fujian province. In addition, due to Japan's occupation of Taiwan, Taiwanese cuisine also features significant culinary influences from Japan. Recently, Taiwanese cuisine has received a certain degree of international

acclaim, and in 2007 more than half of the international tourists in Taiwan listed food as one of the major reasons for visiting the island.

Generally, Taiwanese food is known for its light and fresh taste, with most of the dishes prepared by steaming, blanching and stewing. Rice is considered a staple of the Taiwanese diet and pork, chicken and seafood are the most commonly eaten meats. Dumplings, especially those filled with soup and pork meat, are also very popular. Most meals are cooked in woks, stirred quickly in boiling oil in order to lock in the flavor of the food. Garlic, chili peppers, monosodium glutamate (msg), and scallions are often used for flavoring; in fact, the word for "msg" (wèijīng) means "flavor essence" in Chinese. Because of the mix of cultural influences on the island, food from throughout China, Japan and Southeast Asia is typically found, in addition to native Taiwanese, Hakka and Aborigine culinary traditions.

Snack foods, or "small eats," are also extremely popular in Taiwan. At night markets, such as the Shilin Night Market in northern Taipei, a common snack is chòu dòufu, or "stinky tofu." This fermented tofu gives off a smell similar to that of blue cheese. Whole roasted squid on a stick is also popular, especially in coastal cities such as Kaohsiung. For dessert, shaved ice covered with sweet and condensed milk, syrup and slices of fresh fruit is a popular treat.

Though Taiwan is small, each town or area has its own specialty food item. For example, in Ilan on the northeast coast of Taiwan, the specialty is niúshé bǐng, or cow tongue cookies, named for their appearance, not their ingredients. These dry, flat cookies are made from a mixture of sugar, flour and pork fat. When traveling, it is common for people to buy gifts of specialty food items to take home for their friends and relatives to enjoy.

In addition, restaurants in Taiwan are prized not for their unique dishes, but for their ability to make the same traditional dishes better than anywhere else. Thus, one enjoyable gastronomic festival is the annual "Beef Noodle Soup Competition," where chefs from all over Taipei compete to see who can make the tastiest beef noodle soup, one of the most famous dishes in Taiwan.

Life's Milestones

Weddings are typically lavish rituals in Taiwan. Traditionally, before a couple marries, the bride and groom visit a fortune-teller to ensure that their astrological dates are complementary; otherwise, the marriage may be broken off. However, couples are increasingly refraining from this practice. Most brides wear white, Western-style dresses at their weddings, though the ceremony may still include traditional practices, such as shielding the bride with an umbrella or a covering designed with certain symbols to ward off evil spirits. As in Western cultures, the wedding ceremony is typically a large banquet with lots of feasting and drinking.

In Taiwanese society, the traditional Chinese custom of zuò yuèzi ("sitting out a month") after giving birth is strictly followed. As such, young mothers typically stay for up to a month in hotel-like hospitals, where they are typically fed a special diet of Chinese herbal medicine and taught how to care for their babies. According to traditional superstitions, mothers were not supposed to do certain things that might make them catch cold, such as wash their hair or exercise. However, these rules have been somewhat relaxed more recently.

CULTURAL HISTORY

Art

Taiwanese painting during Japanese rule, which lasted between 1895 and 1945, was influenced by Japanese-style impressionism—a 19th-century art movement largely characterized by visible brush strokes, ordinary subject matter and the innovative use of light. In particular, Taiwanese painting focused on Taiwan's unique landscapes and scenes of local life. After World War II, the influx of artists from Mainland China evoked a shift toward more traditional ink painting.

However, in the late 20th century, a new nationalist movement emerged, and abstract art became popular. Contemporary artists in Taiwan began to use sculpture, interactive digital displays and everyday objects to explore themes of postmodernism, globalization and identity. Many expressive works by new artists such as the sculptor Yang Mao-lin (b. 1953–) can be seen at the Museum of Contemporary Art in Taipei and the Taipei Fine Arts Museum.

Architecture

Traditional Taiwanese architecture reveals a range of styles over the last several centuries, from the early period of Chinese influence during the Ming and Qing Dynasties, to European influence during both Dutch and Spanish colonization, to the era of Japanese occupation. Much of traditional Taiwanese architecture derives from the southern style of Chinese architecture (particularly Southern Fujian), and includes ornamental effects such as wood or clay sculpture and roof decorations in the shape of animals, as well as curved roofs and detailed outlines. In fact, traditional Taiwanese architecture offers a detailed glimpse into ancient Chinese architectural traditions, particularly in its temple design (especially the decorative folk art, which includes the use of colors and calligraphy) and the traditional layout of family compounds, such as the san-ho-yuan (three-section compound), comprised of a central building with two wings.

Drama

Glove puppetry (bùdàixì) is a distinct artistic tradition in Taiwanese folk culture, brought to the island in the 18th century by Chinese immigrants. This folk art originated a century earlier from the Quanzhou and Zhuangzhou areas of the Fujian province in China. Prior to the introduction of television in the 1960s, glove puppetry was one of the leading forms of entertainment in Taiwan. These hand puppets are often very detailed, with artistically carved faces and embroidered costumes. Over the years, glove puppetry styles have evolved to include painted backdrops, Western and Chinese musical accompaniment, electric lighting effects, and larger puppets.

In contemporary culture, many television programs in Taiwan feature glove puppets. Puppet masters must learn many skills, such as the different voices and movement styles that accompany each traditional puppet character, as well as the complicated acrobatics and martial arts performed by the puppets during fight scenes. Though no longer as popular as it once was, glove puppetry is still considered an important folk tradition in Taiwanese art and performance.

Taiwanese film during the country's colonization period was strongly influenced by Japanese styles, such as having a poet-actor narrate during silent films. After the end of the Chinese Civil War (1927–1950), the Koumintang (KMT) government in Taiwan began sponsoring Mandarin-language films that were typically apolitical. These included films in the martial arts genre, as well as romantic melodramas. In the 1980s, faced with competition from popular Hong Kong films, the government-run Central Motion Picture Corporation (CMPC) began sponsoring new, upcoming directors such as Edward Yang (1947–2007) and Hou Hsiao-Hsien (b. 1947–). This became known as New Wave Cinema. Unlike early films, the films of the New Wave film movement focused on realistic portrayals of Taiwanese life and history, as well as the conflict between traditional values and modern materialism.

After the end of martial law in the late 1980s, the seriousness of New Wave cinema relaxed somewhat, and films dealing with lighter, more amusing subjects gained in popularity. A central figure in contemporary Taiwanese cinema is Ang Lee (b. 1954–), who has recently brought Taiwanese films to the forefront internationally. Two of his most popular films include *Eat Drink Man Woman* (1994), which centers on the generational differences in modern Taiwanese society, and *Crouching Tiger, Hidden Dragon* (2000), a celebration of traditional martial arts films. In addition, issues of identity and the conflict between traditional and modern and Eastern and Western still feature prominently in contemporary films, such as in *Betelnut Beauty*

(2000) by Lin Cheng-sheng (b. 1959–). A "betel nut beauty" refers to young woman, typically in revealing clothing, that sell cigarettes in glass enclosed structures along the roadside in Taiwan.

Dance

Taiwan is home to the internationally renowned Cloud Gate Dance Theatre of Taiwan, a modern dance group founded in 1973. Founder Lin Hwai-min (b. 1947–) has been widely acclaimed as one of the most influential choreographers of the 20th century. In addition to studying Chinese opera in Taiwan and classical court dance in Korea and Japan, Lin also studied modern dance in New York under famous choreographer Martha Graham (1894–1991). Lin also studded fiction writing at the famous Iowa Writers' Workshop. Cloud Gate Dance Theatre combines all of these dance and storytelling influences with traditional qi gong exercises, martial arts and calligraphy to create emotional and distinctive performance pieces.

The fourteen recognized indigenous groups of Taiwan also have a rich cultural history of music and dance. A major component of Taiwanese indigenous ceremonies and rituals includes group dances and ballads accompanied by drums, flutes and stringed instruments. Additionally, Taiwanese aboriginal artwork, such as weaving and sculpting, is well-known for its beautiful colors and intricate designs. Since the rise of indigenous people's rights in the 1990s, Taiwanese indigenous artists have focused on both preserving their ancient songs and dances and increasing awareness of their traditions in mainstream Taiwanese society. Aboriginal singers such as A-mei (b. 1972–), of the Puyuma people, and Landy Wen (1979–), of the Atayal tribe, are some recent pop stars in the contemporary Taiwanese music scene.

Music

Like glove puppetry, Taiwanese opera is also a distinct performance art that originated in the folk traditions of early Taiwanese settlers from Fujian. Gradually, these songs were combined with other performance traditions, such as the operatic "cart drum" style of singing found in northeastern Taiwan and the classical Beijing opera. Taiwanese opera is commonly performed on open-air stages during temple festivals and other celebrations. Two traditional Taiwanese musical styles include nanguan and beiguan. Nanguan, a form of chamber music featuring instruments such as the pipa, a plucked string instrument, is typically soft and melodious. Nanguan was brought to the island as early as the 16th century by immigrants from Fujian. Beiguan, which typically features drums and gongs, is louder and more percussive. Beiguan is played in wedding and funeral processions, as well as during Taiwanese operas.

Literature

For the past century, the question, "What does it mean to be Taiwanese?" has been a driving force in both literature and film. Changes in Taiwan's political environment—from Japanese colonization, to the authoritarian rule of the Kuomintang of China (KMT), or the Chinese Nationalist Party, to democracy—have called into question different interpretations of Taiwanese history and identity. Literature has played a key role in expressing the conflicts experienced by those seeking a Taiwanese identity.

During the period of Japanese colonization (1895–1945), when Japanese was the official language of the island, most literature was written in Japanese, though traditional Chinese poetry was also popular. However, when the Chinese Nationalist (KMT) government took control of Taiwan after World War II, it outlawed Japanese and instituted the use of Mandarin Chinese. Since most native Taiwanese did not speak or write Mandarin, this silenced a generation of native Taiwanese writers. As a result, most literature produced during the mid-20th century was written by immigrants from Mainland China. Due in part to censorship and propaganda efforts by the KMT, it was composed mainly of nostalgic stories about the writers' homeland.

As KMT control began to relax, the 1970s saw a rise in "nativist" Taiwanese literature. Nativist literature was written primarily by native

Taiwanese authors. They emphasized Taiwanese culture, history and language, as well as the conflicts between Mainland Chinese immigrants and native Taiwanese. Contemporary writers in Taiwan still address these questions, in addition to such themes as the struggle between tradition and modernity, issues of post-colonization, and frustration at Taiwan's international political ostracism or isolation. Key figures in Taiwanese literature include Hwang Chun-ming (b. 1939–) and Li Ao (b. 1935–).

Children's literature in Taiwan has grown in popularity since the 1990s, and has been influenced by the children's literature traditions of Japan and the US. Children's literature also addresses the issues of identity that are so prominent in Taiwanese society. One example is *Guji*, by Chen Chih-Yuan (b. 1975–), a book about a crocodile raised as a duck. Social problems also figure centrally in other children's books, such as in *The Stray Dogs Around My House and Me* (1997), by Lai Ma, the pen name of Lai Jian-ming. This book addresses the problem of irresponsible pet care in Taiwan and the sad lives of dogs abandoned by their owners.

CULTURE

Arts & Entertainment

The contemporary music scene in Taiwan explores issues of identity and belonging, relating them to the political and cultural obstacles Taiwan faces in the international arena. One prominent example is the heavy-metal band Chthonic, the first Asian band to be featured at Ozzfest, an annual music festival in the US featuring mostly heavy metal music. In addition to rock instruments, Chthonic also employs traditional Chinese instruments such as the pipa (stringed instrument). Touring the US in 2007, Chthonic forcefully campaigned for Taiwan's inclusion in the United Nations (UN). A song written specifically for the campaign, "Unlimited Taiwan," celebrates the unique culture of Taiwan and expresses the desire of Taiwanese people to have their country recognized internationally.

Taiwan has an internationally known film industry. Taiwanese director Ang Lee has found success outside his native country with such films as "Eat Drink Man Woman" (1994), "Crouching Tiger, Hidden Dragon" (2000), and "Hulk" (2003). Most of the country's films are based on novels and short stories written and published in Taiwan. In spite of their quality and diversity, however, Taiwan's writers are little read by the rest of the world.

Tai chi is performed as an early morning ritual throughout Taiwan, both for health and for the beauty of the ritual body motions. Groups gather to perform in city parks, also popular gathering places for folk dancing, Chinese chess competitions, and tea ceremonies. Karaoke (also called KTV) also has become one of Taiwan's most popular recreations in recent years. Young Taiwanese also enjoy ping pong, soccer, basketball, and badminton, and there are several golf clubs in Taipei.

Cultural Sites & Landmarks

Perhaps the most striking landmark in Taiwan is Taipei 101, a 101–floor modern skyscraper that became the tallest building in the world when it was completed in 2004. The building design combines postmodern and traditional elements, and was created to be reminiscent of an ancient Chinese pagoda or a stalk of bamboo. It has eight trapezoidal floors and a tall spire (in Chinese culture, eight is considered an auspicious number). Other architectural landmarks include the National Taiwan Democracy Hall in Taipei, an elaborate blue and white octagonal structure. Formerly known as the Chiang Kai-shek Memorial Hall, its name was changed by former President Chen Shui-bian in 2007 to reflect Taiwan's transition to democracy. The hall's expansive courtyard is often used for markets, celebrations and demonstrations, while the two grand buildings on either side are the National Concert House and the National Theater.

Fort Zeelandia in the town of Anping is another notable landmark. Built by Dutch colonists in 1634, Fort Zeelandia was the last stronghold of the Dutch before the Taiwanese folk hero Koxinga drove them out (1624–1662) in 1662.

One of Taiwan's most famous natural landmarks is the Taroko Gorge, on the eastern side of the country. The famous gorge is located in Taroko National Park, one of Taiwan's seven national parks, and features sheer cliffs and beautiful mountain rivers. Another popular tourist and ecological destination is Sun Moon Lake, in Nantou County. Designated as one of the thirteen national scenic areas in Taiwan—which are selected based on cultural and ecological importance—it is the nation's largest lake. The island in the middle of the lake, Lalu Island, is also considered holy ground for the Thao tribe, one of Taiwan's fourteen recognized aboriginal groups.

The tallest mountain in East Asia, Jade Mountain, is also located in Taiwan. The mountain is part of a protected natural park, and obtaining a pass to climb it requires a lengthy application. Other famous mountains include Snow Mountain and Mount Ali. A popular attraction on Mount Ali is a narrow railway that carries passengers up the mountain to view the sunrise.

Libraries & Museums

The National Palace Museum in Taiwan holds one of the most extensive collections of ancient Chinese art and artifacts in the world. Originally located on the Chinese mainland, the museum's collection was relocated to Taiwan during the final years of the Chinese Civil War. In fact, many argue that if the collection had not been relocated to Taiwan, much of it would have been destroyed during China's Cultural Revolution, a tenuous political and economic power struggle during the 1960s in which certain aspects of culture were forbidden.

In 2003, the National Museum of Taiwanese Literature opened in Taiwan. Its mission is to preserve not only Taiwanese literary traditions, but Japanese and Mandarin literature as well. Taiwan's sole national library is the National Central Library, located in Taipei. Founded in China in 1933, it relocated to Taiwan in 1949. Highlights of its collection include over 12,000 rare books, including written artifacts such as wooden tablets from the Han Dynasty (206 BCE to 220 CE).

Holidays

Republic Day (October 10) is Taiwan's national holiday, commemorating the Chinese Revolution led by Dr. Sun Yat-Tzen in 1911. It is celebrated in Taipei with fireworks and a light show.

Other holidays are based on the lunar calendar. These include Chinese New Year (usually early February), the Lantern Festival on the fifteenth day of the first lunar moon, and the Ghost Festival of the seventh lunar month (usually August or September). During the Ghost Festival, when ghosts walk, no one travels who can avoid it, and no marriages take place. Visiting temples is recommended.

Youth Culture

Taiwanese youth culture is typically on the cutting edge of style in Asia, mixing pop culture from Japan, Korea and the US with distinctly Taiwanese elements. One current trend is to zhuāng kě'ài ("play cute"), which is a particular manner of behavior and speaking often adopted by teenager girls. The trend has transcended into popular culture, where cartoon characters and cute toys and gadgets, such as phone charms, have become popular. In addition, martial arts novels and Japanese-style manga, or comic-book novels, are popular amongst youth, and small, privately-run comic-book libraries can be found all over Taiwan. Video and computer gaming systems, such as Nintendo's Wii, are also trendy.

Well-known Taiwanese pop singers include Jody Chaing, Jay Chou, Cyndi Wong and the all-girl musical group S.H.E. In recent years, Taiwanese pop has opened to external influences, such as rap, rock, and even Mandarin pop. "Idol soap operas", TV shows that feature famous singers, are also popular. Karaoke TV (KTV) lounges have become common hang-out spots where young people gather to sing along to music videos and socialize. Since Taiwan's night markets feature an unending supply of fashionable, inexpensive clothing and goods, young people like to shop for bargains and hang out at night markets.

SOCIETY

Transportation

The transportation system in Taiwan is among the most developed in East Asia. The rapid-transit subway system in Taipei was completed in 2005, and along with extensive bus routes, makes traveling anywhere in Taipei or its surrounding neighborhoods relatively easy and convenient. Kaohsiung, in southern Taiwan, completed its first subway line as of 2008, In addition, several other cities, such as Taichung, are also planning subway lines. The high-speed bullet train (gāotiě) from Taipei to Kaohsiung also began running in early 2007. The bullet train reduces the travel time between the two cities—which are on the northern and southern tips of the island, respectively—from four hours by conventional train to just ninety minutes.

Traffic moves on the right-hand side of the road.

Transportation Infrastructure

As part of the "Four Asian Tigers"—the others being Hong Kong, South Korea, and Singapore—Taiwan has witnessed much industrial and economic growth since the last few decades of the 20th century and the early 21st century. This surging industrialization and growth is particularly evident in Taiwan's transportation infrastructure. For example, the republic introduced its first rapid transit system in 2008 (it opened in the Kaohsiung metropolitan area), a high speed rail, or bullet train, began operations in 2007, and a freeway system was recently constructed in the western corridor. There are also several urban metro lines, and numerous older railways have been repurposed as tourist attractions.

As of the early 21st century, Taiwan had four major ports—Hualien, Kaohsiung, Keelung, and Taichung—and thirty-seven airports, thirty-five of which are paved (2013). They have also

focused on improving cross-strait transport since the mid-1990s.

Media & Communications

The three leading daily newspapers in Taiwan are the *United Daily News, China Times* and *Liberty Times*, with the *Apple Daily* a popular tabloid-style daily. Additionally, the *China Post* is Taiwan's leading English-language newspaper As of 2007, there were over seventy-five television broadcast stations, with the most popular being the China Television Company (CTV), Chinese Television System (CTS) and the Taiwan Television Enterprise (TTV). The Public Television Service (PTS) is the only non-profit TV broadcaster.

Generally, government influence on broadcast is minimal in Taiwan. In fact, the country was rated the freest country in Asia for media freedom every year from 2006 to 2008 in the annual Freedom in the World Survey, conducted by the international organization Freedom House. According to Freedom House, print media in Taiwan is completely independent. However, the links between government officials and broadcast media organizations have sometimes come under question, largely due to the fact that over 100 cable channels are available to Taiwanese citizens.

The Internet in Taiwan is largely unregulated and widely accessible throughout the island. In fact, Taipei's citywide Wi-Fi network is the world's largest such network, covering 90 percent of the city's 2.7 million people as of 20154. In addition, the Taiwanese are some of the most computer-savvy people in the world; as determined by a 2014 government survey, 80 percent of the population is Internet users, while 82.6 percent of Taiwanese families own a computer.

SOCIAL DEVELOPMENT

Standard of Living

As a non-UN member, Taiwan, or the Republic of China, is not represented or ranked on the United Nations Human Development Index, which measures quality of life indicators. However, based on available data, Taiwan would have a very high human development ranking. Nonetheless, many assert that Taiwan's quality of life will not keep pace with the country's well-noted economic achievements.

Water Consumption

According to Taiwan's Water Resources Agency (WRA), water consumption in 2013 amounted to 11 cubic meters of water per person, which represents a gradual decrease since consumption peaked in the 1990s (though the consumption rate remains above the global average). Conservation of water has become an important topic, as total demand is expected to rise and available water resources have become affected by climate change and other geographical and climate factors such as uneven rainfall, rapid runoff, and steep rivers.

Education

Education in Taiwan has changed little from the system available under the Japanese until 1947: the Nationalist government retained the system while eliminating the systemic discrimination Japan practiced against the Taiwanese. Children in Taiwan attend six years of elementary school (including two years of kindergarten), followed by three years of junior high school and three years of senior high. Nine years of education are compulsory, and a ten-year trial compulsory program was recently implemented. Overall, twenty-two years of formal study are supported.

Taiwan's admissions examinations, notoriously high-stress and often blamed for teenage suicide, are being revised and may be replaced. Under the current system, admissions tests administered after junior high determine placement in academically challenging senior high schools, vocational schools, bilateral high, or in five-year junior colleges. After completing secondary education, students face a second battery of admissions tests to determine eligibility for colleges, universities, and institutes of technology.

There are sixty-one public and private colleges and universities in Taiwan today. Taipei

has over twenty universities and colleges, and hosts thousands of international students each year. The average literacy rate for the nation is 96 percent.

As of 2009, and more updated statistics are not yet available, the average net percentage of students matriculating from elementary school is 99.73 percent, while the average for junior high and senior high is 97.63 percent and 95.56 percent, respectively. The total net enrollment rate that same year was approximately 90 percent—89 percent for males and 91 percent for females. The literacy rate in Taiwan was 98.5 percent in 2014, with males achieving 99.7 percent and females achieving 97.3 percent.

Women's Rights

According to traditional Chinese conceptions of the family, women were subordinate to their husbands and were confined to the roles of wife, mother and homemaker. Issues that primarily affected women, such as domestic abuse, were seen as private family affairs. However, drawing on Western feminist ideology, Taiwanese activists began to promote gender equality and women's rights in the 1970s. After the end of martial law in 1987, feminist ideas gained greater public acceptance, and by the late 1990s women's rights legislation was being passed. Some notable legislation includes the Sexual Assault Prevention Act, enacted in 1997; the Domestic Violence Prevention Act, enacted in 1999; and the Gender Equality in Employment Act, passed in 2001.

Today nearly half of the Taiwanese workforce is female. Even though working women are much more common now than they have been in previous decades, Taiwanese women still often face pressure from their families to get married and have children. Also, since child-rearing duties are usually still seen as the woman's domain, mothers are often expected to take care of their children in addition to working a full-time job. This puts a great deal of pressure on modern Taiwanese women, and may be part of the reason why divorce rates in Taiwan doubled between 1993 and 2003 (to 0.287 percent). In addition, as of 2007 over a quarter of Taiwanese women aged thirty-five to forty-four were unmarried.

In many business sectors, such as the service industry, Taiwanese women still only earn about 75 percent as much as men, though this rate is slowly increasing. A government program designed to help divorced or low-income women find employment or start their own businesses was established in 2007. However, as of 2008 it had only aided around thirty women.

The UN's conception of "gender mainstreaming," which stresses equal representation of men and women on decision-making bodies, is increasingly popular in Taiwanese government policy. The Women's Rights Promotion Committee, part of the Executive Yuan, Taiwan's main government body, is committed to ensuring that all committees under the Executive Yuan include both genders, and that neither gender occupies more than two-thirds of the seats in any committee. In 2008, over half of all central government committees had attained this standard, and in the February 2008 legislative elections women took 30 percent of the seats. In 2012, the Executive Yuan forwarded its progress and made certain changes to its organization with the creation of the Department of Gender Equality.

Significant challenges in women's rights still remain, however. Over 60,000 cases of domestic violence, mostly inflicted on women by men, were reported each year from 2005 to 2008. However, in 2000 only 28,000 cases were reported, implying that as more facilities for helping women are established, greater numbers of women are using their services.

Additionally, Taiwan has the highest rate of teen pregnancy in Asia, reaching nearly 1.3 percent in 2005. According to the Taipei Association for the Promotion of Women's Rights, this is due both to a lack of sex education and to traditional attitudes of women's subservience to men, which means young girls are often afraid to stand up to their boyfriends about using protection. However, women's rights organizations, such as the Awakening Foundation and the Modern Women's Foundation, continue to pressure the government to enact new laws and provide more services to help women and victims of abuse.

Health Care

Since 1995, Taiwan has had a National Health Insurance Program (NHIP). Each year, citizens pay graduated, income-based insurance premiums to the government at rates revised every five years. More than 95 percent of the population is covered by the plan.

NHIP covers physician care, hospital costs, prescription medicines and some over-the-counter medications, lab and X-ray charges, dentistry, traditional Chinese medicine, and certain home care and day care services. Patients are charged a co-payment for each service. Physicians often live in apartments above storefront clinics, making their services available to patients after hours.

Life expectancy in Taiwan has increased greatly in recent history. In 2015, average life expectancy was eighty years (seventy-seven years for men and more than eighty-three years for women). Death rates for newborns and women in childbirth have dropped 90 percent (as of 2015, there are less than 4.5 deaths per 1000 live births).

GOVERNMENT

Structure

Taiwan is a constitutional multiparty democracy. Its constitution was adopted in 1946. The government has three branches.

The executive branch consists of the president, who acts as chief of state, and the vice-president, as well as the President of the Executive Yuan (or premier, who is the head of government) and the Vice President of the Executive Yuan (vice-premier).

The legislative branch is the one-house Legislative Yuan, with 225 members. Overseas Chinese citizens and aboriginal peoples are represented in the legislature. All legislators serve three-year terms. The Judicial Yuan consists of justices appointed by the president and approved by the Legislative Yuan.

In spite of its constitution and full government structure, Taiwan is in a unique position. Its government in 1949 was that of the Republic of China in exile, and anti-communist nations accepted that designation. Today, however, not even the island's closest allies offend the government in Beijing by using that name. Although Taiwan, as "the Republic of China," once sat on the United Nations Security Council, it lost that seat to the Chinese government in Beijing and is no longer a member of the United Nations.

In 2005, China passed legislation declaring illegal any movement of a Chinese province to secede. The threat of force against Taiwan seems implicit, although tensions have eased somewhat since that time.

Political Parties

Taiwan has a multi-party political system that has nearly 140 political parties. However, there are only two major political parties—the ruling Kuomintang of China (KMT), or the Chinese Nationalist Party, and the Democratic Progressive Party (DPP). The KMT is the oldest political party in Taiwan, and is a supporter of Chinese unification. The DPP, on the other hand, advocates for Taiwanese independence and identity. Other minor parties include the People First Party (PFP) and the New Party (NP), which make up the Pan-Blue coalition with the KMT, and the Non-Partisan Solidarity Union (NPSU), all of which are represented in the legislature. The NPSU is the only non-coalition affiliated party represented. The other coalition or alliance, the Pan-Green Coalition, consists of the DPP, the Taiwan Solidarity Union (TSU), and the Taiwan Independence Party (TAIP).

Local Government

Taiwan has sixteen hsien (counties), five shih (provincial municipalities), and two chuanshih, which are the special municipalities of greater Kaohsiung and greater Taipei, and which maintain a municipal government and council. Counties are then further subdivided into rural and urban townships, and then county municipalities, while cities and the special municipalities are divided into districts. Local governance at the provincial level consists of a provincial government, headed by a governor, and advisory council. The local governments of cities and counties include a legislature or council, with members popularly elected to four-year terms. Magistrates oversee counties while mayoralties govern cities. Each also serve non-consecutive four-year terms.

Judicial System

The Judicial Yuan ("house") is three-tiered and composed of a Supreme Court, composed of sixteen grand justices and the highest judicial body in Taiwan, and High Courts and District Courts. The second-tiered High Courts represent the provinces and special regions of Taiwan, while District Courts, the lowest courts, function on a city or county level. In recent years, Taiwan has been criticized for what is seen as eroding justice by numerous international observers, particularly the practice of pre-trial detention, which critics allege presumes guilt.

Taxation

Taiwan's highest corporate tax rate is 25 percent, while the personal tax rate ranges from 6 percent to as high as 40 percent. Other taxes include property tax, a stamp duty, and a value-added tax (VAT), levied at 5 percent. Taxes and other revenues account for 16.1 percent of the GDP (2014 estimate).

Armed Forces

The armed forces of the ROC, or Taiwan, consist of the Army, Navy, and Air Force, and three support branches: Combined Logistics Command, Reserve Corps, and Military Police Force. While the armed forces prioritize national defense and non-provocation, public service has recently become a primary task of military personnel. Weapons procurement has also become an increased priority, and Taiwan recently sought to purchase a number of F-16 fighter jets from the US. Taiwan, which maintains a twelve-month period of compulsory service, plans on having an all-volunteer force by 2015, numbering approximately 215,000.

Foreign Policy

Taiwan's foreign policy is primarily focused on gaining and maintaining formal diplomatic recognition from other states. During the 1970s, the People's Republic of China (PRC) ceased its isolationist policy and began to engage with other nations on the condition that they dropped all formal recognition of the Republic of China (ROC), or Taiwan. This resulted in the dismissal of Taiwan's government from the United Nations (UN) in 1971, as well as from other international organizations for which statehood was a requirement.

As of 2015, only twenty-two states, most of them small and under-developed states similar to Tuvalu and the Dominican Republic, recognize Taiwan. In exchange for their diplomatic support, Taiwan provides financial and development support to these states. De-facto embassies, known as Taipei Economic and Cultural Offices, provide all the functions of normal embassies in many countries that do not formally recognize Taiwan, such as the United States (US). As one of Taiwan's closest informal allies, the US is committed to provide for Taiwan's defense under the Taiwan Relations Act of 1979. This act was passed by US Congress after formal ties with Taiwan were severed in order to deter a military attack on Taiwan from China.

As part of its foreign policy efforts, Taiwan annually campaigns to reenter the UN and related organizations such as the World Health Organization (WHO). Taiwan has tried various tactics, such as requesting observer-status only (a condition granted to Palestinian representatives) or entering under the name "Taiwan" instead of the formal "Republic of China." All attempts, however, have failed, due to the veto power that China holds as a member of the UN Security Council (UNSC).

However, Taiwan is able to participate in certain international organizations that do not require statehood for membership, such as the World Trade Organization (WTO). Within this organization, due to pressure from China, Taiwan is known by the title, "Separate Customs Territory of Taiwan, Penghu, Kinmen and Matsu." In addition, Taiwan competes in the Olympics under the name Chinese Taipei. Taiwan has also actively engaged in non-political organizations and events, such as the World Games and the Deaflympics, both of which will be held in Taiwan in 2009.

Another facet of Taiwan's international involvement is disaster relief and humanitarian aid efforts. For example, during the 2005 East Asian tsunami, the government of Taiwan donated $50 million (USD) in relief aid, while private donations from Taiwanese citizens amounted to $20 million (USD). Charities and organizations such as the Buddhist Tzu-Chi Foundation and the Taiwan Root Medical Peace Corps routinely send medical teams to countries like Haiti, the Dominican Republic, Malawi and Mongolia to provide medical assistance and training. Over the past decade, Taiwan has contributed more than $300 million (USD) to ninety-five countries in the form of medical and humanitarian aid.

Relations between China and Taiwan are tense, and the possibility of conflict is always high. This has made the US extremely wary of any disruption in the "status quo" – broadly seen as an indefinite equilibrium where Taiwan does not declare independence, and China does not attack Taiwan. During the presidency of Chen Shui-bian (2000–2008) of the Democratic Progressive Party, relations between China and Taiwan were exceptionally strained. This was due both to China's increasing military threats towards Taiwan, such as the deployment of over 800 missiles on the Chinese coast facing Taiwan and military simulations of an amphibious attack on the island, as well as Chen's strong leanings toward Taiwanese independence.

Upon his election in 2008, Ma Ying-jeou of the Nationalist (KMT) Party made it a top priority to smooth relations on either side of the Taiwan Strait. He enacted such measures as instituting direct flights between Taiwan and China, increasing the number of Chinese tourists granted visas to Taiwan, and allowing limited Chinese investment in Taiwanese companies. Such measures have had a positive impact on relations, even as they generally remain tense.

Human Rights Profile

International human rights law insists that states respect civil and political rights, and also promote an individual's economic, social and cultural rights. The United Nations Universal Declaration on Human Rights (UDHR) is recognized as the standard for international human rights. Its authors sought the counsel of the world's great thinkers, philosophers, and religious leaders, and were careful to create a document that reflects the core values shared by every world culture. (To read this document or view the articles relating to cultural human rights, visit http://www.udhr.org/UDHR/default.htm.)

Taiwan's human rights record has progressed significantly in the past century, in conjunction with Taiwan's increasing democratization. The Taiwanese government expressed full commitment to the UN's Universal Declaration of Human Rights by establishing a National Human Rights Commission in 2001, under the leadership of then-President Chen Shui-bian.

Except for the fact that women are not required to fulfill the mandatory eighteen months of military service, Taiwan adheres fully to Article 2 of the UDHR, which emphasizes equal treatment regardless of ethnicity, gender, religion, etc. However, Taiwanese citizens abroad are sometimes subject to discrimination due to their citizenship. For example, since the UN does not recognize Taiwan's statehood, Taiwanese reporters are forbidden from entering the UN to cover meetings.

In terms of religion (Article 18), Taiwan is one of the most accepting countries in the world. All religious organizations are allowed to meet and practice freely. Taiwan's religious inclusivity can be seen in Taiwanese temples, where Buddhist, Daoist, Confucian, and occasionally Christian figures–in some cases, Santa Claus—are all placed side-by-side.

Though freedom of expression (Article 19) was severely hampered under Japanese occupation and until the end of martial law in 1987, Taiwan is now considered one of the freest countries in Asia. Similarly, whereas in the past freedom of assembly risked police intervention and political dissidents were jailed, today protest marches and sit-ins are quite common. The first occasion of this change was during the Wild Lily Student Movement of 1990, ten months after the Tiananmen Square Massacre in China. During this movement, then-President Lee Teng-hui agreed to meet with student demonstrators instead of cracking down on them. As a result of this meeting, Taiwan held its first democratic elections in 1992 and its first direct presidential election in 1996. Furthermore, Taiwanese citizens practiced their right to assemble again in September 2006 by staging a month-long sit-in to protest government corruption in Chen Shui-bian's administration.

However, with regard to Taiwanese Aborigines, or the indigenous peoples of Taiwan, human rights practices are often called into question. Substandard educational and employment opportunities have given rise to movements by various indigenous representative groups demanding greater rights, including legal protection and the return of native aboriginal lands. Though the demand for land has been unrealized, in 1996 the government promoted the Council of Indigenous Peoples to ministry-level status in the Executive Yuan. Greater coverage of aboriginal culture in school textbooks was instituted in 1998. In the 2008 Legislative Yuan election, six of the 113 seats were held (as legally mandated) by Taiwanese aborigines.

ECONOMY

Overview of the Economy

Taiwan's strong capitalist economy remained largely stable in 1999 as other Asian countries sank into recession. Taiwan relies on China as its largest export partner.

In 2014, the gross domestic product (GDP) was estimated at $1.075 billion USD, with a per capita GDP of $45,900 USD. The unemployment rate was 4 percent (2014 estimate) of a work force of just under 12 million. The majority of people work in industry and services. Only 1.5 percent of the population falls below the poverty line.

Nearly one million Taiwanese do business with mainland China, having invested $100 billion USD in Chinese enterprises. Direct flights from Beijing to Taiwan, without stops in Hong Kong, began in 2005.

Industry

Taiwan's industries include the manufacture of electronics, computer goods, chemicals, iron and steel, machinery, cement, and textiles. Other industrial activities include petroleum refining and food processing.

Taiwan's major exports include computer products, electrical equipment, metals, plastics, rubber products, and textiles. In addition to China, major trading partners are the United States, Japan, and South Korea. Taiwan is also a regional hub for the illegal trade of heroin and methamphetamines.

Labor

As of 2014, Taiwan's labor force was an estimated 11.54 million, the majority of which worked in the services sector. Approximately 5 percent of the available labor force was employed in agriculture. As of 2015, Taiwan's unemployment rate was 4 percent, a drop from the 2012 estimate of 5.67 percent.

Energy/Power/Natural Resources

Taiwan contains limited deposits of coal and natural gas, as well as limestone, marble, and asbestos. Fish and seafood remain important resources. The island's farmland and forests are either too limited or not easily exploited. In the 21st century, Taiwan's chief economic resource lies in its skilled labor force.

In recent years, Taiwan's citizens have increasingly recognized the island's environmental value, creating sixty-seven nationally protected sites (six national parks, eighteen nature reserves, twenty-four forest reserves, twelve coastal reserves, and seven wildlife refuges).

Because of the proliferation of factories along the flat western shoreline, wetlands have been endangered by water pollution and industrial emissions. Other environmental threats include air pollution, raw sewage, low-level radio-active waste disposal, and contamination of drinking water supplies. Moreover, an underground trade in endangered animal species still exists.

Fishing

Taiwan has a highly developed commercial fishing industry and is considered a global leader in aquaculture. As of the early 21st century, Taiwan's fishing industry was approximately a $3 billion (USD) industry, with tuna, squid, mackerel and tilapia comprising the primary exports. However, Taiwan has been asked to reduce its tuna fishing, and the government has recently made attempts to scale back the coastal fishing fleet. Distant waters fishing accounts for nearly three-fourths of total fisheries production in Taiwan.

Forestry

According to the Taiwan Forestry Bureau, as of 1995, forestland occupied nearly 60 percent of the total area of Taiwan, approximately 77 percent of which was national forest. Hardwood forests are the primary forest type of Taiwan, and most wood materials are imported. While the timber industry is expected to grow, the country was the fourth largest importer of tropical logs in the last decade.

Mining/Metals

The production of marble, limestone, dolomite, and natural gas and petroleum are the primary mining activities of Taiwan.

Agriculture

Taiwan's agriculture, largely for domestic consumption, includes rice, corn, fruits, vegetables, and tea. Only one-quarter of the island's area, concentrated mostly on the western plains, is used for farming. Agriculture accounts for less than 2 percent of GDP.

Animal Husbandry

Hogs and poultry, and to a lesser degree, cattle, are raised for meat.

Tourism

Urban Taiwanese are Taiwan's own best tourists, often traveling to the mountains or beaches on summer weekends. Popular sites include Alishan, a mountain resort from which one ascends picturesque Chu Shan or Yu Shan, Taiwan's highest mountain. In Tienhsiang, not far from Taipei, tourists visit Taroka Gorge, which features nineteen kilometers (twelve miles) of sheer cliffs dropping down to a river of whitewater rapids.

Maolin, another mountain village, is surrounded by waterfalls, suspension bridges, and river walks. Nearby is Dona, an aboriginal village, and Dona Hot Springs, a natural spa.

Historic Tainan, the former capital, is a Buddhist pilgrimage center, remarkable for its hundreds of architecturally distinctive temples. Frequent religious parades and festivals take place in Tainan.

The small islands surrounding Taiwan are popular summer destinations. The sixty-four-island archipelago of Penghu offers sandy beaches, grasslands, and fishing villages. Taiwan's oldest temple is in Makung, the only city in the archipelago.

Evelyn Atkinson, Ann Parrish, Micah L. Issitt

DO YOU KNOW?

- Taiwan's national anthem sets music to words from a speech by Chinese leader Sun Yat Sen. He was translating words from Abraham Lincoln's Gettysburg Address: "Government of the people, by the people and for the people."

- The popular drink known as bubble tea, or boba, originated in Taiwan. It combines flavored iced tea with tapioca pearls or coconut jelly, and is sipped through a wide straw.

- The original architecture of Taipei City was designed using the concepts of feng shui to arrange buildings and other objects to achieve the most harmony with the environment. The location of city monuments and the Taipei City Gate still conform to ancient beliefs about feng shui.

Bibliography

Davison, Gary Marvin and Barbara E. Reed. *Culture and Customs of Taiwan.* Westport, CT: Greenwood Publishing Group, 1998.

Kagan, Richard C. *Taiwan's Statesman: Lee Teng-hui and Democracy in Asia.* Annapolis, MD: Naval Institute Press, 2007.

Lary, Diana. *China's Republic.* New York: Cambridge University Press, 2007.

Lee, Shyu-tu and Jack F. Williams, eds. *Taiwan's Struggle: Voices of the Taiwanese.* Lanham, MD: Rowman and Littlefield, 2014.

Rubinstein, Murray A., ed. *Taiwan: A New History* (Expanded Edition*).* Armonk, NY: M.E. Sharpe, 2007.

Wachman, Alan. *Why Taiwan?* Stanford, CA: Stanford University Press, 2007.

Wang, David Der-wei and Carlos Rojas, eds. *Writing Taiwan: A New Literary History.* Durham, NC: Duke University Press, 2007.

Yip, June. *Envisioning Taiwan: Fiction, Cinema, and the Nation in the Cultural Imaginary.* Durham, NC: Duke University Press, 2004.

Works Cited

"A Quick Look for Visitors." *The Government Information Office, Republic of China.* http://www.gio.gov.tw/taiwan-website/2–visitor/quicklook/index2.htm

Chung, Oscar. "The Flavor of Taiwan." *Taiwan Review.* May 2008. pp. 12–17.

Chung, Oscar. "Words and Music." *Taiwan Review.* August 2007. p.22

"Cloud Gate Dance Theatre of Taiwan." www.cloudgate.org.tw/eng

"Country Report: Taiwan." Freedom in the World. *Freedom House.* 2008. http://www.freedomhouse.org/template.cfm?page=22&year=2008&country=7500

"Culture: Everyday Etiquette." *The Kangaroo and the Dragon.* 9 October 2004. http://waze.net/china/etiquette1.php

"Family Life." *Taiwan: Cultural Profiles Project.* 2002. www.cp-pc.ca/english/taiwan/family.html

Gao, Pat. "New Blood, New Buildings." *Taiwan Review.* January 2001. http://taiwanreview.nat.gov.tw/site/Tr/ct.asp?xItem=585&CtNode=119

"Gender Equality." *Taiwan Review.* April 2008. pp. 1–20.

"Gender Equality Committee of the Executive Yuan." http://www.ey.gov.tw/gec_en/cp.aspx?n=11EFF33070D6DF4B.

"Glove Puppetry." Cultural Taiwan. *Government Information Office of Taiwan.* 2006 . www.gio.gov.tw/taiwan-website/5–gp/culture/glove_puppetry/

"Habitation." A Brief Introduction to Taiwan's History and Culture. *Taiwan Provincial Administration Hall.* www.tpg.gov.tw/e-english/history/history-e-7.htm

Her, Kelly. "A Taste of the Night." *Taiwan Review.* May 2008. pp. 18–25

Imai, Gary. "Asian Gestures." Gestures: Body Language and Nonverbal Communication. 1996–97. *California State Polytechnic University*, Pomona http://www.csupomona.edu/~tassi/gestures.htm#asian

Jack, Stephen. "Taiwanese Cuisine." Eating China Blog. http://www.eatingchina.com/articles/taiwanfood.html

Liu, Alexandra. "A New Wave of Indigenous Pop—The Music of Pur dur and Samingad." *Taiwan Panorama.* August 2000. p. 92.

"Members of the Legislative Yuan," *The Legislative Yuan of Republic of China.* Accessed September 23, 2015. http://www.ly.gov.tw/en/01_introduce/introView.action?id=4.

"The Han Nationality Music." Research Institute of Musical Heritage, *National Taiwan Music Center.* http://rimh.ncfta.gov.tw/rimh/en/02_Hlist.asp?cate_id=63

"The Power of a Tsunami." *Taiwan Review.* March 2005. http://taiwanreview.nat.gov.tw/ct.asp?xItem=1056&CtNode=128

"Population for Township and District since 1981." *Ministry of the Interior, Republic of China (Taiwan).* www.moi.gov.tw/english/News_meat.asp?Newsid=321

"The Secret of Lotung Night Market." *Go2Taiwan Blog.* www.go2taiwan.net/blog_content.php?sqno=40

"Social Customs in Taiwan," *Study Abroad International.* 2000–2008. www.studyabroadinternational.com/Taiwan/Taichung/Taiwan_Taichung_Taiwan_customs.html

"Taiwanese Opera." Cultural Taiwan. *Government Information Office of Taiwan.* 2006. www.gio.gov.tw/taiwan-website/5–gp/culture/tw-opera/index.htm

"Taiwan's Culture and Art." *AsianInfo.org.* 2000. www.asianinfo.org/asianinfo/taiwan/pro-art.htm

Teng, Shu-fen. "Seeing the Immortals – The World of Sculptor Yang Mao-lin." *Taiwan Panorama.* June 2008. p. 98

Wang, Audrey. "Have You Eaten Yet?" *Taiwan Review,* 58.5 (May 2008): 5–11.

Wu, DD. "China-Taiwan Relations: Hardly a Crisis." *The Diplomat.* 31 July 2015. http://thediplomat.com/2015/07/china-taiwan-relations-hardly-a-crisis/.

Tropical fruits in the Pacific islands. iStock/chameleonseye

PACIFIC

An Australian stockman on a ranch. iStock/Anne Greenwood

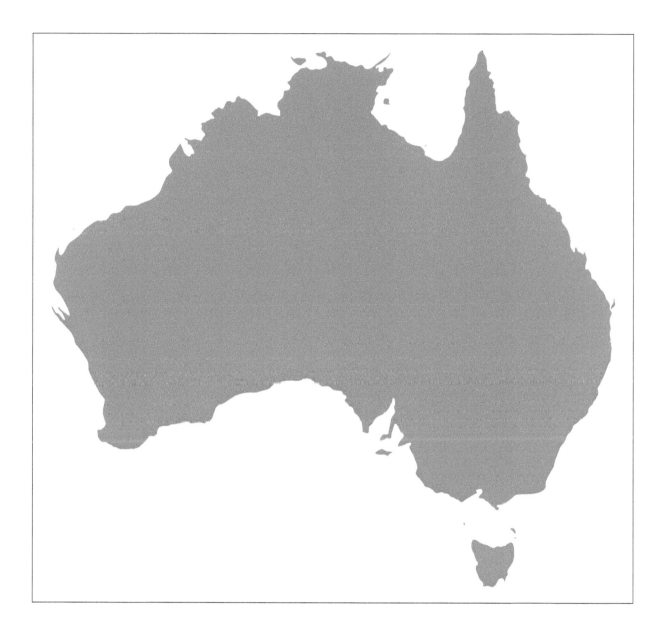

AUSTRALIA

Introduction

The island of Australia lies in the Southern Hemisphere, south of Indonesia and north of Antarctica. The eastern half of the world's smallest continent is surrounded by the South Pacific Ocean; the western half by the Indian Ocean. Australia is divided into six states (New South Wales, Queensland, South Australia, Tasmania, Victoria, and Western Australia) and two territories (Australian Capital Territory and Northern Territory).

The sixth-largest country in the world, the Commonwealth of Australia is known for its strong market economy aided by significant natural resources, and enjoys a worldwide reputation as a tourist destination. Many travelers visit the country for its natural wonders, which include the Great Barrier Reef.

GENERAL INFORMATION

Official Language: English
Population: 23,923,101 (2015 estimate)
Currency: Australian dollar
Coins: The Australian dollar is subdivided into 100 cents; coins of the Australian dollar are available in denominations of 5, 10, 20 and 50 cents, and 1 and 2 dollars.
Land Area: 7,682,300 square kilometers (2,966,152 square miles)
Water Area: 58,920 square kilometers (22,749 square miles)
National Anthem: "Advance Australia Fair"
Capital: Canberra

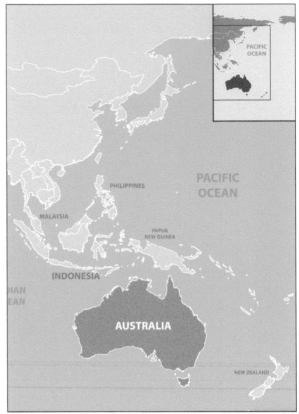

Time Zone: Australia comprises several time zones: GMT +8, GMT +9:30, and GMT +10.
Flag Description: The flag of Australia features the flag of the United Kingdom in its upper hoist (left) side; it takes up roughly one-quarter of the flag's area. The same deep blue background of the UK flag is that of the rest of the flag. Below the UK flag is a seven-pointed white star, known as the Federation Star or the Star of the Commonwealth. On the fly (right) side of the flag are five white stars arranged to resemble the Southern Cross constellation. Four of the stars are larger and feature seven points. One star is smaller and features five points.

Population

Population density in Australia is only about 3 people per square kilometer (seven people per square mile), making it the most sparsely populated continent after Antarctica, and at the opposite extreme of densely populated nearby Asian

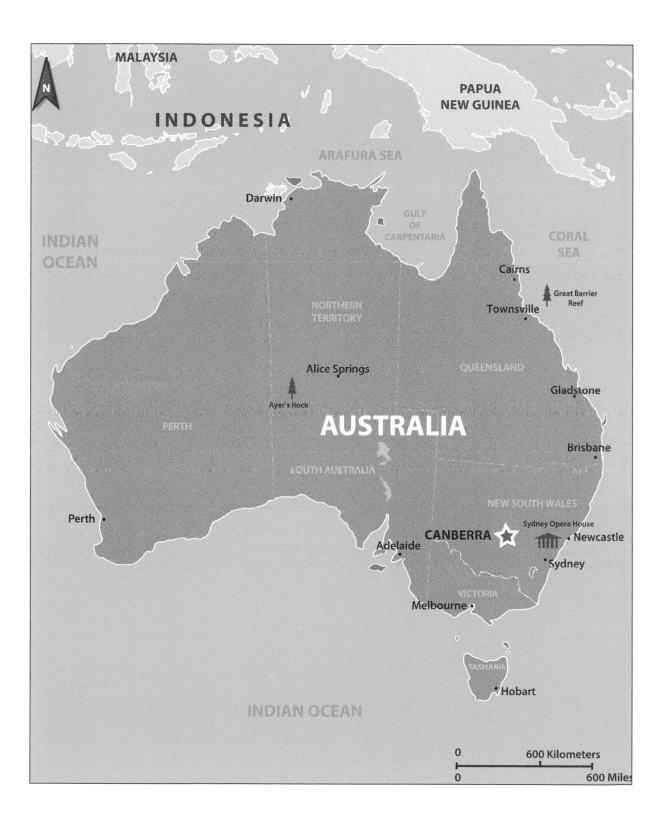

Principal Cities by Population (2015):

- Sydney, New South Wales (4,627,345)
- Melbourne, Victoria (4,246,375)
- Brisbane, Queensland (2,189,878)
- Perth, Western Australia (1,896,548)
- Adelaide, South Australia (1,225,235)
- Canberra, Australian Capital Territory (367,752)
- Newcastle, NSW (308,308)
- Wollongong, NSW (289,236)
- Geelong, Victoria (226,034)
- Hobart, Tasmania (216,656)

neighbors such as India. Australia's land area, in fact, nearly equals that of the United States, but its population of approximately twenty-four million is only a fraction of the U.S. population. In 2015, annual population growth was an estimated 1.4 percent.

As of 2015, slightly more than 89 percent of Australia's population lived in or near urban centers, the vast majority of which are situated on the country's coastline. Large cities on the country's east coast include Brisbane in Queensland, and Sydney in New South Wales (near the smaller capital of Canberra). Other major cities include Melbourne in Victoria, Adelaide in South Australia, and Perth along the southwest coast in Western Australia. New South Wales has the highest population (over 7.2 million in 2012), followed by Victoria (5.6 million in 2012).

Languages

English is the principal language spoken in Australian. Roughly, 18 percent of the population speaks Chinese or other Asian, Arabic, or European languages.

Native People & Ethnic Groups

Australia has been inhabited for approximately 50,000 years. The continent's native people are known as Aboriginal Australians, thought to have migrated from Southeast Asia across a land bridge, and Torres Strait Islanders. Together, these

two distinct groups are known as Indigenous Australians.

Before Europeans settled Australia in the late 18th century, the indigenous population numbered around 350,000. This number was greatly reduced by introduced diseases, forced removal, and genocide. As European settlers established large livestock operations in the Australian outback, aboriginal people were forced into virtual slavery as their lands shrank and their living conditions declined. In 1967, Indigenous Australians were granted the right to be counted in the census, thus receiving greater political and legal representation at the same time.

Approximately 92 percent of Australians are of European descent. Between 1950 and 2000, immigration from Southeast Asian countries (especially Vietnam, Malaysia, and the Philippines) increased significantly. Asians account for about 7 percent of the population. The remaining 3 percent is split about evenly between Aboriginal Australians and people of Middle Eastern descent.

Aboriginal Australians live mostly in the "bush" in Western Australia and the Northern Territory. Most of Australia's Torres Strait Islanders live on the islands off the coast of the Cape York Peninsula.

Religions

Australians are 60 percent Christian, split roughly into thirds between Roman Catholics, Anglicans, and various Protestant denominations. Two and a half percent of residents are practicing Buddhists, 1.3 percent is Hindu, and 2.2 percent is Muslim. In the 2011 census, more than 30 percent noted their religious affiliation as either "unspecified" or "none."

Climate

The north coast of Australia is about the same distance from the equator as Guatemala. Its tropical humid climate is wettest during the summer rainy season (January through March). Temperatures average about 32° Celsius (90° Fahrenheit) in winter and 30° Celsius (86° Fahrenheit) in summer. Highs often exceed 38° Celsius (100° Fahrenheit).

Australia's east and west coastal areas receive about 100 centimeters (40 inches) of rainfall per year. The vast remainder of the country is very dry, with averages of less than 50 centimeters (20 inches) per year.

Southern coastal areas have a temperate climate with a summer average temperature of about 20° Celsius (67° Fahrenheit), and a winter average of about 10° Celsius (50° Fahrenheit). Snow is unusual except on high elevations and on south-lying Tasmania.

Tropical cyclones affect the northeast and northwest coastal areas, most commonly Queensland and Western Australia. The southwest and southeast can experience dry winds from the interior that sometimes fan huge wildfires. One such blaze near Melbourne in 1983 destroyed about 3,700 buildings and killed seventy-six people. A 1994 inferno near Sydney destroyed 205 homes and killed four people, and bushfires in the Australian state of Victoria in 2009 resulted in 173 deaths and the destruction of over 2,030 houses; the latter has since been referred to as the Black Saturday bushfires.

ENVIRONMENT & GEOGRAPHY

Topography

The continent of Australia is a low plateau at about 300 meters (1,000 feet) above sea level, broken by the higher Great Dividing Range running north to south along the heavily populated eastern coastal plain. The highest point of this range is Mount Kosciusko in New South Wales, at an elevation of 2,228 meters (7,308 feet).

Off the northeast coast is the Great Barrier Reef, the world's largest coral reef at about 2,000 kilometers (1,250 miles) long. The entire Australian coastline stretches more than 25,500 kilometers (16,000 miles).

Centrally located Lake Eyre Basin is the country's lowest point, at 15 meters (50 feet) below sea level. Normally a dry salt lake, during exceptionally rainy years it becomes Australia's largest lake at 9,000 square kilometers (3,475 square miles).

From Lake Eyre, other dry lakes and deserts stretch to the western coastal plains, including nearby Simpson Desert (145,039 square kilometers/56,000 square miles), Tanami and Gibson Deserts (310,799 square kilometers/120,000 square miles) in central Australia, and the Great Sandy (388,498 square kilometers/150,000 square miles) and Great Victoria (647,497 square kilometers/250,000 square miles) Deserts to the west, the latter is known for its red sand dunes. About 40 percent of Australia is desert.

Near the town of Alice Springs, at the geographic center of the country, is Ayers Rock (Uluru), one of the best-known Australian landmarks. Believed to be the largest freestanding rock in the world, its red sandstone creates a striking image against its flat surroundings.

The Murray River is the longest river in Australia, running 1,930 kilometers (1,200 miles) from the Great Dividing Range to the southern coast at Spencer Gulf. The 1,867-kilometer (1,160-mile) long Darling River flows into the Murry at Wentworth. Both are major sources of irrigation.

Among Australia's numerous islands, the largest is Tasmania at 68,401 square kilometers (26,410 square miles). Lying 240 kilometers (150 miles) south of Victoria, it is nicknamed Apple Isle for its fruit harvest.

Canberra, the capital, occupies 805.6 square kilometers (311 square miles) of land in the Australian Capital Territory's (ACT) northeastern region, 650 kilometers (404 miles) northeast of Melbourne, and 300 kilometers (186 miles) southwest of Sydney. The ACT has an area of 2,358 square kilometers (910 square miles) and is located in New South Wales, near the southeastern coast of Australia.

Plants & Animals

Eucalyptus trees from the southern coast and pine trees from the east coast are Australia's principal lumber cash crops. Less common trees include oak, ash, and cedar. Australia's floral emblem is the Golden Wattle, a small tree with large fragrant yellow spring flowers.

Nearly half of all Australian wildlife is endemic (found only in Australia). Its fifty species

The duck-billed platypus is native to eastern Australia and the region of Tasmania.

of marsupials include the koala, kangaroo and the Tasmanian devil, a dog-like carnivore found only on its namesake island.

Australia's two distinctive monotremes (mammals that lay eggs) are the platypus, a small furry animal with webbed paws for swimming and a duck-like bill; and the echidna, which resembles a porcupine due to its coat of sharp spines. Baby echidnas are called puggles.

The emu is native to Australia. One of the world's largest birds, it grows up to 2 meters (6 feet) tall. The thousands of species of fish in Australian waters include more than 150 shark species.

CUSTOMS & COURTESIES

Greetings

Australians are generally very friendly, and will greet those they meet with a warm smile and handshake, which are used by both sexes indiscriminately. A single kiss on the right cheek may replace the handshake and is a common practice between women or a woman and a man, but only when the person is known well. "G'day mate" remains the most well-known and frequently used Australian greeting, but common greetings such as "Hello," "Hey," "Nice to meet you," and the like are also very common. Most people will also address each other by name.

Nicknames are frequently used, even when first meeting someone. For example, if your name is Samuel, some Australians will initially greet you as "Sammy" or "Sam," even if you have not indicated a preference. This is perceived as a sign of fondness or friendliness. In business circles, addressing people by their first names is also common instead of more formal titles. Such titles are generally only used by children to figures of authority and by sales and customer service staff in the hospitality and retail sectors.

Gestures & Etiquette

Australians are known for having a relaxed attitude, and teasing and informal behavior or jokes are often considered acceptable social etiquette. In Australian vernacular, or slang, this aspect of culture is called "taking the piss." In particular, visitors may be put off by the way that Australians commonly tease one another with seemingly derogatory remarks. However, it is done as a sign of respect and fondness for the person that is seemingly being "insulted," and is not intended to offend. The best response is to tease the other person back, though when uncomfortable, smiling and changing the topic is acceptable.

Australians also have great respect for a "down-to-earth" and modest personality. As such, wearing what is considered flashy clothes or spending one's money freely is not admired. Their egalitarian, modest nature is also reflected in customs when eating out and drinking. When at a restaurant, bills are expected to be split equally between the group, regardless of the financial status, gender, or race of those present (except in certain business contexts). In addition, buying rounds of drinks, a practice by which everyone takes turns buying drinks for the group, is also a common practice, regardless of one's gender or financial situation.

Eating/Meals

Australians typically eat three main meals a day. This usually consists of a breakfast of cereal or toast in the morning, a cold lunch in the early afternoon—often after noontime—and a hot evening meal, called tea or dinner, between 6:30 and 8:00 pm. "Supper" is considered to be a midnight snack. Schoolchildren also eat a snack commonly called recess or morning tea during a break from class at 11:00 am. Afternoon tea, at around 3:00 pm, is also common. Like many other Western cultures, however, the tradition of three main meals a day is increasingly being eroded in Australia by the prevalence of easily accessible snacks and fast foods. In light of the related obesity epidemic, diets of all sorts (often influenced by the latest American fad) are also popular and may influence dining habits.

Australia's various immigrant populations have also influenced Eating and meal traditions. While British dining traditions were more common during the 1900s, Europeans that arrived in the mid-20th century, along with Asian immigrants that arrived beginning in the 1970s, have brought their own traditions with them. However, one dining tradition unique to Australia is the Aussie barbeque. Consisting of sausages, hamburgers, steak, or seafood cooked on an outdoor grill,and typically served with fresh salad and bread, it remains a popular meal. Often starting at about 5:00 pm and continuing well into the night, it celebrates dining outdoors as a way to enjoy the pleasant Australian climate.

Visiting

Since Australians are generally considered a relaxed and friendly race, a dining or overnight invitation would not be uncommon for visitors. The atmosphere when visiting an Australian's home is generally informal and relaxed. No particular treatment is afforded to guests, and hosts do not expect guests to be particularly well mannered or formal. Guests are usually expected to make themselves feel at home. Helping the host, or at least offering to help, is considered polite.

When invited for dinner, guests should offer to bring a food dish or drink. It is common to bring a bottle of wine for an indoor meal (beer if it is a barbeque) or a dessert item. Any food or drink leftover is generally left with the host and not taken home. In addition, smoking indoors in restaurants in Australia is illegal, and few Australians welcome smoking in their homes.

LIFESTYLE

Family

The typical Australian family is a nuclear one. It is common for children to stay at home for school (boarding school would generally only be considered by families living in rural areas), and during their college studies, as Australian universities are generally not residential. Residential dorm-style accommodations, or sharehouses, are available, but Australians will usually apply to colleges close to home. It is also not customary to stay at home until marriage, and many young people will live with their partner before marriage.

In Australia, the family home is typically for immediate family only. Grandparents and other relatives do not customarily live in the same house (although for some immigrant populations this may differ). The divorce rates and remarriage rates, are high in Australia, as they are in many other Western countries. It is illegal for same-sex couples to marry in all Australian states. Laws vary in each state regarding adoption by same sex couples.

Housing

The single family home remains the most common form of housing in Australia, though apartment buildings are becoming more popular in the larger cities. In a recent national census, it was reported that over 85 percent of Australians resided in a house, with just 13 percent living in a flat, unit, or apartment. The availability of affordable housing is a major concern for many Australians, especially younger ones.

The architectural designs of most houses are based on European and American styles. For example, the triple-fronted brick veneer style popular in America in the mid-20th century is still most common, though many are rendered and repainted to mirror current American architectural trends. There are some architectural styles, however, that reflect the unique climate and geography of Australia, such as the Filligree, Queenslander, and Federation residential styles. The use of native timber and stone and corrugated iron is also considered particularly "Australian."

Food

For the first fifty years of colonization, the food eaten in Australia was strongly British; roast beef or chicken with potatoes and vegetables, as well as bread and butter pudding, were staples. However, increased immigration after World War II has greatly influenced Australian cuisine. Since then, Australian cuisine could be characterized as more multicultural. For example, "modern Australian" cuisine, as cooked in Australia's top restaurants, shows strong Asian influences on a European base, particularly incorporating Thai, Vietnamese and Japanese flavors. Other influences included Italian, Greek, and Mediterranean cuisines, which all arrived in Australia during the mid-20th century.

There are a small number of famous "Australian" foods also. Vegemite is a thick, dark spread used on toast or bread. It was created in the 1920s, originally from the yeast left over from brewing with a strong salty flavor. Anzac biscuits are a traditional Aussie cookie originally sent as care packages by mothers of soldiers in the Australia New Zealand Army Corps (ANZAC) during World War I. They are made out of oats, flour, coconut, butter, and golden syrup. Lamingtons are a distinctive Australian cake, traditionally eaten for morning tea. They consist of sponge cake cut into cubes, dipped in melted chocolate, and then sugar and dried coconut. Damper is a basic bread made by mixing flour, water and a pinch of salt. It is then kneaded into a ball and typically cooked over a campfire. Damper was a staple food mainly in early colonial Australia, but it is still made in modified forms.

Other unusual Australian foods include kangaroo, a red meat similar to venison, and barramundi, a prized sport fish that moves between fresh and salt water. It is typically barbequed and is very expensive due to its elusive nature. Australia is known worldwide for its wine production, particularly its chardonnay (white) and shiraz (red) varieties.

The traditional food of Indigenous Australians, or "bush tucker" as it is sometimes called, revolves around the meat of native animals (including insects and grubs, as well as mammals and fish) and native flora and fauna. However, such food is rarely eaten now, as Indigenous Australians follow a more Western diet.

Life's Milestones

Many milestones that are celebrated in Australia are largely dependent on religion. Since the majority of Australians are Christian, traditions such as baptism, the traditional Christian weddings, and Christian funeral rites are widely practiced. However, more secular versions of these events, such as a garden wedding with a civil celebrant, or a memorial service in a city hall, are becoming increasingly popular in the early 21st century.

Other milestones celebrated by Australians are similar to other Western cultures, and include the eighteenth birthday, which marks the legal age in Australia to vote and consume alcohol. In addition, the twenty-first birthday is also popularly celebrated, and large parties or gatherings with friends and family often mark both birthday occasions. School proms, or formals, are another highlighted event for most Australian youth and typically happen in the final year of high school.

CULTURAL HISTORY

Art

The art of Indigenous Australians has been an important part of their culture throughout their 50,000 years of existence. Painting on leaves, rock and bark, and items carved of wood and rock were all traditional forms of expression. Such works generally centered on "dreamtime" stories—Aboriginal spiritual tales explaining the creation and existence of the world. During the 20th century, new forms of art more accessible to Western audiences were created in Australia, including Aboriginal "dot" paintings. This artistic style consisted of images painted onto canvas using a series of dots.

Since colonization, mainstream Australian art has also emerged as an important feature of Australian culture. Beginning with botanical drawings by colonial explorers, a focus on the Australian landscape has been an enduring feature. Artists of the Heidelberg school in the 1880s—considered to be the formal beginning of a distinctive "Australian" style of art—focused on the natural landscape. Many of Australia's most famous artists have also specialized in images of nature. Brett Whiteley (1939–1992) is famous for his landscapes of Sydney, and Pro Hart (1928–2006) is known for his memorable depictions of the Australian outback, or bush (in Australia, the term "bush" is used to refer to undeveloped territory). Others have focused on Australian history and culture. Sidney Nolan (1917–1992) is famous for his iconic images of bushranger, or outlaw, Ned Kelly; John Brack (1920–1999), is known for his portrayal of modern Australian culture and society.

Architecture

Australian architecture has traditionally been influenced by British architecture. Since Indigenous Australians were largely nomadic, they did not build permanent structures. The earliest architectural structures were built by the British settlers, who tended to use the architectural styles most popular in Britain. This included Georgian architecture and, beginning in the mid-19th century, Victorian architecture. By the early 20th century, a national style had developed. Known as the Federation style, it was an Australian take on the Edwardian style and featured cream-painted decorative timber, tall chimneys, and even Australian motifs such as kangaroos.

In addition, climate and geography have also played an influential part in Australian architecture. For example, the Queenslander, an all-timber housing style raised on piles, was designed to increase airflow in the hot weather and offer protection from floods. From the 1930s onward, American and other international influences have also been apparent. For example, the Californian Bungalow and Spanish Mission styles remain popular in contemporary Australia.

Three of the most famous architectural landmarks in Australia are the Sydney Opera House, the Sydney Harbour Bridge, and the Royal Exhibition Building in Melbourne. The Sydney Opera House is one of Australia's most recognizable buildings and consists of a series of pre-cast concrete shells. The Sydney Harbor Bridge, the main bridge carrying traffic across Sydney Harbor, is another distinctive Australian icon. It is also considered the world's widest longspan bridge. The Royal Exhibition Building in Melbourne is a large exhibition hall that combines elements of the Byzantine, Romanesque, Lombardic, and Italian Renaissance styles. These styles were typical of Victorian architecture popular in Europe at the time of the building's completion in the late 19th century.

The Sydney Opera House and the Royal Exhibition Building are both listed as United Nations Educational, Scientific and Cultural Organization (UNESCO) World Heritage Sites.

Drama

European colonization in the late 18th century introduced theater to Australia. By the late 19th century, several major theaters had been established in cities such as Melbourne, Sydney, and Brisbane, and performances of British plays (particularly those of William Shakespeare) were popular. In 1973, the Sydney Opera House opened; its Drama Theatre, which contains over 500 seats, remains a popular dramatic venue, with the Sydney Theater Company often performing there.

Notable 20th century playwrights include Louis Nowra (1950–), whose works *Albert Names Edward* (1977) and *Inner Voices* (1977) garnered much critical acclaim; Hannie Rayson (1959–), who is known for her play *Hotel Sorrento* (1990), among others; and John Romeril (1945–), whose 1972 play *Bastardy* dealt with themes of racism and other social issues.

In 1906, Australia produced what was considered the world's longest feature film at the time, *The Story of the Kelly Gang*. From the 1890s to the 1920s, several hundred silent films were made in Australia. However, as British and American imports flooded the market during the 1920s, the Australian film industry declined. While some important films were made in the next few decades, such as 1955's *Jedda*, which detailed the story of an Indigenous girl separated from her family, the film industry was considered terminal by the 1960s. Increased funding in the 1970s spurred a film resurgence and between 1970 and 1985, over 400 films were made. Internationally renowned films made during this period included *Picnic at Hanging Rock* (1975) and *Mad Max* (1979). Many of these films dealt distinctly with Australian issues, such as Man from Snowy River (1982), which was based on the bush traditions of drovers, and *Gallipoli* (1981), which was based on Australia's involvement in the First World War. This time period is commonly referred to as the "golden era" of Australian cinema.

Music

Music has been an important part of indigenous culture for thousands of years. "Clan songs," typically songs about the history of a particular clan or tribe that are frequently updated and revised, were commonly sung within clans in a process called manikay. This is the term used by the Yorta Yorta people, Indigenous Australians that lived in the present-day state of Victoria. (Because there are over 100 different languages spoken by Indigenous Australians, such terms often vary). Songlines outline "dreamtime" stories about the creation of the natural world that have been passed down for generations. Sung in a particular order, they have helped indigenous tribes navigate hunting routes because of the way local landmarks are described and have helped document indigenous folklore and spiritual history.

Traditional instruments used in Indigenous Australian culture are the didgeridoo and clapping sticks. The didgeridoo is a hollow tube of wood—usually bamboo or eucalyptus—used as a wind instrument. Beeswax is commonly applied to line the end used as a mouthpiece. Clapping sticks are small sticks of wood that are carved into smooth shapes and painted with ornamental designs. They are clapped together as a percussion instrument.

Folk music has also played an important part in Australia's cultural history. The earliest Australian songs were created by convicts and based on traditional English songs. Often, the lyrics were replaced to describe the long sea journey undertaken by the convicts to reach Australia. Well-known examples of these songs include *Girls of the Shamrock Shore, Bound for South Australia, Botany Bay,* and *Convict Maid.* Traditionally, the fiddle, penny whistle, banjo, and mouth organ were popular accompaniments in folk music.

As convicts and settlers adapted to their new environment, they created songs that described life in their new country. Known as "bush music," such songs featured tales of bushrangers, escaped convicts who lived off the land and stole from free settlers; swagmen, nomadic men who slept under the stars while working on the land; and drovers, who herded livestock. They also featured songs about sheep shearers and gold miners. The language employed in bush music is typically colorful and informal, reflecting the fact that it was typically written by the working class. The most famous example is *Waltzing Matilda,* Australia's unofficial national song about a swagman shearer. Like most folk music, bush songs were passed down as part of oral tradition until the mid-20th century, when they were finally recorded.

Literature

Australian literature has played an important role in forming and expressing Australian culture. Early novels were often set in the outback and tell stories of struggle during the early years of colonization. Historically, this theme of relationship-to-place, the reconciliation of an Australian world and identity, was prevalent in Australian literature. Australia's convict history was also a prominent theme and featured heavily in *For the Term of his Natural Life (1874)*, by Australian novelist Marcus Clarke.

Indigenous Australia is also expressed and explored in several important works by indigenous authors. Aboriginal author Sally Morgan's memoir, *My Place*, played an important role in bringing indigenous issues to the attention of mainstream Australia. Australian author Patrick White (1912–1990) was awarded the Nobel Prize for Literature in 1973, becoming the first Australian to receive the honor. Initially dismissed in Australia, White eventually became known for his portrayal of the Australian middle class. Other authors such as Thomas Keneally (1935–) are known for their treatment of international themes in their work. Keneally's book, *Schindler's Ark (1982)*, was the basis for the 1993 film *Schindler's List*, set in Germany during World War II. Peter Carey (1943–) is another well-known Australian novelist on the international scene.

Poetry has been influential in shaping Australia's cultural history. While many Australian authors have published traditional poetry, the bush ballads of Andrew "Banjo" Paterson (1864–1941) and Henry Lawson (1867–1922) are perhaps the best-known examples of Australian poetry. Both as the lyrics of folk songs and as independent poetry, these lyrical poems describe life in the bush in early Australia. They include Paterson's *Waltzing Matilda* and *The Man from Snowy River*. Les Murray (1938–) is similarly known for a direct style.

CULTURE

Arts & Entertainment

For post-colonial Australia, the arts have been an important tool in helping to form a unique national identity. While many films, novels, and music styles have simply mimicked the trends popularized by international artists, Australia has witnessed the emergence of national styles and an identity separate from Great Britain and America. Artistic themes that have truly developed a sense of national identity include the celebration of Australia's history and landscape and protest songs that focus on Australian Aboriginal or environmental issues. Australian films, music, and literature began to focus on Australian bush

folklore. In this context, they are notable for their ability to help forge an identity and celebrate the nation's history. Acclaimed contemporary Australian novelists include Peter Carey, Tim Winton, and Kate Grenville.

The contemporary arts have also been incredibly important to Indigenous Australians in helping to retain their culture in mainstream Australian society. Historically, Indigenous Australians suffered during the British colonization of Australia. Because of their history, telling the story of their suffering has become just as important to Indigenous Australians as retaining their language and culture. While many contemporary Indigenous Australian artists have moved toward works that are more abstract and away from traditional "dreamtime" images, "dreamtime" imagery is still popular. Famous Indigenous Australian artists include Richard Bell, Emily Kngwarreye, and Clifford Possum Tjapaltjarri.

While international chart-topping groups are undoubtedly popular in Australia, Australians still celebrate their own local musicians. Some have had international careers, including opera singer Dame Nellie Melba, the BeeGees, AC/DC and country singers Slim Dusty and Keith Urban, while others remain popular only in Australia due to their focus on Australian life and issues. Contemporary Australian music with a discernible "Australian" identity includes modern indigenous music by bands such as Yothu Yindi, singers such as Archie Roach and Ruby Hunter, and indie singers such as Paul Kelly, whose work focuses on life in Australia. Notable Australian bands known for writing protest songs include Midnight Oil and the John Butler Trio.

Australians excel at sports such as tennis, cycling, golf, track and field, and auto racing. Famous tennis players include Lleyton Hewitt, Margaret Smith Court, Evonne Goolagong (of Aboriginal descent), Patrick Rafter, Rodney Laver, and John Newcombe. Famed golfer Greg Norman is joined by modern players Adam Scott, Mark Hensby, and Stuart Appleby. Cathy Freeman, an Australian runner of Aboriginal descent, won gold in the 400-meter event in the 2000 Olympic Games in Sydney. Sports such as Australian rules football, cricket, swimming, and soccer, also play a large role in Australian culture.

Cultural Sites & Landmarks

Australia has nineteen sites listed as UNESCO World Heritage Sites, three of which are man-made. The Great Barrier Reef (GBR) is the largest collection of coral reefs in the world and is regarded as one of the seven wonders of the natural world. Located off the coast of northeast Australia, it is comprised of over 2,800 individual reefs and 900 islands that cover 348,000 square kilometers (134,000 square miles). It is home to over 1,500 species of fish and 250 species of birds, as well as sea turtles, whales, dolphins and salt-water crocodiles. However, recent climatic changes have caused substantial episodes of coral bleaching, and rising ocean temperatures are considered a major threat to the reef's existence. In fact, experts have stated that besides climate change, pollution, land use and other environmental issues threaten the health of the reef. In 2015, the site was spared being placed on the List of World Heritage in Danger due to concerns over the health of the reef.

Uluru, also known as Ayers Rock, is a large sandstone formation located in Uluru-Kata Tjuta National Park in central Australia. It is 348 meters (1,142 feet) high and measures 9.4 kilometers (5.8 miles) in circumference. The local Aboriginal people consider the rock formation sacred, and they offer guided tours of the area. Climbing the rock has become a popular activity for those fit enough to withstand its demanding height and the often-severe desert heat.

Fifteen other natural attractions are also listed as World Heritage Sites, including Kakadu National Park in the Northern Territory, with its dramatic gorges and caves; the Purnululu National Park in Western Australia, which contains the famous Bungle Bungle Range of sandstone domes; the Ningaloo Coast, located on the remote western coast, with its underground network of caves and water courses; the Greater Blue Mountains Areas of New South Wales; the Wet Tropics of Queensland; and the temperate Tasmania Wilderness. Fraser Island in Queensland, the largest sand island in the world, and Macquarie Island, a small island located halfway between the Australian mainland and Antarctica, are also listed.

Arnhem Land in the Northern Territory remains a prominent example of Aboriginal culture. Declared an Aboriginal reserve in 1931, it is home to the Yolgnu peoples, among other Indigenous Australian groups, Stunning examples of ancient Aboriginal rock art can also be seen in the caves of the area. The sites of Ubirr, Noulangie, and Nanguluwur are some of the most visited cultural sites there.

The Melbourne Cricket Ground (MCG), referred to as the "G" by locals, is considered by many to be the spiritual home of the Australian sport of cricket. The stadium was home to the 1956 Olympic Games, the 2006 Commonwealth Games, and the Cricket World Cups in both 1992 and 2015. It is perhaps best known as the official home of the national sport, Australian rules football, similar to rugby. The stadium has a 100,000-person capacity.

The crown jewel among the country's arts venues is the Sydney Opera House, first opened in 1973 after nearly twenty years of work on its design, funding, and construction. Its five halls host touring groups, in addition to serving as home to the Sydney Theatre Company, Sydney Symphony Orchestra, and Opera Australia. The unique architecture of the Opera House, on Bennelong Point in Sydney Harbor features white granite tiles set into sail-shaped swooping shells, making it one of Australia's most-recognized landmarks and a favorite tourist attraction.

However, perhaps there is no greater cultural site in Australia than its many beaches. With the vast majority of Australia's population located on the coast, beach life is an integral part of Australian culture. From the bustle of Bondi Beach in Sydney, to the tranquility of secluded Wineglass Bay in Tasmania, the Australian coast may be the best location in which Australian culture is fully appreciated.

Libraries & Museums

Sydney's Australian Museum, opened in 1827, features natural history and anthropology exhibits, as does the Art Gallery of New South Wales, opened in 1874. Melbourne's National Gallery of Victoria, opened in 1859, highlights the country's visual arts. Other museums include the Art Gallery of South Australia in Adelaide, the Queensland Art Gallery in Brisbane, and the Art Gallery of Western Australia in Perth. The National Gallery of Australia, located in the nation's capital, Canberra, houses over 160,000 works of art. The National Gallery has one of the largest assortments of Aborigine, Torres Strait Islander, and Australian art in Australia. Of more interest from a historical perspective, perhaps, is the Heide Museum of Modern Art in Melbourne. Famous modernist Australian artists such as Sidney Nolan, Albert Tucker, Arthur Boyd, and Charles Blackman frequented its historic buildings.

The National Library of Australia was established in 1960 and is the country's largest reference library. The library houses collections of Australian literature, as well as journals, newspapers, rare books, and manuscripts. According to the library's website, it holds close to 10 million items in its overall collection.

Holidays

Official holidays observed in Australia include Australia (National) Day (January 26), and ANZAC Day (April 25), commemorating Australia's entry into World War I. Typical Christian holidays such as Easter and Christmas are also widely celebrated.

Festivals often coincide with holidays; the Montsalvat Jazz Festival is held in Eltham, Victoria, during the Australia Day weekend. The Mount Isa Mines Rotary Rodeo takes place in August in Queensland. The Australian Grand Prix in Melbourne is run in November, and the three-day Sydney to Hobart Yacht Race begins on Boxing Day (December 26).

Youth Culture

Australian youth culture is very much influenced by youth culture in the U.S. with regard to film, music, fashion, and language. The same actors, films, bands, and fashion trends that are popular in America are generally supported in Australia. In fact, American music and films are generally considered "cooler" than Australian ones, which are often more art-house or indie than mainstream. In fact, many older Australians lament the way that Australian youth mimic Americans in their views of life. Young people are also highly technologically savvy and spend much time on the Internet.

There are, however, some trends among young people that may be seen as "Australian." A love of sports such as Australian rules football is a major part of growing up in Australia. Going to see games, following a team, and playing in sports is considered very important. Equally, there is a greater emphasis on the outdoors generally than in other places, including spending time hiking or at the beach. Surfing is also very popular particularly in the northern states of New South Wales and Queensland. Surf culture—as characterized by fashions such as board shorts and flip-flops—is very much alive and is an important part of youth culture in these coastal regions.

SOCIETY

Transportation

Traveling by vehicle remains the most common form of transportation in Australia. In major urban centers, public transportation may be used. This is especially the case in Melbourne, where trains, trams, and buses are readily available, and in Sydney, which has a commuter system, buses, and ferries. Nonetheless, most urban families or residents typically own at least one car, and reliance solely on public transport would be considered rare. In rural areas and territories, travel by car or truck remains the primary form of transport. Notably, given the rising cost of fuel and greater awareness of global warming in the early

21st century, many local and regional councils have begun to improve bicycle lanes and to push for further investment in public transportation.

Because of the expansive distance between the larger metropolitan areas in Australia, the most common mode of transportation between these urban centers is through commercial or private aviation. For example, while rail, bus, and road networks exist, it typically takes one hour to fly from Melbourne to Sydney compared to roughly eleven hours via other means of transportation.

Traffic moves on the left-hand side of the road in Australia.

Transportation Infrastructure

Transportation infrastructure in Australia is well developed, and several major transportation infrastructure projects, including road and rail expansion/construction, have been completed and more continue to be announced. Australia's road network comprises 823,000 kilometers (511,388 miles) and its railways about 37,000 kilometers (22,991 miles). There are over 450 airports in Australia, with the busiest being Sydney Airport, Melbourne Airport, and Brisbane Airport. In 2005, there were over fifty international airlines servicing passengers travelling to and from Australia.

Media & Communications

Australia's media and communications industry is comparable to other modern and affluent countries. Televisions, cell phones, and computers are all widely used, even in rural settings. In fact, 99 percent of households own a television and 94 percent of Australians own a cell phone. As of 2013, over 89 percent of Australians had access to the Internet at home. Ninety-six percent of households with children under fifteen years of age had access while the percentage dropped to seventy-eight for households without children under the age of fifteen. Mobile-only Internet users are also on the rise; 21 percent of adult Australians did not have a fixed Internet connection at the end of 2014. The media is also considered transparent, meaning accusations of censorship or bias based on government or corporate interests are rare.

There are three public broadcasters owned by the government, and three main metropolitan networks. The government-owned channels, ABC, SBS, and National Indigenous Television, run independently of the government, however, and are widely praised for their high quality journalism. In addition, subscription-based programming was introduced in the 1990s with the creation of three providers, Foxtel, Austar, and Optus Television. (Foxtel acquired Austar in 2012). Subscription rates remain relatively low compared to other affluent countries. Community-based programming has been available since the 1980s. Free-to-air digital television was launched in 2001, and high-definition television (HDTV) was launched in 2007. As of March of that same year, only 28 percent of Australian households had adopted HDTV. Changeover to digital television was completed at the end of 2013.

Since July 1997, the telecommunications industry has been open to competition from other carriers, and over ninety carriers have since registered to operate in Australia. The government-owned telecommunications carrier Telstra (formerly Telecom Australia) has been privatized, in stages, throughout the 1990s and 2000s. By the end of the share release in 2006, the government's share was reduced to 17 percent.

There are many national, state and community newspapers, most of which are owned by News Corp Australia, Fairfax Media, and APN News and Media. The only national broadsheet is *The Australian.*

SOCIAL DEVELOPMENT

Standard of Living

Australia ranked second best of all 187 nations ranked on the 2014 United Nations Human Development Index, which measures quality of life indicators.

Water Consumption

Access to improved drinking water sources and sanitation services is very high in Australia, with 100 percent of the population having access to those services.

Education

About half of Australian children begin their education with preschool. State-run schools provide compulsory primary education, although as many as 35 percent of school-age children attend private schools. Of the private schools, 21 percent are Catholic.

Australia boasts nearly 100 percent literacy, thanks to an emphasis on creative solutions for reaching children who live in remote areas. Various forms of communications such as two-way radios and video or online classes are used in order to teach these students.

Some of the largest of Australia's more than forty public colleges and universities include Monash University (founded in 1958) in Victoria, with more than 55,000 students; the University of Sydney, established in 1850; and the University of Melbourne. Schools with an emphasis on technology, such as Queensland University of Technology and Royal Melbourne Institute of Technology (RMIT) University, also enjoy high enrollment.

Colleges receive substantial tax-funded assistance from the Australian government, although that funding declined since the 1980s. During that period, many schools came to rely heavily on foreign enrollments from Singapore and other Southeast Asian countries.

The gender gap in education slightly favors female students in Australia. According to the Australian Bureau of Statistics, between school years three and seven, female students reached more literacy benchmarks in reading, writing, and mathematics than male students did. Female students have higher completion rates, as well, with between 71 and 75 percent completing compulsory schooling between the years 1994 and 2004. For male students, completion rates ranged between 60 and 64 percent during that same period.

Women's Rights

In 1902, Australia became the first country in the world to grant women the right to vote and stand for election. Ironically, twenty and forty-one years passed before a woman was elected to state or federal parliament, respectively, the longest for any Western nation. Since then, women have served as state premiers; the leader of minor political parties, and in 2008, Australia had its first female deputy prime minister and first female governor general (the ceremonial head of state and representative of the Queen). However, up until 2010, a woman had yet to serve as prime minister or opposition leader. Julia Gillard (1961–) served as the first female Prime Minister and Australian Labor Party leader from 2010–2013. The first woman High Court judge was appointed in the 1990s, with several more appointed since. Three out of the seven justices in 2015 were women.

In addition, while outright discrimination, whether racial, gender or sexual, is illegal, many argue that latent discrimination still exists in business and politics, and women's rights groups continue to criticize Australia for the lack of women in high political or corporate positions. Until 2010, when Australia passed a parental leave law, women's rights groups also criticized the Australian government for being the only developed country, apart from the United States, without paid maternity leave.

However, women's rights in Australia are generally considered well protected. Australia has human rights laws that protect the rights of women and give women grounds to sue on the basis of sexual discrimination. Australia has also been a member of the Convention on Elimination of All Forms of Discrimination against Women (CEDAW) since 1983. In 2009 Australia signed the Optional Protocol to CEDAW, which would allow a further legal avenue for sexual discrimination complaints.

Overall, women are generally respected as equals socially and culturally, and are given the freedoms and opportunities one would expect in the modern world.

Health Care

Health care in Australia is similar to that in the United States, with a major difference being that every Australian is eligible for state-funded health insurance. However, quality of life among Aboriginal peoples (including life expectancy, health, poverty, employment, and education) is significantly lower than that of the white Australian population.

Average life expectancy for Australians is eighty-two years; almost eighty-five years for women and almost eighty years for men (2015 estimate). The infant mortality rate is low, at 4.37 deaths per 1,000 live births.

The government's Flying Doctor Service provides health care in remote areas of Australia. It is one of the largest aeromedical organizations in the world, using the latest technology to coordinate care, in concert with air ambulance services.

GOVERNMENT

Structure

Australia's six states are organized under a constitutional monarchy with a bicameral parliament. The British monarch's appointed governor-general serves as the symbolic head of state.

The Prime Minister (PM) is the leader of the majority elected party in the legislature. The Senate is made up of twelve elected representatives per state and two each from the Australian Capital Territory and the Northern Territory, for seventy-six. The House contains about twice as many elected representatives as the Senate, according to the population of each state. Most senators serve six-year terms. House members serve three-year terms. The PM selects Parliament members to form the cabinet, which includes ministers of Defence, Education and Training, Finance and Foreign Affairs.

State governments are also generally bicameral parliamentary systems, while local governing falls to shire councils, borough councils, city, and town councils.

Political Parties

The following political parties are active in Australia as of 2015: the Australian Greens, led by Richard Di Natale and founded in 1992; the Australian Labor Party, led by Bill Shorten and founded in 1891; the Family First Party, led by Bob Day and founded in 2002; the Coalition of the Liberal Party (formed in 1944) and the National Party (1920), led by Malcolm Turnbull (Prime Minister) and Warren Truss, respectively; the Palmer United Party, led by Clive Palmer and founded in 2013; and the Katter's Australian Party, led by Bob Katter and formed in 2011.

The Australian Labor Party won fifty-five seats in the House of Representatives in the 2013 federal election. The Liberal/National Coalition won ninety, and the Greens, Katter's, and Palmer United each captured one seat in the House. The Liberal/National Coalition won seventeen Senate seats, and the Australian Labor Party won twelve Senate seats. The Australian Greens, meanwhile, won four Senate seats.

Local Government

Local governments in Australia are generally referred to as Local Government Areas (LGAs). Local government is single-tiered and generally consists of an elected regional council overseen by a directly or indirectly elected mayor.

Judicial System

The court system of Australia includes a High Court, which consists of a chief justice and six other justices who are appointed by ministers on the Federal Executive Council, as well as a Family Court, Federal Court, and Federal Magistrates Court. There is also an Industrial Relations Courts, as well as State and Territory Courts.

Taxation

As of 2015, the top income tax levied in Australia was 49 percent, while the corporate tax was a flat 28.5 percent. Other taxies levied include a goods and services tax (GST) and a property transfer tax.

Armed Forces

The Australian Defence Force comprises an army, navy, and air force. As of 2015, there were approximately 58,000 active military personnel.

Foreign Policy

As a large country with a small population and a relatively small gross domestic product (GDP), Australia's foremost foreign policy objective has been to establish strategic alliances. As Great Britain's sway in Asia declined following the Second World War, Australia developed closer ties with the United States, which has remained Australia's most important ally in the early 21st century. The Australia, New Zealand, United States Security Treaty (ANZUS) is a military treaty in which all represented nations cooperate on military or defense matters in the Pacific Ocean. In August 2014, the two countries signed the US-Australia Force Posture Agreement at the annual Australia-United States Ministerial consultations (AUSMIN) which paves the way for even closer defense and security cooperation. In addition, Australia and the US maintain a free trade agreement. The U.S. is also one of the top four sources of exports (the first three are China, Japan, and South Korea). The strength of the alliance was tested when Australia committed troops to the U.S.-led wars in Afghanistan and Iraq, despite popular protest.

Maintaining strong relationships with its Pacific neighbors is also a priority for Australia. Indonesia, a largely Muslim country to the north, is considered a particularly important ally to Australia. However, relations between Australia and Indonesia have at times been tested, most recently in 2005 when nine Australians were arrested in Bali for drug smuggling. After the nine Australians, collectively known as the "Bali 9," were convicted, the death penalty was evoked, though eventually commuted for all but two. The two key organizers were executed by firing squad in the spring of 2015. This remains a contentious foreign policy issue, as the death penalty is not given in Australia, and pleas made by the Australian government for leniency have not been met.

Australia led the multi-national INTERFET forces, which intervened as peacekeepers in East Timor in 1999. This multi-national force was acting against Indonesia-led militia as the country had just been officially granted independence from Indonesia. (Australia again sent troops in 2006 to quell rising violence during the East Timor crisis). In 2015, tensions erupted between the two countries regarding the long-running dispute over undersea oil and gas fields access. There have also been two terrorist bombings targeting Australians in Indonesia attributed to Islamic extremists: the bombing of the Australian Embassy in Jakarta in 2000 and the bombing of a largely Australian-patronized nightclub in Bali in 2002, killing ninety-four Australian nationals.

Australia has a close relationship with the island nations of the Pacific. As the wealthiest country in the area, Australia contributes substantial foreign aid to these islands, both in terms of finance and labor. However, some Pacific islands have criticized Australia for trying to exert too much power and influence over them. It is also not uncommon for Australia to voice its opinions strongly regarding the domestic affairs of these island nations. For example, Australia voiced its displeasure with Fiji's military coup and the subsequent interim government formed in 2006. Sanctions that were imposed have since been lifted. Australia has also controversially intervened in the affairs of the Solomon Islands by requesting the extradition of that nation's attorney general for sex crimes committed in Vanuatu in the 1990s. Furthermore, Australia's decision to open an offshore detention facility for asylum seekers in Nauru has also been subject to criticism by other nations, though Nauru received substantial payment and did not object. In particular, the Australian Human rights Commission has issued reports on the serious allegations of the abuse of children at the facility.

Australia's foreign relations with its other close neighbor, New Zealand, have been less dramatic. New Zealand is considered substantially similar to Australia culturally, and the two countries share a friendly rivalry akin to that of Canada and the U.S.

Australia has strong trade relationships throughout much of Asia. China has recently overtaken Japan as the largest export market, with China's appetite for Australian coal, steel and other commodities fueling Australia's current economic growth.

Dependencies

Dependencies (and the year they officially fell under administration) include the Ashmore and Cartier Islands (1934), Christmas Island (1958), the Cocos (Keeling) Islands (1984), the Coral Sea Islands (1969), Heard Island and the McDonald Islands (1947), and Norfolk Island (1914).

Human Rights Profile

International human rights law insists that states respect civil and political rights, and promote an individual's economic, social, and cultural rights. The United Nations Universal Declaration on Human Rights (UDHR) is recognized as the standard for international human rights. Its authors sought the counsel of the world's great thinkers, philosophers, and religious leaders, and were careful to create a document that reflects the core values shared by every world culture. (To read this document or view the articles relating to cultural human rights, visit http://www.un.org/en/documents/udhr/.)

Australia was regarded as a leader in arguing for and forming the UN Universal Declaration of Human Rights, and considers itself a model country when it comes to respecting and protecting those rights. However, Australia's human rights record has not been perfect. The Australian government has been criticized in recent years for its treatment of asylum seekers and the establishment of anti-terrorism laws passed since the September 11, 2001 terrorist attacks.

Australia implemented a policy of mandatory detention for asylum seekers arriving illegally on Australia's shores in the early 1990s. By the end of that decade, it had become a hot political issue when then-Prime Minister John Howard passed a series of laws making it more difficult for asylum seekers to assert their rights. These included a policy of "territorial exclusion," whereby parts of Australian territory (especially islands to the North where people may arrive illegally by boat) are excluded from official Australian territory. As such, asylum seekers who land there do not enjoy the same legal rights as those who arrive on the mainland.

A new temporary visa scheme was also implemented, giving successful asylum seekers who arrived illegally lesser rights than others. This scheme was similar to the so-called "Pacific solution," in which asylum seekers were processed on offshore facilities in Nauru and other Pacific islands where they had less legal rights. These reforms contradict Article 2, which states that everyone has equal rights to the protections outlined, and Article 14, which states that everyone has the right to seek asylum in other countries. While the Australian government has pledged to close the Pacific island facilities, other key aspects of the policy remain.

Australia's anti-terrorism legislation, passed since 2001, has been criticized for the allowance of harsh treatment of suspected and convicted terrorists. Particularly concerning aspects of the legislation include detention procedures and the content of control orders placed on convicted terrorists. These include the length of detention without needing evidence, content of requirements to inform relatives, monitoring of communications with lawyers, lack of access to information regarding control orders, and the harsh conditions of detained individuals. This legislation is considered in violation of Article 3, the right to liberty, and Article 9, freedom from arbitrary arrest and detention.

Concerns about the entrenched discrimination against same-sex couples under Australian law (including access to benefits/entitlements such as superannuation and child support, the inability to marry, and the lack of anti-discrimination legislation on the basis of sexuality) and the poor health and education outcomes for

Indigenous Australians have also been raised by some human rights groups. The lack of anti-discrimination legislation violates Article 7, regarding equal protection against discrimination, and the health and education outcomes violate Articles 25 and 26 regarding the right to health and education. Lastly, criticism has also been leveled at Australia for its failure to chastise its trading partners adequately, including China and Indonesia, for human rights violations.

ECONOMY

Overview of the Economy

Australia has a robust Western-style market economy. In 2014, the gross domestic product (GDP) was estimated at just over $1.09 trillion (USD). Per capita GDP was estimated at $46,400 (USD).

Australia's largest trading partners are China, the United States, and Japan.

Industry

Services account for about 68 percent of GDP, led by property and business services. Manufacturing makes up about 6.5 percent of GDP.

Commodities account for more than 50 percent of exports. Coal is the leading export by value followed by iron ore, nickel, copper, and aluminum. Australia is among the world's top producers of gold and the largest volume producer of diamonds.

The mining industry during the 1970s and 1980s relied on Japanese investment and demand, particularly for iron ore. Expansion of China's economy from 1995 to 2005 again increased demand for raw materials.

Labor

Unemployment dropped from 5 percent in 2004 to about 4.5 percent by 2008. By 2014, Australia's unemployment rate was an estimated 6.1 percent.

Energy/Power/Natural Resources

Globally, Australia was the largest net exporter of coal and the twelfth largest exporter of natural gas in 2014. The country also exports hydrocarbon.

Fishing

The Australian Fishing Zone (AFZ) covers 8.1 million square kilometers (3.08 million square miles), making it the third largest fishing zone in the world. There are over twenty Commonwealth fisheries; their total annual production value is $300 million (USD). Important fish species include the southern blue fin tuna, the northern prawn, the eastern tuna, and billfish.

Forestry

Australia contains 3 percent of the world's forests, with 16 percent of the continent covered in forest. Over 66,000 people are employed in forest industries, which bring in around $22 million (USD) each year. The two main sources of lumber are eucalyptus trees from the southern coast and pine trees from the east coast. Oak, ash, and cedar are other, less-common species.

Mining/Metals

Australia is the world's largest coal exporter. Other abundant mineral resources include bauxite, copper, tin, iron ore, gold, silver, uranium, nickel, tungsten, mineral sands, lead, and zinc. Gemstone deposits include diamonds, opals, topaz, and sapphires. Most of the country's mining takes place in Western Australia and Queensland.

Due in part to a reliance on coal for about 75 percent of its power generation, Australia has a high level of greenhouse gas emissions. Deforestation has slowed, however, helping to reduce some pollutants.

Agriculture

Agriculture accounts for only 3.7 percent of Australia's GDP. In 2014, total agricultural receipts were $51 billion (USD). Agricultural receipts were led by beef at $14.7 billion (USD), followed by wheat ($8 billion (USD), dairy, vegetables, fruits, lamb, and wool. Australia leads the world in wool exports. Fruit crops were led by grapes, largely destined for the wine industry, at about $1.003 billion (USD).

Animal Husbandry

In 2015, there were approximately 1.6 million head of dairy cattle and 29.3 million head of meat cattle. That same year, there were approximately 72.6 million head of sheep and 4.8 million head of pigs. In addition, there were around 482 million chickens raised for meat in addition to chickens used for egg production.

Tourism

The 2000 Olympic Games, held in Sydney, boosted tourism to nearly 5 percent of GDP. Levels in 2002–2003 fell to about four percent but still accounted for about half a million jobs and a contribution of $32 billion USD to the economy. Receipts were about 75 percent from domestic tourists, and 25 percent from international guests. The 2015 tourism industry forecast was positive with an expected growth of 3.5 percent for the coming year.

Tourists stay at beachside resorts in Cairns in order to visit the Great Barrier Reef. Other resorts line much of the east coast. The central desert region, known as the "bush" or the "Outback," is also popular with tourists that are more adventurous.

Alice Ashbolt, John Pearson, Jamie Aronson,
Jael Bridgemahon

DO YOU KNOW?

- The Australian War Memorial was first planned as a tribute to Australian soldiers lost in World War I, particularly during the ill-fated Gallipoli campaign, and closes each day to the strains of "Last Post," the Aussie equivalent of "Taps." The last survivor of the Gallipoli Campaign, Alec Campbell, died in 2003 at the age of 102. He was given a state funeral.

- Australia was first sighted by Europeans in 1606. The Dutch called the island New Holland. In 1770, Captain James Cook claimed the island, which he called "New South Wales," for Great Britain. The name Australia is derived from the Latin word "australis" ("southern"); usage of this name dates to the late 18th century.

Bibliography

Australian Bureau of Statistics. www.abs.gov.au.

Australian Government, Culture Portal. www.acn.net.au.

Australian Government, Department of Foreign Affairs and Trade. www.dfat.gov.au.

Australia's Official Travel Website. www.australia.com.

Karl, Roland F., Berghoff, Jorg, Mussig, Jochen and Bolch, Oliver. *Australia: Continent of Contrasts.* Germany: Bucher, 2007.

Kleinert, Sylvia and Margo Neale, eds. *Oxford Companion to Aboriginal Art and Culture.* South Melbourne: Oxford University Press, 2001.

Murray, Peter. *The Saga of the Sydney Opera House.* London: Spon Press, 2003.

Penney, Barry. *Australia - Culture Smart!: A Quick Guide to Customs and Etiquette.* London: Kuperard, 2006.

Ryan, Judith, et al. *Imagining Australia: Literature and Culture in the New World.* Cambridge, MA: Harvard University Press, 2004.

Welsh, Frank. *Australia: A New History of the Great Southern Land.* London: Allen Lane/Penguin, 2006.

Works Cited

"Advancing the National Interest," Foreign Policy Whitepaper, 2003, http://australianpolitics.com/foreign/elements/2003_whitepaper.pdf

"Australia: first name or title? Addressing others with respect" http://www.executiveplanet.com/index.php?title=Australia:_First_Name_or_Title%3F

Australia-New Zealand Relations http://en.wikipedia.org/wiki/Australia-New_Zealand_relations

Australian Bureau of Statistics, www.abs.gov.au

Australian Clearinghouse for Youth Studies, Culture and Subculture http://acys.info/youth_facts_and_stats/culture

Australian Electoral Commission, Election 2013, http://results.aec.gov.au/17496/Website/SenateResultsMenu-17496.htm

"Australian food and drink," Australian Government Culture and Recreation Portal, http://www.cultureandrecreation.gov.au/articles/foodanddrink/

Australian Government, Australian Institute of Family Studies, http://www.aifs.gov.au/index.html

Australian Government Culture Portal http://www.australia.gov.au/information-and-services/culture-and-arts

Australian Government, "Marriage and Family in Australia" http://www.aph.gov.au/house/committee/laca/Famserv/chap2.pdf

Australian Government, Office for Women, http://www.ofw.facsia.gov.au/index.htm

Australian Government, "Women in Politics" http://www.cultureandrecreation.gov.au/articles/womeninpolitics/

"Australians get mobile," Australian Communications and Media Authority, http://www.acma.gov.au/theACMA/engage-blogs/engage-blogs/Research-snapshots/Australians-get-mobile

"Australian Residential Architecture Styles" http://www.homedesigndirectory.com.au/articles/ArchitecturalStyles.shtml

"East Timor Battles Australia over Petroleum Pipeline," *The Wall Street Journal*, September 24 2015, http://www.wsj.com/articles/east-timor-scraps-sea-border-talks-with-australia-1443084994

"Elements of Australian Foreign Policy," http://australianpolitics.com/foreign/elements/

"Food and drink," Aussie Info.com http://www.aussie-info.com/identity/food/index.php

Great Barrier Reef Marine Park Authority, Australian Government, http://www.gbrmpa.gov.au/corp_site.

Heide Museum of Modern Art, Official Website, http://www.heide.com.au/heide_education.php

History of Australian Telecommunications Industry, http://www.caslon.com.au/austelecomsprofile2.htm

"Indigenous Australian Art," Wikipedia http://en.wikipedia.org/wiki/Australian_Aboriginal_art

"Letter to Australian Prime Minister Kevin Rudd," Human Rights Watch, November 2007, http://hrw.org/english/docs/2007/12/17/austra17574.htm

"Linguists Say Australian Youth Talk like Americans," Courier Mail, http://www.news.com.au/couriermail/story/0,23739,23963981-3102,00.html

Meat & Livestock Australia, Industry Overview, http://www.mla.com.au/About-MLA/Cattle-sheep-goat-industries/Industry-overview/Cattle

Melbourne Cricket Ground Official Website, http://www.mcg.org.au/

National human Rights Action Plan, http://www.humanrightsactionplan.org.au/nhrap/focus-area/womens-rights

"Our Changing Climate," Great Barrier Reef Marine Park Authority, Australian Government, http://www.gbrmpa.gov.au/corp_site/info_services/publications/misc_pub/climate_change_vulnerability_assessment/our_changing_climate

"Royal Exhibition Building," UNESCO World Heritage site, http://whc.unesco.org/pg.cfm?cid=31&id_site=1131

"Social etiquette in Australia" http://www.convictcreations.com/culture/socialrules.htm

"Sydney Opera House," Culture and Recreation Portal, Australian Government, http://www.cultureandrecreation.gov.au/articles/sydneyoperahouse/

"Sydney Harbour Bridge," Culture and Recreation Portal, Australian Government, http://www.cultureandrecreation.gov.au/articles/harbourbridge/

Tasmanian Wilderness World Heritage Area, Parks Tasmania information site, http://www.parks.tas.gov.au/wha/whahome.html

"Television in Australia," Wikipedia, http://en.wikipedia.org/wiki/Television_in_Australia#Broadcasting

"Trade at a glance," Department of Foreign Affairs and Trade, http://www.dfat.gov.au/trade/tag/index.html#sect03

Ultimate Guide to Australian sharks, Australian Geographic, July 10 2013 http://www.australiangeographic.com.au/topics/wildlife/2013/07/ultimate-guide-to-australian-sharks

Uluru Official Website, http://www.environment.gov.au/parks/uluru/

Victoria Facts: Royal Exhibition Building and Carlton Gardens, http://www.about-australia.com/facts/victoria/history/royal-exhibition-building-and-carlton-gardens/

"World-Australian senate to Advise Moving Families," TIME September 1 2015, http://time.com/4018253/abuse-australias-detention-nauru-asylum-refugees/

Bula Men. iStock/HDCineman

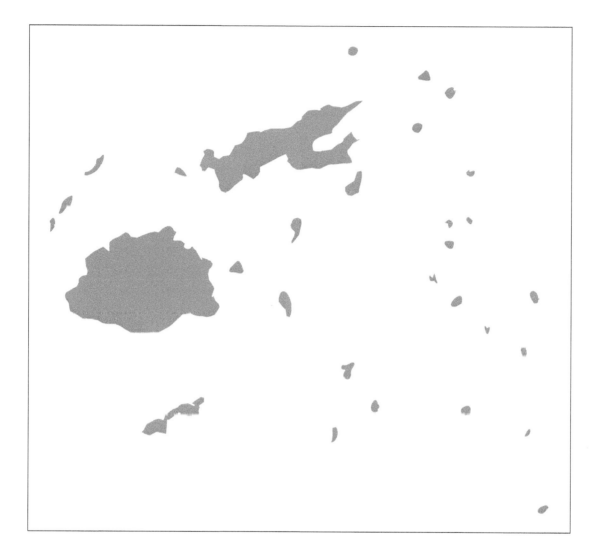

FIJI

An Introduction

The Republic of the Fiji Islands is an independent, archipelagic nation in the Pacific Ocean that consists of hundreds of islands and islets. It is located approximately 2,000 miles northeast of Australia and 3,000 miles southwest of Hawaii. Excluding Australia and New Zealand, Suva, the island nation's capital, is the largest urban center in the South Pacific.

Today, the island nation is a popular tropical tourist destination, especially among citizens of Asia, Australia, and the United States. However, the country has experienced political turmoil and military tension in recent years, which has created unrest and concern about the possibility of violence.

Historically, Fijian art has been functional as much as it has been decorative. Traditional Fijian art forms include basket weaving, jewelry, pottery, weaponry, dance, and storytelling.

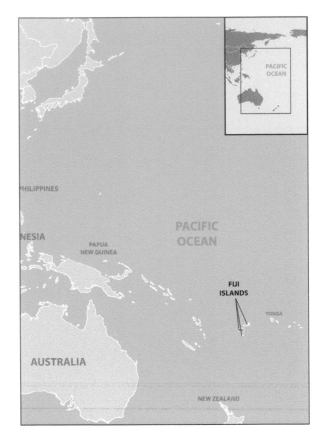

GENERAL INFORMATION

Official Language: English
Population: 877,000 (2013 estimate)
Currency: Fijian dollar
Coins: The Fijian dollar is subdivided into 100 cents. Coins are available in denominations of 5, 10, 20, and 50 cents and 1 dollar.
Land Area: 18,274 square kilometers (7,056 square miles)
National Anthem: "God Bless Fiji"
Capital: Suva
Time Zone: GMT +12

Flag Description: The flag of Fiji is light blue. It features a small version of the Union Jack, or flag of Great Britain, in the top left corner. This remains on the flag despite the fact that Fiji gained independence from Britain in 1970. The right section, or "fly" portion, of the flag depicts the Fijian shield-of-arms.

Population

About one-tenth of the citizens of Fiji live in the capital of Suva. Half of the population lives in rural areas comprised of many small farming or fishing villages. Population density is 48.22 people per square kilometer (119 per square mile).

The population is evenly divided between rural and urban areas. Nasinu, with approximately 90,000, is the largest city. Suva and Nausori are the second and third largest urban centers, with populations of about 85,345 and 62,073, respectively. Population growth on the Fiji islands was estimated at 0.7 percent in 2014.

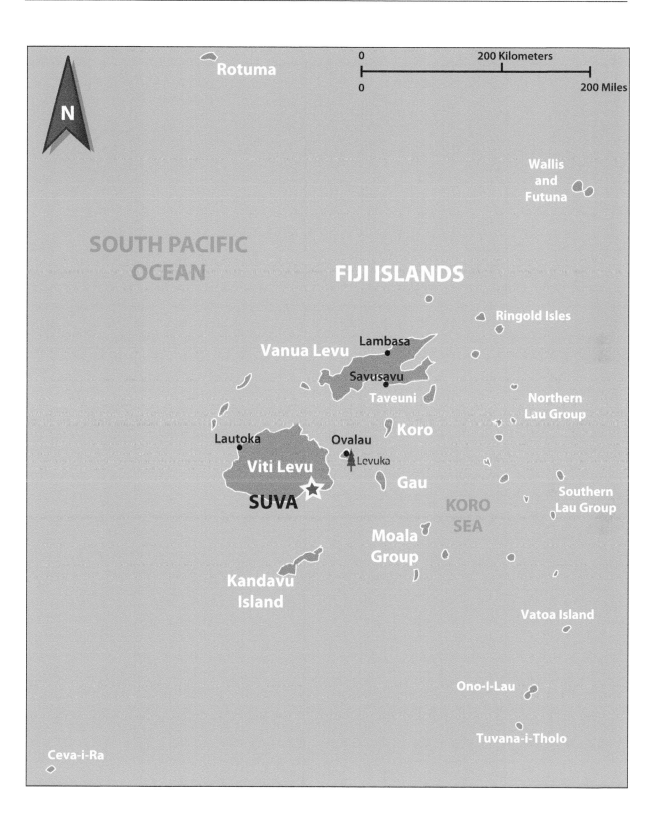

Principal Cities or Towns by Population (2012 estimates):
- Nasinu (89,522)
- Suva (85,345)
- Nausori (62,073)
- Lautoka (56,892)
- Nadi (49,930)

Ethnically, Fiji is dominated by two groups. Fijians account for 50 percent of the population, and are mainly of Melanesian and Polynesian descent. Indians are the second largest ethnic group, accounting for 46 percent of the population. The remaining percentage of the population consists mainly of descendants from Chinese, European, and other Pacific Islander backgrounds.

Languages

Most Fijians speak English, the country's official language. However, native Fijians speak Fijian to each other. Fijian is classified as an Austronesian language also known as Malayo-Polynesian. The large Indian population generally speaks Hindi, an Indo-European language spoken widely in Northern and Central India. The Indian slaves who worked on the British plantations brought the language to the islands.

Native People & Ethnic Groups

Polynesians (arriving around 1500 BCE) and Melanesians (arriving around 500 BCE) first settled Fiji. Bloody tribal warfare between these groups during the 19th century earned Fiji the nickname the "Cannibal Islands." Europeans began to settle in Fiji soon after.

Eventually Fiji would become a British colony, and the Indian population was introduced. Today, Fijian culture is said to resemble the Polynesian culture more than the Melanesian culture.

Religions

Religion in Fiji is divided along ethnic lines. Most of the native Fijians consider themselves Christians; 37 percent of the population is Methodist and 9 percent is Roman Catholic. Approximately 34 percent of the population (primarily Indians) practices the Hindu religion. Muslims account for about 7 percent of the population.

Religious activity in Suva is largely centered on the Methodist and Roman Catholic branches of Christianity, although the city's Indian population is split between those of Hindu and Muslim faith.

Climate

Fiji has a tropical climate with an average annual temperature of 25° Celsius (77° Fahrenheit). Summer lasts from December to April, with temperatures reaching 32° Celsius (90° Fahrenheit). During these hot months, Fiji also gets most of its rain. Areas on the windward side of the mountains can expect about 330 centimeters (130 inches) of rain annually, while areas on the leeward side receive about 250 centimeters (98 inches) per year.

ENVIRONMENT & GEOGRAPHY

Topography

The Republic of the Fiji Islands is made up of 332 islands, 110 of which are populated. The total land area is 18,270 square kilometers (7,054 square miles) which is about the size of the American state of New Jersey.

Viti Levu and Vanua Levu are two of the larger islands, accounting for 85 percent of the total land area. These islands are of volcanic origin, with elevations ranging from sea level to the top of Mount Tomaniivi on Viti Levu, which is the highest point in Fiji at 1,324 meters (4,344 feet). In contrast, many of the smaller coral islands barely rise a few meters above sea level.

Rivers flow from the mountainous islands. The Rewa is the largest river on Viti Levu, and flows for more than 160 kilometers (just over 99 miles). There are three other major rivers on Viti Levu: the Sigatoka, Nadi, and Ba. The largest river on Vanua Levu is the Dreketi.

Almost half of the islands are covered by forests. The mountainous islands have two distinct ecosystems due to the trade winds. Generally, there are rainforests on the eastern sides of the mountains, where more rain falls, and grassy plains on the western sides, which receive less rain.

Plants & Animals

Fiji is a land of lush vegetation. More than 3,000 plant species have been identified there. Many of these plants are used for food, medicine, or building materials. Ota is an edible fern also used in the construction of traditional Fijian houses. The sap of a tree fern called balabala was once used to treat headaches. Other widely used native plants include bamboo, mangroves, hardwood trees, and coconut palms.

As one might expect from a group of tropical islands, there are nearly seventy-five different species of birds in Fiji, and an abundance of snakes and lizards. Fiji's coral reef is among the largest in the world, surrounding nearly all of the islands. There are two native species of mammals in Fiji: rats and bats. Animals such as cattle, dogs, horses, and sheep were all introduced by settlers.

CUSTOMS & COURTESIES

Greetings

English is the official language of Fiji, and most everyone speaks it. Fijian and Fiji-Hindi are also taught in schools, and both native Fijians and Fijian Indians may also speak their own dialect. As such, typical English language greetings are common, as are greetings in Fijian (the national language of native Fijians) and Fiji-Hindi (the national language of Fijian Indians). In addition, there are over 300 different dialects spoken by native Fijians throughout the many islands, and Fijian Indians may speak an Indian dialect, such as Gujarati, Tamil, Telugu, or Punjabi.

One of the more common and informal greetings in Fiji is "Bula" ("Hello," or "Welcome"), followed by "Ni sah yandra" ("Good Morning").

The phrase "Ni sa moce" (both "Goodbye and "Goodnight") is a common farewell phrase. In Fiji-Hindi, the greeting for both hello and goodbye is "Namaste." Additionally, it is common to address Fijians by their first name, even in a business setting or when speaking to someone of authority. Generally, Fijians are very friendly, even to strangers, and it is common for visitors and locals alike to wave and smile and call "Bula" when passing someone on the street.

Gestures & Etiquette

Throughout Fiji, modest dress is customary, and even expected of tourists and travelers. It is common for men and women to wear a sarong (a large wrap around clothing or sheets of fabric), also called sulas, or other clothing that covers the legs. It is considered disrespectful to wear a hat or sunglasses when entering a village, building, or residence, In addition, proper etiquette requires the removal of shoes before entering a household.

Generally, Fijians are modest people, and typically refrain from loud or excited conversation and gestures. For example, raising one's voice, standing akimbo (with one's hands on the hips), and pointing during conversation, particularly towards another individual, are all considered inappropriate or rude. It is also against traditional custom to touch another Fijian on the head, including children.

Out of custom, Fijians generally welcome visitors to eat or share something with them. It is perfectly polite to decline such invitations. In addition, timeliness is not particularly important to Fijians. The phrase "Fiji time" is commonly used to note that meetings, appointments, and other scheduled events almost never start on time.

Eating/Meals

In traditional villages, breakfast was eaten early before attending to the daily obligations, largely related to fishing or agriculture. In the midmorning, the men would return to the village to stoke the lovo, or traditional Fijian oven, and the women would prepare the main meal of the day, usually served mid-afternoon. After the main meal, leisure time or further work would be done until nighttime. A smaller dinner or supper would then be eaten later at night.

However, as villagers and urban Fijians move away from the traditional farming and fishing lifestyles, eating habits are changing. Generally, mealtimes are no longer fixed, and snacking between meals is common. This is partly because of the growing prevalence of fast food and other convenience foods, which encourage greater snacking and meals on the go, particularly in urban areas. However, it is also because food is such a significant part of socializing.

When visiting friends, food will usually be served, and it is polite to accept. The social aspect of food also means that meals tend to be eaten together. As such, many families will not begin to serve until all of the family (and any guests) are present. With people working different hours, and a greater variety of social occasions, this means meal times are more erratic. Traditionally, the village would all cook and share food together for each meal. While in some villages this may still occur, cooking is generally done by each family individually, both in villages and in cities.

Indian Fijians also practice many Indian meal traditions. For example, in some parts of India, men and women eat separately, and in some Indian Fijian families, this still occurs. Additionally, many villagers eat with their hands, in which case a bowl of water for washing one's hands is provided. Villagers will generally sit on the ground in a circle, and not at a table with chairs.

Visiting

A visit to a traditional Fijian village customarily involves the presentation of a sevusevu—a gift of kava, the traditional drink, produced from the roots of the kava plant—to the village chief. The presentation usually takes place at the chief's residence, and other village men may attend, thus creating a social occasion. Typically, the kava is served by grinding up the kava into a powder and mixing it with water. It is then poured into the hollowed shell of half a coconut and shared.

While kava is an acquired taste, it is polite for strangers or travelers to drink from the cup when offered.

Exchanging gifts is not an integral part of Fijian culture, but giving a gift to thank someone for their hospitality or other generosity may be done. Practical gifts are considered more appropriate and are more appreciated, particularly in rural areas. However, there are no cultural obligations for reciprocal gift giving. Additionally, as Fijians are generally warm and friendly people, food is typically offered to a visiting guest. It is considered polite to accept this offering, particularly if food is given as a gift.

LIFESTYLE

Family

amily is considered very important in Fijian culture, and spending time with and looking after family members is a priority. Traditionally, Fijians have many children and stay close to their extended families, making for large family gatherings. In traditional village life, the "second" family of all Fijians is the village itself, emphasizing the importance of community. Additionally, villagers customarily eat and share food together every night and know all about events in each other's lives. The support offered by all of the villagers to each other and the sense of community is profound. As village life becomes less traditional, the idea of family has maintained an even greater role in society.

While arranged marriages were common in traditional Fijian villages to foster good relationships between clans, they are becoming increasingly uncommon among native Fijians. Indian Fijians, who have the Indian traditions of arranged marriages, may still practice them.

In urban centers, as women gain more independence and pursue careers of their own, couples are marrying and having children later.

Housing

Housing in traditional Fijian villages is simple and communal in style. Houses, or bures, are traditionally single-room buildings with bamboo woven walls and thatched roofs. Kitchens and bathrooms are usually housed separately and are often used communally. Kitchens are equipped with lovos, or deep-earth ovens. In fact, the underground lovo cooking process remains a popular culinary tradition in contemporary society. Villages typically have no electricity or hot water, although such facilities are becoming more common. Less traditional villages may include houses made out of corrugated tin and wood, often of varying designs and colors, with two rooms instead of one. Almost all houses in rural Fiji are located within villages; very few are isolated.

More than 40 percent of Fijians now live in cities, which have Western-style housing and modern facilities. Old British-style buildings still exist from the colonial era, as well as newer apartment-style buildings and residences. Wealthy Fijians may have large houses with many rooms and modern amenities and technology.

Food

Generally, the cuisine in Fiji developed from the use of simple and native ingredients, incorporating Polynesian, Chinese, Indian, and European influences. Some of the most common ingredients shared among the islands include vegetables such as yams, cassava, and taro, and fruits such as plantains, coconuts, and bananas. Many dishes are centered on meat, including beef, pork, and poultry, as well as seafood. Many of the spices typically used in Fijian cuisine were influenced by the culinary traditions of India and China and may include chilies, garlic, ginger, turmeric, and cumin, in addition to soy-based sauces.

Native Fijians traditionally eat mostly fish, fresh fruit, and vegetables and nuts. Wild pigs and chickens are also eaten; the latter is often reserved for special occasions. Whether cut, shaved, pressed, dried, or used as a cream or milk, coconut features prominently. Local dishes include kakoda, a dish of marinated, steamed fish served with coconut cream and lime, and kassaua, cooked tapioca with coconut cream, sugar, and mashed bananas. The lovo feast, where a range of meat, fish, vegetables, and fruit are cooked in the traditional lovo oven, is another highlight. Dairy was not available for many years, and many Fijians remain lactose intolerant.

The Indo-Fijian diet is more Indian in style. While dishes have been abridged throughout the years so that most are now distinct from their Indian counterparts, they still use similar cooking styles and ingredients, including flat bread, rice, and vegetables made into Indian-style curries and other dishes. Meat is eaten when available; although religious traditions may restrict its type—Indian Hindus will not eat beef and Indian Muslims will not cat pork.

The native drink of Fiji, kava (or yagona), is also a distinct feature of the Fijian diet. Made from the root of the kava pepper plant, it is dried and ground up and water is added. It has the consistency of muddy water, with a slight aniseed flavor.

Life's Milestones

The vast majority of ethnic Fijians are Christian, and their celebrations of life's milestones are rooted in Christian traditions, including christenings, weddings, and funerals. Additionally, both Christmas and Easter are widely celebrated. Weddings, in particular, incorporate more Western-style traditions, including white wedding gowns. For Indo-Fijians, Indian customs such as large, traditional weddings are common, as are the religious ceremonies and customs of their Hindu, Sikh, or Islamic faith.

Some Fijian traditions regarding death are still practiced, particularly in rural areas. A traditional Fijian funeral lasts many days. For the first four or five days after the death, family and friends gather together and place mats and tabua, the teeth of a sperm whale, on the body. The body is buried and a burial ceremony is held. Further ceremonies happen again, on the fourth and tenth nights after the burial. One hundred nights later, the Vakataraisulu ceremony is traditionally held. During this ceremony, items are lifted off the gravesite and the grave is cemented over. A final ceremony is held one year later.

Birthdays are not typically celebrated with much fanfare in Fijian culture. When a couple's first child is born, both sides of the family generally gather to celebrate, but ordinary birthdays are not a significant event. However, with increasing exposure to Western culture, this is slowly changing.

CULTURAL HISTORY

Art

Traditional art in Fiji is reflected in the historic artisanship and artistry of practical items such as weaponry, ceramics, and clothing. Fijians developed a reputation for creating efficient and aesthetic weaponry. Often, these weapons, which included spears and clubs, were painstakingly engraved and decorated. Wooden clubs were the most common weapon for many years, and were given complex engravings and even inlaid with whale ivory. The carving of canoes was another highly regarded and elaborate traditional art in Fiji culture based in practicality and not aesthetics.

Fijian housewares are also noteworthy for their artistry. Traditionally, skills were passed down from generation to generation, with different areas specializing in different skill sets. Cooking pots, basins, and water containers were traditionally made out of clay, using an ancient technique involving a river pebble, paddle, and bonfire. Pots could be plain or decorated with natural objects such as shells, and then varnished. Other bowls would be carved out of wood and have four legs so they could stand upright. Large bowls often took the form of a turtle, and shallow bowls used by priests were made in the shape of a heart or crescent. All were decorated with complex engravings. Mats and baskets were also made, woven together from the leaves of pandanus plants and coconut trees.

Decorative textiles and jewelry making are also significant traditional arts in Fiji. Bark cloth, or "tapa" cloth, is made from the bark of the mulberry tree. The bark is stripped from the tree, dried, beaten into a cloth, and used for clothing. It is decorated with various geometric designs, either stenciled or hand-drawn onto the cloth. Historically, these designs were unique to the family or village of the wearer, but in recent times have expanded into wider design types.

Traditional jewelry materials often included a whale's tooth. For example, Fijians used a whale's tooth as the centerpiece of their tabua talisman, a ceremonial piece of jewelry used for spiritual purposes. Many of these crafts are still considered living arts, and form a significant part of the island nation's tourist and trade industry.

While the fine arts such as painting and sculpture did not develop in Fiji until contemporary times, they are rooted in the rock paintings of Fiji's limestone cliffs. The origins of some Pacific rock art are largely unknown, but these cliff paintings are similar to the Polynesian art styles that developed over the centuries in the Pacific Rim. In addition, body painting was a popular and often daily traditional art in Fiji. Special designs were reserved for ceremonies or times of war, and henna tattoos were particularly popular.

Architecture

Traditional architecture in Fiji, and throughout the Pacific islands, was not complex nor a particular art form. Instead, it was largely practical, and influenced by climate and the availability of materials. Traditional houses, or bures, were often one-room bamboo structures with thatched roofs. Leaves and reeds were also used in the construction of these simple structures. Many such houses remain, largely for tourist and aesthetic purposes. Modest one- or two-room structures made out of corrugated tin or other types of wood are more common today.

During Fiji's colonial period, its architecture was largely influenced by European styles. British colonial architecture is particularly evident in government and public buildings. The arrival of the British in the 19th century also ushered in more Western-style housing, such as apartments and freestanding dwellings. Recently, modern architectural designs, typically blended with tropical or traditional Fijian aesthetics, are increasingly common in urban areas.

Drama

Cinema in Fiji developed only as recently as the early 21st century, with the Fiji Islands Audio Visual Commission (FIAVC) Act of 2002. The aim of the act is to promote the audio and visual arts in Fiji and to attract filmmakers and production studios to Fiji through tax incentives. In addition, 2004 marked the debut of the first native feature film, *The Land Has Eyes*, directed by Vilsoni Hereniko (b. 1954–). It is also the first Fijian film to be submitted for consideration for an Academy Award.

Music & Dance:

The traditional music of Fiji consists mostly of vocal music and rhythmic accompaniment. It is performed during worship services and in a variety of traditional dances. In church, the choral music is generally rich and has many harmonies sung simultaneously. Typically, it is accompanied by traditional percussion instruments, including wooden drums, clap sticks, hand clapping, and foot stomping. Some foreign instruments may also be used, such as the guitar, ukulele, and mandolin.

The various traditional forms of dance remain an integral part of Fijian society, and are still widely practiced today. The meke is perhaps the best known, and comprises a number of forms of dance and music. Each meke is typically practiced by a group of dancers, called the matana, and set to music. It is mostly rhythmic musical accompaniment, traditionally performed on the lali ni meke, a wooden drum; the derua, bamboo tubes used for stomping on the ground or on mats; as well as foot stomping, clap sticks, and hand clapping. Often these accompaniments are complemented by chanting or singing. The musicians performing in the meke are called the vakatara.

Generally, dancers participating in the meke are all-male or all-female groups, dancing the same movements in unison. Men's dances include war dances, fan dances, and dances performed sitting down. They are generally very vigorous and aggressive, with much chanting and stamping. Women's dances include standing, sitting, and fan dances, and are generally slow and graceful, with lots of wrist, hand, and body movements. They often tell ancient stories and folk songs, and are accompanied by poetry. Male performers are dressed in full warrior costume while female performers are dressed in traditional skirts and jewelry.

Meke are composed and performed according to many rituals. For example, each meke is led by one man, called the dau ni vucu, who is responsible for coordinating the dance and accompanying movement, as well as any costumes, extra instruments, and poetry and songs. This man must have undergone a ritual, led by the local priest, to qualify.

Musical instruments may also have purposes that are more practical. For example, the lali drum, a large wooden drum with a sound that can travel for many miles, was traditionally used to announce significant events, such as wars, births, and deaths, through distinctive rhythmic patterns. The conch shell, with a hole cut into its side, is also used as a trumpet to signify special events. Both are still widely used in contemporary society.

Literature

Fiji has a strong oral tradition of storytelling that has held a greater place in the island nation's cultural history than written or recorded literature. Traditional Fijian stories typically concentrate on ancient myths, fables, and legends, such as creation stories and legends that explain the natural world. Popular legends include the story of Vuvu, a girl swallowed by a great fish and taken across the sea, and Dakuwaqa, a legend about the spirit that entered a shark. In addition, many of these stories and legends were also incorporated into the chants and songs sung as part of the meke. These oral traditions are now being written and codified in an attempt to preserve them.

Poetry also became an important literary device used to tell these many stories. It is recited, chanted, or sung as part of meke, or alone, as people gathered for recitations. Religious poetry, often rooted in Christianity, is old often recited or chanted at church. The literature of ethnic Fijians still often uses the traditional stories, while a second style of literature, known as Indo-Fijian literature, is quite different. Written by the ethnic Indians who were sent to Fiji as indentured laborers in the 1800s and their descendants, this literature focuses on that particular period in history and the oppression and struggle that was involved. More recently, Fijian literature has incorporated more Western-style devices, with writers increasingly writing in English since the latter half of the 20th century.

CULTURE

Arts & Entertainment:

With over 300 distinct islands—complete with separate dialects and cultural practices—and a large concentration of two distinct ethnicities, creating a cohesive national identity has been an ongoing challenge in Fiji. However, the contemporary arts have played a pivotal role in establishing the cultural and national identity of Fiji. In recent years, national identity has become a prominent theme in Fijian art, and the continued performance and practice of diverse and traditional artistic practices—from the meke to the skilled artisanship of traditional handicrafts—helps to shape cultural identity while maintaining a strong link with the past.

For Indian Fijians, literature in particular has been critical to their distinct cultural and national heritage. The shaping and importance of Fijian identity and its mixed culture, in general, is explored in the works of contemporary poets and writers such as Mohit Prasad and Teresia Kieuea Teaiwa. Another prominent Indo-Fijian writer is Satendra Nandan (1940–), an accomplished essayist, poet, and novelist who writes about modern Fiji, particularly from his view as a participant in Fijian politics (he served two years as the Minister of Health and Social Welfare, among other positions within government). In addition, *The Indo-Fijian Experience* chronicles significant works by Indian Fijian writers on the issue of identity.

The practice of ancient artistic traditions by ethnic Fijians remains an important way to preserve culture. Fijian-style music is still performed in church and at festivals and celebrations, and contemporary Fijian music groups still commonly sing in traditional Fijian styles. For example, the Qaliwai Trio tours the country performing traditional-style Fijian music, including some of the classic songs. The trio is one of the most popular groups in the country.

The contemporary arts have also been a critical way to galvanize power in the Fijian political system. Racial tensions have always existed between the ethnic Fijians and Indo-Fijians. Since independence in 1970, this conflict has influenced four separate military coups. The unique ability of the arts to bring people together, ignite passion, and help form a national or cultural identity has also helped to create these distinct racial and political divisions. Conversely, many Fijians argue that art is also the most powerful way to bring Fijians together.

Marching bands, parades, and beauty pageants are trademarks of the three city festivals held each year in Fiji. Nadi, known for its horseracing, is the home of the Bula Festival held each July. Suva is known for the Hibiscus Festival, held in November. Nicknamed the "Sugar City" for its sugar growing and processing industry, Lautoka celebrates the Sugar Festival each September.

Because of the varied religious and ethnic groups on the island, Fijian religious festivals are diverse. Festivals to celebrate Christmas, Diwali, and the prophet Mohammed are joined by a host of secular events held each year. Christmas is celebrated in Fiji, much as it is in the United States. Diwali is the Hindu festival of lights and celebrates the triumph of good over evil.

Cultural Sites & Landmarks

Fiji's natural environment and tropical climate are perhaps the most attractive qualities of the island nation and its rapidly developing tourist industry. The islands, of which there are more than 300, are surrounded by coral reefs and an abundance of marine life—over 1,000 species of fish can be found among the soft coral—offering world-class diving. The pleasant weather and beaches are also complemented by other geographical attractions, such as mountain ranges, rainforests, rivers, and caves.

However, Fijian traditions and ceremony continue to thrive in the villages and islands, providing a glimpse of the traditional way of life of Fijians. For example, many villages continue to stage traditional performances of meke, in addition to pottery and weaving demonstrations. There are numerous cultural and historic sites outside of the traditional Fiji villages, including the Fiji Museum and the Cultural Center at Orchid Island.

In the major cities of Suva and Nadi, there are many religious buildings, most notably Christian churches, Hindu temples, and Islamic mosques. These include the largest Hindu temple in Fiji, the Sri Siva Subramaniya Temple, located in Nadi. Landmarks in Suva include Suva City Library and the Government House, both examples of British colonial architecture, as well as the University of the South Pacific (USP). In addition, the government of Fiji has submitted the township and island of Levuka, Ovalau, for consideration as a World Heritage Site as designated by the United Nations Educational, Scientific and Cultural Organization (UNESCO). Considered the birthplace of modern Fiji, Levuka is historically significant as a colonial settlement and port.

Libraries & Museums

The Fiji Museum, which contains the largest collection of Fijian artifacts in the world, is located in the capital's botanical gardens. Collections range from prehistoric artifacts to the country's experience during World War II. The museum also contains a reference library and a collection of art from local artists.

The Fiji government's Legal Deposit Library houses all materials published within the country. Along with the Sir Alport Barker Memorial Library, it makes up the country's National Archives. Significant libraries are also maintained at the Fiji Institute of Technology (FIT), the University of the South Pacific (USP), and the Fiji School of Medicine.

Holidays

Fiji gained its independence from England on October 10, 1970. The anniversary of this event is commemorated each year on the national holiday known as Fiji Day. Other public holidays include Ratu Sir Lala Sukuna Day (May 30), in honor of Fiji's most prominent modern political leader.

Hindu holidays observed in Fiji include Diwali (October or November), the festival of lights; Holi (February or March), the festival of colors; and Ram Naumi (March or April).

Christian holidays, such as Christmas and Easter, as well as Muslim holidays like the Prophet Mohammed's birthday (July) are also celebrated.

Youth Culture

With the gradual urbanization of the population, and increased access to technology, a more global youth culture is emerging in Fiji. This exposure has made Fijian youth aware of more Westernized styles and images that are very different to the traditional way of life in Fiji. For example, one American study has found that since the introduction of television, the incidence of eating disorders among teenage girls has risen dramatically.(In Fiji, women have always desired to be reasonably big and curvy, and being thin was highly unattractive).

While this increasing urbanization has generally affected the music, trends, and recreational activities of youth in Fiji, it remains a phenomenon only for the few relatively wealthy or urban Fijians. In the country's urban areas, movie cinemas show films in English and Hindi (Bollywood films and music are very popular among Indo-Fijians), and Internet cafes allow youth to connect socially and play computer games. However, 60 percent of youth still live in rural areas, and access to technologies such as television and the Internet are still very limited in the early 21st century.

Although school attendance is not compulsory, attendance among children, aged six to fourteen is around 98 percent. However, beyond school, youth unemployment continues to be an issue in Fiji. Recently, the government has made efforts to assist young Fijians in finding employment. In terms of activities, one major focus of Fiji youth is rugby union. This particular sport remains the predominant recreation among Fiji youth, as well as the majority of the population. For example, even though television was only introduced in Fiji in 1994, it was brought it into the country three years earlier so that Fijians could view the rugby world cup. Other outdoors activities such as swimming, fishing, and football (soccer) are also popular among youth.

SOCIETY

Transportation

Walking remains the main form of transportation for local Fijians, and the ownership of vehicles is generally limited to urban and wealthy citizens. In urban areas, taxis are available. Buses are the main mode of public transportation on larger islands. For travel between islands, boats and ferries are most common. Automobile traffic in Fiji travels on the left side of the road.

Transportation Infrastructure

While a number of roads remain unpaved, mostly in remote areas, the network of highways is generally well maintained, largely due to Fiji's importance as a tourist destination. Fiji also has a private railway system, which is operated by the sugar industry, specifically the state-controlled Fiji Sugar Corporation (FSC). As such, it is not available for passenger travel.

There are two international airports in Fiji, with frequent flights to Australia, New Zealand, North America, Europe, and some Asian ports. Lambasa, Lautoka, and Suva are the three main ports.

Media & Communications

As a remote Pacific Island, and with a population traditionally reliant on subsistence agriculture and fishing, Fiji has been relatively slow to adopt communications technologies. The traditional form of communication between islands was the coded beating of drums and blowing of horns. Since colonization, a substantial number of newspapers and radio stations have been operating in all three national languages, and are accessible in all areas of Fiji. Other forms of communications technology, however, are less prevalent.

Fiji received access to television in 1994. The national public TV station is Fiji TV, which also has a satellite, pay-to-view service, provided by Sky Fiji, with over 25 channels. Local programs are provided in Fijian, Hindi, and English. The government estimates that over 60 percent of the population has television sets. Progress has also been made in recent decades to improve access to telephone lines on the islands. In the early 21st century alone, an estimated 288 villages were connected, but still only 72 percent of villages have access to telephone service. By 2015, cell phones outnumber landline phones. As of 2014, there were 181,800 internet users in Fiji, or around 21 percent of the population. Radio is the most popular source for entertainment and news, particularly on remote islands. The Fiji Broadcasting Network (FBN) operates five stations. Commercial stations broadcast in English, Fijian, and Hindi.

Media policy in Fiji is very modern and open. The constitutional right to freedom of expression is recognized and protected, and there have been no recent accusations of undue censorship.

SOCIAL DEVELOPMENT

Standard of Living

Fiji ranked 88th out of 187 countries on the 2013 United Nations Human Development Index, which measures quality of life and standard of living indicators.

Water Consumption

Fresh water is readily available on most of Fiji's islands. Many Fijians collect rainwater from roof systems that are subsequently used for household cooking and chores. Wells are also used, but some islands face pollution issues related to groundwater. The Fijian Public Works department oversees Suva's water infrastructure at the city's Wailuku Water Treatment Plant.

Education

Primary school education in Fiji is compulsory, with eight years of free education provided by the government. School for children in grades nine through twelve is not free, but some financial assistance is available.

Approximately 94 percent of the population over the age of fifteen can read and write. The capital of Suva is home to the University of the South Pacific and the Fiji School of Medicine. There are also many vocational and technical schools located in Suva.

Women's Rights

In traditional Fijian society, gender roles were very segregated and women had very little power. They were responsible for domestic duties, while the men worked, socialized, and made the majority of the decisions. However, as Fiji has modernized, its attitude toward women has also changed. Women are now an integral part of the modern workforce and achieve a standard of equality roughly equivalent to that in most countries. Furthermore, there are as many as eighteen female company directors, and multiple government programs to assist in the empowerment and equality for women, including a special government ministry for women, and a National Women's Advisory Council. Additionally, women have a literacy rate of 92 percent (compared to men at 96 percent).

Health Care

The national government of Fiji is responsible for providing its citizens with reasonable low cost health care. The Ministry of Health is responsible for the operation of urban and rural public health facilities, disease control research, administration of nursing homes, and health education.

GOVERNMENT

Structure

The Fijian political system has a history of instability due to the rivalry between native Fijians and Indians. Fiji has had two racially-motivated coups since gaining its independence in 1970. Although native Fijians claimed victory in the elections of 1987, the government was seen as being dominated by the Indian minority. A coup ensued resulting in a change in power. In 1999, the first Indian prime minister was elected, leading to yet another coup. The leader of the coup demanded that political power be guaranteed for the indigenous population. Due to international pressure, the coup was overturned.

Today, Fiji employs three branches of government: executive, legislative, and judicial. The president, who acts as chief of state and is elected by the Great Council of Chiefs to a five-year term, heads the executive branch. The Great Council of Chiefs is made up of the highest-ranking members of the traditional tribal system. The president appoints a prime minister, who acts as the head of the government.

The legislative branch consists of the Senate and the House of Representatives. The Senate has thirty-four seats and the House of Representatives has seventy-one seats, roughly two-thirds of which are reserved for the islands' various ethnic groups.

Political Parties

Fiji is home to a collection of small political parties that form coalitions in parliament (the Fijian Parliament consists of a house and senate). House leaders are elected representatives, whereas senators are nominated to their seats by governmental entities. Parliamentary coalitions include the Fiji First Party, the United Fiji Party (SDL), the Social Democratic Liberal Party, and the National Federation Party.

Local Government

Local government in Fiji is organized differently in urban and rural areas of the country. Urban areas have city and town councils, while rural areas have advisory councils. The island of Rotuma established its own island council in 1978.

Judicial System

The judicial branch consists of the Supreme Court, Court of Appeal, High Court, and Magistrates'

Courts. The Supreme Court is the highest court in the land, with the judges appointed by the president.

Taxation

The Fiji Inland Revenue and Customs Authority (FIRCA) oversee the Fijian taxation system. Fijians pay a variable income tax that ranges from 7 to 21 percent. Customs duties on goods entering Fiji range from 5 to 32 percent. Taxes are also collected by the Fijian government from cruise vessels, visiting yachts, and commercial vessels. The country's social security system is overseen by the Fiji National Provident Fund, which also administers disability and life insurance to Fijian citizens.

Armed Forces

The Republic of Fiji Military Forces (RFMF) consists of an infantry regiment and navy. A relatively small military, it is estimated at 3,500 strong, along with 6,000 reservists.

Foreign Policy

Fiji became an independent country in 1970 and has since pursued an active role in international affairs. It sees itself as a strong role model for other Pacific islands. It is a member of a number of international bodies, and plays a very active role in the South Pacific Forum.

The most important relationships it has are with its most significant trade partners: Australia, New Zealand, and India. It also highly values its relationships with its Pacific island neighbors, the Commonwealth of Nations—a voluntary organization consisting of independent states, many of which are former British colonies, and of which Fiji is a member—and the United States. Fiji has also prioritized forging stronger economic and trade relationships with its Asian neighbors to the north, particularly through its "Look North" policy. Notable memberships include the Asian Development Bank (ADB), the World Trade Organization (WHO), the International Labour Organization (ILO), and the UN, of which Fiji was the 127th member.

However, numerous military coups (and consequent illegal governments) have strained Fiji's foreign relations with Australia, New Zealand, the Commonwealth, and the U.S. These coups (two in 1987, one in 2000, and another in 2006) have resulted in the island nation's suspension from the Commonwealth and the negation of foreign aid. (After failing to meet a deadline to hold national elections by 2010, Fiji was fully suspended in September of 2009.) Fiji has also been involved in several disagreements with its Pacific neighbors, most notably a territorial dispute with Tonga and a trade dispute with Vanuatu that involved a ban on certain Fijian exports. In addition, Fiji was criticized for its decision to withdrawal from an international forum of Pacific island leaders in September 2008.

On March 14, 2014, the Commonwealth Ministerial Action Group voted to change Fiji's full suspension from the Commonwealth of Nations to a suspension from the councils of the Commonwealth, allowing them to participate in a number of Commonwealth activities, including the 2014 Commonwealth Games. The suspension was lifted in September 2014.

Human Rights Profile

International human rights law insists that states respect civil and political rights, and promote an individual's economic, social, and cultural rights. The United Nations Universal Declaration on Human Rights (UDHR) is recognized as the standard for international human rights. Its authors sought the counsel of the world's great thinkers, philosophers, and religious leaders, and were careful to create a document that reflects the core values shared by every world culture. (To read this document or view the articles relating to cultural human rights, visit http://www.udhr.org/UDHR/default.htm.)

In general, Fiji has a strong human rights profile, and is not singled out by human rights groups for systemic abuses. In 1997, the island nation established the Fiji Human Rights Commission, an independent body formed under the republic's constitution. The parliament passed the

Human Rights Commission Act 1999 two years later. However, human rights abuses have been reported, largely stemming from the country's various military coups and the governance of interim governments.

Many human rights organizations, most notably Amnesty International, have alleged that human rights have deteriorated since Fiji's last military takeover in 2006. In particular, the interim government has been accused of arbitrary arrest and detention, a violation of Article 9 of the UDHR; poor treatment of prisoners, a violation of Article 5; curtailing the rights to freedom of expression, a violation of Article 19; and freedom of movement and assembly and association, violations of Article 13 and 20, respectively. The coups themselves may also be criticized as violating the human right to governance by peaceful and fair elections and representation, a violation of Article 21.

Other human rights issues in Fiji have arisen simply because the island nation is undeveloped in terms of infrastructure and economy. As such, housing shortages, widespread poverty, and health issues have led to discrimination against those living in unstable or poor living conditions. This constitutes a violation of Article 25, which articulates the right to an adequate standard of living. With poor infrastructure in many remote villages and increasing urbanization in less remote areas, the increasing informal or squatter communities with no access to clean drinking water, sanitation and waste disposal are of concern. The Human Rights Commission investigated this issue in May 2008, and the government is continuing its efforts to improve the health and quality of life of its people.

Lastly, Fiji still maintains a 1944 law that criminalizes sexual acts between men, even though the 1997 constitution bans discrimination based on sexual orientation. However, a 2005 court ruling found this law to be unconstitutional, while maintaining that such acts are still illegal in public. While the government maintains that the country's views against homosexuals are now relaxed, many international rights groups claim that hostility against homosexual men is still prevalent.

Migration

A significant number of native Fijians continue to leave the islands for opportunities in North America and Australasia (Australia, New Zealand, New Guinea, and neighboring islands). Increasing political tensions and increasing incidents of social unrest have resulted in more Fijians choosing to emigrate overseas.

ECONOMY

Overview of the Economy

Economically, Fiji is full of contradictions. Its natural resources make it one of the healthiest economies of the Pacific Islands; however, almost half of the population survives on subsistence farming. The farming and processing of sugar accounts for a third of the country's industrial activity. Estimated gross domestic product (GDP) per capita was around $4,606 (USD) in 2013, with agriculture contributing 11.7 percent, industry, 18.1 percent, and services, 70.2 percent.

Unemployment is estimated at approximately 8.8 percent of the workforce, with most of the workers employed in the islands' larger cities. Many do not participate in the cash economy at all, choosing to live on what they can grow themselves. Fiji's main trading partners are Australia, New Zealand, and India, as well as Japan and England.

Industry

The two mainstays of the Fijian economy are the sugar and service industries. The service industry employs nearly 57 percent of the workforce. About 28 percent of the workforce is employed in agriculture, forestry, and fishing. The demand for Fiji's forest resources has increased significantly in recent years.

Industrial pursuits include mining, manufacturing, and construction. Industry employs approximately 15 percent of the workforce. Gold and silver are the main exports of the mining industry, while the garment industry is the flagship enterprise of the manufacturing interests.

Labor

In 2013, Fiji's unemployment rate was an estimated 8.8 percent. Agriculture is the largest employment sector, particularly sugar production. However, many of those who are included in the country's agricultural sector work in the realm of subsistence farming. An increasing number of Fijian's are employed in the country's growing tourism industry.

Energy/Power/Natural Resources

Fiji has considerable natural resources, including an abundance of marine life and timber. Gold and copper are also mined in small quantities, and there are potential offshore oil resources. Hydropower serves as a source of energy for the islands.

Although it is known as a tropical paradise, Fiji is facing some pressing environmental issues. The oceans that border Suva and other large cities are becoming polluted; the demand for timber has resulted in deforestation and soil erosion; and erosion has, in turn, caused damage to the coral reef, as the silt runoff smothers the living coral.

The government has reacted by protecting parts of Fiji. Bouma National Heritage Park has been established to protect nearly the entire island of Taveuni. The Fijian government has also signed international environmental agreements concerning a wide range of issues including ozone, marine life, and deforestation.

Fishing

Fiji's fishing industry represents an integral part of the country's economy and culture. Among the species harvested in the waters surrounding the islands include barracuda, marlin, and tuna. In 2008, the country's fishing industry provided an estimated $200 million annually to Fiji's overall GDP. In recent decades, the government has sold fishing licenses to foreign-based vessels in the effort to increase revenue. However, the incursion of foreign fishing fleets into Fijian waters constitutes a major challenge to the future of the Fiji fishing industry and threatens the livelihood of many native Fijians.

Forestry

Hardwood trees are one of the primary natural resources of the island nation of Fiji and account for an estimated 1.1 percent of the country's GDP. Over 50 percent of the Fijian islands are forested, and the country's forestry industry is growing. Timber is Fiji's third-largest export commodity. The country's Department of Forestry continues to oversee the modernization of the island's forestry industry and ensures that the resources are used in an environmentally sustainable manner.

Mining/Metals

Fiji has small but rich deposits of silver and gold, as well as other mineral resources such as copper, lead, zinc, and gravel. Limestone is mined for cement production. Political stability has hampered mining production and investment in the early 21st century. In 2010, a Chinese mining company announced plans to begin bauxite mining in Fiji.

Agriculture

In Fiji there are a large number of people who participate in subsistence level farming and produce no goods for export. There are also large commercial plantations that grow sugarcane, coconuts, cassava, sweet potatoes, and bananas. Sugarcane is the most widely grown commercial crop, while rice is widely grown by subsistence farmers.

Following a tropical cyclone in March 2010, the Fiji government allocated $2.6 million to help rehabilitate the agricultural sector.

Animal Husbandry

Fijian farmers raise cattle, sheep, horses, and goats. However, the animals are raised for domestic consumption. Although fish exports are an important part of the Fijian economy, the country does not export economically significant numbers of livestock.

Tourism

Roughly 658.000 tourists visit Fiji each year. The tourism industry adds over $700 million USD to the economy annually. Fiji's sometimes-unstable political environment and severe weather have caused some disruptions in this vital industry in the past. Two coups in the late 1980s not only affected tourism, but also caused a great migration of skilled Indian workers out of the country.

The capital of Suva, on the southeast coast of Viti Levu, is the most sophisticated urban center in the country. It is the political and administrative hub for the island chain and has many modern as well as colonial era architectural offerings.

The main attraction for tourists visiting Fiji is the city of Nadi, on the western side of Viti Levu. Set against a mountainous backdrop, Nadi is widely considered the most beautiful spot in the country. It relies almost entirely on income from tourism, and as such offers, nearly everything a tourist could need. Tourists and pilgrims alike visit the city's Sri Siva Subramaniya temple, as it is the largest Hindu temple in the Southern Hemisphere.

Many of the smaller islands provide excellent snorkeling and other outdoor activities. As some small islands do not receive many visitors, it is customary to ask for the chief's permission to visit certain villages.

Alice Ashbolt, Christopher Stetter, M. Lee

DO YOU KNOW?

- Because Suva city receives so much rainfall throughout the year, Suva residents refer to the western region of the island of Vita Levu, which is extremely dry in comparison, as "the burning west."

- On display in the Maritime section of the Fiji Museum is the rudder of the HMS Bounty, a British ship made famous due to a mutiny in 1789.

Bibliography

Becker, Anne E. *Body, Self and Society: The View from Fiji.* Philadelphia: University of Pennsylvania Press, 1995.

Katz, Richard. *The Straight Path: A Story of Healing and Transformation in Fiji.* New York: Addison-Wesley Publishing Company, 1993.

Ravuvu, Asesela. *Vaki I Taukei: The Fijian Way of Life.* Suva: Pacific Studies of the University of the South Pacific, 1983.

Ryan, Paddy. *Fiji's Natural Heritage.* Wollombi: Exisle Publishing, 2000.

Stanley, David. *Moon Fiji* (Moon Handbooks). Berkeley: Avalon Travel Publishing, 2011.

Starns, Dean, et al. *Fiji (Travel Guide).* Oakland, CA: Lonely Planet, 2012.

Troost, J. Maarten. *Getting stoned with savages: a trip through the Islands of Fiji and Vanuatu.* New York: Broadway Books, 2008.

Wright, Ronald, *On Fiji Islands.* New York: Viking, 1986

Works Cited

Australearn, Fiji http://www.australearncanada.org/ destinations/fiji/cities/

"Background to Fiji's four coups." http://news.bbc.co.uk/1/ hi/world/asia-pacific/6209486.stm

Cotton, Caroline. "Everywhere is Home: Rhythms of Native Life in Fiji." Accessed at http://www. transitionsabroad.com/listings/living/articles/living_in_ fiji_rhythms_of_native_life.shtml.

Ewins, Rod, "Fijian Art." http://www.justpacific.com/fiji/ fijianart/artintro.pdf

"Fiji." CIA World Factbook http://www.cia.gov/library/ publications/the-world-factbook/geos/fj.html

"Fiji". Nations of the world: a political, economic, and business handbook. 14th ed. Amenia, NY: Grey House Publishing, 2014

"Fiji 2015". Index of economic freedom http://heritage.org/ index/country/fiji

Fiji FAQs and Fiji Facts http://www.fiji-faqs.com/index. cfm/city/20/suva.html

"Fiji GDP and economic data". Global finance http:// gfmag.com/global_data/fiji-gdp-country-report

Fiji Government Online Portal http://www.fiji .gov.fj/

"Fiji Houses." Polynesian Cultural Centre. http://www. polynesia.com/fiji/fijian-houses.html

Fiji Human Rights Commission. http://www.humanrights.
   org.fj/

"Fiji: internet usage, broadband, and telecommunications
   reports." Internet World Stats. http://internetworldstats.
   com/sp/fj.htm

"Fiji Islands Art Guide" http://www.fiji-island.com/tourist-
   information/arts.html

"Fiji Music." http://www.janesoceania.com/fiji_music/
   index.htm

"Fiji – Report on Human Rights Practices, 2010." http://
   www.state.gov/g/drl/rls/hrrpt/2010/eap/154384.htm

"Fiji tax profile 2014." KPMG http://home.kping.com/
   content/dam/kping/pdf/2015/03/fiji-tax-profile-2014.pdf

"Fiji telephones." Trip advisor http://tripadvisor.com/
   travel=g299331-s605/fijitelephones.html

"Fiji Village Etiquette," Bula Fiji (Fiji Visitor's Bureau).
   http://www.bulafiji.com/page.php?id=11

"Fiji Village Guides." http://pacific-travel-guides.com/fiji-
   islands/eco-tourism/village.html

"Fiji Visitor's Bureau." http://www.bulafiji.com/index.php

"Fijian Art, Essays, and Papers/" http://www.justpacific.
   com/fiji/fijianart/index.html

"Fijian Myths and Legends." http://www.upei.ca/~meincke/
   fijimyth.htm

"Human Rights Watch – Fiji." http://hrw.org/
   doc/?t=asia&c=fiji

"Language," Rob Kay's Fiji Guide. http://www.fijiguide.
   com/Facts/language.html

Madraiwiwi, Ratu Joni. "Governance in Fiji: The interplay
   between indigenous tradition, culture, and politics."
   http://epress.anu.edu.au/ssgm/global_gov/mobile_
   devices/ch15.html

Oceanic arthttp://www.britannica.com/EBchecked/
   topic/424484/Oceanic-art/14316/Fiji-Tonga-and-Samoa

"The people. Fiji Guide." http://fijiguide.com/page/the-
   people

Tamata, Apolynia, "The Story of the Fijian Story-teller."
   http://www.usp.ac.fj/fileadmin/files/others/vakavuku/
   fijianstoryteller.doc

"Vocal music of the Fiji Islands." http://encarta.msn.com/
   media_461519190/vocal_music_of_the_fiji_islands
   .html

"Women, Peace and Security Resources: Fiji." http://www.
   peacewomen.org/resources/Fiji/fijiindex.html

KIRIBATI

Introduction

The Republic of Kiribati (pronounced KIR-i-bas or KIR-i-bati) is a combination of three island groups (the Gilbert Islands, the Phoenix Islands, and the Line Islands) located in the South Pacific Ocean, about halfway between Hawaii and Australia. Comprised of thirty-three coral atolls, the country covers an ocean area roughly equal to the size of the continental United States, halfway between Australia and Hawaii. More than twenty of the islands are inhabited. The Gilbert Islands, named for British mariner Thomas Gilbert, along with the Phoenix Islands and the Line Islands became a British protectorate by 1892 and a colony by 1915. The Japanese captured the area during World War II and several bloody battles between U.S. and Japanese forces occurred on the Makin (now called Butaritari) and Tarawa atolls in 1943. The country gained its independence from the United Kingdom on July 12, 1979 and took the new name, Republic of Kiribati.

Kiribati is renowned for its picturesque scenery and wildlife, but contains few natural resources. The United Nations' Development Policy and Analysis Division (DPAD) has considered the country a least developed country (LDC) since 1986. In addition, pollution caused by overpopulation and lagoon latrines, particularly on the Tarawa atoll, have threatened the attractive natural environment, and as ocean levels have continued to rise in the early twenty-first century, the islands are becoming increasingly smaller and uninhabitable.

GENERAL INFORMATION

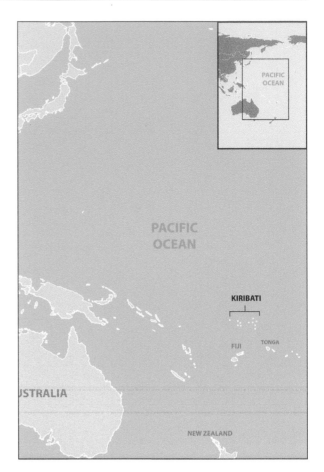

Official Language(s): English
Population: 105,711 (2015)
Currency: Kiribati dollar
Coins: The Kiribati dollar is pegged to the Australian dollar. Coins are available in denominations of 5, 10, 20, and 50 cents, and 1 and 2 dollars.
Land Area: 811 square kilometers (313 square miles)
National Motto: Te Mauri, Te Raoi ao Te Tabomoa (Health, Peace and Prosperity)
National Anthem: "Teirake Kaini Kiribati" ("Stand Up, Kiribati")
Capital: Tarawa
Time Zone: GMT +12; in 1995, Kiribati proclaimed all of its islands are under a single time zone, even though some are on the other side of the International Date Line.
Flag Description: Kiribati's elaborate flag design consists of a rising golden sun with nineteen

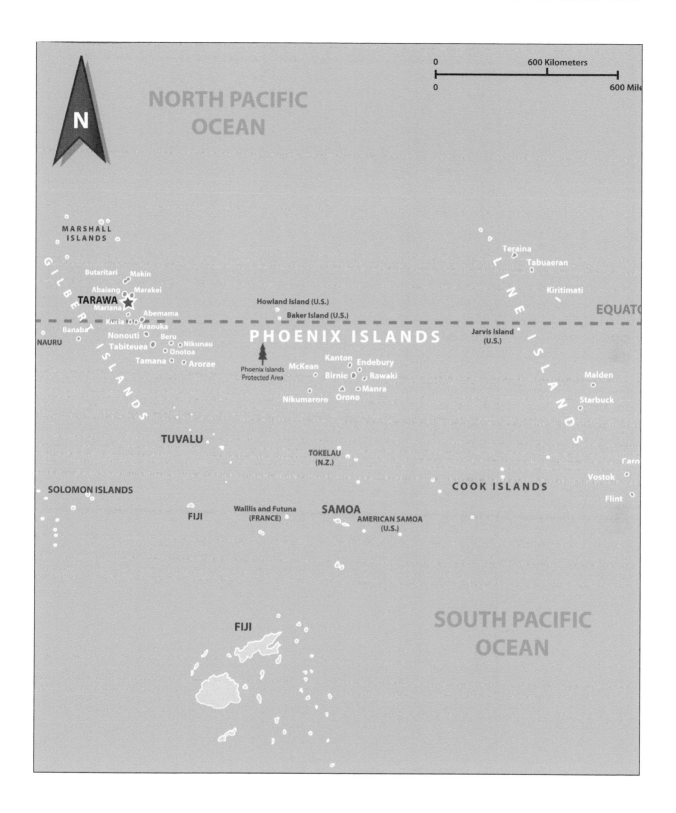

Principal Cities on South Tarawa Island (2010):

- Betio (15,755)
- Bikenibeu (6,568)
- Teaoraereke (4,171)
- Bairiki (3,524)
- Eita (3,061)
- Bonriki (2,355)

straight and wavy rays against a dark red field (or background). Above the rising sun (which is half concealed beneath the waves) is a golden frigate bird in flight. The flag's lower half is dark blue, and consists of three horizontal wavy stripes of white, representing the three island groups. Concepts symbolized by the flag include power, freedom, and native culture, including Kiribati dance patterns.

Population

Kiribati's population, known as I-Kiribati, is overwhelmingly of Micronesian ethnicity, with I-Kiribati comprising 89.5 percent and mixed I-Kiribati ethnicities at 9.7 percent. The Tuvaluan, who are of Polynesian origin, account for 0.1 and other ethnicities account for .8 percent of the population.

Approximately 90 percent of the population lives on the Gilbert Island chain; about 50,182 inhabit the islets of South Tarawa, according to the 2010 census, and approximately 15,755 live on Betio (BE-so) islet. The amenities and educational opportunities available in the capital, as compared to the underdeveloped outer islands, draw South Tarawa's large population. In fact, over half of Kiribati's population lives on South Tarawa, and many have moved there from the outer islands. Overcrowding and unsanitary conditions in South Tarawa have led to government-sponsored relocation programs, but continued high population growth has undermined these efforts.

The population is young, with nearly 31 percent of people in Kiribati under the age of fourteen, and just over 65 percent between the ages of fifteen and sixty-four. Average life expectancy

at birth is sixty-eight years for women and sixty-three years for men (2015 estimate).

Languages

While English is the official language, I-Kiribati is widely spoken. The language is part of the Austronesian linguistic family and related to the Micronesian and Polynesian languages. Missionaries from Hawaii, notably Hiram Bingham II (1831–1908)—the first to translate the Bible into I-Kiribati—invented the written language, which uses the 'ti' letter combination to make the 's' sound.

Native People & Ethnic Groups

The islands of Kiribati were first settled by Micronesian people as early as 3,000 BCE. Later arrivals included Polynesian people from Fiji, Tonga, and Samoa. Because of intermarriage and intermixing, the modern population is comprised of a blending of these ethnic groups.

The ancient inhabitants of Kiribati were warlike people, clad in woven armor made of coconut fiber (coir) and armed with shark-tooth swords (trunun). A seafaring people, it is believed that they traveled long distances in outrigger canoes. Europeans began arriving in Kiribati during the 16th century, with the British claiming the islands in the late 19th century.

Religions

Missionaries during the 19th century, especially after 1852, introduced Christianity to the islands. More than 55 percent of the population practices Roman Catholicism. Over 33 percent are adherents of the Kempsville Presbyterian Church, while 4.7 are Mormon, and two percent are Seventh Day Adventist. As of 2015, there was also a small (2.3 percent) Baha'i population, as well.

Climate

Kiribati's climate is tropical, with hot and humid conditions moderated to some extent by trade winds. Because the islands straddle the equator, temperatures are relatively stable, and the country does not experience seasons. Proximity to the equator also brings a blindingly bright midday sun to all the islands. The average year-round temperature is 28° Celsius (83° Fahrenheit). Southeast trade winds blow from March to November, and the wetter westerly winds blow through the rest of the year.

Annual rainfall totals range from 117 centimeters (46 inches) on Onotoa to 311 centimeters (122 inches) on Butaritari. The islands north of the equator have their wettest season from June to November, while those to the south experience heavy rainfall between November and April. In addition, while the country experiences occasional typhoons, there is no designated typhoon or monsoon season. Cyclone Pam, a Category 5 tropical cyclone, indirectly affected Kiribati in March 2015, causing great damage due to heavy flooding.

The climate of South Tarawa is tropical and characterized by hot and humid weather. Its average annual temperature for South Tarawa is roughly 28° Celsius (82° Fahrenheit), though temperatures can typically be 10° lower on the islands in the North Pacific Ocean. The islands experience occasional droughts and strong winds from the ocean.

ENVIRONMENT & GEOGRAPHY

Topography

Kiribati consists of three island groups: the Gilbert Islands, the Phoenix Islands, and the Line Islands, which together are spread over 3.5 million square kilometers (1,351,357 square miles). In general, the country consists of coral atolls with extensive offshore reefs. White sand beaches and deep lagoons create a stunning landscape.

There are no rivers in Kiribati, but some islands have freshwater lagoons. Kiritamati (Christmas Island), the largest coral atoll in the world, accounts for 50 percent of the country's land mass.

The islands are all low-lying, making them exceptionally vulnerable to rising sea levels. Scientists have suggested that the islands of Kiribati may one day have to be abandoned before the sea covers them. The highest point in the country is an unnamed point on Banaba, at 81 meters (266 feet) above sea level.

South Tarawa is located on the mast-shaped atoll of Tarawa, one of the thirty-two atolls (a ring-shaped coral island that partially encloses a lagoon) and lone raised coral island that form the nation of Kiribati. Located in Micronesia—a vast region in the Pacific Ocean encompassing hundreds of small islands—Kiribati is separated by the equator, with islands in both the North and South Pacific Oceans. South Tarawa itself is a part of the Gilbert Islands, which consist of sixteen of Kiribati's thirty-three island masses, and is situated roughly 2,800 miles northeast of Australia, and 2,500 miles southwest of Hawaii.

South Tarawa consists of a horizontal line of islets, all of which are inhabited. The Southern branch of Tarawa, stretching from the islet of Betio to the islet of Bonriki, makes up the region that is South Tarawa. The larger islets of South Tarawa are connected by causeways and the smaller ones are reached by boat. South Tarawa is one of the most populated regions of the South Pacific, with 3,184 people per square kilometer (8,247 people per square mile), and spans 15.76 square kilometers (6.08 square miles).

The islets of South Tarawa are located at an average altitude of three to six meters (ten to twenty feet) above sea level and—with ocean levels rising in recent years—the land mass of South Tarawa has been reduced, further worsening the issue of overpopulation. In addition, the construction of the causeways running between the islets has also reportedly altered ocean currents, also making the islets more susceptible to immersion. In 2000, the World Bank estimated that nearly one-quarter to one-half of South Tarawa would be underwater by 2050. Because coastal erosion has also become a serious concern, the Ministry of Environment, Lands and Agriculture Development (MELAD) has begun planting mangrove and ironwood trees, whose root systems strengthen coastal areas and provide shelter for the development of coral.

South Tarawa's dense population, the changing of the tidal currents due to causeway construction, an overloaded sewage system, and other waste management concerns have made it very susceptible to pollution. Natives and visitors are often discouraged from swimming in the water, and pollution has lowered the number of fish available for consumption, a particular difficulty for a nation that relies on the sea for food.

Plants & Animals

The prevalent coconut palm not only provides food for the I-Kiribati, but is also the source of the country's main exports. Other common plants found on the islands include the Starbuck Island Daisy, bunchgrass, seaside scrub, banana trees, mangroves, and pandanus trees, whose fruit is important to the I-Kiribati diet.

Wildlife is scarce on dry land in Kiribati. Common animals include the Polynesian rat, seabirds, and a few species of lizards. Up to 8 million sooty terns migrate through Kiritimati (Christmas Island) each year. Other bird species typically spotted on the islands include tropicbirds, boobies (related to gannets), frigate birds, and noddies (a member of the tern family). Birds endemic to Kiribati are the endangered Bokikokiko, also known as the Kiritimati Reed Warbler (Christmas Island Warbler).

Marine life is abundant around all the islands. Land crabs thrive on Kiritimati (Christmas Island). Pacific bonefish, gray sharks, marlins, and stingrays also abound in the ocean surrounding Kiribati.

CUSTOMS & COURTESIES

Greetings

English is the official language of Kiribati and is used in all administrative and educational functions. Most islanders also speak I-Kiribati, or 'Gilbertese,' a language in the Austronesian lan-

guage group that is descended from the original language of the Kiribati natives. The main greeting used is "Mauri" ("Hello," also "Welcome"), with another basic greeting being "Ko na mauri" ("You be well"). Some might alternatively ask, "Ko uara?" ("How are you?"). Shaking hands is the common gesture of greeting. New acquaintances tend to limit contact to handshakes, while friends and family frequently embrace.

Gestures & Etiquette

The I-Kiribati are characteristically modest and conservative, and emphasize appropriate clothing, such as knee-length dresses for women. The I-Kiribati also consider the head to be the most important part of the human body and feel it is unacceptable to touch a person's head without permission, particularly the crown. Pointing is also considered disrespectful, and it is more common for I-Kiribati to point by inclining their head and indicating with their noses. Additionally, direct eye contact, particularly with an elder or other figure of advanced status is considered inappropriate. To signify agreement, I-Kiribati might raise their eyebrows, a gesture that some cultures use to signify surprise. Raised eyebrows also signify acceptance and approval. Lastly, public affection is frowned upon, and unmarried men and women are not supposed to be alone together.

Food is the most important commodity on Kiribati and islanders take the distribution of food seriously. Family members follow a strict protocol regarding the distribution of food and may take offense to guests taking food out of turn or eating more than warranted by the person's social status. If given the choice to eat first, the guest should always offer a small amount of food to the dominant male in the group.

Eating/Meals

The I-Kiribati generally have their daily meals whenever food is available. For example, the first meal of the day for villagers is usually when the agricultural workers of the family return home after their first shift, usually bringing coconut sap and fish with them. The family may not eat again until the late evening, when the workers return from the second coconut harvest. Tidal phases may also affect eating customs, and some families may eat in the middle of the night, when many of the island's fish are caught. This traditional late night meal is called te tairaa, and usually consists of fresh fish or leftovers from the evening meal. Even in urban areas, it is not uncommon for families to rise in the late night or early morning to eat a meal of fish before returning to sleep.

Island residents in the modern urban environment may take meals similar to those in Western countries—such as breakfast, lunch, and dinner—while those living in villages and rural areas eat on a different schedule. Generally, breakfast is light fare and may consist of tea, bread, fish, and rice. Lunch may also typically consist of fish and rice, while canned meats and other dishes might be served for dinner. Meals might also consist of leftovers from the previous meal.

Most I-Kiribati meals are traditionally served family style, with the women of the house bringing the food to the children and men who are gathered. Only after the men have begun eating will the women sit to join in the meal. The oldest male is usually served first and males are given their choice of any of the food available before women and children. When food is scarce, women may be left with only remnants from the meal they have prepared. The entire family customarily eats together, often including extended family members. Respect for elders and guests remains an important part of the traditional island culture of Kiribati. Elder males and guests are also given special priority during meals.

Visiting

The I-Kiribati make a point of inviting friends and family into their homes on a regular basis. Because agriculture is difficult in Kiribati and food scarcity is a major concern for many families, offering food to guests is considered an important gesture of generosity. As such, I-Kiribati may take offence if a person, even a stranger, refuses to join them for a family meal.

A guest will often be offered their choice of food from the communal dish. In standard I-Kiribati etiquette, the guest should then break off a piece of food and offer it to the elder male in the home. After the elder male has accepted and eaten the offering, the rest of the family will then commence eating. Visitors should not eat until full, as this is might be perceived as an indication of selfishness. However, pretending to be sated is an act of appreciation visitors might bestow upon their hosts.

It is not expected for guests to bring presents when visiting a home, but most hosts will appreciate small items of food, sweets, liquor, and other small gifts. It is also considered appropriate for guests to bring toys or candies for the host's children. Guests typically avoid extravagant gifts, as this may be off-putting and call attention to the family's financial status.

LIFESTYLE

Family

The nuclear family is the primary unit of I-Kiribati society and the mwenga, or home, traditionally consists of a couple, either married or unmarried, and their children. Polygamy was once common in Kiribati, but has been replaced by monogamous partnerships, as natives have been converted to Christianity. Marriage rates continue to be high on the islands in comparison to European and North American nations, and divorce is uncommon in Kiribati, though it has become more common in the twenty-first century. Many marriages also continue to be arranged, especially in rural areas. Following marriage, the wife usually moves to live with the husband's extended family or tribe.

The extended family system is important to I-Kiribati culture and forms the basis of the island's clans and tribes. Young couples rely on parents, grandparents, and other members of the clan to help with child rearing and other assistance, such as food or money. Each extended family has a unimane, or elder male, who is the traditional leader of the tribal group. The unimane is the tribal executive and gives council at the maneaba, or meeting house, which is at the center of the territory controlled by the tribe.

The unimane from each tribe may meet with groups of traditional leaders gather to discuss issues affecting the island and society as a whole. While church organizations and political organizations have begun to eclipse the traditional authority of the unimane, the traditional leaders of each group and family still exercise significant influence in the lower levels of island politics through cooperative lobbying.

Housing

Modern structures are gradually replacing the traditional I-Kiribati home, which was an open-sided, thatched rectangular hut. Modern houses constructed of brick or concrete block instead of wood are now common, and corrugated metal has begun to replace thatched fronds as the primary roofing material. Urban districts such as Christmas Island and Tarawa also contain apartments and shared housing units. Rural homes and structures will commonly still use natural resources, such as bamboo for floors; coral or pandanus wood for support beams; and coconut husks, called coir, for floor mats and even mattresses. Family compounds traditionally have separate buildings for sleeping, socializing, cooking, and storage.

In rural areas, villages take the form of irregular groups of houses surrounding some natural feature, such as a productive agricultural area or a source of water. Most villages are located near the ocean, and may contain a makeshift dock made from wood and stone. At the center of the village, the community constructs a mwaneaba, or meeting house. This is usually an open-sided building where community members gather for group activities, celebrations, and to discuss issues affecting the community. Indoor plumbing is uncommon in rural areas and several families may share central sanitary and cooking facilities.

Families may also cooperate to build and maintain small gardens and pens for livestock.

Food

The cuisine of Kiribati is similar to other Pacific and Polynesian cuisines, and relies heavily on locally grown starches and imported foods, such as canned meats and the fruits and vegetables that do not grow well in Kiribati's sandy soil. Seafood, coconut, pandanus fruit, breadfruit, yams, and taro are primary ingredients of traditional dishes, and rice is a staple dish served with meals. The giant, elephant-ear-shaped leaves and starchy corm of the taro plant are eaten roasted or boiled, often with banana and coconut. Taro is also boiled and mashed as a side dish, and ingredients used to flavor the taro include coconut milk, spicy peppers, salt, and fish oil. In places that lack refrigeration, fish and other seafood may be salted and dried or smoked for preservation. Pork and chicken are also common and curry dishes are popular. A common delicacy is palusami, which is coconut cream with curry powder and sliced onions wrapped in taro leaves.

Fish is the most common protein source on the islands. The most common preparation for fish, especially white fish, is to boil the fish meat and serve with starchy breadfruit or yams. Another common preparation is to roast fish meat wrapped in coconut leaves, over an open fire. Fish is often seasoned with salt, coconut milk, and spicy peppers. I-Kiribati prepare pork in the same way as fish, either roasted or boiled and usually served with breadfruit or other vegetables. Coconut is included in both savory and sweet recipes and is often used to make broth or sauce for entrees. It is customary for the I-Kiribati to combine sweet flavors whenever fish is served. Relishes incorporating coconut and banana are eaten with salty or oily fishes, such as porpoise, mullet, and salt cod.

Among many recipes for pandanus, a group of plants that is commonly used in Southeast Asian and Oceanic cooking, I-Kiribati have developed a drink known as te kabubu. The concoction is made by mixing water with the dried meat of the pandanus fruit. The meat of the fruit is then subjected to a complex process involving steam cooking and roasting in coconut leaves until a dry mash is produced. This desiccated pulp is then ground by hand into a powder, which is mixed with water to make a drink. Te kabubu was originally developed to accompany religious ceremonies and is still used in ceremonial functions. The drink has a purgative property—it can induce vomiting if taken in significant quantity—but also contains many of the most essential vitamins and minerals and used for sustenance, particularly when food becomes scarce.

Another drink common in Kiribati is the coconut toddy, which is made from the sap of the coconut flower. Coconut sap is usually harvested in the morning by making an incision at the base of the coconut flower and allowing the sap to drain into a collection vessel. Sap is usually collected immediately before sunrise and again just before sunset. In its raw form, and mixed with water, the sap makes a sweet drink that is high in nutrients. Within fifteen hours of harvesting, coconut sap begins to ferment and I-Kiribati also consume the fermented coconut sap for its intoxicating qualities.

Life's Milestones

Approximately 96 percent of I-Kiribati is Catholic or Protestant. Most individuals on the islands follow the traditional Christian rites of passage including baptism, marriage, and funerary customs. Social gatherings in Kiribati, called botakis, are held for most milestones and for basic reasons, such as engagements, birthdays, or visits. These gatherings range in scale and may be island-wide or involve the meeting of a few friends and family. These gatherings traditionally include speeches, singing, dancing, and other events that are held in the mwaneaba (meeting house).

The birth of a new child is a cause for celebration since it significantly enhances the prestige and social stature of the parents within I-Kiribati society. Members of the extended family will often pay the parents a visit, bringing

gifts or money to aid the couple with expenses. The family spares little expense to provide a feast of rare foods and invites both family and friends to the celebration. Families sometimes choose to roast an entire pig at the baptism celebration, representing a significant investment on the part of the family.

Marriage marks the traditional transition to adulthood. While most marriages take place with the aid of a protestant or Catholic minister, traditional tribal customs are also observed. The bride and husband usually wear traditional I-Kiribati wedding clothing and the parents arrange many marriages. However, arranged marriages are decreasing amongst youth in the twenty-first century. In I-Kiribati custom, the husband makes an offering of land for permission to marry the bride. Land ownership has also been important in I-Kiribati culture, and this traditional wedding gift custom is still observed in Kiribati, especially among rural populations.

The I-Kiribati funeral is a blend of Western and traditional tribal custom. Most families hold a wake for the deceased and invite a large number of their extended family to attend. Family members share food and socialize at the wake followed by a celebration with dancing and singing to accompany the ceremonies. Family members will commonly invite the family pastor or priest to give a blessing at the funeral, but may also pay homage to the traditional tribal gods. Livestock like beef and pork is rarely consumed on a daily basis in Kiribati, but is often eaten at funerals and other special occasions. Neighbors and friends will usually contribute meat to the feast at the wake.

CULTURAL HISTORY

Art

Traditional I-Kiribati weaving techniques are part of the nation's cultural heritage, but are maintained primarily by inheritance. Traditionally, mothers pass on the art to their children. Some professional I-Kiribati weavers sell woven blankets, clothing, and other goods to tourists through markets in South Tarawa or other venues. Weavers utilize the leaves of the pandanus and coconut plants to create a variety of crafts, from clothing and mats to household decorations and ceremonial items. Other traditional art forms include elaborate string figures, wooden baskets, and shell jewelry.

Music & Dance

Kiribati is known throughout the Pacific Islands for its music, which includes a variety of folk songs and complex group dances. Possessing only a few traditional instruments, early I-Kiribati musicians tended to concentrate on vocalizing, such as chanting, and percussion. In a typical song, a single singer might carry the key melody, while a group of singers sang the chorus. The I-Kiribati used their own bodies as percussion instruments, as well as a variety of drums, made from wood and dried gourds, sticks, and the conch shell.

Many of the early songs and dances created in Kiribati were used to accompany religious, social, and cultural ceremonies. For example, the te kaimatoa and te taubwati are two patterned dances similar to Western line dancing in that they are performed in groups standing in parallel rows. The te buki (swaying hip dance) is performed by a synchronized group of dancers, usually women, as a chorus of men provide percussion by striking wooden boxes or clapping their hands in rhythmic patterns. Many of the songs focus on spiritualism or relate to daily activities, such as canoe building or fishing. Traditional love songs were also popular. While contemporary I-Kiribati musicians may use modern instrumentation, including guitar, drums, and electronic instruments, most I-Kiribati musicians retain the traditional skills of their ancestors.

The unique dance styles of Kiribati have influenced dancers across the Pacific and are considered an essential part of I-Kiribati cultural heritage. Kiribati had no written language to preserve the cultural heritage of its peoples, so music and dances were used to tell stories, transmitting information about history and culture.

Many dance styles retain this communicative, ceremonial function. The stick dance, reserved for festivals and other community celebrations, was developed as an accompaniment to stories told by village elders.

I-Kiribati dancers must learn to control each part of their bodies and to coordinate closely with the music. The movements of the arms, legs, hands and the expressions of the face are all performed in concert with changes in the music. The facial expressions are especially important in I-Kiribati dancing, as they are used to enhance the communicative message of the music. I-Kiribati dancers are also known for their unique head movements, which are often compared to the movements of native bird species. Men and women traditionally dance in rows or groupings that are divided by gender.

CULTURE

Arts & Entertainment

While the I-Kiribati are exceedingly proud of their native artistic accomplishments, the government lacks the resources to provide funding for artistic projects. In addition, artists lack the supplies necessary for creative forms of expression such as painting. Most artists work in traditional art forms, and fund their work by selling their crafts in South Tarawa and through online vendors. While government funding and assistance is limited, a number of private organizations provide funds for artists whose work promotes native culture.

I-Kiribati dancing, which is similar to dance styles in Hawaii and elsewhere in the Pacific region, is considered part of the nation's cultural heritage. As such, it is supported through government programs that promote and fund dancing education. In addition, the public school system includes basic art, music, and dance classes for children in a joint effort to promote fitness and maintain the traditional culture of the island natives.

Self-defense and traditional martial arts are also central components of I-Kiribati culture and national heritage. In traditional I-Kiribati society, men were expected to train in combat skills and become warriors. The first tribes that formed on the islands used single-combat to settle disagreements and establish the dominant hierarchies between clans. Combatants wore armor woven from coir (coconut fiber), and they fought with swords made from woven plant reeds studded with sharks' teeth, which created a serrated edge.

In addition to ceremonial dueling, the I-Kiribati developed several indigenous martial arts styles, which have been passed through private tutelage for centuries. Unlike Asian martial arts, I-Kiribati martial artists do not use kicking attacks, but instead emphasize fast hand movements to overwhelm opponents. In addition to unarmed combat, I-Kiribati martial artists utilize sticks, swords, and spears as weapons. The martial arts of Kiribati are largely defensive, teaching students to anticipate and react to attacks from their opponents.

The martial arts of Kiribati were not known outside of the island until the twentieth century, as they were kept secret within I-Kiribati clans. Several prominent families developed their own unique techniques, which have since developed into distinct schools of martial arts training. The government of Kiribati considers the island's martial arts to be an important component of the nation's cultural heritage. Though they are considered important to the cultural environment of the nation, I-Kiribati martial arts are in danger of extinction, as fewer students choose to train in the higher levels.

Sports, especially canoe racing, soccer, and volleyball, are popular in Kiribati. A soccer tournament takes place every year on New Year's Day.

Cultural Sites & Landmarks

The capital region, South Tarawa, is a collection of small islets strung across one of the larger atolls in the Kiribati island chain. The town of Bairiki, an island that forms part of the Tarawa administrative district, is the site of the nation's largest airport and contains some of Kiribati's primary cultural attractions. These include the Bairiki National Stadium and the remnants of colonial architecture left on the islands. The town also contains a campus of the University of the South Pacific (USP).

As a Pacific island nation, Kiribati is home to an expanse of beautiful oceanic lagoons, tropical forests, and rich marine habitats and ecosystems, many of which have been preserved in the North Tarawa Conservation Area. Kiribati is also home to the Phoenix Islands Protection Area (PIPA), considered one of the largest marine protected areas in the world, with 40,825,000 hectares (157,626 square miles). The conservation area, which consists of eight atolls and two submerged reefs, was inscribed in 2010 as a World Heritage Site list administered by the United Nations Educational, Scientific, and Cultural Organization (UNESCO). To establish the reserve, Kiribati used funding and technical aid donated by the New England Aquarium in Boston, Massachusetts, and Conservation International. It is also believed that the island of Nikumaroro, part of the Phoenix Islands, is the site where famed but ill-fated pioneer aviator Amelia Earhart (1897–1937) landed during her attempted flight around the globe in 1937, the year she disappeared.

Libraries & Museums

The Cultural Museum (Te Umanibong) on Tarawa contains a collection of artifacts relating to the history of the islands. The museum features ceremonial artifacts from the founding tribes of Kiribati, as well as artifacts from the British and military operations conducted on Kiribati during World War II. In fact, the Kiribati island group experienced some of the Pacific region's most fierce fighting during World War II, and physical remnants of the war, such as pillboxes, coastal guns, and wreckage, can still be seen. In addition, the island nation is home to several war memorials, including the United States Marines War Memorial, the Japanese War Memorial, and the Coast Watchers Memorial, the latter dedicated to twenty-two British coast watchers beheaded by the Japanese.

The Kiribati National Library and Archives, overseen by the Ministry of Education, is located in Bairiki and is the country's largest library.

Holidays

Kiribati celebrates its independence on July 12 with a parade in Tarawa. Kiribati obtained its independence from the British on this date in 1979. The country also observes International Women's Day on March 8 and Youth Day on the first Monday in August. Christian religious observances, like Good Friday, Easter, and Christmas Day are also celebrated in Kiribati.

Youth Culture

It is estimated that young people comprise approximately 52 percent of Kiribati's national population. Children are held in high regard in I-Kiribati culture and the government takes care to support and foster a productive and stimulating culture for its youth. There are many youth organizations throughout the country, including Bairiki-based Kiribati National Youth Council, while the both Catholic and Protestant organizations remain active in establishing youth programs and activities. The government's commitment to youth is expressed through a national holiday—National Youth Day on August 10—that involves festivals and workshop programs throughout the country. Moreover, the government initiated a National Youth Policy, (2011–2015); with an eye to ensuring young adults develop the spiritual, physical, and social wherewithal to contribute constructively to the nation, while curbing substance abuse. In Tarawa and other areas, legislators invite teenagers and younger children to participate in roundtable discussions wherein children are asked to comment on the state of the nation and to give their opinions on national issues.

Football (soccer) and volleyball are the most popular youth sports in Kiribati, with basketball and tennis becoming increasingly popular. The public school system also encourages involvement in sports though a physical education program. Beach life is central to I-Kiribati culture. Most children in Kiribati learn from an early age to swim and participate in water sports, including competitive diving and recreational snorkeling. Many I-Kiribati teenagers also begin working in the tourism industry at a young age, helping to provide tours to visitors or working in retail districts near popular tourist destinations.

SOCIETY

Transportation

There is no public transportation system and all buses, which are usually smaller minivans, are privately owned. The downtown area of Tarawa is the only place on the islands where visitors can find taxi and minibus services, and the road network is fairly developed there. The government does not regulate prices for taxis and buses, and fares are generally arranged in advance. Rented vehicles, such as trucks, are more common on outlying islands. Traffic moves on the left-hand side of the road.

Transportation Infrastructure

Kiribati's transportation infrastructure is characterized as inadequate and rudimentary. Ferry service is generally available between main islands and there are twenty-three airports in Kiribati, four of which have paved runways. The remaining airports are small, domestic airfields. Bonriki International Airport, in Tarawa, is the nation's largest airport and serves four airlines. It is the primary arrival point for international visitors. Air Kiribati, founded in 1995, and Coral Sun Airways, established in 2009, are the nation's two domestic air service providers, while Fiji Airways and Air Marshall Islands offer flights into and out of Bonriki International. Cassidy International Airport, located on Kiritimati Island (Christmas Island), was one of the nation's largest international airports until deteriorating runway conditions led Air Pacific, the only airline it serves, to discontinue flights to and from the airport in September 2008. Air Pacific resumed flights to and from Cassidy in May 2010, following runway repaving. Within Kiribati, visitors can obtain shorts flights from many of the nation's smaller airports for travel between islands. Kiribati has no railway system.

Media & Communications

The government protects the freedom of the press and media organizations are allowed to freely and openly criticize the government and state policy. In fact, watchdog organization Freedom House has ranked Kiribati's press as "Free" since it began its global classifications in 1998. Kiribati has two privately owned newspapers, *Kiribati Newstar*, which provides local and international news coverage on a weekly basis, and the *Kiribati Independent*, which is published every two weeks. *Te Uekera* is the government-owned weekly, established in 1982. There are also a number of private publications, like *Te Mauri*, produced by the Protestant Church and some international organizations operating in the country. A government office, the Broadcasting and Publications Authority (BPA), operates the nation's largest radio station, Radio Kiribati, which is the primary source for news throughout the country. However, BBC and Radio Australia signals are also received.

Satellite television coverage and Internet are available in the cities. The government does not restrict foreign media and has no laws in place to restrict Internet communication or access. As of 2014, there were an estimated 12,200 Internet users, representing slightly less than 12 percent of the population. Telecom Services Kiribati Limited (TSKL) remains the only national telecommunications provider. In April 2009, another regional telecommunications provider, Digicel, cancelled plans to establish service in Kiribati, citing interference from the government telecommunications agency.

SOCIAL DEVELOPMENT

Standard of Living

Kiribati ranked 133rd out of 187 countries on the 2014 United Nations Human Development Index, which measures quality of life and standard of living indicators based on 2012 data.

Water Consumption

South Tarawa is the urban part of Kiribati, and the only region with running water and basic sanitation. According to 2015 statistics from the World Health Organization (WHO), approximately 66.9 percent of the population has access to an improved source of drinking water, while an estimated 39.7 percent have access to improved sanitation.

Education

Education is free and compulsory in Kiribati from ages six to fourteen. Secondary education is available to most students. Most of the islands' schools are run by missionary or religious organizations, such as the Roman Catholic Church and The Church of Jesus Christ of Latter-day Saints. Many of these, however, are being incorporated into the system under Kiribati's Ministry of Education. Qualified and experienced teachers are in short supply in Kiribati.

Advanced schooling is available at the Tarawa Technical Institute and the Kiribati Teacher's College. The University of the South Pacific (USP), based in Suva, Fiji, has a Kiribati campus, while the Marine Training Center in Tarawa prepares students for service on international ships.

According to UNESCO, in 2009, the school life expectancy (in number of years attended) was 7.1 for female students and for 6.8 male students.

Women's Rights

In Kiribati, men are traditionally more respected than women are. They are considered dominant to women and are expected to be the primary earners in the family. Because of the traditional norms regarding gender roles, women face discrimination in hiring and are often paid less than their male counterparts are. Certain professions, including education and administrative assistant positions, remain open to women. There are no laws on the penal code prohibiting discrimination based on gender, which prevents legal measures to ensure equal treatment.

The penal code contains provisions that address rape and spousal rape, and women's rights organizations found that Kiribati police are generally effective in enforcing the law in cases where women were willing to press charges. While domestic abuse is not specifically mentioned in the penal code, laws covering assault are effectively extended to cover domestic violence. In 2010, the Kiribati government published a study on violence against women, which revealed that 68 percent of Kiribati women had experienced one or more forms of domestic violence. Both internal and non-governmental organization (NGO) investigations indicate that domestic abuse is related to the high level of alcohol abuse on the islands. While the police and courts effectively prosecute abusers brought to trial, women's rights organizations report that prosecutions are uncommon because of social prohibitions that discourage women from reporting abuse. Some reports indicate that police often counsel women to attempt to solve the issue through mediation rather than divorce and/or prosecution.

Health Care

Quality health care is scarce in Kiribati. Most medical care is provided by visiting medical groups from Australia. Medicines are in short supply. Vitamin A deficiency, HIV/AIDs, diabetes, and dysentery are prevalent on the islands. Kiribati's infant mortality is relatively high, at 34.26 deaths per 1,000 live births.

The population suffers from malnutrition due to a poor diet and unsanitary living conditions. Most homes do not have toilets, so lagoons are often polluted with human waste. In 2015, population growth was estimated at 1.15 percent, a drop from 2.5 percent in 2005. Still, this positive rate challenges the country's slim resources.

GOVERNMENT

Structure

On Christmas Day of 1777, British Captain James Cook arrived at Kiritimati, also called Christmas Island. British Captain Thomas Gilbert visited the islands in 1788, and named

them the Gilbert Islands, after himself. In 1892, the Gilbert Islands became a British protectorate. The United States also claimed the Phoenix and Line Islands.

During World War II, the Japanese occupied Tarawa and other islands in the archipelago. US troops invaded and retook Tarawa in November 1943 in one of the bloodiest battles of the war in the Pacific. The Allied attack on Tarawa was the first large amphibious landing in World War II.

After World War II, the island remained under British control until the 1960s, when they were granted self-government. Full independence came on July 12, 1979. That year, the United States relinquished the Phoenix and Line Islands.

Today, Kiribati is a democratic republic. The Beretitenti (president) is both chief of state and head of government and is elected by simple majority vote from among members of the legislature. The unicameral legislative branch is known as the Maneaba Ni Maungatabu (House of Assembly). It has forty-six members, forty-four of which are elected by popular majority vote (often in two rounds) to four-year terms. The president is limited to three four-year terms and can be removed from office by a majority vote of the Maneaba.

Political Parties

Political parties in Kiribati are rather informal and loosely grouped. Currently, the country's major political parties are the Boutokaan Te Koaua (Pillars of Truth), which won fifteen seats in the 2011 parliamentary elections; the United Coalition Party, which attained ten seats; and the Maurin Kiribati Party, which achieved three seats. The remaining seats went to independent candidates. Other political parties include the Maurin Kiribati Party (MKP), Maneaban Te Mauri (Protect the Maneaba), the National Progressive Party, and the Kiribati Tabomoa Party.

Local Government

The country is divided into six administrative units, including Banaba, Central Gilberts, Line

Islands, Northern Gilberts, Southern Gilberts, and Tarawa. It is further divided into single-tiered eighteen rural (or island) and three urban (or town) councils. Each of the inhabited islands maintains a council. An elected chief councilor, holding office from two to four years, heads each council.

Judicial System

Kiribati's judicial system is based on a combination of English common law and customary law. The court system consists of the High Court, the Court of Appeal, and twenty-six magistrates' courts, operated on a district basis. The High Court maintains jurisdiction over constitutional issues. All judges, including the High Court's chief justice, are appointed by the president, with consultation from the Public Service Commission (PSC).

Taxation

Tax rates in Kiribati are high, with 35 percent the top corporate and personal income tax rate. Import duties and other taxes, such as a departure tax and value-added tax (VAT), are also levied.

Armed Forces

Kiribati maintains no armed forces, except for a police force, and relies on neighboring New Zealand and Australia for matters of national defense. The constitution prevents the formation of armed forces.

Foreign Policy

The Republic of Kiribati, which consists of thirty-three atolls, has largely avoided international disputes and managed to establish itself as a productive member of the international community since achieving independence in 1979. Kiribati joined the United Nations (UN) as a full member in 1999 and has since joined a number of UN groups focusing on issues that directly affect the Pacific region. Kiribati is also a member of the International Monetary Fund (IMF), the World Bank, the Commonwealth, the Pacific Islands Forum, and Asian Development Bank (ADB), among other international and regional institu-

tions. Only four countries—Taiwan (Republic of China), Australia, New Zealand, and Cuba—maintain diplomatic representation in Kiribati (in Tarawa). Cuba, specifically, provides medical aid; encourages Kiribati students to study medicine in Cuba; and, under Raúl Castro, signed a cooperation agreement to facilitate advances in healthcare.

Kiribati's primary foreign relations goal is to secure the economic prosperity of the islands, promote sustainable development, and build functional economic and diplomatic partnerships in the Pacific region. Kiribati has also joined with the international community in efforts to control global warming. In the early 21st century, President Anote Tong (1952–) warned that his nation would be under water by 2050 due to climate change. To this end, Kiribati concentrates its diplomatic efforts within the Pacific Community and the Pacific Islands Forum, both groups established by the UN. The nation does not maintain its own military and relies on New Zealand and Australia for national defense. Kiribati has also developed a strong relationship with Japan, which has become the nation's most significant source of development aid.

Kiribati's only significant international dispute was a disagreement with France. In 1995, France decided to renew its nuclear testing program in French Polynesia. Kiribati and New Zealand broke off relations with France in protest and were later joined by the island nations of Nauru and Tuvalu. After France resumed testing, Japan, New Zealand, and Australia banned French products. France discontinued testing in 1996 under significant pressure from the international community and mounting evidence, that testing in the 1960s and 1970s had led to an increase in thyroid cancer on the islands nearest to the testing sites.

Human Rights Profile

International human rights law insists that states respect civil and political rights and promote an individual's economic, social, and cultural rights. The United Nations Universal Declaration on Human Rights (UDHR) is recognized as the standard for international human rights. Its authors sought the counsel of the world's great thinkers, philosophers, and religious leaders and were careful to create a document that reflects the core values shared by every world culture. (To read this document or view the articles relating to cultural human rights, visit http://www.ohchr.org/EN/UDHR/Pages/Introduction.aspx.)

Human rights monitoring agencies have found that the government of Kiribati is committed to the rights of citizens and that the penal code is generally effective in addressing human rights issues. Child and domestic abuse are among the most pressing issues facing Kiribati. The government lacks the resources to address abuse in rural communities.

Kiribati has a single detention facility, and juveniles under sixteen and criminals charged with minor crimes are not generally held with the prison's general population, which in 2013 numbered 141, four of which were women. This number, however, represents overpopulation, as the facility's maximum capacity is 125. Those charged with minor offenses are most often released on bail before trial and children under sixteen years of age may be held within detention centers for no more than one month before release. However, there is no separate facility to house juvenile offenders, which is a violation of the UDHR and the guarantee of special status for women and children. Kiribati is currently working with the UN to improve the juvenile justice system. In practice, penal system employees and police generally have ensured the safety of under-age offenders and few juveniles were forced into the nation's primary detention system.

While Kiribati has a public court system that handles all civil and criminal offenses, some tribes living in rural areas maintained a traditional tribal court system. Under this system, presiding village elders recommend punishments for those accused of crimes. While the tribal system is not legal under the penal code, the government has insufficient resources to prohibit the practice in rural areas and within remote island populations. In addition, while the government is committed to protecting children, lack of resources

also prevented police from effectively monitoring family welfare in rural areas. Alcoholism is common in Kiribati and contributes to high rates of domestic abuse. The Kiribati Police Force has established a special branch to investigate and address domestic issues, including child abuse.

Child neglect is a serious problem and aid organizations report that many Kiribati children are malnourished and lack basic resources. While there are aid programs in place, aid workers have difficulty distributing aid and food to rural populations and many parents fail to seek aid when in need. While there are no laws against prostitution, underage prostitution—below the age of twenty—is considered illegal. Human rights monitoring agencies report that the lack of laws preventing prostitution has facilitated underage prostitution.

ECONOMY

Overview of the Economy
Kiribati remains one of the poorest countries in Oceania. In 2014, the per capita gross domestic product (GDP) was estimated at $1,700 (USD). The economy relies heavily on aid from Australia, the United Kingdom, Japan, New Zealand, and China; this aid accounted for 43 percent of the government's finances in 2013. Development has been hampered by the lack of skilled workers and the country's remote location.

Fees paid by foreign fishing vessels and money sent home by I-Kiribati working in other countries are also economically significant. Out-of-country workers send home remittances amounting to around 6 percent to the country's GDP. South Tarawa is the urban area of Kiribati, giving it a comparatively large wage economy.

Industry
Industrial activity in Kiribati is light, but still contributes 9.2 percent to the GDP and occupies 10 percent of the labor force. Some companies make coconut oil from copra for export. Clothing and footwear is also manufactured. The country's phosphate mines, which were booming before

independence in 1979, are almost completely depleted and no longer commercially viable.

Sales of off-coast fishing licenses make up a large portion of the economy. Kiribati's main exports are copra (dried coconut meat, from which coconut oil is pressed), sea salt, and seaweed, while food comprises approximately one-third of the country's imports. In addition, South Tarawa houses a diesel power plant and a small light industry sector, which manufactures textiles, furniture, and beverages, mainly for domestic consumption. Kiribati's major export partners are France, Japan, the United States, and Thailand.

Labor

The country's labor force is severely underemployed, while official unemployment figures stand at nearly 31 percent, affecting almost one-third of the population. Over 60 percent of all wage-earning jobs in Kiribati are located in South Tarawa, with most of these jobs in the area of public administration. Only 16 percent of the country's population works for formal wages, leaving control of South Tarawa's economy to the fishing industry. Many citizens, especially those on the outer Islands, rely on subsistence farming, the selling of handicrafts, and remittances (money sent by family working abroad).

Energy/Power/Natural Resources

Historically, Kiribati's most important natural resource has been the phosphate deposits on the island of Banaba. However, these deposits have been depleted since 1979, leaving the country's economy dependent largely on the public sector, foreign fishing licenses, and humanitarian aid.

The country's only other natural resource is the abundance of marine life found in the waters surrounding the islands, something the country has begun seeking to protect. While the fish, particularly tuna, in Kiribati's waters attract fishing vessels from other nations, Kiribati has begun to restrict fishing in certain areas in order to allow the reefs to regenerate. The hope is that, in the end, diving, snorkeling, and other ecotourism will begin to fill the gap.

However, environmental pollution continues to be a concern in Kiribati. Most of the population lives in unsanitary conditions, and sewage is often released directly into lagoon waters. South Tarawa's dense populations, the changing of the tidal currents due to causeway construction, an overloaded sewage system, and other waste management concerns have exacerbated an already significant problem. Natives and visitors are often discouraged from swimming in the water, and pollution has lowered the number of fish available for consumption, a particular difficulty for a nation that has traditionally relied on the sea for food.

Fishing

Kiribati's rich fishing grounds represent the country's primary natural resource, with fishing licenses accounting for nearly half of the country's revenue. Tuna is the primary commercial catch. The country also exports seaweed and aquarium fish. In 2014, President Anote Tong closed commercial fishing for 12 nautical miles around the southern Line Islands in order to allow the reefs and tuna population to recover.

Agriculture

The majority of Kiribati's population survives by subsistence farming and agricultural products represent 26.3 percent of the country's GDP. However, just 2.5 percent of the islands' land is arable. Crops of breadfruit, papaya, taro, pandanus, and coconut are grown in the generally poor soil. Bananas are grown on Butaritari, and there are coconut plantations on some of the uninhabited Line Islands. Seaweed is harvested to be made into emulsifiers and pharmaceuticals. Mining and forestry are of little or no significance to the island nation's economy.

Tourism

Despite a lack of tourism infrastructure, tourism provides about one-fifth of the country's gross domestic product and makes up a significant part of the economy. Still, in 2013, the World Bank estimated that just 5,900 overnight visitors came to Kiribati, which is an increase of 1,000 people from 2012. Attractions such as the World War II landmarks on Betio islet—rusting landing craft that were beached during the US invasion of Tarawa from November 20–23, 1943, along with Japanese artillery, can be seen on South Tarawa as well—and the scenic qualities of all of the islets of Tarawa draw visitors to the islands. The coral reefs surrounding the islands also make Kiribati a popular destination for divers. Other favorite tourist activities include snorkeling and sport fishing. The Bonriki International Airport, which is the hub for Air Kiribati and Coral Sun Airways and services Fiji Airways and Air Marshall Islands, makes South Tarawa the easiest destination for tourists. Most foreign tourists visit Tarawa and Kiritimati (Christmas Island). The Phoenix and Line Islands are, at present, still not serviced by any airline, although Coral Sun Airways seeks to remedy this.

Micah Issitt, Roberta Baxter, Anne Whittaker,
Savannah Schroll Guz

DO YOU KNOW?

- In January 1995, Kiribati proclaimed that the International Date Line would be adjusted so that all of its territory would be in the same time zone (specifically, the same day).

- Kiribati has a higher sea-to-land ratio than any country in the world. It is also the world's largest atoll country, with thirty-three landforms in total: thirty-two atolls and one raised coral island.

- During World War II, Tarawa was first occupied by Japan and then by Allied forces. It became the gateway between the Americas and the Philippines during the war, and the center of fighting in the South Pacific.

Bibliography

Asian Development Bank. *Economic Cost of Inadequate Water and Sanitation: South Tarawa, Kiribati.* Manila, Philippines: Asian Development Bank, 2014. Pacific. https://chaseonline.chase.com/MyAccounts.aspx Studies Ser.

Brash, Celeste, Brett Atkinson, et al. *South Pacific.* Oakland, CA: Lonely Planet Press, 2012.

Carey, Melissa. *Islanders and Education, The I-Kiribati Experience: An Indigenous Ethnographic Approach.* Saarbrücken, Germany: Lambert Academic Publishing, 2011.

CIA & State Department. *Kiribati Country Studies: A brief, comprehensive study of Kiribati.* Covington, WA: Zay's Publishing, 2012.

Hezel, Francis X. *The New Shape of Old Island Cultures: A Half Century of Social Change in Micronesia.* Honolulu, HI: U of Hawaii P, 2001.

Icon Group International. *The 2016 Kiribati Economic and Product Market Databook.* Las Vegas, NV: ICON Group International: 2015.

Levy, Neil M. *Micronesia.* 5th ed. New York: Avalon Travel Publishing, 2000. Moon Travel Handbooks Ser.

MacDonald, Barrie. *Cinderellas of the Empire: Towards a History of Kiribati and Tuvalu.* Fiji: U of South Pacific P, 2001.

Rapaport, Moshe. *The Pacific Islands: Environment & Society.* Rev. ed. Honolulu, HI: U of Hawaii P, 2013.

Sherrod, Robert. *Tarawa: The Incredible Story of One of World War II's Bloodiest Battles.* New York: Skyhorse Publishing, 2013.

Stanley, David. *Moon Handbooks South Pacific.* 8th ed. Berkeley, CA: Avalon Travel Publishing, 2004.

Wycoff, Anne, ed. *Fanning Island, Republic of Kiribati.* Montréal, Canada: CMS World Media, 2003.

Works Cited

"Kiribati Country Profile." *BBC News.* BBC, 14 Dec. 2011. http://news.bbc.co.uk/2/hi/asia-pacific/country_profiles/1168527.stm.

Bureau of East Asian and Pacific Affairs. "US Relations with Kiribati." *U.S. Department of State.* U.S. Department of State, 9 Feb. 2015. Web. http://www.state.gov/r/pa/ei/bgn/1836.htm.

Bureau of Democracy, Human Rights, and Labor. "Kiribati." *Country Reports on Human Rights Practices for 2013*. Washington, DC: US State Department, 2014. PDF.

Central Intelligence Agency. "Kiribati." *The World Factbook*. Central Intelligence Agency, 2015. Web. https://www.cia.gov/library/publications/the-world-factbook/geos/kr.html.

Development Policy and Analysis Division. "Kiritbati." *Least Developed Countries: LDC Factsheets*. DPAD, 2015. Web. http://www.un.org/en/development/desa/policy/cdp/ldc/profile/country_100.shtml.

Freedom House. "Kiribati." *Freedom in the World 2015*. Freedom House, 2015. Web. https://freedomhouse.org/report/freedom-world/2015/kiribati.

Howard, Brian Clark. "Pacific Nation Bans Fishing in One of World's Largest Marine Parks." *National Geographic*. The National Geographic Society, 16 Jun. 2014. Web. http://news.nationalgeographic.com/news/2014/06/140616-kiribati-marine-park-commercial-fishing-ocean-protection/.

"Kiribati." *World Travel Guide*. Columbus Travel Media, Ltd., 2015. Web. http://www.worldtravelguide.net/kiribati.

"Kiribati for Travellers." *Kiribati National Tourism Office*. Ministry of Communication, Transport and Tourism Development, 8 Oct. 2013. http://www.kiribatitourism.gov.ki/.

Republic of Kiribati Ministry of Internal & Social Affairs. *Kiribati Family Health and Support Study: A study on violence against women and children*. Noumea, New Caledonia. Secretariat of the Pacific Community,

2010. PDF. http://countryoffice.unfpa.org/pacific/drive/KiribatiFamilyHealthandSafetyStudy.pdf.

———. *National Youth Policy 2011–2015*. Tarawa, Kiribati: Ministry of Internal & Social Affairs, 2011. PDF.

Sparks, B. "Odd Fighting Units: Kiribati Warrior of Micronesia." *Warfare History Blog*. B. Sparks/Blogger, 20 Mar. 2013. Web. http://warfarehistorian.blogspot.com/2013/03/odd-fighting-units-of-world-history.html.

'Taxation.' *Ministry of Finance & Economic Development*. Government of Kiribati, 18 Jul. 2015. Web. http://www.mfed.gov.ki/our-work/taxation.

UN Development Programme. "Table 1: Human Development Index and its components." *Human Development Reports*. UNDP, 2015. Web. http://hdr.undp.org/en/content/table-1-human-development-index-and-its-components.

UNESCO. "Phoenix Islands Protected Area." UNESCO World Heritage Sites. UNESCO World Heritage Centre, 2015. Web. http://whc.unesco.org/en/list/1325.

UNESCO Institute for Statistics. "School life expectancy: Kiribati." *UNdata*. United Nations Statistics Division, 16 Apr. 2015. Web. http://data.un.org/Data.aspx?q=Kiribati+school&d=UNESCO&f=series%3aSLE_1%3bref_area%3aKIR.

World Health Organization. "Countries: Kiribati." *World Health Organization*. WHO, 2015. http://www.who.int/countries/kir/en/.

World Bank. "International tourism, number of arrivals." *The World Bank Data*. The World Bank Group, 2015. Web. http://data.worldbank.org/indicator/ST.INT.ARVL

Aerial view of Atoll reefs in the Marshall Islands. iStock/Robert_Ford

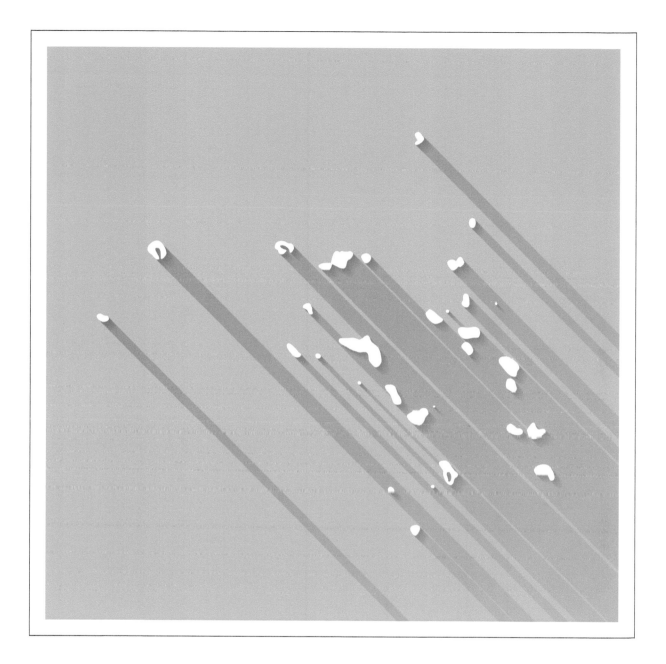

MARSHALL ISLANDS

Introduction

The Republic of the Marshall Islands consists of 1,225 islands grouped into twenty-nine atolls, and five individual islands. The atolls are composed of coral accumulations that cling to the crater rims of volcanoes long submerged in the Pacific. The country is located about 4,100 kilometers (2547 miles) southwest of Hawaii and 3,000 kilometers (1,864 miles) northeast of Papua New Guinea, in the North Pacific Ocean. The republic is often referred to as simply the Marshall Islands and sometimes RMI. The Marshall Islands is the smallest country among the American-affiliated countries of Micronesia. The Marshall Islands is both home to part of the US Missile Defense System, located at US Army Kwajalein Atoll Reagan Missile Test Site, and one of the five sites vital to successful operation of the worlds Global Positioning System (GPS).

The Marshall Islands have a complex history of foreign rule. Between the eighteenth and twentieth centuries, they were claimed in succession by Spain, Germany, Japan, and finally the United States. As part of a United States Trust Territory, some of the islands in the Bikini and Enewetak Atolls were used for nuclear testing between 1946 and 1958, something for which the Marshall Islands government still seeks compensation. Today, the Marshall Islands are an independent state led by a constitutional government. Collectively, the country's citizens are known as Marshallese.

The Marshallese are known for their skilled canoe building and ocean navigation. The ocean is an essential part of Marshallese culture. Residents of the capital of Majuro enjoy some imported modern amenities and utilities. However, they still live a relatively traditional lifestyle.

The economy of the Marshall Islands continues to face many challenges. In addition, global warming has resulted in rising sea levels and the deterioration of coral reefs, which threaten the nation's very existence. As of 2015, some islands are just one meter above sea level.

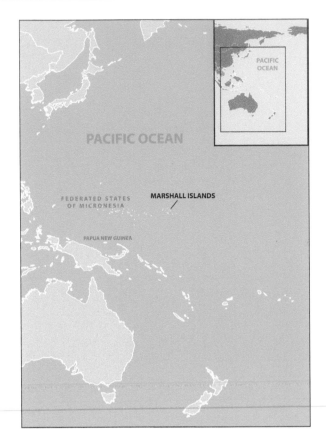

GENERAL INFORMATION

Official Language: Marshallese, English
Population: 72,191 (2015 estimate)
Currency: United States dollar (USD)
Coins: The U.S. dollar is divided into cents; 100 cents are equal to one dollar. There are 1, 5, 10, and 25-cent coin denominations. In addition, a fifty-cent coin and a one-dollar coin is also available, but are used rarely.

Population of the Marshall Islands by Atoll (2014):

- Majuro (31,000)
- Ebeye (15,00)
- Kwajalein (13,500)
- Arno (1,794)
- Ailinglaplap (1,729)
- Jaluit (1,788)
- Wotje (859)
- Namu (780)
- Mili (738)
- Ebon (706)
- Enewetak (664)

Land Area: 181 square kilometers (70 square miles)
National Anthem: "Forever Marshall Islands"
Capital: Majuro
Time Zone: GMT +12
Flag Description: The flag of the Marshall Islands features a two-color triangular band that runs diagonally from left to right. Blue represents the Pacific Ocean. In the bicolor band, the orange stripe represents the Ralik Chain, sunset, and courage, while the white stripe symbolizes the Ratak Chain, sunrise, and peace. This rising, bicolor band is also intended to reference the equator. In the flag's upper left hand corner, there is a white star with four larger rays at its cardinal points and twenty smaller rays. The star's four points symbolizes the Christian cross, while the twenty-four total rays represent each electoral district.

Population

Just under half of the population of the Marshall Islands lives on the island of Majuro. A large percentage, nearly one-quarter of the population, also live on the 80-acre Ebeye Island, which has become known as the "ghetto of the Pacific." Half of the population on Ebeye is under the age of fourteen. The capital is spread across the islets of Delap, Uliga, and Darrit (known as DUD) in the Majuro Atoll. Collectively, these are the most populous of the roughly sixty islets that make up the Majuro Atoll.

In recent decades, people from the outer islands have moved to the more populous centers in search of employment, particularly at the US military base. Many young Marshallese work abroad, in Hawaii, Guam, or the United States. Although many people are migrating from the Marshall Islands, the country has one of the highest birth rates in the world, at three children per woman. The country's rapid population growth has raised concerns about whether or not the islands' natural resources can sufficiently provide for its people. In 2015, water and electricity to the native populations are inconsistent, with water arriving only two to three days per week.

The population of the Marshall Islands is young. In 2015, an estimated 36 percent of the population was under age of fourteen and another 60.38 percent was estimated to be between the ages of fifteen and sixty-four. Life expectancy at birth is seventy years for males and seventy-five years for females (2015 estimate). Population density is high, at more than 300 people per square kilometer (more than 100 people per square mile). According to the 2011 census, the highest population density continued to be on Ebeye, with 31,013 per square kilometer (80,117 per square mile).

Languages

The two official languages of the Marshall Islands are English and Marshallese. Although English is the official language of the Marshallese government and is taught in the public school system, more than 92 percent of the population also speaks Marshallese. Marshallese, of the Malaysian/Polynesian family of languages, has evolved into two distinct dialects: ratak in the east and ralik in the west. The two dialects have only minor differences and speakers from the east and west can readily understand each other. While most Marshallese speak English, Marshallese is commonly used across the islands. Some residents of the Marshall Islands also speak Japanese.

Native People & Ethnic Groups

Humans arrived in the Marshall Islands thousands of years ago, though the precise date is unknown.

Expert sailors and navigators, the region's first settlers most likely arrived by outrigger canoe, using waves and currents to navigate over the surrounding waters and creating charts for other mariners. The modern-day population of the Marshall Islands maintains a rich tradition of songs about their ancient ancestors.

Today, Marshallese comprises about 92 percent of the population of the Marshall Islands. The remaining 8 percent consists of minority ethnic groups and includes Americans, Micronesians, Filipinos, Chinese, New Zealanders, Australians, Kiribati, Koreans, and Fijian.

Religions

There is no official religion in the Marshall Islands. However, over half of the population (54.8 percent) is Protestant Christians and members of the United Church of Christ. Other Christian denominations on the islands include Assembly of God (25.8 percent), Roman Catholic (8.4 percent), Bukot nan Jesus (2.8 percent), and Mormon (2.1 percent). Other Christian denominations, such as Baptist and Pentecostal, together comprise 3.6 percent. Religions with a small percentage of adherents on the Marshall Islands include Baha'i, Jehovah's Witness, Judaism, and Islam.

Climate

The climate of the Marshall Islands is tropical and the weather is often hot and humid. Temperatures fluctuate little and the average temperature is approximately 27° Celsius (80° Fahrenheit). The northern islands are typically cooler and drier than the southern islands. The months from January to March are drier, and the summer months are characterized by calm seas and still winds. The wet season lasts from May to November of each year. From time to time, the islands will experience typhoons, a type of cyclone, although these are relatively infrequent. Average annual rainfall is 3,444 millimeters (136 inches). On April 19, 2013, the Marshall Islands government declared a state of emergency over a prolonged drought, which particularly affected the northern atolls, where 6,834 people were impacted and subsistence agriculture severely compromised. This state of emergency ended in September 2013, as rains resumed and drought conditions eased.

In recent years, the government of the Marshall Islands has also declared a state of emergency over flooding caused by swell waves and extreme high tides generated by off shore tropical storms. Increasing sea levels caused by global warming have also resulted in growing concerns related to severe flooding in Majuro and other areas of the country.

ENVIRONMENT & GEOGRAPHY

Topography

The Marshall Islands consist of two parallel atoll chains. The chains stretch out over 1,287 kilometers (800 miles). The northeastern chain is called Ratak, or Sunrise, and includes the Mili, Majuro, Maloelap, Wotje, and Likiep atolls. The southwestern chain is called Ralik, or Sunset, and contains the Jaluit, Ailinglaplap, Kwajalein, Rongelap, Bikini, Enewetak, and other atolls. The Kwajalein Atoll is the largest in the world.

The atolls are made of coral, and form C-shaped lagoons. White beaches lie along the lagoons and coral reefs are located just offshore. The highest point on the Marshall Islands is an unnamed point on the Likiep Atoll and is 10 meters (33 feet) above sea level. The average height of the atolls is 2 meters (7 feet) above sea level. However, climate change has caused water levels to rise and many islands are just 1 meter (3.3 feet) above sea level. The country's total coastline measures 370.4 kilometers (230.2 miles).

The capital, Majuro, is also called DUD (Darrit, Uliga, Delap). The city is actually built on three islands in the Majuro Atoll and is connected by a road.

Plants & Animals

Coconut palms are among the most common trees found throughout the Marshall Islands.

The coconut crab found in the Marshall Islands is related to the hermit crab.

Smaller plants and vegetation grows on some islands, while others are mostly bare. Common plant life includes breadfruit trees, taro, pandanus, arrowroot, yams, banana trees, and cassava.

The marine life in the waters surrounding the Marshall Islands is diverse and includes whales, dolphins, porpoises, 250 species of reef fish, and several species of marine turtles. Birds and sea birds are abundant, but the only native mammal is the Polynesian rat. There are also several types of lizards, coconut land crabs, reef shrimp, and one snake species found on the islands. Several species of longhorn beetles and sea spiders are endemic to the Marshall Islands. Two native bird species, the Wake Rail and the Ratak Micronesian Pigeon are, as of 2015, extirpated.

CUSTOMS & COURTESIES

Greetings

Traditionally, the handshake was not a common gesture of greeting on the islands though Westerners introduced the custom. In the Marshall Islands, however, handshakes generally last longer than in Western cultures.

The Marshallese use the term "Yokwe" (also "Iokwe") as a general greeting. The word translates as "love," or "love to you," but is also used to express "hello," "goodbye," and a number of other sentiments. Another greeting commonly used is "Itok im mona," which translates as "come and eat." Inviting visitors to share food or a drink is considered a polite way to extend a greeting, even if it is not a literal invitation. Names are not commonly used during greetings, and the Marshallese will often use a general expression, such as "motta" ("friend"), as a substitute. When conversing, the Western understanding of personal space is often disregarded, and the Marshallese make frequent contact with their hands.

Gestures & Etiquette

There is a complex, but not openly or strictly enforced system of social stratification in Marshallese culture that helps to establish roles within the society. Reverence for age and experience translates into a system of social conventions, under which younger people are expected to address elders in a deferential and respectful manner. In addition, the traditional model of Marshallese life is a system within which children are always expected to take social cues from older members of society.

The Marshallese are affectionate with friends and family, often holding hands and embracing. However, there are accepted cultural guidelines that govern contact between members of the opposite sex. Young men and women are not allowed to display affection in public. Marshallese are also highly conservative in conversation regarding personal, sexual, or physical topics, and they make less use of hand gestures than do Western speakers. In fact, the Marshallese may be offended by relatively emotive and energetic conversation.

Eating/Meals

Marshallese culture is closely tied to the traditional foods harvested from the environment. Seafood is a major component of the local diet and has become one of the cornerstones of Marshallese culture. In addition, rocky soil and poor mineral content makes agriculture difficult and only a few vegetables are produced in significant quantity. However, tropical trees, such as the coconut, are able to anchor into the rocky soil and provide fruits and nuts. Coconuts are important, not only as an ingredient in Marshallese food, but also as a raw material for equipment, crafts, and architecture.

Most Marshallese customarily eat two or three meals a day, corresponding to breakfast, lunch, and dinner. Unlike many cultures, Marshallese have few foods reserved for a specific time of day and virtually any component of local cuisine may be eaten at any time of day. Fish is nearly always a central component of the largest meal of the day, though it is prepared in numerous ways. Food, including fish, beef, various poultry, and vegetables, is generally cooked on an outdoor fire or in an oven built into the ground.

Many Marshallese eat meals with their fingers and rarely use utensils. However, silverware is used at restaurants. Some families sit on the floor while eating or on mats, called jaki, which are woven from pandanus leaves. Shoes are generally removed before stepping on the jaki. Meals are customarily served on communal dishes, from which people help themselves.

Visiting

Social visits are an important part of Marshallese culture. Many would consider it unusual for an individual to go for an entire week without visiting friends or family. Reciprocity is also an important component of social communication. Individuals who are invited to a friend's home are expected to extend a return invitation for sometime in the near future.

Because of the considerable difficulty, some families face in obtaining food, sharing food with friends and family is considered one of the most important gestures of kinship and affection. Hosts typically spare little expense to provide food and drink for guests, who are expected to show their appreciation by eating as much as possible.

Visitors might bring small gifts for their hosts to celebrate the occasion. Food, candy, and household items are commons gifts, as well as small toys or treats for children. Guests will often bring a dish to contribute to the meal.

LIFESTYLE

Family

Traditionally, few Marshallese own property individually and most territory is owned collectively by a jowi, or clan. Each jowi consists of several families united through blood or bonds among the elder females of each family within the clan. In the past, the clan controlled a certain territory under the supervision of an alap (clan elder) who managed the clan's property. Each clan also had an iroij (chief) who had final authority over decisions that affect the entire clan. Within the clan's territory, each family was given its own property. Ownership of the land itself was inherited according to a matrilineal system, with the highest-ranking woman of each clan designated as the property owner.

Men and women often first set up housekeeping and live together in a common-law marriage, called koba, before legally marrying. While each nuclear family in the clan system functions as an independent unit, each family within a clan also works with other clan families for the benefit of the entire clan. A family's firstborn child is seen as an important sign of status and the family traditionally gives their firstborn child special consideration in food and resources. Married couples usually move onto the land of the wife's family, as their offspring will carry the wife's name and clan affiliation. Members of both the husband and wife's family remain closely associated and assist with childrearing and in sharing resources. Informal adoptions are also common, and extended families will take responsibility for the children of others when necessary. Occasionally such adoptions are outside bloodlines.

A Marshallese clan will usually contain more than one family line, representing associations between the female leaders of several families. This may extend for several generations. The paternal line is linked by blood and the traditional kin group of the Marshall Islands includes both members of the female's clan and members of the male's paternal line, all cooperating for mutual benefit. In traditional Marshallese culture, it was considered taboo for members of different clans to marry, but such restrictions have relaxed in the modern era.

Housing

The vast majority of Marshall Islands residents live in the islands' urban areas. Most Marshallese live in simple houses that are constructed from a combination of wood and concrete blocks with corrugated tin roofs. On the Kwajalein and Majuro Atolls, apartment-style housing or low-cost single unit homes are common. In rural zones, housing is concentrated along productive coastal fishing zones or along rivers, lakes, and natural water features. Houses are heavily clustered because suitable land is in limited supply.

Before concrete blocks were brought to the islands, Marshallese used woven plant fibers and wood from the breadfruit tree to build their huts. Some Marshallese still live in these traditional huts made from thatched plant materials. While indoor plumbing and heating have become more common, many islanders still use outdoor sanitary facilities and rely on fire for heat and light.

Food

Seafood is the mainstay of Marshall Island's cuisine. Tropical fruits and nuts also constitute one of the most important components in native dishes. Over the years, Marshallese food culture has absorbed elements of Japanese, Malaysian, and European culinary traditions.

The Marshallese use red snapper, tuna, cod, and a variety of other fish to cook fish steaks, one of the most basic entrees in the local cuisine. The steaks are cooked with peppers and salt and sometimes rubbed with citrus or fruit for extra flavor. Another common preparation is to cook steaks of fish or chunks of chicken or pork in banana leaves over an outdoor fire pit. The banana leaf covering concentrates the heat and imparts a soft texture to the meat. Other types of seafood, like clams, oysters and other mollusks, also feature prominently in local cuisine. Fried or boiled oysters are often served in a simple preparation with salt, citrus, and a side of roasted breadfruit. Meat from fish or marine invertebrates may also be served minced and dried, with garlic and salt for flavor.

Breadfruit, although part of the mulberry family, is used much like a vegetable and is one of the most common produce items in the Pacific. The meat of the breadfruit is served boiled or roasted and then salted. It usually appears in Marshallese cuisine as a side dish, but is also eaten as a snack. Coconut is used in both savory and sweet dishes and is a common component in Pacific cooking. Chunks of coconut are often cooked with fish or pork and may also be used to sweeten a savory vegetable dish. Coconut milk may be mixed with peppers and onions to create a spicy sauce for fish and other meats. Breads with chunks of coconut, cooked in coconut milk, are a common dessert item.

Because of limited resources, many Marshallese families survive on imported processed and canned foods, eating few vegetables and little fresh fish. This has contributed to a host of health problems among the population.

Life's Milestones

Most Marshallese—more than 54.8 percent as of 2015—are Protestant and follow traditional Christian rites of passage, including baptism, marriage, and funerary customs. However, the Marshallese have also maintained a number of tribal traditions and customs marking the various stages of life.

A child's first birthday, known as the keemem in Marshallese, is one of the most important traditions in Marshallese culture. The parents of the child host the celebration at their home, spreading mats made of palm fronds in front of their door to invite guests into the house. The family may spend days or even weeks preparing for the keemem, weaving plates and decorations from dried pandanus leaves and preparing food and other elements of the party. Traditionally, the families of both parents contribute to the celebration, bringing toys, presents, and food. This event is often a large affair, with members of the extended clan and even residents from nearby islands invited to the party.

At the keemem celebration, members of the family, clan elders, and relatives traditionally give speeches and the guests engage in singing and dancing. The family's pastor also customarily attends and gives a birthday blessing to the child. In Marshallese custom, it is believed that if the baby's clothing disappears at the keemem, the baby will be blessed with good luck. The parents hang the baby's clothing on a clothesline at the party and, following the pastor's blessing, guests celebrate by "stealing" the baby's clothing, often stripping the child until it is wearing nothing but a diaper.

Marriage is the traditional marker of the transition to adulthood and the newly married are given enhanced status within the clan. Marshallese children usually marry from within the same clan or to members of other, related clans. Marriage to "cousins," who may be related by blood or are seen as cousins from another associated clan, is common and seen as a way to increase the stability and status of the clan. Marriage ceremonies bear characteristics of both Christian tradition and tribal custom. Before marriage, men and women often live together for several years in a tradition called koba, wherein the couple is supposed to grow accustomed to living with one another before engaging in marriage and starting a family. Many couples have children while living in koba and typically choose to formalize their relationship through marriage later.

Marshallese funerals also contain elements of both Christian and tribal customs. For example, the initial gathering for a funeral is close to the European tradition of a wake, except that guests drop small amounts of money into the coffin for the deceased to use in the afterlife. Family and friends gather next for a funeral, which is generally a somber and simple affair. It is attended by elders from the clan, in addition to members of the deceased's immediate family. In traditional Marshallese custom, it is believed that the spirit of the deceased leaves the body after death. Members of the family and clan usually gather approximately five to six days after the burial for another celebration, with food and music to celebrate the departure of the deceased's soul.

CULTURAL HISTORY

Arts & Crafts

The Marshall Islands is home to numerous craft traditions that date back to the ancestral tribes of the islands. Native artisans often used materials taken from the natural environment. These include a variety of wood, leaves, and grasses, and objects harvested from the sea such as coral, shells, and stones, all of which figure prominently as raw materials. Even as Marshallese artisans lacked official patronage throughout the islands' development, their artistic traditions were maintained by later generations. This can be attributed to the fact that much of the Marshallese craft traditions are functional.

Marshallese women developed many of the islands' most prominent craft traditions. Marshallese women have been weaving leaves and dried plant fibers for centuries, using them to create clothing, such as headbands, hats, and household items, including woven baskets and mats. These same raw materials were also used in building early Marshallese homes. Over the centuries, weavers began using plant materials to make decorative implements and ritual objects. Using various substances found on the island, weavers were able to dye palm and coconut fronds to create colorful sculptures. The Marshallese are also known for their handmade patterned stick charts, traditionally used for navigating the islands and their swells.

Marshallese weaving techniques have spread throughout the Pacific and influenced artisans living on nearby islands. In fact, Marshallese woven crafts became renowned throughout the Pacific as the finest such handicrafts. In the twentieth century, artisans learned to capitalize on the tourism industry, selling native crafts, such as woven bags, decorative fans, and ornaments. Seashell jewelry is likewise sold through the markets in Kwajalein and Majuro and other retail stores across the islands. Today, some craftspeople have been able to find an international market for their goods by selling them through mail order and online vendors.

Architecture

The downtown area of Majuro, the capital, combines modern architecture with traditional Marshallese buildings and a few buildings of Japanese and American design from the nation's colonial period. Traditional Marshallese buildings in the city's residential districts are simple structures without extensive utilities or modern conveniences. Administrative buildings are more elaborate structures constructed from stone or cement block. Most of the city's oldest buildings are built entirely from wood, though many have fallen into disrepair from exposure.

Canoe Building

Historically, the Marshallese are known for their canoe making, since such transportation was essential to their lifestyle for centuries, even dating back to ancient times. They mastered the art of canoe building long before Europeans set foot on the islands. Over the centuries, they became known as some of the best canoe makers in the Pacific. In fact, Marshallese canoes can sail closer to the direct wind current than modern craft that use of synthetic sails and hull materials.

The pinnacle of Marshallese design is the outrigger canoe, traditionally carved from the trunk of a breadfruit tree. The outrigger canoe consists of a carved wooden passenger chamber, which may hold one or more passengers and a small amount of cargo; an attached rig provides balance and increases speed. There are three different types: the walap is a larger version that can carry several dozen passengers and reach a length of more than 30 meters (100 feet); the tipnol is a sailing version used for the open ocean; and the kōrkōr is a small paddle canoe used for lagoon fishing and sailing.

The shipbuilding traditions of the Marshallese are passed from one generation to the next through the effort of professional artisans. They may take one or more students each year, teaching them the traditional and modern building techniques and how to use them to navigate ocean currents. Few shipbuilders use the ancient techniques developed by the early Marshallese craftspeople, and modern watercraft may include imported wood and sails made from synthetic cloth. (Traditionally, sails, which are triangular in shape, were made from dried and treated pandanus leaves.) However, the tradition of carving breadfruit canoes and weaving sails from dried pandanus leaves is considered part of the nation's cultural heritage. These techniques are still taught by skilled artisans to students in hopes of preserving the techniques for posterity.

Music

The "roro," or traditional chant, is an important part of traditional Marshallese music, and usually involve ancient legends. Each consists of four to six lines that are chanted in a deep tone, first beginning slowly, and speeding up with each repetition. Depending on the roro contents or theme, they may be performed in a call-and-response style. Traditional music also uses a unique type of drum, which is shaped like one side of an hourglass. The traditional dance of the Marshall Island is call "beet." Beet involves complex movements and rhythms and is influenced by Spanish folk dance.

Modern popular music is also enjoyed on the islands. Popular bands on the island perform country music and rock and roll classics as well as their own blend of the Marshallese sound and contemporary styles.

Literature

Early traditional Marshallese stories were compiled by Jane Downing (1962–) and Dirk H. R. Spennemann in the volume *Marshallese Legends and Traditions*. Downing has also published English versions of other Marshallese stories, including "The Whale and the Sandpiper" and "The Hermit Crab and the Needlefish." In 2003, Daniel A. Kelin II and Nashton T. Nashon published *Marshall Islands Legends and Stories*. Another popular book that takes place in Marshall Islands is *Melal: A Novel of the Pacific* by Robert Barclay.

Tattooing & Body Adornment

The Marshallese were practicing the art of tattooing before the arrival of the first foreigners to the islands. This tradition of body adornment was initially developed as a ceremonial practice, marking the transition to adulthood for both women and men. The various designs convey clan affiliation and status and symbolize the connection of the islanders to the natural environment, with motifs that mimic the sea turtle's carapace and sharks' teeth. The traditional Marshallese tattoo ceremony could last more than a month, with the subject spending part of each day receiving their tattoos. While men were tattooed over their entire bodies, most women were only tattooed on their arms, shoulders, and thighs. Clan leaders received the most elaborate designs and were also tattooed on their faces to conceal signs of aging.

Most Marshallese tattoo designs use a combination of dark dots and lines, arranged into different patterns to symbolize elements of the environment. The body of the individual was divided into certain zones, which are often given nautical names. For example, the section of a man's chest from the sternum to the naval was called the "mast." Early tattoo artists used a makeshift needle made from fish bone, which was driven under the skin with a small mallet. Friends and family usually surround the subject during the process while ritual drums and music are played in the background.

While some Marshallese continue to practice the traditional tattoo ceremony, it has become less common and fewer families demand that their children undergo the process. Marshallese descendants living abroad brought their traditional designs into the tattoo industry, and many tattoo artists around the world now create "Pacific-style" tattoos for their clients. Even in the traditional Marshallese ceremony, some now use modern tattoo equipment and synthetic ink, which are less expensive and easier to procure.

CULTURE

Arts & Entertainment

The Marshall Islands are known for the traditional handicrafts produced by the local population. Baskets, as well as woven wall hangings, belts, purses, and mats are made from pandanus leaves by Marshallese women. Marshallese men are skilled in woodcarving, canoe building, and constructing the unique stick charts that show ocean currents and are used for navigation. The Marshalls Handicraft Shop, a shop on Majuro, sells a wide variety of local crafts. The shop has revived traditional handicrafts and given the Marshallese a place to sell their handiwork.

The sport of rugby is popular in the Marshall Islands, as is tennis and cricket. Sports Stadium in Majuro is home to the Marshall Island's national soccer team, which is not affiliated with FIFA. The islands also have a national basketball team.

Cultural Sites & Landmarks

Majuro is considered the cultural and economic capital of the Marshall Islands, and is home to half of the country's population. The city contains the island nation's most significant retail district, as well as numerous traditional open-air markets. Significant cultural sites include the Alele Museum, which provides a tour of Marshallese history that spans the prehistoric societies of the islands' original residents to the use of the Bikini Atoll as a nuclear test site by the United States military. The area is also home to the College of the Marshall Islands (CMI), the national postsecondary school.

The Laura islet of Majuro contains several historic landmarks, including the Peace Park Memorial, which was constructed by the Japanese to honor their fallen World War II soldiers. Near the memorial is the 1918 Typhoon Memorial, which commemorates more than 200 Marshallese who died during that devastating storm.

Outside of Majuro is the Likiep Historic District, a village that contains fifteen buildings built between the late nineteenth century and the early twentieth century (1880–1937) by German colonists who settled in the Marshall Islands in 1859. Several small commercial and religious buildings remain as testament to the German copra industry. The German colonists were interested in harvesting copra, the dried meat of the coconut, which they shipped back to Germany and sold to other European countries. German colonialism and the coconut trade greatly influenced Micronesia, particularly in terms of socio-economics and land tenure, architecture, and the advent of Christianity.

Many of the islands that make up the island nation are largely undeveloped and contain numerous protected natural zones. The Mili Atoll, for instance, has a large and diverse coral reef ecosystem that is home to thousands of fish and marine invertebrate species. Large populations of sharks, rays, and dolphins rely on the reef habitat for food and as breeding habitat. The Marshall Islands government has established a nature conservancy surrounding the Mili Atoll. Another key area for biodiversity is the Bikini Atoll, largely undisturbed since first used as a nuclear testing site in the mid-twentieth century. The Bikini Atoll's lagoon also remains home to sixteen sunken warships still accessible to divers.

The Northern Marshall Islands Atolls is a collection of seven largely uninhabited atolls that have been preserved as natural parks. The islands are lined with coral reef habitat, which is home to thousands of species. Several species of marine reptile, including the rare green turtle, use the shores of the islands to breed. Unlike many of the Pacific Islands, the Northern Atolls have no introduced plant life. They are considered one of the last existing examples of the native Pacific Islands ecosystem.

In 2005, the Likiep Village Historic District, the Mili Atoll Nature Conservancy, and the Northern Marshall Islands Atolls were submitted for tentative entry to the World Heritage Site List, maintained by the United Nations Educational, Scientific, and Cultural Organization (UNESCO). As of 2015, these three sites were still on the World Heritage List Tentative List. In 2010, however, the Bikini Atoll Nuclear Test Site was inscribed to commemorate the sixty-seven nuclear tests carried out in the area between 1946 and 1958, including the first-ever 15-megaton hydrogen-bomb test explosion in 1952, called "Castle Bravo." This test alone sent five ships to the bottom of the lagoon and created the 6,500-foot Bravo crater.

Libraries & Museums

The Alele Museum, located in downtown Majuro, functions as a historical and ethnographic museum, with displays and information about the history of the islands and their inhabitants. Among the museum's displays is an exhibit on the development of canoe technology in Micronesian culture. The museum also contains the Joachim DeBrum collection of 2,500 photographic prints, which depict traditional Marshallese life from 1880 to 1930.

Holidays

Official holidays observed in the Marshall Islands include Memorial Day and Nuclear Victim's Remembrance Day (March 1); Constitution Day (May 1); Labor Day (first Monday in September). Also celebrated are Manit Day (last Friday in September); Independence Day (October 21);

President's Day (November 17); Gospel Day, which is similar to Thanksgiving but has greater emphasis on church services (first Friday in December); and Christmas Day (December 25).

Many holiday celebrations include dancing and singing. Aging Week, the last week in May, features displays of traditional Marshallese crafts, medicines, and cookery. Fisherman's Day, celebrated on the first Friday in July, marks the beginning of an annual game-fishing tournament. Another traditional cultural festival, Alele Week, is held during the last week in August.

Youth Culture

Marshallese youth typically form their first friendships within their clan, and generally only forge outside friendships after they begin attending school. Like many other young adults, many Marshallese teenagers also work, most often in the retail industry or in family businesses. While many youth might find employment at a young age to earn recreational money, a large number do so to help the family. Youth culture is highly influenced by the culture and trends of North America and Europe, and Marshallese youth enjoy a variety of imported music, fashion, and films. English is the official language, and American trends and fashions are perhaps more popularly emulated. Sports are also a popular for both socialization and recreation, and include tennis, football (soccer), and softball.

Marshallese youth face many new challenges in the early twenty-first century. As the family structure on the Marshall Islands began to change in the late twentieth century, including a rising divorce rate, the rate of teenage suicide increased sharply, to what the government called epidemic proportions. This rising suicide rate was largely attributed to significant depression, the leading causes of which were family crisis and lack of resources. Studies have also suggested that the Marshall Islands, like other islands in Micronesia, has a rapidly increasing rate of teen pregnancy. In 2008, government groups began working with several NGOs to address, more effectively, teen pregnancy through outreach and education programs across the islands.

SOCIETY

Transportation

There are no regular public buses and shared taxis are common. Automobiles travel on the right-hand side of the road in the Marshall Islands, although Majuro has only one road. Visitors are advised to arrange the cost of their trip in advance, as there are no regulations governing taxi rates. Public transportation in most outlying islands is nonexistent.

While all inhabited islands have ports, only private commercial transport is typically available. Private boats may offer short trips between islands for a modest fee. Air Marshall Islands, the domestic carrier headquartered in Majuro, offers domestic flights from Majuro to all of the populated islands.

Transportation Infrastructure

There is an estimated 65 kilometers (40 miles) of paved roads in the Marshall Islands, with many back roads leading into rural areas. On the major islands, which include Majuro and Kwajalein, the roads are paved in asphalt, while roads on the other atolls are usually made of stone, coral, or laterite (a residual red soil). There are no railways

The islands have thirty-five airports, five of which have paved runways. Marshall Islands International Airport, also known as Amata Kabua International Airport, is located in Majuro and serves United Airlines, Air Marshall Islands, Nauru Airlines, and Japan Airlines, which charters scuba-tour flights.

Media & Communications

The government of the Marshall Islands respects the freedom of the press and allows media organizations to criticize openly government policy without reprisal. Because English is the official language, foreign English language media is popular in the country and supplements locally produced print and broadcast offerings. Freedom House, a government and media watchdog group, has classified the Marshall Islands press as "free" since it began its *Freedom in the World* surveys in 1999.

There are two locally produced newspapers in the country. The government-owned *Marshall Islands Gazette*, which is published on a monthly basis, produces news, official information and some entertainment coverage. There is also a private newspaper, *Marshall Islands Journal,* which is published on a weekly basis and provides both news and entertainment coverage. The *Marshall Islands Journal* is produced as a dual language publication in both English and Marshallese.

There are two television stations available in the Marshall Islands. The largest, MBC TV, is a state-run station providing news and public service programming, as well as several shows rebroadcast from international English language stations. AFN Kwajalein, which is produced by the U.S. military, provides news and entertainment programming, including rebroadcasting popular American programming. Satellite television is available in most urban areas and has largely supplanted local programming. Three radio stations—one state-owned (V7AB "Radio Marshalls"); one a private, religious station (V7AA "The Change 104.1"); and one run by the US military (AFN Kwajalein)—are also available.

The majority of telecommunications are provided by the Marshall Islands National Telecommunications Authority, of which the government has significant ownership. As of 2014, 11.7 percent of the population was internet users.

SOCIAL DEVELOPMENT

Standard of Living

The Marshall Islands are not ranked on the United Nations 2014 Human Development Index, which measures quality of life indicators (based on 2012 data). However, it was considered to be in the medium human development division of the index, where it was last listed in 1998.

Water Consumption

There is a severe shortage of fresh water in the Marshall Islands, the main source of which is

rainfall. Although Majuro has a 36.5 million gallon reservoir, studies have suggested that volume should be doubled in order to supply water to the country's growing population. Nevertheless, UNICEF reports that, in 2011, the urban areas in the Marshall Islands had 93.3 percent access to improved water sources, while rural areas had 97.4 percent access. Improved sanitation facilities were less pervasive, with just 84.5 percent of the urban population enjoying such access and only 56.2 percent of rural populations with the same access.

In addition, the Pacific Islands Applied Geoscience Commission has reported that power supply to the island's public utility infrastructure needs to be improved. The country's water system also has problems with pollution, due largely to the lack of reliable sanitation systems. Although work has been done to improve the existence of water-borne diseases in home water catchments, significant challenges remain.

Education

In the past, young Marshallese had no formal schooling and learned primarily from their families and communities. The Boston Missionary Society established missionary schools on twenty-two of the atolls in 1857, and these continued through World War II. Once the Marshall Islands came under American administration, a Department of Education was formed, and education through the high school level was offered.

Eight years of free and compulsory education is available for all Marshallese. English is the language of instruction.

The College of the Marshall Islands (CMI) offers courses in teacher training and nursing. In addition, the University of the South Pacific has a small campus in Majuro. The College of the Marshall Islands was recently accredited by the Western Association of Schools and Colleges (WASC) region of the Accrediting Commission for Community and Junior Colleges (ACCJC). The College of Micronesia—Majuro—was established in 1989 and operates as a satellite campus for the larger institution.

The average literacy rate in the Marshall Islands is high, at 93.6 percent among men and 93.7 among women. However, the U.S. Department of State has reported that quality and availability of education resources in the country remains a significant barrier to economic improvement.

Women's Rights

The traditional male-dominated culture of the Marshall Islands is an obstacle to establishing equal protection for women under the penal code. In cases of abuse, spousal rape, and other domestic issues, women are often reluctant to prosecute for fear of social and community criticism and reprisal. Women United Together Marshall Islands (WUTMI) is the nation's largest non-governmental organization (NGO) addressing women's rights and operates under the umbrella of the organization Pacific Women Shaping Pacific Development, known simply as Pacific Women.

Rape is illegal and carries penalties of up to twenty-five years imprisonment. Spousal rape is specifically addressed in the penal code and WUTMI observers found that the government aggressively addressed cases involving rape. Spousal abuse and other forms of domestic violence are believed to be common, but were not appropriately addressed by authorities until the passing of the Domestic Violence Prevention and Protection Act of 2011, which makes spousal abuse a criminal offense and provides additional safeguards for women through the implementation of protection orders. According to WUTMI reports, 60 percent of women have been victims of abuse in the home. To decrease the frequency of domestic abuse, workers with WUTMI and other human rights organizations are active in passing out literature and presenting educational seminars to inform women of their rights.

While traditional Marshal Island's culture is based on a matrilineal system of inheritance and property ownership, reports from the WUTMI indicate that women often own property in name only while a male relative assumed effective control over the family's property and finances. Traditional male dominance has also prevented many women from obtaining advanced positions within society. However, women frequently owned and operated private businesses, and WUTMI reports indicate that the number of women seeking private employment has increased in the twenty-first century. For example, women have occupied positions in the Marshall Island's legislature and in the judicial branch of the government, although their numbers are still few. As of the 2011 elections, while seven women ran for legislative seats, just one was elected. Reports indicate that, overall, women are less likely than men to be hired when applying for positions and earn less, on average, than male counterparts. Moreover, while the legal minimum age for women to marry is sixteen, the U.S. Department of State and UNICEF indicate that six percent of girls are married by the age of fifteen.

Health Care

The health of the Marshallese is impacted by diabetes, dysentery, obesity, high blood pressure, and malnutrition. The World Health Organization estimates that 90 percent of hospital admissions in 2014 were due to type-2 diabetes-related complications. On some islands, children suffer blindness due to a lack of vitamin A. The infant mortality rate is high, at 20.66 deaths per 1,000 live births.

The population of the Marshall Islands also faces a unique health situation due to nuclear testing on some of the atolls. Cancer is the main disease related to these tests. The United States has paid compensation claims of $63 million (USD) to 1,500 people affected by radiation. Lack of qualified medical personnel, including doctors and nurses, is a continuing problem throughout the islands, with just 0.44 doctors and 2.7 hospital beds to every 1,000 people. The largest hospital is the Majuro Hospital, which employs 65 percent of all the Marshall Islands' health workers, according to the World Health Organization. Ebeye's hospital employs 27 percent of the country's health workers.

GOVERNMENT

Structure

British Captain John Marshall mapped the Marshall Islands in 1788, providing them with their English name. After being controlled by Germany and Japan, the Marshall Islands became part of the United States' Trust Territory of the Pacific Islands in 1946. The U.S. used the Bikini and Enewetak atolls for nuclear testing until 1958.

On July 12, 1978, the Marshallese voted for self-government as a Trust Territory of the U.S. A constitution was approved and a government was installed on May 1, 1979. It achieved full sovereignty from the U.S. on October 21, 1986.

In October 1986, the United States and the Marshall Islands entered into a Compact of Free Association that gave the islands approximately $1 billion (USD) over fifteen years, along with compensation for the effects of nuclear testing. The United States is also responsible for the islands' defense. In May 2004, an amended agreement was approved and considerations to the country were increased.

The Republic of the Marshall Islands is a constitutional government. The executive branch includes the president, who is both chief of state and head of the government. The president is elected from the ranks of the Nitijela (Parliament), and the president chooses the executive cabinet from its members. The president serves a four-year term and is not subject to term limits.

The Marshall Islands' legislature is bicameral. The Council of Iroij, consisting of clan twelve chiefs, administers matters of custom and tradition on the islands. They specifically advise the presidential cabinet and review laws to be sure they are in accordance with clan practice. The Nitijela has thirty-three members, called senators, who are elected to four-year terms. Majuro has five seats, Kwajalein has three, Ailinglaplap, Arno, and Jaluit have two each, and the other regions have one seat each. The inhabited islands each have a mayor and an island council to handle local affairs.

Political Parties

There are no formal political parties in the Marshall Islands, as none of the organizations running for office has headquarters, designated party structures, or official platforms. However, two major political groups have competed in recent general elections. These organizations include the United Democratic Party and Aelon Kein Ad, which is a led by a group of traditional Marshallese chiefs. However, neither group is incorporated under law. The general elections held on the islands in 2003, 2007, and 2011 were non-partisan elections.

Local Government

On atolls of the Marshall Islands that are considered municipalities—of which there are twenty-four—an elected mayor and a traditional chief oversee issues of government. The mayor oversees local environmental protection, building projects and utilities.

Judicial System

The judicial system of the Marshall Islands is based on British and U.S. common and customary law. Judicial branches include the Supreme Court, the High Court, and district and community courts. A Traditional Rights Court decides land disputes.

Taxation

Local governments on the Marshall Islands charge a sales tax that ranges from two to four percent. New businesses in tourism, manufacturing, and fishing that register with the Office of the Minister of Finance are exempted from having to pay a gross revenue tax for a period of five years. However, the government also offers exemption for other industries, such as mining, in exchange for a royalty fee. On-shore businesses play a 3 percent gross revenue tax, while non-resident, offshore businesses are exempt from taxes. Individual taxes include an 8 percent annual income tax that increases to 12 percent after the first $10,400 earned.

Armed Forces

The defense of the Marshall Islands is the sole responsibility of the United States. The country has no standing army of any kind.

Foreign Policy

While recognized as a free and sovereign nation, the Marshall Islands has a special relationship with the U.S., defined under the terms of the Compact of Free Association (COFA) put into place in 1986 and renegotiated between 1999 and 2003. Under the terms of the compact, which was approved by popular vote in 2004, the U.S. agreed to provide $57 (USD) million in annual assistance to the Marshall Islands until 2024. The U.S. also provides Marshallese citizens access to some federal programs, such as the U.S. postal system and the Small Business Administration, and the Marshallese may travel to the U.S. without a visa. In addition, the Marshall Islands allows the U.S. to remain the sole military presence on the islands, while the U.S. provides the islands with defense. Prior to the first COFA signed in 1986, the formal establishment of the Republic of the Marshall Islands in 1979, the island nations was a Trust Territory of the U.S.

In accordance with the free association agreement, the U.S. takes complete responsibility for the safety and security of the Marshall Islands. The Marshall Islands government is free to form economic, diplomatic, and trade agreements with any nation, so long as such associations do not threaten the security of U.S. military forces operating on the islands. The Marshall Islands is a member of prominent international organizations and institutions, including the United Nations (UN), which it joined as a member state in 1991, and the International Monetary Fund (IMF). The Marshall Islands also participates in several international organizations and forums aimed at protecting natural resources in the Pacific and in developing financial independence for the islands.

Human Rights Profile

International human rights law insists that states respect civil and political rights and promote an individual's economic, social, and cultural rights. The United Nations Universal Declaration on Human Rights (UDHR) is recognized as the standard for international human rights. Its authors sought the counsel of the world's great thinkers, philosophers, and religious leaders and were careful to create a document that reflects the core values shared by every world culture. (To read this document or view the articles relating to cultural human rights, visit http://www.ohchr. org/EN/UDHR/Pages/Introduction.aspx.)

The Marshall Islands is a functional democratic system with a strong record of protecting the rights of citizens. However, human rights monitoring organizations have identified several areas of concern, including prison conditions, women's rights, human trafficking, and insufficient protection of workers in the manufacturing and agricultural industries.

Government reports indicate that poor prison conditions in the Marshall Islands are a result of a general lack of resources for prison maintenance. According to observers, prisoners lacked adequate access to sanitary and medical facilities, a violation of Article 5 of the UDHR, which guarantees freedom from inhumane treatment. In addition, observers found that juveniles are sometimes housed with the adult prison population, placing them at increased risk for rape and violence. This is a violation of Article 25, guaranteeing special status for women and children.

While the government of the Marshall Islands is committed to child welfare, there are insufficient resources to effectively monitor child welfare in rural areas. The nation's child and family services divisions are concentrated in urban areas and larger towns. While the law requires teachers and other childcare workers to report suspicion of abuse to police, reports are uncommon.

Some monitoring agencies have reported that persons of Chinese descent face discrimination on the Marshall Islands and police and government officials are reluctant to address abuse. Other reports indicate that the law does not adequately protect homosexual and transgender persons, who are often victims of discrimination because of societal norms prohibiting open homosexual behavior. Discrimination based on sexual orientation, nationality, and creed is prohibited under the penal code.

While national law mandates a minimum wage for private and public sector work, worker's rights organizations have argued that the minimum wage is not sufficient to provide for family welfare. In addition, some workers' rights organizations have argued that the government does not adequately enforce the wage laws. Many workers, particularly in the industrial and agricultural industries, work in poor conditions, posing a risk to their health and welfare. The Marshallese labor office sets national standards for working conditions, but lacks the resources to ensure that workers are protected from dangerous conditions, especially in rural areas.

The United States had also put the Marshall Islands on the U.S. State Department's Tier 2 Watch List in its 2013 and 2014 *Trafficking in Humans Report* because the country has failed to put measures in place to halt the practice. Because the Trafficking Victims Protection Act only allows a country to remain on the Tier 2 Watch List for two consecutive years, the Marshall Islands was moved to Tier 3 in the 2015 report. However, the U.S. State Department indicates in the 2015 report that RMI still does not comply with the minimum standards for the elimination of trafficking, there have been no prosecutions of traffickers in the previous four years, and only one investigation was launched in 2013.

ECONOMY

Overview of the Economy

The economy of the Marshall Islands relies on assistance from the United States. The Amended Compact of Free Association links the two countries. Under this agreement, the U.S. provides aid through 2024, when a trust fund will take over payments. Under the revised Compact, the RMI will receive $1.5 billion (USD) in economic aid. Such revenue accounts for approximately 70 percent of the Marshall Islands' gross domestic product (GDP).

Many basic necessities, including rice, meat, tobacco, equipment, and petroleum, are imported to the Marshall Islands, along with luxury items such as cola and coffee. In fact, imports expenditures exceed export income. For example, in 2013, exports were recorded at $53.7 million (USD), while imports were $133.7 million (USD). Most of the technology, motor vehicles, and industrial machinery are also imported. The U.S. and Japan remain the island nation's most important trading partners.

In recent years, the economy has suffered due to government downsizing (the government employs more than half the workforce), drought, and a decline in tourism revenue. In 2014, the per capita GDP was estimated at $3,300 (USD).

Overseas workers also make a significant contribution to the economy of the Marshall Islands. The Compact of Free Association allows Marshallese to join the U.S. military, and many do. In fact, the Marshall Islands surpasses any single U.S. state in enlistee numbers.

Industry

Industry in the Marshall Islands is limited to tuna and coconut processing and handicrafts manufacturing. Investors hope to diversify the economy by starting clam and black pearl farms, although this plan has yet to take hold. In addition, there are plans to build a fishing services center for ships at Majuro. Approximately 600 ships are registered by the Marshall Islands, generating $1 million (USD) in revenue each year.

The United States' Kwajalein Missile Range contributes heavily to the local economy, paying $32 million (USD) in annual salaries and $15 million (USD) in rent. The government also employs over 30 percent of the Marshallese workforce.

Energy/Power/Natural Resources

The Marshall Islands' most important natural resource is the ocean that surrounds the country, particularly the marine life and minerals in the deep seabeds surrounding the atolls. The biggest environmental problem facing the Marshall Islands is the radioactive contamination of the atolls where the United States has conducted nuclear testing. Other environmental problems include a lack of potable water; pollution of lagoons, particularly Majuro lagoon, from sewage and fishing ships; and drought. In 1997–98, the islands experienced such severe drought that people in Majuro had access to clean water only one day a week.

Fishing

The majority of the Marshall Islands' fisheries revenue comes from foreign fishing licensing. Fishing, nonetheless, remains vital to the economy of the islands. Sport fishing, although part of the tourism industry, also contributes revenue to the economy.

Forestry

While 12 percent of RMI's landmass is urban and developed, the Marshall Islands have an estimated 70 percent of forest cover thanks to coconut plantations and agroforests, according to the U.S. Department of Agriculture Pacific Northwest Research Station.

Mining/Metals

Minerals, such as cobalt and manganese, have been discovered in the deep seabeds around the atolls, but these deposits have not yet been mined.

Agriculture

Much of the Marshall Islands' agriculture is done at the subsistence level. Nearly 51 percent of available land is used for agricultural purposes, with 7.8 percent cultivated and planted, 11.7 percent in permanent pasture, and 31.2 percent in permanent crops. Coconut palms are the top

cash crop, contributing 4.4 percent to the country's GDP. Other important agricultural products include breadfruit, tomatoes, melons, sweet potatoes, yams, and taro.

Animal Husbandry

Livestock includes pigs and chickens, and these are largely kept for family and community subsistence purposes rather than for export. Generally, the island cannot provide for other livestock.

Tourism

The Marshall Islands are renowned among tourists for the excellent diving and sport fishing available in the surrounding waters. The abundant marine life and the plethora of shipwrecks bring adventurous divers from around the world to the country. The Majuro Atoll is a particularly popular spot for diving and ocean exploration, and boasts a wide diversity of marine life. Day trips are also taken to nearby Bikini Atoll, the site of U.S. nuclear weapon testing in the mid-20th century. The atoll is home to a number of sunken ships available for wreck diving, including the USS Saratoga, which is the world's largest ocean wreck available for diving.

As of 2015, the tourism industry employs a small sector of the work force, and that percentage is expected to grow as the sector expands. As of 2012, the World Bank indicated that just 4,600 overnight tourists visited the Marshall Islands, suggesting there is significant room for industry growth.

Micah Issitt, Roberta Baxter, and Savannah Schroll Guz

DO YOU KNOW?

- The Marshall Islands are often called the "Pearl of the Pacific," because its twenty-nine coral atolls resemble a string of pearls when viewed against the blue backdrop of the Pacific Ocean.

- The area around Majuro Atoll has long been prized for its aquatic biodiversity, but the Marshall Islands also contain a variety of habitats for migratory and littoral bird species. Approximately eighty-four species of bird have been catalogued on the islands, including several that are endemic to the region and five that are globally endangered.

Bibliography

Booth, Thomas. *Micronesia: The Marshall Islands.*
Winston Salem, NC: Hunter Publishing, 2012. Hunter
Travel Ser.

Brash, Celeste, Brett Atkinson, et al. *South Pacific &
Micronesia.* Oakland, CA: Lonely Planet Press, 2012.

Hezel, Francis X. *The First Taint of Civilization: A History
of the Caroline and Marshall Islands in Pre Colonial
Days, 1521–1885.* Honolulu, HI: U of Hawaii P, 2000.
Pacific Islands Monograph Ser.

———. *The New Shape of Old Island Cultures: A Half
Century of Social Change in Micronesia.* Honolulu, HI:
University of Hawaii Press, 2001.

———. *Strangers in Their Own Land: A Century of
Colonial Rule in the Caroline and Marshall Islands.*
Honolulu, HI: University of Hawaii Press, 2003. Pacific
Islands Monograph Ser.

Kelin, Daniel A., II, ed. *Marshall Islands Legends and
Stories.* Honolulu, HI: Bess Press, Inc. 2003.

Levy, Neil M. *Micronesia.* 5th ed. New York: Avalon
Travel Publishing, 2000.

Rapaport, Moshe. *The Pacific Islands: Environment &
Society.* Rev. ed. Honolulu, HI: U of Hawaii P, 2013.

Rudiak-Gould, Peter. *Surviving Paradise: One Year on a
Disappearing Island.* Oakland, CA: Andy Ross Agency,
2013.

Works Cited

BBC. "Marshall Islands Country Profile." *BBC News.*
BBC, 12 Sept. 2015. http://news.bbc.co.uk/2/hi/asia-
pacific/country_profiles/1167854.stm.

Bureau of Democracy, Human Rights and Labor. "Marshall
Islands." *Country Reports on Human Rights Practices
for 2014.* U.S. Department of State, 2015. Web. http://
www.state.gov/j/drl/rls/hrrpt/humanrightsreport/index.
htm#wrapper.

Bureau of East Asian and Pacific Affairs. "U.S. Relations
with Marshall Islands." *US Department of State.* US
Department of State, 4 Feb. 2015. Web. http://www.
state.gov/r/pa/ei/bgn/26551.htm.

CIA. "Marshall Islands." *The World Factbook.* Central
Intelligence Agency, 2015. Web. https://www.cia.gov/
library/publications/the-world-factbook/geos/rm.html.

Freedom House. "Marshall Islands." *Freedom in the World
2015.* Freedom House, 2015. Web. https://freedomhouse.
org/report/freedom-world/2015/marshall-islands.

Economic Policy, Planning, and Statistics Office. *The RMI
2011 Census of Population and Housing Summary and
Highlights Only.* Majuro, Marshall Islands: RMI Office
of the President, 2012. PDF.

"Marshall Islands Courts System Information." *Pacific
Islands Legal Information Institute.* University of the
South Pacific, 2001. Web. http://www.paclii.org/mh/
courts.html.

"Marshall Islands: Drought—May 2013." *ReliefWeb.*
United Nations Office for the Coordination of
Humanitarian Affairs, 2015. Web. http://reliefweb.int/
disaster/dr-2013–000053-mhl.

Marshall Islands: Pearl of the Pacific. Marshall
Islands Visitor's Authority, 2013. Web. http://www.
visitmarshallislands.com/

Spennemann, Dirk H.R., ed. "Culture." *Marshalls: Digital
Micronesia.* Charles Sturt University, Australia/Dirk H.
R. Spennemann, 2005. Web. http://marshall.csu.edu.au/
Marshalls/Marshalls_Culture.html.

U.S. Department of Agriculture Forest Service. "Marshall
Islands." *Pacific Northwest Research Station.* USDA
Forest Service, 27 Oct. 2014. Web. http://www.fs.fed.us/
pnw/rma/fia-topics/state-stats/Marshall-Islands/index.
php.

U.S. Department of State. "Marshall Islands." *Trafficking
in Persons Report 2015.* US Department of State, 2015.
Web. http://www.state.gov/j/tip/rls/tiprpt/2015/index.
htm.

UN Development Programme. "Table 1: Human
Development Index and its components." *Human
Development Reports.* UNDP, 2015. Web. http://hdr.
undp.org/en/content/table-1-human-development-index-
and-its-components.

UNICEF. "Marshall Islands." *UNICEF Statistics.* UNICEF,
2013. Web. http://www.unicef.org/infobycountry/
marshallislands_statistics.html.

"Visiting the RMI." *US Embassy of the Republic of
Marshall Islands.* RMI Embassy, 2005. Web. http://
www.rmiembassyus.org/Visiting%20the%20RMI.htm.

"Women United Together Marshall Islands (WUTMI)."
Pacific Women Shaping Pacific Development. Australian
Government/Secretariat of the Pacific Community,
2015. Web. http://www.pacificwomen.org/pacific-links/
women-united-together-marshall-islands-wutmi/.

World Bank. "International tourism, number of arrivals."
World Bank Data. The World Bank Group, 2015. Web.
http://data.worldbank.org/indicator/ST.INT.ARVL.

———. "Paying Taxes in Marshall Islands." *Doing
Business.* The World Bank Group, 2015. Web. http://
www.doingbusiness.org/data/exploreeconomies/
marshall-islands/paying-taxes/.

World Health Organization West Pacific Region. *Human
Resources for Health Country Profile: Marshall Islands.*
Geneva, Switzerland: World Health Organization, 2014.
PDF.

MICRONESIA,
Federated States of

Introduction

Located in the northern part of the Pacific Ocean between Hawaii and Indonesia, the Federated States of Micronesia (FSM) are part of the geopolitical region known as Oceania, and part of the larger island grouping known as Micronesia. The Federation's 607 islands are collected into four major island groupings that are represented by the states of Chuuk (formerly Truk), Kosrae (formerly Kosaie), Pohnpei (formerly Ponape), and Yap.

Once a part of the Trust Territory of the Pacific Islands under United States administration, the Federated States of Micronesia achieved near full independence in 1986. The United States has pledged to continue to supply economic aid until at least 2023.

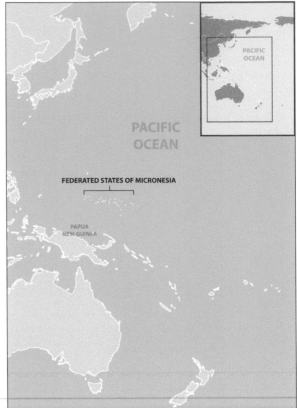

GENERAL INFORMATION

Official Language: English
Population: 103,000 (2012 estimate)
Currency: United States dollar
Coins: The U.S. dollar is divided into cents, and 100 cents are equal to one dollar. There are 1, 5, 10, and 25-cent coin denominations. In addition, a 50-cent coin and a 1-dollar coin is also available, but are rarely used.
Land Area: 702 square kilometers (271 square miles)
National Motto: "Peace, Unity, Liberty"
National Anthem: "Patriots of Micronesia"
Capital: Palikir (on Pohnpei)
Time Zone: GMT +11

Flag Description: The flag of the Federated States of Micronesia is light blue, which represents the Pacific Ocean. In the center of the flag are four white stars, representing Chuuk, Pohnpei, Kosrae, and Yap.

Population

Most of the Federation's residents live in or around the urban centers located in each state. The FSM have a high immigration rate and its annual population growth rate is just 0.26 percent. However, beginning in the 1990s, there have been a growing number of expatriates settling in the FSM. These include citizens from the United States, Europe, and Asia.

Languages

Although the official language of the Federated States of Micronesia is English, a variety of regional languages is also commonly spoken. These languages include Trukese, Pohnpeian,

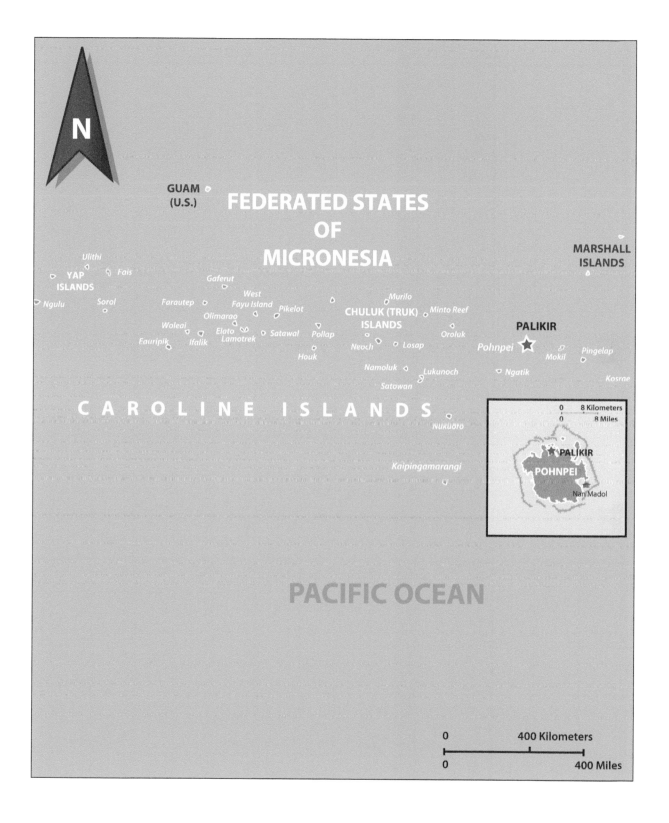

**Principal Cities by Population
(2012 estimates):**

- Weno (17,747)
- Palikir (7,747)
- Kitti (7,743)
- Nett (6,375)
- Madolenihmw (6,293)
- Tol (5,654)
- Kolonia (4,396)
- Fefen (4,024)
- Tonoas (3,762)
- Uman (2,847)

Yapese, Kosrean, Ulithian, Woleaian, Nukuoro, and Kapingamarangi.

Native People & Ethnic Groups

Micronesia's earliest inhabitants likely came by outrigger canoe to settle on the island of Yap anywhere between 4,000 and 2,000 years ago from the Philippines and Indonesia. Later peoples traveled from the islands of Melanesia to populate the rest of Micronesia's current territory.

The Federated States of Micronesia are home to nine primary ethnic groups derived from the islands of Micronesia and Polynesia. Of these, the Chuukese and Pohnpeian groups make up the overwhelming majority. Pohnpeians represent about a quarter of the national population, in fact, and a small number of Polynesians live on the Kapingamarangi atoll (an atoll is a coral island enclosing a lagoon) of Pohnpei State. Social groupings in Micronesia are organized primarily around clans in which extended families, including close relations and adopted individuals, live together.

Religions

The islands' residents are overwhelmingly Christian. About 50 percent of the population, most of them residents of Yap, practice Catholicism, with about 47 percent of the remainder practicing some form of Protestantism. Buddhists comprise 0.7 percent of the popula-

tion. Freedom of religion in the FSM is protected under the constitution.

Climate

The Federates States of Micronesia lie within a tropical climate zone. All of the states, but particularly the islands in the eastern part of the Federation, experience heavy rainfall throughout the year. There are also occasional severe typhoons during typhoon season, from August to December. Destructive storms are uncommon on Pohnpei, unlike in the western extremities of the FSM. The island is situated on the southern edge of a typhoon zone. In 1905, a typhoon blew through the area destroying the old capital of Kolonia.

Temperatures on the islands hover at an average of 27° Celsius (81° Fahrenheit) throughout the year.

ENVIRONMENT & GEOGRAPHY

Topography

The Federated States of Micronesia are spread over an expanse of the Pacific Ocean about 5,000 kilometers (3,000 miles) west of Hawaii and 3,000 kilometers (2,000 miles) east of the Philippines. Papua New Guinea lies about 1,500 kilometers (about 1,000 miles) to the north.

Most of Micronesia's 607 islands are volcanic, creating rugged landscapes with steep cliffs, deep valleys, and dense, tropical vegetation. Volcanic peaks are covered in upland rainforests.

Unlike the islands of the other three states, Yap was created by a ridge in the Asian tectonic plate, and is covered in gentle, rolling hills. The Federation's hundreds of islands create a wealth of lagoons, harbors, coral atolls, and volcanic outcroppings.

Pohnpei accounts for half of the Federation's land mass.

Plants & Animals

Micronesia's upland forests, rich volcanic soil, and tropical climate make the islands home to a huge variety of plant and animal species, many of which are found nowhere else on earth. Micronesia's remote location in the Pacific Ocean means that there are very few mammals native to the islands. Those that are endemic are endangered by the destruction of forested lands for human cultivation. Environmental organizations are working to protect the Chuuk, Mortlock Islands, Pohnpei, and Marianas flying fox. These indigenous fruit bats can have a wingspan of up to 1 meter (3 feet) and can be seen wheeling about the islands' skies at dawn and dusk.

The Federated States are also home to the Polynesian sheath-tailed bat, and the dugong, a manatee-like marine animal. On Pohnpei, a few remaining Asian deer are found in unpopulated areas.

Micronesia coastal areas and rainforests are the habitat for a wealth of lizards, skinks, and geckos, though no snakes inhabit the islands. The majority of Micronesia's animal life, however, comes in the form of insects, particularly mosquitoes, gnats, and cockroaches.

The waters off the Micronesian islands are home to a variety of coral, a big draw for scuba divers. These waters also provide the habitat for sea turtles, lionfish, stingrays, whales, sharks, and barracuda.

CUSTOMS & COURTESIES

Greetings

Because of the friendliness of the Micronesian people, warm greetings accompanied by a smile are the norm regardless of social standing or age differences. Although some variations occur across the island grouping, nearly all greetings share a certain degree of informality. One common greeting across the islands is "Where are you coming from?" or "Where are you going?"

People on the islands on Yap, Chuuk, or Pohnpei may hail others, particularly visitors and passers-by, with the common phrase of "Budoh mongoi" ("Come and eat"). This is an invitation rather than a simple greeting, and requires the one greeted either to take some food or to decline by saying "I am full." Other greetings are also common in each of these island groups. For example, the greeting "Kaselehlie" ("Hello") is frequently used on Pohnpei, while the Chuukese may offer "Ran annim" ("Good morning"). On the Yap islands, "Kafel" ("It was good") is often used in both greeting and leave taking. A common exchange between friends is "Mogethin?" ("What did you come here for?").

Inclining one's head in greeting is a common Micronesian practice. To greet someone passing by, Micronesians may catch someone's eye and nod or raise their eyebrows. Western practices such as hand shaking have only a limited presence on the islands; instead, Micronesians often bow when meeting others. However, the use of the English language greetings is widespread.

Gestures & Etiquette

Although the federation has a casual, informal culture, certain behaviors are expected of people depending on their sex, age, and status. Family members of the opposite sex follow set patterns of seating and interaction. For example, women are required to sit below the level at which male relatives are seated. On traditional islands such as Yap, women are also expected to bow to men when walking past them. If a man passes a woman, tradition demands that that woman crouch until he has gone by. As the most traditional of the islands in the FSM, Yap also has a social caste system requiring lower status members to defer to higher status members. The island favors modest dress, with women often wearing long skirts to cover their thighs.

Micronesians avoid walking between two people who are talking to each other. If splitting up a chatting pair is unpreventable, a deep bow accompanied by a request to pass (such as "excuse me") is customary. Similarly, at a gathering where many people may be seated on the ground, it is considered rude to step over someone else. Instead, a Micronesian walks around anyone sitting, being careful not to step between those who may be talking to one another. When sitting, polite behavior calls for women to curl their legs to one side and men to cross their legs.

Because much of Micronesian culture is based on the idea of sharing, the offering and acceptance of food and drink are important social gestures. Only when a person is genuinely quite full from a recent meal should an offer of food be refused. Additionally, beverages should always be welcomed. Failing to offer food to visitors may be perceived as a breach of etiquette.

In Micronesia, maintaining eye contact is considered rude. Instead, Micronesians make eye contact only momentarily while conversing before generally focusing away from the other person. Typically, Micronesians look downward or at a point away from others' faces when talking. Eye contact between men and women is generally considered a flirtatious gesture.

Eating/Meals

While mealtime practices vary somewhat from island to island, some customs are culturally pervasive across the federation. For example, Micronesian men traditionally retain responsibility for catching or harvesting food while women prepare the food. Usually, women and older girls also clean up after the meal, and any extra food is typically shared with family and friends. On most islands, meals rarely appear at set times, For example, Pohnpeians typically eat when hungry rather than waiting for a specific time, while on Kosrae and Yap, two and three meals per day are the norm, respectively.

Most Micronesians use utensils to eat. On the islands of Chuuk, eating with the hands is still relatively common at family meals, although utensils are typically used at restaurants. The concept of sharing that underlies Micronesian meals can also be seen in the use of communal plates in addition to individual plates. Banana leaves and coconut husks sometimes serve as extra plates and cups. Talking during meals is frowned upon, as is it believed to interfere with eating.

Traditionally, feasts hold great significance in Micronesian culture. These grand meals often mark important events, such as birthdays, holidays, and funerals. In fact, one of the first adult responsibilities taken on by young people is helping stage these events. At feasts, foods are varied and plentiful. For example, Yapese feasts may feature not only breadfruit and fish, but also pig, chicken, and lobster. Etiquette dictates that guests at a feast take home any leftovers to share with others or to eat on following days.

Visiting

Because of the close family and social ties common on Micronesia, visits to the homes of family and friends are frequent occurrences. In fact, neglecting to visit someone for an extended period may be considered rude. Some visits may be prompted by events such as childbirth or illness, while others are simply a chance to engage in a favorite Micronesian activity: chatting. Since Micronesians often honor Sunday as a day of rest, that day is a popular choice for visits.

Usually, Micronesians simply stop by one another's homes without making formal arrangements beforehand. Food and drink are typically offered to visitors upon arrival. A courteous guest either accepts this offer or politely declines. Often, social visits take place outside, with both hosts and visitors sitting on woven mats. Many Micronesians have a special open-air house used for entertaining and leisure activities. If a social gathering occurs in this usually simple building, people sit on the ground against the walls. The head of the household may sit in the doorway, although others generally do not linger in doorways so as not to block others from entering or exiting the room.

Adults and young people—even relatives— do not participate in the same social groups, although older people may entertain children by telling them stories from Micronesia's oral tradition. Adult Micronesians enjoy playing cards and board games while talking with friends and family. Children often play together on the beach or in the ocean.

LIFESTYLE

Family

Traditionally, Micronesian society centers on the family rather than the individual. Thus, Micronesians perform most day-to-day activities, such as eating and working, alongside others in their families. Families often live on extended compounds, with several generations sharing a large plot of land. Micronesian bloodlines on many islands are matrilineal, meaning that family relationships pass through from a mother to her children. For this reason, family compounds are generally made up of people related through their female relatives. When a Micronesian woman marries, her new husband joins her family compound. The couple then claims a portion of the land as their own. On some islands, such as Kosrae, couples may instead decide to live with the groom's family.

On traditional islands, relationships are close knit and family elders are highly respected. Older or infirm members of the family are typically cared for by younger generations. Many children are raised not by their parents, but by extended relatives. Aunts and uncles are commonly called by the words for "mother" and "father" by their nieces and nephews, regardless of whether they are actually raising them.

On capital islands where Western lifestyles have become more common, these traditional ties have begun to wane. Families are more likely to live in independent nuclear family groups and have less contact with extended family members.

Housing

The type of housing in which a Micronesian lives relies somewhat on the available resources of their particular island. On main islands, cement houses with glass windows and flat tin roofs are common. These homes may have electricity, providing residents the capability to have some basic cooking appliances such as rice cookers.

In outlying islands, homes are more likely to be constructed of inexpensive local wood or of woven mats. These mats are used not only as the exterior walls of huts, but also as also as simple walls dividing the interior space. On some islands, thatched roofs made of the fronds of native plants are very common. These roofs are attached after the completion of the rest of the building using nun, a locally produced rope made of coconut husks. Although electricity is rarely available on islands with these types of homes, some families have generators to provide power.

The Micronesian family compound typically contains several independent houses, each the property of an independent family unit. Compounds also are home to shared, free-standing kitchens with kerosene stoves or clay ovens. On hot nights, Micronesians may sleep in the shared building commonly used for entertaining.

Food

Fresh fish is widely available and inexpensive throughout the federation, making it a staple for all Micronesians. Traditionally, fish is baked in a charcoal or clay oven. Years of Japanese occupation influenced Micronesian cuisine, and the Japanese combinations of raw fish and rice known as sushi and sashimi are popular fish preparations. Tropical fruits such as papayas, coconuts, and bananas are also common on the islands and are often served as a dessert or eaten as a snack. Despite a relatively brief growing season, breadfruit is the most popular fruit. With a starchy texture not unlike that of a potato, the breadfruit serves as the basis for many Micronesian dishes. Breadfruit can be baked and eaten plain, or stuffed with meat such as chicken or Spam, which is widely consumed in the islands due to its long shelf life.

After the seasonal breadfruit, taro—a vegetable with both edible roots and leaves—is the most widespread plant food on the island. Grown year round, taro makes up an important part of the Micronesian diet. One traditional preparation of taro, called rodimadok, makes use of both the root and the leaf. First, grated taro root is wrapped in a taro leaf pouch and baked. The pouch is then opened and the baked root is mixed with a little coconut milk or water and sugar. A more complex taro recipe, pilolo in mwehng, also combines grated taro root with water and sugar. Some coconut cream and cornstarch are added to this mixture, which is then rolled into balls and baked to make a sweet taro roll.

In recent years, increased consumption of American-style foods has begun causing significant health problems for Micronesians. Diet-related diseases such as diabetes and obesity have risen as Micronesians have developed a taste for sugary or fatty imported foods.

Life's Milestones

Family plays a significant role in Micronesian society. Although the practice of arranged marriage has declined, relationships are typically formalized only after agreements are made among a couple and their families. Church ceremonies of greater or lesser size have largely replaced the traditional grand feast that once marked a marriage.

Traditionally, women on many Micronesian islands reside at the local depal, or women's house, during, and for several days following, childbirth. Female family members from both sides of the family typically assist with births. Exceptions to this practice occur on Pohnpei, where a trained medical doctor often oversees a birth, and on Kosrae, where only a women's mother is required to be present. Because of the traditionally high infant mortality rate, the birth of a child is often not celebrated until that child's first birthday.

Death is as much a community affair as birth. A deceased person is usually kept in the home for no more than two days before the funeral. During this mourning period, visitors come to comfort the family. Women display their grief by wailing loudly. Typically, the deceased is placed on a woven mat inside a painted coffin and buried in a grave. On some islands, a large feast follows the funeral.

CULTURAL HISTORY

Traditional Arts & Crafts

Although the fine arts such as painting and sculpture never took hold in Micronesia, artisans of the past were skilled woodworkers. Carved human figures were sometimes used to decorate community men's houses, where adult males relaxed and talked. More often, craftspeople made functional items such as bowls and dance paddles, as well as decorative items such as jewelry.

On the islands of Chuuk, one of FSM's four states, carved wooden rods known as love sticks were vital to traditional courtship methods. Each Chuukese man owned a uniquely carved love stick, some reaching up to 4 meters (13 feet) in length. During the night, a man who was interested in a particular young woman traveled to her home and slid the stick through the hut's thatched wall in an attempt to wake her. Upon awakening, the young woman felt the carvings on the love stick to determine the identity of her caller. Then, she signified her interest by pulling the stick into the hut in invitation, shaking it to show that she would come out to meet him, or pushing the stick out altogether to show her lack of interest. This traditional practice has largely fallen out of favor.

On Yap, where islanders have long been recognized for their navigational prowess in simple canoes, wooden charms called hos were considered vital aids to the safety of a journey for centuries. Micronesians believed that these charms contained powerful magical abilities to control the weather and keep dangerous storms at bay during a canoe voyage. Craftspeople carved a charm from a block of wood into a stylized human form and tipped it with stingray spines. These sharp additions were both the source of the charm's name and its weather-controlling powers. Before each voyage, a navigator invoked his hos by chanting to the yalulawei, a group of local sea deities. The charm then came aboard ship, where it resided in a place of honor along with offerings to the yalulawei. After the successful completion of a voyage, the hos went back to the main canoe house—the only land location that could contain its magic.

One of the more historic and prominent arts of the islands is weaving. The backstrap loom, a simple weaving instrument made of sticks and rope, was probably introduced to the islands by travelers from Southeast Asia. Taking its name from the strap that secured it to the waist of the weaver, the backstrap loom was highly portable and able to make a wide variety of fabric objects, including clothing, mats, and baskets. Evidence suggests that use of the backstrap loom in Micronesia predated the arrival of Europeans by hundreds of years.

Micronesian women soon became sophisticated weavers, and the textile arts rose to great prominence within Micronesian culture. On Pohnpei, a specially woven sash known as the tor came to symbolize status and power. This sash was worn by both men and women over the traditional Micronesia fiber skirt. Each prominent Pohnpeian family owned a specific combination of color and pattern, a concept not unlike the European crest of arms. Duplication was prohibited, and someone caught wearing a tor to which he or she had no familial right could be put to death. By the early 20th century, the influence of Christian missionaries had led to a decline in backstrap weaving and its associated garments.

Architecture

Much of the architecture of FSM is a blend of elements both traditional and modern. The capital of Palikir, for example, built expressly as a governmental administrative center to replace the adjacent town of Kolonia, was designed so that the new administrative complex would harmonize with the surrounding landscape. To do so, Palikir's designers laid out a series of low-rise buildings landscaped with native flora. The modern buildings also incorporate elements of traditional Micronesian building styles, including the use of numerous columns for both structural and aesthetic purposes. In addition, the main thoroughfare was built in an east-west direction to take advantage of natural lighting as well as the cooling trade winds.

Dance & Music

The traditional dancing of Yap constitutes one of the most important traditional Micronesian art forms. Dancing holds such prominence in Yapese society, in fact, that villages typically have a special area called a dancing circle set aside for performances. Some Yapese even assert that a person who cannot dance cannot truly call him or herself Yapese. On Yap, parents teach their children dances from a young age, and people of all ages, sexes, and castes perform these dances. Some common dances include the stick dance, the standing dance, and the marching dance. Groups, sometimes of mixed gender and sometimes of men or women, perform all of these dances only. Feasts and special occasions call for dancing, as do dance contests held between different villages.

Dance provides the impetus for another art form: the dance paddle of Pohnpei. These wooden paddles are inscribed with geometric designs and further decorated with leaves from the pandanus tree. In the traditional Pohnpeian paddle dance, sound and movement combine with cultural heritage. Four rows of dancers—two of women and two of men—perform together, each with a specific type of dance. During the performance, dancers chant stories from the Pohnpeian oral tradition.

This mixture of chanting and tapping forms the basis for traditional Micronesian music, which has little history of instrumentation. Music is often performed as an accompaniment to dance rather than as a stand-alone art form, and traditionally tells stories from the islands' past. Western influence on Micronesia's arts can be heard in the local music. Christian church hymns accompanied European missionaries to the islands, and today Micronesians continue to enjoy signing those hymns. Choral groups of all ages and sexes often perform at churches and festivals.

Literature

In Micronesia, folklore and Truk (Chuuk) Island mythology had flourished for at least several centuries before the arrival of Spanish explorers in the sixteenth century. The presence of a ruling elite graced with ample leisure time encouraged the growth of storytelling and poetry. The lack of a written language meant that those stories and poems were held in the somewhat fluid oral tradition. On the islands of Chuuk, it was believed that the vocation of storytelling came from Anulap, a Micronesian deity representing both magic and knowledge. These storytellers underwent formal training to learn both folklore and magic.

Recurring themes in Micronesian folklore were often related to contemporary problems of the society and were tied to the surrounding sea. Creation tales told of the formation of the world from the heavens and explained the shape and geographical distribution of the many Micronesian islands. One tale attributed this scattering of land to the actions of a displeased giant. At the heart of many stories is the trickster, often in the form of a semi-divine youth or a rat, a character that is common in the folklore of other indigenous cultures.

During the twentieth century, increased Westernization led to the gradual loss of these stories among younger generations. By the 1970s, researchers had found that few young Micronesians were familiar with the stories of their ancestors. A resurgence of interest in Micronesian heritage seems likely to have somewhat improved local knowledge of the tales.

CULTURE

Arts & Entertainment
As Micronesia came under the influence of various European and Asian powers during the nineteenth and twentieth century, many of the nation's ancient art forms fell out of practice. However, with the movement toward increased independence in the latter half of the twentieth century came renewed interest and participation in traditional cultural expression. Today, the arts community celebrates Micronesian heritage through the revival of traditional art, dance, and music. For example, traditional dancing remains an important part of life within Micronesian clans, particularly in Yap, the Federation's most traditional region. Men and women dance separately in traditional dances built around shaking and shuffling movements, sometimes including chanting.

On the islands of Chuuk, the art of woodcarving remains a vibrant and productive art form. The well-known tapwanu masks produced on the Mortlock islands are the only masks created in any of the Micronesian islands. The traditional breadfruit wood has now been replaced by hibiscus wood, and the carvings themselves have been christened "devil masks." Originally intended to serve both decorative and magical purposes, the masks have become popular souvenirs in recent years. Chuukese love sticks, although now rarely a part of courtship ritual, are also still produced for the souvenir market.

Cultural Sites & Landmarks
Nan Madol, a large archeological site located just off the southeast coast of Pohnpei, is one of most historically significant and widely known places in modern Micronesia. Built of a series of over ninety artificial islets, or small islands using megalithic architecture, Nan Madol is sometimes called "the Venice of the Pacific" for its extensive canal system. Residents and visitors traveled the city's canals in canoes, winding between platforms built atop coral reefs. As the seat of power for rulers of the Saudeleur Dynasty (roughly 500–1450 CE), the city offered impressive sights such as a massive fortified complex known as Nan Dowas. Although vegetation and natural forces have left parts of this island city inaccessible to modern visitors, many burial sites, ceremonial centers, and other places of interest are still accessible among the massive ruins.

The island of Pohnpei is also home to the Pohnpei State Botanical Garden, with seven hectares (eighteen acres) of both native and imported plants ranging from pepper plants to mahogany trees. Kolonia's Spanish Wall once marked the edge of the nineteenth-century Fort Alfonso XIII. Today, it forms the outfield fence of the Spanish Wall Ballfield, Pohnpei's baseball diamond.

Although lesser known, the Lelu Ruins on Kosrae are a historic and cultural site of great importance in the Pacific. Developed about 1400 CE, Lelu served as the Kosraean capital. Its architectural similarities to Nan Madol have led to scholars to believe that Lelu builders contributed greatly to the design and construction of the other city. Today, visitors walking through the complex on the original coral and rock pathways can view Posral, the ruins of the royal complex, and Insaru, the site of the royal burial ground. In residential areas, dwellings loom on high, stacked foundations and protective walls skillfully built without mortar stand up to roughly six meters (twenty feet) tall. Located in the center of the modern town of Lelu, the ruins offer a readily accessible, striking vision of Kosrae's past.

The Chuuk islands offer some land based sights in addition to the extensive underwater wreck diving off the coast. In Weno, Chuuk's capital, visitors can examine both traditional arts and crafts and a vast collection of World War II artifacts—the islands were the site of a major naval battle in 1944—at the Chuuk Enthographic Exhibition Center. North of Weno, Mount Tonachau rises 228 meters (750 feet) above ground. Locals believe the mountain to be haunted, and legend claims that the son of traditional Micronesian hero Soukatau constructed a meetinghouse on the summit. On the Yap islands, visitors can tour the islands on ancient stone walkways connecting villages such as Okaaw and Kadaay. These small settlements allow visitors to observe the traditional Micronesian way of life.

Libraries & Museums

The small Lidorkini Museum, in Pohnpei, contains many of the artifacts from the Nan Madol archaeological site. The Kosrae State Museum, located in the town of Tofol, contains many artifacts from the lesser-known site of the Lelu Ruins. The Kosrae Museum also boasts many artifacts from other eras of the island's history.

Holidays

Micronesians celebrate most of the major holidays celebrated in the United States: Christmas, New Year's, Easter, Halloween, and even Thanksgiving. In addition, each state has its own holidays. Kosrae celebrates Liberation Day (marking the American defeat of the Japanese army in World War II) on September 8. Yap celebrates Yap Day during the first week in March, when traditional dancing and sporting competitions take center stage.

The Federation as a whole celebrates Constitution Day on May 10 and Independence Day on November 3. Yap residents periodically hold mitmits, village-sized feasts in which one village hosts another, and everyone is treated to dancing, singing, and the exchanging of gifts.

Youth Culture

Since many young people leave school after the eighth grade, Micronesians take on a number of adult responsibilities at a young age. Girls typically help care for younger siblings or practice traditional weaving techniques while boys assist with the household hunting and fishing. When not working, teenaged Micronesians—particularly those on the less traditional capital islands—often enjoy watching television, listening to music, and participating in sports such as basketball and track and field.

Because Micronesian society frowns on the open mingling of unrelated men and women, young Micronesians typically do not have dates in public places. Instead, a young man visits the home of the woman in whom he is interested. Sometimes friends of the couple have arranged these visits; other times, the man knocks on the woman's window and asks her to come out. This style of secret dating, sometimes called nightcrawling, harkens back to the traditional use of love sticks in years gone by.

SOCIETY

Transportation

Walking remains the primary method of transportation for many Micronesians, and on smaller islands, automobiles may be practically nonexistent. The little automobile traffic that is on the islands travels on the right-hand side of the road.

Within Micronesia, independent islands are connected by water or air. A system of ships known as "field trips" make slow journeys carrying cargo and local passengers from island to island every few weeks. These ships typically travel from a main port such as that of Pohnpei or Yap to that of a distant island, and return along the same path. Along the way, the field trip ship typically stops for a period—between a few hours and a few days—at a number of smaller ports. Shorter water trips may be undertaken by motorboat or even canoe. Each group of islands has its own airport, and small aircraft service many outlying islands.

Transportation Infrastructure

Throughout the islands, unpaved roads are common. On the main islands, some roads have been covered with crushed coral or stone. An estimated 40 kilometers (25 miles) of Micronesia's estimated 240 kilometers (150 miles) of roads were paved.

Media & Communications

The main islands receive commercial television and radio broadcasts. Three television channels and fifteen radio stations have over-the-air broadcasts, with cable service providing additional television channels. There are an estimated 2,800 televisions in Micronesia. Micronesia has no daily newspapers. Weekly publications include the Pohnpei Business News, the Island Tribune, and Micronesia Weekly. The federal government publishes the National Union, a bi-weekly newsletter.

Mass communications have been slow to come to Micronesia. Telephone and basic Internet service are available on the four main islands, but are —like electricity—uncommon at best in outlying islands. In 2014, there were approximately 29,370 Internet users in the FSM, representing slightly more than 28 percent of the country's population. Residents of the main islands of Pohnpei, Yap, and Kosrae also have cell phone service, and by 2005, cell phone users had exceeded landline users. Shortwave and two-way radio services, as well as satellite stations, enable Micronesians on even small islands to communicate with one another and receive information about emergencies, such as typhoons.

SOCIAL DEVELOPMENT

Standard of Living

The Federated States of Micronesia is ranked 124th out of 187 nations on the United Nations Human Development Index for 2013. Life expectancy is high, at an average of seventy years of age. The infant mortality rate is 19.47 deaths per 1,000 live births. A little more than one-quarter of Micronesia's residents live below the poverty line.

Water Consumption

Given the amount of rainfall on the islands, the availability of water is not a problem on the Federated States of Micronesia. Although safe drinking water is available in urban areas, the country's public water infrastructure can be unreliable. Many rural areas still obtain water from streams and from rain catchments. The most significant threat to the FSM's water supply remains pollution from animal and human sources.

Education

Micronesian children are required to attend primary school through the eighth grade. The

U.S. Peace Corps still plays an active role in providing teachers, although the islands have been adding more citizens to the nation's supply of teachers.

Education is compulsory from ages six to fourteen. There are five secondary schools, one per island, where students complete their curriculum of science, mathematics, language arts, social studies, and physical education. There are also private secondary schools for those able to pay. The College of Micronesia and the University of Guam provide university level and post-graduate educations in the region. Many of Micronesia's university educated residents receive their degrees from American institutions with educational grants and financial aid from the U.S. government.

In spite of the islands' limited educational resources; the Federated States of Micronesia boasts an adult literacy rate of approximately 89 percent, slightly higher among men than women do.

The FSM continues to contend with the problem of "brain drain," which is the phenomenon of educated people opting to flee the country for opportunities abroad. An estimated 1,000 islanders have left in recent decades. Efforts to improve employment opportunities on the islands are aimed at reversing emigration trends.

Women's Rights

Micronesian women receive the same formal education and have the same employment opportunities as men. However, in Micronesian cultural society, women retain a subservient position to men. Although some traditional practices, such as the isolation of menstruating women, have greatly declined, women are still perceived through traditional gender roles. Despite a legal ban on gender discrimination, sexual harassment remains legal and common. Women in more urbanized areas lack the protections given by traditional culture, bringing new problems to which Micronesians have found few solutions.

In Micronesia, neither spousal abuse nor spousal rape is a crime, and domestic abuse was both widespread and severe throughout the islands. Women face a greater threat of spousal abuse in areas where the traditional interrelations with extended family members have declined. In the absence of brothers, fathers, and uncles, women have fewer ready resources for support and protection than in the past. Increasingly, extended families are disinclined to intercede on the behalf of abused relatives, placing abused women in a weaker and more dangerous position than those of earlier generations. Further, the government does not sponsor shelters for victims of domestic abuse, nor have private organizations risen to fill that void. Most cases of domestic abuse go unreported due to a combination of factors. Micronesians typically see spousal abuse and neglect as a private matter, and many families discourage abused women from seeking outside assistance. The possibility to reprisals from the abuser also deters women from reporting on the situation to the authorities.

Outside of the context of marriage, rape is a serious crime in the federation and carries stiff consequences. Anecdotal evidence suggests that rape and other attacks on both citizen and foreign women in Micronesia are common, although few cases are reported to the authorities. This is likely due to the traditional subservience of women, and a culture that readily believes that single women living or moving about alone may be inviting trouble. Micronesian law does not prohibit prostitution, but the practice seems relatively rare.

The islands are home to several community-based women's organizations. These groups seem to be encouraging the move away from traditional gender roles by promoting the intellectual, social, and cultural development of women. In 2005, women's organizations assembled in Pohnpei to celebrate International Women's Day chose to forego traditional agricultural and dance contests in favor of speeches about the formation of each group, exemplifying the changing role of such organizations.

Women have equal access to education, and are increasingly taking advantage of these opportunities. In 1973, women composed only about one-third and less than one-quarter of high school and college students, respectively. Two decades later, both percentages had risen to nearly one-half. Private sector and government positions are open to women, and many women hold low- to mid-level government jobs. However, women are underrepresented in the upper levels of Micronesian government. As of 2008, no women served on the legislature at the state level, and no women held seats in the national legislature. This situation seems likely to improve due to the increasing number of women running for elective office.

Health Care

Micronesia has no national health care system. A small number of health clinics are scattered throughout the islands. Most health care is provided through the four hospitals located on major islands. Medical supplies are often scarce in some of these hospitals, and care varies widely.

GOVERNMENT

Structure

Various peoples throughout their thousands of years of history have ruled Micronesia's islands. Spain was the first modern Western empire to claim Micronesia, but whaling ships frequently stopped at the islands during the 1800s. Diseases brought by the whalers killed half of the population on Pohnpei in 1854 and decimated the population of Kosrae. In 1899, Germany purchased the islands from Spain and relocated many of the inhabitants to coconut plantations that were established on land seized by the German government.

Germany lost the islands to Japan during World War I. Japan invested in the islands' infrastructure, settled Japanese citizens throughout the area, and made plans to annex the islands. The economy flourished under the Japanese, but

the Micronesians were second-class citizens. The Japanese military bombed Pearl Harbor on December 7, 1941. In 1944, the U.S. responded by bombing Japanese ships in Chuuk Lagoon. World War II saw heavy fighting between U.S. and Japanese forces throughout Micronesia until Japan's defeat, and Micronesia's infrastructure and economy were destroyed.

After the war, the United Nations gave administrative rights over the states of Chuuk, Pohnpei, Yap, and Kosrae to the U.S. in the form of a Trust Territory. Beginning in 1946, the United States cordoned off Micronesia and begin the intense testing of nuclear bombs over the Marshall Islands. Experts are still studying the long-term effects of these tests on Micronesia's residents.

Micronesia formed its first congress in 1965, though the country remained under executive control of the U.S. government. An investigation later revealed that the congress had been under surveillance by the CIA. A group of Peace Corps volunteers who arrived from the U.S. in the 1960s helped mobilize Micronesians to demand self-government. In 1978, the four states voted to share a constitution. The Federated States of Micronesia was established the following year.

In 1982, the Federated States and the U.S. government entered into a fifteen-year agreement in which the U.S. gave the Micronesian government sovereign authority except with regard to foreign relations, and promised economic aid. The United States received the right to maintain its military bases in the islands. The agreement took effect in 1986. In 1999, a Compact of Association replaced the agreement and declared Micronesia a U.S. protectorate. The Compact has since been renewed until 2023.

The Federated States of Micronesia has a constitutional government that operates under a Contract of Free Association with the U.S. that was last amended in May 2004. The country's unicameral congress has fourteen members, ten of whom are elected by popular vote within their districts to two-year terms. The other four members represent one of the Federation's states for four-year terms. The congress elects the president and vice president from among the four representatives of the states.

Political Parties

There are no political parties in the Federated States of Micronesia. The country's parliamentary representative democratic republic is rooted in the country's constitution, which was ratified in 1979. Since 1979, elections for government roles in the FSM have been non-partisan.

Local Government

The constitution of the FSM does not require states to establish a local government. However, local governments must establish democratic laws and are not allowed to collect taxes on trade between islands. Prior to 1979, some FSM islands had governments in place. The constitution stipulated a five-year period for the establishment of the larger system. Municipal governments oversee tax collection and infrastructure development in each state. Chiefs that have the ability to veto decisions made by higher echelons of the government oversee rural areas.

Judicial System

The judicial system of the FSM is based on the United States. The Supreme Court of the FSM is considered the highest court in the country, consisting of a chief justice and five associate justices. State courts oversee judicial matters on each of the FSM main islands.

Taxation

The Customs and Tax Administration (CTA) oversees taxes. All products imported into the Federated States of Micronesia are taxed. Revenue taxes are collected from foreign businesses operating on the islands. The CTA also collects a national income tax and administers the FSM's social security system.

Armed Forces

The Federated States of Micronesia have no standing military forces. The defense of the islands is the responsibility of the United States military.

Foreign Policy

At the time of Micronesia's independence in 1979, the United States retained control of the federation's foreign affairs. However, with the finalization of the Compact of Free Association (COFA) between the U.S. and Micronesia in 1986, the federation gained full control over its external affairs. Since that time, Micronesia has largely dictated its own foreign policy and handled its own international relations. Today, it holds formal diplomatic ties with over fifty-five nation states, ranging from the neighboring Marshall Islands and Palau to distant territories such as Croatia and South Africa. The United Nations (UN) welcomed Micronesia as a member nation in 1991.

Much of Micronesia's foreign policy is aimed at developing strong relationships with other nations in its region. In 1988, the federation opened formal diplomatic relations with Japan; since that time, the latter nation has become the second largest foreign aid donor, and the countries' respective heads of state have paid official visits to each other. Micronesia also established diplomatic ties with China in the late 1980s, and in 2004, the two nations reaffirmed their relationship to encourage increased cooperation. Because of its ties with China, the federation does not formally recognize Taiwan, or the Republic of China (ROC)

Despite the great physical and cultural differences between them, the federation and Israel have maintained a long friendship. Israel assisted the growing nation during the early years of Micronesia's independence. Over the ensuing years, Israel and Micronesia have worked together on areas of mutual interest such as agriculture and health care. In return for this show of Israeli support, the federation has generally supported the continued independence and regional aims of Israel.

In September 2008, representatives from Micronesia, along with those of nine other Pacific island nations, traveled to Cuba to participate in a bilateral, or mutual, ministerial meeting. At this gathering, the nations discussed the growing problems faced by small island nations as the result of global issues such as climate change and shortages of food and energy. The eleven countries represented also agreed to increase cooperation in education, health care, and recreation.

The close ties between Micronesia and the U.S. have somewhat informed the federation's foreign policy. The U.S. is the largest foreign aid donor to Micronesia, providing both direct economic aid and indirect developmental aid, particularly through the presence of Peace Corps volunteers. Under the renewed free association agreement with the U.S., Micronesia gave the U.S. full control of its national security. Because of this protectorate, Micronesia itself maintains no military forces, instead relying on those of the U.S. In fact, some citizens of the federation have joined the U.S. military and have fought on behalf of the U.S., in such conflicts as the recent wars in Iraq and Afghanistan.

Human Rights Profile

International human rights law insists that states respect civil and political rights, and promote an individual's economic, social, and cultural rights. The United Nations Universal Declaration on Human Rights (UDHR) is recognized as the standard for international human rights. Its authors sought the counsel of the world's great thinkers, philosophers, and religious leaders, and were careful to create a document that reflects the core values shared by every world culture. (To read this document or view the articles relating to cultural human rights, visit http://www.udhr.org/ UDHR/default.htm.)

Overall, Micronesia's human rights record is a positive one and Micronesians enjoy basic human rights that are guaranteed under the federation's 1979 constitution. For example, there are constitutional prohibitions against discrimination based on race, language, or sex, and Micronesian law also barred discrimination in public employment based on disability. Religious freedom is formally acknowledged in the constitution and the creation of a state religion is prohibited under Micronesian law. Although the freedoms of speech and press as outlined in the UDHR are not specifically identified in the Micronesian constitution, these freedoms are in practice. Cultural and academic rights are also freely practiced in the nation and no law or practice bars full citizen participation in society. Nonetheless, traditional Micronesian culture has stymied the full human rights development that the UDHR demands. Furthermore, laws limit the abilities of non-citizens to own land or take certain jobs, and foreigners find it practically impossible to obtain Micronesian citizenship despite length of residency or marital status.

Despite these many human rights successes, some areas provide ample room for improvement. Although not as common as in the past, arranged marriage is still an accepted Micronesian practice. Because their families may contract young men and women in Micronesia into marriage, the federation fails to meet the standards of marital freedom set by the UDHR. Due to a lack of legal protections, workers' rights also failed to meet fully UN standards, although the prevalence of family-owned businesses and public employment limited most violations in practice.

Throughout the nation, relaxed access to governmental proceedings generally suffered due to the low number of media outlets and lack of sufficient staff to handle information requests. In 2007, accusations of election fraud stemmed from voting discrepancies in the parliamentary election balloting that took place on the islands of Chuuk. Because the state and national listings of registered voters did not agree, many Chuukese were unable to vote in the election. However, it seems likely that this problem stemmed from administrative errors rather than from an active attempt to disenfranchise voters. Past political problems in the state of Chuuk have included election violence and government corruption, generally relating to financial matters.

ECONOMY

Overview of the Economy

Micronesia's economy is primarily agricultural. About two-thirds of those employed in the country are government employees. There is also a small amount of construction on the islands. Other industries are related to the region's marine life and tourism: fish processing, cultivation of marine life, and craft items constructed from shell, wood, and pearls. Micronesia's estimated per capita GDP is $3,185 (USD).

Industry

In the capital of Palikir, the modest manufacturing sector includes fish processing plants and textile factories. Most of the area's exports, which account for only a fraction of the gross domestic product (GDP), include seafood products, coconut derivatives, black pepper, and other handicrafts and goods. These are primarily destined for markets in Japan, Hong Kong, Guam, and the United States.

Energy/Power/Natural Resources

Micronesia's most valuable natural resource is its coastal waters. A little less than 3 percent of the country's land is arable. However, the country does have tropical forests, marine products, phosphate, and deep-seabed minerals.

In recent years, the island of Pohnpei has increased the planting and harvesting of a traditional plant, sakau, which is marketed in the United States and Europe as the health supplement kava.

Fishing

Tuna provides a significant amount of revenue for the nation, approximately $200 million (USD)

annually. While the country has ownership over the tuna stock harvested in its waters, though, domestic participation is almost nonexistent.

Forestry

Although most of the FMS is forested, there is no significant forestry industry on the islands and deforestation is not an issue.

Mining/Metals

The FMS is home to large offshore supplies of manganese. However, the mining of this material takes significant industrial technology. As of 2010, no efforts to mine actively the FSM's manganese supply have begun.

Agriculture

Subsistence farming is common in Micronesia. Primary harvests include tropical fruits, vegetables, and sweet potatoes. Farmers cultivate and sell black pepper, coconuts, cassava (tapioca), and betel nuts.

Animal Husbandry

The FSM has no significant livestock industry. Poultry and pigs are the most common livestock raised for food.

Tourism

Micronesians hope that a growing tourist trade will help them become less dependent on U.S. aid in the future. The islands' dramatic coastlines, picturesque uplands, and diverse coral reefs are a draw for Western tourists willing to make the long journey across the Pacific.

Chuuk Lagoon (formerly called Truk Lagoon) was the scene of the largest naval loss in history when U.S. forces attacked the Japanese navy stationed there during World War II. Scuba divers flock to the area to explore the wreckage that litters the seabed.

Vanessa Vaughn, Amy Witherbee,
Beverly Ballaro

DO YOU KNOW?

- Only an estimated sixty-five of the FSM's 607 incorporated islands are inhabited.

- Micronesia's monitor lizards can grow up to six feet long.

- Nan Madol, on Pohnpei, is the 13th century ruins of a city made of stacked basalt stone under the Saudeleur Dynasty.

- Prior to the use of international currencies, the traditional currency of Yap was the rai, a stone carved into a disc with a hole through the middle. Rai could be up to four meters (twelve feet) in diameter and could weigh as much as 4,535 kilograms (five tons). Every Yapese village has some rai on full view, with each piece still owned by individuals and occasionally used for commercial transactions. Value is now determined by not only size of the rai, but also by its history and age.

Bibliography

Ashby, Gene. *Some Things of Value: Micronesian Customs and Beliefs.* Eugene, OR: Rainy Day Press, 1989.

Brower, Kenneth. *Micronesia: The Land, the People, and the Sea.* Baton Rouge: Louisiana State University Press, 1981.

Cole, Geert, et al. *South Pacific and Micronesia (Travel Guide).* Oakland, CA: Lonely Planet, 2006.

Hezel, Francis X. *Making Sense of Micronesia.* Honolulu, HI: University of Hawaii Press, 2013.

Kluge, P. F. *The edge of paradise: America in Micronesia.* New York: Random House, 1991.

Works Cited

"Human Rights Report: Federated States of Micronesia." U.S. Department of State: Diplomacy in Action. United States Department of State. http://www.state.gov/g/drl/rls/hrrpt/2010/eap/154393.htm.

"Arable land (% ofland area)". World Bank. http://data.worldbank.org/indicator/AG.LND.ARBL.ZS

Art of the Pacific Islands. Pacific Territories Grant. Pacific Resources for Education and Learning. http://www.prel.org/programs/pcahe/PTG/documents/SaipanBox2.pdf

Ashby, Gene. *Some Things of Value: Micronesian Customs and Beliefs.* Eugene, OR: Rainy Day Press, 1989.

"China, Micronesia to promote bilateral ties." Consulate General of People's Republic of China in San Francisco. http://www.chinaconsulatesf.org/eng/zhuanti/taiwan/twnews/t80582.htm

"Collection of Local Recipes." Island Food Community of Pohnpei. http://www.islandfood.org/recipes/recipes.htm

"Country profile: Micronesia." BBC News. . http://news.bbc.co.uk/2/hi/asia-pacific/country_profiles/1300849.stm

"Cuba and Pacific Strengthen Co-operation." Radio New Zealand International. http://www.rnzi.com/pages/news.php?op=read&id=42076

"Education system in Micronesia". Foreign credits. http://classbase.com/countries/micronesia/education-system

"Federated States of Micronesia". *Nations of the world: a political, economic, and business handbook.* 14th ed. Amenia, NY: Grey House Publishing, 2014.

"Federated States of Micronesia." Office of Insular Affairs. U.S. Department of the Interior. http://www.doi.gov/oia/Islandpages/fsmpage.htm

"FSM Statistics." Division of Statistics. Government of the Federated States of Micronesia. http://www.spc.int/prism/country/fm/stats/

"General Information on the FSM." Government of the Federated States of Micronesia. http://www.fsmgov.org/info/index.html

"Japan-Micronesia Relations." Ministry of Foreign Affairs of Japan. http://www.mofa.go.jp/region/asia-paci/micronesia/index.html

Kjellgren, Eric. *Oceania: Art of the Pacific Islands in the Metropolitan Museum of Art.* New York: Metropolitan Museum of Art, 2007.

Levy, Neil M. *Moon Handbooks: Micronesia.* Emeryville, CA: Avalon Travel Publishing, 2003.

"Mayan Textiles: Backstrap Looms." The Fabric of Mayan Life: An Exhibit of Textiles. Sam Noble Oklahoma Museum of Natural History. http://www.snomnh.ou.edu/collections-research/cr-sub/ethnology/mayan/Technology/Backstrap.html

"U.S. relations with thr Federated States of Micronesia." U.S. Department of State: Diplomacy in Action. United States Department of State. . http://www.state.gov/r/pa/ei/bgn/1839.htm.

"Micronesia, 1900 AD to Present." Heilbrunn Timeline of Art History. The Metropolitan Museum of Art. http://www.metmuseum.org/toah/ht/11/oci/ht11oci.htm

"Micronesia: Eating and Recipes." CountryReports.org. http://www.countryreports.org/people/recipe.aspx?countryid=161

"Micronesia, Federated States of." *World Data Analyst.* Encyclopedia Britannica. http://www.world.eb.com.ezproxy.libraries.wright.edu:2048/wdpdf/Micronesia.pdf.

"Micronesia, Federated States of." The World Factbook. Central Intelligence Agency. https://www.cia.gov/library/publications/the-world-factbook/geos/fm.html.

"Micronesia-Israel Relations." Jewish Virtual Library. http://www.jewishvirtuallibrary.org/jsource/Politics/Micronesia.html

"Micronesian Seminar." Micsem.org. http://www.micsem.org/home.htm

Mitchell, Roger E. *Micronesian Folktales.* Nagoya: Asian Folklore Institute, 1973. http://www.nanzan-u.ac.jp/SHUBUNKEN/publications/afs/pdf/a263.pdf

"Nan Madol." Heilbrunn Timeline of Art History. The Metropolitan Museum of Art. http://www.metmuseum.org/toah/hd/nmad/hd_nmad.htm

"Pacific and Cuba meet to discuss co-peration." Radio New Zealand International. http://www.rnzi.com/pages/news.php?op=read&id=42045

Poignant, Roslyn. *Oceanic Mythology.* London: Paul Hamlyn, 1967.

"Road to Riches." BBC News. http://news.bbc.co.uk/hi/english/static/road_to_riches/prog2/tharngan.stm

Sehpin, Masaleen. "International Women's Day Celebration draws crowd." *The Kaselehlie Press* 17 Mar. 2005. http://www.fm/news/kp/2005/03_8.htm

"Tor (Sash)." Collections Online. Museum of New Zealand. http://collections.tepapa.govt.nz/objectdetails.aspx?oid=205813&coltype=pacific%20cultures&regno=ol002156/3

Williams, Ian. "Even Micronesia and Marshall Islands Desert U.S.-Israeli Anti-Palestine Campaign at United Nations." *Washington Report on Middle East Affairs, April/May 1999.* http://www.wrmea.com/backissues/0499/9904070.html

Tuna fish at market. iStock/noblige

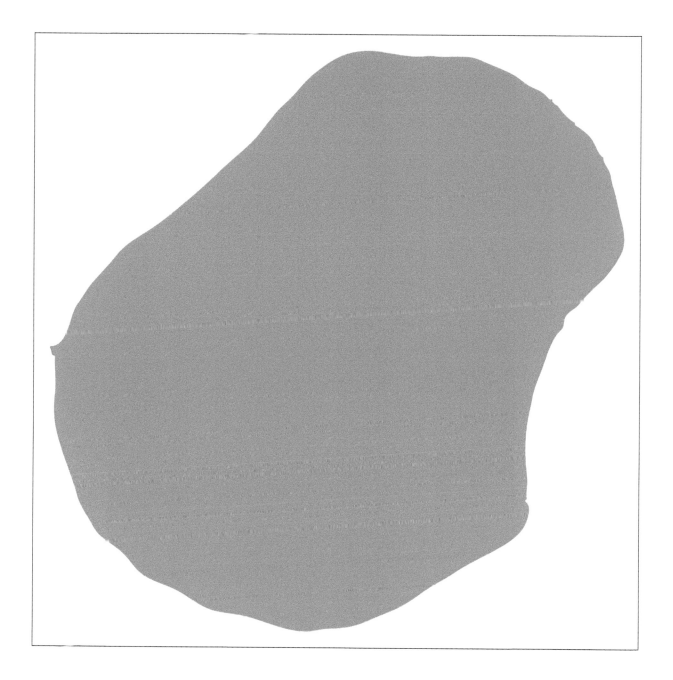

NAURU

Introduction

Nauru is officially known as the Republic of Nauru. It is a small island nation in the South Pacific, located 40 kilometers (25 miles) south of the equator. When the island gained its independence from Australia in 1968, it became the smallest independent republic in the world.

English Captain John Fearn was the first European to land on Nauru, and he called it Pleasant Island. Today, the island faces dire ecological conditions as the result of a century of mining phosphates for fertilizer. The island was once rich in petrified bat and bird guano, which is high in phosphates. With the deposits depleted, the Nauruans face national bankruptcy and personal poverty. Most of the island is uninhabitable, and almost all food and water must be imported.

Nauru is the only republic in the world that does not have an official capital; the Yaren district acts as the de facto capital of small the island nation.

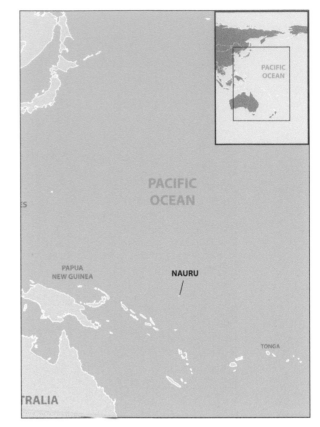

GENERAL INFORMATION

Official Language: Nauruan, English
Population: 9,540 (2015 estimate)
Currency: Australian dollar
Coins: 1 Australian dollar is subdivided into 100 cents; coins of the Australian dollar are available in denominations of 5, 10, 20 and 50 cents, and 1 and 2 dollars.
Land Area: 21 square kilometers (8.1 square miles)

National Motto: "God's Will First"
National Anthem: "Nauru Bwiema" ("Nauru Our Homeland")
Capital: No official capital; government offices are in the Yaren district
Time Zone: GMT +12
Flag Description: The flag of Nauru depicts the island's geographical location, and consists of a dark blue field, representing the Pacific Ocean, with a horizontal golden stripe, representing the Equator, running through the center. Nauru itself is represented as a twelve-pointed white star and sits in the lower hoist quarter, below the line, representing Nauru's geographical position of 1° below the Equator. The color white symbolizes the phosphate once abundantly found on the island, while the twelve points of the star represent the island's original twelve tribes.

Population

Of the roughly 9,540 people living in Nauru, nearly 4,859 reside in Yaren. Ethnically, Nauruans

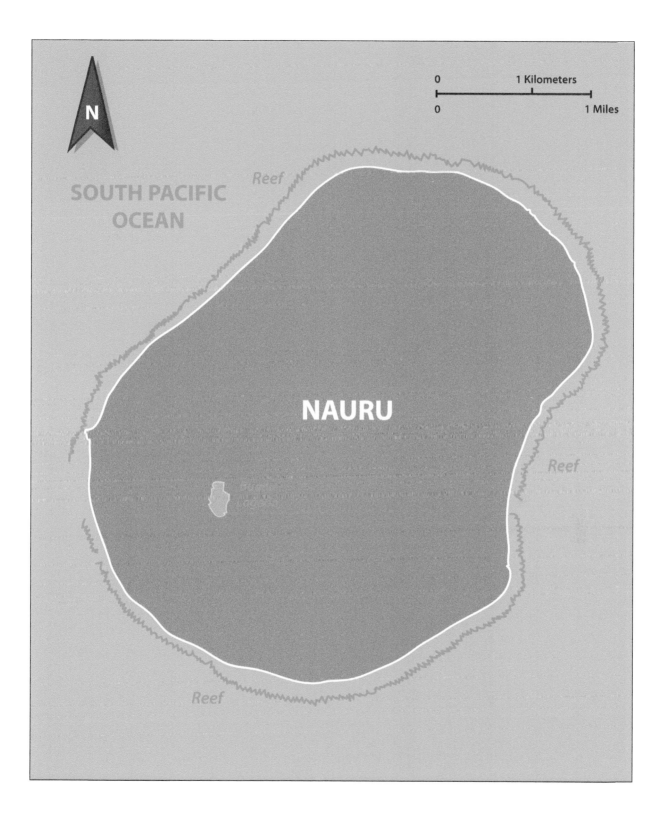

Principal Regions by Population (2005):*

- Yaren (4,859) (2012 estimate)
- Denigomodu (2,827)
- Meneng (1,830)
- Aiwo (1,092)
- Yaren (820)

* Due to its small size, Nauru has no cities, and is divided into fourteen inhabited regions; census data is not necessarily current.

are a mixture of Polynesian, Melanesian, and Micronesian. Ethnic groups living on the island include Nauruans (58 percent of the population), Pacific Islanders (26 percent), Chinese (8 percent), and Europeans (8 percent). Most, if not all, non-Nauruans are connected with the phosphate industry, as laborers, executives, or financiers.

Nauru's entire population is concentrated on the narrow strip of coastline around the perimeter of the island. The population density is 649 people per square kilometer (1,681 people per square mile). The government hopes to ease overcrowding by developing cleared areas on the central plateau, where phosphate-mining operations have been conducted for nearly a century.

The island nation had an estimated population growth rate of 0.555 percent in 2015. As of the last census, 32 percent of the population was fifteen years of age or younger.

Languages

The remoteness of the island isolates the population as well as the language. The national language, Nauruan, does not resemble other Polynesian and Micronesian languages, and is spoken by almost 96 percent of the population. Although Nauruan is the official language, English is the language of government and commerce, and is widely spoken or understood.

Native People & Ethnic Groups

Nauruans, descended from Polynesian explorers, are the island's native population. They are organized into twelve traditional clans.

Religions

About 66 percent of Nauruans belong to the Nauruan Protestant Church. Another third are Roman Catholic. Missionaries arrived on the island in the late 19th century, and the Nauruans were quickly converted to Christianity.

Climate

Nauru has a tropical climate, making for warm, humid, and breezy weather with little variation. Daytime temperatures are between 24° and 34° Celsius (75° and 93° Fahrenheit). Humidity is steady at 80 percent. The northwest trade winds blow from March through October.

Rainfall varies widely. Some years, the island receives a total of 190 to 200 centimeters (75 to 79 inches) of rain. Westerly monsoons are responsible for the wet season November through February. Other years see extensive droughts.

Phosphate mining has changed the very climate of Nauru. The bare rock exposed by mining retains heat and dries up moisture, lengthening, intensifying and increasing the number of droughts.

Nauru's elevation is so low that if the greenhouse effect results in a rise in ocean levels, the entire island could be submerged.

ENVIRONMENT & GEOGRAPHY

Topography

Nauru is an oval coral island surrounded by a reef. The island lies in the South Pacific Ocean, 40 kilometers (25 miles) south of the equator and 4,000 kilometers (2,500 miles) northeast of Sydney, Australia. Its nearest neighbor, another island of phosphate rock, is Banaba (Ocean Island) in Kiribati, 300 kilometers (186 miles) to the east. The Yaren district is the center of government, and is situated in the southern left corner of the oval-shaped island.

Nauru has a narrow, sandy beach around its perimeter. In the center of the island is the

The male frigatebird inflates a bright red pouch to attract females during mating season.

phosphate plateau, or "topside." This area's guano deposits have been depleted, and mining operations have left strange-looking coral pinnacles all over the plateau. The surrounding coral reef is exposed at low tide. Because of the danger posed by the reef, ships anchor at sea, and passengers and cargo are shuttled by barge to shore. The island's highest point, at 61 meters (200 feet), is on the rim of the phosphate plateau.

Plants & Animals

Like many other Pacific islands, Nauru did not have a rich biology even before humans arrived. Today, most native plant species are extinct, and the destruction of habitats has greatly diminished the bird population.

One plant that does well is the pandanus. Other names for this medium-sized tree (usually 15–25 feet tall) include "screw-pine," "tourist pineapple" and "hala." Thriving in poor soil and saltwater conditions, it is common to tropical Pacific islands. The fruit is eaten, and the long leaves yield a fiber often used by Pacific islanders for weaving. The pandanus also has some medicinal properties.

Also growing in the coastal area are some coconut palms. The Buada lagoon has a surrounding fertile area that supports bananas and some vegetables.

Only a few species of birds live on Nauru permanently, but many species visit seasonally. Some local species are the frigate bird, the noddy (black tern), and the Nauru canary (a nightingale reed warbler). The frigate bird is the national bird and is sometimes kept as a caged pet.

Although there are no native mammals, rats, cats and mice have arrived with travelers. Packs of wild dogs roam the central plateau.

CUSTOMS & COURTESIES

Greetings

The official language of Nauru is English, although Nauruan is also cited as an official language. While English is spoken and widely understood among most Nauruans, Nauruan, an Oceanic language, is the traditional language of the people. Chinese Pidgin English is also spoken. However, modern Nauruan youth speak English almost exclusively. There are several options for exchanging greetings in Nauru, including "Ekamir Omo" ("Greetings" or "hello") and "Omo Yoran" ("Good morning").

Gestures & Etiquette

The key feature of Nauruan etiquette is generosity. To that extent, giving prized possessions to another is seen as a great moral act in Nauruan society. This traditional practice created a constant circulation of material goods throughout Nauru. As a result, Nauruans are disciplined to show little attachment to material goods. If a prized possession is lost, a public showing of distress is considered inappropriate. (Weeping is even discouraged during periods of mourning.) In general, Nauruans do not show extreme emotions publicly, instead relying on subtle acts such as joking or teasing.

Historically, Nauru has been known for maintaining a harmonious environment. In fact, upon first sighting, the island was named "Pleasant Island." Violence, or rather a show of harshness, is discouraged and considered bad etiquette. In addition, it was customary for Nauruans and other island cultures in Oceania to give only positive answers, though this tradition has faded in recent years. This affected the decision making of the island, as all decisions had to be reached unanimously. This delicate level of harmony also is found in courtship between Nauruans. Love relationships are thought of as a game, with the early stages of a relationship defined by an exchange of sweet talk and kind gestures. Traditionally, these kind gestures included brushing another's hair.

Eating/Meals

Traditional Nauruan society was based on fishing, and meal times were regulated by the return of the anglers. While Nauruans eat smaller meals whenever they desire, this custom is still practiced to an extent. Another feature of Nauruan mealtimes is that the meals are always plentiful and shared. It is very typical for the extended family, along with the neighbors, to be invited to share a meal.

Nauruans traditionally eat communally, and spread the food out in large bowls on a large mat, around with the diners are seated. They do not usually face one another, as giving each person his or her privacy while eating is considered good etiquette. Traditionally, Nauruans eat carefully with their hands, taking small bites. This is seen as a form of respect for the anglers who bring in the food.

Visiting

The idea of harmony also extends to visiting. Some Nauruans consider appearing hurried as disrespectful or rude. Generally, both entering and leaving another's home is a drawn-out process. When Nauruans do leave another's home, their departure is conducted in such a way that it is not noticed. It is also typical for Nauruans to bring presents when they visit one another, as they have a strong tradition of gift giving.

LIFESTYLE

Family

In the past, Nauruan tribes were based on a matrilineal line and inheritance was from the mother. In this system, women held most of the authority and daughters were prized over sons. To some extent, women remain the authoritative figure in Nauruan culture, and are in charge of all the important decisions in the family and in the tribe. Traditionally, intermarrying within one's own tribe was forbidden, but these rules have relaxed.

The tribes are typically divided into a three-tier hierarchy. The wealthiest class is the temonibe, which has the power to make decisions. The amenangame is a similar class, but does not have the ability to make decisions. The itsio is the lowest class, comprised of people who are not allowed to have possessions (although they are not considered slaves). They generally take on servant positions, but are usually treated well.

Housing

Traditional Nauruan homes were constructed using the resources of the island, and thatched roofs and walls made from coconut leaves were typical. With the discovery of phosphate in the island's inner plateau, Nauruan homes, most of which were owned by the government, began to be constructed with modern materials. They also included such amenities as electricity and running water.

In Nauru's post-phosphate boom, Nauruan homes are characterized as cramped—the average household size in 2002 was six—and are constructed using cinder blocks. (As of the 2007 Nauru Demographic and Health Survey, the average Nauruan household had approximately 6.1 members, with nearly 70 percent of households headed by a male figure.) Some of the homes use corrugated asbestos sheeting on roofs and as the sheeting ages and become increasingly weathered, the asbestos fibers pose a potential health threat to those living in such homes. Nearly all the homes have small yards, though the ground surrounding the homes appears talc-like due to the increasing droughts that plague the island. The keeping of livestock is common, and waste is often stored in yards due to the expense in exporting trash off the island. In recent years, there have been a number of electricity outages and sanitation issues.

All Nauruans own small pieces of the island. The tiny tracts—some are the size of a double bed—were divided by the government and allotted to the people. It is common for all Nauruans to know the location of their piece of the island, no matter how small or uninhabitable it might be.

Food

Seafood and the coconut are central to the cuisine of Nauru, and are traditional staples of the local diet. Commonly consumed meats include chickens and pork, and practically all feasts feature a roasted pig as the central dish. With the advent of the mining industry, the traditions of fishing waned, and a large amount of food is now imported. The reliance on the mining industry, coupled with this vast change of diet, has led to Nauru's stature as the world's most obese nation as of 2007. At the time of the survey, the adult population of Nauru had an obesity rate of 94.5 percent.

Raw fish has been a traditional staple of Nauruan cuisine for centuries. Nauruans prize the emorr, a flying fish, and the ibiya (milkfish) for their innards. The emorr lives primarily on zooplankton and the ibiya consumes mostly microorganisms, making the insides of the fish safe to eat. The fatty flesh of the itibab (tuna) and the eae (bonito) are also eaten raw. (Generally, the fattier the flesh, the better it tastes.) Another type of fish that is consumed raw is the red fish, found in the depths of the ocean. These types of fish are quite oily and considered the best tasting by most Nauruans. The red fish are often served during feasts, celebrations, and other festive events. Raw fish is commonly served with the flesh of the coconut.

While certain species are simply eaten raw, fish that are considered less tasty are often cooked, usually by broiling over a fire. The fire is sometimes made with coconut shells, giving the fish a specific flavor. Shellfish, collected on the beach and eaten almost immediately, are also broiled over the fire. Using a ground oven is another method of cooking fish. The Nauruan ground oven is similar to those found in Hawaii. Ground ovens consist of a pit lined with stones, and then covered with a mixture of coconut husks and wood. Once only coals remain, the fish, sometimes covered in leaves, is placed on the hot stones. The oven is covered with a special mat, which is held down by large stones. Octopus, sharks, eel, and tuna are examples of seafood often cooked in the ground oven.

The coconut, a staple ingredient of the traditional Nauruan diet, is used for its flesh, juices, and sap, from which syrup is made. The climate of Nauru is also suitable for other varieties of fruit, including the pandanus fruit. However, this fruit has disappeared from the Nauruan landscape. In the past, a special cake called an edongo was made from pandanuses. To make this cake, the flesh of the fruit is first put on hot coals. Next, the skin of the fruit is removed and a jelly is made from the fruit. This jelly is then spread over a tray and dried in the sun. At night, the jelly is returned to the oven. This process continues for three days until the jelly, which resembles a sheet cake, hardens to the point where it can be broken off. To make a cake that is truly admirable, one would also add bits of a previous cake to the jelly as it hardens. The cake was used to cure common ailments such as stomachache and diarrhea.

Life's Milestones

Marriage customs have changed in present-day Nauru. Traditionally, the families arranged marriages, and it was the family of the young woman who made the proposal to the family of the young man. After the initial proposal, each family showered the other with gifts in a playful, yet competitive, way. Traditionally, the bride was also expected to be a virgin.

Funeral ceremonies have also changed over the years. Contemporary Nauruan funerary traditions have a Christian-style burial, but in the past, funeral arrangements depended on ones social class. For example, the bodies of servants were often discarded in caves, while most Nauruans were wrapped in a mat and buried at sea. However, upper-class Nauruan families had a very unique ceremony in which they would keep the body in the attic, rubbing it daily with oils until all the flesh had been worn away. Regardless of social class, it is a Nauruan custom to refrain from mourning the dead; the proper display of emotion after the death of a loved one is simply a smile.

CULTURAL HISTORY

Art

Due to Nauru's isolated location and its relatively small population, little is known about the artistic traditions of the island. However, Nauruans do have several unique artistic practices, including the making of string figures. This complex process involves the creation of intricate designs on the hand with closed loops of string. String figures (which are also made by neighboring islands in Oceania) began as only a few patterns that were passed down from generation to generation. Occasionally, new patterns would be added or an existing pattern would be altered until they began to multiply and became part of competitions held on the island. The object of string making is to create the most complex pattern possible, and a typical competition would last two to three days.

The more complicated string figures often involved the assistance of three to four people. Hands, necks, feet, and teeth were used to create these complex designs. The making of string figures began to resemble performance art. Traditionally, competing in string figure making was an activity only practiced by men. While women would make string figures, they mainly did so in the home, passing on special patterns to their daughters. Some of the figures were made while telling stories, particularly myths and legends, and some involved chanting while they were being made.

The art of string figures has died out considerably as the culture of Nauru changed during the 20th century. The attention paid to string figures by the outside world, particularly among cultural anthropologists, resulted in a revival of the art form in the 1930s. Some new designs were created and the activity enjoyed a sort of renaissance. Quite a few of the string figures were carefully sketched out, collected, and then published in order to help preserve the art form.

Nauruans also make many handicrafts such as woven baskets and mats. As in other Micronesian cultures, women carefully wove these items. Nauruan women were quite skilled in fiber arts, creating pieces that can be found in the world's most prestigious museums. They often fashioned these handicrafts from either coconut leaves or the leaves of the pandanus tree, producing a weave that is more delicate in nature. The different tribes that inhabit Nauru have their own weaving patterns, and it is considered improper to copy the designs of other tribes. The leaves of the coconut and pandanus trees have also been used to make several other aesthetic and functional items, including skirts, jewelry, headbands, and brooms. Often, these decorative items were embellished with flowers, coral beads, and feathers. It was also common for the women to dye the fibers to embellish the geometrical patterns.

One popular item that was used by Nauruans to carry personal items was the egadakua, a woven basket shaped into a box adorned with handles. The baskets were also associated with childbirth, as the materials used to assist with the birth were usually carried in this type of basket. These baskets were often embellished with designs marking to which family or tribe the carrier belonged. Decorations were also added to indicate the rank of the carrier. For example, shark teeth were often used as a special adornment to indicate these associations.

Perfume

Nauruans value beauty and cleanliness, and perfume making is a treasured tradition. Fragrances are added to lotions, potions, and steam. One of the most common forms of perfume is made from coconuts and applied to the body as a lotion. The coconut oil is scented with various flowers, which are added to the lotion mixture before it reaches boiling temperature. As the cream settles back into oil, the flowers are removed. Despite the influx of modern perfumes becoming available to Nauruans in recent decades, this traditional perfume remains the most popular. Another traditional method of scenting coconut oil was to use a heart-shaped fruit called dedagoda that washed up on the shore after storms. The fruits contain a nut, which is dried and then made into a powder that can be added to the coconut oil. However, these fruits are no longer found.

While lotions are the most popular form of perfuming one's body, another way Nauruans have perfumed themselves is through drinking potions. By drinking a fragrant mixture, one will emit a pleasant odor for days. These potions are generally only used for special occasions. The mixture usually has a coconut juice base, and the fragrance is added by using certain flowers or leaves. To make steamed perfumes, a ground oven is used to heat up stones, and flowers and leaves are then placed on the stones. Women, covered in some sort of fabric, stand over the stones to let the perfume encompass their bodies. Traditionally, steamed perfumes were used during and after menstruation.

Drama

One of the most popular traditions of Nauru is the telling of myths and legends. These stories have been handed down from generation to generation to preserve certain aspects of Nauruan culture. Certain Nauruan myths focus on the cosmos, particularly the moon and stars. The focus on these celestial themes suggests that pre-Christian Nauruans might have observed a religion based on the worship of the moon. Another category of myths focuses on the unexplainable or the supernatural world.

One of the most popular myths tells the story of a mother and her three sons. After refusing to heed their mother's warnings about swimming in the ocean, they drift off and must be rescued by the youngest brother after he has grown large enough to swim after them. After finding his brothers, they roam the ocean, only to be mistaken for fish by nearby villagers. When the youngest brother is captured and eaten, the mother collects his bones (bones are considered the most revered part of the dead by Nauruans), and the boy comes back to life. He then exacts his revenge on the fishers who had captured him. This legend serves as a reminder to Nauruans of the power of fish and the importance of listening to one's mother.

Music & Dance

The music and dance customs of Nauru are rooted in the island's Micronesian heritage. The traditional music is often characterized as rhythmic, and dances often accompany important customs, such as those involving fishing or traditional feasts. However, German colonial occupation (1888–1914)—German colonial authorities banned traditional dance in the late 19th century—Japanese occupation during World War II, an early 20th-century population decline (due to an influenza epidemic), and the phosphate mining industry have all contributed to the disruption of native music and dance customs and practice. Music and dance is still associated with festivals, holidays, and the welcoming of visitors to the island.

Literature

One of the country's most popular poets is Joanne Gobure (1982–), who writes most of her poetry in English. The content of her work often focuses on Christian themes. Her most popular poem to date is titled, "A Beautiful Prayer." The poem received quite a bit of attention among Christian websites and forums. It is a meditation on the Gospel of John, intertwining the themes of this 15th-century writing with the author's personal experiences. The poem uses simple word choice and is organized with simple line breaks. Another famous Nauruan writer is Margaret Hendrie (1924–1990), who penned the nation's national anthem, "Nauru Bwiema." The anthem was officially adopted when the nation declared its independence in 1968. Unlike Gobure, Hendrie chose to write in Nauruan.

CULTURE

Arts & Entertainment

Economic problems overshadow the arts in Nauru. With an estimated unemployment rate of over 20 percent in the early 21st century, fostering the arts is not a priority for the government. There is no particularly large or active arts community in Nauru.

In addition, many of the artistic traditions of the past suffered as the population have dramatically changed in the last several decades. Two of the traditional tribes of Nauru died out in the 20th century. By the end of World War II, the population of Nauru had dropped to only 1,500. Some Nauruans do continue to make traditional handicrafts for export and for visitors, but the industry is not thriving.

Australian Rules football (soccer) is the national sport. The game involves two teams of eighteen players who compete on a pitch shaped like a cricket oval. This game is so popular that children have been named after football stars. Nauru also has an Olympic weightlifting team, established in 1994. Marcus Stephen (1969–), elected president in December 2007, has won numerous gold and silver medals in the sport. Other weightlifters of note are Sheeva Peo and Yukio Peter.

Nauruans sometimes hunt the noddy, or black tern, a local bird. Fishing is also popular. Birds and fish caught by Nauruan sportsmen are usually eaten.

Cultural Sites & Landmarks

Nauru, at just 21 square kilometers (8.1 square miles), is considered the world's smallest island nation. As a result, the tiny island does not have many significant cultural sites. Outside of the island's history of phosphate mining and role during World War II, its natural beauty is perhaps the nation's most renowned attraction. Beautiful coral pinnacles adorn the east coast of the island, though the shoreline of Nauru is generally rocky and devoid of beach areas. Some of the inner areas of the island also contain cliffs, which provide a view of the entire island.

One of the most interesting locations on the island is the gutted plateau of the inner island, called "Topside," which makes up approximately 80 percent of the landscape. After a century of phosphate mining, the area has become uninhabitable and features deep pits and towering limestone pillars. (Nauru's phosphate deposits were formed over thousands of years, and the substance was mainly produced by the solidification of oceanic microorganisms and bird droppings.) It is a constant reminder of the extreme environmental impact of phosphate mining. Because most of the island features this moonlike landscape, there is not enough space for the growing population.

There are several sites on the island that document the years of Japanese occupation during World War II. The Japanese controlled Nauru from August 26, 1942, until September 13, 1945. Among the ruins is a hospital built by the Japanese inside a natural sinkhole. During this time, tunnels were dug out, the floors were covered with wooden planks, and a large fan ventilated the entire area. However, in 1988 the sinkhole was filled with rocks and other debris. There have been efforts to uncover this area and promote it as a tourist attraction. Another interesting attraction is the site of a B-52 bomber wreck. The plane's wreckage is among the coral pinnacles of the plateau.

Libraries & Museums

The regional University of the South Pacific maintains a campus on Nauru, located in the Aiwo district, which has a library facility. Museum artifacts concerning Nauru are typically grouped in larger collections focusing on Micronesian art and culture, and are spread out over a large group of national museums. At one point, the now defunct Nauru Phosphate Corporation built a small museum, called the Nauru Museum or Nauru Military Museum, listed in travel guides as one of the island's top attractions. As of 2009, the museum, which contained WWII wreckage and artifacts, remained closed.

Holidays

Official holidays include Independence Day (January 31), Constitution Day (May 17), and

National Youth Day (September 25). Angam (Homecoming) Day, October 26, commemorates the times when the island's population has exceeded 1,500 people. This is thought to be the minimum number necessary for survival.

Youth Culture

All children are required to attend school from the ages of six to fifteen. However, the educational system, due to lack of funding and resources, is not very reliable. As a result, the youth of Nauru have a high illiteracy rate. In addition, because higher education is limited on the island, many young Nauruans go to university in Australia. The Nauruan government does assist those wanting to further their education with special grants for study abroad. When students do graduate from the Nauruan education system, job opportunities are extremely limited. While potential plans to rehabilitate the island's inner plateau could lead to many new employment opportunities for youth, there are also programs in place to help those young people who do not finish school get the training they need in order to obtain employment.

Sports are quite popular among Nauruan youth, with Australian Rules football being the most popular. The sport began to be played in Nauru during the 1930s, and there is a national league run by the Nauru Australian Football Association (NAFA). The league has seven senior teams and five junior teams currently competing. The teams play in the island's only stadium, the Linkbelt Oval, the surface of which is crushed phosphate dust. The nation also has a team that plays internationally. The other most popular sport in Nauru is weightlifting. The nation has successfully competed in the Commonwealth Games, as well as the Olympics.

SOCIETY

Transportation

As a small island nation, transportation in Nauru mainly consists of walking, private automobile, or motor scooter. As of 2008, there were approximately 2,000 registered vehicles, but no public transport (including taxis) or car rental service. There is an airport with a paved runway, with service by Our Airline (formerly Air Nauru), the national carrier, to other nearby islands, as well as Hong Kong, Japan, Australia, New Zealand, and the Philippines. Our Airline operates only one Boeing aircraft.

Traffic moves on the left-hand side of the road.

Transportation Infrastructure

The transportation infrastructure of Nauru is limited. There is one airport, the Nauru International Airport, located in the Yaren district. As of the turn of the 21st century, the roadways throughout Nauru, which mainly consist of one paved road circling the island (ring road), totaled about 30 kilometers (18 miles). A small railway services the phosphate mining industry. The Nauru government, in their 2009 revised National Sustainable Development Strategy, lists the maintenance of roads as a long-term goal (2025) and the provision of private-sector public transportation and port refurbishment as short-term goals (2012).

Media & Communications

Nauru's constitution allows freedom of expression, although some stipulations are included in the case of protecting national security. Despite this allowance, Nauruan law does not include protections for freedom of information. This has resulted in problems with the government not allowing certain documents to be revealed in the past.

There are only a few media outlets in Nauru, and the tiny island nation does not have a daily news publication. The government does publish a weekly called the *Nauru Bulletin*, *the Central Star News*, and the *Nauru Chronicle*. There is one publication operated by an opposition group, called the *People's Voice*. In addition, there is a state-operated radio, Radio Nauru, and a state-owned television station, Nauru Television (NTV). These stations distribute some foreign media, including Radio Australia and programming from New Zealand and the British Broadcasting Corporation

(BBC). As of 2006, an estimated 88 percent of Nauruan households had televisions, but only 52 percent owned working radios.

While there is no Internet censorship, access remains extremely limited due to insufficient infrastructure. As of 2005, less than 3 percent of the population is considered Internet users. However, as of 2004, the island was reported to have two Internet cafés providing access for a small fee.

SOCIAL DEVELOPMENT

Standard of Living

When profits from phosphate mining were high, the government provided national healthcare and education, keeping the literacy rate above 90 percent. Since then, with the economy in decline, these public services have diminished. The United Nations Human Development Index, which measures quality of life and standard of living indicators, did not include the nation of Nauru in the 2014 list (which is based on 2013 data). Nonetheless, the island nation is considered to have a medium human development rating.

Water Consumption

According to the 2015 Nauru Demographic and Health Survey, seven in ten households use improved toilet facilities, and 65 percent of households had improved sanitation facilities. In addition, approximately 96 percent of the survey's respondents reported that they had access improved water sources, with rainwater listed as a primary source, with most households responding that they treated water—in most cases, through boiling—to protect against contamination.

Education

Education is free, and it is compulsory for children between the ages of six and sixteen. Primary school lasts for seven years, and secondary school lasts up to four years. The island supports several small schools, including pre-primary, primary, secondary, and vocational institutions. According to the 2007 Nauru Demographic and Health Survey, completion rates for secondary education were low—15 percent for girls and 11 percent for boys. In addition, net attendance for primary school was 88 percent, decreasing to 60 percent at the secondary educational level.

Nauru has no university, but it maintains an extension center of the University of the South Pacific (Suva, Fiji). The island's average literacy rate is roughly 99 percent.

Women's Rights

Traditional Nauruan society was based around a matriarchal system, and having a daughter was considered better than having a son. Women generally enjoyed a more authoritative societal role than men enjoy, and were in charge for nearly all major decisions.

However, modern conditions are not quite as favorable for some for women.

Nauruan law grants equal rights and freedoms to both men and women, and the main factor affecting women's rights in Nauruan society is the impoverishment of the small island nation. While there are no laws that prevent women from participation in politics, it is rare for a woman to hold a prominent public office. For example, in the April 2008 parliamentary elections, there were four women candidates; however, none of them was elected. Women have held such high positions as the head of the presidential counsel and the head of civil service. The Women's Affair Office has been established to help women gain access to professional opportunities, including encouraging the production of traditional crafts. The office also gives out two scholarships a year, sending recipients to Suva (the capital of Fiji) to participate in workshops designed to educate women in areas such as home economics.

Sexual crimes against women are thought to be common, but data on their frequency is unavailable. Nauruan law identifies rape as a crime punished in some case by life in prison. Although not identified specifically as a crime, authorities do investigate spousal rape, and charges have been filed in these cases. Issues of domestic abuse are sometimes settled within the family or the larger community; police do intervene if disputes reach a heightened level.

Health Care

The average life expectancy in Nauru is sixty-six years—sixty-two for men and seventy for women (2015 estimate). The relatively short life expectancy is blamed on a junk food diet resulting in a high incidence of diabetes, heart disease, and obesity. Diabetes afflicts about 30 percent of adults over twenty-five and about 50 percent of senior citizens on the island. This is one of the highest rates of diabetes in the world.

In the 1970s, life expectancy in Nauru was even shorter than it is today. Men could expect to live no longer than fifty years, the shortest lifespan in the Pacific Islands group. The improvement is attributed to preventive health care and education.

Another major cause of death is automobile accidents. The island has only one paved road, but most families own at least one car.

Health care is free to residents of Nauru. There are 1.5 doctors per 1,000 people. The annual health expenditure per capita is $1,015 (USD).

GOVERNMENT

Structure

Nauru is a republic with a constitution that has been in force since January 31, 1968. The voting age is twenty. Suffrage is universal, and voting is compulsory.

Executive authority rests with the president, who is both the chief of state and the head of government. The president is chosen by Parliament from among its members and serves for three years or until a vote of "no confidence." The president appoints a cabinet of four or five members from among the members of Parliament.

The eighteen-member Parliament is a unicameral legislature, elected by popular vote. The members of parliament are elected for up to three years, but they can lose their seats in case of a "no-confidence" vote. No-confidence votes are frequent, and have resulted in almost continuous changes of government since independence. Several presidents and members of Parliament have lost elections or been forced out of office on charges of corruption or for such social errors as refusing to apologize. The June 2010 Nauruan parliamentary elections resulted in a hung parliament, as there was no clear majority.

Before becoming a self-governing nation, Nauru was overseen by German and Australia. German annexed the island in 1888. After Germany's defeat in World War I, the League of Nations awarded trusteeship of Nauru to Australia, New Zealand, and the United Kingdom. After World War II, the United Nations confirmed the trusteeship, with Australia as administrator.

In 1968, Nauru gained its independence. In 1999, it joined the United Nations. The district of Yaren is internationally accepted as Nauru's capital, though it has never been made the official capital. The country's government, including parliament, ministries, and administrative offices are located there. The international airport is there as well.

Political Parties

Nauru is traditionally perceived as a non-party (or non-partisan) democracy, but maintains several political parties, including the Democratic Party of Nauru (DPN), founded in 1987; the Nauru First (Naoero Amo), often considered the only formal party; and the Centre Party, which has not maintained a parliamentary seat since 2003.

Local Government

The country is subdivided into fourteen administrative districts (Aiwo, Anabar, Anetan, Anibare, Baiti, Boe, Buada, Denigomodu, Ewa, Ijuw, Meneng, Nibok, Uaboe, and Yaren). Some community and local affairs are handled by the Nauru Island Council, which has limited responsibilities.

Judicial System

The highest court of Nauru is the High Court of Australia, which can hear appeals from the Supreme Court of Nauru, which hears both civil and criminal cases. Underneath the Supreme Court is a Family Court and District Court. The judicial system is based on British common law.

Taxation

There is no income or corporate tax in Nauru. There is, however, an airline departure tax and a 7 percent tax on all goods.

Armed Forces

Nauru has no armed forces. Per an informal agreement, the country is dependent upon Australia for matters of national defense.

Foreign Policy

Nauru was first annexed by Germany and then controlled by Australia. After brief occupation by Japan, Nauru was back under the control of Australia. The tiny island nation finally gained its independence in 1968, and subsequently joined the Commonwealth of Nations, which consists of former British colonies. As a designated special member of this international organization, Nauru is allowed to take part in all activities, with the exception of meetings between heads of government. Additionally, Nauru became a member of the United Nations (UN) in 1999, and holds membership in the Pacific Islands Forum, the South Pacific Commission (SPC), the African, Caribbean and Pacific Group of States (ACP), and the South Pacific Applied Geoscience Commission (SOPAC). Nauru also recently joined the South Pacific Tourism Organization (SPTO).

Nauru has a unique relationship with Australia and remains highly dependent on substantial financial aid from the country. In fact, with the economy and environment of Nauru having suffered due to years of phosphate mining, Nauru even filed a lawsuit against Australia in the International Court of Justice (ICJ). The suit was filed because of damages associated with phosphate mining during the time the island was under Australian jurisdiction. The case was settled out of court in 1993. The Australian government agreed to pay $107 million (AUD) to Nauru. Additionally, Australia also promised to assist Nauru with rehabilitating its devastated environment.

Nauru has also served as the temporary detainment center for Afghan refugees who were prevented from entering Australia. The refugees were attempting to seek asylum in Australia due to the conflicts in both Afghanistan and Iraq, and were intercepted by the Australian government.

The government then constructed a deal with Nauru to open up a detention center. Approximately 1,200 refugees were initially held in the center, but by 2006, there was only one refugee on the island. However, in September 2008, the Australian government placed seven Burmese refugees in the center while working on their application for asylum. Eighty-two Sri Lankan refugees were also transferred to Nauru in March 2007. The center was eventually closed in February 2008, and the remaining Sri Lankans were taken to Australia. Nauru was given aid in the form of grants and other support in exchange for housing the refugees.

As Nauru's phosphate resources completely diminished in 2006, the nation scrambled to forge relations with countries in order to obtain aid. In 2002, the country entered diplomatic relations with China, severing its recognition of Taiwan (Republic of China) as a country. In exchange, China had promised the nation $130 million (USD) in aid. However, in 2005, Nauru once again began relations with Taiwan, ending its relationship with China. Nauru took further steps to solidify its relationship with Taiwan when it opened an embassy in 2007 in Taipei. While relations between the United States and Nauru are friendly, the United States maintains no official diplomatic offices on the island.

Nauru has opposed missile defense shield propositions by the United States due to fears that missile testing would cause debris to fall on the island.

Human Rights Profile

International human rights law insists that states respect civil and political rights, and promote an individual's economic, social, and cultural rights. The United Nations Universal Declaration on Human Rights (UDHR) is recognized as the standard for international human rights. Its authors sought the counsel of the world's great thinkers, philosophers, and religious leaders, and were careful to create a document that reflects the core values shared by every world culture. (To read this document or view the articles relating to cultural human rights, visit http://www.udhr.org/UDHR/default.htm.)

The Nauruan constitution generally upholds human rights as outlined in the UDHR. The few reported human rights grievances involved the refugee processing and detention center opened by the Australian government, but administrated by the Nauruan government. Afghani, Burmese, and Sri Lankan asylum seekers were held in the center from 2001 until March 2008. During this period, the Human Rights and Equal Opportunity Commission (HREOC) was denied permission to view conditions inside of the detention center, and it remains unknown what conditions the refugees were kept in. (Australia was also possibly in violation of the UDHR due to Nauru's refusal of visits from human rights organizations.)

During their stay on Nauru, the refugees were prevented from fully exercising their rights due to lack of access to lawyers, friends, and family, as well as their respective religious organizations. The mental heath of the refugees is also said to have deteriorated during their stay at the Nauruan detention center. However, when the Nauruan government first entered agreements with Australia to house the refugees, Nauru agreed, in correspondence with Article 14, that it would not deport refugees to their former countries of residence if this action would threaten their lives or liberty.

While the Nauruan constitution allows for freedom of expression, there is a lack of independent media outlets. The only non-government owned and operated publication is the *People's Voice*. Another area of concern is government transparency, as the constitution does not provide access to government documents. Thus, it has been difficult for the public to gain access to government information. During the 2007 elections, an independent group observed that the government did not provide information on certain election issues, and did not provide the people with proper voter education materials.

Other human rights matters include issues of discrimination. While ethnic Chinese make up only 5 percent of the population, this group has often been the target of various acts of theft and assault. However, Nauruan authorities cite these acts as economically motivated rather than rooted in discrimination against the ethnic Chinese. Another issue involves the outlawing of sodomy. However, this law has not been enforced and discrimination against homosexuals is not common.

ECONOMY

Overview of the Economy

After 1968, when Nauru gained its independence, the Nauruans were among the richest people in the world. Nauruans grew wealthy from the sale of their phosphate reserves; labor was imported from Kiribati and Tuvalu. During its peak as a guano mining empire, Nauru boasted the second-highest gross national product (GNP) per person in the world, after Saudi Arabia.

However, changes over the years have made Nauru one of the most dramatically shifting economies in the world. Phosphate exports declined in the 1990s when the Australian market collapsed and Asia was in financial crisis. In recent years, with phosphate deposits running out, the per capita gross domestic product has fallen to $2,500 (USD) (2006 estimate).

Knowing that the deposits would be exhausted, Nauru had invested heavily in trust funds. However, fraud, poor investments, and government corruption nearly bankrupted the country. Nauru has been forced to sell off its international real estate holdings in order to pay its debts. In an attempt to save money, the government has frozen wages, privatized some government agencies, reduced the staffs in others, and closed some overseas consulates.

The government has also had to resort to more creative methods of supporting its economy and generating revenue such as the sale of fishing rights in its water zone for profit. In 2001, Nauru agreed to house two Australian refugee camps for payment, though Australia has discontinued the use of the detention centers.

In 2006, scientists discovered the possibility of continued phosphate mining on the island, though the national debt has continued to increase. In response, the Yaren district has begun a revised economic program with import and export, tourism, fishing and banking as the chosen industries to replace the depleting phosphate mines.

Nauru receives foreign aid from New Zealand, Japan, China, and Taiwan, which intervened to fund a new airline so commercial imports could resume after the government declared bankruptcy in 2004.

Industry

For decades, Nauru's only industry has been phosphate mining. With phosphate deposits running out, one possible source of income in the future is coconut products. In the mid-19th century, Nauru produced as much as a million pounds of copra (dried coconut meat) for export.

Labor

According to statistics released from the U.S. Department of State, Nauru's labor force participation rate was 78 percent in 2006, less than 1 percent of which was subsistence workers. Unemployed workers numbered 1,588 that same year. In 2015, the unemployment rate was twenty-three percent.

Energy/Power/Natural Resources

Nauru's only natural resource is petrified guano, the droppings of bats and seabirds. Guano contains high-quality phosphate, which is used in fertilizer. Rainwater is collected in roof storage tanks, and an outdated desalinization plant provides a small amount of fresh water for the island's inhabitants.

Fishing

The country continues to lack a local commercial fishing base. Nauru's EEZ (exclusive economic zone) totals 320,000 square kilometers (123,552 miles), and the county has licensing agreements to allow several purse-seine foreign vessels to operate, including those from Japan, Taiwan, China, and the Republic of Korea. (Purse-seining vessels are fishing boats that use long nets, often 1 mile long, to encircle and catch tuna.) As of March 2010, there were also approximately thirty-nine American purse-seiner fishing vessels licensed to fish in Nauru waters.

Tuna conditions are excellent in the waters off Nauru, and tuna catch-control measures have been implemented in 2010 to help protect against the overfishing of big-eye tuna.

Mining/Metals

Phosphate mining has dominated Nauru. High-quality phosphate from petrified guano deposits was discovered in 1899, and mining began in earnest in 1906. The agreement to mine Nauru was made between the German and British governments. Though not required to by the agreement, the Germans chose to pay the Nauruan landowners a fee for the phosphate mined on their land.

The deposits are almost depleted, and Nauru is conducting studies to determine the feasibility of mining secondary and residual deposits of phosphates.

Agriculture

Nauru has virtually no arable land, except for the narrow coastal strip. Some small-scale agriculture is practiced. Coconuts are the principal crop, with up to 1,600 metric tons produced annually.

Other agricultural products include tropical fruits (bananas, pineapples, and pandanus), vegetables, and coffee. Most agricultural activities occur at the subsistence level.

Animal Husbandry

Some small Nauruan farms raise pigs and chickens (eggs). Agricultural activity, including the raising of livestock, is extremely limited on the island due to a lack of water resources and grazing land.

Tourism

Nauru has very little tourism, and has not developed a tourism infrastructure. However, tourism is considered one of the possibilities for revitalizing the nation's economy in the future. Three are only two main hotels in operation on the island.

There are some good beaches on Nauru, particularly in Anibare Bay. Swimming, however, can be dangerous because of the strong, unpredictable currents. Facilities for golf and tennis are available, and it is possible to walk around the island in a day.

Charter boats are available for deep-sea fishing or diving. Divers can enjoy the coral reef that surrounds the island, or they can explore the many World War II-era shipwrecks on the ocean floor. Because of the deep water close to the shore, fishing is excellent. Marlin, sailfish, wahoo, and yellowfin tuna may be caught just off the beaches, due to the deep water close to the shore.

Kianoosh Hashenzadeh, Ellen Bailey,
Anne Whittaker

DID YOU KNOW?

- There is only one football pitch (field) on the island. Because there is no grass, the pitch consists of guano powder spread over crushed rock. Pitch markings are made with oil.

- Yaren sponsors Nauru's national holiday, Angam Day. The word "Angam" is translated as "Homecoming." Also called the "Day of Fulfillment," it is reserved for celebrating the two times in Nauru's history when the population recovered from dwindling below the minimum number of people needed on the island for survival, which is 1,500.

Bibliography

Petit-Skinner, Solange. *The Nauruans.* San Francisco: MacDuff Press, 1995.

This American Life. "253: The Middle of Nowhere." *This American Life:* Public Radio International, 2007.

McDaniel, Carl N. and John M. Gowdy. *Paradise for Sale: A Parable of Nature.* Berkeley, CA: University of California Press, 2000.

Kayser, Alois. *Nauru One Hundred Years Ago: 1. Pandanus.* Suva, Fiji: University of the South Pacific Centre on Nauru, 2002.

———. *Nauru One Hundred Years Ago: 2. Fishing.* Suva, Fiji: University of the South Pacific Centre on Nauru, 2002.

Works Cited

"Human Rights Report: Nauru." Human Rights Report. U.S. State Department. http://www.state.gov/g/drl/rls/hrrpt/2008/eap/119050.htm.

Australia, Amnesty International. "Human Rights Situation Deteriorating on Nauru." 2007. Amnesty International Australia. April 24 2009. http://www.amnesty.org.au/news/comments/2733/.

"Background Note: Nauru." http://www.state.gov/r/pa/ei/bgn/16447.htm.

"Cooking in Nauru." Food & Beverage. http://www.gowealthy.com/gowealthy/wcms/en/home/articles/travel/food-and-beverage/Cooking-in-Nauru-1209889635179.html.

"Ethnologue Report for Nauru." http://www.ethnologue.com/show_country.asp?name=nauru.

Freedom House, Freedom of the Press - Nauru. Online. UNHCR Refworld, available at: http://www.unhcr.org/refworld/docid/478cd5372.html

Gajda, Stan. "Preserving Historic Sites." 1996. Nauru Phosphate Corporation. http://74.125.95.132/

search?q=cache:HxtdZIi5BzsJ:www.pacificwrecks.com/
people/visitors/gajda/nauru/protect.pdf+japanese+occup
ation+of+Nauru&cd=8&hl=en&ct
=clnk&gl=ca&client=firefox-a.

"Joanne Gobure." http://en.wikipedia.org/wiki/Joanne_
Gobure.

Kayser, Alois. *Nauru One Hundred Years Ago:* 1.
Pandanus. Suva, Fiji: University of the South Pacific
Centre on Nauru, 2002.

———. *Nauru One Hundred Years Ago*: 2. Fishing. Suva,
Fiji: University of the South Pacific Centre on Nauru,
2002.

"Margaret Hendrie." http://en.wikipedia.org/wiki/
Margaret_Hendrie.

"Nauru." Ed. The Commonwealth. http://www.
thecommonwealth.org/YearbookHomeInternal/138866/.

"Nauru." Lonely Planet. http://www.lonelyplanet.com/
nauru.

"Nauru." Country Profile. BBC News. http://news.bbc.
co.uk/2/hi/asia-pacific/country_profiles/1134221.stm.

"Nauru - Education." Encyclopedia of the Nations. http://
www.nationsencyclopedia.com/Asia-and-Oceania/
Nauru-EDUCATION.html.

"Nauru - Transportation." http://www.nationsencyclopedia.
com/Asia-and-Oceania/Nauru-TRANSPORTATION.html.

Petit-Skinner, Solange. *The Nauruans*. San Francisco:
MacDuff Press, 1995.

"Population Distribution." Nauru Bureau of Statistics.
http://www.spc.int/prism/country/nr/stats/Census/popn_
distribution.htm.

"Republic of Nauru." Hitchhikers Guide to the Galaxy.
BBC. http://www.bbc.co.uk/dna/h2g2/A634646.

Streib, Lauren. "World's Fattest Countries." Forbes.com,
2007.

This American Life. "253: The Middle of Nowhere." This
American Life: Public Radio International, 2007.

NEW ZEALAND

Introduction

New Zealand is a series of islands located 2,012 kilometers (1,250 miles) southeast of Australia in the South Pacific Ocean. It is a former British colony, and currently a Commonwealth Realm. The country consists of two large islands and a host of smaller islands. It is known for its beauty, its artistic contribution to the world of film, and for its indigenous Polynesian Maori culture.

Wellington is the capital and governmental seat of New Zealand. Home to the national opera, symphony and ballet, as well as the film industry, it is referred to as the country's culture capital. Wellington is known for being a metropolitan tcity with a small town feel.

People from New Zealand are sometimes affectionately referred to as Kiwis, a nickname borrowed from a species of flightless bird native to the country. The bird is also New Zealand's national symbol.

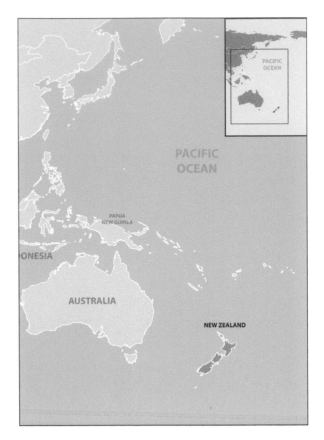

GENERAL INFORMATION

Official Language: English and Maori
Population: 4,438,393 (July 2015)
Currency: New Zealand Dollar
Coins: The New Zealand Dollar is subdivided into 100 cents. Coins come in denominations of 10, 20, and 50 cents, and come in denominations of one and two dollars.
Land Area: 267,710 square kilometers (103,336 square miles)
Water Area: 1,609 square kilometers (2,784 square miles)

National Anthem: "God Defend New Zealand"
Capital: Wellington
Time Zone: GMT +12
Flag Description: The flag of New Zealand features a deep blue background with the UK flag situated in its upper hoist (left) side, taking up approximately one quarter of the flag. On the fly (right) side of the flag are four red, five-pointed stars, each of which is edged in white. The cluster of stars represents the Southern Cross constellation.

Population

New Zealand has a young, growing population. The average age is thirty-six years, and the population is growing at a rate of slightly under 1 percent. Although New Zealand is known for its natural beauty, more than 86 percent of the population lives in urban areas. The capital is Wellington, but the most populous city is Auckland. The population density of New Zealand is low, at roughly fifteen people per square kilometer (thirty-nine per square mile).

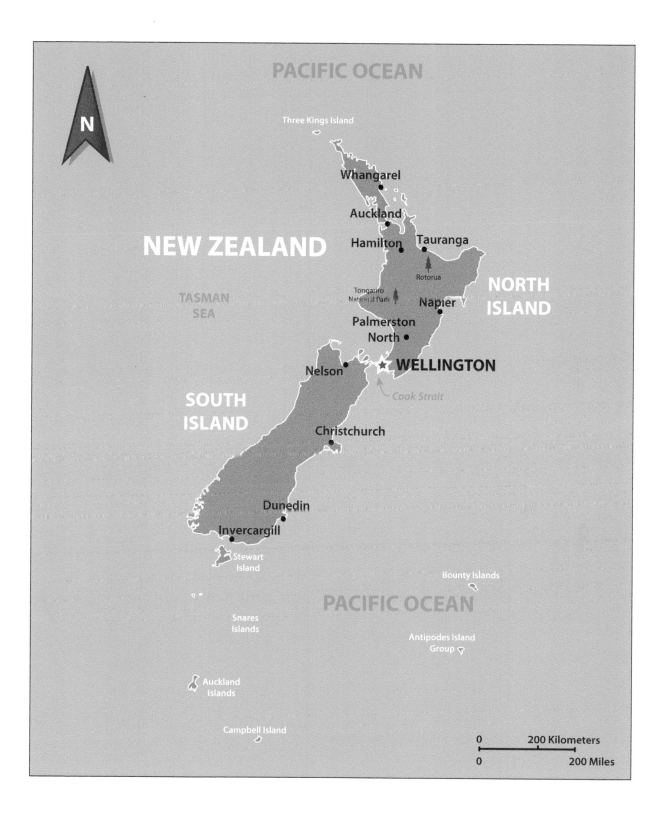

Principal Cities by Population (2012):

- Auckland City (434,699)
- Manukua City (430,144)
- Christchurch (385,663)
- North Shore City (280,323)
- Waitakere City (213,184)
- Wellington (193,525)
- Hamilton (172,429)
- Tauranga (125,477)
- Dunedin (112,470)

As New Zealand has become more modernized, internal migration has been from rural to urban areas. Auckland and Christchurch are the two largest cities. According to early 21st century estimates, the population of the greater Wellington area is between 370,000 and 460,000, and the population of the city proper is 193,525.

Wellington's population is older than that of New Zealand as a whole. Approximately 18 percent of the population in Wellington is under the age of fifteen. In New Zealand, 19 percent of the population is under fifteen years old. The elderly population is also small.

Even though relatively few of Wellington's residents identify as Maori (between 4 and 12 percent), the indigenous group's presence is still felt in the city. Almost 82 percent of the population claims European ancestry, about 12 percent claim either Pacific or Asian ancestry, and many claim membership in more than one ethnic group. About 20 percent of Wellington's population is comprised of immigrants.

Languages

New Zealand recognizes both English and Maori as official languages. Maori is an Austronesian language, and few natives are fluent, since Maori was banned in New Zealand schools in the late nineteenth century. Today, the language is being revived through government funding and its use in many schools. Some small segments of the population speak other European or Polynesian languages.

Native People & Ethnic Groups

The native Maori represent the largest minority in New Zealand, at nearly 8 percent of the total population. They first settled in New Zealand sometime during the first millennium. Some modern Maori groups refer to themselves as "tangata whena" ("people of the land").

In 1840, the Maori entered into a treaty giving Great Britain sovereignty over the region. When the British began to colonize New Zealand, land disputes with the Maori grew into wars. By 1872, the Maori were defeated and their population had declined drastically. More than 100 years later, in 1975, the government created the Waitangi Tribunal to address Maori grievances and investigate land claims. The Maori are is still represented poorly in the country's health, labor, education, and crime statistics, despite population growth, and having largely integrated into New Zealand's European-dominated society.

In addition to an indigenous population, 70 percent of New Zealanders are of European ethnicity, including English, Irish, Scottish, German, Scandinavian, Croatian, and Dutch. East Asian and Pacific Islanders each account for roughly 6 percent of the population. Many East Asian immigrants arrived during New Zealand's gold rush in the 1860s. Many Pacific Islanders migrated from Tonga, Fiji, Tokelau, Niu, the Cook Islands, and Samoa.

Religions

A majority of New Zealanders are Christian. The Maori are known as more ardent followers of their faith. The Maori have their own belief system, but there are two major Maori Christian churches, the Ringatu Church and the Ratana Church, that have small but active memberships.

Climate

New Zealand is located in the Southern Hemisphere, so its seasons are opposite those in the Northern Hemisphere. The warmest months are January and February, and the coldest are June and July. Temperatures tend to be slightly warmer in the north than the south, but with the exception of the extreme north and south locations, most temperature variations are minimal.

The average low temperatures range from 2° Celsius (35° Fahrenheit) in the south to 8° Celsius (46° Fahrenheit) in the north. Auckland, on the North Island, has an average high temperature of 23° Celsius (73° Fahrenheit) while Christchurch, on the South Island, has an average high temperature of 21° Celsius (71° Fahrenheit).

The east coast receives much more rain than the west coast because of the mountains, which serve as a natural weather barrier. For example, Christchurch, to the east, receives about 64 centimeters (25 inches) of rainfall per year, while Hokitika, to the west, receives about 290 centimeters (114 inches) annually.

Wellington is extremely windy. The high winds and 497 kilometers (309 miles) of coastline on the Cook Strait make Wellington a premier surfing destination. Two of the best-known surfing breaks in the city occur in Lyall Bay and Palliser Bay. Furthering the appeal of surfing as a sport is the fact that the average Wellington resident lives less than 3 kilometers (1.86 miles) from the ocean.

ENVIRONMENT & GEOGRAPHY

Topography
New Zealand's two main islands (the North Island and the South Island) are the second and third largest in the thousands that make up the South Pacific island chain. They are separated by the Cook Strait. The country's total land area of 267,710 square kilometers (103,336 square miles) makes it roughly the same size as Japan. Many small, uninhabited islands are also part of the country. These include the Chatham Islands, Auckland Islands, Antipodes Islands, Bounty Islands, Kermadec Islands, and Stewart Island.

The North Island is characterized by its many large volcanoes, including Mount Ruapehu, which erupted as recently as 1996. Just off the east coast is White Island, which is actually the peak of a submerged volcano. The North Island

also contains several thermal areas such as geysers and hot mud flats.

Wellington City, located on the southern tip of the North Island, is capital city with a total area of just 290 square kilometers (111.9 square miles.), but boasts more restaurants per capita than New York, and more open land per capita than any other city in the world.

The Southern Alps run almost the entire length of the South Island. Mount Cook, at 3,754 meters (12,316 feet) above sea level, is the highest point in New Zealand. There are also a number of rivers, many of which are fed by the glaciers. The Southern Alps contain more than 300 glaciers, the largest of which is Tasman Glacier.

Offsetting the mountainous region are the Canterbury Plains, the country's largest lowland expanse. The hills and flatlands of Otago Plateau give way to the neighboring Fiordland National Park to the west. This is where the southernmost foothills of the Southern Alps meet the coast to form a series of narrow deep-water inlets.

The country's largest lakes include Lake Waikaremoana, Lake Taupo, and Lake Wanaka. With an area of 606 square kilometers (234 square miles), Lake Taupo is the country's largest. It rests in the middle of an inactive volcano and drains into New Zealand's largest river, the Waikato.

Plants & Animals
There are roughly 2,000 species of native plants in New Zealand, and national parks protect most of the country's lush vegetation. One of the more distinctive plants is the pohutukawa, also known as the "New Zealand Christmas tree," which is filled with bright red flowers each December. Trees commonly found in the forests include rimu, beech, tawa, matai, and rata. Ferns and flax are also prevalent. The mountainous areas produce alpine and subalpine herb fields, and scrub and tussock.

The islands of New Zealand formed before the evolution of mammals, and their isolation meant that only flying mammals would be able to thrive. Therefore, the bat is the island's only native land mammal. With no predatory mammals, birds and reptiles flourished. Birds did not need to fly to survive, and many built their nests on the ground.

Unique animals found in New Zealand include the tuatara, a prehistoric lizard, and the weta, a giant insect similar to a cricket.

Today, New Zealand is home to many species of flightless birds. The morepork, tui, weka, and kea are a few of the most common native birds found on the islands. Pigs, goats, possums, dogs, cats, deer, and sheep have all been introduced, with damaging effects. Many native plant and bird species face extinction because of plants and animals that have been introduced to the country.

CUSTOMS & COURTESIES

Greetings

In general, New Zealanders disdain formality, and this casual nature is typically reflected in their greetings. People in New Zealand commonly greet one another by saying "G'day" ("Good day") or other casual expressions similar to "Hello" or "Good morning." Other common expressions are "Cheers" ("Thanks or good-bye"), "Ta" ("Thank you"), and "Later" or "Catch you" ("See you later").

New Zealanders have adopted many Maori phrases. "Kia ora" is widely used and can mean anything from "Hello," "Good day," or "Good health" to "Good-bye," "Thank you," or "Good luck." "Tena koe" is common when greeting one person and means "Greetings to you." The Maori custom of raising both eyebrows as a sign of recognition is also becoming more common among New Zealanders.

In addition, many New Zealanders use handshakes when meeting someone for the first time, particularly in business or formal situations. Maori commonly greet other Maori with a hug or a hongi, which is the pressing of noses and foreheads. It is a sacred tradition that signifies the sharing of the breath of life. It is not customary for non-Maori to use this greeting unless a Maori initiates it.

Maori also use an elaborate set of greetings in business meetings and traditional ceremonies. These involve the powhiri, a formal welcome that can last up to three hours. Visitors are called to an area in front of the meetinghouse and instructed where to sit. They then listen to several speeches and songs. Afterwards, a member of the visiting group will give a short speech explaining the purpose of the visit. The visitors then line up and walk to their hosts. They then shake each person's hand, kiss one of their cheeks, and hongi.

Gestures & Etiquette

New Zealanders have a strong national pride and appreciate when people recognize their country's distinct traits. They often are offended when they are referred to as, or considered similar to, Australians. Overall, New Zealanders are generally regarded as friendly, but somewhat reserved with people until they get to know them. They consider modesty an important attribute. As such, they commonly dislike, or disapprove of, flashy behavior or arrogance. In fact, they use the term "tall poppy syndrome" to describe their lack of respect for people who brag, try to stand out or act as if they are better than others are. The term derives from the cutting of tall poppies to match the height of the other poppies in a field or garden.

New Zealanders often consider people who act overly friendly or direct as aggressive and intrusive. Likewise, they prefer not to discuss personal issues with people they have just met. They also dislike extended eye contact and excessive physical contact such as backslapping.

Social rank and position are of generally of little importance to New Zealanders, mostly because their country is egalitarian. People seldom use titles, such as "mister" or "sir," and prefer to call people by their first names. Dress also is understated, and casual clothing is worn for all but the most formal occasions. For example, it would not be considered uncommon for a university vice president and a university janitor to dress in a similar fashion.

Certain behaviors also have unique meanings in New Zealand. For example, it is considered rude for a non-Polynesian person to sit at a higher level than a Polynesian does. In addition, Maori customs specify strict rules of etiquette when visiting a marae, which are sacred places in Polynesian society. While rules may vary by region, some of the most common rules include the following: enter only with permission, take shoes off before entering, turn cell phones off, do not sit on any surface where food has been prepared, do not talk loudly, and do not walk in front of people who are talking.

Eating/Meals

In New Zealand, most people typically eat three meals a day. Breakfast is the first meal of the day and is eaten before work or school. Lunch usually is eaten between 11 am and 1 pm, and the evening meal, or tea, is eaten between 6 and 8 pm. Families often eat the evening meal together. Dishes are served family-style, with everyone at the table helping themselves from platters of food placed on the table. Some families pray before their meals, but this tradition has become less common in recent years. At large Maori gatherings where food is served, it is customary for an elder to give a blessing before the meal. Visitors are often asked to sing a song after the meal as a thank you or sign of appreciation for the food and hospitality.

In addition, many people have a cup of tea with cakes or cookies during the afternoon. Not to be confused with the evening meal, this snack is called afternoon tea. An evening snack is called supper. New Zealanders also commonly use the continental custom of holding their knife in the right hand and the fork in their left. When they have finished eating, they place the knife and fork parallel along the side of the plate with the handles facing to the right.

Visiting

New Zealanders are hospitable and enjoy having people over for meals and gatherings. It is common for guests to be invited for tea (the evening meal) or a barbie (barbeque). Guests may be asked to "bring a plate," which is a plate of food or dish to be shared with others. Written invitations are rare, and most people will offer an invitation in person or by telephone.

New Zealanders expect visitors to make themselves at home. Houses are casual and there generally is no English-style parlor or front room. People may take their shoes off before or immediately after entering the house, but practices vary by household. The host often will show visitors around the home by giving them a room-by-room tour. Gift giving is not required, but guests can bring a small gift. However, a large or expensive gift may make the host feel awkward. Gifts such as flowers or chocolate are generally given for formal dinner parties.

Guests to Maori houses will experience different customs. Maori place a high regard on food and the head. Thus, they never pass a plate of food over someone's head. They also do not place objects such as jackets on a table or chair where food may be served. They also do not sit on pillows used for the head.

LIFESTYLE

Family

Typically, New Zealand households consist of a nuclear family, though Maori and Polynesian households may include extended family members. In the past, the traditional family was two parents and two children. Today, childless families are becoming more common, with almost 50 percent of households consisting of a single person or a couple with no children. Single-parent households also are more common. In fact, New Zealand has the third highest number of single-parent households in the world, with over 18 percent of all households consisting of one parent and a child or children.

Marriage rates are declining as divorce rates are increasing in New Zealand. In addition, many couples are getting married for the first time at a later age than in the past. In the 1970s, almost one-third of all brides were teenagers. However, in 2006 the median age of women entering marriage for the first time was twenty-eight; the median age for a man entering his first marriage is thirty. Many couples live together without getting married. Women also are waiting to have children until they are older, and are having fewer children than in the past.

Maori families are part of a tribe, or iwi. Due to increased mobility, tribal members no longer live in the same region as they did in the past. They do retain strong ties to their tribe, though, and members of a tribe often return to their tribe's meeting place for ceremonies and other tribal gatherings.

Housing

New Zealanders have a high rate of home ownership, with over 66 percent of the population owning their own home. Most houses are detached, or stand-alone, buildings, typically set on a quarter of an acre or less. A common house is a one-story, timber building with a front and back yard. It may have two or three bedrooms. In recent years, new homes are being built with up to six bedrooms. Most houses also have gardens. Townhouses and apartments are more prominent in cities, where space is more limited. Once uncommon, apartments in high-rise buildings are becoming more widespread in metropolitan areas.

Most homes have plumbing and electricity. In some remote rural areas, homes are not connected to a water supply, and residents collect rainwater and store it in a tank on the roof. Central heating is also not standard, and the majority of homes are heated by electricity. People also burn wood and use bottled gas as heating sources.

Some New Zealanders own vacation homes. In North Island, these homes are called bachs, short for bachelor homes. In South Island, they are called cribs. These are small homes built of inexpensive materials and designed to provide only the most basic shelter.

Food

New Zealand's cuisine reflects the diversity of its multicultural population—Asian, Polynesian, and European. Its British heritage dominated most food choices until the 20th century. The mainstay of most diets typically consisted of beef, lamb and venison, potatoes, vegetables such as peas, carrots, and cabbage, and British dishes such as fish and chips (lightly battered and deep fried pieces of fish, traditionally cod, and potatoes) and meat pies. In the 1950s, many immigrants began arriving in New Zealand, especially from Asian and Pacific Rim countries. They introduced ethnic cuisines to New Zealanders, and prepared New Zealand's natural resources, such as fish and fruits, in new ways. As a result, fish gained in popularity, as did Mediterranean cuisine.

Today, New Zealanders eat a wide variety of foods. Meat and fish, including pork, cervena (venison), salmon, crayfish, oysters, mussels, scallops, paua (abalone) and tuatua (a shellfish native to New Zealand) are common in many dishes. The most popular takeout food is a variation of the traditional fish and chips, in which shark, hoki, or tarakihi is used. Meat pies, which are sold in stores and on street carts, are another favorite staple. They are small individual pastries often filled with steak, mince (a fine blend of dried herbs and fruits or meat), or vegetables. A typical British meal of roast lamb with baked kumara, a sweet potato, also remains popular.

Two popular fish dishes are abalone patties, also called paua steaks, and whitebait fritters. Abalone patties are freshly caught abalone marinated with crushed kiwi fruit and fried for one to two minutes. Whitebait fritters are tiny fish eaten whole. They are dipped in a light batter of whipped egg white and fried for one minute. A hangi is a Maori meal prepared for large groups or special gatherings. Layers of meat, fish, and vegetables are wrapped in cabbage leaves and cooked in an earth oven, or an underground pit lined with hot stones.

In addition, a popular dessert—called pudding—is pavlova. Named for the famous Russian ballerina, pavlova is a meringue shell made of egg whites, sugar, vanilla, and cornflower topped with whipped cream and fruit, such as kiwi, passion fruit, or strawberries.

Another favorite desert is hokey-pokey ice cream, which is vanilla ice cream with chunks of caramel candy mixed in.

Life's Milestones

Many of New Zealand's customs follow those of Western cultures. For example, the birth of a child is announced in the newspaper, and gifts are often given for the new baby. Teens can obtain a driver's license when they are sixteen, and a twenty-first birthday is celebrated with a large party.

Wedding customs are also similar. Brides usually wear white, and the groom customarily wears a tuxedo or suit. They have a best man, maid of honor, and bridal party, and gift requests are made through gift registries. Before the wedding, brides often attend a hen party, similar to a bachelorette party. The groom is typically thrown a stag party, similar to a bachelor party. These gatherings are usually same-sex parties where the future bride and groom engage in fun activities. Many wedding ceremonies are held outdoors in gardens, parks or on the beach. The ceremony is followed by a reception with food, music, and dancing. In the past, the traditional wedding cake was a multilayered fruitcake with white icing. However, chocolate and other flavored cakes are replacing fruitcake.

Funerals for non-Maori are also similar to Western customs. Traditional Maori funerals, on the other hand, take place over several days. Tribal members, friends, and relatives gather to process their grief not only for the person who has just died, but also for others who have died in the past. The term "tangihanga" is used to describe this process. Tangihanga are held at the marae, home, or funeral parlor. Once a person passes away, family members usually stay with the body at all times until it is buried. The body is then placed in an open coffin, and mourners are invited to touch, hug, or kiss the body to express their grief. People tell stories and share their memories for several days, and they often leave koha, or money, to help the family with funeral expenses.

CULTURAL HISTORY

Art

New Zealand's early culture has its roots in the traditions of both its indigenous Maori people and later British settlers. Traditional Maori art includes carving, weaving, and tattooing. Many Pacific nations had a tradition of carving, and the Maori continued this craft when they came to New Zealand in the 13th century. Using shells and sharp stones, they carved ornate designs out of stone, bone, and wood to create canoes, pendants, ceremonial objects, sculptures, and wooden meetinghouses. Later, they carved tools from stone and used steel tools.

The Maori used the native flax plant to plait and weave cloth, baskets, and other objects. They also integrated the Eastern Polynesian tradition of tattooing into their culture. The process of tattooing was known to the Maori as Tā Moko ("to tap or strike"), and was used a way to signify social status or mark a rite of passage. Artists cut intricate patterns into the skin and then rubbed pigment into the cuts. The tattoos featured traditional designs similar to those used in carvings. Men often had full-face tattoos, or moko. Traditionally, women could only tattoo their chin, nose, and upper lip. Maori art declined during the 19th century, when European missionaries tried to suppress the Maori culture. Maori art experienced a renaissance after the 1960s, with the wider resurgence of Maori culture and identity.

Early painters in New Zealand were largely influenced by European styles and mainly painted landscapes, portraitures, and religious scenes. When modernism was introduced in the 1950s, painting styles such as expressionism, cubism, and abstractionism became popular. However, beginning in the late nineteenth century, many New Zealanders tried to create a distinct style of art that was considered unique to New Zealand. Prominent New Zealand artists during this period include Toss Woollaston (1920–1998), Colin McCahon (1919–1987), William Sutton (1917–2000), and Rita Angus (1908–1970).

Architecture

Prior to European colonization, Maori architecture mainly consisted of "wharenui" or "whare," which were communal meeting houses fashioned from wood. Many European architectural styles found their way to New Zealand over the course of the 19th and 20th centuries. In fact, certain areas clearly exemplify specific architectural movements, such as the town of Napier. After much of the town's buildings were destroyed in an earthquake in 1930, a flurry of construction resulted in a widespread Art Deco and Spanish Mission style. Other prominent architectural styles include Victorian, Baroque, Edwardian, and Gothic. The Auckland Supreme Court, built in the 1860s, as well as Old St. Paul's church in Wellington, reflects a Gothic style. The town of Oamaru, the buildings of which were constructed during the gold rush boom in the 1870s, features a distinct Victorian architectural style.

Music

Songs and musical composition were (and remain) strongly linked to Maori heritage, religion, and social customs. There were many different types of song, with each having its own specific purpose and place in the culture. Karakia were spells, sung rapidly and in monotone, giving the impression of an unbroken flow of sound.

Whakaaraara Paa, or "watch songs," were sung by those guarding the villages to alert the villagers of danger. These watch songs were also sung before an important social event of ritual to capture the attention of a wide audience. Paatere were songs composed by women in response to their being slandered by gossip. A form of retaliation, the songs were written in the form of a dialogue and performed by groups of singers who accompanied the music with gestures and facial expressions. Paatere were very detailed accounts of the wronged woman's lineage; the songs also named those who had been involved in the slandering.

Maori instruments include the porutu, rehu, and kooauau, all of which resembled flutes. Percussion instruments include the tookere, pakuru, and the rooria. The Maori also devised several types of trumpet-like instruments, such as the puutoorino and the teetere (flax trumpet).

Drama

The first motion picture show in New Zealand appeared in 1896, but it was many years before New Zealand developed a thriving film industry. In fact, few films were produced before the 1970s, and most were documentaries about New Zealand or feature films based on Maori stories or culture. In 1978, the government began funding films and established the New Zealand Film Commission. This led to a boom in filmmaking that continues today. Several highly acclaimed films are *The Piano* (1993), *Once Were Warriors* (1994), and *Whale Rider* (2002). In addition, the filming of the *Lord of the Rings* trilogy (2001–2003) in New Zealand placed the country's film industry on the map, as it helped create a skill base in the local film community.

Dance

Dance has long been an important part of Maori culture. Traditionally, songs, chants, and dances told stories, expressed ideas, and passed on beliefs and knowledge. Kapa haka is a Maori performance art form that combines songs, chants, and dance. Dance styles include haka, poi, and waiata ā-ringa. Haka is the Maori word for dance, but today it is primarily used to refer to a Maori challenge or posture dance performed by men. For example, the All Blacks rugby team has been performing the haka before every match since 1888. Poi is usually performed by women, and the dancers tell a story through arm movements and swinging a poi, a ball on a string. In waiata ā-ringa, dancers tell a story through the actions of their hands, feet, and legs. Facial expressions are also an important part of each dance style, and in haka, dancers stick out their tongues in a display of defiance.

New Zealand dance encompasses both European and Maori traditions. During the early 20th century, New Zealanders enjoyed ballet performances by European troupes. In 1953, Poul Rudolph Gnatt (1923–1995) founded New Zealand's first ballet company, the Royal New

Zealand Ballet. It performs both classical and contemporary dances. Contemporary dance companies formed in the following decades: Limbs Dance Company was formed in 1977 and toured the country until 1989; Footnote Dance Company was founded in 1985; Commotion was founded in 1990; and Black Grace Dance Company was established in 1995. Pioneering and contemporary choreographers include Mary Jane O'Reilly, Douglas Wright, and Michael Parmenter.

Literature

The earliest literature to come out of New Zealand was nonfiction. European explorers wrote travel accounts, journals, and descriptions of New Zealand primarily for audiences in Great Britain. New Zealand literature also includes Maori oral traditions and legends, which were written down by early European settlers.

In the early 20th century, New Zealand authors began writing for both New Zealand and British audiences. Since there were no publishing houses in New Zealand, books were published in Great Britain. Nonfiction books at the time focused on New Zealand history, plants and animals, and colonial life. Short stories were also popular, and appeared in New Zealand's many newspapers and magazines. Two popular New Zealand authors of short stories were Katherine Mansfield (1888–1923) and Frank Sargeson (1903–1982), the pen name of Norris Frank Davy.

By the 1930s, a nationalist movement had risen to prominence. New Zealanders had recently gained their independence and were more interested in developing their own culture than in adopting that of the British. It was during this time that New Zealand strengthened its own literary voice and developed a strong literary tradition. Poetry and novels flourished, and addressed themes of cultural identity and postcolonial life. Notable poets include Allen Curnow (1911–2001), Kendrick Smithyman (1922–1995), and James K. Baxter (1926–1972). Novelists include Barry Crump (1935–1996), who wrote semi-autobiographical comic novels; Noel Hilliard (1929–1997), who depicted racial

discrimination in *Maori Girl*; Sylvia Ashton-Warner (1908–1984), who wrote about her experiences teaching Maori children; and Janet Frame (1924–2004), who is renowned for her autobiographies and for developing a unique narrative.

New Zealand writers during the latter half of the 20th century continued to write about life in New Zealand, but increasingly questioned historical accounts, particularly focusing on racial and social issues affecting the Maori. In 1973, Witi Ihimaera wrote *Tangi*, the first novel written by a Maori; it was named the Wattie Book of the Year, New Zealand's highest literary award at the time. In 1985, Keri Hulme wrote *The Bone People*, which won international acclaim and awards. Maori writer Alan Duff's novel *Once Were Warriors* (1990) depicts an urban Maori family.

Other accomplished Kiwi writers include Janet Frame, Margaret Sutherland, Fiona Kidman, Maurice Gee, Witi Ihimaera, Vincent O'Sullivan, and Owen Marshall.

CULTURE

Arts & Entertainment

The New Zealand government is an active supporter of the arts. It has established numerous agencies to promote New Zealand's cultural identity and to make its culture accessible to all citizens. The primary national agency for the arts is Creative New Zealand. It provides support for professional and emerging artists and arts organizations through grants, scholarships, fellowships, residencies and awards. It funds fine arts, visual arts, literature, music, dance, and theater.

Despite its funding, the government takes a hands-off approach to controlling art. It encourages cultural diversity and creative expression. It also seeks to reflect the cultures of its multicultural population. In recent years, there has been a resurgence of Maori and Polynesian pride. Multicultural arts activities and programs are flourishing, and many art organizations, including Creative New Zealand, have Maori arts boards and teams devoted specifically to developing, preserving, and promoting Maori arts.

The Centre for New Zealand Music Trust (SOUNZ) promotes music by New Zealand composers. It sponsors a music information center for both consumers and composers of music. Playmarket is an agency that supports playwrights through advisory services and competitions. In addition, the New Zealand Book Council promotes reading through programs such as Meet the Author, Words on Wheel, and Writers in School that bring writers to diverse and distant locations throughout New Zealand. The primary dance organization in New Zealand is Dance Aotearoa New Zealand (DANZ). It offers educational and recreational programs in a diverse range of dance styles. It also sponsors festivals, such as Polyfest. Like many other groups, one of its primary goals is to strengthen relationships with the Maori to encourage dance development.

A group whose primary purpose is to promote contemporary Maori arts is Maori Arts New Zealand, or Toi Maori Aotearoa. It covers a wide range of arts including music, dance, drama, visual arts, writing, carving, weaving, Tā moko, tikanga and traditional waka. It sponsors Maori artists as well as international exchanges with other indigenous artists. It holds workshops, exhibitions, festivals, and performances. The Tautai Contemporary Pacific Arts Trust provides support to contemporary Pacific artists. Most of these artists are visual artists from diverse backgrounds who share a Pacific heritage. One of the purposes of the group is to provide these artists a means to deal with the transitional issues related to developing a new cultural identity in New Zealand.

In addition, Arts Access Aotearoa provides programs that allow for creative expression by individuals with disabilities, at-risk youths and elders, prisoners and disadvantaged migrants. Its artists are part of the outsider art movement, which is made up of artists who have no formal art training and are outside the mainstream of society. It sponsors exhibitions of their creations in public spaces.

Although it produces relatively few films, the contemporary New Zealand film industry has earned a reputation for high-quality films as well as outstanding directors. Many films have earned international attention and won notable awards, including the Academy Award.

Some of the country's most prominent directors are Roger Donaldson, director of *Sleeping Dogs, Smash Palace,* and *The World's Fastest Indian*; Jane Campion, who directed *The Piano*; and Peter Jackson, who directed *King Kong* and *Heavenly Creatures*, in addition to the *Lord of the Rings* trilogy. Other notable directors are Vincent Ward, director of *Vigil* and *The Navigator*; Lee Tamahori, who directed *Once Were Warriors*; Christine Jeffs, director of *Rain* and *Sylvia*; and Niki Caro, who directed *Whale Rider* and *North Country*. Wellington is the center of the film industry in New Zealand, and is affectionately known as "Wellywood."

The country's many popular festivals focus on food and wine, art, music, sports or music. Some of the more popular events include the Summer City Programme, a collection of festivals held in Wellington; the BMW Wine Marlborough Festival in Blenheim; and the New Zealand Festival, a month-long celebration of New Zealand's culture.

Cultural Sites & Landmarks

New Zealand is a country of stunning natural beauty and diverse landforms, including beaches, lakes, mountains, waterfalls, forests, and volcanoes. It is home to fourteen national parks and more than 1,000 other parks and reserves. It is no surprise, then, that some of New Zealand's most popular cultural attractions are its nature areas, in addition to the many Maori heritage sites.

One of the most popular parks is Tongariro National Park, which sits on a volcanic plateau on the North Island and has three active volcanic mountains. The area was the ancestral home of the Ngati Tuwharetoa tribe, who consider the mountains their ancestors. In the 19th century, other tribes also claimed ownership of the mountains. Fearing the mountains would be sold and divided, the tribal chief gave the land to the New

Zealand government in 1887. It later became New Zealand's first national park. Today, the park features many diverse landscapes that attract hikers, skiers and other recreationalists. A crater lake is at the top of one mountain and a desert sits at the base of another. The park is a United Nations Educational, Scientific and Cultural Organization (UNESCO) World Heritage Site for both its natural and cultural value.

Another popular park is Fiordland National Park on the South Island. A vast wilderness area, the park is noted for its rugged mountains, glacial-carved fiords, lakes, forests, and glaciers. It is part of Te Wahipounama, a huge UNESCO World Heritage Site that encompasses several national parks. Called Te Wai Pounamu ("greenstone waters") by the original Maori inhabitants, Te Wahipounama is largely untouched by human development. The area is of cultural significance to the Maori, who consider the mountains and valleys their ancestors.

Many tourists visit the Rotorua region for its geothermal activity. Volcanic activity in the Whakarewarewa Thermal Valley has resulted in geysers, hot springs, and pools of bubbling mud. According to Maori legend, the goddesses of fire, Te Pupu and Te Hoata, created these thermal features when they first emerged from the earth. The largest geyser, Pohutu (Maori for "splash"), erupts several times a day and spouts up to 30 meters (98 feet). It is always preceded by Prince of Wales Feathers, which spouts up to 12 meters (39 feet). The smaller geyser was originally named Indicator, but it was renamed in 1901 to honor a royal visitor.

The Rotura region is considered the center of Maori culture. Cultural sites and attractions include recreated Maori villages, carved meetinghouses and a buried village. The Te Puia cultural center promotes the Maori culture through cultural tours and performances, arts festivals and educational activities. It includes a visiting center and the New Zealand Maori Arts and Crafts Institute, which teaches traditional carving and weaving.

Wellington was officially declared a city in 1886. It was named in honor of Arthur Wellesley, first duke of Wellington, who had helped colonization efforts. Wellington also became the new capital and governmental seat for the country. Today, a building known as the Beehive, nicknamed for its distinctive shape, is one of two major parliamentary buildings in Wellington. The other, the Parliament House, is less interesting architecturally, but is the actual meeting place of the country's parliament.

The car-free section in the center of the Cuba Street Mall is home to a playground, coffee shops, and bars. One of the most famous landmarks in Wellington is the Bucket Fountain in the Cuba Street Mall. The fountain was refurbished in 2003. Wellington also has a large botanical garden. Since the release of Peter Jackson's *Lord of the Rings* movie trilogy, many locations used for the films have become tourist attractions. Mount Victoria, Seatoun, Hutt Valley, and Dry Creek Quarry were all used for various scenes in the films. The beaches of Gallipoli, and specifically the Ataturk Memorial, are also major tourist attractions and the sites of yearly pilgrimages.

Libraries & Museums

The Museum of Wellington City and Sea, situated in the harbor, contains numerous exhibits about the city's maritime history, including accounts of the Wahine ferry disaster, which killed fifty-one people in 1968. The Museum of New Zealand, called Te Papa, is also located in Wellington, and includes many Maori artifacts. There are also two major art museums, the City Gallery Wellington and the Academy Galleries.

Established in 1965, the National Library of New Zealand serves as the country's legal deposit. It features extensive collections of books, manuscripts, periodicals, ephemera, oral histories, and government publications.

Holidays

Official holidays observed in New Zealand include Waitangi Day (February 6), which commemorates the signing of the Treaty of Waitangi between the Maori and the British in 1840. This holiday is also known as New Zealand Day. ANZAC (Australia and New Zealand Army

Corps) Day, celebrated on April 25, commemorates all Australians and New Zealanders who have died in wars, with special emphasis on those who perished at Gallipoli in World War I.

Youth Culture

Although New Zealand is physically isolated from the rest of the world, New Zealand youth are often exposed to other cultures through their own international travels and through foreign visitors to New Zealand. For example, many young people participate in an Overseas Experience, or OE, in which they travel or work in another country after they have completed school.

The youth culture in New Zealand is heavily influenced by the U.S. and by the Pacific Rim. In urban areas, a Pacific Island culture has developed in recent years. There has also been a resurgence of Maori pride. By blending traditional Polynesian and Maori elements with modern ones, young artists have created a unique look often called urban Pacific chic. This culture has its own fashion, music, and streetwear, and has been adopted by many urban youth. In addition, hip-hop, rap music and traditional Polynesian and Maori chants and sounds have created a new musical style called haka, or haka rap. Popular musicians include singer-songwriters Bic Runga and Anika Moa.

SOCIETY

Transportation

Most New Zealanders own their own vehicle—88 percent of households have at least one car—and generally use their vehicle as their primary mode of transportation. Cars are so popular that as of 2006, over 15 percent of households owned three or more cars. Buses provide local transportation within major cities, though some cities also have trolleys and electric trains. Public transportation is generally not a popular alternative.

For long distances, most people drive or fly. An excellent network of roads and airports exists throughout New Zealand, connecting urban and rural areas. Due to New Zealand's rugged terrain,

flying is a quick and efficient way to travel, and almost every city and large town has an airport with several airlines offering air service. Air travel has largely replaced rail and bus transportation, both of which are relatively slow for long distances. In addition, ferries carry cars and passengers between the North and South islands.

Traffic in New Zealand moves on the left-hand side of the road.

Transportation Infrastructure

The transportation infrastructure of New Zealand is well developed in the early 21st century. There are over 10,000 kilometers of state highways, which carry approximately 35 percent of the country's traffic, as well as 82,000 kilometers of local roads. There are over 100 airports with the largest being Auckland International Airport; Wellington Airport and Christchurch Airport are also significant. Public transportation takes the form of railway, bus, and ferry transport. Some areas have more developed public transportation infrastructure, such as Wellington, Auckland, and Christchurch.

Media & Communications

New Zealand is unique in that it has no national newspaper. Instead, it has a high number of local (and metropolitan) daily newspapers—twenty-eight in 2006. In addition, more than 2,000 magazines are published there. New Zealand also has a high number of radio stations. The state-owned Radio New Zealand broadcasts commercial-free news, music, talk shows, and other programs. There are also over 200 commercial radio stations. Two companies control commercial radio: Radio Network and RadioWorks.

Both the state and private companies control television. The state-owned Television New Zealand (TVNZ) operates four channels, TV One, TV2, and TVNZ 6 and TVNZ 7. TVWorks operates two national channels, TV3 and TV4. Sky Television, a subscription-based television company, provides over thirty channels to subscribers. Maori Television is a government-funded station that promotes Maori culture. In 2007, Freeview was launched. Freeview is a consortium of TVNZ, Maori Television, and private television and radio broadcasters providing free service via satellite and a digital system.

New Zealanders have eagerly embraced other telecommunications. As of 2014, over 1.85 million people have access to a telephone, 5.1 million percent have access to a cell phone, and 91.5 percent have access to the Internet.

SOCIAL DEVELOPMENT

Standard of Living

New Zealand ranked seventh on the 2014 United Nations Human Development Index, which measures quality of life and standard of living indicators. Statistics show that in the capital, Wellington's residents enjoy the twelfth highest quality of living in the world.

Water Consumption

Access to improved drinking water sources and sanitation services is very high in New Zealand, with 100 percent of urban and rural populations having access to improved drinking water and 88 percent of the rural population having access to improved sanitation systems.

Education

It is mandatory for New Zealand children between the ages of five and sixteen to attend school. Public education is free, with relatively few people choosing to attend private schools. Primary school lasts for eight years. Generally, students transfer to specialized school for their last two years. Secondary education is usually a five-year program and is free for students until age twenty.

The University of Auckland is the largest of New Zealand's eight universities. The universities are located in the major cities, as are most of the technical and vocational institutions.

The gender gap in education tends to favor female students. Research has indicated that educational outcomes of male students are generally lower than those of female students. In 2002, 59 percent of undergraduate students were female, while male students accounted for 41 percent of enrollment. In 2004, male students still accounted for only 41 percent of undergraduates. At the university level, however, male students are overrepresented in the study of engineering and architecture, while female students are overrepresented in the study of education and health (2004).

Women's Rights

In New Zealand, many women's rights are protected through legislation that bars discrimination due to gender. New Zealand was the first country in the world to grant women the right to vote (in 1893). It also passed an Equal Pay Act in 1972 to provide equal pay for men and women doing the same job. Women serve in the military and in all branches of the government. They also hold many of the nation's highest political offices, including that of the prime minister.

Almost 60 percent of women in New Zealand who are of working age are in the workforce. Despite the Equal Pay Act 1972, most women's earnings are less than those of male coworkers are. As of 2006, the average hourly wage for women was 85.8 percent of that earned by men. In addition, women have fewer employment opportunities than men do, and they typically work in lower-paying industries, such as hospitality and services, that require little education and experience. These positions pay significantly less than male-dominated professions. Many women also work part-time because of childrearing responsibilities or the inability to find full-time work.

The government has initiated programs to narrow the gender gap in pay, provide more economic opportunities for women, and improve women's well-being and work-life balance. It recently passed legislation providing paid parental leave for women as well as paid leave for pregnant women for medical care and pregnancy-related activities. The government is also expanding early childhood education and childcare options to allow for greater participation in the workforce by women. The government also provides supplemental income to assist low-income families. More women are pursuing higher education, and the government provides financial assistance, including low-interest loans, to enrolled students.

Maori and Pacific women generally earn far less than non-minority women do. Government programs seek to improve employment opportunities for minority women through training programs, apprenticeships, and skills development. They also fund programs for the development of small businesses owned and operated by minority women. They also have instituted programs that provide more access to health care and mental health services for women, particularly minority, elderly and rural women.

Many women in New Zealand have been victims of domestic violence. In 2000, over 50 percent of all homicides were related to domestic violence. Maori women are almost twice as likely as other women to have experienced violence from a partner or spouse. The Domestic Violence Act was passed in 1995 to help protect anyone who is subject to physical, psychological, or sexual abuse by a family member, relative, caretaker, guardian, or partner. The government provides funding for women's shelters, rape crisis centers, counseling, and violence-prevention programs.

Although minority women have significantly less advantages than non-minority women do, overall, women in New Zealand have opportunities similar to those of other developed countries. According to a 2007/2008 UN report, New Zealand ranked nineteenth among 177 countries on the Gender Empowerment Measure. This takes into consideration women's economic power and political participation in a given country. In comparison, Canada ranked fourth and the U.S. ranked twelfth.

Health Care

New Zealand offers a wide variety of health and disability services. Most citizens have access to modern hospitals, pharmacies, and doctors. The country has a liberal social welfare system, offering benefits to the sick, elderly, disabled, unemployed, and single parents.

All New Zealanders receive free medical care at local hospitals, and those with financial need may receive subsidized care from primary health facilities.

Life expectancy at birth is nearly eighty-four years for women and seventy-nine years for men (2014 estimate).

GOVERNMENT

Structure

New Zealand's government functions under a parliamentary democracy with a prime minister as head of government. The Queen of England is the symbolic head of state, and is represented by a governor-general.

After general elections, the leader of the majority party in Parliament is appointed prime minister. The prime minister appoints a cabinet, whose ministers run the daily operations of government and sit on the Executive Council to advise the governor general. The constitution requires the governor general to abide by the recommendations of this council.

Parliament consists of the 120-member House of Representatives entrusted with the power of making laws. Members are elected every three years, and several seats are reserved for Maori candidates.

The governor general is charged with appointing all judges. The hierarchical court system includes a Court of Appeal, High Court, and District Courts. While Court of Appeal decisions are usually final, those decisions can sometimes be appealed to the Privy Council in England.

Political Parties

Political parties in New Zealand include the National Party, which won sixty seats in the 2014 general election; the Labour Party, which won thirty-two seats; the Green Party, which won fourteen seats; the New Zealand First, which won eleven seats; the Maori Party, which won two seats; and several other parties that won one seat each.

Local Government

Local government in New Zealand comes in the form of twelve regional councils and, below them, seventy-three territorial authorities, which include fifty-seven district councils, sixteen city councils, and four unitary authorities (which govern the four regions that do not have regional councils). Regional councils oversee civil defense, regional land transport planning, and resource management, while territorial authorities oversee public health and safety, as well as road and water infrastructure.

Judicial System

The court system of New Zealand comprises a Supreme Court, the Court of Appeal, the High Court, and district courts.

Taxation

The top income tax rate in New Zealand was 38 percent in 2009. The corporate tax rate is 30 percent. A goods and services tax (GST) is also levied.

Armed Forces

The New Zealand Defence Force comprises an army, navy, and air force. There are approximately 9,000 active military personnel in the early 21st century.

Foreign Policy

Historically, New Zealand's closest ties have been to Great Britain. Many of the country's original European settlers were from Great Britain, and New Zealand exported many of its products there. In 1973, Great Britain joined the European Economic Community, allowing for the free flow of goods among member countries. As a result, New Zealand established relationships with countries in Asia and the Pacific Islands. This helped it to become less dependent on Great Britain and to solidify its place as a member of the Pacific community.

A core objective of New Zealand's foreign policy is to promote a prosperous global market. It supports activities that foster strong economic conditions within New Zealand and its neighboring countries. It signed the Closer Economic Relations (CER) free trade agreement with Australia in 1990, which allows for unrestricted trade between both countries. The agreement is also known as the Australia New Zealand Closer Economic Relations Trade Agreement (ANZCERTA). In addition, New Zealand is also a member of many international organizations, including the Asia-Pacific Economic Cooperation (APEC), Asian Development Bank (ADB), the International Bank for Reconstruction and Development (IBRD), and Organization for Economic Co-operation and Development (OECD).

New Zealand is an active participant in organizations that work to promote security and peaceful relations in the Pacific. It is a founding member of the United Nations (UN) and helped establish the Five Power Defence Arrangements (FPDA), a series of relationships that also includes the UK and Australia. As a part of these arrangements, New Zealand, Australia, and the UK are committed to consult one another in the event of an attack or threat on Malaysia or Singapore. In recent years, this group has added humanitarian aid to its security mission, and provided help in disasters such as the 2004 Indian Ocean earthquake that resulted in a deadly tsunami.

New Zealand's opposition to nuclear testing in the South Pacific has often defined its foreign policy and relations. In 1984, it refused to allow nuclear-powered or nuclear-armed ships to enter its waters. Shortly afterward, it declared itself a nuclear-free country. This resulted in its removal from the Australia, New Zealand, United States Security Treaty (ANZUS) by the United States. This defense treaty states that if any of the three countries were attacked in the Pacific, the others would come to its assistance. Australia still honors its pact with New Zealand, but relations between the U.S. and New Zealand are strained.

In 1985, the environmental activist group Greenpeace planned to protest France's testing of nuclear weapons in the Pacific. However, in a controversial act, French operatives bombed and sunk Greenpeace's ship. New Zealand denounced the bombing and attempted to prosecute all involved. These actions helped New Zealand earn a reputation as a pacifist country, and to gain an identity separate from Great Britain.

New Zealand's military consists of its army, navy, and air force. There is no conscription—enlisting in the military is voluntary. New Zealand's military has been involved in many peacekeeping activities, but it has not sent any troops to engage in active warfare since the Falklands War in 1982. Peacekeeping troops have participated in missions in East Timor, Sierra Leone, Mozambique, Papua New Guinea, Afghanistan, and other international "hot spots" in the Pacific, Middle East, Europe, and Asia.

Dependencies

The dependencies of New Zealand include the island of Niue, which has been self-governing in free association with New Zealand since 1974 and the island of Tokelau, a former British protectorate that fell under the administration of New Zealand in 1925. In addition, the Cook Islands, another former British protectorate that fell under the administration of New Zealand in 1900 and in 1965 became a self-governing territory in free association with New Zealand is also a dependency.

Human Rights Profile

International human rights law insists that states respect civil and political rights, and promote an individual's economic, social, and cultural rights. The United Nations Universal Declaration on Human Rights (UDHR) is recognized as the standard for international human rights. Its authors sought the counsel of the world's great thinkers, philosophers, and religious leaders, and were careful to create a document that reflects the core values shared by every world culture. (To read this document or view the articles relating to cultural human rights, visit http://www.udhr.org/UDHR/default.htm.)

New Zealand has a generally positive human rights record. It has formally committed to honoring the rights specified in the UN's Universal Declaration on Human Rights, as well as other treaties established under the UN Charter and the International Labour Organization (ILO). It passed the Human Rights Act 1993 and the Human Rights Amendment Act 2001, both of which protect people from discrimination and other human rights abuses.

The Human Rights Act and the Human Rights Amendment Act are generally in line with all of the articles of the UDHR. They allow free expression of thought and assembly, the right to worship as one chooses, free movement, and freedom from torture or cruel and unusual punishment. They provide for protection under the laws of the country and allow for participation in government through direct participation or through freely chosen representatives.

These acts do allow for some exceptions. For example, they are in agreement with Article 2, which prohibits discrimination based on a personal characteristic, such as sex, race, or religion, unless policies and practices allow for justifiable discrimination. An example of justifiable discrimination includes separate restrooms based on sex. Women are allowed to serve in the armed forces, but they may be given preferential treatment based on their gender and excused from active combat roles.

The acts also allow exceptions to Article 23, which grants people the right to work and to free choice of employment. The acts allow employers for national security work to deny employment to individuals based on national origin, religious or political beliefs, mental health disability, or relationship to a particular person. They also allow members of parliament and other political bodies to hire political advisers based on their political beliefs.

New Zealand strives to ensure that the human rights of all people, especially members of minority groups, are protected. It passed the Maori Language Act of 1987, which established Maori as one of the official languages of New Zealand. This allows for greater participation in cultural affairs by Maori-speaking members of the community and is in line with Article 27, which protects the right for all people to participate in the cultural life of the community.

In 2004, New Zealand issued a formal assessment of human rights in New Zealand in the document "Human Rights in New Zealand Today." Based on its findings, it established the New Zealand Action Plan for Human Rights Priorities for Action 2005–2010 to review areas of concern and make improvements as necessary. Some of the areas it addresses include protecting the rights of transgendered people, teaching sign language to all schoolchildren to ensure greater communication among hearing and hearing-impaired individuals, and prohibiting the inappropriate use of seclusion in mental health services. It also is working to decrease the high rate of violence against women.

ECONOMY

Overview of the Economy

New Zealand's economy depends largely on its modernized agricultural sector. Although it contributes less than 10 percent of the gross domestic product (GDP), it occupies roughly 1 percent of the labor force, making it a highly efficient industry.

Tourism is one of Wellington's major industries, which also fuels growth and employment in related fields such as retail. Other important industries in the Wellington economy include film, fashion, manufacturing, biotechnology, and education. Although much of the farmland in the surrounding area (particularly in the south of the city center) has been developed, the northern end of the Wellington district is still home to several farms which produce fruits and vegetables, dairy, sheep and cattle. The harbor is a major economic hub, where Wellington imports petroleum products, motor vehicles, minerals, and exports meats, in addition to wood products, dairy products, wool, and fruit.

In 2014, New Zealand's GDP was estimated at $198.1 billion (USD), with a per capita GDP of $35,200 (USD).

Industry

New Zealand has made great progress in transforming itself from an agrarian to an industrial economy. Today, the country enjoys a good mix of manufacturing and services combined with a strong agricultural industry.

New Zealand's economy relies a great deal on export earnings. New Zealand's most important industries include food processing, wood and paper products, textiles, banking and insurance, and tourism. The agricultural, horticultural, forestry, mining, energy, and fishing industries account for more than half of New Zealand's total export earnings. Industry contributes 26.6 percent of GDP, and services contribute 69 percent (2014 estimate).

Another major industry, covering approximately 322,000 hectares (796,000 acres) of land, is possum control. Possum are not native to New Zealand, and are considered pests because of their detrimental impact on native wildlife.

Labor

The labor force of New Zealand comprised approximately 2.45 million people in 2014. The unemployment rate that same year was 5.4 percent.

Energy/Power/Natural Resources

New Zealand's most important natural resource is the land itself, followed closely by its water resources. More than half of the land is used for crops or grazing, and 30 percent is forested, while the many rivers and lakes are valuable sources of hydroelectric power. Wellington's high winds spurred an interest in wind energy in the early 1990s, and as a result, a large wind turbine was built in 1993. The turbine has since become a symbol of the city, visible from miles away in most directions. The turbine supplies eighty homes with power.

Fishing

With approximately 15,000 kilometers (9,320 miles) of coastline, New Zealand's fishing industry plays a significant role in the country's economy. In 2008, the total value of seafood exports was nearly $1 billion (USD).

Forestry

Roughly, 24 percent of New Zealand is indigenous forest. Common tree species include kauri, beech, rimu, tawa, and taraire. The forestry industry is growing. In fact, it contributed 2.8 percent of the country's GDP and employs over 17,000 workers (2009). Forestry products are exported to countries such as China, Australia, and Japan.

Mining/Metals

The islands are not rich in minerals, with small deposits of gold, coal, limestone, and iron ore. There are some offshore natural gas deposits, and smaller quantities of oil can be found both on shore and off.

Agriculture

Major crops grown in New Zealand include wheat, barley, potatoes, pulses, and vegetables, accounting for less than 5 percent of the total agricultural output. Fruits from the exotic (kiwifruits and tamarind) to the ordinary (apples and pears) are also important to the agricultural sector.

Animal Husbandry

The climate in New Zealand allows for almost continual grass growth, which is ideal for raising farm animals. Deer (raised for venison) and sheep are the country's most important livestock products. In 2006, there were approximately 1.6 million deer in the country. New Zealand produces more mutton than any other country, and is the world's second-largest wool producing country. In addition, farmers in New Zealand raise large amounts of cattle, goats, and pigs. Dairy products account for nearly one-third of all farm output. There were approximately 5.2 million dairy cattle in 2006.

Tourism

Each year New Zealand attracts nearly 2 million visitors, generating roughly $3.8 billion (USD) in revenue. Approximately 370,000 people were employed in the tourism industry in 2012. Tourism revenue accounted for 14 percent of the GDP between 2008 and 2012.

The country's largest cities of Wellington and Auckland provide cultural attractions as well as natural beauty. The Northland province is the center of Maori and Pakeha culture and history, not to mention some of the most beautiful beaches and best diving spots in the world. Adventurers and ecotourists are drawn to the dramatic landscapes of Otago and Southland, which offer whitewater rafting, parasailing, bungee jumping, and other outdoor activities.

Barb Lightner, Christopher Stetter,
Alex K. Rich

DO YOU KNOW?

- New Zealand declared its independence from Great Britain on September 26, 1907.
- The Maori name for New Zealand is Aotearoa, roughly translated as "land of the long white cloud."
- Wellington is the southernmost capital in the world.

Bibliography

Belich, James. *Making Peoples: A History of the New Zealanders, From Polynesian Settlement to the End of the Nineteenth Century.* Honolulu, HI: University of Hawai'i Press, 2002.

De Roy, Tui, and Mark Jones. *New Zealand: A Natural History.* Buffalo, NY; Richmond Hill, Ont.: Firefly Books, 2006.

Denoon, Donald, Philippa Mein Smith and Marivic Wyndham. *A History of Australia, New Zealand, and the Pacific.* Oxford, UK; Malden, MA: Blackwell Pub., 2000.

Fischer, David Hackett. *Fairness and Freedom: A History of Two Open Societies: New Zealand and the United States.* New York: Oxford University Press, 2012.

Gillespie, Carol Ann. *New Zealand.* Philadelphia, PA: Chelsea House, 2005.

King, Michael. *The Penguin History of New Zealand.* New York: Penguin Books, 2003.

Mason, Jeffrey Moussaieff. *Slipping into Paradise.* New York: Ballantine Books, 2004.

Mein Smith, Philippa. *A Concise History of New Zealand.* Cambridge; New York: Cambridge University Press, 2005.

Nile, Richard, and Christian Clerk. *Cultural Atlas of Australia, New Zealand, and the South Pacific.* New York: Facts on File, 1996.

Sinclair, Keith, ed. *The Oxford Illustrated History of New Zealand.* Auckland; New York: Oxford University Press, 1997.

Te Kanawa, Kiri, and Michael Foreman. *Land of the Long White Cloud: Maori Myths, Tales, and Legends.* New York: Arcade Pub., 1989.

Works Cited

"About Pay and Employment Equity. Pay and Employment Equity." Department of Labour. http://www.dol.govt.nz/services/PayAndEmploymentEquity/pccu/index.asp

"About Radio New Zealand." Radio New Zealand. http://www.radionz.co.nz/about.

"Action on the Transgender Inquiry: Executive Summary." Commission's Work. Human Rights Commission. http://www.hrc.co.nz/home/hrc/introduction/actiononthetransgenderinquiry/resources/executivesummary.php.

Arts Access Aotearoa. http://www.artsaccess.org.nz/.

"The Australia, New Zealand and United States Security Treaty (ANZUS Treaty), 1951." U.S. Department of State. http://www.state.gov/r/pa/ho/time/cwr/102768.htm.

"Background Note: New Zealand." U.S. Department of State. http://www.state.gov/r/pa/ei/bgn/35852.htm

Boddington, Bill, and Didham, Robert. "Busy making other plans: increases in childlessness in New Zealand. http://www.stats.govt.nz/NR/rdonlyres/DE8BA7D2-E8CC-44C4-88FD-40DF08195A4B/0/Article.pdf

Butler, Susan. *New Zealand—Culture Smart!: A Quick Guide to Customs and Etiquette."* London: Kuperard; New York: Distributed by Random House, 2006.

Byrnes, Giselle M. "ANZUS." World Book Online Reference Center. http://www.worldbookonline.com/wb/Article?id=ar724180.

Byrnes, Giselle M. "New Zealand, History of." World Book Online Reference Center. 2008. http://www.worldbookonline.com/wb/Article?id=ar389523.

Byrnes, Giselle M. "New Zealand." World Book Online Reference Center. http://www.worldbookonline.com/wb/Article?id=ar389520.

Central Intelligence Agency. *The World Factbook.* New Zealand. https://www.cia.gov/library/publications/the-world-factbook/geos/nz.html.

Centre for New Zealand Music Trust (SOUNZ). http://sounz.org.nz/.

"Cheese takes the cake at weddings." The Dominion Post. July 10, 2008. http://www.stuff.co.nz/4613461a19716.html

Chesters, Graeme. *Culture Wise New Zealand: The Essential Guide to Culture, Customs & Business Etiquette.* London: Survival, 2007.

"Communications." New Zealand High Commission. http://www.nzembassy.com/aboutmore.cfm?CFID=4603240&CFTOKEN=99686852&c=14&l=56&i=5498&p=477.

"Company Profile." Sky. http://www.skytv.co.nz/company-profile.aspx.

"The Competition Arrives." Inside TVNZ. Television New Zealand. http://tvnz.co.nz/view/page/826505/823807.

Cultural Policy in New Zealand. http://www.mch.govt.nz/publications/cultural-policies/index.html#_Toc71523742.

"Dance Styles and Props." http://www.tki.org.nz/r/arts/dance/discover_dance/maori-genres_e.php.

DANZ (Dance Aotearoa New Zealand). http://www.danz.org.nz/about_danz.php.

"Defence." New Zealand High Commissioner. http://www.nzembassy.com/aboutmore.cfm?CFID=4603240&CFTOKEN=99686852&c=14&l=56&i=5504&p=478.

"Defence Portfolio Briefing to the Incoming Government 2005." The New Zealand Ministry of Defence. http://www.defence.govt.nz/reports-publications/election-brief-2005/introduction.html.

Demographic Trends: 2007 Reference Report. http://www.stats.govt.nz/analytical-reports/dem-trends-07/default.htm.

"Dining Out – Food in New Zealand." New Zealand History Online. http://www.nzhistory.net.nz/culture/no-pavlova-please/dining-out.

"Discovering Dance: Maori dance." Te Kete Ipurangi (TKI) – The Online Learning Centre. http://www.tki.org.nz/r/arts/dance/discover_dance/maori_e.php.

Domestic Violence. Family Court of New Zealand. http://www.courts.govt.nz/family/what-familycourt-does/relationships/domestic-violence.asp.

Dyson, Ruth. Action Plan for New Zealand Women. Ministry of Women's Affairs. 2004. http://www.mwa.govt.nz/news-and-pubs/publications/actionplanReportFinal.pdf.

"Economic Rationales for Narrowing the Gender Pay Gap, The." National Advisory Council on the Employment of Women. http://www.nacew.govt.nz/publications/quality/women/index.html.

"Five Power Defence Arrangements (FPDA)" British High Commission Kuala Lumpar. http://www.britishhighcommission.gov.uk/servlet/Front?pagename=OpenMarket/Xcelerate/ShowPage&c=Page&cid=1058537122554.

Fodor's Exploring New Zealand, 4th ed. New York: Fodor's Travel Publications Inc., 2008.

Fodor's New Zealand, 2007 ed. New York: Fodor's Travel Guides, 2007.

"Foreign Policy and Overseas Aid." New Zealand High Commissioner. http://www.nzembassy.com/aboutmore.cfm?c=14&l=56&CFID=4603240&CFTOKEN=99686852&i=5503&p=478.

Freeview Channels. http://www.freetv.co.nz/freeview.html.

"Gnatt, Poul Rudolph." Dictionary of New Zealand Biography. http://www.dnzb.govt.nz/dnzb/default.asp?Find_Quick.asp?PersonEssay=5G11.

Gordon, Fenn. *The Touring Manual: a guide to touring the performing arts in New Zealand.* Creative New Zealand. 2003. http://www.creativenz.govt.nz/files/touring.pdf.

"HAKA," from *An Encyclopedia of New Zealand,* edited by A. H. McLintock, originally published in 1966. *Te Ara—The Encyclopedia of New Zealand.* http://www.teara.govt.nz/1966/H/Haka/AllBlackshaka/en.

Harper, Laura, et al. *The Rough Guide to New Zealand.* 5th ed. London, 2006.

"History." Wellington City Council. http://www.wellington.govt.nz/move/innovative/history.html

"The History of Mediaworks NZ." http://www.mediaworks.co.nz/Default.aspx?tabid=38.

"The History of Television Broadcasting." New Zealand Television Broadcasters' Council. http://www.nztbc.co.nz/story.html?story_history.inc.

"Hongi ~ Embrace." Tourism New Zealand. http://www.newzealand.com/travel/about-nz/culture/powhiri/the-ceremony/hongi-embrace.cfm.

"Households." Statistics New Zealand. http://www.stats.govt.nz/products-and-services/new-zealand-in-profile-2007/households.htm.

"Housing." New Zealand High Commission. http://www.nzembassy.com/aboutmore.cfm?CFID=4603240&CFTOKEN=99686852&c=14&l=56&i=5495&p=477.

"Housing and Property in New Zealand." New Zealand High Commission. http://www.nzembassy.com/info.cfm?CFID=6016642&CFTOKEN=24662889&c=14&l=56&s=go&p=61686.

"Hulme, Keri." World Book Online Reference Center. 2008. http://www.worldbookonline.com/wb/Article?id=ar749817.

Human Development Report. 2007/2008 Report. Gender empowerment measure. United Nations. http://hdrstats.undp.org/indicators/279.html

"Human Rights Act." Human Rights Commission. http://www.hrc.co.nz/home/hrc/abouthumanrights/humanrightsinnewzealand/humanrightsact.php

"The Human Rights Act 1993: Guidelines for Government Policy Advisers." http://www.justice.govt.nz/pubs/reports/2000/hr_act/index.html.

"Human Rights Action Plan: New Zealand could be world leader in human rights." Human Rights Commission. http://www.hrc.co.nz/home/hrc/newsandissues/actionplannzcouldbeworldleader.php.

"Human Rights and Seclusion in Mental Health Services." Human Rights Commission. http://www.hrc.co.nz/home/hrc/newsandissues/seclusioninmentalhealthservices.php.

Internet Movie Database. http://www.imdb.com/.

"Introducing New Zealand: Film Industry History." Film New Zealand. http://www.filmnz.com/introducing-nz/film-industry-history.html.

Janaki, Kremmer. "Pacifist, Anti-Nuclear New Zealand Marches to Its Own Drummer." *World and I.* Dec. 1, 2005. p 32.

"Kapa Haka." http://www.maori.org.nz/waiata/.

Maori Arts New Zealand. http://www.maoriart.org.nz/.

New Zealand Book Council. http://www.bookcouncil.org.nz/index.html.

"Maori Culture." Tourism New Zealand. http://www.newzealand.com/travel/about-nz/culture/culture-maori-culture.cfm.

Maori Language Commission. http://www.tetaurawhiri.govt.nz/english/about_e/.

"Maori Society and Culture." New Zealand Embassy. http://www.nzembassy.com/aboutmore.cfm?CFID=4603240&CFTOKEN=99686852&c=14&l=56&i=5482&p=477.

"Maori Television." New Zealand On Air. http://www.nzonair.govt.nz/maori_television.php.

McClure, Margaret. "Auckland." *Te Ara—The Encyclopedia of New Zealand.* http://www.TeAra.govt.nz/Places/Auckland/Auckland/en.

McKinnon, Malcolm. "Bay of Plenty places." *Te Ara—The Encyclopedia of New Zealand.* http://www.TeAra.govt.nz/Places/BayOfPlenty/BayOfPlentyPlaces/en.

McKinnon, Malcolm. "Volcanic Plateau." *Te Ara—The Encyclopedia of New Zealand.* http://www.TeAra.govt.nz/Places/VolcanicPlateau/VolcanicPlateau/en.

MediaWorks. http://www.mediaworks.co.nz/.

"Michael Parmenter Awarded Creative New Zealand Choreographic Fellowship." *Art News* Oct 26, 2005.

Creative New Zealand. http://www.creativenz.govt.nz/node/3878

Mitchell, Adrian. "New Zealand Literature." World Book Online Reference Center. 2008. http://www.worldbookonline.com/wb/Article?id=ar389540.

"Modern Radio." Mediascape. http://www.mediascape.ac.nz/cms/index.php?page=history-3.

Molloy, Les, in collaboration with the New Zealand Department of Conservation. *Wild New Zealand*. Cambridge, MA: MIT Press, 1994.

Molloy, Les. "Protected areas." *Te Ara—The Encyclopedia of New Zealand,* updated Sept. 20, 2007. http://www.TeAra.govt.nz/TheBush/Conservation/Protected Areas/en.

New Zealand, 6th ed. New York: DK Pub., 2006.

New Zealand, 13 ed. South Yarra, Vic., Australia; Berkeley, CA: Lonely Planet, 2006.

"New Zealand." CIA Factbook. https://www.cia.gov/library/publications/the-world-factbook/geos/nz.html#Econ.

"New Zealand." *Encyclopædia Britannica*. 2008. Encyclopædia Britannica Online. http://www.britannica.com/EBchecked/topic/412636/New-Zealand.

"New Zealand—Culture, Etiquette, and Customs." Kwintessential Cross Cultural Solutions. http://www.kwintessential.co.uk/resources/global-etiquette/new-zealand.html.

"New Zealand: Housing." CultureGrams World Edition. 2008. ProQuest. http://ezproxy.ahml.info:2763/world/world_country_sections.php?contid=8&wmn=Oceania&cid=112&cn=New_Zealand&sname=Housing&snid=27

"New Zealand: Transportation and Communications." CultureGrams World Edition. 2008. ProQuest. http://online.culturegrams.com/world/world_country_sections.php?contid=8&wmn=Oceania&cid=112&cn=New_Zealand&sname=Transportation_and_Communications&snid=20.

New Zealand Action Plan for Human Rights Priorities for Action 2005–2010. http://www.hrc.co.nz/report/actionplan/0foreword.html.

"New Zealand Airports." http://www.newzealand.com/travel/getting-to-around-nz/getting-to-nz/airports/airports_home.cfm.

"New Zealand Culture: Maori Culture." The University of Waikato. http://www.waikato.ac.nz/international/students/general/culture.shtml.

New Zealand Department of Conservation, "Fiordland National Park." http://www.doc.govt.nz/templates/PlaceProfile.aspx?id=38468.

New Zealand Department of Conservation, "International visitor numbers to selected National Parks." http://www.doc.govt.nz/templates/openpage.aspx?id=44861.

New Zealand Department of Conservation, "Rotorua's geothermal treasures." http://www.doc.govt.nz/templates/page.aspx?id=33673.

New Zealand Department of Conservation, "Tongariro National Park." http://www.doc.govt.nz/templates/PlaceProfile.aspx?id=38487.

New Zealand, Ministry of Tourism, "Tourist Activity: Maori Cultural Tourism," Updated March 2008. http://www.tourismresearch.govt.nz/Documents/Tourism%20Sector%20Profiles/Maori%20Culture%2003-2008.pdf.

New Zealand, Ministry of Tourism, "Tourist Activity: Nature-Based Tourism," Updated April 2008. http://www.tourismresearch.govt.nz/Documents/Tourism%20Sector%20Profiles/NatureBasedTourismApril2008.pdf.

"Newspapers and Magazines." New Zealand High Commission. http://www.nzembassy.com/aboutmore.cfm?CFID=4603240&CFTOKEN=99686852&c=14&l=56&i=5492&p=477.

"NZ Defense Policy: Major Projects." The New Zealand Ministry of Defence. http://www.defence.govt.nz/defence-policy/major-projects.html.

O'Connor, Damien. "The future is bright for Te Puia, a Rotorua Maori tourism icon," April 28, 2006. http://www.beehive.govt.nz/release/future+bright+te+puia+rotorua+maori+tourism+icon.

Oettli, Peter H. *CultureShock! New Zealand: A Survival Guide to Customs and Etiquette.* Tarrytown, NY: Marshall Cavendish, 2006.

"Our Work: Arts Organisations." Creative New Zealand. http://www.creativenz.govt.nz/our-work/organisations/national.html.

Penrith, Deborah, and Kelly, Susan. *Live & Work in Australia and New Zealand.* 4th ed. Oxford. Vacation Work, 2005.

Phillips, Jock. "Beach culture." *Te Ara—The Encyclopedia of New Zealand.* http://www.teara.govt.nz/EarthSeaAndSky/RecreationSeaAndSky/BeachCulture/5/en

Phillips, Jock. "Ordinary Blokes and Extraordinary Sheilas." *Te Ara—The Encyclopedia of New Zealand,* updated 1-Oct-2007. http://www.TeAra.govt.nz/NewZealanders/NewZealandPeoples/TheNewZealanders/en.

Playmarket. http://www.playmarket.org.nz/home.

"Population." Official website for Auckland, New Zealand. http://www.aucklandnz.com/VisitorInformation/StoryofAuckland/ArticleDisplay.aspx?ID=11166&SubGroup=Key_Facts&Island

"Population." Official website for Wellington, New Zealand. http://www.wellingtonnz.com/about_wellington/wellington_facts/population.

Principal Dailies (New Zealand), in Europa World online. London, Routledge. Arlington Heights Memorial Library. http://www.europaworld.com/entry/nz.dir.155.

"Public Transport." http://www.energywise.govt.nz/yourtravel/a-to-b/public-transport.html.

"Quick Stats About New Zealand: Households." Statistics New Zealand. http://www.stats.govt.nz/census/census-outputs/quickstats/snapshotplace2.htm?type=region&id=9999999&tab=Households?p=y&js=y.

QuickStats National Highlights. Transport. Statistics New Zealand. http://www.stats.govt.nz/census/census-outputs/quickstats/snapshotplace2.htm?type=region&id=9999999&tab=Transport?p=y&js=y.

Resources. Human Rights Commission. http://www.hrc.co.nz/home/hrc/resources/resources.php.

Rotorua's Official Website. http://www.rotoruanz.com/.

Rough Guide to New Zealand, The, 5th ed. London: Rough Guides: Distributed by the Penguin Group, 2006.

Sinclair, Keith, editor. *The Oxford Illustrated History of New Zealand.* Auckland; New York: Oxford University Press, 1997.

Stewart, Carol, "Hot springs, mud pools and geysers." *Te Ara—The Encyclopedia of New Zealand.* http://www.TeAra.govt.nz/EarthSeaAndSky/HotSpringsAndGeothermalEnergy/HotSpringsMudPoolsAndGeysers/en.

"Sustainable and safe land transport: Trends and Indicators." Land Transport NZ. http://www.landtransport.govt.nz/performance/2007/docs/trend-1.pdf http://www.landtransport.govt.nz/performance/2007/docs/trend-2.pdf http://www.landtransport.govt.nz/performance/2007/docs/trend-6.pdf http://www.landtransport.govt.nz/performance/2007/docs/trend-8.pdf.

Swarbrick, Nancy . "Creative life." *Te Ara—The Encyclopedia of New Zealand* http://www.teara.govt.nz/NewZealandInBrief/CreativeLife/1/en.

Swarbrick, Nancy, "National Parks." *Te Ara—The Encyclopedia of New Zealand.* http://www.TeAra.govt.nz/TheBush/Conservation/NationalParks/en.

"Table 6.03: Area, Estimated Resident Population and Population Change." Demographic Trends 2007. http://www.stats.govt.nz/NR/rdonlyres/B26C4F7D-B32C-4412–8B61-C1778DCBCED5/0/Chapter6_Subnationalpopulationestimates.pdf

"Tangihanga." Kōrero Maori. http://www.koreromaori.govt.nz/forlearners/protocols/tangi.html

Tautai Contemporary Pacific Arts Trust. http://www.tautai.org/home.php.

Te Ahukaramū Charles Royal. "Whenua—How the Land Was Ahaped." *Te Ara—The Encyclopedia of New Zealand.* http://www.TeAra.govt.nz/EarthSeaAndSky/Geology/WhenuaHowTheLandWasShaped/en.

"Television Broadcasting in New Zealand." Discussion Document. Digital Television. Minister of Broadcasting, Hon Marian Hobbs. http://www.executive.govt.nz/minister/hobbs/digital/background.htm.

"Tikanga: Tangihanga Procedures." Maori.org.nz. http://www.maori.org.nz/Tikanga/default.asp?pid=sp45&parent=42.

"Transport." New Zealand High Commission. http://www.nzembassy.com/aboutmore.cfm?CFID=4603240&CFTOKEN=99686852&c=14&l=56&i=5490&p=477.

"Transport." QuickStats National Highlights (Aug 9, 2007). Statistics New Zealand. http://www.stats.govt.nz/census/2006-census-data/national-highlights/2006-census-quickstats-national-highlights-revised.htm?page=para012Master.

Tunku Abdullah, Tunku Ya'acob. "FPDA Remains Relevant with Broadened Role to Reflect New Security Threats." ADJ July & August 2006. pp 4–7. http://www.shpmedia.com/images/ADJ%20July%20&%20August%202006%20FPDA%20article.pdf.

UNEP, World Conservation Monitoring Centre, Te Wahipounamu—South West New Zealand data sheet. http://www.unep-wcmc.org/sites/wh/swnz.html.

UNEP, World Conservation Monitoring Centre, Tongariro National Park data sheet. http://www.unep-wcmc.org/sites/wh/tongarir.html.

UNESCO, "World Heritage List." http://whc.unesco.org/en/list.

UNESCO, World Heritage, "Te Wahipounamu—South West New Zealand." http://whc.unesco.org/en/list/551.

UNESCO, World Heritage, "Tongariro National Park." http://whc.unesco.org/en/list/421.

Universal Declaration of Human Rights. http://www.udhr.org/UDHR/default.htm.

U.S. Department of State. New Zealand. Country Reports on Human Rights Practices – 2006. http://www.state.gov/g/drl/rls/hrrpt/2006/78785.htm.

"Wedding Cakes Today." http://www.weddings.co.nz/features/cakes-today.php.

"Wellington." World Book Online Reference Center. http://www.worldbookonline.com/wb/Article?id=ar597760.

"What paid and unpaid leave is available and when does it start?" Employment Relations. Department of Labour. http://www.ers.dol.govt.nz/parentalleave/employees/what-is-available.html.

Wilson, John. "Families and Households." *Te Ara—The Encyclopedia of New Zealand,* updated 23-Sep-2007. http://www.teara.govt.nz/NewZealandInBrief/Society/3/en.

Wilson, John. "Government and Nation." *Te Ara—The Encyclopedia of New Zealand,* updated Sept. 23, 2007. http://www.TeAra.govt.nz/NewZealandInBrief/GovernmentAndNation/en.

PALAU

Introduction

The island Republic of Palau is one of the world's smallest and youngest sovereign states. It became a fully independent state on October 1, 1994.

Palau consists of more than 300 islands in six groups, making up the western archipelago of the Caroline Islands in Micronesia. Situated in the North Pacific Ocean, Palau lies 500 miles (800 kilometers) east of the Philippines, 4,450 miles (7,150 kilometers) southwest of Hawaii, and 720 miles (1,160 kilometers) south of Guam. Palau is probably the first chain of Micronesian islands to be settled, and was a major battleground during World War II, when the United States seized the islands from the Japanese.

The republic boasts the greatest biodiversity in Micronesia. Sea life flourishes in the waters around the islands—2,000 species of fish, 300 species of coral, sea grass, and a stingless jellyfish that is believed to exist only in Palau all flourish. Palau is also home to more than 140 species of birds.

Palau is a matrilineal society organized around a clan structure, meaning that obligations, inheritance and descent are traced through the mother. Although modern patriarchy has affected Palauan society, women are still strong and active in economic, social and political affairs.

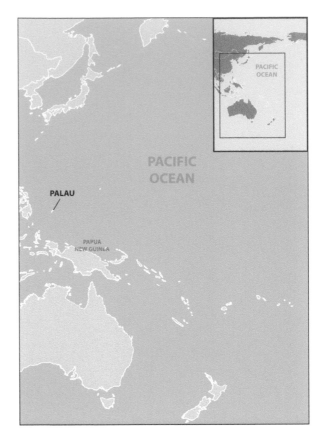

GENERAL INFORMATION

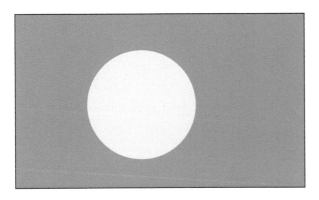

Official Language: Palauan, Sonsoralese, Tobi, Angaur, Japanese, English (varies by island)
Population: 21,265 (2015 estimate)

Currency: U.S. Dollar
Coins: Coins are issued in denominations of 1, 5, 10, 25 and 50 cents. There is also a 1 dollar coin.
Land Area: 459 square kilometers (177 square miles)
National Anthem: "Belau Rekid" ("Our Palau")
Capital: Melekeok
Time Zone: GMT +9
Flag Description: The flag of Palau consists of a sky blue field, representing independence, with a yellow disc placed slightly off-center (towards the hoist side) representing the moon (symbolizing national unity and destiny). (The moon itself symbolizes love and tranquility, among other concepts.)

Population

Of the nation's more than 300 islands, only nine are populated. Most Palauans live on the island of Koror (Oreor), which served as the interim capital while a new capital, Ngerulmud, was being built in the state of Melekeok, on the island of

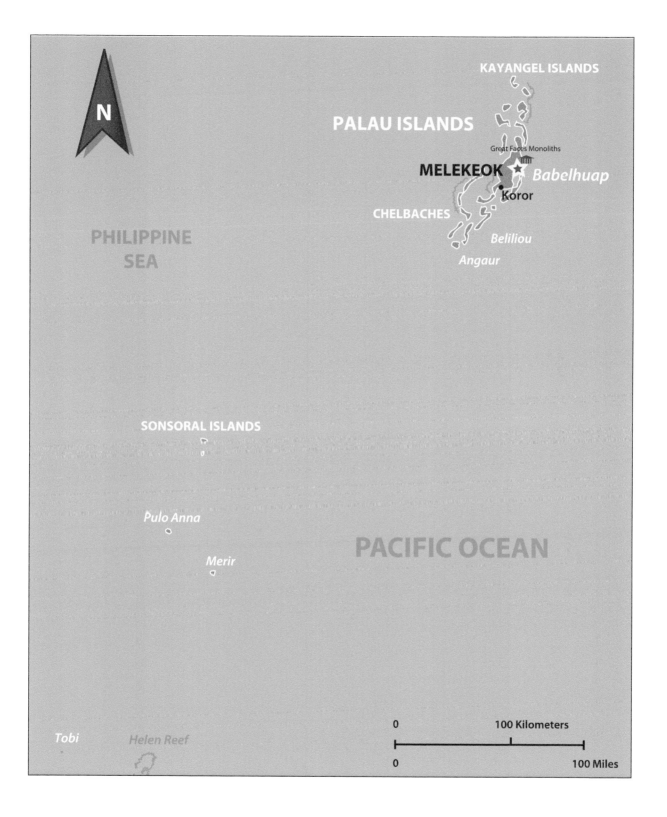

N

KAYANGEL ISLANDS

PALAU ISLANDS

Great Faces Monoliths

MELEKEOK Babelhuap

Koror

CHELBACHES

PHILIPPINE
SEA

Beliliou

Angaur

SONSORAL ISLANDS

Pulo Anna

PACIFIC OCEAN

Merir

Tobi Helen Reef

0   100 Kilometers

0   100 Miles

Principal States by Population (2012):
- Koror (11,665)
- Airai (2,537)
- Pelelieu (489)
- Ngaraard (453)

Babelthuap (Babeldaob). In 2012, a national census measured the population of Koror at 11,665. The main airport is in Airai, on Koror. Population density is forty-four persons per square kilometer (115 persons per square mile). Most of the inhabitants who do not live on Koror live in villages scattered across the habitable islands, where they primarily pursue subsistence farming or fishing.

Nearly 75 percent of Palauans are Micronesian, with mixtures of Malayan and Melanesian. Filipinos are the largest minority group, at 16.3 percent of the population. Other ethnic groups include Chinese, Japanese, and Carolinian (from the Caroline Islands).

Laws and custom have equal importance in Palauan life. In most of Palau, an unmarried person is considered a child and unable to accept responsibility. However, because of laws and constitutional provisions, an eighteen-year-old "child" can vote, a twenty-one year-old "child" can purchase alcohol, and a thirty-five year-old "child" may be elected to public office.

Clans are still the basic organization of society. Palau is matrilineal, meaning that obligations, inheritance and descent are traced through the mother. Although modern patriarchy has affected Palauan society, women are still strong and active in economic, social and political affairs.

Languages

Numerous languages are spoken in Palau, and official languages vary from island to island. English is the official language everywhere, and Palauan is official on most islands. The exceptions are Sonsoral, where Sonsoralese is the official language; Tobi, where Tobi is official; and Angaur, where Angaur and Japanese are official.

Native People & Ethnic Groups

Palau is believed to be the earliest-settled island group in Micronesia. According to archaeological evidence, humans may have arrived in Palau thousands of years ago from Southeast Asia. The exact origins of the early Palauans is unknown, but cultural anthropologists suggest that they might have come from any of a variety of locations around the South Pacific, including Melanesia, Micronesia, Polynesia, Australia, or Asia. Most Palauans today are descendants of these original settlers.

Today, ethnic tensions are growing as immigrants flock to Palau. The number of immigrants and tourists has mushroomed from since the 1970's. Almost all tourism and fisheries are operated by non-Palauans. The resentment of native Palauans has sometimes led to unequal treatment of foreigners, in spite of legal guarantees of equality.

Religions

Palau has no official religion, but many Palauans are Christians. An estimated 49.4 percent of the people are Catholic, and 30.9 percent are Protestant. Nearly 9 percent of the people are adherents of Modekngei, an indigenous, marginally Christian religion that emphasizes Palauan traditional culture and values. Jehovah's Witnesses comprise just over 1 percent of the population.

Climate

Palau's tropical climate is hot and humid. The average annual temperature is 27° Celsius (82° Fahrenheit), with little seasonal variation. Average relative humidity is 82 percent.

As is the case with the temperature, there is little variation in rainfall, although the months between May and November are considered the "wet" season. On average, the islands receive 373 centimeters (146 inches) or rainfall each year. Although Palau lies outside the main typhoon path, it is sometimes hit by damaging storms.

ENVIRONMENT & GEOGRAPHY

Topography

Palau consists of more than 300 islands in six groups, making up the western archipelago of the Caroline Islands in Micronesia. Situated in the North Pacific Ocean, Palau lies 500 miles (800 kilometers) east of the Philippines, 4,450 miles (7,150 kilometers) southwest of Hawaii, and 720 miles (1,160 kilometers) south of Guam.

Palau's chain of islands stretches for 400 miles (650 kilometers), with a total coastline of 944 miles (1,519 kilometers). There are eight main islands, the largest of which is Babelthuap (Babeldaob). Other large islands include Koror (the capital), Arakabesan, and Malakal. A highway connects Koror and Malakal.

The islands are surrounded by a coral reef. The fertile, volcanic northern islands are covered with trees. The southern islands are coral, and most are too rugged to be inhabited. Babelthuap has mountains, including the country's highest point, Mount Ngerchelchuus, at 794 feet (242 meters) above sea level.

Babeldaob is the largest of the 343 islands which form the archipelago of Palau. The village of Melekeok, the interim capital, covers 7 square kilometers (2.7 square miles) directly along the coastline of the island. The new national capital, Ngerulmud, and the former capital, Koror, are also located in the state of Melekeok.

Plants & Animals

Palau boasts the greatest biodiversity in Micronesia. In the waters around the islands, 2,000 species of fish, 300 species of coral and several species of sea grass flourish. Palau is also home to more than 140 species of birds, including 16 endemic species. Of the 1,260 plant species in Palau, 109 are endemic. Endangered or threatened animal species in Palau include the Micronesian megapode, the Micronesian scrubfowl and the Japanese night heron.

Land mammals include two endemic bat species, the Palau Fruit Bat and the rare sheath-tailed bat, an insect-eater. The saltwater crocodile is threatened by hunting and loss of habitat. The ocean is alive with sharks, turtles, dolphins, anemones, corals, sponges, octopus, sea urchins, clownfish, lionfish, eels, goatfish, idol fish, jellyfish, manta rays, snails, clams, sea cucumbers, starfish, squid and many other forms of marine life.

Some of the many bird species found in Palau include frigate birds, egrets, petrels, flycatchers, parrots, rails, fantails, shearwaters, herons, bitterns, boobies, plovers, crakes, cranes, gulls, cormorants, the Pacific black duck, lorikeets, eagles, falcons and mynas.

It is believed that Palau was once almost entirely covered by forest. Today it is an estimated 87.6 percent forested. Six species of palm trees are native to Palau, including the ancient cicada palm. Other trees include coconut and other palms, betel, ironwood, breadfruit, the Brazilian rubber tree, the Siamese cassia, hibiscus, pandanus, and various broadleaf hardwoods. Introduced species include kapok, species of orchid trees, India rubber trees, Panama cherry trees and pink trumpet trees. Mangrove swamps flourish, though some have been damaged by clearing for taro-growing.

Common plants include the rare wild orchid, pink lady, white ginger, devil's fig, Bengal trumpet, water hyacinth, mint weed, molasses grass, Java plum, wild basil, several species of violets including the Philippine violet, Madras thorn, and love-in-a-mist.

CUSTOMS & COURTESIES

Greetings

A handshake is the common gesture of greeting in Palau, and may extend to the gentle grasping of the forearm. Greetings and conversations are typically carried out within an arm's length, and personal contact such as holding hands and touching another's arm while conversing may be common. However, Palauans generally remain reserved when meeting or interacting with someone whom they do not know well. A simple nod or bow shows respect for elders, who are customarily greeted first.

The two official languages of Palau are Palauan (also called Belauan) and English. Common greetings include "Alii" ("Hello"), "Ungil tutau" ("Good morning"), "Ungil cho-dechosong" ("Good afternoon"), and "Ngera chised" ("What's the latest?").

Gestures & Etiquette

Like many cultures, Palauans frequently use demonstrative gestures to communicate. For example, they point using their mouths or with their finger, and to beckon someone, they might sweep the hand in a downward motion. In addition, the signaling of "yes" or a similar affirmation may be done by raising one's eyebrows.

Palau is a matrilineal society, meaning that descent traditionally follows the female lineage of a family. As such, women have maintained considerable power in the community at large. To that end, it is not uncommon for women to initiate dating (though a man usually asks the woman). Social etiquette also includes respect and deference for elders and conservative attire within villages and urban areas. Palauans generally do not also appreciate declined invitations to a gathering; it is considered better to accept an invitation and not attend to decline outright.

Other important aspect of social etiquette in Palau involves the tradition of chewing the betel nut, which is a green palm nut. The nut is customarily sprinkled with powdered lime and wrapped in a leaf from a pepper tree. (More experienced chewers tend to heavily coat their nuts with lime, which can cause a burning sensation in the mouth of a novice chewer.) Chewing the betel nut eventually causes one's teeth to turn red. However, it is considered rude or inappropriate to comment on this habit. Palauans enjoy sharing chew with others, and it is considered a valuable social activity to sit and chew while talking.

Eating/Meals

In Palauan culture, sharing food is a regulatory and celebratory event that occurs within clans and villages. Gathering over food is generally how Palauans maintain close kinship ties and cultural obligations, such as the celebrations of birth. During Palau's period as a protectorate of the United States, which lasted from the conclusion of World War II in 1945 until 1994, restaurants became increasingly common in urban areas. In rural areas, traditional cuisine is still common. Much of the food was traditionally grown and harvested by women. In the early 21st century, individuals or families continue to farm most of the food in rural Palau, while a great deal of the food in the larger cities is imported.

When possible, Palauans might generally eat three meals per day, though mealtimes are generally informal. Utensils may be used, though traditional foods are customarily eaten with the hands. For breakfast, light fare is typical and may consist of un-yeasted breads along with coffee. For lunch, often the heaviest meal, and dinner, taro in soup or on a plate with fish is common, while meals such as roasted pork are eaten occasionally. Sandwiches, influenced by European and American colonial history, are also commonly eaten. Because it is easily grown on the islands, taro root is one of the most common foods and also serves a historically nutritional need. Staple foods and diets also vary somewhat among the many Palauan islands. For example, a pumpkin and coconut soup called subliwal is a tradition in Ngiwal, a small village in Babeldaob. Sea cucumber, called cheremrum, is a specialty in Ngeremlengui, one of the island nation's sixteen states.

Visiting

The atmosphere for social visits in Palau is generally casual, with guest typically arriving and staying late. (Punctuality, however, may be expected in formal and business situations,) The focal point of a visit is often the sharing of a meal, a social tradition among clans that dates back centuries. Socializing might also take place in an open-air structure reserved for visits. Weekends are a particularly popular time for visiting and sharing food, and Palauans generally welcome the chance to introduce outside visitors to their traditions. Reciprocity and the ceremonial exchanging of gifts also remains a traditional part of Palauan culture. It is also customary for visitors to remove their shoes when entering another's living space.

LIFESTYLE

Family

The traditional Palauan family is matrilineal, meaning the family and larger clans extend from the mother's lineage, called telugnalek. Ten clans constitute an entire village, a tradition which is still practiced. The village is then governed by a council of chiefs chosen among the ranking clans, with a parallel female council also formed to act in an advisory role. Women have traditionally held a substantial amount of power within Palauan culture, and continue to be largely responsible for a clan or village's finances, as well as the division of land. Nuclear families, however, are now more common among younger generations.

Before the introduction of modern conveniences and the importing of food, families spent substantial time fishing and farming. Men learned how to read the tides and currents for the best fishing, while men remained on land to attend to agrarian duties and child rearing. Marriage, along with the adoption of children into a family, was traditionally undertaken for the sake of land and wealth (a practice which continues in the early 21st century). The mother's brother has also had a traditionally powerful role, as he maintained power similar to that of the father of the family.

Housing

Traditional housing in Palau was rectangular in shape and consisted of wood and thatched roofs. Larger houses were often built on wooden platforms that were raised off the ground on stone. Palm fronds and pandanus leaves were used to construct the roofs of the traditional bai, or male meetinghouse, and bamboo (for the flooring) and coconut husks (the fiber was made into rope) were also common materials. Houses tended to

be ornately decorated. A small cooking house or structure was traditionally separated from the main house. Traditional houses also contained a sacred place known as the cheldeng, where valuables were kept and spirits were believed to reside.

Most contemporary housing is Palau is modernist in nature, and may borrow from Japanese architecture, though some traditional principles are still used. The majority of houses are made of concrete blocks or wood and metal sheeting, and roofs are typically corrugated cardboard. Though most homes house single families, some apartment buildings house multiple families. Some Palauans chose to live on houseboats, called "live-aboards." Clan members continue to help finance the construction costs of clan-members' homes.

Food

The fruit of the banana, citrus, and coconut trees, along with taro, fish, and pigs and cattle, form the culinary basis of traditional Palauan cuisine. Local fruits are generally incorporated into every meal, and mild spices are used to add the unique flavors of Palauan dishes. Taro is one of the most common foods on the islands, and can be added to coconut soup, baked into chips, and mashed into cakes. Other traditional Palauan foods include copra (coconuts), sweet potatoes, yams, and cassava (tapioca). Seafood such as fish and shellfish are staples, and pork and chicken are the most commonly eaten meats. In recent years, imported rice has become a popular staple.

One Palauan specialty is fruit bat, which is typically cooked whole and served in a broth. Other specialties include the giant turtle and green turtle (called melob), and smoked fish, which, along with pork, is commonly wrapped in taro leaves and steamed. A favorite dessert is coconut, whose milk is preferred to animal milk. Coconuts also favor prominently in desserts, such as coconut milk shakes and coconut ice cream. The culinary influences of both American and Japanese cuisine are also becoming more commonplace, including the prevalence of salads and sandwiches made with roasted pork. Larger

The fruit bat is native to Palau and is featured in their famous bat soup.

cities such as Koror also feature numerous Asian restaurants that serve Japanese sushi, traditional Indian food, and Korean specialties.

Life's Milestones

While most Palauans are Christian, and observe rites of passage in the Christian faith, several traditional Palauan ceremonies continue to mark major life events. These include a birth ceremony called omersurch, the ceremony that marks a couple's first house, called ocheraol, as well as funeral services known as kemeldiil.

Marriage in Palau is called chebechiil, and the wealth of the prospective bride's family continues to be an important factor to the prospective groom's family. As such, the parents of both the bride and groom must agree to the marriage of their children first. When a man wishes to marry a woman, his cousin, or father traditionally accompanies him to the woman's home for the sake of respectability. The prospective groom then sits to the left of the door, signaling the reason for his visit. The accompanying

relative leaves the home when the visit is successful. The man, however, stays at the home of his future in-laws. About two months' later, the future bride's parents send food to the groom's parents announcing the ceremony, which all family members attend. The ceremony involves the groom's family giving money to the bride's parents, the final proof of marriage. Throughout the married couple's life, the man continues to have financial obligations to the wife's family, and the wife provides food for her relatives during certain occasions.

CULTURAL HISTORY

Art

Traditional Palauan art served both functional and spiritual purposes. Craftsmen were chosen in Palau, and only a few people in a village practiced such skills as canoe building, woodcarving, basketry, and jewelry making. The canoe was essential for transportation, and early Palauans built special canoes for every occasion. Larger canoes were used for battle and were as long as 18 meters (60 feet). Canoes were traditionally shaped with crescent-shaped stems and hulls and had double-hulls. Because of their cultural importance, canoes also served as models for shrines on the Palauan islands. Palauan men also carved many other types of objects, such as bowls, large food containers with inlaid shells, and plates.

Palauan women were traditionally the basket weavers. They also wove mats for sleeping and sitting, and sails, used for larger canoes, out of coconut palms and pandanus leaves. Jewelry in traditional Palau revealed wealth the wealth of women who wore certain items. For example, women showed social status by wearing articles that were used for money, such as beads. Bead currency, called udoud, was made from glass beads or high-fired clay. These beads were used in articles such as necklaces. More recently, necklaces that reveal status are made with black and pink coral, a more recent form of Palauan currency.

Architecture

The Pacific island nation of Palau is known for its prehistoric architecture, most notably the Palauan terraces (the sculpting of earth) and ancient stonework. One of the most famous terraced sites is the earthworks at Babeldaob, the largest island. The terraced hills and flattened hilltops were not necessarily used for agrarian purposes. Because the sculpted earth slopes inward toward a center hill, the retention of rainwater for crop cultivation is a plausible explanation for their creation. However, because of the presence of "crown and brim" structures, which are the primary characteristics of sculpted hills, many speculate Palau's ancient terraced earthworks were also used as defensive measures. Some terraces contained stonework, such as pathways and platforms. It is believed that the construction of these sites peaked between 1000 and 1400 CE, and their exact creation, functions, and abandonment remain a mystery.

Also located on Babeldaob are ancient stone sculptures collectively called the "Great Faces." These carved megaliths (large monumental stones) are specifically located in the capital of Melekeok. The stone carvings reveal a type of grimacing face that covers the entire side of a stone. All of the stones, of which there are nine, face the sea, and only two have been repositioned from their original location. They range between 1 meter (3 feet) and 2.4 meter (8 feet) tall, and their placement mimics traditional Palauan architectural themes. For example, some of the stones at this site and others on the island form corners of an area, with other stones situated at the front, as if to guard the site. Another greater grouping of smaller sculpted megaliths is located at Badrulchau, the northernmost tip of Babeldaob.

Prehistoric Irrai Village, in the south of Babeldaob, contains terraced hills near a bay. Still visible are the pathways throughout the village, stone bulkheads and boat landings, and stone platforms. The stone pathways connect the platforms that exist throughout the village. A bai, or men's clubhouse, was also part of this village. The bai is considered one of the finest examples of Micronesian architecture. It was traditionally built with heavy wooden planks carved without non-metal, traditional tools, and coconut rope was used to tie the structure together. The bai was often perched on a platform of stone and included four corner posts, each of which signified a chief in the village. The chiefs would use these corner posts for support during their meetings. Women were not allowed to enter a bai, which would frequently have carvings of women on the end gables to warn women not to enter. In one type of bai, Palauan young adults were taught Palauan ways of hunting, carpentry, and fishing. In another type of bai, only the chiefs held important meetings. It is believed that the stone structures at Badrulchau were used in ancient versions of the traditional bai.

Music

In addition to storytelling, Palauan culture also valued chanting and dance. Traditionally, those of high social status and authority within the village chanted songs about historical events that were important to the village culture. They would also use chants to socially reprimand a villager for uncharitable deeds and behaviors. Such chants involved parody, and the public audience and comical situation helped lessen the severity. Chants also held special spiritual significance for Palauans, and were used to call an ancestor or a mythological god. The language used in such chanting usually did not consist of everyday speech.

Dance

Dance and music are truly intertwined in Palau's culture. Dance usually accompanied chants, and dancing was often a traditional mainstay at ceremonies such as weddings. Proper form and movement were essential for communicating the message of the dance, which could be about a successful harvest or battle. Dances, along with chants, were also essential to Palauans for communicating with the spirit world. The dance has a pair of elements: the "mother" dance, called delal a ngloik, which deals with more serious issues, and a humorous element, called beluulchab. Men traditionally learned dances at the bai, while women learned them at home.

Dancers also traditionally adorned themselves with certain costumes, as well as flowers and shell jewelry. Women and girls wear two-piece skirts made from treated hibiscus bark, which are colored according to their family or clan. The specific movements of the dancers, such as hip movements and the bending of the knees, emphasizes the skirt. While a substantial amount of Palauan culture, including dancing and chanting was almost lost or waned during colonial rule, many are now beginning to pass these traditions on to new generations.

Literature

Because no common written language existed in Palau until the 1970s, Palauans passed their history and folklore to other generations through oral traditions such as storytelling. They related events, traditions, special occasions, and daily situations. More recently, storyboards, which are wooden panels that feature carved or painted cultural stories and myths, have developed special cultural significance for Palauans. They were also carved and painted onto long panels or beams inside the men's clubhouse, called a bai. Examples of these stories include creation myths, such as the origin of human life and of the breadfruit tree in Palau, and historic events, such as typhoons and battles. Storyboards also contained morals in the stories of daily life.

CULTURE

Arts & Entertainment

Traditional dances are still performed in Palau. Dancers adorn themselves with flowers and use their movements to pass along stories and traditions of childbirth and marriage. Though men perform dances, such as a traditional dance involving two sticks struck together to form rhythmic beats, women are the primary performers. In their role as traditional dancers, women maintain their prominent cultural roles in Palau's matrilineal society while simultaneously passing

along traditional culture to younger generations. Dance changed in 20th-century Palau. One of the more common contemporary dances is called matamatong, which is a marching-type dance that is considered to have originated during the 20th century. Dancers emulate a march and mimic typical marching refrains.

Contemporary music began appearing on the islands in the mid-1980s. Palauan popular music includes forms generated from early 20th-century melodic Palauan love songs, called derebechesiil. These songs recall Japanese control of the islands by their Japanese folk flavor. Popular music from the U.S. and Europe also grew in popularity, though lyrics are typically in Palauan or a combination of Palauan and Japanese or English. The younger generation tends to listen to the contemporary pop music that is influenced by Europe and America. The typical pop band has guitars, drums, keyboards, and synthesizers. However, a vocalist accompanied by a keyboard player is more common in Palau. Popular music now even accompanies the ngasech, a birth ceremony that customarily features traditional Palauan music.

Palauans compete internationally in sports as well, such as table tennis, swimming, volleyball, softball, wrestling, weightlifting, baseball, basketball, outrigger canoeing, and track events.

Cultural Sites & Landmarks

The culture of Palau and its many landmarks have evolved distinctly from the country's Pacific environment. The waters that surround Palau are rated one of the Seven Wonders of the Underwater World by Conservation, Education, Diving, Awareness, and Marine-research (CEDAM) International. The archipelagic nation of more than 300 islands and islets covers more than 160 kilometers (100 miles) of sea that includes unique coral reefs, endemic marine life, and deep ocean that allows for diving depths of 305 meters (1,000 feet). In fact, about 1500 species of fish and 700 species of coral have been recorded around the islands, and diving remains one of the island nation's most important tourist draws. The island also contains exceptional biodiversity and landmarks on land, as well, including the tallest waterfall in Micronesia. Located near the main commercial state of Koror is the Ngardmau Waterfall, which drops 217 meters (713 feet) from Mount Ngerchelchuus, which is itself known for its estimated seventy species of orchids.

Palau is also famous for its Rock Islands, which include nearly 300 limestone and coral rocks jutting out of the sea. Also called Chelbacheb, the islands are shaped like mushrooms because the waves have worn away their bases. Numerous types of sea life find refuge in the Rock Islands, including stingless jellyfish that are believed to exist only in Palau. In fact, Jellyfish Lake (or Ongeim'l Tketau), a saltwater lake which contains up to 10 million jellyfish, lies within one of the Rock Islands. Though it is a completely enclosed lake, it once was open to the ocean, making it accessible to jellyfish. The surrounding waters of Rock Islands are also renowned for their deep blue holes and crystal caves that lie underneath the many islands.

Palau's numerous cultural and historic sites include the Belau National Museum, established in 1955, and the Chades er a Mechorei, a pre-colonial causeway. The national museum in Koror offers exhibits of Palau history and culture, such as examples of traditional stone and shell money and native art. The Chades er a Mechorei, a causeway built before Europeans arrived, is one of Palau's best-preserved sites. Placed on the Palau Register of Historic Places in 1995, the causeway sits at the edge of the village of Airai. People from throughout Palau constructed different parts of the structure without the use of modern technology. It is believed that the causeway demarcates the border between two Palauan chiefdoms, the Reklai and the Ibedul.

Like many island nations throughout Micronesia, Palau was the stage for fierce fighting in the Pacific theater of war during World War II. As a result, the archipelagic nation contains a wealth of World War II heritage sites, wreckage, and memorials. The Palau island of Peleliu, in particular, was the site of a large battle between American and Japanese military forces. The island still contains numerous memorials, battlefields, and monuments erected to those who died in the battle, including the Peleliu WWII Memorial Museum. Remnants of the fierce fighting, such as Japanese concrete bunkers and cannons, are still extant. Peleliu is also home to a German lighthouse from World War I.

Libraries & Museums

Libraries in Palau include the Palau Public Library and the Palau Community College Library, both in Koror. In 2010, the Palau Association of Libraries, which comprises public and state libraries, among other institutional repositories, received a $39,980 grant from the Institute of Museums and Library Services to assess library collections in the island republic.

The Belau National Museum in Koror is the national museum of Palau. Established in 1955, it is considered the oldest museum in Micronesia, with its collections ranging from natural history and anthropology to arts and material culture. Exhibits include Palauan art, Palauan canoes, Palau's historical role in World War II, as well as a number of outdoor exhibits such as WWII relics, carved limestone sculptures, and a botanical garden. The Peleliu WWII Memorial Museum, located on Peleliu Island, commemorates the Battle of Peleliu, one of the most controversial and costly battles in the Pacific Theater.

Holidays

Palauans celebrate many typical American holidays, including Thanksgiving and Labor Day. Other official holidays observed in Palau include Youth Day (March 15), Senior Citizens' Day (May 5), President's Day (June 1), Constitution Day (July 9), Independence Day (October 1), and United Nations Day (October 24).

Youth Culture

Playing sports and attending sports events are very important to Palauan youth. A concerted effort is currently underway in the schools to make physical education resources more comprehensive, including volleyball, badminton, and football (soccer). Both young boys and girls also spend ample time playing basketball, softball. Westernization is prevalent among the youth culture of the dominant and larger islands, particularly pop music and dance trends. However, there is a concerted effort among many island young adults to preserve the traditional culture, including music, dance, storytelling, and native foods. Many Palauan young people are engaged in more American- and European-influenced activities, such as dancing in clubs. However, youth throughout Palau are also getting involved in organized community service organizations to develop programs that only engage young adults in cultural programs.

SOCIETY

Transportation

There is no public transportation throughout the Republic of Palau, and most travel around the main islands is usually done by automobile. Taxis are available in Koror, which is also the only city on the islands with a shuttle bus service. Travel between the islands is mostly handled by private boat services.

The Palau International Airport, at Airai, carries passengers to and from Manila and Guam, and smaller airports with unpaved runways run scheduled flights to and from Angaur and Pelelieu. Three airlines offer international service, and three domestic airlines carry passengers from Pelelieu to Angaur.

Drivers travel on the right-hand side of the road in Palau.

Transportation Infrastructure

Overall, Palau has a well-developed infrastructure. The island has seen much recent activity in its transportation infrastructure, such as the 2006 completion of the 53-mile (85-kilometer) "Compact Road" circling the island of Babeldaob, due to foreign assistance, particularly the U.S. Trust Territory Capital Improvement Program (CIP). Malakal Commercial Port is the country's commercial port facility.

Media & Communications

Media and communications on the islands are fairly limited. There are no regional television stations based on Palau. Cable television is popular, consisting of American programming—on a six-day delay—and satellite programming in real time. There are several independent newspapers, mostly published weekly, and six radio stations, one of which is government-owned. The Palauan media is generally allowed to freely express views and opinions.

The Palau National Communications Corporation (PNCC) operates all telecommunications services. As of 2014, an estimated 19,100 Palauans were using mobile cellular phones, and since 2006, satellite dishes handle a wireless broadband network. Internet service in the republic is low but growing rapidly. As of 2013, there were an estimated 6,560 internet users, about a third of the population.

SOCIAL DEVELOPMENT

Standard of Living

Palau ranked 60th out of 187 nations on the 2013 United Nations Human Development Index, which measures quality of life and standard of living indicators.

Water Consumption

Surface water run-off, particularly watersheds, is the primary source of water production in Palau, while smaller, outlying islands depend on groundwater and rainfall. The Koror/Airai Water Treatment Plant supplies water to approximately three-fourths of the Palauan population. In addition, rainwater catchment systems are typical among most households.

In 2010, the Asian Development Bank stated that Palau had the highest rate of water usage in the Pacific region, and needed to manage its water resources in a more cost-effective manner. Recently, discussions of water resource management in Palau have turned to desalination as a way of improving the island nation's limited resources.

Education

Children make up roughly 29.9 percent of the population of Palau. They receive free education from elementary through high school, and attendance is compulsory for children up to the age of sixteen. Generally, the educational system is modeled after the American educational system, and runs from kindergarten through the twelfth grade.

Palau maintains one government-run high school as well as a number of private, church-affiliated high schools; as of 2013, Palau has sixteen public elementary schools and two private elementary schools, five private high schools, and one community college. Palau public schools had an official enrollment of 2,322 students for the 2013–2014 school year. In addition, the community provides opportunities for non-formal education, recreation and cultural expression. Progress is being made in securing equal rights and providing supportive services for disabled children.

The average literacy rate is 99.5 percent (99.5 percent among men and 99.6 percent among women).

Women's Rights

Women have traditionally maintained an important cultural and social role in Palau's matrilineal culture. Women remain influential in inheritance and property rights, and serve in traditional advisory roles within villages and clans. However, certain abuses, such as the trafficking of persons, domestic violence, and instances of rape, have been reported.

Sexual harassment is illegal in Palau, yet social and culture pressures result in underreporting. Trafficking in women (and some men) remains an ongoing issue. Women are typically brought from the Philippines and China to work in Palau as prostitutes and hostesses, or as domestic servants in homes. The government imposes heavy fines and prison sentences for those charged with trafficking, but it has lacked sufficient expertise and resources to combat the problem. Palau has offered some of the trafficked victims other employment options in the country.

In 2013, no rape or sexual abuse charges were reported; however, this is once again indicative of underreporting. In addition, women's groups reported that only a small percentage of domestic violence cases were reported, as many women are reluctant to press charges. No shelters for abused women exist in Palau, but the government is engaging in education campaigns to prevent future domestic violence.

In 2015, the national women's conference held its seventeenth meeting. This year's conference theme was "Equal rights and equal opportunity for women." As of the same year, half of the country's four supreme court justices are women. However, zero out of the countries twenty-five legislators are women.

Health Care

While education is fully subsidized by aid from the United Nations Educational, Scientific and Cultural Organization (UNESCO) and the United States, health care is not. The country has roughly two private medical clinics and one public hospital. In addition, medical personnel are isolated from each other and lack opportunities for training.

Palau is faced with the challenge of dealing with diseases typical to developing countries, such as dengue fever, as well as conditions which arise from a modern lifestyle, such as alcoholism and cancer. Major problems include mental illness and an increasing rate of suicide. Palau's mental illness rate is almost twice the normal rate, especially among young males.

Life expectancy is increasing, from sixty-nine years in 2000 to an estimated seventy-three years in 2015; seventy years for men and seventy-six years for women. The infant mortality rate was thirty-two deaths per 1,000 live births in 1980. In 2015, it was estimated at eleven deaths per 1,000 births.

Maternal health is especially good in Palau, with only three maternal deaths in the decade between 1984 and 1994. The high quality of obstetrical services is credited, as well as the availability and widespread use of contraceptives.

GOVERNMENT

Structure

Palau became a fully independent state on October 1, 1994. It has a constitutional government in free association with the United States. Suffrage is universal at age eighteen. For administrative purposes, the country is divided into sixteen states.

The president is chief of state and head of government. The president and vice-president are elected on separate tickets by popular vote; they each serve four-year terms.

The bicameral parliament is the Olbiil Era Kelulau (OEK), literally, "House of Whispered Decisions." It is also known as the Palau National Congress. The Congress consists of a House of Delegates and a Senate. Both the sixteen delegates and the nine senators are elected by majority vote in single seat constituencies. Both delegates and senators serve four-year terms.

Political Parties

Palau has no political parties and no political pressure groups.

Local Government

There are sixteen traditional municipalities in Palau, designated as states. Each state has the authority to elect heads of state and legislatures. As each state varies, local governance may consist of governors, traditional chiefs or elders, or high ranking clans. In addition, a Council of Chiefs, made up of traditional chiefs from Palau's sixteen states, advises the president.

Judicial System

The Supreme Court is the highest court. It consists of one chief justice and three associate justices who serve lifetime appointments until mandatory retirement at age sixty-five. The legal system is based on Trust Territory laws, acts of the legislature, common law and customary laws. The equality of customary and written laws sometimes causes confusion.

Taxation

Palau has a low to moderate taxation structure. The primary taxes levied are revenue tax, wage and salary tax, and import duties. There are no corporate or property taxes.

Armed Forces

The island republic of Palau maintains no armed forces. After signing into a Compact of Free Association in 1994, Palau is dependent upon the United States for defense and security matters for fifty years. In 2015, a small American military presence of thirteen soldiers, operating as a Civic Action Team (CAT), is deployed in Palau.

Foreign Policy

Palau gained full independence from being a protectorate of the United States in October 1994, and has since developed diplomatic ties with numerous Pacific countries, especially Japan, Australia, and Taiwan. At independence, the Republic of Palau joined the Compact of Free Association (COFA), which, along with the Federated States of Micronesia (FSM) and the Republic of the Marshall Islands (RMI), is an agreement with the United States. Ratified in 1993, the agreement provides Palau with access to many U.S. programs, economic aid for fifteen years, and military defense. In return, the United States gains certain defense rights, such as missile testing in specific areas and military access. Under the compact, Palauans are also able to serve in the U.S. military. The aid enables Palau to enjoy a per capita income well over twice that of the Philippines and many other places in Micronesia. About half of the islands' inhabitants work for the government. Palau's internal economy is based on subsistence agriculture, fishing, and tourism.

Two months after achieving full independence, Palau was admitted to the United Nations (UN). The country also holds membership in other prominent international organizations and institutions, including the International Monetary Fund (IMF), the Asian Development Bank (ADB), the

South Pacific Commission (SPC), the Forum Fisheries Agency, and the South Pacific Forum (SPF). The island nation also maintains key relations with the European Union (EU), with the latter particularly addressing Palau's energy needs through the European Development Fund (EDF).

Like many other Pacific nations, Palau is actively involved in global environmental matters, particularly climate change, which is projected to have a devastating effect on the Pacific region. The Palauan government has worked with sixteen Pacific Island nations to encourage their ratification of the Kyoto Protocol on global warming, as Palau and a great number of Pacific islands and coastal nations are under threat from rising ocean levels. In 2006, Palau became the first nation to host the Taiwan-Pacific Allies Summit. Palau is also a key leader in the 2005 Micronesia challenge, a program which aims to conserve 20 percent of forest land and 30 percent of coastal waters by 2020.

Human Rights Profile

International human rights law insists that states respect civil and political rights, and promote an individual's economic, social, and cultural rights. The United Nations Universal Declaration on Human Rights (UDHR) is recognized as the standard for international human rights. Its authors sought the counsel of the world's great thinkers, philosophers, and religious leaders, and were careful to create a document that reflects the core values shared by every world culture. (To read this document or view the articles relating to cultural human rights, visit http: //www.udhr.org/UDHR/default.htm.).

Generally, the Palauan government has respected the rights of the republic's citizens. As a constitutional republic, elections are conducted in a free and fair manner, and Palauan citizens elect a president and other government representatives, including a legislature, every four years. Section 1 of the Palauan constitution guarantees citizens the freedom of conscience and religion, and Section 2 guarantees the freedoms of free speech, press, and peaceful assembly, as well as

for redress of grievances. Citizens are all guaranteed equal protection under the law and the right to a fair trial, and are protected against search and seizure. The Palauan government is also forbidden from depriving any citizen of life, liberty, or property without due process, and cannot discriminate on the basis of gender, race, language, belief, age, or social status. The constitution further prohibits torture and inhumane punishment, as well as the exploitation of children. Lastly, Section 13 of the Palauan constitution guarantees the equality between men and women and the right to marry.

While Palau's human rights record is generally good, some key challenges and human rights abuses have been reported. In 2014, the U.S. State Department identified government corruption, discrimination, and abuse of foreign workers as Palau's most significant human rights problems. Palau has seen an increase in foreign workers since the turn of the 21st century. However, these workers, who are non-citizens, are prohibited from buying land or from becoming citizens. Foreign workers have also regularly reported acts of discrimination and are frequently targets for various crimes. Palauan authorities have reportedly not pursued crimes against foreign workers, who have also faced discrimination in all facets of their lives in Palau, including at work, in education, and when attempting to access social services. Also, when foreign workers sought to leave a poor work environment, their employers reportedly either took their passports or verbally threatened them.

Other human rights challenges in Palau include human trafficking and domestic abuse.

ECONOMY

Overview of the Economy

The government is the major employer in Palau, and also provides many social services. In recent years, tourism has grown in importance. Most farming is done at the subsistence level, and Palau imports much of its own food.

In 2015, the per capita gross domestic product (GDP) was estimated at $16,300, more than double what it was in 2008.

Industry

Industries in Palau are small, consisting of tourism, construction, craft items and garment making. In 2014, Palau exported an estimated $19.1 million (USD) worth of goods, mostly tuna. Japan receives most of the country's tuna exports. Other exports include shellfish, copra and clothing.

Labor

Labor is concentrated in the major industries of tourism, agriculture, and subsistence fishing. The tourism industry is growing rapidly. In 2005, the unemployment rate was 4.2 percent. Palau had an estimated 4,000 foreign workers in 2014, mostly from the Philippines (65 percent), as well as China and Vietnam.

Energy/Power/Natural Resources

Palau's natural resources include forests, small amounts of minerals such as gold, marine resources such as fish in the surrounding waters, and other mineral deposits in the deep seabed.

Environmental concerns facing Palau include inadequate sewage facilities, coral- and sand-dredging operations which threaten marine habitats, illegal fishing and over-fishing.

Fishing

The fishing industry is concentrated on the offshore fisheries for tuna and its related species, such as skipjack tuna, yellowfin tuna, and bigeye tuna. However, Palau's primary source of revenue involving fishing is the selling of licenses to foreign fishing vessels. It is estimated, in fact, that approximately $200 million (USD) in fishing profits are exported by foreign companies who are licensed to fish in Palau waters.

Agriculture

Less than 11 percent of the land in Palau is arable. Most farmers grow food for their own consumption. Coconuts are the chief cash crop. Other crops include cassava, taro and sweet potatoes.

Other agricultural products include copra (dried coconut meat, from which oil is extracted), eggs, fruit, vegetables, betel nuts, livestock and poultry. The fish catch includes sturgeon, groupers, crabs, wrasses, tuna, mackerel and shellfish.

Tourism

Tourism is a major part of Palau's economy. Visitors to the country bring in over $70 million annually. Attractions include cultural and historic sites and cultural centers, such as Ngarachamayong Cultural Center and Ngirngemelas Square, both on Koror, and Chades er a Mechorei, an ancient causeway. History enthusiasts may view artifacts from World War II on the islands of Paleliu and Angaur. Other attractions include Jellyfish Lake, with its clouds of sting-less jellyfish, the Palau Aquarium and the world-famous Rock Islands, a group of mushroom-shaped, foliage-covered islets.

Favorite activities for tourists include diving and snorkeling (Palau has been named one of the "seven underwater wonders of the world"), dolphin encounters, and canoe tours. Because of its magnificent scenery, Palau has become a favorite spot for honeymooning.

Kathryn Bundy, Ellen Bailey

DO YOU KNOW?

- The 2004 season of the television show *Survivor* was filmed in Palau.
- The late Jacques Cousteau, legendary French marine explorer and inventor of the aqualung, enjoyed diving at Palau's Ngemelis Wall. In his opinion, it was one of the world's best dive walls.
- Palauans do not need visas or permits to visit, live in, or work in the United States.

Bibliography

Abels, Birgit. "Performing Palauan Identity: Popular Music in the Western Carolines." *New Zealand Journal of Research in Performing Arts and Education: Nga Mahi a Rehia.* http://www.drama.org.nz/ejournal_single. asp?ID=38.

Abels, Birgit. *Sounds of Articulating Identity. Tradition and Transition in the Music of Palau, Micronesia.* Santa Cruz, CA: Logos, 2008.

Hollywood, Mike. *Papa Mike's Palau Islands Handbook.* iUniverse, Inc, 2006

Kaeppler, Adrienne L. *The Pacific Arts of Polynesia and Micronesia.* New York, New York: Oxford University Press, 2008.

Levy, Neil. *Moon Handbooks Micronesia.* Berkeley, California: Avalon Travel Publishing, 2003.

Morgan, William N. *Prehistoric Architecture in Micronesia.* Austin, Texas: University of Texas Press, 1989.

Rechebei, Elizabeth D. *History of Palau: Heritage of an Emerging Nation.* Palau: Ministry of Education, 1997.

Works Cited

Abels, Birgit. "Performing Palauan Identity: Popular Music in the Western Carolines." http://www.drama.org.nz/ ejournal_single.asp?ID=38. *New Zealand Journal of Research in Performing Arts and Education: Nga Mahi a Rehia.*

"Background Note: Palau." http://www.state.gov/r/pa/ei/ bgn/1840.htm. February 25, 2008. *U.S. Department of State.*

"Chades er a Mechorei." http://www.visit-palau.com/thingstodo/activity_description. cfm?activityID=11C1CC. *Visit Palau.*

"Constitution of the Republic of Palau." http://www. paclii.org/pw/legis/consol_act/cotrop359/. *Palau Constitutional Convention,* January 28–April 2, 1979, Koror, Palau.

"Culture of Palau." http://www.visit-palau.com/aboutpalau/ art.html. *Visit Palau.*

"International Inspiration—Palau." http://www.uksport.gov. uk/pages/international_inspiration_-_palau/. *UK Sport.*

"Micronesia." http://www.trip-n-tour.com/Destination/ Micronesia.aspx. *Trip-N-Tour: The Dive/Travel Experts of the Pacific.*

"Missionaries." http://www.pacificworlds.com/palau/ visitors/mission.cfm.

Morgan, William N. *Prehistoric Architecture in Micronesia.* Austin, Texas: *University of Texas Press,* 1989.

"Palau." http://www.wondersoftheallworld.com/palau.html. *CEDAM International.*

"Palau." http://www.mnsu.edu/emuseum/cultural/oldworld/ pacific/palau.html.

"Palau." The World Factbook. https://www.cia.gov/library/ publications/the-world-factbook/geos/ps.html#Comm. *Central Intelligence Agency.*

"Palau." *Dances of Life.* http://piccom.org/home/ dancesoflife/palau.html. *PBS.*

"Palau." http://www.culturecrossing.net/basics_business_ student_details.php?Id=8&CID=158. *Culture Crossing.*

"Human Development Reports: Palau." http://hdr.undp.org/ en/countries/profiles/PLW. *United Nations Development Programme.*

"Palau." http://data.un.org/CountryProfile. aspx?crName=Palau. *UN Data.*

"2014 Investment Climate Statement: Palau." http://www. state.gov/documents/organization/228600.pdf. *U.S. Department of State.*

"Country Reports on Human Rights Practices for 2014: Palau." http://www.state.gov/j/drl/rls/hrrpt/ humanrightsreport/index.htm#wrapper. *U.S. Department of State*

"Palau." http://www.citypopulation.de/Palau.html. *City Population.*

"Statistical Yearbook." http://palaugov.org/wp-content/ uploads/2014/07/2013-ROP-Statistical-Yearbook.pdf. *Republic of Palau Ministry of Finance.*

A traditional Papuan woman. iStock/andersen_oystein

PAPUA NEW GUINEA

Introduction

The Independent State of Papua New Guinea (PNG) is located in the South Pacific Ocean, roughly 200 kilometers (124 miles) north of Australia. The country occupies the eastern part of the island of New Guinea, the second largest non-continental island in the world. It also encompasses the islands of the Bismarck Archipelago, some of the Solomon Islands, and other small islands.

Papua New Guinea is renowned for the abundant diversity of its indigenous cultures, languages and animal life. There are more than 700 spoken dialects, and perhaps an even greater number of ethnic groups. Nearly 200 species of mammals have been discovered on the islands, and still much of the mountainous tropical terrain is unexplored.

GENERAL INFORMATION

Official Language: English
Population: 6,672,429 (2015 estimate)
Currency: Papua New Guinean kina
Coins: 100 toea equal one kina. Coins are available in denominations of 5, 10, 20, and 50 toea, and 1 kina.
Land Area: 452,860 square kilometers (174,850 square miles)
Water Area: 9,980 square kilometers (3,853 square miles)
National Anthem: "O, Arise All You Sons"
Capital: Port Moresby
Time Zone: GMT +10

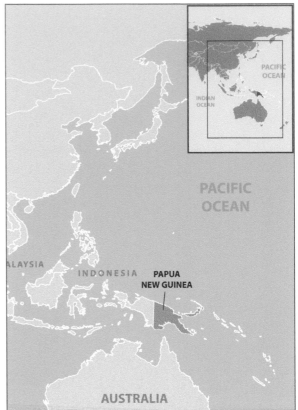

Flag Description: The flag of Papua New Guinea is a bicolor flag divided diagonally from the top hoist (or left) side. The bottom triangle is black, and features the Southern Cross constellation, consisting of five white stars. The top triangle, occupying the fly, is red, and features a yellow bird of paradise design. The flag's design symbolizes the country's emergence into nationhood.

Population

The population of Papua New Guinea is divided into thousands of different communities, divided along the lines of language, family, and tribal custom. Indigenous peoples inhabit the remote interior of the country, and are often isolated from each other by mountains.

Approximately 87 percent of the population lives in rural areas, although more and more Papua New Guineans are moving to urban areas. The population of the capital, Port Moresby, was measured at 364,125 in the 2011 census. Most of the city's residents live in poverty, a problem

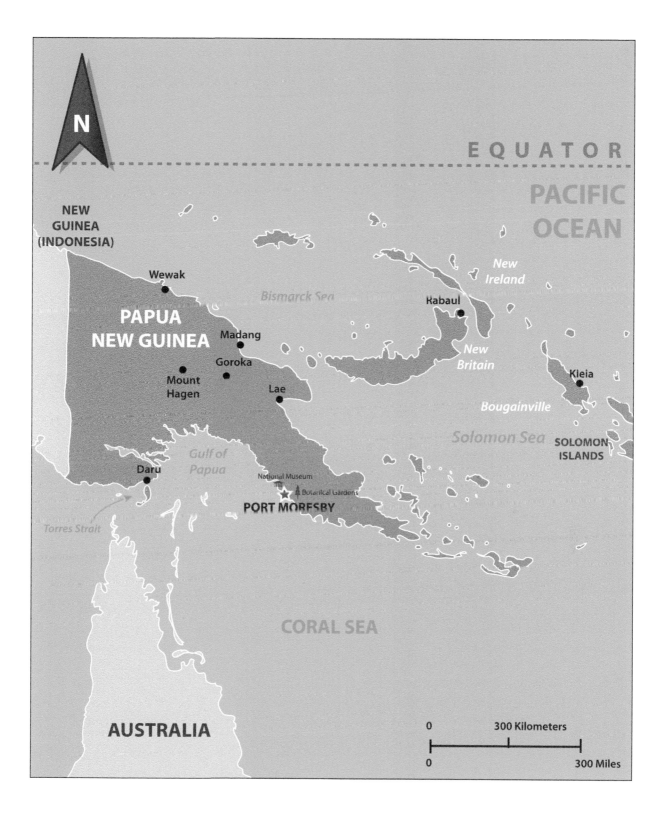

Principal Cities by Population (2011):

- Port Moresby (364,125)
- Lae (148,934)
- Wewak (37,825)
- Madang (35,971)
- Mt. Hagen (29,765)

exacerbated by an influx of migrants from rural areas. Most arrive in the capital in search of economic opportunity but, once in the capital, cannot afford to leave. The lack of road and rail links, between Port Moresby and other parts of the country, forces passenger traffic to flows primarily through the city's international airport.

The population is young, with more than half between the ages of fifteen and sixty-four. Life expectancy at birth is sixty-nine years for women and sixty-five years for men.

Languages

There are over 700 dialects spoken throughout the country, some estimates put the number as high as 850, about 12% of the world's total. English is an official language, but it is only spoken by approximately 2 percent of the population. The other two official languages are Tok Pisin also called Melanesian Pidgin and which is widely spoken, providing a common language for most inhabitants, and Hiri Motu, or Pidgin Motu.

Native People & Ethnic Groups

It is thought that humans first arrived on the island about 50,000 years ago. These people, the ancestors of the modern Papuans, survived by fishing and hunting; later arrivals, probably Melanesians, took up farming. In addition to these two groups, there are small populations of indigenous Pygmies living in the interior of the country.

New Guinea Papuans comprise the majority of the population of Papua New Guinea. The islands and the eastern coast are populated by people of Melanesian, Micronesian, and Polynesian descent, together accounting for

about 15 percent of the population. According to the United Nations Development Programme, within these sub-groupings, PNG is home to approximately 200 distinct tribal groupings (with more than 850 ethnic groups, with that number sometimes reported as high as 1,000). With such diversity, the population is often classified by four distinct ethnic groups: Papuans (from the south), New Guineans (from the north of the main island), Islanders, and Highlanders. As such, no ethnicity predominates.

The Port Moresby region has traditionally served as home to two major ethnic groups: the Motu people, who lived along the coastal areas, and the Koitabu, who lived inland. The ancient roots of the Motu people are on display in a number of villages adjoining the capital's urban sprawl. The Motu people, who originally controlled the territory in which the Port Moresby is located, continue many traditional cultural practices, such as building many of their dwellings on stilts on the edge of the waters from which they made their living as traders and fishermen. Intermarriage has led to an extensive mingling of these two groups. Port Moresby is also home to other indigenous populations as well as a significant number of Western expatriates, especially Australians.

Religions

There is no official religion in Papua New Guinea. More than half the population is Christian, either Protestant (69.4 percent of the country's total) or Catholic (27 percent). Indigenous beliefs, including ancestor worship and belief in spirits, are also widespread.

Climate

Since it is close to the equator, most of Papua New Guinea experiences a tropical climate. The temperatures range from 21° to 32° Celsius (70° to 90° Fahrenheit) in the coastal regions. In the mountainous areas, frost can occur, and it occasionally snows on Mount Wilhelm.

The northwest monsoon blows from December to April, with drier southeast winds arriving from May to October. The Milne Bay region receives an average of 508 centimeters (200 inches) or rain each year, while Port Moresby receives about 115 centimeters (45 inches).

Port Moresby's climate is influenced by its location in the rain shadow, or precipitation shadow, of the Owen Stanley Range, a mountain range that blocks the downpours that drench nearby regions during the rainy season. Coupled with the sheltering effects created by offshore coral reefs, these mountains also help protect the harbor from inclement weather patterns approaching the capital from a northwesterly direction.

ENVIRONMENT & GEOGRAPHY

Topography

Papua New Guinea shares its western border with the Irian Jaya province of Indonesia, its neighbor on the island of New Guinea. Hundreds of offshore islands, including the Bismarck Archipelago, Manus, Buka, Bougainville, the Louisiade Archipelago, and others, account for roughly 15 percent of the country's total land area.

The interior mainland of Papua New Guinea is dominated by the Bismarck, Victor Emanuel and Owen Stanley mountain ranges. The porous limestone rock absorbs rainwater, so there are no streams in this part of the country. The country's highest point is at the peak of Mount Wilhelm, 4,509 meters (14,793 feet) above sea level.

Between the mountain ranges are the highland valleys, where most of the population is concentrated. The southern region is characterized by its many rivers, as well as Milne Bay. Major rivers include the Fly, Kikori, Markham, and the Ramu. The Fly River is 1,127 kilometers (700 miles) long; roughly 70 percent of its length is navigable.

The southwest coast is one of the largest swamp areas in the World, draining into the Gulf of Papua. Rising 61 meters (200 feet) above the swamp is the area of grassland known as the Oriomo Plateau.

Because of its location along the Pacific "Ring of Fire," PNG experiences frequent earthquakes and mudslides, and its islands have active volcanoes. Some of the smallest islands are coral atolls.

Plants & Animals

Papua New Guinea's vegetation varies according to elevation. Rainforests cover about 85 percent of the country, and include about 200 different types of trees, such as mahogany, laurel, oak, and hoop pine. Mangrove and sago palms grow in the swamp areas, and pine trees are found on the mountain slopes. Above 1,650 meters (12,000 feet), alpine grasses and flowers flourish.

Wild life is abundant throughout the country. Nearly 200 species of mammals have been discovered living in Papua New Guinea. Many mammals are nocturnal, and about one-third of them are marsupials, including tree kangaroos, cuscuses, and wallabies.

Colorful birds thrive in Papua New Guinea. Birds of paradise were hunted almost to extinction and today are protected by law. Crocodiles, pythons, and black-and-white banded sea snakes are also found near the country's rivers.

The coral reefs surrounding New Guinea support thriving marine life, including whales, dolphins and sea rays.

CUSTOMS & COURTESIES

Greetings

Urban Papua New Guineans typically shake hands when greeting. In rural areas, the traditional greeting of clasping hands is common. When greeting a village chief, elder, or leader, custom dictates that one should bow to show respect and deference. While physical greetings are generally similar across islands, villages and communities, verbal greetings can be complicated by linguistic differences. It is believed that there are as many as 850 separate languages spoken in the country. However, the official languages are English, Tok Pisin, and Hiri Motu (or Pidgin Motu), and English is taught in the school and customarily used for business. Tok Pisin (or Melanesian Pidgin), a form of Pidgin English, is perhaps more commonly spoken than English. It allows members many villages, islands, and communities to communicate and engage in trade.

Common Tok Pisin greetings and phrases include "Welkam" or "Mipela Welkam Yupela" ("Welcome"); "Monin tru" or "Gutpela monin" ("Good morning"); "Avinun tru" or "Gutpela avinun" ("Good afternoon"); "Gutpela nait" ("Good evening"); "Gude" or "Halo" ("Hello"); and "Husat nem bilong yu?" ("What is your name?"). People also tend to stand close to one another, as personal space is generally not over-valued when socializing.

Gestures & Etiquette

The people of Papua New Guinea customarily communicate with their bodies. For example, they may nod their heads and clasp their hands in greeting, and close friends and family may greet one another by putting their hands on the other's waist. Characteristic gestures include pointing with their chin rather than a finger or hand, and bowing in deference to a chief or elder. In addition, personal space and privacy are not traditionally maintained between friends, family members, and close acquaintances.

Social customs and etiquette are traditionally based on a belief in reciprocity and hospitality. Examples of reciprocity include competitive feasting between villages and the sharing of betel nuts (buai) between friends. Since families build social relationships and support systems by engaging in feasting exchanges with other families, the inability to reciprocate gifts, aid, or meals (possibly due to a lack of resources) often makes relationships between individual families and villages impossible.

Papua New Guineans also have a flexible sense of time and schedules, a characteristic similar to other Pacific cultures. Locals refer to the phenomenon of Melanesian time to explain how they value flexibility over punctuality. For example, people are expected to stop and chat with friends and acquaintances (referred to as

wantoks, or ones who speak the same language), even if the personal exchange makes them late for an event or meeting.

There are a few taboos in PNG that influence customs, behavior, and etiquette. Local belief forbids walking or stepping over food or sleeping people, which would make the food or person unclean. In addition, people do not generally ask or use first names. Social etiquette and custom also dictates that women dress modestly—women customarily cover their legs with skirt or fabric wrap. In some instances, women refrain from interacting with people outside of their kin group or villages. Public contact between men and women, such as public affection or holding hands, is also frowned upon, and avoiding eye contact with strangers is generally the norm.

Eating/Meals

In rural areas and villages, people generally eat two main meals each day. Rural Papua New Guineans mostly grow their own food, while those in urban areas commonly plant kitchen gardens and purchase whatever fruit and vegetables they cannot grow themselves. People living in urban areas may also eat at restaurants and kai bars (fast food bars). In addition, small markets and grocery stores generally sell staples such as rice, canned meats, and tea. Boiling or roasting food over an open fire is a common cooking method, and tea and snacks of sugarcane, coconut milk, and fruit are eaten during the workday.

Mumu pits (earth ovens) are common at celebrations in both rural and urban areas. A common eating custom at large-scale ceremonial occasions such as weddings involves the slaughter and roasting of hundreds of pigs. Families and villages, lead by their chiefs, also engage in competitive feasting. Village chiefs may host other exuberant and lavish events with feasting, dancing, singing, and drumming in an effort to build their group's status over neighboring families and villages.

Papua New Guineans value hospitality and reciprocity. When invited to a home or village for a meal, feast, or celebration, custom dictates that a reciprocal invitation will be made. There are few food related taboos except for the belief that a man should not eat in front of his in-laws. In addition, villages with chiefs have particular dining rules and customs; for instance, food is always set aside for the chief and his family.

Visiting

In Papua New Guinea, individuals, families, and whole villages visit one another on a regular basis. The society is based on reciprocity and hospitality, and the practice of visiting serves the important social function of building relations and trust. In addition, because the country lacks a government safety net for its citizens, Papua New Guineans rely on neighboring families and villages for support instead of the government. People build and strengthen their exchange relationships by engaging in acts of reciprocity, such as competitive feasting between villages and the sharing of betel nuts (buai) between friends. These acts of reciprocity and hospitality build familiarity, trust, and obligation.

When visiting a home, male visitors will usually be treated with greater hospitality and respect than female visitors. Also, food is traditionally served first to chiefs and elders. Due to the social importance of reciprocity, guests are expected to bring a gift for their hosts, such as rice, canned meat, tea, salt, sugar, or cooking oil. Guests are usually offered plates of food or snacks of fruit. In some instances, guests will be given much more food than they can consume during their visit, and it is customary to distribute the extra food to those in the household or village. Visitors and hosts do not traditionally exchange words of thanks at the end of a visit; instead, visitors express appreciation and gratitude to their hosts by giving and receiving gifts, as well as extending a reciprocal invitation to their hosts.

Large-scale competitive feasting visits between villages and chief communities may correspond to harvest times, but small-scale social visits occur throughout the year. Families and villages unable or unwilling to reciprocate a social gesture will not be able to maintain the relationship.

LIFESTYLE

Family

Family is considered the social safety net of Papua New Guinean society. The traditional notion of family is expanded to include an ever-growing kin group or clan. Membership in a kin group implies obligations and responsibilities. Villages include one or more families living in adjacent houses. Families traditionally share meals, chores, and ceremonial occasions. People, such as migrants, may join a kin group if they contribute to the life and work of the group.

Marriages tend to be arranged and based on trade and social relations, and husbands and wives must come from outside the kin group or clan. Desirable husbands are based on their work ethic and health, as wells as their resources, as they are required to pay a substantial bride price. Polygamy (the practice of having more than one wife) is legal and common, and divorce is uncommon. Unfulfilled marriages most often end through desertion or suicide.

Modernization and urbanization are transforming family relationships in the early 21st century. Due to urban migration, particularly to find works, many Papua New Guineans cannot readily participate in reciprocal family events and chores. As a result, they may lose their familial safety net or clan membership.

Housing

The majority of the population lives in small, traditional villages and rural areas. In fact, subsistence-based societies are the norm, and their preservation is acknowledged in the national constitution. Papua New Guineans tend to prefer village life with its relative safety and opportunities for strong local bonds and farming. Traditionally, villages covered the main island and 600 small neighboring islands. These villages were historically connected through trade and marital relationships. Towns and cities were rare until colonization, and the largest urban areas (with approximately 20,000 residents or more) include Port Moresby, Lae, Madang, Mt. Hagen, Wewak, and Goroka.

In villages, houses are made out of locally available materials such as bamboo and local hardwood. Bamboo is split into strips and weaved together to form walls or floors. Roofs may be made of palm fronds. Houses tend to be single-story structures. Round houses are common in Highland areas, while stilt houses are common in coastal or swamp areas. Stilt houses, also called pile dwellings, may be built on the shore or directly over the sea or swamp. Houses made of bamboo and indigenous hardwoods require upkeep and replacement on an ongoing basis due to insects and weather damage. All village or rural homes have gardens or farm plots. In urban areas, there has been a shortage of housing, resulting in an increase in substandard houses and informal settlements (or shantytowns).

People tend to own village land collectively. Individuals and families are expected to participate and contribute to village life, or risk being turned out of the village. Some villages and towns have their roots in colonial or post-colonial business ventures such as plantations or mines. These early towns were built to house hundreds of workers. In some colonial towns, larger-scale institutional housing structures, such as boarding houses or small apartment complexes, remain.

Food

Traditional cuisine in Papua New Guinea is based on staple foods such as starchy vegetables (sago, yams, taro, rice, and sweet potato), edible wild greens (kumu), fruit (coconut, mango, pineapples and banana) and meat (pork, fowl, and fish, as well as bush meat such as marsupial, cassowary, and turtle). Curry powder, ginger, black pepper, and salt, along with locally grown onions and tomatoes, are commonly used to flavor dishes. Food availability and delicacies vary widely by region. For example, coastal areas have fish and salt from the sea to use in their cooking while inland areas have kaukau (sweet potatoes) and swampy areas have mud clams. In urban areas, Chinese and Indonesian flavors are increasingly popular.

Traditional cooking methods include the mumu pit (earth oven) and clay pots over open

fires. Small kerosene stoves are also increasingly common in villages. Mumu pits, particularly favored for ceremonial events and large groups, are large pits dug into the ground filled with rocks and fire. Food, usually wrapped in leaves or placed inside green bamboo, is placed on the hot rocks to cook.

Traditional dishes include mumu, dia, mud clams, chicken pot, and bully beef. Mumu is both a much-loved national dish and a cooking method. A classic Mumu includes pig meat, sweet potatoes, rice, and wild greens cooked in a fire pit. Dia is a classic dish of sago root, bananas, and coconut cream. Mud clams are often prepared with fern leaves and coconut cream. Chicken pot is a one-pot recipe often cooked on an open fire. Ingredients include one chicken, oil, sweet potato, green onions, pumpkin tips, corn, coconut cream, curry powder, and salt. The bully beef recipe, also known as corned beef, includes canned meat which became popular in the area during World War II. Bully beef is made with a tin of corned beef, tomatoes, coconut cream, and rice. Coconut cream, which appears in many traditional recipes, is made by mixing and straining coconut flesh and water.

Life's Milestones

Important life milestones in PNG include the welcoming of an infant into the clan or village, initiation into adult society, and funerary traditions. When infants are a year old, the clan and village holds a feast to celebrate and welcome the infant into the group. The process of welcoming young men and women into adult society is marked with an initiation ceremony. Male and female initiation ceremonies involve seclusion, fasting, contact with spirits and ancestors, and body transformation. Teenage boys are traditionally only welcomed into adult society only after spending time in one of the men's secluded houses. Teenage girls traditionally enter adult society after seclusion in a menstrual hut or the payment of a bride price.

Papua New Guineans hold mortuary ceremonies when a person dies. Mortuary ceremonies have different components depending on the perceived reasons for death. For example, Papua New Guineans treat the death of a young person very differently than the death of an elder. Death in old age is considered natural, expected, and often welcome, while the death of a young or middle-aged person as a sign of wrongdoing or spirit or ancestral displeasure. The mourning period for a loved one traditionally ends with the performance of a ceremony called tepurukari in which mourners offer money and food to the deceased's relatives.

CULTURAL HISTORY

Art

Papua New Guinea is an extremely diverse nation with an estimated 850 spoken languages and over 1,000 traditional cultures. This complexity is evident in Papua New Guinean art, which is equally as diverse. It includes ancient wood carving techniques, weaving technology, weaponry, ritualistic jewelry making, textile art, and even currency. One particularly renowned art in Oceania is bark cloth, which consists of traditional costumes or clothing made from tapa cloth woven from the bark of trees. Artisans also used shells, tusks, animal teeth, and bird feathers to decorate their ritual costumes, including headdresses, and jewelry. In addition, much the characteristic art is primitive in nature; this is because the artists and cultures historically developed their techniques and crafts in relative isolation.

The artistic traditions of the nation were rooted in the needs and social practices of everyday life. Indigenous tribes developed artistic techniques such as woodworking and ceramics to create the items needed for daily village life. Thus, functional items such as wooden plates, clay pots for cooking, and bamboo vessels for water storage or drinking represent early artistic endeavors. The basis for art forms was also religious and spiritual, and included mask carvings (representing powerful spirits), ceremonial shields and spears, and sculptures such as fertility statues. The tribes of the Sepik region are particularly known for their ornate carvings,

depicting local fauna, spirits, or abstract designs, and Sepik art and architecture is often considered symbolic of the overall cultural heritage of Papua New Guinea.

Arts and culture are also shaped by the nation's colonial past and relatively modern independence. (Papua New Guinea achieved its independence in 1975.) In an effort to build its post-colonial national identity and culture, Papua New Guinea's new government, along with financial aid from Australia, invested heavily in visual arts and architecture. A national art school was established to help local artists and architects learn and combine traditional and modern techniques. Students of the school participated in the design of the National Parliament, the National Museum, and the Papua New Guinea Banking Corporation (PNGBC) building. Government buildings also display the murals and sculptures of local artists.

Some of the more distinguished artists of the contemporary era include Mathias Kauage (1944–2003), considered the country's best-known artist and Timothy Akis (1944–1984), considered the country's first exhibiting artist. Kauage is often referred to as the "founding father" of Papua New Guinea's indigenous art movement and was even awarded the Order of the British Empire (OBE).

Architecture

The Sepik region in Papua New Guinea is known for its traditional architecture. The area is dotted with traditional villages situated against the banks of the Sepik River and its tributaries. Much like Sepik art, which is known for its ornate carvings and abstract nature, the architecture of the Sepik region, is often characterized by elaborate woodcarvings and ornamentation. This distinct style of architecture is perhaps best represented by the "haus tambaran," or spirit house.

Built in a highly elaborate manner, these houses typically featured facades, or exterior walls, decorated with ancestral figures or supports carved in the likeness of clan spirits or ancestors. Other architectural features included triangular gables and roofs shaped like saddles. Houses were also raised on stilts.

The Abelam of the East Sepik province of Papua New Guinea are particularly known for their "spirit house" architecture. The Upper Sepik River Basin, owing to its cultural heritage, including these gabled spirit houses, is a tentative UNESCO World Heritage Site.

Music

In Papua New Guinea, music is an important part of all village rituals and celebrations. During the 20th century, music and dance that accompanied village celebrations was called "sing-sing" (or singsing) in Tok Pisin (Papua New Guinea's pidgin language). In some areas, these sing-sings have evolved into competitive events between clans and villages. Papua New Guinea's traditional tribal music has been shaped—and silenced—by religious missionaries, as well as periods of German, British, and Australian colonization.

During the nineteenth and much of the 20th century, German, British, and Australian colonial authorities, as well as Christian missionaries, occupied Papua New Guinea. This foreign presence sought to change many aspects of traditional tribal life, including music. However, missionaries and colonial authorities were unsuccessful in their efforts to ban or limit sing-sing rituals and events in tribal villages. These ceremonies, which included dance, music, costumes, and oratory, served as a vehicle for cultural preservation and cultural resistance during colonization.

Instruments used in traditional or tribal folk music include the slit-drum (garamut); bamboo mouth harps; shell whistles; water gongs; wooden stamping tubes; skin-covered drums (kundu); paired flutes; gourd horn (kanggur); slit-gong; wooden trumpets (kurudu); and twelve foot bamboo trumpets (dige). Traditional instruments are made from locally available resources such as lizard skin, coconut shells, clay, bamboo, palm fronds, shells, and local hardwoods. Particular instruments and songs are also associated with particular tribes, regions, and ceremonial uses. For example, the twelve-foot bamboo trumpets

are used almost exclusively during initiation ceremonies in the Madang region or district. In Tangu, the sound of the slit-gong announces the beginning of important events.

Christian missionaries introduced the church hymn and mouth organ to villages during the 19th-century, while Western occupation in the 20th century introduced popular Western musical styles and instruments.

Dance & Drama

Dance and drama are used and enjoyed in formal and informal ways throughout Papua New Guinea. The Raun Theater and the National Theater were established in the 1970s to bring traditional Papua New Guinean culture to the stage. The Raun Theater troupe performs traditional legends and stories, usually by local authors and playwrights. The stories deal with initiation ceremonies, sago-palm harvesting, indigenous practices such as traditional healing and rain making, and social practices such as feasting, courtship, and hunting. The theater troupe performs both domestically and internationally.

In rural areas, dance and dramatic performances are often didactic and accompany healing, feasting, and magical rituals. Often, dances or dramatic performances consist of a variety of different practices, including not just movements and storytelling, but other artistic processes such as oration and singing (thus they were called singsings). For example, tribal chiefs engage in competitive oratory and speeches during competitive feasting events. Notable cultural dances, or sing-sings, include the elaborate and costumed fire dance (also referred to as a snake dance), performed by members of the Baining tribe to celebrate birth, harvest, and initiation. In the dance of the Wigmen of the highlands' Huli culture, decorated wigs of real hair are worn.

Literature

Historically, Papua New Guinea has fostered a predominantly oral rather than written literary tradition. With over 800 documented tribal languages and a loosely defined pidgin language called Tok Pisin (or Melanesian Pidgin), formal literature has been scarce. Instead, tribes have developed oral histories and traditions regarding clan genealogy, initiation rites, funeral chants and speeches, and magic spells. Throughout the 20th century, cultural anthropologists and Papua New Guinean cultural centers have recorded and written down samples of traditional oral history and folklore.

Papua New Guinean folklore is part of a larger body of literature called Melanesian folklore. Melanesian folklore includes stories from Papua New Guinea, Solomon Islands, Vanuatu, and New Caledonia. Common folklore themes or topics in Melanesian folklore include mythology, cargo cults (a magical belief that salvation will come from the arrival of material goods), sexuality, and childhood. Melanesian folklore also contains trickster tales, which are common in indigenous oral traditions and typically feature a clever trickster hero who might embody an entire culture.

Following Papua New Guinea's independence from Australia in 1975, Papua New Guinea's few published writers worked to grow and nurture Papua New Guinean literature. In addition, the Bureau of Literature, Department of Information and Extension Services began publishing collections of stories of village life or retelling of folktales. The bureau also holds writing classes and sponsors literary competitions and visiting writers.

CULTURE

Arts & Entertainment

The role of the arts reflects the country's modern culture, historic traditions, collective experience, and social consciousness. After independence, the people of Papua New Guinea have actively used the arts to build their post-colonial national identity and culture.

A wide variety of traditional arts and crafts are practiced by the diverse cultural groups throughout the country. Unique cooking pots and bowls, along with intricate shields, spirit masks, and bright clothing are all produced by the country's indigenous groups. Wood carving and basket weaving are also practiced.

The literary and musical traditions in Papua New Guinea are kept alive by oral storytelling and elaborate religious rituals. The traditional Papua New Guinean celebration known as "sing sing," which combines music, dance, elaborate costumes, feasting, and drama, is an important part of the country's cultural life.

British and Australian influences have made rugby and football (soccer) the most popular sports among Papua New Guineans.

Cultural Sites & Landmarks

In 2008, the United Nations Educational, Scientific and Cultural Organization (UNESCO) recognized the Kuk Early Agricultural Site as a cultural World Heritage Site. It is a protected area of 116 hectares (286 acres) of swamp in western New Guinea. Archaeological excavation has shown that the ancient site has been inhabited by humans for nearly 10,000 years. The Kuk Early Agricultural Site represents and illustrates the transition that humans in the area made from plant gathering to agrarian efforts, such as farming bananas, taro, and yam. It contains evidence of cultivation mounds, drainage ditches, and wooden farming tools, and also shows changes in agricultural practices over time.

Papua New Guinea is also renowned for its undeveloped, diverse terrain and for abundant tribal cultures. UNESCO is considering many of these culturally and environmentally important sites for inclusion on the World Heritage List. These include the Kikori River Basin and the Great Papuan Plateau, which covers 6 percent of the nation's landmass, and the rugged Kokoda Track (also known as the Kokoda Trail) and Owen Stanley Ranges. Both of these are proposed as mixed sites distinguished for their biodiversity and geographical importance, as well as for their cultural landscapes. The latter was the site of a famous World War II battle between the Australians and the Japanese in 1942. Other proposed sites include the Milne Bay Seascape, which incorporates uninhabited coral atolls and islands; the Sublime Karsts of Papua

New Guinea, which feature distinct landscapes and sparse human activity; and the Upper Sepik River Basin, recognized for its diverse habitats and tribal cultures.

Port Moresby is home to the National Museum and Art Gallery, which features one of the world's most renowned collections of indigenous art, as well as extensive anthropological, archeological, and natural science exhibits. The National Museum encompasses the Department of Modern History Museum, which is dedicated to 20th-century events in Papua New Guinea. The museum also features significant collections of World War II and other military artifacts. It also contains an extensive photography collection documenting the islands' wartime experience. The Port Moresby (Bomana) War Cemetery also reflects the toll of the war on the island, as it contains the remains of nearly 4,000 British Commonwealth fighters who were casualties of the Allied effort to defend the territory from Japanese invasion.

In addition, the Port Moresby's National Botanical Gardens houses one of the world's largest orchid collections. Originally affiliated with the adjoining University of Papua New Guinea, the gardens contain a wide sampling of tropical vegetation indigenous to the region. Other attractions in the capital include the National Parliament building, which combines elements of traditional design within a modern architectural framework. It was built in 1984 in the style of a traditional haus tambaran or "spirit house" (an ancestral place of worship). In small villages, the spirit house is an elaborately decorated ceremonial structure around which tribal life revolves.

Libraries & Museums

The Papua New Guinea National Museum and Art Gallery is comprised of three different museums, including the main museum in Waigani, the War Museum (also called Modern History premises) in Gordons, and the JK McCarthy Museum in Goroka. The museum houses anthropological and archaeological collections, war artifacts, and contemporary art pieces. The War Museum,

which was established in 1978, houses a notable collection of war relics from World War II. The J.K. McCarthy Museum houses six galleries of artifacts and specimens from the Highlands of Papua New Guinea, including wooden bowls, stone mortars, blades, ceremonial objects, and talismans.

The National Library of Papua New Guinea was founded in 1978 and is located in the capital of Port Moresby. Five years prior, in 1973, the Papua New Guinea Library Association was founded.

Holidays

In addition to most major Christian holidays, Papua New Guineans celebrate their independence from Australia on Independence Day (September 16). As a former British colony and member of the Commonwealth of Nations, Papua New Guinea also observes the birthday of the reigning British monarch.

Youth Culture

A large discrepancy has developed between urban and rural youth in Papua New Guinean society. Young people living in urban areas experience very different lives than their counterparts in traditional communities. Urban youth tend to socialize within traditional wantok (referring to language or tribal) groupings, and youth gangs have become a growing problem in urban areas. These urban gangs, called raskols, compete for territory and members. As a result, youth and gang violence have quickly become part of a larger urban culture of lawlessness.

The culture of rural youth, who mostly live in traditional villages, continues to be characterized by adherence to rooted customs such as gender-based chores and expectations, including initiation rituals. Generally, early 21st-century trends among the country's youth population include Western pop music and clothes with company logos. Popular sports include rugby, football (soccer), cricket, softball, and basketball.

Education in PNG is generally non-compulsory between the ages of six and fifteen. School attendance continues to be a challenge in the 21st century. It was estimated in 2012 that enrollment in primary school was at 60 percent, 63 percent among men and 57 percent among women. Many parents pull their children from school due to poverty and child labor. Numerous organizations, such as the International Red Cross and London's Commonwealth Youth Program, are working to increase educational and social opportunities for Papua New Guinea's youth.

SOCIETY

Transportation

Locals travel on land throughout the country on personal transport vehicles such as a bus, flatbed truck, or pickup truck. Taxis are common in urban areas such as Port Moresby. Traffic moves on the left-hand side of the road.

The main ports and terminals are located in Kimbe, Lae, Madang, Rabau, and Wewak. Boat travel and connections between islands are extensive. However, transport boats and ferries between islands rarely have sufficient life preservers or lifeboats for emergencies.

Transportation Infrastructure

Travel in Papua New Guinea is slow and limited. The large majority of runways and roads are unpaved. In 2011, Papua New Guinea had an estimated 11,000 kilometers (6,835 miles) of waterways, and 9,349 kilometers (5,809 miles) of roadway—with the Highlands Highway (Okuk Highway) being the main highway. There are 561 airports (540 of which are unpaved), and the country's international airports are in Port Moresby and Lae; the country's national airline is Air Niugini.

Media & Communications

Media and communications outlets and infrastructure are challenged by the island geography and mountainous terrain, as well as the existence of approximately 850 different ethnicities and languages. Radio remains the dominant medium, and there is a state-run national radio station, as well as provincial stations. Television

is also becoming increasingly popular, despite limited coverage areas, and includes the state-run National Television Service. There are fifty-six radio stations (1998) and three television broadcast stations. The constitution protects freedom of speech and press. While media outlets are able to express a wide variety of opinions and perspectives, newspaper editors have reported incidents in which government officials have tried to sway coverage through intimidation. The two daily newspapers are *The National* and *Post-Courier*, both of which are foreign-owned.

International assessment of Papua New Guinea's communications system is that the services and access are limited and minimal. The state-owned Telikom PNG Limited is the national telecom provider. As of 2014, only 2 percent of the population used landline telephones, and Telikom PNG expects the nation to have full access to telecommunication services by 2020. As of that same year, it was estimated that roughly half of Papua New Guineans have cell phones; there were also an estimated 164,500 Internet users, representing 2.5 percent of the population.

SOCIAL DEVELOPMENT

Standard of Living

In 2013, Papua New Guinea was ranked 157th out of 187 countries on the United Nations Human Development Index, which measures quality of life indicators. In 2015, life expectancy is approximately sixty-seven years—69.3 for females and 64.8 for males.

Water Consumption

Water supply and sanitation in urban areas is overseen by the PNG Waterboard. However, approximately 87 percent of the population resides in rural areas, and, only 33 percent of the rural population has access to improved drinking water sources. Further, only 13 percent have access to improved sanitation services. Overall, only 40 percent of the PNG population has access to improved water, and only 19 percent have access to improved sanitation services. More often, the primary source of drinking water in rural areas remains rainwater or other natural sources such as water drawn from shallow wells or taken from creeks and rivers.

Education

Free and compulsory primary education in Papua New Guinea starts at age seven and lasts for six years. Secondary education is available for most students. Education is administered by the government, with the help of Christian missionaries who have been operating schools in the region since the 19th century. Higher educational institutions include the University of Papua New Guinea, founded in 1965 and located in the capital, and the University of Technology at Lae. The adult literacy rate is 64.2 percent.

Papua New Guinea has been working with foreign governments and NGOs to help improve the country's educational system. It was estimated in 2012 that enrollment in primary school was at 60 percent, 63 percent among men and 57 percent among women. Aside from financing, a lack of qualified teachers and adequate classrooms remains a significant issue.

Nonetheless, PNG has made some strides in improving enrollment and the overall educational system in recent years. For example, according to the Australian government, the school completion rate for enrolled children up through the eighth grade was 56 percent in 2009, up from 45 percent in 2007. In addition, the net enrollment rate for basic education in 2009 was 63 percent, up from 52 percent in 2007.

Women's Rights

Despite equality under the law, women face gross inequalities in Papua New Guinea. In rural areas, tribal customs allow for women to be treated significantly different than men. For example, village or tribal courts that find women guilty of adultery tend to send women to jail, while men found guilty of adultery often receive little censure or punishment. Social custom also allows for women to be purchased as brides, and in some instances, tribes or clans will exchange or

offer women to resolve disputes or debts. Women are also more likely than men to be illiterate, uneducated, and unemployed, and are traditionally depended upon for domestic responsibilities. In urban areas, a woman may employ a member of her extended family so that she can work outside of the home.

Social problems faced by Papua New Guinean women include violence, prostitution, and sexual harassment. Violence against women is an ongoing concern, and domestic and sexual abuse and police misconduct toward women is increasing in urban areas. This is exacerbated by the fact that women tend to under-report incidents of abuse. In villages and certain rural areas, traditional values tend to limit domestic abuse and violence against women. However, village custom dictates that the crime of rape should be settled through material compensation rather than criminal punishment. In addition, the majority of women in the nation's prisons are incarcerated for the crime of physically attacking or murdering another woman. Prostitution is illegal but very common, and sexual harassment continues to be a serious problem that prevents women from reaching high levels of education or employment.

The role and treatment of women in Papua New Guinea's society, culture, and political life is slowly changing because of the work of international women's rights organizations, as well as social and economic changes. Organizations actively working to improve women's rights in Papua New Guinea include the Australian International Development Assistance Bureau (AIDAB), the United Nations Development Program (UNDP), the International Red Cross, and the ADB, which is working to undertake a gender assessment on which to base development programs and education campaigns. These organizations work to provide women with small business loans, educational opportunities, local political knowledge, and family planning education. Women's rights organizations also encourage women to engage in social change. The Ministry of Community Development is the government agency directly responsible for gender equality issues affecting women.

Health Care

Quality health care continues to be scarce in rural areas of Papua New Guinea. Only one-third of the population has access to improved drinking water, and the immunization rate is very low. Diseases such as typhoid, diarrhea, whooping cough, measles, malaria, and tuberculosis are prevalent. The infant mortality is high, at 38.55 deaths per 1,000 live births (2015). The government is committing money to improve health care, especially in more isolated areas.

GOVERNMENT

Structure

Today, Papua New Guinea is a constitutional monarchy. The chief of state is the British monarch, represented in the country by a governor-general. The prime minister, usually the leader of the majority party, is the head of the government. Officials of the cabinet, or National Executive Council, are appointed by the governor-general.

The unicameral National Parliament is the country's legislature. Its 111 members are elected to five-year terms. For administrative purposes, the country is divided into a national capital district, nineteen provinces, and one autonomous region.

Papua New Guinea is a member of the Commonwealth of Nations, the United Nations, the World Bank, the Asian Development Bank, the Non-Aligned Movement (NAM), and occupies an observer position in the Association of South East Asian Nations (ASEAN).

Political Parties

Papua New Guinea has a large number of political parties, and the Papua New Guinean government is traditionally ruled by coalitions of two or more parties that unite to form a majority coalition. Following the general elections of 2012, not one party won even one quarter of the seats and only two parties won over 10 seats. Sixteen seats went to independents. The People's National Congress Party gained the most seats—twenty-seven—and the Triumph Heritage Empowerment Party won the second most, twelve.

Other major parties represented in Parliament include the Papua New Guinea Party, the National Alliance Party, the United Resources Party the People's Action Party, the People's Democratic Movement, and the United Resources Party.

Local Government

Aside from the national level, governance on PNG occurs at both the provincial and local level. Overall, there are nineteen provinces and ninety-one districts (as well as the capital area of Port Moresby). Further subdivided, there are 26 urban local-level governments, called LLGs, and 300 rural local-level governments, made up of councilors. The head of a LLG is either state-appointed or elected by the councilors. Matters of local governance are overseen by the minister of provincial and local government affairs.

Judicial System

The highest court in Papua New Guinea is the Supreme Court, which sits five judges. Below the Supreme Court is the National Court, which hears civil and criminal cases, can interpret the constitution, and otherwise has unlimited jurisdiction. Other established courts include district and local-level courts, military and taxation courts, land courts, and traffic courts, among other lower level courts. PNG's judicial or legal system is based on English common law.

Taxation

The Papua New Guinean government levies personal income and corporate taxes at high rates; the top income tax is 42 percent. Additional taxes include a value-added tax (VAT), interest tax, and excise taxes.

Armed Forces

The Papua New Guinea Defence Force (PNGDF) is made up of a land force, a small air operations force, and a small maritime force. The armed forces have received significant training and assistance from Western nations such as Australia, New Zealand, and the United States. Core services of the PNGDF include border security, maritime responsiveness, maintaining public order, nation-building, and disaster relief.

Foreign Policy

Papua New Guinea's relations with other nations, especially neighboring countries in the Pacific, tend to be positive. It tends to maintain moderate positions on most international issues and is the recipient of extensive bilateral and multilateral foreign aid. Notable nations and organizations involved in developmental aid programs with PNG include Australia, Japan, the United States, and the People's Republic of China, as well as the European Union (EU), the United Nations (UN), the Asian Development Bank (ADB), the International Monetary Fund (IMF), and the World Bank. As of 2015, the country maintains diplomatic relations with fifty-six countries, and holds membership in the Asia-Pacific Economic Cooperation (APEC) forum, the ASEAN Regional Forum (ARF), the Secretariat of the Pacific Community (SPC), and the South Pacific Regional Environmental Program (SPREP), among other prominent foreign institutions.

Australia is a significant bilateral provider of economic aid to PNG. For example, Australia donates an estimated $332 million (USD) annually to support project development. Australia and PNG also established the Enhanced Cooperation Program (ECP) in 2004 to facilitate Australia's efforts to contribute law enforcement officials to PNG's national police force. The ECP was developed as a means of addressing the growing urban violence and lawlessness. Other neighboring countries, such as New Zealand, are also committed to helping address growing problems of corruption, lawlessness, and land rights issues. The United States is also considered a vital developmental partner, and U.S. investment focuses on healthcare and educational aid, including HIV/AIDS training programs and school building projects. The United States also contributes to environmental protection efforts and the development of the national police force.

Papua New Guinea has ongoing international disputes with Indonesia over illegal immigrants, smuggling, and narcotics. It has also been the target of international censure over the government's inaction regarding human trafficking. The country remains one of the main destinations for Filipino, Thai, and Chinese women and children who have been forcibly enslaved as prostitutes and servants.

Human Rights Profile

International human rights law insists that states respect civil and political rights, and promote an individual's economic, social, and cultural rights. The United Nations Universal Declaration on Human Rights (UDHR) is recognized as the standard for international human rights. Its authors sought the counsel of the world's great thinkers, philosophers, and religious leaders, and were careful to create a document that reflects the core values shared by every world culture. (To read this document or view the articles relating to cultural human rights, visit http://www.udhr.org/UDHR/default.htm.).

PNG has an overall positive human rights record. However, areas of human rights abuses do exist, and include government corruption, excessive police force, and tribal violence. Freedom of religion is protected, but religious education, with a distinct Christian focus, is taught in public schools, and non-Christian students may be excused from class but are not offered any equivalent religious instruction. Media outlets are able to express a wide variety of opinions and perspectives. However, newspaper editors have reported incidents in which government officials have tried to sway coverage through intimidation. Other infringements included poor prison conditions and the violation of privacy rights.

Discrimination against women and minorities remains a huge concern in PNG. For example, social custom, rather than constitutional law, often shapes family rights, and marriages are often arranged without the bride's consent. Polygamy is legal, and divorce, though legalized, is discouraged, and marriages frequently end through suicide or desertion. Homosexuality is criminalized, and despite constitutional protections, children, people with disabilities, and members of certain tribes and clans consistently face legal and social discrimination.

ECONOMY

Overview of the Economy

In 2014, the gross domestic product (GDP) per capita was estimated at $2,400 (USD), with approximately 37 percent of the population living below the poverty line.

The economy relies on exports of copper, gold, and oil, as well as agricultural products such as coffee and tea. Gold, copper and oil comprise two-thirds of the export earnings. Approximately 85 percent of the population practices subsistence agriculture, and the agriculture sector makes up an estimated 26.3 percent of the GDP.

With its seaport and international airport, Port Moresby is the country's major point of transit for the exports produced by the surrounding area's dairy farms, rubber plantations, and livestock ranches. Coffee, plywood, timber, and gold are other important exports that pass through the city.

Industry

Mining is Papua New Guinea's main industry. Other important industries include tourism, and the processing of food (especially coconuts) and wood products.

Port Moresby's industrial base consists primarily of sawmilling operations, breweries, concrete factories, and plants for the manufacture of handicrafts as well as the processing of tobacco and food items. The capital is also home to the nation's first petroleum refinery.

Labor

According to the CIA Factbook, the workforce of Papua New Guinea was estimated at 4.171 million in 2014. Approximately 85 percent of the labor force works in the agricultural sector.

Energy/Power/Natural Resources

Papua New Guinea is rich in mineral resources. Development of the country's oil and natural gas reserves is still in the early stages, but this sector is predicted to become a large part of the economy. The Panguna Copper Mine on Bougainville Island is the largest copper mine in the World, and the Porgera Gold Mine in Enga Province is the largest outside of South Africa. However, the country also faces environmental problems due to toxic dumping from mining activity.

Fishing

Port Moresby's natural harbor and its proximity to rich fishing grounds have made the fishing industry a key component of both the local and national economy. The trade in tuna, much of it destined for Japanese markets, is the mainstay of commercial fishing operations, and the harvesting of shrimp also generates significant income.

Forestry

About 63.1 percent of the land is forested. Tropical timber provides a valuable export item, and the primary forestry products are raw logs, veneer sheets, plywood, woodchips, and processed or sawn timber, the majority of which are exported. However, the processing of tropical timber in PNG comes at the expense of the country's dense rainforests; it is estimated that between 1972 and 2002, nearly one quarter of rainforests in PNG were degraded or destroyed through logging operations. According to more recent satellite photos depicting deforestation in PNG, it is estimated that the country could lose half of its trees by 2021 without the implementation of sustainable forestry or conservation.

Mining/Metals

Papua New Guinea possesses a wealth of mineral resources, but the mountainous terrain makes robust extraction difficult. Nevertheless, the Panguna Copper Mine produces 2 percent of the World's copper. Recent discoveries of oil and natural gas reserves in the Gulf of Papua have spurred development in the mining industry.

Agriculture

Subsistence farming provides a living for 85 percent of the population. Less than 3 percent of the land is arable, and most of the soil is of poor quality; slash-and-burn agriculture has contributed to the lack of good farmland. The government is trying to educate farmers in the use of modern methods, including fertilizers and crop rotation.

Most Papua New Guinean farmers grow yams, sweet potatoes, sugarcane and pineapple. Because yams can be stored for long periods, they are an important crop for the small farmer. Commercial crops, which have become more important in recent years, include coffee, tea, bananas, coconuts, cassava, and cocoa. There are also rubber plantations in the south of the country.

Tourism

Because Papua New Guinea lacks extensive transportation, communication, and other necessary infrastructure, tourism has not been a large part of the country's economy. Political unrest and high crime rates, particularly in Port Moresby, have kept many tourists away.

However, tourism is increasing rapidly. The warm waters and coral reef surrounding the island make Papua New Guinea an ideal destination for divers; World War II-era wreckage may also be viewed in the waters off the country's coast. Outdoor enthusiasts also enjoy whitewater rafting and hiking along the Kokoda Track.

Papua New Guinea is served by international airports in Port Moresby and Lae; the country's national airline is Air Niugini. In 2013, an estimated 174,000 non-residents visited Papua New Guinea, more than double the 2006 total.

Simone Isadora Flynn, Roberta Baxter

DO YOU KNOW?

- Portuguese explorer Jorge de Meneses was the first Western explorer to reach Papua New Guinea in 1526.

- The Panguna Copper Mine is twice as wide as San Francisco's Golden Gate Bridge.

- In the centuries predating the arrival of Europeans in the Port Moresby area, Port Moresby's arid climate and poor soil prevented the local Motu people from raising sufficient crops. As a result, the Motu became expert sailors, who bartered clay pots and other implements for food grown by the villages with which they traded. The Motu canoe fleets, called hiri, were commonly manned by several hundred men. As many as 20,000 clay pots might be traded in the course of a single trading expedition.

Bibliography

Salak, Kira. *Four Corners: One Woman's Solo Journey into the Heart of Papua New Guinea.* Washington, DC: Counterpoint, 2001.

Smith, Michael French. *Village on the Edge: Changing Times in Papua New Guinea.* Honolulu: University of Hawaii Press, 2002.

St. Louis, Regis, et al. *Papua New Guinea.* Oakland, CA: Lonely Planet, 2012.

Telban, Borut. *Dancing through Time: A Sepik Cosmology.* New York: Oxford University Press, 2004.

Waiko, John Dademo. *A Short History of Papua New Guinea.* New York: Oxford University Press, 2014.

West, Paige. *Conservation Is Our Government: The Politics of Ecology in Papua New Guinea.* Durham, NC: Duke University Press, 2006.

Works Cited

Allen, Bryan. "Papua New Guinea National Census 2011." *Australian National University.* http://ips.

cap.anu.edu.au/sites/default/files/IB-2014–44-Allen-ONLINE.pdf.

"Background Notes: Papua New Guinea." *U.S. Department of State*. http://www.state.gov/r/pa/ei/bgn/2797.htm.

Brinkhoff, Thomas. "Papua New Guinea: City Population." http://www.citypopulation.de/PapuaNewGuinea.html.

"Culture of Papua New Guinea." *Countries and Their Cultures*. http://www.everyculture.com/No-Sa/Papua-New-Guinea.html.

"Death: The Last Taboo." *Australian Museum Online*. http://www.deathonline.net/remembering/mourning/oro.cfm.

"Etiquette in Papua New Guinea." *Travel Etiquette*. http://www.traveletiquette.co.uk/PapuaNewGuineaEtiquette.html.

"Human Development Reports: Papua New Guinea." *United Nations Development Programme*. http://hdr.undp.org/en/countries/profiles/PNG.

"International tourism, number of arrivals." *World Bank*. http://data.worldbank.org/indicator/ST.INT.ARVL?page=1.

"Music Archive for Papua New Guinea." *Southern Cross University* (n.d.). http://www.scu.edu.au/schools/sass/music/musicarchive/PNGArchive.html.

"Nationalism and Papua New Guinea Writing." *Australian Quarterly* 43.2 (1971).

"Papua New Guinea." *CIA World Fact Book*. https://www.cia.gov/library/publications/the-world-factbook/print/pp.html.

"Papua New Guinea." *Encyclopedia of the Nations*. http://www.nationsencyclopedia.com/Asia-and-Oceania/Papua-New-Guinea.html.

"Papua New Guinea." *UN Data*. http://data.un.org/CountryProfile.aspx?crName=Papua%20New%20Guinea.

"Papua New Guinea." *UNESCO World Heritage List*. http://whc.unesco.org/en/statesparties/pg.

"Papua New Guinea." *Women's Organizations*. http://www.distel.ca/womlist/countries/papuanewguinea.html.

"Papua New Guinea." *World Atlas*. http://www.worldatlas.com/webimage/countrys/oceania/pg.htm.

"Papua New Guinea." *Culture Crossing*. http://www.culturecrossing.net/basics_business_student.php?id=160.

"Papua New Guinea: Country Reports on Human Rights Practices." *U.S. Department of State*. http://www.state.gov/g/drl/rls/hrrpt/2006/78787.htm.

"Papua New Guinea." *World Directory of Minorities* (n.d.). http://www.faqs.org/minorities/Oceania/Papua-New-Guinea.html

"Papua New Guinea Artists." *National Geographic Music*. http://worldmusic.nationalgeographic.com/worldmusic/view/page.basic/country/content.country/papua_new_guinea_854.

"Papua New Guinea Index." *International Constitutional Law*. http://www.servat.unibe.ch/law/icl/pp__indx.html.

"Papua New Guinea (PNG) National Museum." *Pacific Wrecks*. http://www.pacificwrecks.com/restore/png/museum.html.

"Papua New Guinea." *UNICEF*. http://www.unicef.org/infobycountry/papuang_statistics.html#117.

Rubin, Don and Ghassan Maleh. "The world encyclopedia of contemporary theatre." London: *Taylor & Francis*, 1999.

Shelly, Louise, ed. "Papua New Guinea Cookbook." *Wewak: Port Moresby Community Development Group, Inc. and Wirui Press*, 1976.

Slone, Thomas. "An annotated bibliography of Melanesian Folklore." http://members.tripod.com/~THSlone/PNGFB.html.

Ceremonial tanoa (bowl) and fue (fly-whisk) from Samoa. iSock/samoankiwi

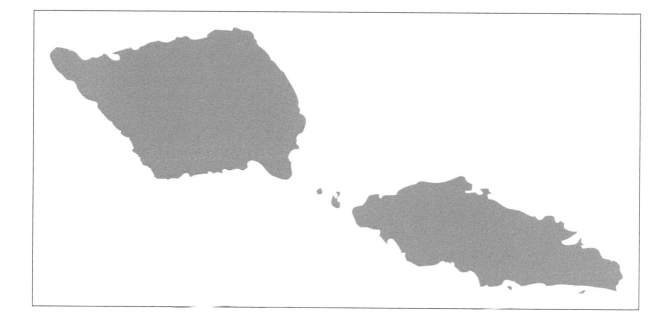

SAMOA

Introduction

Samoa, previously named Western Samoa and sometimes referred to as Independent Samoa, is one of the smallest countries in the world. It is a nation built on ten small islands located in the South Pacific, near New Zealand and Australia. It is part of the continental grouping of Oceania. Samoa is a separate nation from American Samoa, a U.S. territory made up of several small islands to the east of Samoa. The people of Samoa, called Samoans, form a community of self-sufficient farmers.

Samoa is a polite society steeped in tradition and hierarchy. Even when tensions and conflict arise, Samoans will use traditional rituals and customs to resolve matters. Tattooing is an important ritualized custom in Samoan culture that involves full community participation. Tattoo artistry is a highly revered skill, and intricate distinctive designs are created for men and women.

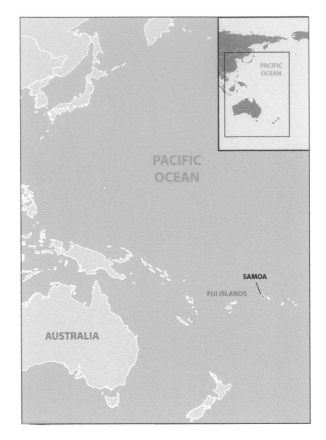

GENERAL INFORMATION

Official Language: Samoan and English
Population: 197,773 (2015 estimate)
Currency: Samoan tala
Coins: The Samoan tala is divided into 100 sene. Coins are available in denominations of 1, 2, 5, 10, 20 and 50 sene, and 1 tala.
Land Area: 2,821 square kilometers (1089 square miles)
Water Area: 10 square kilometers (3.86 square miles)

National Motto: "Fa'avae i le Atua Samoa" ("Samoa is founded on God")
National Anthem: "The Banner of Freedom"
Capital: Apia
Time Zone: GMT -11
Flag Description: The flag of Samoa consists of a red background or field with a blue canton (rectangle) in the upper hoist (left-hand) side. The Southern Cross constellation, made up of five white stars—four large, one small—sits in the canton. The traditional colors of red, blue, and white symbolize loyalty or courage, patriotism or freedom, and purity, respectively.

Population

Samoa has the largest Polynesian population of any country. Over 92 percent of the population in Samoa is of full Polynesian heritage. Roughly, 7 percent of the island's inhabitants are Euronesian, meaning that they are of Polynesian and European descent. The remaining minority of the population is mostly European.

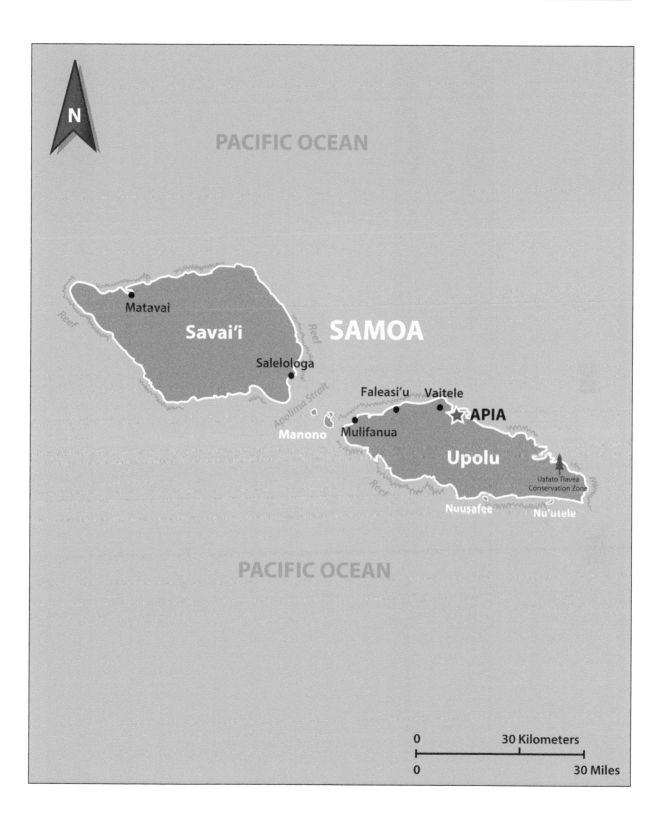

Principal Cities by Population (2011):

- Apia (36,735)
- Vaitele (7,182)
- Faleasi'u (3,745)
- Vailele (3,647)
- Le'auva'a (3,168)

The European population in Samoa is mainly the result of Germany's occupation of the islands during the First World War, and New Zealand's guardianship over the islands in the years before Samoa gained independence in 1962. The capital of Apia is home to more minorities, including a large Chinese population, and is Samoa's only urban city. The Tuamasaga district, which covers the central portion of the island of Upolu and includes the capital, is the most populous district at 89,582 (2011). The largest island of Samoa, Savai'i, has an estimated population of 47,948 (2011).

The people of Samoa live in villages throughout the islands. Samoan society is based on the importance of family and agriculture. In a system that is separate from the national government, Polynesians use community councils to direct local affairs.

In 2015, the islands' population growth rate was estimated at of 0.58 percent. The urban population accounts for 19.1 percent of Samoa's total population, with an urbanization rate of -0.24%.

Languages

Although English and Samoan are both considered official languages, Samoan is the designated national language of the islands. Samoan is predominantly spoken, but most Polynesians know some English and use it primarily in business, when trading with New Zealand and Australia, for example.

Native People & Ethnic Groups

Samoa has a large Polynesian population—an estimated 92.6 percent—with small minorities of both Euronesians (7 percent) and Europeans (less than 1 percent). Although Samoa has been inhabited and controlled by many groups of people, the predominant Polynesian culture has existed there for nearly 2,000 years. It is believed that the original inhabitants came from western territories, and settled on the island of Upolu. It is difficult to know the cultural habits of the original people because the Christian missionaries who later came to the islands have had such a strong influence on Polynesian lifestyle.

Religions

Nearly every person in Samoa is Christian. Several denominations of Christianity are represented, the largest being Protestant Congregational (about 31.8 percent), Roman Catholic (about 19.4 percent), Methodist (about 13.7 percent), and Mormon, or Latter Day Saints (about 15.2 percent). Other represented denominations include Seventh-Day Adventist and Assembly of God. Christianity has had an enormous impact on the islands' culture, which was previously based on the worship of many gods. Many traditional religious elements remain, but some traditional Polynesian practices were forbidden by the missionaries who brought Christianity to the region.

Climate

Because of Samoa's tropical climate, the islands experience hot weather year-round. The average temperature is about 26° Celsius (79° Fahrenheit). Rather than cold and warm seasons, there is a wet season during which there is substantial rainfall, and a dry season that lasts for the majority of the year.

Due to its location, mountainous terrain, and extensive coastline, Samoa is constantly threatened by major storms. These windy storms are usually tropical cyclones that have killed many people and caused a good deal of destruction throughout the islands.

ENVIRONMENT & GEOGRAPHY

Topography

Samoa's area covers ten volcanic islands. Therefore, the terrain is mountainous and covered with high slopes and ridges that extend to the shores.

The majority of the country is divided between the two main islands, Savai'i and Upolu, which were formed by volcanic eruptions. The remaining area is spread across the eight smaller islands, but only two of these, Manono and Apolima, are inhabited. Samoa's highest point is Mount Silisili on the island of Savai'i. Silisili reaches a height of 1,866 meters (6,122 feet) at its peak.

Plants & Animals

Samoa has a tropical climate, and is therefore home to a large number of plant and animal species. Palm trees are found along the shore, while the mountains are surrounded by rainforest areas. Dozens of species of birds surround the islands, in addition to flying foxes, skinks, porpoises, dolphins, and lizards. Land and sea turtles are found along the shores, and over 900 species of fish contribute substantially to Samoa's agricultural economy.

On the land, the rainforest is home to nearly seventy-five species of tropical vegetation, many of which are used as herbal remedies and medicines. Researchers around the world work with Samoan vegetation in the search for new medicines. The surrounding Pacific Ocean contains numerous varieties of coral reefs.

CUSTOMS & COURTESIES

Greetings

Greetings in Samoan culture customarily depend on social status, setting, and whether or not a formal or informal activity is involved. "Talofa" ("Hello") is a greeting that occurs when people have never met before, or if they have not seen each other for a long period. The greeting is often heard when locals interact with foreigners, and is rarely heard in a village where residents interact on a regular basis. "Malo" ("Hi") is a colloquial greeting, with the proper response being "Malo lava." Shaking hands during greetings may also be commonplace, a custom that was most likely adopted from Western culture.

Ceremonial greetings are the most complex form of greeting featured in Samoa and a testament to how multifaceted the Samoan language is. This greeting is reserved for a person of high status and can only take place when the various high-ranking adults have sat down in the front area of a house. Ceremonial greetings typically involve two parts: the first involves one person welcoming the other person to the house, and the second involves a polite response. The actual language used in the greeting depends on the people involved and the situation.

Gestures & Etiquette

Interactions in Samoa reflect the country's intricate traditional values, and are influenced by differences in status. During a ceremonial greeting, there is generally no eye contact between any of the individuals involved in order to preserve and show disparities in rank. A ceremonial greeting may be completed in its entirety without any eye contact. Instead, all the members involved in the greeting will generally concentrate on an area of the room that is markedly different from the location of the party they are addressing.

The clothing of Samoa indicates an understanding of modesty that diverges greatly from that of the Western world. The lavalava (or lava-lava) is an essential item in the Samoan wardrobe. It is a large, single piece of cloth that is used by both men and women, who wrap it around themselves like a skirt. Most Samoans prefer brightly-colored attire, and will wear shirts and blouses with floral designs on top. During official occasions and more formal events, men will wear a darker lavalava constructed from the same material as a Western suit. Men will usually combine this with a button-up shirt, tie, and formal suit coat. For women, formal events usually entail wearing a puletasi, a type of two-piece, long dress popularized by Christian missionaries.

Understanding Samoan concepts of modesty is necessary when following Samoan etiquette. Women who live in more rural settings will often carry out their daily chores shirtless. Other areas of the body must be covered at all times though, and it is considered especially improper if the region between a person's calf and his or her thigh is exposed. Some villages that lead a traditional way of life have forbidden any women from wearing pants. Generally, swimsuits are banned from villages.

Samoa is a polite society steeped in traditions and hierarchy. Even when tensions and conflict arise, Samoans will use traditional rituals and customs to resolve matters. Samoans will avoid violent confrontations when possible, and will try to maintain a peaceful community in even high stress situations. Samoan culture does not tolerate anyone who is prone to angry outbursts in public as it is considered rude and weak behavior. Instead, Samoans are expected to keep their negative emotions to themselves.

Eating/Meals

Samoans eat two or three meals per day. It is rare for Samoans to converse a lot during meals, especially due to etiquette that does not allow hosts to begin a meal until their guests have finished eating. Community is important during mealtimes, and offering other people to share before eating in their presence is considered a sign of good manners. Although guests do not have to finish everything on their plates to show respect, it is courteous to taste everything and handle the food with respect. Sunday is an important religious day for the Samoan community, and most traditional Sunday meals are cooked in the umu, a cooking method involving a hearth and heated stones. For many Samoans, prayers are said before each meal.

For Samoans, kava is an important ritualized drink that is presented to special guests. It is traditionally drunk at the beginning of village meetings and important ceremonies. Kava is made out of the roots of a pepper plant that have been ground up. The concoction has a soothing effect. When a person receives kava, a few drops of the drink are dripped on the ground while the words "ia manuia" ("Let there be blessings") are spoken. This act symbolizes restoring the earth with the kindness embodied in the kava.

Modern Samoans, especially in urban areas, have adopted a more Western-influenced diet, giving up the daily intake of fresh fish, taro, and fruits that are traditionally eaten during mealtimes. Medical practitioners have connected this change in diet with a rise in diabetes and obesity.

Visiting

There is a specific protocol that must be followed when receiving guests. Depending on the guest, a family or the village will prepare for the visitor's arrival. Ula (a flower wreath meant to hang around one's neck) is readied, as is food made especially for the occasion. The guest's welcome ceremony can range from informal to highly ritualized, with the tone of the ceremony determined by the guest's rank and the context of the visit.

When entering a Samoan's home, it is considered impolite to walk across a mat inside with shoes. If the other guests are not wearing shoes, they should be removed at the door. If one walks in front of another person, it is proper protocol to bow slightly. While it is generally considered impolite to stand when speaking to a person sitting, it is even more important that a guest receives and accepts whatever his or her Samoan host offers. Even if everyone else is sitting on the floor, the visitor should sit on a chair if it is offered. When guests are seated on the floor, it is expected that they cross their feet and legs, in an effort to prevent their feet from pointing at others.

Gifts are generally warmly received, and a failure to accept a gift can be misconstrued as an insult directed at the gift-giver. Gifts will also be given to people who are considered to have higher status than the giver. Mats and food are frequently offered as gifts, and there is no expectation that a gift should be given in return. In the instance of an orator, who has delivered an impressive welcome speech or greeting, it is considered polite to offer a large cash sum in public to compensate him for his skills. In addition, the majority of families in Samoa are Christian, and many homes will hold an evening vespers service, during which time the family congregates to pray and read the Bible together.

LIFESTYLE

Family

The Samoan concept of family extends far beyond the nuclear family. It is understood that a Samoan will not only be loyal to immediate family, but will also remain equally loyal and supportive of extended family members. A Samoan family, referred to as a Samoan a'iga, involves all the people connected by the same common ancestor. Each village consists of a few a'iga, and the power that each a'iga holds within the village is determined by its size. Every Samoan a'iga will have one or a few matai (chiefs) who govern the family.

Communities are largely regulated by a strong dedication to family life. If an individual does not adhere to village rules and customs, his or her entire family may face punishment and suffer the judgment of the rest of the village. Samoans control their actions and abide by village laws largely due to the fear of shaming their family if they misbehave. If an individual hurts or commits an offense against another person, especially a young woman or an elderly person, then it can be interpreted as a crime against the victim's entire family. In this way, a failure to adhere to village laws affects the whole community.

Housing

Urban areas in Samoa, such as Apia, offer a range of housing options. These include homes modeled after modern Western homes, colonial houses, and traditional Samoan houses. Beyond the urban areas, traditional Samoan architecture is predominant. The traditional Samoan home is a fale, or a hut that is thatched with sugarcane leaves and elevated on stilts. The design of the huts demonstrates a cultural emphasis on community. Fales are open with no walls, and this symbolically and physically shows the community that there are no secrets between families. Samoans sometimes lower coconut palm blinds over the open sides of the fale. The blinds have a dual purpose of creating a sense of privacy during the nighttime, and preventing rain from entering the hut during tropical rainstorms.

Food

Food in Samoa is simple, with little seasoning or spices. Samoans often enjoy their food if it is consumed in a more natural state, the way the ingredients were found in the wild. Meals will often involve fresh fish, meat from local animals, or canned meat. The fish and meat is accompanied by taro root, which is most often boiled, and rice that has been cooked with coconut milk. Although Samoans do not often eat much fruit during mealtimes, cooked green bananas and breadfruit are popular. Breadfruit is a large, round yellow fruit that grows on local trees.

There are several ways that Samoans cook their food. Umu is a traditional cooking hearth with stones placed over a fire pit. After the fire has weakened to the point where it is glowing embers, Samoans will set foods like breadfruit, green bananas, taro, and fish onto the stones. The food is covered with banana palm leaves, where it continues to cook. Another method of cooking is referred to as oka. In preparing oka, a fish is separated into small pieces and is mixed with onions, salt, lemon juice, and coconut cream. The acidity of the lemon slowly cooks the fish, which will sit in this mixture until it is ready to be eaten.

Lu'au is a particularly popular Samoan dish. In lu'au taro is combined with coconut cream and then tied up into taro leaves. This concoction of taro and coconut is then cooked in an umu. After the dish is cooked, the leaves are unwrapped and the baked contents are consumed.

Life's Milestones

For Samoans, adhering to fa'a Samoa, or a traditional Samoan lifestyle, is central to preserving their community. While the older generation enjoys the privileges and respect that come with fa'a Samoa, the younger generation must abide by conventional approaches to courtship before marriage. Even though larger towns tolerate a Western approach to dating, which involves un-chaperoned social interaction, remote and more traditional villages expect their villagers to closely follow Samoan customs.

The traditional courtship process involves a soa (or a go-between), who will impart the young man's interest to the young woman. Societal expectations usually prevent the young man and woman from any physical contact in public, including kissing or holding hands. Instead, the young man is required to court the woman in front of her family members. The courtship process shows respect for the woman's family and eliminates any suspicion of improper activity. The young man should bring presents for the family and food—usually something cooked on the umu, the traditional Samoan cooking hearth.

CULTURAL HISTORY

Art

For Samoans, the art of tattooing is an important, ritualized custom. The pe'a, or full body tattoo, used to be a necessary step in receiving the title of matai, which is traditionally bestowed to the head of an extended family group. It is an intensive and painful procedure that takes weeks to complete. The custom of receiving the pe'a involves more than just one tattooist (known as the tufuga). There are usually up to six helpers or apprentices that aid the tattoo artist by mixing the dye, wiping away the blood, cleaning and sharpening the instruments, and holding the skin tight.

The community also fully participates in the process. For example, young women from the village are employed to calm and distract the person being tattooed. The women will hold down the man's body, massage his head, and entertain him with songs in order to prevent him from focusing on the pain. Samoan culture looks down upon a man who becomes noticeably affected by pain, whether it is by whining or crying out. Such behavior during the tattoo process is seen as less masculine by the rest of the village and risks criticism from elders, peers, and family members.

Tattooing is a highly revered skill in Samoan culture, and the tattoo artist is traditionally well compensated for his services. The tattoo artists must be adept at using a number of tools, including the sausau, a two-foot long mallet used to impress the designs of the tattoo into a person's skin. Some of the combs used include the autapulu, which is a wide comb used to fill in the large areas of solid dye, and the ausogi'aso laititi, which is used to make refined lines. The dye process involves burning lama nuts, which are large, oily seeds taken from the native candle-nut tree. The soot from the burned nuts is later collected and ground using a pestle.

The tattoo process is broken into five sessions. In the first session, the ano le tua (or the height that the tattoo will reach on the man's body) is determined. The tattoo is always designed to show above a man's lavalava – the traditional dress of the Samoan people. A pe'a body tattoo will cover a man's thighs, his lower back, his posterior, his abdomen, and his groin area. Although women also receive tattoos, the ritual for men is much more comprehensive; the designs for the men are much more intense, with sizable regions of solid dye being imprinted into their skin. The tattoo design for women is referred to as malu. It covers the area from a woman's upper thighs to the point directly below her knees. In contrast to the male tattoos, it is lighter and more delicate.

The weaving of fine mats is another art form that is intrinsic to daily life in Samoa. Weaving is a traditionally feminine skill passed down from generation to generation. Many of the mats use plant fibers from the leaves of the common coconut tree and pandanus plants. Between the two, mats produced from the pandanus are considered finer and more valuable. The way that the pandanus is prepared and used to create a mat depends on what type of mat is being made. The finer the mat, the more processing techniques the pandanus will have to undergo.

'Ie toga is believed to represent the highest standard of mats. In Samoa, mats have been traditionally viewed as a bartering tool, in the same way that currency is used, and the 'ie toga is considered the most valuable item in a Samoan exchange. The process preparing the pandanus plant for 'ie toga is particularly complex. First, the spines of the pandanus must be removed, and then the leaves are sectioned into separate batches, which are boiled in water for five to ten minutes. After the boiling process is complete, the dull underside of each leaf is removed from the shiny, top layer and thrown away. The remaining part of the leaves is then attached to sticks and tied together into small bunches. These batches of leaves are left in the sea to bleach for three to five days. When the bundles are removed, they have turned a lighter, shinier color. The design of the mat is simple, and is valued for its soft silk-like texture and delicacy.

An 'ie toga can take months or years to finish. Often, one generation may begin the process of weaving a traditional 'ie toga only to have the next generation complete the process. The 'ie toga reflects the value that Samoan culture places on community and a shared sense of history. As an 'ie toga ages and is passed through more hands, it becomes linked to more community events and its inherent worth increases. During marriages, the family of the bride will present 'ie toga to the groom's family. A family's status can be measured in the amount of 'ie toga they own and are able to give to another family. 'Ie toga is also given in instances of ifoga, a ritual in which one individual asks forgiveness from another.

Architecture

The predominant structure of traditional Samoan architecture is the fale, which is the traditional Samoan house. Generally, the fale is an open and oval-shaped thatched hut with a light timber frame, providing protection from the main elements of sun and rain (and to retain cool temperatures inside). The house's beams or rafters are held together by rope, and blinds made from woven palm leaves or fronds are substituted for walls. (As stated previously, the blinds have a dual purpose of creating a sense of privacy during the nighttime, and preventing rain from entering the hut during tropical rainstorms.) Other traditional construction materials include coral gravel and posts made of hardwood. The majority of fales were destroyed after a massive hurricane swept over the island nation in 1964. Reconstruction of houses after the hurricane consisted of cement blocks, representing a significant change in Samoan architecture.

Other traditional structures, or types of fale, include the Fale tele (big house), Afolau (long house), Faleo'o (small house), and Tunoa (cook house). The advent of colonialism brought more modern styles of European architecture, as represented in the colonial buildings in Apia and the island nation's various churches, such as the historic Catholic Church in the village of Safotu.

Drama

Samoan drama or theater can be traced to fiafias, which are traditional Samoan meals or festive occasions accompanied by dancing and singing. (The term, which is used throughout the Pacific region, can be translated as "celebration" or "joy or as "get-together.") In the capital of Apia, these shows are now mostly held for the purposes of tourism, and feature dancing and singing.

Another important aspect of Samoan drama or theater is the act of clowning, or comic theater. Often, comic acts of clowning would occur at special gatherings, such as weddings, or public events, such as fundraising. These can be in the form of comical dances, which are usually improvised. There are also more formalized or scripted performances featuring rehearsed comedic sketches. These may be political in nature, as a means of criticizing government officials. (Because deference for authority is important in Samoan society, these performances were often the only outlet for critical free speech against government.)

Music

Samoa's contact with the Western world has developed and influenced its musical culture since the colonists and missionaries arrived in the 19th century. The country's evolving musical tastes shows how Samoans were able to accept and modify foreign traditions to meet the standards and aesthetics of their own culture. Europeans introduced Samoa to the choirs and church hymns (called pese lotu) in the late 19th century. Choir singing soon became more popular than the traditional form of communal singing that involved songs accompanied by the percussive beat of the fala (a mat that is beaten with sticks). Activity of the United States Marines on Samoa during World War II further encouraged Samoans to embrace Western music. Each generation welcomed the new musical trends coming from overseas, and these trends continued to reach Samoa with increasing speed as radio and other forms of communication were made accessible to the islands. A way that Samoans still utilize foreign music and make it their own is to take a Western song and create a Samoan cover version. This process oftentimes involves creating a more upbeat tempo and a distinct "Samoan" sound, in addition to translating the lyrics into the Samoan language.

American pop music is a major influence in Samoa's musical history and evolution. The frequent migration of citizens between Samoa and Hawai'i led to a cultural exchange, with the 'ukulele and guitar becoming two of the most prevalent instruments. Modern Samoan musicians will often use an electronic keyboard now to simulate the sounds of various instruments and create more progressive versions of classic Samoan songs. There are also traditional Samoan songs that have been modernized in other ways, and some will be remixed in a manner related to Pacific island reggae. Besides remixing, these new interpretations of old songs will often still incorporate some traditional elements, such as through the use of traditional instruments like the pate (a hollow log that creates a distinctive, loud percussive sound).

Hip-hop music has been a useful medium of political expression for Samoans. In 1990, three Samoans established a hip-hop group named The Mau, a name that referred to an early 20th-century political group that advocated for Samoa's independence from German and New Zealand colonialism. The hip-hop group adopted the same motto as the political Mau movement: "Samoa mo Samoa" ("Samoa for Samoans"). The group focused on issues regarding Samoan nationalism, history, and the Samoan diaspora (displaced community) in the United States and fused it with elements of the American Black Power movement. This blend shaped the style of other Samoan hip-hop groups that followed, and many

hip-hop artists now combine Samoan traditions with American influences.

Dance

Music and dance have always been intricately connected to Samoa's traditional way of life. Songs and dances are ways communities can further bond with each other. They are also a means of heralding events, mourning losses, and maintaining a collective history and heritage. Modern Samoa has been plagued with economic difficulties, and tourism has also emerged as a way for Samoans to preserve their cultural and artistic traditions and ensure financial support. For example, the fiafia used to be a theatrical presentation reserved for a village's special occasions. During the fiafia, various groups would compete in a friendly manner through song and dance, progressively trying to outshine the other groups. In modern Samoa, fiafias have been adapted to a hotel environment, which is the place where they are usually performed.

A fiafia will usually involve the siva and sasa – two of the most popular Samoan dances. In the siva dance women softly sway their hands, hips, and feet to convey a story. The sasa dance is named after the Samoan term meaning "slap," and is meant to portray everyday happenings for traditional Samoans. During the sasa dance, both men and women form rows and complete a series of fast-paced movements, slapping areas of their bodies in sync with percussion instruments and themselves. This dance is performed together as a group, with men and women sitting and standing at different points in the dance.

In the past, the Samoan islands have served as a useful liaison, or connecting point in passing on cultural trends. A dance movement that Samoa helped transmit to other countries is known as "popping," a style of hip-hop dance that synchronizes the rhythm of the music with a dancer's movements, and contortions. In this way, New Zealand dancers learned popping styles when they visited Samoa and were exposed to dance techniques that were originally learned in the U.S. Samoans picked up these novel dance techniques when they visited or lived among American-Samoan communities.

Literature

Samoa's literary heritage is rooted in the island nation's oral traditions—the poems, songs, and family genealogies—that were passed down through generations. Many early myths and legends dealt with great journeys over sea as well as creation stories. In one traditional Samoan myth, the god Tagoloa made the islands and created humans from worms. (With the later arrival of Christian missionaries, many Samoan myths, such as creation stories, shifted to reflect a Christian influence.)

Later, as Samoa's written literature developed, Albert Wendt (1939–) emerged as one of the island country's preeminent writers. Wendt is credited with publishing one of the first novels by a Pacific Islander with 1973's *Sons for the Return Home*. He has also authored numerous poems and plays, and won the 1980 New Zealand Wattie Book of the Year Award with *Leaves of the Banyan Tree* (1979), a three-generation epic set in Samoa. Another notable Samoan writer is Sia Figiel (1967–), who won the Commonwealth Writers' Prize for fiction in 1997 for the South East Asia/South Pacific region for the novel *Where We Once Belonged* (1996).

CULTURE

Arts & Entertainment

Entertainment in Samoa is largely based on tradition and religion. Music is an important part of religious practice. Polynesians are particularly known for their singing voices and musical ability. Brass band performances are popular, and are most often performed by Samoa's official police band.

Music is a substantial element of Samoa's most significant artistic performance, the fiafia. The fiafia is a traditional blend of dance, music, and live entertainment that is now an important part of popular culture. Traditional Polynesian dances such as the sa sa, the siva and the taualuga

are included in the fiafia. While dance was once an integral part of the religious practices of the Samoan islands, it was altered and censored by Christian missionaries. Dance is now primarily a form of entertainment, and has been stripped of its religious significance.

Although Polynesian folklore is kept alive by the oral tradition in Samoa, there is a strong interest in written literature. Because of the high literacy rate and the proliferation of the arts, Polynesian literature is widely read. One of Samoa's most famous inhabitants was the Scottish author Robert Louis Stevenson (1850–1894), whose works are celebrated on the islands.

Cultural Sites & Landmarks

A strong devotion to fa'a Samoa (the Samoan way of life) regulates how Samoans interact with their surroundings. The Uafato Tiavea conservation zone is considered evidence of how Samoa's traditional indigenous lifestyle and lush landscape live in harmony. The area contains marine wildlife, untouched coral reefs, and rare flora and fauna that are not found in more developed regions of the country. As the largest rainforest in the Pacific, the conservation zone features a diverse range of animal species, in addition to the unspoiled scenery. The area's topography has inspired a number of myths that explain how certain geographical features came into existence. Such stories connect the people with the landscape, and are necessary in understanding the local culture. For example, the legend of Fatutoama explains the location of a series of large stones. Fatutoama's story relates her husband's failure to share a shark that he had caught with the rest of his family. His entire family ultimately faces the consequences of his actions; his wife and children turn into stones and he turns into a coral reef.

Fagaloa-Uafato is located within the conservation zone's boundaries and, according to excavations, is one of the oldest human settlements in Samoa. Research shows that clay from the area was used in the creation of a special type of pottery, referred to as Lapita pottery. Communities that live in the area continue traditional modes of conservation in order to care for the surrounding forests and ocean. Some protective measures include, limiting hunting and contact with the natural resources, and prohibiting the use of poisons or pesticides on the plants and wildlife.

Savai'i is Samoa's largest island, with a size that exceeds all other Samoan islands combined. It is referred to as the "soul of Samoa," since it has been more resistant to modernization and is considered the best example of traditional Samoan living. The island is an active volcano, and was reported to have erupted in 1911. Savai'i has a number of noteworthy topographical features. The Puemelei mound, also known as "the Star Pyramid," was built around 1100 to 1400 CE, according to data extracted from archeological digs. The approximate date of its construction makes it the oldest structure in Polynesia. It is also the largest structure from any Polynesian island, with a height reaching around twelve meters (39 feet). It is constructed entirely of natural basalt stones, a volcanic rock found on Savai'i.

Robert Louis Stevenson, who wrote the classic novels *Kidnapped* (1886*)* and *Treasure Island* (1883)*,* lived in Samoa, for the last four years of his life. He was well loved by locals and became known as tusitala ("teller of tales"). His former home, a restored colonial building called Vailima, is now a museum commemorating his life in Samoa. His grave is located just below the 475-meter (1,559-foot) summit of Mt. Vaea, which overlooks Vailima and the rest of Apia.

Libraries & Museums

The National Museum of Samoa (Falemata'aga o Samoa), located in the capital of Apia, holds several hundred items of ethnographic, archaeological, and biological importance in Samoa, including modern art pieces, historical photographs and documents, plant specimens, and historical artifacts such as canoes, pottery, and prehistoric tools dating to before 1000 BCE. Due to the museum's small stature—it occupies three rooms in a government building—many of its most important pieces are also safeguarded abroad.

Public library service in Samoa dates back to the mid-20th century, and now includes over forty libraries. The Nelson Memorial Public Library, officially opened in 1960, serves as the national depository. Academic libraries are located at the National University of Samoa and the University of the South Pacific, Alafua Campus. There are also numerous special and school libraries throughout Samoa.

Holidays

There are few indigenous celebrations outside of Christian holidays, which are observed in Samoa. On June 1, Polynesians celebrate their Independence Day. The nation officially gained independence from New Zealand on the first day of 1962, but Samoa's people choose to commemorate the day in June so that New Year's Day could remain a separate festival. In celebrating their independence, Polynesians participate in group dances and songs, horse and boat races, and large feasts.

Youth Culture

For many young Samoans, hip-hop culture plays a significant role in their daily lives. The popularity of hip-hop has increased as the ties between Samoa and the United States have strengthened. This intensification of relations and culture between the two countries is mainly due to the migration of young people that have traveled back and forth between Samoa and the United States. Hip-hop as both a dance and musical culture has been a way for Samoan youths to connect, despite the physical distance between the two countries. Additionally, young people have been able to preserve their heritage and maintain a sense of cultural pride by incorporating aspects of Samoan culture into hip-hop, and vice versa.

SOCIETY

Transportation

Buses are a popular mode of transportation and they often carry more passengers than the legal limit allows. In these situations passengers must si'i, or sit on someone else's lap. The buses typically run without a formal timetable and often begin their route early in the morning. There are few buses that run at night, and the frequency of buses depends on the destination's accessibility and size. It is generally easier to catch a bus to a popular destination than it is to find one heading to a remote village.

In 2009, Samoa became the first country in roughly forty years to transition from driving on the right-hand side of the road to driving on the left-hand side. The switch was the result of the enacted Road Transport Reform Act 2008. However, the decision was protested widely—for example, it is argued that 14,000 of Samoa's estimated 18,000 vehicles are designed for right-hand driving—it was made because the country wants to import cheaper cars that have the steering wheel on the right side. Reduced speed limits, road maintenance, a three-day ban on alcohol, and a two-day holiday accompanied the switch.

Transportation Infrastructure

Samoa has become increasingly easier to navigate by road. As of 2001, there was an estimated 2,337 kilometers (1452 miles) of roads, 332 kilometers (206 miles) of which were paved. As of 2013, Samoa had four airports, only one of which with a paved runways. Faleolo Airport is Samoa's main airport. In 2015, there are international flights to Samoa from Australia, Fiji, the United States, New Zealand, American Samoa, and Tonga.

Media & Communications

There are a few radio stations in Samoa, which serve an important role in communicating with locals who do not have access to other forms of media and communication. As of 2009, there were five national television stations, one state run and four private. *Samoa Times* and *Samoa Observer* are two of the main dailies. As of 2014, there were an estimated 27,600 Internet users.

The national radio station is 2AP. Every evening 2AP broadcasts information regarding significant events, such as births, deaths, family events, and noteworthy political happenings. Oftentimes

this is the only way for remote villages to know when an emergency has occurred or is about to occur. In 2008 the government announced plans to privatize Radio 2AP, which some critics argued has compromised Radio 2AP's value, since the new owners have decreased the station's signal strength making Radio 2AP unavailable to certain villages.

Within the Samoan legal system, members of the independent media are given the freedom of press and the freedom of expression. Nevertheless, there have been cases where the government has limited the media from discussing controversial political topics. In these instances, the government has restricted the freedom of the press by creating strict controls on what can and cannot be reported.

SOCIAL DEVELOPMENT

Standard of Living

The country ranked 106th out of 187 countries on the 2013 United Nations Human Development Index, which measures quality of life indicators.

Water Consumption

Approximately two-thirds of Samoa's water supply is sourced from surface water, while one-third comes from groundwater. The national service supplier, the Samoa Water Authority (SWA), operates five treatment plants and, as of 2009, services about 88 percent of the population. In rural and isolated areas, rainwater harvesting is practiced, while other villages operate their own water services. In addition, an estimated 91.1 percent of the rural population has access to basic sanitation, while 93.3 percent of the urban population has access.

Education

Schools are free in Samoa. Children are required to attend Samoa's numerous elementary schools, and often continue their education at the high school and college levels. The National University of Samoa has several campuses throughout the islands.

The Mormons operate a large academy in Samoa as part of the Mormon temple there. Secular education is also provided. In addition to classroom instruction, schools often broadcast lessons on the radio for students at home.

The government runs most schools. In 2008, government-run schools accounted for 84 percent total enrollment (by provider) at the primary level, and 60 percent total enrollment at the secondary level. (That same year, mission schools increased their share at the secondary level, to 38 percent total enrollment by provider.) In 2010, the student-to-teacher ratio at the primary level was 30; at the secondary level, it was 21. Overall, female students have a higher participation rate than male students between the ages of five and fourteen. The national participation rate in 2013 for that age group is 95.3 percent.

The literacy rate in Samoa is very high and nearly 99 percent of Polynesian adults can read and write in Samoan. Of the literate population, about half can also read and write in English.

Women's Rights

Under the Samoan constitution, women have equal rights. In the past, however, traditional Samoan culture has encouraged and maintained a subordinate role for women in society, and Samoan women have historically endured a minor status in their family and village. The position of women in modern Samoan society is now changing, and more women are gaining significant posts in government and business. In 2015, there are still only two women seated in parliament; however, five women serve as the chief executive officers (CEO) of government organizations. The government also established measures to further incorporate women into the workforce. Under the Ministry of Women, Community, and Social Development, the government created a number of literacy and training programs to assist women who did not complete their high school education. The title of matai, or village chief, will sometimes be bestowed to women, although this is often not the case.

While abuse of women is prohibited, domestic abuse is a common occurrence. Societal expectations and the traditional position of women allow instances of domestic violence to largely go unchecked by village communities and the government. Many cases are unreported due to social attitudes and the fear of further abuse should the situation be made public. Abuse is considered a prevalent problem in Samoan society, but is only considered punishable if there are visible signs of bodily harm. When taken to court, any person indicted in a case involving domestic abuse could face prison terms lasting a few months to a year. In addition, reporting a rape is still quite discouraged by Samoan society. Rape in the Samoan court system is treated as a serious offense, and the cases that come to trial are not taken lightly. If a man is convicted of rape, he can face a punishment of two years to life in prison.

A domestic violence unit has been established by the Ministry of Police in conjunction with several non-governmental organizations (NGOs) that battle domestic abuse throughout the country. The primary NGO combating domestic violence in Samoa is Mapusaga O Aiga Samoa (MOA). The unit and the NGOs have worked together to develop anonymous hotlines, and shelters for victims. They have also made counseling sessions and support groups available to victims.

Health Care

Polynesians enjoy full national health care as provided by the government. There are certain fees associated with specific patients and treatments. Residents either go to the general clinic or are treated by visiting nurses on the islands. Immunization, care for the elderly, and emergency treatment are available to all of Samoa's residents.

GOVERNMENT

Structure

Samoa is a constitutional monarchy. The government is based directly on the government of Great Britain, and it includes a parliament, the fono, as its legislative branch. The head of state, a native chief called the O Le Ao o Le Malo, oversees the fono. The O Le Ao o Le Malo's powers are extremely limited, and he is in many ways a figurehead.

The fono, which sits for a five-year term, essentially runs the government, and contains a forty-nine member cabinet that is elected by Polynesians, representing forty-one constituencies. Only the matai of Samoa's villages are allowed to campaign for a seat in the fono, which meets daily at the Fale Fono.

Political Parties

There are a number of political parties in Samoa. The party to which a matai belongs is represented in the fono once he gains a seat. Political parties include the Human Rights Protection Party (HRPP), which has been the country's dominant party since the 1980s, and as of 2015 holds twenty-nine of the forty-nine seats in the fono. Tautua Samoa, which, as of the last elections in 2011, is the main opposition party (they won thirteen of forty-nine seats). Other parties include the Samoa Party (founded in 2005), the Samoa Progressive Political Party, and the Christian Party.

Local Government

Polynesians use the Samoan word matai, which means "chief," to refer to land owners at the village level. In Samoa's eleven designated districts, there are 362 villages, in which Polynesian families live on privately owned farmland. This land is overseen by a family's matai. The role of the matai also extends beyond the family. Matai meet in Samoa's government center, known as the Fale Fono, where they participate in the national government as a representative body.

Overall, local governance is divided among twenty-six urban local governments and 286 rural local governments, and eighty-nine districts and nineteen provinces. The Minister of Internal Affairs oversees local government issues.

Judicial System

The judiciary consists of a Supreme Court (with six judges), a district court, and a court of appeal headed by overseas judges. A Land and Titles Court hears customary land ownership issues and matters regarding matai titles. Local village councils also have a judiciary function. Samoa's legal system is based on the English legal system.

Taxation

Taxes levied in Samoa include excise taxes and a value-added tax (VAT). As of 2014, twenty-seven percent is the highest tax rate for both corporate and income taxes.

Armed Forces

There are no armed forces in Samoa, and the country is dependent on New Zealand and Australia for national defense. The Samoan police are responsible for maritime patrolling.

Foreign Policy

New Zealand and Samoa have had close ties since the former occupied the latter during World War I in 1914. Because of a friendship treaty signed in 1962, the year of Samoa's formal independence, the countries have maintained strong relations, and New Zealand remains one of Samoa's leading trading partners. Under the treaty, Samoa is allowed specific requests, such as asking New Zealand to serve as an international representative of Samoan interests. Since Samoa does not have an official army, the country is also allowed to request aid from New Zealand's armed forces. New Zealand established a Samoan quota scheme whereby 1,100 Samoans can immigrate each year to New Zealand via a lottery process.

Despite its small population, the island nation has participated in a number of international organizations, including the United Nations (UN), the World Health Organization (WHO), and the International Monetary Fund (IMF). The country has an active membership in the Pacific Islands Forum (PIF), the Secretariat of the Pacific Community (SPC), and the Secretariat of the Pacific Regional Environment Program (SPREP), the latter of which is located in Samoa. Samoa is also an active participant in the South Pacific Forum (SPC). At the forum, the country has voiced important matters related to the nation's well-being, such as nuclear testing in the Pacific region, and environmental issues regarding fishing and forestry sectors. Another concern for Samoa is its desire to nurture economically beneficial relationships with its Pacific Island neighbors.

Samoa has taken part in the Regional Assistance Mission to Solomon Islands (RAMSI) in July 2003 where it has volunteered a small police force for RAMSI's use. Samoa has also employed its police in peacekeeping missions located in Sudan, Liberia, and East Timor. In September 2008, Samoa took part in a series of meetings between Cuba and Samoa, meant to increase cooperation between the two countries. Since Cuba and Samoa are both small islands, the issue of climate change and how rising water levels may affect island nations is a shared interest.

Samoa opened embassies in China and Japan in January 2009. Both countries have served as sources of economic aid in the past. China has helped Samoa expand its infrastructure and create development programs to help its weakened economy. Besides aid, the People's Republic of China (PRC) has cancelled previous debts, provided free anti-malaria drugs, and eliminated tariffs on exports. In return, under the "One China" policy, Samoa has aligned itself with Chinese policies and agreed not to conduct diplomatic relations with Taiwan. In 2008, after a series of controversial riots erupted in the Autonomous Region of Tibet, the head of the Samoan legislative body announced that Samoa supported China's response to the riots and recommended that other nations not intervene.

Human Rights Profile

International human rights law insists that states respect civil and political rights, and promote an individual's economic, social, and cultural rights. The United Nations Universal Declaration on Human Rights (UDHR) is recognized as the standard for international human rights. Its authors sought the counsel of the world's great thinkers,

philosophers, and religious leaders, and were careful to create a document that reflects the core values shared by every world culture. (To read this document or view the articles relating to cultural human rights, visit http://www.udhr.org/UDHR/default.htm.).

The Samoan government generally adheres to the principles set forth in the UDHR, but has been charged with failing to respect the rights of women and individuals who do not have matai (chief) status. The government has also been accused of limiting the rights of the media and the religious freedoms of its citizenry, and allowing for poor living conditions at state prisons. In addition, while Samoan law formally allows the freedom of religion. Samoan tradition usually prevails over law.

In each Samoan village, a family will have a matai, who acts as the family leader and representative. The matai form the village fono, or village council, which formulates and upholds the collective values of the village. Under this political hierarchy, the matai select the village's religious beliefs and denomination, and establish what rituals they must follow. A failure to follow the religion that the matai have chosen can lead to serious consequences; villagers can be forced to pay fines, undergo an ifoga apology ceremony, or in more extreme cases, they can face expulsion from the village.

Article 19 covers the notion that each person has the right to receive ideas from various media without the government censoring or altering the content. Samoa is a largely Christian nation since missionaries began espousing their beliefs in the 19th century. In 2011, a census recorded nearly the entire population as Christian. Although Samoans have altered Christian traditions to fit their own rich spiritual history, the Church holds significant sway in modern Samoa. In 2006, the country's principal censor banned the controversial Hollywood blockbuster, *The Da Vinci Code*. The film implies that Mary Magdalene was Jesus' wife—a suggestion that the censors believed would affect the faith of younger Christians. The censor reportedly acted within the authority granted to him by the Samoan constitution's film act.

Article 29 states that each person's rights may be limited by the law only to the extent that will ensure the rights of others while maintaining a fair social order. The U.S. Department of State in 2014 reported that Samoan prison facilities were inadequate and did not meet basic standards of living. One concrete cell with a gravel floor will hold anywhere from twenty-six to thirty inmates. The majority of cells lack toilets, and have little lighting or ventilation. Some underage youth that were sentenced as juveniles have been reportedly held in the same area as adult inmates due to limited resources.

ECONOMY

Overview of the Economy

Samoa's per capita gross domestic product (GDP) was an estimated $5,200 (USD) in 2014.

Samoa has low inflation rates and low national debt, and is not dependent on industry for its economic survival. Most of the manufacturing jobs in the workforce are related to agricultural goods, which are used internally. As of 2014, an estimated 58.5 percent of the economy was based on services, 30.1 percent on manufacturing, and 11.4 percent on agriculture. Agriculture, however, accounts for the majority—90 percent—of exports, and two-thirds of the workforce.

Industry

Significant industries in Samoa include auto parts manufacturing, food processing, and building materials. Exports include automotive parts and clothing. As of 2014, the industrial production growth rate was estimated at 1.5 percent.

Labor

Unemployment does not really exist in Samoa, mostly due to the fact that most Polynesians are self-sufficient and do not need to hold a job in order to live. The agricultural sector dominates the labor force, employing two-thirds of

the Samoan workforce, which was estimated at 48,580 in 2012.

Energy/Power/Natural Resources

Samoa's islands are small and natural resources are few. As a result, Samoa remains dependent on neighboring nations for many of its needs. Even existing resources are in danger. Hydroelectricity is fundamental to Samoa's industry, accounting for over a quarter of its electricity; because of the strong currents flowing around the islands, hydroelectric power is perhaps Samoa's most sustainable energy resource.

Fishing

Fishing is considered a natural resource, since the fishing industry feeds most Polynesians. As of 2000, most fishing households—an estimated 70 percent—retained their catch. Tuna (albacore, yellowfin, bigeye, and skipjack) is a significant catch and Samoa's most popular fish export. Inshore fishing yields crabs, lobsters, sea urchins, and shellfish.

Forestry

Dense hardwood rainforests cover some areas of the islands, but the demand for the rare woods has raised concerns that logging and deforestation will irreversibly damage the islands' ecosystem.

Agriculture

Much of Samoa's economy and revenue is based on agriculture, and the vast majority of the workforce is engaged in the agricultural sector. Agriculture is responsible for 90 percent of Samoa's major exports, which include fish, bananas, coconut cream, coconut oil, coffee, beer, clothing, and copra. Most goods are exported to Samoa's primary trading partners, which include American Samoa, New Zealand, Fiji, Australia, Japan, South Korea, and the United States.

Devastating cyclone storms typical of the South Pacific region can cause large setbacks in agricultural output, potentially damaging the economy.

Animal Husbandry

Animal husbandry covers the breeding, feeding, housing, and management of livestock. Common livestock in Samoa include poultry, pigs, sheep, and cattle.

Tourism

Over100,000 people visit Samoa each year, accounting for over half of the country's GDP.

The tourism industry has been on the rise in recent years.

Regular destinations for tourists include the Mulinuu tombs, which house the remains of past royalty, and Vailima, the former home of author Robert Louis Stevenson that now serves as the residence of Samoa's head of state.

Danielle Chu, Richard Means

DO YOU KNOW?

- The last volcanic eruption in Samoa happened in 1911, when Mount Silisili on the island of Savai'i erupted. The volcano is still considered active today.

- In 2000, Polynesian geography students found an active underwater volcano off the eastern shores of Samoa, and named it Vailulu'u.

- Samoa and the surrounding Samoa Islands were once known as the Navigators Islands, because the Polynesian people were known for being excellent canoe builders.

Bibliography

AhChing, Peter Leiataua. *Polynesian Interconnections: Samoa to Tahiti to Hawaii.* Lulu Press, 2005.

Blackburn, Mark. *Tattoos from Paradise: Traditional Polynesian Patterns.* Atglen: MSchiffer Publishing, Ltd., 1999.

Field, Michael J. Mau: *Samoa's Struggle for Freedom.* Auckland: Polynesian Press, 1991

Fraser, Marie. *In Stevenson's Samoa.* London: BiblioBazaar, 2008.

Lahaye, Mary E. *Letters from Samoa: Life, Love and Lore of the Manu'a Islands.* Irvine: Interncon Publishing, 2004.

Matsuda, Matt K. *Pacific Worlds: A History of Seas, Peoples, and Cultures.* New York: Cambridge University Press, 2012.

Mead, Margaret. *Coming of Age in Samoa.* New York: HarperCollins Publishers, Inc., 1928.

Smith, Stephen John. *The Samoa (N.Z.) Expeditionary Force, 1914–15: an account based on official records of the seizure and occupation by New Zealand of the German Islands of Western Samoa.* Ferguson & Osborn, 1924.

Stevenson, Robert Louis. *A Footnote to History (Eight Years of Trouble in Samoa).* London: BiblioBazaar, 2009.

Turner, George. *Samoa: A Hundred Years Ago and Long Before.* London: BiblioBazaar, 2007.

Works Cited

AAP. Samoa bans Da Vinci Code film. 22 May 2006 http://news.ninemsn.com.au/article.aspx?id=102603 .

Australian Government - Department of Foreign Affairs and Trade. Samoa Country Brief .. http://www.dfat.gov.au/GEO/samoa/samoa_brief.html.

CIA - The World Factbook. Samoa. 4 November 2015 https://www.cia.gov/library/publications/the-world-factbook/geos/ws.html.

City Population. Samoa. http://www.citypopulation.de/Samoa.html.

Duranti, Alessandro. "Language and Bodies in Social Space: Samoan Ceremonial Greetings." American Anthropologist (1992): 657–691.

Gell, Alfred. Wrapping in Images: Tattooing in Polynesia. Oxford: Royal Anthropological Institute of Great Britain and Ireland, 1997.

Henderson, April K. "Dancing Between Islands: Hip-hop and the Samoan Diaspora." Basu, Dipannita and Sidney J. Lemelle. The Vinyl Ain't Final: Hip-hop and the Globalisation of the Black Popular Culture. Ann Arbor, 2006. 180–199.

HyperWar Foundation. Hyperwar: History of USMC Operations in WWII, Vol. 1: Pearl Harbor to Guadalcanal, Part II. http://www.ibiblio.org/hyperwar/USMC/I/USMC-I-II-3.html#fn8.

Immigration New Zealand. Samoan Quota Scheme. 31 March 2008. http://www.immigration.govt.nz/migrant/stream/live/samoanquota/.

Little Jr., Elbert L. and Roger G. Skolmen. Common Forest Trees of Hawaii (Native and Introduced). 20 August 2008. http://www.ctahr.hawaii.edu/forestry/Data/Common_Trees_Hawaii.asp.

Mallon, Sean. Samoan Art and Artists: O Measina a Samoa. Honolulu: University of Hawaii Press, 2003.

Oceanside Museum of Art. Worn with Pride - Tatau (Tatoo). 2002. http://www.oma-online.org/worn_with_pride_04.html .

Polynesian Cultural Center. Samoa : Samoan Houses. http://www.polynesia.com/samoa/samoan-houses.html.

Samoa.co.uk. Samoa - Dance. http://www.samoa.co.uk/dance.html .

———. Samoa - Food and Drink. http://www.samoa.co.uk/food&drink.html .

———. Samoa - Transport. http://www.samoa.co.uk/transport.html.

Taylor, Alan. Polynesian Tattooing. Laie: Institute for Polynesian Studies, Brigham Young University - Hawaii Campus, 1981.

UN Women. Samoa. http://asiapacific.unwomen.org/en/countries/fiji/co/samoa.

UNESCO World Heritage Centre. Fagaloa Bay - Uafato Tiavea Conservation Zone. http://whc.unesco.org/en/tentativelists/5090/.

UN Data. Samoa. http://data.un.org/CountryProfile.aspx?crName=Samoa?.

United Nations Development Programme. Human Development Reports: Samoa. http://hdr.undp.org/en/countries/profiles/WSM.

U.S. Department of State. Human Rights Report: Samoa. http://www.state.gov/g/drl/rls/hrrpt/2008/eap/119055.htm.

U.S. Department Of State. Samoa -Country Reports on Human Rights Practices. http://www.state.gov/g/drl/rls/hrrpt/2006/78789.htm.

U.S. Department of State. Samoa - International Religious Freedom Report. http://www.state.gov/g/drl/rls/irf/2007/90152.htm .

U.S. State Department. Samoa 2014 Human Rights Report. http://www.state.gov/documents/organization/236684.pdf.

Vitchek, Andre. A Tale of Two Samoas. 23 May 2008. http://www.fpif.org/fpiftxt/5242.

World Bank. Data by Country. http://data.worldbank.org/indicator/ST.INT.ARVL.

Skulls and shell money on Skull island, part of the Solomon Islands. iStock/Tammy616

Solomon Islands

Introduction

The Solomon Islands, which are comprised of nearly 1,000 islands, lie in the South Pacific Ocean. For nearly a century, the country was a protectorate of Great Britain, and obtained its independence in 1978.

The history of the Solomon Islands dates to ancient times. Archaeological evidence suggests that hunter-gatherer groups, most likely representing Melanesian ethnic families, were present on the larger of the Solomon Islands by 1000 BCE. More recently, Solomon Islanders were distinguished during World War II for their efforts in rescuing and caring for downed Allied airmen.

The largest island, Guadalcanal, was the scene of some of the fiercest fighting of World War II, and its shores are littered with the wrecks of ships and planes. Today, the nation continues to develop its economy and infrastructure, although it is hampered by civil unrest.

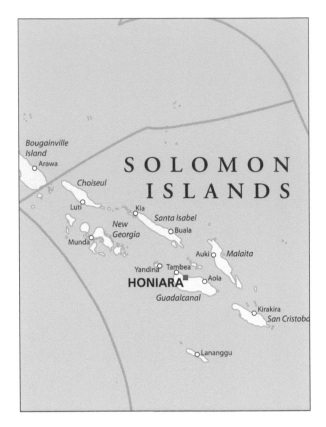

GENERAL INFORMATION

Official Language: English
Population: 622,469 (2015 estimate)
Currency: Solomon Islands dollar
Coins: Circulated coins are available in denominations of 1, 2 5, 10, 20, and 50 cents and 1 dollar.
Land Area: 27,986 square kilometers (10,805 square miles)
Water Area: 910 square kilometers (351 square miles)
National Motto: "To Lead is to Serve"

National Anthem: "God Save our Solomon Islands"
Capital: Honiara
Time Zone: GMT +11
Flag Description: The flag of the Solomon Islands features a blue and green field split diagonally by a rising yellow line. The blue field, situated on top, represents water; the green field, situated on the bottom, represents fertility; and the yellow line symbolizes sunshine. Five white stars, each with five points and arranged in an "X" pattern, are displayed in the upper hoist (right) side, in the blue field, representing the five main groups of islands.

Population

An estimated 95.3 percent of Solomon Islanders are classified as Melanesian, an ethno-linguistic group that includes inhabitants of a number of islands in the South Pacific. The remaining population is mostly represented by the Micronesian and Polynesian ethnic groups, and a further small

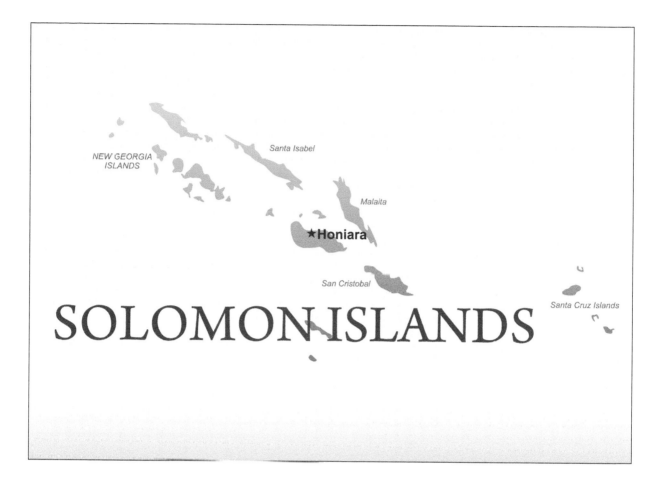

Principal Cities by Population (2009):

- Honiara (64,609)
- Tandai Ward (10,605)
- Auki (5,105)
- Malango Ward (4,636)
- Gizo (3,547)
- Noro (3,365)

percentage is represented by immigrant groups from Asia, Australia, and Europe.

In the capital Honiara, the ethnic stratification is more diverse, as the city has served as a major settlement for immigrants. The population of Honiara was measured in the 2009 census at 64,609 and continues to grow given the countries urbanization rate of 4.25 percent (2015).

Most Solomon Islanders live on the coast; an estimated 77.7 percent reside in rural areas. The population density is about twenty-two persons per square kilometer (fifty-eight persons per square mile). Less than 400 of the approximately 1,000 islands are inhabited. The island nation is estimated to have a population growth rate of just over 2 percent.

Languages

English is the official language of the Solomon Islands, but the language has developed into a number of English-Creole dialects, the best known of which is Solomon Island's Pidgin, or Solomon Pijin. Various Melanesian dialects are spoken by over 80 percent of the population. English is the official language of the government and the school system, and 84 percent of the nation's adults are literate. Honiara has a significant population of Chinese residents, gathered in an ethnically homogenous part of the urban area where Chinese dialects are commonly spoken. Overall, it is estimated that there are over one hundred indigenous languages or vernaculars spoken in the country.

Native People & Ethnic Groups

It is believed that Melanesians from New Guinea settled the Solomon Islands in pre-

historic times. Today, most native Solomon Islanders live in rural villages. The first Europeans to see the Solomon Islands were the Spanish in 1568. The islands became a German protectorate in 1885 and a British protectorate in 1893.

The Japanese occupied the Solomon Islands during World War II. Solomon Islanders, along with Australians and Europeans, formed the Coastwatch, a resistance group that rescued downed Allied airmen and shipwrecked sailors, prisoners of war, missionaries and civilians. (Solomon Islanders rescued Lt. John F. Kennedy when his PT boat was destroyed in 1943).

After World War II, many of the Malaita islanders (Malaita is the largest island of the populous Malaita Province) moved to Guadalcanal, the country's largest island. The mixture was not peaceful, as the different ethnic groups, including village groups, in the Solomon Islands often do not get along. In this case, the tensions eventually led to armed conflict between the two groups. At one time, the prime minister was kidnapped by the militant Malaita Eagle Force and forced to resign. Peace was not restored until 2003, when Prime Minister Sir Allen Kemakeza asked Australia to help disarm the militia and maintain order in the country.

Religions

The Solomon Islands have no established church. Christianity is the predominant religion, practiced by an estimated 95 percent of the population, with a plethora of denominations represented. The Church of Melanesia constitutes the largest denomination, followed by Roman Catholics and other Protestant denominations. In addition, about 4 percent of the population holds indigenous beliefs, and there are Bah'ai and Muslim groups. In some cases, Christian beliefs are held in conjuncture with traditional or indigenous beliefs.

Climate

The Solomon Islands have an equatorial climate, with little variation by season. Usually, the islands experience trade winds, but typhoons are not uncommon. Fortunately, the storms are rarely destructive. Earthquakes are frequent, and volcanoes occasionally erupt.

Humidity is high, and temperatures average between 21° and 32° Celsius (70° and 90° Fahrenheit). The average temperature in Honiara is 27° Celsius (81° Fahrenheit) year-round. Rainfall is heavy, with different areas of the country receiving between 150 and 500 centimeters (60 and 200 inches) each year. Honiara's average rainfall is 216 centimeters (86 inches).

ENVIRONMENT & GEOGRAPHY

Topography

The Solomon Islands is an archipelago in Melanesia, in the southwestern Pacific. The nation includes most of the Solomon Islands group, but Bouganville, Buka and a few smaller islands are part of Papua New Guinea, to the west. Also part of the country are the Oton Java Islands (Lord Howe Atoll), Rennell Island, and the Santa Cruz Islands.

The capital of the Solomon Islands is Honiara. It is located on Guadalcanal, the largest and undoubtedly the most famous of the islands, because of its history during World War Guadalcanal covers an area of 6,475 square kilometers (2,500 square miles).

Most of the islands are volcanic, with rugged mountains and a covering of tropical plant growth. Nearly every island has a ridge of mountains in the center, rising as high as 1,200 meters (4,000 feet). One side of the island is a sharp slope to the sea, while the other has a gentle slope to a coastal strip. More than 87 percent of the land is forested. Some of the islands, especially the outlying ones, are atolls (ring-shaped coral reefs).

The highest point in the country is Mount Makarakomburu, at 2,447 meters (8,028 feet) on Guadalcanal. Lake Tenggara, on Rennell Island, is the largest lake in the South Pacific. The country has no major rivers.

Plants & Animals

The coral reefs surrounding the Solomon Islands abound with marine life, from the coral itself to requiem sharks. Dolphins, prawns, crayfish, tuna, slugs, crabs, eels, clown fish and giant clams inhabit the reefs. However, dead or dying coral reefs are an environmental concern facing the country.

The Solomon Islands have the second highest (after Papua New Guinea) diversity of land animals of any place in the Pacific. In fact, although the Solomon Islands rainforest covers only 7 percent of the planet's surface, it contains more than three-quarters of the world's plant and animal species.

The country boasts 130 species of butterflies, thirty-five of which are endemic (native only to the Solomon Islands). In addition, eight of the seventy-two reptile species are endemic, including the giant prehensile-tailed skink and the keeled monitor lizard. Four of the 173 species of birds are endemic to the Solomon Islands, including the Ghizo white-eye, which is listed as critically endangered. In addition, nineteen of the fifty-three mammal species are endemic.

The Solomon Islands is home to parrots, coconut crabs, malaria-carrying mosquitoes, crocodiles, twenty-five species of frogs and thirty-four species of bats.

A total of 2,780 species of plants grow in Solomon Islands. Breadfruit trees, coconut palms, oil palms, Polynesian chestnut, and 230 species of orchids (at least thirty of them endemic) flourish in the tropical climate. Mangrove forests and sea grass provide important marine breeding grounds.

Problems include the water hyacinth, which is growing so lavishly that it is choking rivers. The asagao, or morning glory, has smothered large portions of the coastal rainforest on Makira and is threatening other islands.

Cats, both domestic and feral, are not native to Solomon Islands. When cats began threatening the bird population on Simbo Island, bird owners began killing cats. Cane toads, introduced in the mid-1800s, have destroyed large numbers of indigenous frogs.

CUSTOMS & COURTESIES

Greetings

As the Solomon Islands are a diverse nation, the mode of greeting varies according to ethnic group. English is the official language, but Solomon Islanders generally use the Pijin phrase "Halo" ("Hello"), with variations used for addressing more than one person. (Pijin belongs to the English Creole language family.) This greeting may be accompanied by a firm handshake—a fairly recent adoption—and close friends or family may embrace or kiss. However, Solomon Islanders are generally reserved, and many men, especially those belonging to the older generations and in outlying areas, do not appreciate physical contact between strangers and female family members, as such contact is still considered taboo.

Some cultures may still employ traditional methods of greeting. The Tikopia culture, for example, uses the traditional "nose kiss" as a form of formal greeting. This is governed by a strict set of rules, subject to the social status of the two parties involved. For example, a nose-to-nose or nose-to-cheek greeting is only allowed between those of the same social status, while elders are greeted by a nose kiss to the wrist. Chiefs were customarily created by pressing one's nose to the leader's knee. With the introduction of Christianity to the islands, many of these traditional practices waned.

Gestures & Etiquette

Solomon Islanders are generally characterized as reserved yet easygoing, which is evident in their gestures and social etiquette. For example, eye contact, particularly prolonged contact, is avoided, and distance is established when conversing with strangers. Intimacy between the sexes is generally avoided in public, and often considered impolite. Islanders may also converse using gestures; for instance, a question may be answered with the raising of eyebrows, which mean "yes."

Respect, particularly for elders, is considered a very important quality. The elderly are always addressed in a respectful manner and they are always obeyed unquestioningly. Each local culture also has its own social hierarchy in which certain groups of people are accorded respect by virtue of their status in society. The importance of respect and humility in island life is also seen in day-to-day behavior. Swearing, for instance, is prohibited, public displays of anger are frowned upon, and confrontational and socially awkward situations are generally avoided altogether. Additionally, interpersonal and inter-group conflicts are traditionally solved through bargaining and compromise, with compensation paid to the family of those wronged.

Other unique aspects of the local culture include the handling of negotiations and transactions and the concept of time. Negotiations are traditionally based on the preservation of the relationship. To that end, a seller may respectfully lower the price of a good or commodity, while the buyer might respectfully offer a higher price. Traditionally, time is perceived as a commodity that cannot be quantified. As such, punctuality is not particularly stressed, and there is no general sense of being rushed.

Eating/Meals

Eating patterns in the Solomon Islands vary. Three meals per day is a common practice (though lunch may be generally skipped), and these meals are often substantial, especially in rural areas. Breakfast is light, usually consisting of leftovers, and the evening meal is the main meal of the day. Traditionally, women are responsible for meal preparations, and the main meal is usually a family affair (though among some groups, women and men eat separately). Generally, meals are eaten at home for the majority of the population.

In urban homes, tables are becoming more common, but are generally absent in rural homes. Meals may be eaten quickly and in silence, as making noise or talking during a meal is considered rude. The traditional way of eating is with the hands; in urban areas, however, utensils are commonly used. In addition, many Solomon Islanders, even those in villages, also use commercially manufactured pots and dishes instead of traditional wooden food bowls.

Visiting

Solomon Islanders are a hospitable people and visiting is an important part of their culture. Villages traditionally maintain a special hut reserved for visitors, and it is customary to greet the chief first when visiting a neighboring village or island. If a visitor is brought food, this signals that they are welcome, and may be invited into the chief's hut. During visits, women are expected to avoid houses in which men are entertaining.

In the rural villages, visiting is not common during the day, when most people are tending to farm work. Thus, visits occur in the early evening, upon returning to the village, particularly as meals are prepared. However, visitors generally leave when meals are served, since mealtime is a private family affair in many rural areas. The visiting may then resume after the evening meal has been concluded.

There is a strong tradition of gift giving in the Solomon Islands. When a gift is offered, it is customarily accepted. For the islanders, wealth lies not in hoarding, but in giving to others. A gift creates a relationship between the giver and the receiver, and the latter becomes obliged to pay it back. In the highlands especially, this obligation is taken particularly seriously.

LIFESTYLE

Family

The extended family is the most important social unit in the Solomon Islands and is a source of social stability. Traditionally, the family functions as a single unit and family allegiances supersede all loyalties. In its modern form, the family plays an important role in business as well as socio-political alliances. Additionally, the term wantok ("one talk') refers to speakers of the same language. It is used to refer to non-kin with whom one shares social origins and to whom one owes allegiance. Refusing a request of help is tantamount to bringing shame on the entire family.

The clan is an extension of the family. Known as laen in Pijin, this is an alliance of families who believe they have descended from a common ancestor. (Traditionally, if the ancestor is mythical, such as a particular bird or animal, that animal is not hunted by the clan.) The structure of the family and clan varies from island to island, and each clan is headed by a chief. The majority of the clans are patriarchal, but some are matrilineal. In these clans, inheritance passes through the maternal line, and the most important figure in the family might be the maternal uncle.

Traditionally, couples had a large number of children, but modernization and urbanization have reduced this number. Extended families remain close. Cousins, for example, are considered siblings, and uncles exercise paternal authority. Living patterns also vary with different families and clans. In some cases, parents live with their younger children while older boys share one house; in others, men and women sleep in different houses. This structure of social organization and the importance of the family have led to the historical absence of any concept of private property. In the Solomon Islands, ownership has always been a concept linked intimately with that of family and clan.

Housing

Even though an increasing number of people are living in urban areas, eight out of ten people still live in rural areas in the Solomon Islands. While some of these villages have been somewhat modernized, the rural lifestyle is still traditional. These villages are small—usually less than 100 people—and typically situated near water. Every village has a church, perhaps a school, and a number of ceremonial and custom houses. In the village, the houses face each other in two rows with a path down the middle. Houses vary in size and shape, but are generally small and constructed using the same traditional methods. Almost every house maintains a garden.

The majority of houses are rectangular and divided into rooms using walls and partitions.

Generally, the framework is constructed by lashing together light poles with coconut fronds, the walls are made with bamboo or thatch, and the roof is thatched with the leaves of the sago palm. The floor could be thatched, made out of betel nut bark or wooden plants, or simply beaten earth. The house may also have a veranda (roofed open porch) and the kitchen is separate from the main building. Houses rarely have windows, and there is usually a hole in the roof to allow smoke to escape. Houses are generally furnished simply; the beds are raised platforms with mats and there are hardly any chairs or other furniture.

In coastal areas, houses may be supported on stilts or built upon artificial islands. These islands are created on shoal passages using boulders which are brought from the reefs, and are usually large enough to accommodate a single house. Some villages today have buildings constructed out of sawn wood and corrugated iron. In many towns, buildings constructed out of fibro-cement and cement brick are becoming increasingly common. In the suburbs of Honiara, the capital, the houses are made using a combination of traditional and modern methods. Honiara is also ringed with a number of squatter settlements as a result of increasing urbanization and a lack of housing resources.

Food

The traditional diet of Solomon Islanders is simple and consists largely of root crops, fruit, nuts, fish, and the occasional meat (mostly pork or chicken). Fruits and vegetables are freshly grown. The most commonly eaten vegetables include taro roots and leaves, yams, cassava (manioc), breadfruit (ulu), and sweet potato (kumara). Breadfruit and yams are the most popular of these. Other common vegetables include the qeta, a turnip-like root vegetable. Qeta is a luxury food, and there are special qeta mashing sticks and bowls which are reserved for this purpose.

Vegetables are often eaten with rice, meat or fish. Poi, for instance, is made of cooked and fermented taro root, and is eaten either with meat or fish, or in the form of porridge. Kara is a popular snack; it is made with coconuts, cassava and corned beef. The cassava and the coconuts are grated and the juice and cream respectively are squeezed out. On a banana leaf, the corned beef is placed between layers of cassava and coconut cream. It is then covered with another leaf and either baked or steamed.

Solomon Islanders use a variety of methods to prepare their food, including frying, baking, and boiling. Two distinctive methods include using an earthen oven, called a mumu, and bamboo cooking. A mumu is essentially a hole in the ground which is lined with stones and covered with sticks. Food, wrapped in leaves, is placed on stones, which have been heated by a fire. Then more hot stones are placed on top of the food and the whole is covered with large leaves, creating an effective oven. Whole pigs, for example, are cooked in these pits. Bamboo cooking involves placing food inside a section of fresh bamboo, the ends of which are sealed with banana leaf plugs. An additional leaf is tied over the end, and the bamboo is then rotated over hot coals until it turns brown.

Tropical fruit is an important part of the island diet, and many local fruits and vegetables are used in the making of desserts. The papaya is commonly eaten, while coconuts and pineapples are also popular. One common dessert is made with bananas and other exotic fruits, wrapped in cassava and served with whipped cream or caramel. Coconut milk is a popular drink in the islands, and the betel nut, which is a mild stimulant, is chewed by almost every islander. Called kaikai buai, the betel nut is added to a mustard stick and crushed coral lime, and the mixture produces a mild reaction when eaten.

Life's Milestones

Elaborate ritual governs every stage of island life. In many local cultures, an expectant mother was sent either to special maternity islands or into the bush prior to birth. Usually, the husband paid two or three women to accompany her and bring her food. During this period, she was not allowed to receive visits or touch crops, and delivered the baby herself. She was welcomed back into the village only after forty days. If either she or the baby died, their bodies were left untouched and unburied as they were believed to be cursed. Even today, although most women travel to the mainland to deliver their baby, the ritual remains relevant. An expectant mother is not touched during the birthing process and cuts the umbilical cord herself. She wraps the baby in pandanus leaves and returns to the village in a canoe. The new mother then spends a month in the women's house, where she observes certain dietary restrictions. Her return to the village is marked by a feast, but this is not attended by married men.

Marriage has traditionally been perceived as an alliance between two families or clans and is almost always arranged. Once an agreement is reached between the families, a bride price is decided (traditionally, shell money or livestock) and paid by the prospective groom to the bride's family, followed by a celebration. In some cultures, the bride then accompanies the groom's family, and spends the next few months with her prospective in-laws. She then returns to her own island and waits to be summoned on the actual wedding day. This is marked by a lavish feast at the bride's island.

Burials are usually marked with a feast during which the family mourns the deceased. In some cultures, faces are blackened or special ornaments are worn as signs of mourning. The funeral is usually held on the same day as the death and there are several different methods of burial. In the past, the dead were sometimes buried in an upright position, with the head and shoulders left above the ground. Chiefs were sometimes buried in their canoes, and the skulls of important people were displayed in the village custom houses. Some coastal people disposed the body off into the sea after an appropriate ceremony, while some highland cultures left the body in the trees. Sometimes, the coffin containing the body was hung from the ceiling of the hut. After a few months, the bones were removed and buried. Today, however, the body is simply buried, and the grave marked with an engraved

headstone, or cremated. Every village generally has its own burial ground.

CULTURAL HISTORY

Art

Although the Solomon Islands have a rich cultural history, their artistic tradition has been mostly limited to craft making. Historically, there has been no major development of the visual or plastic arts on the islands. Similarly, illiteracy has limited the literary arts on the islands to the oral tradition of storytelling. This age-old tradition is an important part of village life, as it is the primary vehicle by which history and ancestral tales are passed down from generation to generation.

The islanders have developed a high level of mastery of their folk art. Traditionally, these crafts have been either utilitarian or ceremonial, and include carving, shell-work, weaving, bamboo plaiting, and the art of weaponry. Craft-making techniques vary from island to island, and certain islands are known for particular crafts. Guadalcanal Province, for example, is known for its woven textiles, which include sturdy bags, trays, mats, and baskets made out of the asa vine. This work is collectively known as bukaware. Bellona Island is also renowned for its small woven pandanus bags.

The islands' woodcarving tradition extends from domestic items such as bowls, walking sticks, and combs to the figureheads and hulls of war canoes. In recent years, the islanders have also started to carve non-traditional items such as models of birds, fish, and humans, as well as miniature war clubs, masks, and canoes for tourists. The nguzunguzu, from Western Province, are perhaps the most distinctive examples of local carving. These are anthropomorphic prow figureheads used to decorate war canoes. Small in scale, these carvings were elaborately decorated with shell inlay. Western Province is also known for its carvings of sharks and dolphins and of anthropomorphic creatures such as the popular kareimanu, a creature half-shark and half-man. Woodcarving in the western districts is usually done in brown-streaked kerosene wood or black ebony.

The islands are also known for their shell-work, which includes ornaments, jewelry, and even currency. The province of Malaita is known for its shell currency, which are small discs of red and white shell, often made into strings or necklaces of bush twine. In the past, tiny shell fishhooks were made out of turtle shell and mother-of-pearl. Shell-work is now mainly used to make jewelry. Round breastplates, for instance, are made out of clamshell with super-imposed turtle shell in filigree work. Other shell jewelry items include rings for arms and legs, light bangles, and small pointed sticks used as a nasal or ear piercing.

Weapon making has a long history in the Solomon Islands. While created essentially for their functionality, weapons are also beautifully designed and elaborately decorated. The most common weapon is the bow (and accompanying arrows). The bow is made from palm wood, with vegetable fiber used as string. The arrows are not usually feathered and are made out of cane, with the points being carved out of hard wood or human bone. Shields are usually small and constructed with wicker or wood, and then elaborately decorated with ornate shell work. War clubs are carved out of a single piece of wood and their shell-inlay decoration gives the effect of gold work.

Architecture
Traditional island architecture in the Solomons varies throughout the islands, and consisted of local materials. This included sago palm leafs, used as thatching, hardwood and betel nut palms, and pandanus, woven into mats. Timber was used to construct the fames, and vines were often employed to help secure the structure. Wood also served as floor covering. In rural construction, kitchens were typically separate from sleeping quarters. As with many Pacific Island nations, modern architecture remains a new and still-developing concept.

Music
Music and dance have traditionally played an important role in the lives of the islanders and are an integral part of feasts. Traditional songs are chants that usually tell stories. Thus, the songs might be about well-known events, such as a war or natural disasters, or imitate the sounds of nature, such as birdcalls. They might also be epic songs, telling stories of folk heroes, or war chants. The singers usually sit in two rows and may shake hand-held rattles while singing. The narrative songs of the male singers may also be accompanied by clapping sticks.

The panpipes are a popular instrument and consist of bamboo or reed pipes bundled together. These tubes may be open at both ends or closed at the lower end. The bundle is held steady and produces a gentle, woodwind sound. The bamboo band was invented in the western Solomons in the 1920s. The instrument is similar to the panpipes, and consists of about fifteen to twenty horizontal pieces of bamboo, of varying length, joined together. The player strikes these on the open end with a rubber thong, usually to the accompaniment of a guitar or ukulele.

The drum is another important instrument in traditional culture. It is an object of prestige and is kept in the hut of the chief. The drum that is native to the Solomon Islands resembles a large wooden pillar-box and is made out of a single piece of tree trunk. Other instruments include castanets or rattles, which are usually made of nuts or seeds tied on a string. These are worn around the ankle and beaten by continual stamping.

Dance
Traditional island dances have been handed down for generations and vary from island to island. Usually, the dancers at the feasts wear special ornaments, headdresses, or flowers, and may carry sticks decorated with feathers. The dances are usually danced by young men, although there are some dances for women. However, men and women do not dance together. Each dance is composed of four or five intricate movements,

with a pause in between. The most common dance is danced by two rows of dancers, each row being led by an expert. They weave in and out, face each other, retire and then return, all the while playing their ankle-worn rattles. Other traditional dances are performed while squatting, using only the head and the arms.

Dance has traditionally been perceived as a serious art. Today, traditional dance on the islands has lost its cultural significance, mainly as a result of increased foreign influence. Similarly, traditional music has also lost some of its appeal with the advent of the radio and other media. Contemporary youth prefer Western popular music or Western-inspired local music to traditional sounds and styles.

Literature

The literary arts have seen a marked development in the recent history of the Solomon Islands. In the 1950s, a number of local writers published notable works of poetry and prose. In 1984, the Solomon Islands Creative Writers' Association (SICWA) was formed by a group of academics and scholars to encourage an artistic genre that was not part of the indigenous tradition. It held writers' workshops for students and encouraged all genres of literature. After a period of dormancy, this organization was revived in 2008 and began publishing a literary magazine. Notable contemporary writers include Rexford Orotaloa (1956–), John Saunana (1945–2013), considered the first native novelist, and poet Jully Makini (1953–).

CULTURE

Arts & Entertainment

The arts have been slow to develop in the Solomon Islands, but today there are a number of art museums and galleries, mainly in Honiara and in other urban centers. The Solomon Islands National Museum in Honiara celebrates the traditional arts. Its exhibits focus on archeology, architecture, traditional dance, and artifacts of cultural importance, such as body ornaments and shell and feather currency. An exhibit known as Cultural Village is located behind the center and features eight traditionally constructed houses, each representing the culture of one of the islands' provinces. The National Art Gallery and Cultural Center and the King Solomon Arts and Crafts Center are also located in Honiara.

The visual arts are beginning to flourish in the islands. The contemporary artists of the Solomon Islands participate in the renowned Festival of Pacific Arts, which takes place every four years in a different Oceanic country (the Solomon Islands hosted the festival in 2012). The South Pacific Contemporary Art Competition is also held annually in an effort to encourage a culture of visual arts in the region. Within the islands themselves, organizations and festivals such as the Artist Association of the Solomon Islands and the Solomon Islands Youth Arts Festival celebrate and promote local artists. One burgeoning contemporary artist is Ake Lianga (1975–), whose works feature birds and animals from his native islands.

Local music is also celebrated and preserved. Indigenous music is celebrated at the Wantok Music Festival, while prominent hotels in Honiara host weekly panpipe performances by the most popular contemporary panpipe bands like the Narasirato Pan Pipers. Other contemporary artists, such as Sammy Saeni, who performs as Sharzy, have successfully created unique music stylings that incorporate indigenous and contemporary styles such as reggae.

Tennis and soccer are popular sports throughout the islands, and attract young athletes to qualifying competitions for the Olympic Games. Michael Leong (1986–) is the top tennis player from the islands and a Davis Cup contender. The Solomon Islands belong to the Oceania Football Confederation, and the national team competes in the Olympics. Golf and basketball organizations hold events in the islands throughout the year. Honiara boasts a seaside golf course under palm trees.

The Western Province holds a week-long Festival of the Sea in December. Community teams participate in war-canoe racing, fishing, and other oceanic competitions.

Cultural Sites & Landmarks

The Solomon Islands have a number of natural and historical landmarks. One of these natural sites, East Rennell, was designated as a World Heritage Site by the United Nations Education, Scientific and Cultural Organization (UNESCO) in 1998. East Rennell makes up one-third of Rennell Island, the southernmost of the Solomon Islands and the world's largest raised coral atoll. The site covers a total area of 370 square kilometers (142 square miles), including Lake Tegano, the largest fresh water lake in the insular Pacific. The lake is brackish and contains about 200 limestone islands. Rennell Island is covered with dense forest and is home to a number of endemic plant and animal species, including rare orchid species. Other natural landmarks include the Mataniko and Tenaru Falls, perhaps two of the most beautiful waterfalls in the South Pacific region.

The Solomon Islands are steeped in history, ranging from the ferocious headhunting tribes that populated the islands' Western Province to the monuments and wreckage leftover from World War II. There are several skull shrines dedicated to the traditional practice of headhunting still extant throughout the Solomon Islands, most notably on Skull Island, a small island of New Georgia. During the Second World War, the Solomon Islands were the site of bitter fighting between the Japanese and the Allied forces. Relics from the war are still scattered throughout the islands' jungles and waters. The islands are also home to some prominent war memorials, including the United States Memorial and the Japanese Peace Memorial. Other important WWII landmarks include Bloody Ridge, Alligator Creek, and Red Beach. Kennedy Island is named after U.S. President John F. Kennedy (1917–1963), who, as a young naval officer, arrived there with his crew in August 1943 after their boat sank.

The island hosts an annual Kennedy swim to commemorate the event, attended by open water swimmers from around the world.

Libraries & Museums

As the cultural capital of the Solomon Islands, Honiara's libraries, universities, and museums contain a wealth of information about the islands' history and native culture. The National Museum offers a large collection of cultural and artistic attractions including examples of native Melanesian art. The National Art Gallery contains historic and modern artwork representing both Melanesian and Polynesian culture. The Honiara Cultural Center is a small, privately owned museum dedicated to the preservation of native Melanesian culture and contains reconstructions and preserved specimens of native clothing, art and architecture.

Holidays

Official holidays observed in the Solomon Islands include the Queen's Official Birthday (June 6), and Independence Day (July 7). In addition, most traditional Christian holidays are celebrated.

Youth Culture

The contemporary youth culture of the Solomon Islands, especially in the urban centers, seems to be a hybrid of traditional and Western cultures. In the rural areas, youth are immersed in a largely traditional culture. There is a strict social hierarchy in these areas, and young people are rigidly controlled by elders, limiting a specific youth culture. There are a limited number of available activities, and sport is generally the most popular pastime among rural youth. Many villages have outdoor volleyball nets and hold rugby games. Other popular sports include netball and football (soccer).

Many youth are migrating to urban centers. However, this has proven to be problematic, as there are not enough educational or employment opportunities to accommodate them. As a result, youth become dependent on kin, and those that simply hang about have been labeled "liu." Due to globalization and heightened tourism, more urban youth are also exhibiting behaviors attributed to Western culture, such as casual socializing between genders and the consumption of alcohol. Western fashions and music are also becoming increasingly popular amongst urban youth, though many still cling to or incorporate elements of native culture.

SOCIETY

Transportation

The primary mode of transportation in the Solomon Islands is by sea, with dinghies and single-hulled canoes most commonly used. Simple dugout canoes are used on rivers. In the interior, walking is also a common mode of transportation. Most villages are connected by bush tracks, and the villagers are used to walking long distances. Road and air travel are also being developed, but public minibuses are only available in Honiara. The road system in the islands is not very extensive and automobiles were introduced in Honiara only in the 1990s, mostly as second-hand imports from Asia. Urban centers are also served by taxis. The islands' only international airport is Henderson Airport, and there are few direct flights.

Traffic moves on the right side of the road.

Transportation Infrastructure

The road network of the Solomon Islands only encompasses thirty islands and stretches an estimated 1,390 kilometers (864 miles). Only about one-fifth of the population has access to land transportation. Most land transport is based on the islands of Malaita and Guadalcanal, and only 11 percent of rural areas are connected by suitable roads. Overall, an estimated 23 percent of villages or towns have road access, while an estimated 32 percent are accessible by sea. A further 40 percent of villages are only accessible by tracks or tails, while only 5 percent are accessible by river. Transportation services are typically small-scale in nature. Roadways in the capital of Honiara have recently been sealed or resurfaced.

Media & Communications

Traditionally, due to a high rate of illiteracy, a vast number of languages, and poor television reception, the radio has been the primary and most influential communications medium. The Solomon Islands Broadcasting Corporation (SIBC) operates a public radio service, including the national stations Radio Happy Isles and Wantok FM, and the provincial station Radio Happy Lagoon. The Australian and Taiwanese governments have provided significant technical assistance to the SIBC, and the former has sponsored programs aimed at promoting peace. There are no local television services in the islands, but satellite dishes pick up international news services and Australian programs

There is one daily newspaper, the English-language *Solomon Star*, and two prominent weekly newspapers, the *Solomons Voice* and *Solomons Times*. The press is relatively free and unbiased. During the coup staged in the islands in 2000, some journalists were persecuted, and their working conditions deteriorated. However, this is no longer the case, and the government generally respects the constitutional provisions for the freedom of speech and expression.

Solomon Telekom is the sole provider of telecommunication services in the islands, but the government has opened up the telecom market for more competition. Internet use is growing rapidly, and there are many Internet cafés around the islands. As of 2014, there were an estimated 46,400 Internet users. Although this number covers only 7.6 percent of the population, it is more than five times the total of Internet users as recently as 2007.

SOCIAL DEVELOPMENT

Standard of Living

The Solomon Islands ranked 158 out of 187 countries on the 2013 United Nations Human Development Index.

Water Consumption

An estimated 93 percent of urban households have access to an "improved" water supply or resource (which includes protected wells or springs, standpipes, or rainwater collection), while access in rural areas was at 77 percent. However, contamination during storage, collection, and transportation of water, particular rainwater, remains an issue; it is believed a small amount of households actively treat their drinking water. In addition, an estimated 70 percent of residences lack access to private or improved sanitation facilities, and the number increases to 85 in rural areas.

Education

Education is not compulsory in the Solomon Islands. Primary education is offered for children between the ages of six and twelve, though the majority of children attend school around the ages of eight and nine. According to the United Nations, the net attendance rate for primary school is 94 percent. Secondary education is available for students until age sixteen or seventeen. Generally, at the age of thirteen, enrollment rates decline significantly for all children.

Slightly less than half of the Solomon Islands' 350 primary and twenty secondary schools are "national" schools, operated by the government or by churches. The others are "provincial schools," operated by provincial assemblies. They provide vocational education, especially in agriculture. The Solomon Islands Centre of the University of the Pacific is located in Honiara. Also, scholarships are provided for students to attend university abroad. Many Solomon Islanders attend universities in Fiji and Papua New Guinea.

The average literacy rate in the Solomon Islands is estimated at 84 percent.

Women's Rights

Women occupy a curious position in Solomon Islands society. While they make significant societal contributions as mothers and in the workforce, and form the backbone of the kinship system, they usually remain unappreciated, and often suppressed. This is particularly evident in rural areas, where there is a strict division of tasks between men and women. Women are responsible for domestic and agrarian tasks, as well as child rearing. They are also generally expected to perform laborious task such as collecting firewood and water, and are trained for these tasks from an early age. Thus, even in their youth, they are trained for a role of subordination.

However, many women do not perceive their roles in society to be necessarily degrading, particularly in matrilineal cultures where women own land and inheritance occurs along the maternal line (though decision-making rests with men). Often, they are proud of their roles within the family structure and kin group. In fact, it is argued that the high social and economic value placed on women is reflected by the bride-price system. A woman's own family will not let her go until a sufficiently high price has been paid for her, thus compensating for their financial loss. However, the system of bride-price also reinforces her subordinate role in society. Moreover, it is one of the primary reasons behind the high rates of domestic violence and abuse of women in society, since the husband has essentially paid for his wife. In most island cultures, however, if a woman is abused by her husband, male family members have a right to demand compensation.

Recently, with increased education and exposure to Western influences, many women are beginning to question this traditional role, though gender equality is far from being realized. While more women are receiving an education, it is usually at the primary level. Women also lack prominence in the political sphere but are beginning to take part in local and national politics. In 1984, a woman was elected as a prominent civil servant and fourteen women contested in the 1994 general elections. Although these numbers are small, they are still significant compared to other Pacific island nations. Female participation in the national work force is still significantly less than that of men, however. As of 2015, the UN estimated that only 60 percent of the entire female population was engaged in employment, significantly less than their male counterparts. In particular, women find it difficult to attain higher-level positions because of widespread gender discrimination. Women are also twice as likely as men to be uneducated. The professions of nursing and teaching have a large number of female workers, but they remain at the junior levels.

Health Care

An estimated 80 percent of the population of the Solomon Islands has access to basic health services. However, doctor-to-patient ratios are low and health services in rural areas consist mainly of health or nursing stations. As of the early 21st century, there are eight provincial hospitals and three private hospitals.

Major causes of death include respiratory diseases, diarrhea and malaria, which is a major health issue. In recent years, the incidence of diabetes has increased tenfold. This increase is attributed to a change to "modern" eating habits in urban areas.

Average life expectancy in the Solomon Islands is seventy-five years; seventy-two years for men and seventy-eight years for women (2015 estimate). The annual health expenditure per capita is roughly $106 (USD).

GOVERNMENT

Structure

The Solomon Islands is a parliamentary democracy. The British monarch is the head of state, represented by a governor-general whom the monarch appoints.

The governor-general is advised by a cabinet. At the head of the cabinet is the prime minister, who is elected by the legislature and other ministers. The other ministers in the cabinet are appointed by the governor-general, with the advice of the prime minister.

The legislative branch consists of the unicameral National Parliament. There are fifty members in the legislature, elected to four-year terms by popular vote. The Solomon Islands has universal adult suffrage for adults twenty-one years and older.

Political Parties

The Solomon Islands has a multi-party system and political parties must form coalition governments; however, the system is often perceived as weak and constantly shifting. There are six prominent parties, and after the 2014 general election, no political party won more than seven seats; thirty-two seats went to independents. Parties represented in government as of 2015 include the Democratic Alliance Party (DAP), the Kadere Party of Solomon Islands (KPSI), the People's Alliance Party (PAP), the Solomon Islands People First Party (SIPFP), the Solomon Islands Party for Rural Advancement (SIPRA), and the United Democratic Party.

Local Government

The Solomon Islands is composed of nine provinces and the capital of Honiara, constituting ten administrative divisions. Provincial governance is overseen by the minister for provincial government, and consists of councilors, who serve four-year terms, and mayors and provincial premiers, who are elected by the councilors and assembly members. Urban councils operate under provincial governments. The city council of Honiara, elected to four-year terms, is overseen by the Department of Home Affairs; there is also a town council for Noro, located in the Western Province.

Local government is structured under three legislative acts: the Provincial and Local Government Act, the Local Government Act, and the Honiara City Council Act. Provincial governments retain responsibility for transportation, infrastructure, health and education matters, while the Honiara City Council has taxation and revenue-raising related powers and is responsible for a wide range of services.

Judicial System

The judicial system consists of a high court and magistrate's court, as well as a network of custom land courts spread throughout the various islands.

There is no supreme court in the Solomon Islands. Judicial power rests with the minister for justice and legal affairs in the cabinet.

Taxation

The top income tax in the Solomon Islands is 40 percent, while the top corporate tax rate is 30 percent (35 percent for foreign companies). Other taxes include property tax, insurance tax, and an excise on tobacco and beer.

Armed Forces

The Solomon Islands does not maintain a military or armed forces for the purpose of national defense. Following the unrest and ethnic conflict that has plagued the country since 1998, the Regional Assistance Mission to Solomon Islands (RAMSI), led by Australia and consisting of other Pacific nations (now fifteen overall), arrived in 2003 to intervene and restore peace. Following the riots that plagued the 2006 general election, RAMSI forces were bolstered. The country does maintain a police force, the Royal Solomon Islands Police Force (RSIPF), and receives assistance from the PPF (Participating Police Force), composed of other Pacific nations. As of 2015, RAMSI forces remain in the country for supplementary policing purposes.

Foreign Policy

The Solomon Islands achieved independence from Great Britain in 1978, and the foreign policy of the islands is still in the process of maturation. The island nation's foreign relations are mostly influenced by national security—the Solomon Islands have no military—and economic development. The Solomon Islands is a developing country and heavily dependent on international aid. International trade relations with the United States and China are important, and the country has focused on encouraging foreign direct investment in recent years.

The island nation is active both internationally and regionally. The Solomon Islands joined the United Nations (UN) in 1978, as well as the Commonwealth of Nations (which consists of former British colonies). It also holds membership in the International Bank of Reconstruction and Development (IBRD), the International Monetary Fund (IMF), and the European Economic Community/African, Caribbean, Pacific Group (EEC/ACP). Regional organizations of which it is a member state include the Secretariat of Pacific Communities (SPC), the Pacific Islands Forum (PIF), and the Melanesian Spearhead Group (MSG).

Relations between the Solomon Islands and both Papua New Guinea (PNG) and Austria have been strained. The rebellion and secession of the island of Bougainville—the largest island of the Solomon Islands group—from PNG in the late 20th century led to an influx of refugees into the Solomons and several attacks on the northern Solomon islands. After a 1998 peace treaty and the normalization of the border in 2004, relations between the two countries have remained cordial. Australia has provided substantial economic and technical assistance to the islands, and plays a significant role in the Regional Assistance Mission to the Solomon Islands (RAMSI). However, some Solomon leaders have accused Australia of using this developmental aid and political power as leverage and interfering in the domestic affairs of the island nation.

The Solomon Islands enjoys strong bilateral relations with the United Kingdom (UK). Until 2004, the UK was sponsoring a regional aid program in the islands. The UK continues to be the largest multilateral donor of funds—through the European Union (UN)—to the islands, contributing almost 15 percent of total developmental aid. The Solomons also formed strong diplomatic relations with the United States after gaining independence. The U.S. government funded the construction of the Solomon Islands Parliament building and has provided technical and humanitarian assistance. However, trade relations between the two nations remain weak. In 2015, U.S. exports to the islands were less than 5 percent of the total exports, and the Solomon Islands' exports to the United States were negligible.

In the early 21st century, the Solomon Islands has established a comparatively aggressive "look north" policy aimed at establishing trade and diplomatic relations with more countries as a means of increasing trade and securing aid. As a result, the islands have developed relations nations such as Cuba, Switzerland, and the Republic of China (ROC, or Taiwan). They are also one of only a few countries which recognize Taiwan as an independent nation. In return for this recognition, they have received substantial aid. The Solomon Islands government has also introduced a series of investment incentives and guarantees to attract foreign direct investment.

Human Rights Profile

International human rights law insists that states respect civil and political rights, and promote an individual's economic, social, and cultural rights. The United Nations Universal Declaration on Human Rights (UDHR) is recognized as the standard for international human rights. Its authors sought the counsel of the world's great thinkers, philosophers, and religious leaders, and were careful to create a document that reflects the core values shared by every world culture. (To read this document or view the articles relating to cultural human rights, visit http://www.udhr.org/UDHR/default.htm.)

The human rights situation in the Solomons dramatically deteriorated at the beginning of the 21st century after civil and ethnic tension resulted in armed conflict in 1998. The situation worsened with a coup d'état in June 2000. Without the military to enforce the rule of law during the national emergency, the security situation worsened, and the victims of the situation were largely innocent civilians. There were a large number of arbitrary abductions and arrests, and those imprisoned faced torture, rape and even murder. Ethnic minorities and women were targeted with abuse and the crisis was worsened by the fact that police forces, like rebels, also perpetrated human rights abuses, including the forced displacement of thousands of people and looting and burning. The rebel army, known as the Isatabu Freedom Movement (IFM), is also believed to have recruited and trained child soldiers.

The human rights situation has significantly improved since the end of the ethnic conflict. The government generally upholds the protection of human rights as declared in the constitution. In addition, some of those who perpetuated human rights abuses during the conflict have been brought to justice. However, some causes for concern do remain. In 2006, for example, there were allegations made by several prisoners that they were mistreated and tortured while being questioned by police. Discrimination and violence against women also remains a significant problem, and in recent years, with a worsening HIV/AIDS endemic, there has been a rise in the practice of black magic and sorcery. This is usually directed against women, who are violently abused, tortured and even buried alive in the name of exorcising supposed demons. Women and disabled people are discriminated against in the workplace.

ECONOMY

Overview of the Economy

The economy of the Solomon Islands collapsed in the early 21st century due to a combination of government debt and domestic turbulence between ethnic and political groups. As a result of this unrest, many international businesses left the nation. Honiara was severely affected by the economic downturn; many of the city's key businesses were force to close and tourism dwindled.

In April 2007, the World Bank assisted the government in establishing a new strategy for economic growth, known as the Agricultural and Rural Development Strategy (ARDS), which provided $200 million over a five-year period to be invested in rural infrastructure development and the expansion of jobs in Honiara and surrounding communities. In 2014, the country's gross domestic product (GDP) was estimated at $1.155 billion (USD), with a per capita GDP of $1,900 (USD).

Approximately 75 percent of the population is employed in agriculture, fishing, or forestry, accounting for over 50 percent of the nation's gross domestic product (GDP). Cocoa, fish, and palm oil are among the nation's chief exports and are generally shipped to China, which receives over 60 percent of the nation's products. Italy and Australia are also important export partners. The nation's most substantial export is timber. Industrial plants around Honiara process harvested wood and food products into exportable goods.

The services industry, which includes tourism, employs approximately 20 percent of the nation's workforce and accounts for about 38 percent of the GDP. In Honiara, a majority of residents are employed in services or hospitality industries. The tourism industry is not based in Honiara, but the city serves as a major hub for tourists traveling to other destinations throughout the islands.

Industry

Major industries on the islands include forestry (for fuel and industrial wood), preparation of frozen fish, production of coconut oil and palm oil, copra (dried coconut meat), electricity production, and limited mining (mostly for gold and silver).

Exports total approximately $493.1 million (USD) annually. The major exported commodities include timber copra, fish, and cocoa.

Labor

In 2007, the Solomon Islands had an estimated labor force of approximately 202,500, with the majority of the population—about 75 percent—working in the agricultural sector, mainly subsistence farming. The services sector constituted about 20 percent of the population, while industry and manufacturing employed about 5 percent.

Energy/Power/Natural Resources

The Solomon Islands' natural resources include fish, phosphates, and trees. The islands have considerable deposits of minerals such as gold, nickel, zinc, lead, and bauxite, but these are relatively unexploited.

A threat is economic development, including mining and logging operations. Many of the people of the Solomon Islands are poor and use their natural resources to help improve their lives. Forests provide building materials, firewood, hunting, fishing and materials for handicrafts. Traditional medicines are also found in the forests, and many people use these to supplement Western medicine. As the population grows, the forests suffer. However, the rainforest can also be a resource for developing herbal medicines and pharmaceuticals.

Electricity is provided by the Solomon Islands Electricity Authority (SIEA); as of 2010, the SIEA provides only an estimated 22 percent of the population with electricity.

Fishing

Tuna is the primary catch of the Solomon Islands' fishing industry, and the industry largely operates as a joint venture with Japan. Under certain agreements, both bilateral and multilateral, nations such as the Republic of Korea and Taiwan also fish Solomon Islands territory. In 2009, to bolster the domestic tuna fishing industry, the Solomon Islands government announced plans to dissolve bilateral agreements and to establish several major onshore fishing companies that would be involved not only in processing catches, but on the production side as well (labeling, packaging, etc.) As of 2015, the town of Noro in the Western Province is the center of the country's onshore fisheries sector.

Forestry

Logging in the Solomon Islands has experienced a decline in the early 21st century after a boom in the 1990s. As of 2011, it was estimated that logging represented about 46 percent of government revenues. Unsustainable logging, deforestation, and illegal logging remain huge concerns and have had severe environmental impacts.

Mining/Metals

Gold mining was once a small-scale operation at the Gold Ridge Mine—it yielded just over 200,000 ounces of gold between 1998 and 2000, providing nearly 30 percent of the national income—but the turn-of-the-century conflicts afflicting the island nation led to the abandonment of operations. The mine is now operated under the control of an Australian-based mining company. The Solomon Islands also has nickel and copper deposits, and undersea mining is being explored.

Agriculture

Only 2 percent of the land in the Solomon Islands is cultivated. Most farming takes place in the lowland forests. Traditionally, fruit trees were planted, with yams and greens beneath. These plantings provided food during long droughts or after damaging storms. Recently, though, soil fertility has declined, probably from over-planting. Now, when a disaster strikes, such as the long drought of 2004–05, many people face starvation unless relief aid arrives.

On the other hand, when there is no disaster, the islanders have access to a greater diversity of foods than in the past. Today's major agricultural crops include coconuts, oil palm trees, rice, cocoa beans, sweet potatoes, yams, taro, vegetables, melons, and other fruit.

Animal Husbandry

Solomon Islanders keep cattle and pigs, and, to a lesser extent, goats and poultry, as well as bees; as of 2008, the company had about 500 beekeepers. It is estimated that over half of the households keep pigs. The number of cattle in the country declined significantly after the civil unrest of the early 21st century.

Tourism

Tourism in the Solomon Islands saw a decline at the beginning of the century due in part to the country's violent ethnic conflict. However, it has been on the rebound since. Improvements in tourism infrastructure include an increase in international airline connections and the 2009 opening of the Heritage Park Hotel in Honiara, the country's first international business standard, or upscale, hotel. Tourism outside Honiara has also been progressing with an influx of foreign investment. In 2014, approximately 24,400 tourist arrivals were estimated.

The Solomon Islands have many attractions for tourists. Divers enjoy viewing the wreckage of ships and planes in the waters surrounding Guadalcanal, especially in the Ironbottom Sound channel (so named because of the large number of Allied and Japanese warships and planes that were sunk there during World War II). Attractions in Honiara include Chinatown, the Point Cruz Yacht Club and the National Museum. Marovo Lagoon, in the Western Province, is the world's largest island-fringed lagoon.

John F. Kennedy's PT-boat base on Munda Island has been turned into a tourist site. Plum Pudding Island, the tiny atoll that Kennedy swam to when his PT boat was rammed in 1943, has been renamed Kennedy Island.

Eco-tourism, including island-hopping, bird watching, and village visits, is also beginning to develop in the Solomon Islands. Lake Tenggano, on the eastern end of Rennell Island, is listed as a World Heritage Site by the United Nations Educational, Scientific and Cultural Organization (UNESCO).

Izza Tahir, Ellen Bailey, Micah Issit

DO YOU KNOW?

- The capital's name "Honiara" came into use in English as an attempt to pronounce the Melanesian term "Naho-e-ara," meaning "facing the east and southeast wind." The winds that hit the city are important to the year-round climate, as they provide heat during the rainy season and cooler temperatures during the dry season.

Bibliography

Alailima, Fay. *New Politics in the South Pacific*. Rarotonga (Cook Islands): Institute of Pacific Studies, University of the South Pacific, 1994.

Ansell, Nicola. *Children, Youth and Development*. New York: Routledge, 2005.

Bollard, Alice A. and Anthony R. Walker. *Givers of Wisdom, Laborers Without Gain*. Suva: Institute of Pacific Studies, 2000.

Coates, Austin. *Western Pacific Islands*. London: Her Majesty's Stationary Office, 1970.

DeRouen, Karl R. and Paul Bellamy. *International Security and the United States*. Westport (CT): Praeger Security International, 2008.

Green, Richard. *The Commonwealth Yearbook 2006*. London: Nexus Strategic Partnerships, 2006.

Howarth, Crispin. *Variaiku: Pacific Arts from the Solomon Islands*. Canberra: Australian National Gallery, 2011.

Kent, Janet. *The Solomon Islands*. London: Clarke Doble & Brendon, Limited, 1972.

Lal, Brij. V. and Kate Fortune. *The Pacific Islands Encyclopedia*. Honolulu: University of Hawaii Press, 2000.

Massey, Brent. *Where In the World Do I Belong?* S.I: Jetlag Press, 2006.

Moore, Clive. *Happy Isles in Crisis*. Canberra, ACT: Asia Pacific Press, 2005.

Morris, Desmond. *The Naked Woman*. New York: Thomas Dunne Books, 2005.

Ogashiwa, Yoko S. *Microstates and Nuclear Issues*. Rarotonga (Cook Islands): Institute of Pacific Studies, University of the South Pacific, 1991.

Oliver, Douglas L. *A Solomon Islands Society*. Cambridge: Harvard University Press, 1955.

Works Cited

"Background Note: Solomon Islands." *U.S. Department of State*. http://www.state.gov/r/pa/ei/bgn/2799.htm#foreign

"Country Profile: Solomon Islands." *BBC News*. http://news.bbc.co.uk/2/hi/asia-pacific/country_profiles/1249307.stm#media

"Data by Country." *World Bank*. November 4, 2015. http://data.worldbank.org/indicator/ST.INT.ARVL

"East Rennell." *World Heritage*. http://whc.unesco.org/en/list/854

"Human Development Reports: Solomon Islands." *United Nations Development Programme*. November 3, 2015. http://hdr.undp.org/en/countries/profiles/SLB

McKinnon, Rowan et al. *Papua New Guinea and the Solomon Islands*. Footscray (Vic): Lonely Planet Publications, 2008.

"RAMSI." *Ramsi*. November 4, 2015. http://www.ramsi.org/

"Solomon Islands." *UN Women*. November 4, 2015. http://asiapacific.unwomen.org/en/countries/fiji/co/solomon-islands

"Solomon Islands." *WHO*. November 3, 2015. http://www.who.int/countries/slb/en/

"Solomon Islands." *City Population*. November 3, 2015. http://www.citypopulation.de/Solomon.html

"Solomon Islands." *Ship for World Youth Alumni Association*. July 2007. http://www.swyaa.org/Handbook/Solomon_Islands.htm

"Solomon Islands." *The World Fact Book*. November 3, 2015. https://www.cia.gov/library/publications/the-world-factbook/geos/bp.html

"Solomon Islands." *U.S. Department of State*. November 3, 2015. http://www.state.gov/g/drl/rls/hrrpt/2006/78791.htm

"Solomon Islands." *World Travel Guide*. http://www.worldtravelguide.net/country/253/communications/Australia-and-South-Pacific/Solomon-Islands.html

"Solomon Islands: A Forgotten Conflict." *Amnesty International*. March 6, 2000. http://www.amnesty.org/en/library/info/ASA43/005/2000

Solomon Islands Visitor Bureau. http://www.visitsolomons.com.sb/solomons/export/sites/SVB/Attractions/Index.html

"Solomon Islands." UN Data. November 3, 2015. http://data.un.org/CountryProfile.aspx?crName=Solomon%20Islands

Stanley, David. *Moon Handbooks South Pacific*. Emeryville (CA): Avalon Travel, 2004.

Waite, Deborah. "TOTO ISU (NguzuNguzu)." *Tribal Arts*. http://www.tribalarts.com/feature/solomon/index.html

Welkam Honiara. March 27, 2009. http://www.welkamhoniara.com/

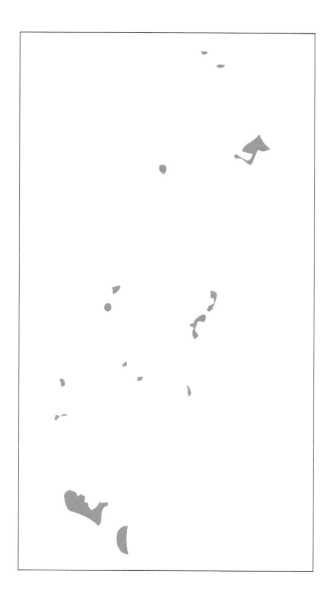

TONGA

Introduction

The Kingdom of Tonga is an archipelago of approximately 170 islands in the Pacific Ocean. There are four main groups of islands within the archipelago: Tongatapu, He'apai, Vava'u, and the Niuas. Although fewer than forty islands are inhabited year-round, most of them are developed for agriculture, adapted for tourism, or protected as wilderness.

Tonga is the only monarchy in the Pacific and the last remaining Polynesian kingdom; its royal family traces its ancestry back a thousand years.

GENERAL INFORMATION

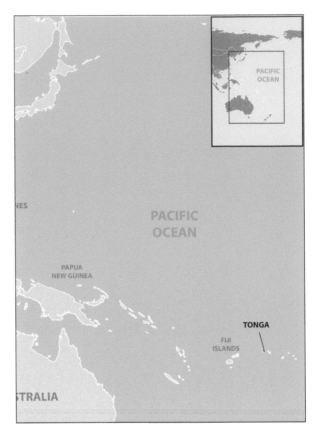

Official Language: Tongan, English
Population: 106,501 (2015 estimate)
Currency: Pa'anga
Coins: The pa'anga is subdivided into 100 seniti. Circulated coins include denominations of 1, 2, 5, 10, 20, and 50 seniti, and 1 pa'anga (though the 1¢ and 2¢ coins are rarely used).
Land Area: 717 square kilometers (276 square miles)
Water Area: 30 square kilometers (12 square miles)
National Motto: "Koe Otua mo Tonga ko hoku tofi'a" ("God and Tonga are my heritage")
National Anthem: "Ko e Fasi Oe Tu'i 'Oe Otu Tonga" ("O Almighty God Above")
Capital: Nuku'alofa
Time Zone: GMT +13
Flag Description: The flag of Tonga is red with a white canton, or upper hoist (left) quarter. Within the white canton is a centered red cross that does not touch the canton's edges.

Population

Tongans are Polynesians. On all the islands, only about 2 percent of the population is non-native (most of these are of European descent or Chinese). The Polynesian language and culture is remarkably uniform, given the number of islands in Tonga and the geographical distances between them. Approximately two-thirds of Tonga's population lives in or near the capital, Nuku'alofa, on the main island of Tongatapu; roughly 23.7 percent of the population is urban. Of the island nation's 170 islands, only thirty-six are believed to be inhabited, though that number has been estimated to be as high as forty-eight.

Languages

Tongans are bilingual. Tongan is universally spoken, and English is the language of education and international commerce. Both are officially

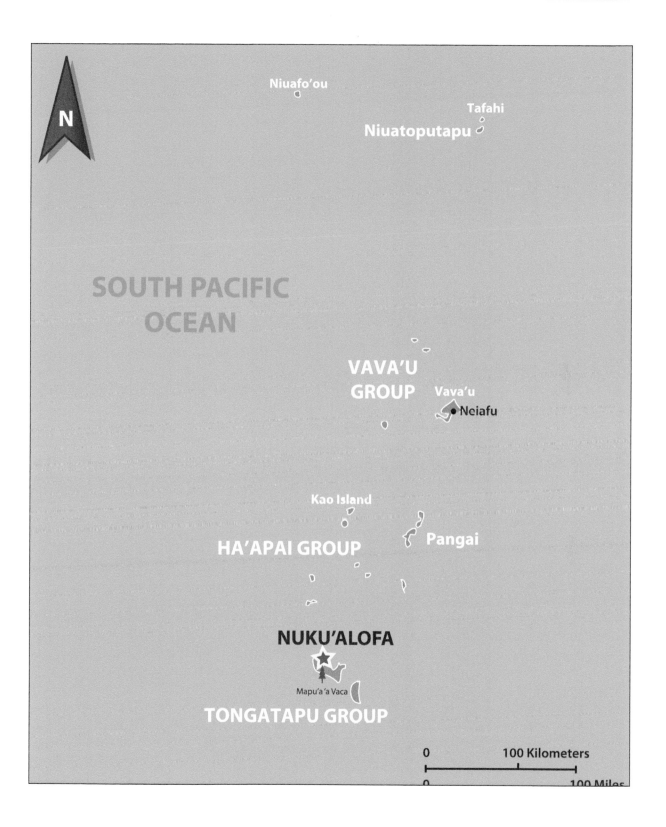

Principal Cities by Population (2011):

- Nuku'alofa (24,229)
- Neiafu (4,057)
- Haveluloto (3,465)
- Tofoa-Koloua (3,526)
- Vaini (3,235)
- Pangai-Hihifo (2,055)
- Pea (2,079)
- Ha'ateiho (2,561)
- Lapaha (2,077)
- Fua'amotu (1,722)

recognized. English is also widely spoken in tourist areas.

Native People & Ethnic Groups

Although Tonga may have been inhabited as early as 3000 BCE, carbon-dating has confirmed a human presence on the islands only since 1100 BCE. Polynesians are descendants of the Lapitas, who arrived in Tonga about 3,500 years ago, first settling on Tongatapu near the present capital. Most anthropologists believe the Lapitas originated in Asia. Their descendents became warriors, attacking neighboring islands and at times extending the Tongan empire to Samoa and parts of Fiji.

Religions

Religion plays an important role in Tongan culture and in the social fabric of the capital, Nuku'alofa. As a result of the efforts of missionaries, Protestant Christianity is the dominant faith (64.9 percent). In 1822, missionaries introduced Christianity to Tonga. In time, they converted Taufa'ahau, king of Ha'apai, and most of his people. Taking the Christian name George, Taufa'ahau later united Tonga and became its first king. Today there are also small groups of Mormons (16.8 percent), Baha'i and Muslims on the islands.

Observation of the Sabbath is enshrined in Tonga's national constitution. As of midnight Saturday, all commercial and recreational activi-

ties in the capital cease until Monday morning. However, foreign visitors are exempted from this. Fines or jail time often await those Tongans who indulge in swimming, sports or other forbidden pursuits. Some members of the Tongan parliament have made attempts to relax these restrictions, but their efforts have been unsuccessful.

Climate

Tonga's climate, though tropical, is mild compared to other Pacific islands. There are essentially two seasons: the warm season from December to May, and the cool season from May to December.

Temperatures in winter (July to September) vary from 17° to 22° Celsius (62° to 71° Fahrenheit). In summer (December to April), temperatures hover between 25° and 33° Celsius (77° and 91° Fahrenheit). Summers can be humid, but trade winds and the island's distance from the equator have moderating effects. Most of Tonga's rainfall occurs in late summer.

Because Tonga lies directly on the cyclone and typhoon path in the South Pacific, storms pose threats, especially between January and March. Serious storms sweep through the area every few years. Volcanic activity on Fonuafo'ou is also a cause of concern.

ENVIRONMENT & GEOGRAPHY

Topography

The Kingdom of Tonga is an archipelago of approximately 170 islands in the Pacific Ocean. The small islands rise and sink, varying the total count of islands from year to year. Tonga lies south of Samoa, southeast of Fiji, and more than 1,000 kilometers (600 miles) east of New Caledonia.

Most islands in Tonga are limestone, formed from ancient coral reefs. Others are of volcanic origin, with limestone on top of layers of lava. Either way, the result is fertile soil. The country's coastline measures 419 kilometers (260 miles).

The islands vary dramatically. Some contain active volcanoes, while others have inactive volcanoes with crater lakes, or volcanic cones and barren lava flows. Some, particularly the Niuas and 'Eua, feature tropical rainforests. Others feature sandy beaches, wide farm fields, or sea cliffs.

The highest point in Tonga is on Kao Island, which rises to an elevation of 1,033 meters (3,389 feet) above sea level. The island of Nomuka, once prized by sailing ships for its fresh water, consists almost entirely of a large, brackish lake. Three islands in the southern Vava'u group (Hunga, Kalau, and Fofua) surround a lagoon so calm it could be a lake.

Tonga's largest city and major port is its capital, Nuku'alofa. It more closely resembles a large town rather than a city, and sits astride a narrow isthmus. To the north lies the Pacific Ocean, and to the south is the Fanga'uta Lagoon.

Nuku'alofa features a deep-water harbor, which plays a key economic role as the center for Tonga's agricultural exports. Offshore coral reefs provide a measure of shelter for Nuku'alofa's port. It is, nonetheless, vulnerable to both cyclones and earthquakes, the threat of which influenced the port's design.

Plants & Animals

The archipelago is known for its flowering tropical plants, including the scarlet heilala, frangipani, and several native species of hibiscus. Giant ferns flourish in rainforests and beside inland lakes.

Flying foxes ride thermal currents above the cliffs of 'Eua. Fruit bats have protected status throughout Tonga. There are two native species of iguana found on the islands. Notable bird species include the red shining parrot, the blue-crowned lorikeet, and the incubator bird, so named because it uses warm volcanic mud for incubating and hatching its eggs.

The coral reefs show much variety; hard and soft corals and the rare black coral all flourish, providing shelter for over 100 species of tropical fish.

The flying fox bat is protected by royal decree in Tonga, making it one of the few places it can be found today.

Pollution and deforestation are threats on many islands, due to the growing population and technological change. Marine ecology is also under siege: some coral reefs have been damaged by shell and coral collectors and by starfish depredation. Over-hunting threatens native sea turtles. Tonga, therefore, has established seven protected areas (five of them marine parks) to preserve plants and animals in their habitats.

CUSTOMS & COURTESIES

Greetings

Tongan men will typically greet each other with a handshake. Tongan women might greet close acquaintances and family by kissing them on the cheek; otherwise, they might simply nod or also shake hands. Men may shake hands with women in a business setting, but touching between the sexes, especially in public, is not common. Tongan and English are both the official languages, and common Tongan greetings include

"Mālō e lelei" ("Hello") and "Fēfē hake?" ("How are you?").

Gestures & Etiquette

Tongans are generally characterized as a friendly, but class-conscious people. (Tonga is often referred to as the "Friendly Islands.") Eye contact is customary between social equals, but Tongans will look down when they believe they are dealing with someone of a higher class. Tongans also generally refrain from touching while talking, and conversations are typically held at an arm's length. In addition, displays of public affection are highly discouraged, and women and men generally avoid contact.

Tongans are also considered conservative in matters of dress. Women are expected to wear skirts that are at least knee-length, and may also be expected to keep their shoulders covered as well. Tourists are also expected to wear conservative clothing when they leave the beach or other swimming areas. Expectations, however, are not as strict for men.

As Tonga is the only sovereign monarch among the Pacific Ocean's island nations, there are certain rules of etiquette that apply to the relationship between royalty and the public. All members of the royal family in Tonga are treated with particular deference. For example, Tongans will make sure they are physically lower than a member of the royal family, and may often accomplish this by sitting or kneeling. Additionally, at an event where Tongan royalty will be present, the public is expected to be seated before their arrival.

Eating/Meals

Traditionally, Tongans ate two meals per day, though often the midday meal was the main meal. Meals include locally grown starches, such as yams and cassava, as well as fruits and vegetables, fish, and meats such as chicken and pork or canned meats. Families often eat together and traditionally sat on woven mats, still common in outlying villages. Furniture is more common in urban areas. While utensils are generally available, it is customarily not considered rude to eat using one's hands. Traditionally, it is inappropriate to stand while eating or drinking.

The kava ceremony is one of Tonga's most-celebrated customs. Kava is a drink made from the kava plant (from the pepper family). It has a number of medicinal qualities and is also considered a mild intoxicant. Kava drinking often takes place at a "kava kalupa," or kava club. Kava clubs are usually reserved for men, and feature a four-legged bowl containing a mixture of ground-up kava and water. Kava is also a traditional part of important events. For example, kava is served when a royal title is being bestowed, and a wedding is often not valid until the bride has drunk some kava given to her by her groom. The arrival of visitors is also celebrated with kava.

Visiting

Visits in Tonga are generally unannounced and visitors are expected to remove their shoes before entering a home. Refreshments are generally offered and gifts are welcomed, but not expected. Traditionally, gifts are not opened in the presence of the gift-giver, and refusing a gift may be taken as an insult. Flowers are generally reserved for special occasions, leaving food and traditional crafts as more appropriate gifts for social visits.

LIFESTYLE

Family

Tongan families are generally sociable and close-knit. Nuclear families are becoming more common in Tonga, but traditional households often include grandparents and other extended family members. Elders are given high priority, and men continue to traditionally serve as heads of the family. Family sizes are also increasing in urban areas in recent years as family members from outlying areas are migrating for work and opportunity.

Housing

A traditionally-built Tongan house is called a fale, and is typically made of wood, often from coconut trees. The roof is made of either coconut or sugarcane leaves, or sometimes tin. Inside, the floors are covered with mats, and rooms are separated with curtains. For many Tongans, a house is primarily used for sleeping or shelter, as most activities occur outdoors. Fales are still found in very rural areas and small villages. Traditional Tongan villages also had separate work and meeting houses, with the kava ceremony held in the latter. In cities and larger towns, Western-style houses and materials are more common.

Food

Tongan cuisine is similar to other Polynesian cuisines, with seafood, locally-grown starches and fruits and root vegetables, and pork and chicken forming their primary staples. Starches such as taro, yams, and cassava fill out many meals, and coconuts, which are also one of Tonga's major exports, are part of many recipes. However, arable land is limited and certain foods are only grown seasonally. Thus, Tongans, like many Pacific Islanders, have made imported, durable processed foods part of their diet, and canned meat is a common ingredient in many dishes.

Lu Pulu, one of Tonga's most common dishes, is made from canned corned beef that is mixed with onion, tomato, coconut milk, then wrapped in banana or taro leaves and baked. 'Ota 'Ika is chunks of raw fish that have been marinated in lemon juice, then mixed with coconut cream and vegetables such as carrots, cucumbers, and tomatoes. Faikakai Ngou'a is a popular dessert, and there are numerous ways to make it. Basically, the dish consists of chunks of taro or breadfruit, over which is poured a caramel-like sauce made from coconut milk and sugar. Topai, a dish of doughy dumplings served with a sugar and coconut syrup, is considered the national dish.

Life's Milestones

As Tongans became Christian, they adopted the rituals associated with that religion, including christenings and Christian weddings and funerary traditions. However, some traditional remnants remain. Tongan wedding ceremonies may be performed by a priest or minister, but can include traditional elements such as wearing of Tongan mats and a kava ceremony. Wedding parties can also last as long as three days. When someone dies, relatives lower in status to the deceased may cut their hair. People wear black for amounts of time that vary according to their relationship to the dead. At the funeral itself, emotion is traditionally expressed through "tangi," or crying with words, and breast-beating.

The tradition of circumcision still remains in Tongan culture. Tongan boys mark their entry into manhood by being circumcised when they reach puberty. The procedure used to be carried out on groups of boys by a village elder, but now is done by doctors in health clinics. The occasion is still typically marked by a celebratory feast, and the young men regard the event with pride. In the past, boys used to be tattooed from their hips to their thighs to show they had become men, but this traditional aspect is rarely practiced today.

CULTURAL HISTORY

Art

Traditionally, wood carving in Tonga encompassed aesthetic items such as sculpture and functional items such as canoes and weaponry. Sculpture in Tonga historically focused on deities. The figures were traditionally squat in proportion, with thick bodies and short, powerful legs, and were carved out of wood and ivory as opposed to stone. Wooden sculptures were not typically ornate—the facial features are the bare minimum, with simple slits for the eyes and mouth. However, this minimalism created a "blankness" that was believed to convey the ominous and powerful nature of the deities the sculptures represented.

Tongans also carved ivory figures believed to represent goddesses or important female ancestors. These figures were thought to hold the power of that spirit and were often kept in temples or shrines. Many of these figurines contained a hole that indicated that they were worn by important women in the village during special ceremonies. Though these sculptures were carved from ivory, they were generally not white, but a golden, light tea color. This color was created by rubbing the figurines in coconut oil and holding them over a fire stoked with sugarcane. Smaller ivory figures were likely strung together and worn as a necklace. The size of these ivory figures is likely an indication of the rarity of ivory.

After the Europeans arrived in the 19th century, they successfully converted the Tongans to Christianity. As a result, the Tongans destroyed many of the figures they had carved, condemning them as false idols. A number of the ones that survived were actually collected by the Europeans themselves and sent back to Europe. Thus, small numbers of these traditional sculptures now exist.

The Tongan prowess in carving is also evident in functional items such as canoes and war clubs. Tongans carved giant canoes that they used to travel throughout the Tongan archipelago. To secure enough wood, they would trade with other island kingdoms. Tongans also carved paddle-like clubs used for fighting, called moungalaulau. These war clubs were made from a tough wood called ironwood, which was also used in Tongan architecture. The clubs were formed with a stone adze (an axe-like tool), then inscribed with intricate designs by a tool with a shark's tooth point. The clubs were typically divided into sections, with each section featuring a different pattern, such as zig-zags, cross-hatching, or herringbone. The Tongans also carved war clubs from coconut stalks. Wooden bowls for kava, a common Tongan drink, and other functional items also provide examples of Tongan carving.

In addition to carving, Tongans were also known for their skill in weaving, which is traditionally done by women. They are perhaps best known for their ngatu cloth. Ngatu is the Tongan version of tapa, a type of bark cloth commonly made throughout the Pacific Islands. The Tongans traditionally used the bark from the paper mulberry tree. Other Polynesian islands used different bark, such as breadfruit tree bark, to make their cloth. Ngatu is also distinguished from the other tapa by its use of colors and patterns. The distinctive patterns on the ngatu cloths are created with a kupesi, a design mat made from coconut blossoms. The new ngatu cloth is laid on top of the kupesi and then painted with a dye, imprinting the patterns. The colors from the dyes come from different barks and flowers. A cloth may then be finished by painting a black or brown border around some of the parts of the designs.

Ngatu became an integral part of Tongan culture and was worn at weddings and funerals. Ngatu cloth was also worn by dancers at ceremonies, and, when presented as a gift, was a way of showing respect. Tongan women still make ngatu in almost the exact same way, with few technological advances. Pandanus and coconut leaves are also used in traditional Tongan weaving, which basically consists of an interlocking weaving method. Both materials are woven into a variety of functional and household items, including mats, baskets, canoe sails, clothing, and even children's toys, and instruments.

Dance

Important events in Tonga, such as weddings, funerals, initiation ceremonies, and visits from other chiefs, were historically celebrated with dancing. During Tonga's large-scale conversion to Christianity, Methodist missionaries forbade these traditional dances, and traditional Tongan dancing waned. However, Catholic missionaries allowed the Tongans to preserve their traditional dancing. One of the most important dances is a traditional group or line dance known as the laka-laka. The term means, "to step briskly or carefully," and the dance incorporates sung speeches and polyphonic instrumentation. The movements are generally energetic, and the dance customarily involves a large group of people. It underwent a revival in the 20th century, and has since been proclaimed an Intangible Cultural Heritage (ICH) by the United Nations Educational, Scientific, and Cultural Organization (UNESCO).

Another preserved dance is the me'etu'upaki, which literally means "dance, standing with paddles." The popular paddle dance is traditionally performed by men in large groups. The paddles, called paki, have a small handle and are tapped against the hand to create a rhythm; at other times, the paddles are twirled or spun. The dancers move in patterns around each other to the accompaniment of drums and a chorus of singers. Their personal movements are generally small and precise, and consist of stepping in place, pointing and tapping their toes, crossing their feet, and jumping lightly. The traditional dance was once performed at many types of events, but now is primarily reserved for occasions involving the royal family.

The 'otuhaka is another traditional dance that has survived since ancient times. It is performed while sitting, and was believed to have been ignored by early Europeans, accounting for its preservation. The dancers are positioned in a gently curved row, and perform mostly by using their arms and hands. The dancers' arms are held close to their bodies, rather than open. Most of the movements are done by rotating the lower arms and the wrists, with a flexibility and grace that is considered quite demanding. The gestures are meant to tell an ancient story. While the dance was traditionally accompanied by a tafua, a percussion instrument consisting of bamboo sticks wrapped in a mat, it is now usually performed to vocal music or other kinds of drums. Other Tongan dances include traditional war dances, such as kailao, and a form of kailao is still performed by Tonga's national rugby team prior to matches.

Music

The origins of traditional Tongan music are ancient, and date back to the telling of the first Tongan fables. These ancient fables included sung passages and remnants of songs. Traditional music has been preserved in Tonga, and is still played at funerals, weddings, or ceremonies involving royalty. However, after Tongans converted to Christianity, European church music became prevalent in Tonga. Some Tongan musical styles were incorporated into these Western hymns.

The Tongans also created a number of distinctive traditional instruments, including the fangufangu, a bamboo flute that is played through the nose. One end of the flute is placed in the right nostril as the left nostril is held closed. Only four notes can be played on a noseflute, but those notes vary according to the size of the pipe. Musical variety is also created by having several musicians playing together. The noseflute also served a variety of ceremonial functions, and was traditionally used to awaken royalty. Other Tongan musical instruments include the mimiha and the slit-gong. The mimiha is a panpipe made from reeds lashed together with coconut fibers. The slit-gong is a hollowed-out log used in traditional pieces. It also substituted for a church bell in some small communities. Numerous types of drums are also used in Tongan music and Tongans often used their bodies in a percussive manner by clapping and snapping their fingers.

Literature

Tonga has mainly had an oral culture; because poetry and stories were more likely to be told through song and dance, there is little historical literature. One of the first written anthologies of Tongan history was written in the early 20th century, when anthropologist Edward Winslow Gifford (1887–1959) published *Tongan Tales and Myths* in 1924, a collection of Tongan folklore. Epeli Hau'ofa (1939–2009), a Tongan who was born in what is now Papua New Guinea, was a prominent sociology professor who is also probably Tonga's best known writer. His books *Tales of the Tongu* and *Kisses in the Nederends* are affectionate satires of the people of the South Pacific and their interaction with outsiders.

CULTURE

Arts & Entertainment

Tonga's most famous art is probably the lakalaka, a narrative dance that presents folk tales and heroes in spectacle, sound, and motion. The dancers, which can number in the hundreds, sing the story as they act it out, mainly through expressive motions of their hands and feet.

A large number of contemporary Tongan artists have established themselves as expatriates, after immigrating to other countries. One such artist is Kulīmoe'anga "Stone" Maka, who immigrated to New Zealand in 1997. He combines Western stylized art, such as abstraction, with Tongan traditions. For example, he created one painting with smoke from fires built with Tongan plants such as cabbage tree, sugar cane, paper mulberry and candlenut. His works have been exhibited throughout the Pacific region. Samiu Napa'a, who moved to Auckland in 1997, is another Tongan who has had work exhibited in New Zealand.

Tonga has been most successful in producing musicians. Church choirs are taken very seriously and perform at a very high level. String bands, consisting of guitar, banjo, ukulele, and bass, are very common, and play at special occasions such as weddings and parties. They produce a gentle, soft, rhythmic music of the type that is found throughout the Pacific Islands. The musicians usually sing along as they play. Reggae has become a very popular form of music in Tonga, and hip-hop has increasingly been adopted by young Tongans.

Cultural Sites & Landmarks

Most of Tonga's historic sites and landmarks are natural wonders formed by the nation's archipelagic geography. One of the most spectacular natural spots is Mapu'a 'a Vaca, a giant group of blowholes dotting the southwest coast of Tongatapu, Tonga's largest island. Located at the top of sea caves, these blowholes erupt in a spectacular plume of water when waves crash into the cave. This site also has historic significance. Mapu'a 'a Vaca translates to "the chief's whistles," and it was believed that an ancient Tongan chieftain used to spend hours listening to the waves whistling through the blowholes.

'Eua is the second largest island in the Tongatapu group, and vastly different in character from the other islands. It is considered the least developed island of Tonga and has a substantial range of tropical rainforest with a variety of flora and fauna. The island also features a rough, hilly landscape that provides excellent mountain-climbing and hiking, as well as an extensive network of caves. 'Eua is also home to the ruined 'Anokula Palace, built by the king off Tonga on a steep cliff—it drops 120 meters (393 feet) to the beach—in 1983. The island also features a national park, 'Eau National Park, which contains approximately 450 hectares (1,111 acres) of tropical forest and a variety of exotic birds and plants. It is also considered the oldest island in the Tongan archipelago, and one of the oldest islands overall in the Pacific region.

Tofua Island is another island that stands out for its biodiversity and history. Located in the Ha'apai group of islands, which are found north of Tongatapu, Tofua is essentially an active volcano. However, it also contains a large strip of rainforest with exotic birds and plants and a giant freshwater lake. The famous mutiny on the *Bounty*, a British Royal Navy ship, took place near Tofua in 1789. A group of sailors took control of the ship and cast the captain, William Bligh (1754–1817), and his loyalists adrift. Bligh and his crew managed to make it to Tofua, where they took refuge in a cave. However, one of the crew was stoned to death by the native inhabitants, and the discovery of the cave and the crewmember's grave remains a contested part of anthropologic lore.

In addition to the natural sites found in the islands of Tonga, Tongatapu also features two especially fascinating man-made structures. Mu'a, a village near Tonga's capital, Nuku'alofa, served as the ancient capital of Tonga, from about the thirteenth to the 19th century. One of its villages, Lapaha, is the site of a royal burial ground, where twenty-two giant tombs still stand. The pyramids are built from earth and supported by large, coral stone slabs. The structures are extremely well-built, an amazing feat considering they were erected with few mechanical tools.

The Ha'amonga 'a Mau'i Trilithon is another spectacular site in Tongatapu. The trilithon is composed of three giant coral limestone slabs.

Two of the slabs stand vertically, with the third laying across the top, connecting the two. It is somewhat similar to Britain's famous Stonehenge. Built in the early 13th century, the structure was thought to be an archway marking the entrance to a royal compound. According to one legend, the king who built it had two sons, and in a bid to encourage unity, composed the structure to show their connection to each other. Marks on top of the stones also show that the stones may have been placed to correlate with the movement of the sun.

Libraries & Museums

The Tonga National Museum is located at the Tonga National Cultural Centre, which officially opened in 1988. The museum houses numerous artifacts relating to Tongan history, including ancient war clubs, traditional woven baskets, and a turtle given to the king of Tonga by English explorer James Cook. The museum also has a permanent exhibit of Lapita pottery.

The Kingdom of Tonga has no official or formal national archives. As of 2004, the Tonga Library Association oversaw fifteen high-school level libraries, nine middle-school level libraries, and eleven primary school libraries, as well as six libraries at the kindergarten level and five at the tertiary level (higher education). The library at Tonga College, in particular, contains more than 4,000 volumes, and over 2,000 periodicals.

Holidays

Independence Day (June 4) commemorates Tonga's freedom, achieved in 1970, from being a British protectorate, a status essentially imposed on the kingdom in 1896.

The King's Birthday (July 4) initiates the weeklong Heilala Festival; the brilliantly colored heilala, Tonga's national flower, coincidentally blossoms on or about the royal birthday. Flaming torches line the coast of Tongatapu in celebration of both events.

Easter is celebrated throughout Tonga, along with Good Friday and Easter Monday, as a public holiday. Celebrations include special church services as well as passion plays, concerts, choir festivals, and other events.

Youth Culture

Like many Pacific island nations, the youth of Tonga are becoming more westernized. Global trends are increasingly influencing popular culture through the Internet, and socializing, listening to popular music, and sports all remain important facets of youth culture. Football (soccer) and rugby, in particular, are the most popular sports, both in terms of spectatorship and participation. American football is also popular, as a number of Tongans have made it to the college and pro level in the US. Education in Tonga is free and compulsory up until the age of twelve. After this, only minor fees are charged for secondary education, and many postsecondary scholarships are foreign-funded. Overall, Tonga has maintained a high literacy rate—an estimated 98 percent.

One of the distinct aspects of Tongan youth culture in recent years is the growth of the Help Youth Pursue Emancipation, or HYPE, movement. The movement was started by Tongan university students who were dismayed by the rising problems in Tonga among youth, including crime, death, and increased dropout rates. The movement urges young people to shed negative cultural expectations and to create social action by pursuing their dreams in a positive way. HYPE sells wristbands that are black, which represents the shadows young people can often feel they are living under, such as the shadows of the authorities and older people. The movement has spread onto the Internet and throughout the Pacific region, and young Tongan celebrities, such as athletes or musicians, can be spotted wearing the symbolic black wristbands.

SOCIETY

Transportation

In Tonga's urban areas, taxis and buses are the common mode of public transportation.

However, bus service is generally limited to the islands of Tongatapu, Lifuka, Foa, and the Vava'u island chain. In outlying and rural areas, walking and riding bikes or scooters is common. Ferry service is also available and can be quite variable. However, ferries customarily do not operate on Sunday. Flying remains the easiest way to travel around the Tonga archipelago. Fua'amotu International Airport is located on the main island of Tongatapu.

Traffic travels on the left-hand side of the road.

Transportation Infrastructure

The country's infrastructure is reasonably strong and well developed, with an extensive network of paved roads connecting urban centers and six airports. Since the national airline went bankrupt in 2004, two small independent airlines have taken over domestic flights. In August 2008, it was announced that Tonga, along with other Pacific Island chains, would benefit from a $200 million (AUD) Pacific Region Infrastructure Facility, co-launched by Australia and New Zealand. It is also funded by the Asian Development Bank (ADB) and the World Bank. The early priority would be to improve transportation infrastructure throughout the island nation. As of 2014, there were 13 airports in Tonga, only one having a paved runway.

Media & Communications

The dominant media in Tonga is owned by the state. The *Tonga Chronicle* is a weekly state-run newspaper, and the privately owned *Times of Tonga* is published in New Zealand. There are no daily newspapers and several monthly and weekly magazines are also published. Most monthly or bi-monthly magazines are church related.

The state-owned Tonga Broadcasting Commission runs two TV stations and two radio stations. While private media generally offers oppositional views, self-censorship is practiced and journalists have been threatened with criminal charges. In 2004, the Tongan government was accused of trying to "Tonganize" the media

by passing an amendment to the constitution that limited press freedom, particularly to safeguard the Tongan monarchy's image. Pro-democracy media is most often the target of government crackdowns

Tonga Communications Corp (TCC) is the country's national telecommunications provider. In 2002, Tonga allowed a second and private mobile telephone provider. A lack of a fiber optic submarine cable has hindered Tonga's information and communication technologies. As of March 2008, there were an estimated 8,400 Internet users, up from an estimated 2,900 in 2002.

SOCIAL DEVELOPMENT

Standard of Living

The Human Development Index rank for Tonga in 2014 was 100th out of 195 countries. According to statistics from the United States government, one in four citizens lives below the poverty level.

Water Consumption

Tonga's primary water resources are groundwater (urban areas) and harvested rainwater (rural areas). In general, the majority of the population has access to improved or safe drinking water (99.6 percent of the total population) and sanitation (91 percent of the total population).

Education

In Tonga, literacy is defined as the ability to read and write in both Tongan and English. According to this standard, more than 99 percent of the total population is literate. Per the 2014 census, the literacy rate of youth aged fifteen to twenty-five was 99.3 percent for males and 99.4 percent for females.

Primary education is compulsory and free for children between the ages six and fourteen. The majority of secondary schools on the islands are religiously-affiliated. Two secondary schools noteworthy for their prestige and history are Topou College, founded in 1866 and now the oldest and largest boys' college (secondary school) in the South Pacific; and Queen Salote College, a girls' secondary school named for the queen and patron of education who ruled from 1918 to 1965.

Institutes of higher learning include the Community Development and Training Center (CDTC), the Tonga Institute of Higher Education (TIHT), Tonga Institute of Education (TIOE), the Institute of Science and Technology, and the Tonga Maritime Polytechnic Institute. The University of the South Pacific runs an extension program in Tonga, offering most of its regular programs. A private, unaccredited university, Atenisi Institute, includes a Foundation for the Performing Arts. By 2007, about 40 percent of post-secondary training was provided by non-governmental or private agencies and institutions.

Women's Rights

Tonga is a conservative and paternalistic society where women continue to face challenges and rights abuses. One of the more notable challenges that Tongan women face involves inheritance and property rights. Under Tongan law, a woman can hold land, but only a male relative can inherit it. Thus, if a woman's husband dies, and there are no male relatives, she is allowed to remain on the family's land, but only if she does not remarry or become involved with another man. Additionally, a widow and her daughters have less right to family property than any illegitimate male children the father might have had.

Domestic and societal violence against women is a growing concern in Tongan society. While domestic violence is against the law in Tonga, international monitoring agencies allege that incidents are underreported and often unpublicized. Spousal rape is also not addressed under the law, and therefore not punishable. When there are reports of domestic abuse, very few women choose to prosecute their abusers because Tongan society frowns on such action. The police have a domestic violence unit, and if a woman reports abuse, she and the abuser are offered counseling. In addition, several non-governmental organiza-tions (NGOs) and churches offer shelters and counseling services for abused women.

Women's roles in Tongan society have generally been confined to wife and mother, and women generally are confined to working in traditional fields such as weaving. Women are also underrepresented politically, and women that do hold high governmental positions typically came from Tongan nobility or have royal connections.

A number of organizations that focus on improving the lives of women have appeared in Tonga in recent years. The Catholic Women's League has worked to gain more legal rights for women, and the Tonga Trust, an NGO, helps women better their standard of living by improving the condition of their homes and creating access better water supplies, particularly in outlying villages. Fefinc'i Fonnua 'O Tonga provides leadership training and teaches women how to run small businesses. Furthermore, segments of Tongan society have actively opposed a UN Convention that would create equal rights for women. The Convention on the Elimination of all forms of Discrimination Against Women (CEDAW) has been met with organized marches and signed petitions.

Health Care

Tongan health care is overseen by the Ministry of Health, which provides free medical and dental care for all citizens, oversees the distribution of pharmaceuticals throughout the islands, and organizes health education programs. Average life expectancy among Tongans is seventy six years; nearly seventy-eight years for women and seventy-five years for men (2015 estimate). In 2014, Tonga ranked 100th on the Human Development Index.

Few tropical diseases are common in Tonga. A successful government-sponsored immunization, water purification, and sanitation program has limited once-common infectious diseases such as typhoid. However, cancer, circulatory and digestive diseases, and diabetes are rising sharply, probably due to changes in Tongans' lifestyle and increased dependence on imported processed food.

Four hospitals serve Tonga, with one in each of the three main island groups. The hospital in Nuku'alofa is the largest, most up-to-date facility, but for advanced medical care, patients are airlifted to American Samoa. Tongan health professionals must receive advanced specialized training in other countries.

GOVERNMENT

Structure

The Kingdom of Tonga is a hereditary constitutional monarchy. United as a kingdom in 1845 by George I Topou, it adopted a constitution in 1875. A British protectorate from 1900, it achieved independence in 1970 and is a member of the Commonwealth of Nations. Its constitution was revised in 1967, strengthening the influence of the monarch. All literate, tax-paying men may vote, as may all literate women over twenty-one.

The executive branch consists of the king as chief of state, a prime minister as head of government, a deputy prime minister, and a twelve-member cabinet. When the king presides over the cabinet in person, it is known as the Privy Council.

The legislative branch is the unicameral Fale Alea (legislative assembly). It has thirty members, of whom nine are elected by popular vote to three-year terms. The assembly also includes the twelve cabinet officers.

The judicial branch consists of a Supreme Court appointed by the king and a Court of Appeals comprised of the chief justice of the Supreme Court and the Privy Council. Tonga's laws are based on English law.

The Kingdom of Tonga has three administrative divisions coinciding with the three largest island groups: Ha'apai, Tongatapu, and Vava'u. Their governors, appointed by the king, are members of the Privy Council.

Political Parties

In Tonga, political parties must be registered as "incorporated societies." Of the four registered parties, the most prominent is perhaps the Tonga Human Rights and Democracy Movement. But in the 2010 elections, the Democratic Party of the Friendly Islands won 12 seats in the legislative assembly, while the Independents held 5 seats. The People's Democratic Party, the Sustainable Nation-Building Party, and the Tongan Democratic Labor Party currently are not represented in the assembly, with the other nine seats held by noble representatives.

Local Government

Tonga is divided into five divisions—Tongatapu, Vava'u, Ha'apai, 'Eua, and Ongo Niua—and subdivided into twenty-three districts. Elected district and town officials represent local governance in Tonga. Some villages maintain councils that assist district and town governments. In addition, the island groups of Ha'apai and Vava'u each have a governor.

Judicial System

Tonga's judicial system is based on English common law. It consists of a Supreme Court, Court of Appeals, a Land Court, and Magistrates' Court. There is also a Privy Council, made up of the monarch, cabinet, and two governors. The Chief Justice serves from overseas, and the Privy Council serves as the Court of Appeals when he is present.

Taxation

Tonga began reforming its system of taxation in the early 21st century. Personal taxation is non-progressive and levied at a 10 percent rate. Overall, the tax base is small. The standard corporate rate is 30 percent. The bulk of tax revenue comes from sales taxes, custom duties, and port and services taxes. Taxes and other revenues account for 29.2 percent of the annual GDP.

Armed Forces

The Tonga Defense Services (TDS) serve as the Pacific island nation's armed forces. The land force consists of the Tonga Royal Guards, established in 1860, and the Royal Tongan Marines. There is also a navy and air defense force.

Foreign Policy

As a small, developing state, Tonga relies heavily on foreign assistance. In fact, in 2005, an estimated 39 percent of the country's gross domestic product (GDP) came from remittances, and ten years later the percentage remained high, second only to tourism. Imported energy, such as petroleum products, environmental issues, such as the effects of climate change, and economic sustainability all figure prominently into Tonga's foreign relations and activities. Australia is Tonga's principal bilateral provider of international assistance. The island nation also maintains cordial relations with New Zealand. Overall, Tonga enjoys good relations with most foreign countries and is particularly active in the Pacific region. Tonga hosted the Pacific Islands Forum in October 2007.

Internationally, Tonga is often considered a proactive island nation. The country holds membership in the United Nations (UN), the International Monetary Fund (IMF), the World Bank, and other important international institutions. In 2007, Tonga became the 151st member of the World Trade Organization (WTO). Tonga is also an active supporter of anti-terrorism worldwide, and was a supporter of the United States-led Iraq War, and deployed Tongan soldiers to Iraq in 2004. King George Tupou V (1948–2012) instituted a "Look East" foreign policy that focused on developing stronger ties with China and other Southeast Asian nations. (As a result, Tonga is opposed to Taiwanese independence.) The current king, George Tupou IV, has continued his brother's policies. Tourism, aviation, trade and security are primary ventures that Tonga has begun exploring with China.

Tonga continues to maintain good relations with the US. Since there is a large contingent of Tongan expatriates living in the US, cooperation between the two nations is mutually beneficial. The US also provides training to the island nation's defensive unit, the Tonga Defense Service (TDS). This five-hundred person unit includes a light infantry and a small amphibious unit. (Australia and New Zealand also have agreements to provide additional support if nec-

essary, and the United Kingdom's military has exercised with Tongan troops as recently as 2000.) In addition to deployment in Iraq in 2004, Tongan troops have participated in the multinational peacekeeping force in the Solomon Islands.

The closest thing Tonga has had to an international incident in recent history is the strange episode of the Republic of Minerva. In the early 1970s, Michael Oliver, an American businessman and activist, decided to create a city-state that would operate under libertarian ideals. He chose the Minerva Reefs, south of Tonga, as the location for an island nation that would support about 30,000 people. Construction had already begun on the city when the Republic of Minerva was declared an independent nation in January 1972. Almost everyone in the world ignored the declaration—except Tonga. Although reports differ about what kind of force Tonga brought to the Minerva Reef, the result was that, in June 1972, a contingent landed on the reef, took down the Republic's flag, and claimed the area for Tonga. Since that time, Fiji has maintained it does not recognize Tonga's claims over the reefs. However, many claim that the reefs have largely been reclaimed by the sea.

Human Rights Profile

International human rights law insists that states respect civil and political rights, and promote an individual's economic, social, and cultural rights. The United Nations Universal Declaration on Human Rights (UDHR) is recognized as the standard for international human rights. Its authors sought the counsel of the world's great thinkers, philosophers, and religious leaders, and were careful to create a document that reflects the core values shared by every world culture. (To read this document or view the articles relating to cultural human rights, visit http://www.udhr.org/UDHR/default.htm.).

The Tongan constitution grants many of the standard human rights outlined in the UDHR. However, its overall record is generally perceived as poor. Most notably, the government, as a constitutional monarchy, does not grant it citizens the right to change the government. International monitoring agencies have also criticized Tonga for the inability of its citizens to gain access to state information. The state has also attempted to control the media and limit freedom of the press. Other problem areas included freedom of religion and societal discrimination. While freedom of religion is generally allowed, only religious programming within the "mainstream Christian tradition" is allowed by the Tongan Broadcasting Commission (TBC). However, the TBC will take announcement of activities by other religions, such as the Baha'i faith, and other religions are not prohibited from broadcasting on private networks. Other societal problems include no standard provisions that guarantee accessibility for the disabled, and discrimination against homosexuals and foreign nationals, such as Chinese workers.

It was reported in 2009 that Tonga had an emigration rate of approximately 33 percent, and more recent statistics are not available as of 2015. North America was the primary destination for Tongan migrants (having increased dramatically in the last half of the 20th century), with an estimated 35.8 percent of Tongan emigrants residing there.

ECONOMY

Overview of the Economy
With no substantial industrial base, Tonga's economy is based almost entirely on agriculture, fisheries, and tourism. Because of high unemployment and inflation, young Tongans often find work in other countries, usually New Zealand and Australia. The funds they send home contribute significantly to Tonga's economy and migration is largely seen as an economic benefit to Tongan households. In 2014, Tonga's per capita gross domestic product (GDP) was estimated at $4,900 USD. The annual GDP of 2014 was estimated at $500 million USD. Tonga receives economic aid from both Australia and New Zealand.

Industry
Tonga's principal industries, tourism and fishing, show annual production growth rates of less than 1 percent, which is a decreased percent for the last decade. The government is actively encouraging commercial fishing. Until recently, fishing was for family meals and tourist sport.

Tonga's chief trading partners are the United States, New Zealand, Japan, Fiji, and Australia. Tonga participates in the Pacific Island Countries Trade Agreement, a regional free-trade agreement signed in 2002.

Labor
In 2006, the formal working population (those aged fifteen through sixty-four) totaled 67,079; however, in 2007, the actual labor force consisted of 39,960 and has dropped to an estimated 33,800 in 2011. Youth unemployment remains a growing concern in the island nation, but overall unemployment in 2011 was only 1.1 percent.

Energy/Power/Natural Resources
Tonga's natural resources are limited to fish and fertile soil. Offshore oil explorations have so far proved futile.

Fishing
The commercial fishing industry, a vital sector of the economy, and the country's small domestic fleet consists of five corporations and nearly twenty vessels, mostly operating from Tongatapu. Red snapper and tuna are the primary commercial catch. Key inshore resources include sea cucumber, seaweed, giant clams, and lobster.

The depletion of certain native species and overfishing in nearshore waters remains a growing concern.

Agriculture
Agriculture is central to Tonga's economy and makes up 27.5 percent of the labor force (2006 estimate). The port of is the primary point of transit for Tongan agricultural exports, especially coconuts and coconut-derived products. Other key exports include squash pumpkins, bananas,

vanilla beans, sweet potatoes, coconuts, cassava, ginger, handicrafts and seafood products, especially tuna and seaweed.

Tonga has long supplied much of the world's vanilla beans. Most are grown on vanilla plantations in western Tongatapu. Tongan coffee, praised by tourists, is new to the international market. Grown organically in volcanic soil at low altitudes and abiding by fair trade practices, it is sold throughout the world.

Tourism

British Captain James Cook, who visited the islands of Tonga in the 18th century, named them the Friendly Islands. Tonga's tourist industry has successfully revived the name to encourage visitors. Following a ten-year development program, tourism now contributes approximately 16 percent of the GDP annually to the economy, and the sector is growing, with a 2024 goal of 22 percent of the GDP. However, following the 2008–2009 global financial crisis, tourism experienced somewhat of a decline; in 2010, the Ministry of Tourism was expecting only eleven cruise ships to arrive in Tonga, down from twenty-three the previous year. The tourism sector has since rebounded.

Tourists enjoy the natural diversity of the islands and the recreational activities available, including ocean and freshwater fishing, whale-watching, scuba diving, snorkeling, surfing, swimming, beachcombing, and birdwatching. Visitors can also explore coral reefs, archeological sights, rainforests, volcanoes, and limestone caves.

Kirsten Anderson, Ann Parrish,
Beverly Ballaro

DID YOU KNOW?

- The name Nuku'alofa, Tonga's capital city, means "abode of love" in Tongatapu.

- Because of the "Tonga Loop" in the International Date Line, Tonga was the first country in the world to greet the 21st century and the new millennium.

- Pigs are considered an important symbol of Tongan society, and the killing of a pig warrants a hefty fine and, in some cases, vigilante justice is often carried out.

- During one of his visits to Tonga, James Cook presented the king with a tortoise. Named Tu'i Maila, the tortoise was between 188 and 192 years old when it died in 1965.

- Taufa'ahau Tupou IV, the former king of Tonga, is believed to have been the first Polynesian to earn a law degree in the South Pacific.

Bibliography

Arbeit, Wendy. *Tapa in Tonga*. Honolulu: University of Hawaii Press, 1995.

Dale, Paul. *The Tonga Book*. Martinsville, IN: Fideli Publishing, 2008.

McLachlan, Craig, et al. *Rarotonga, Somoa, and Tonga*. Oakland, CA: Lonely Planet, 2012.

Morton, Helen. *Becoming Tongan: An Ethnography of Childhood*. Honolulu: University of Hawaii Press, 1996.

St. Cartmail, Keith. *The Art of Tonga*. Honolulu: University of Hawaii Press, 1997.

Small, Cathy A. *Voyages: From Tongan Villages to American Suburbs*. Ithaca, NY: Cornell University Press, 1997.

Wood-Ellem, Elizabeth. *Queen Salote of Tonga: The Story of an Era (1900–1965)*. Honolulu: University of Hawaii Press, 2001.

Works Cited

"Battle of Women's Rights Continues in Tonga." 25 May 2015. http://www.radionz.co.nz/international/

programmes/datelinepacific/audio/201755533/battle-of-women's-rights-continues-in-tonga.

Fletcher, Matt and Nancy Keller. *Lonely Planet: Tonga.* Victoria: Lonely Planet Publications. 2001.

http://anapesi.blogspot.com/2008/09/hype-movement.html

http://anapesi.blogspot.com/search/label/HYPE

http://encarta.msn.com/encyclopedia_761564527/Tonga_(country).html

http://encarta.msn.com/encyclopedia_761564527/Tonga_(country).html

http://news.bbc.co.uk/1/hi/world/asia-pacific/country_profiles/1300742.stm

http://orca.byu.edu/Reports/Journals/2003%20Final%20reports/_fhss/johnsonk.pdf

http://projects.prm.ox.ac.uk:8080/pcs/noteshow_public.php?num=0&pid=300&id=20

http://projects.prm.ox.ac.uk:8080/pcs/noteshow_public.php?num=8&pid=300&id=20

http://samiunapaa.wordpress.com/exhibitions/

http://whc.unesco.org/en/tentativelists/5167/

http://wnnbreakingnewsportal.wordpress.com/2009/03/11/tongan-women-seek-gender-perspective-in-reform-process/

http://www.adb.org/Documents/Books/Country_Briefing_Papers/Women_in_Tonga/chap6.pdf

http://www.amnesty.org/en/region/tonga

http://www.arthistory.upenn.edu/trouble/clubs/tongasamoa/samoatonga1.htm

http://www.britannica.com/EBchecked/topic/422213/Nukualofa

http://www.britannica.com/EBchecked/topic/424484/Oceanic-art/14316/Fiji-Tonga-and-Samoa

http://www.brookvaleps.nsw.edu.au/PROJECTS/tongan/living.html#Housing

http://www.cabinetmagazine.org/issues/18/newfoundlands.php

http://www.culturecrossing.net/basics_business_student_details.php?Id=12&CID=205

http://www.fijitimes.com/story.aspx?id=112135

http://www.frommers.com/destinations/tonga/3039020157.html

http://www.janesoceania.com/polynesia_music/index.htm

http://www.jstor.org/pss/849801?cookieSet=1

http://www.lonelyplanet.com/tonga/transport/getting-there-around

http://www.manukau.govt.nz/default.aspx?id=7697

http://www.matangitonga.to/article/category_index85.shtml

http://www.metmuseum.org/toah/ho/10/ocp/ho_1979.206.1470.htm

http://www.metmuseum.org/toah/ht/10/ocp/ht10ocp.htm

http://www.mfat.govt.nz/Countries/Pacific/Tonga.php

http://www.newsfinder.org/site/more/tonga/

http://www.nma.gov.au/cook/artefact.php?id=265

http://www.nytimes.com/2001/08/05/travel/frugal-traveler-encounters-in-the-kingdom-of-tonga.html

http://www.pacifica.info/en/islands/tonga/transport.php

http://www.pacific-travel-guides.com/tonga-islands/tours/blowholes.html

http://www.planet-tonga.com/HRDMT/

http://www.polynesia.com/tonga/houses-and-village-life.html

http://www.polynesia.com/tonga/houses-and-village-life.html

http://www.polynesia.com/tonga/houses-and-village-life.html

http://www.questia.com/PM.qst?a=o&d=59670204

http://www.state.gov/g/drl/rls/hrrpt/2004/41662.htm

http://www.state.gov/g/drl/rls/hrrpt/2005/61629.htm

http://www.state.gov/g/drl/rls/hrrpt/2008/eap/119060.htm

http://www.state.gov/r/pa/ei/bgn/16092.htm

http://www.state.gov/r/pa/ei/bgn/16092.htm

http://www.swarthmore.edu/x16802.xml

http://www.teara.govt.nz/NewZealanders/NewZealandPeoples/Tongans/4/ENZ-Resources/Standard/2/en

http://www.teara.govt.nz/NewZealanders/NewZealandPeoples/Tongans/4/ENZ-Resources/Standard/3/en

http://www.tonga.islands-travel.com/handicrafts.html

http://www.tonga.islands-travel.com/handicrafts.html

http://www.tongaatoz.com/a.html

http://www.tongaholiday.com/index.php?page_id=10

http://www.tongaholiday.com/index.php?page_id=19

http://www.unesco.ru/files/docs/clt/kazan/kaeppler-expert-en.pdf

http://www.unhcr.org/refworld/country,,,,TON,45b632e02,48d5cbcfc,0.html

http://www.world-food.net/scientficjournal/2007/issue3/pdf/food/f5.pdf

Lal, Brij V. and Kate Fortune: *The Pacific Islands: An Encyclopedia.* Honolulu: The University of Hawaii Press. 2000.

Kaeppler, Adrienne. "Tongan Dance: A Study in Cultural Change." *Ethnomusicology.* Vol. 14, No. 2 (May 1970): pp. 266–277.

"Sub-Regional Office for the Pacific Islands TCP/TON/3302: Migration, Remittance, and Development Tonga." *Food and Agriculture Organization of the United Nations.* April 2011. http://www.fao.org/3/a-an477e.pdf.

"Travel & Tourism: Economic Impact 2014 Tonga." *World Travel & Tourism Council.* http://www.wttc.org/-/media/files/reports/economic%20impact%20research/country%20reports/tonga2014.pdf.

TUVALU

Introduction

Tuvalu's four coral reef islands and five atolls lie scattered across 580 kilometers (360 miles) of the South Pacific Ocean, about half way between Hawaii and Australia. The nation's eight original islands include Nanumea, Niutao, Nanumaga, Vaitupu, Nukufetau, Funafuti, Nukalaelae, and Nui. In fact, "Tuvalu" means, "eight standing together," and refers to the first eight islands of the country. The ninth island, Niulakita, was not settled until the 1950s.

Tuvalu gained its independence from Great Britain in 1978, and it is the world's fourth smallest nation. Residents of Tuvalu are known as Tuvaluans.

GENERAL INFORMATION

Official Language: Tuvaluan, English, Samoan, Kiribati
Population: 10,869 (July 2015 estimate)
Currency: Australian dollar
Coins: Tuvalu mints its own coins, which come in denominations of 1, 2, 5, 10, 20, and 50. A Tuvaluan dollar also exists only as coinage.
Land Area: 26 square kilometers (10 square miles)
National Motto: "Tuvalu mo te atua" ("Tuvalu for the Almighty")
National Anthem: "Tuvalu mo te atua" ("Tuvalu for the Almighty")
Capital: Funafuti
Time Zone: GMT +12

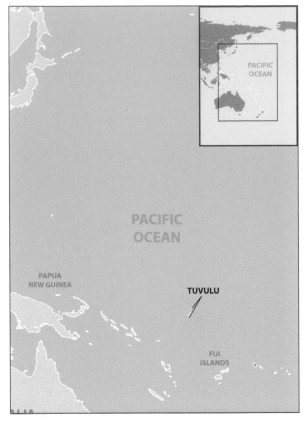

Flag Description: The flag of Tuvalu is based on the British ensign (featured in the top corner, hoist side), and features a blue ensign (sky blue) design, with a body of nine yellow stars representing Tuvalu's nine islands. Generally, the stars are geographically arranged, with some pointing up.

Population

The most populous atolls are Funafuti and Vaitupa, the only cities with other 1,000 inhabitants, and nearly half of Tuvalu's population lives in the Tuvaluan capital of Funafuti, on Funafuti Atoll. The life expectancy in Tuvalu is approximately sixty-four years for men and just over sixty-eight years for women (2015 estimate). The average age is approximately twenty-five years old. Tuvalu's birth rate is nearly twenty-four births per 1,000 people, with an infant mortality rate of nearly thirty-one deaths per 1,000 live births (2015 estimate).

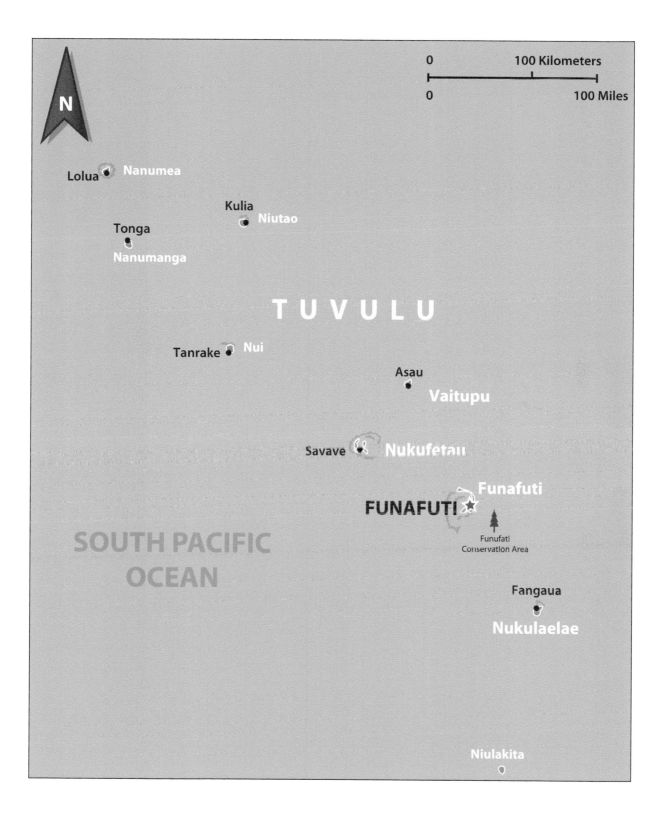

Principal Cities by Population (2012):

- Funafuti (6,025)
- Vaitupa (1,555)

Languages

Because the country's islands can be isolated from each other, Tuvaluan dialects are unique to locations. Furthermore, the present inhabitants of the island of Nui still speak I-Kiribati, which is a different language from that spoken on the other islands.

Native People & Ethnic Groups

Tuvalu's small population is ethnically 96 percent Polynesian and about 4 percent Micronesian. Early Tuvaluans probably came to the islands in waves from Polynesian Samoa, Tonga, and Uvea. The Micronesian peoples of the Nui Atoll, of which there are about 600, are thought to be of Kiribati (or Gilbertese) origin.

In 1986, a team of scuba divers off the coast of Nanumaga Atoll found a cave about 40 meters (131 feet) below the surface of the water, in which they found traces of human civilization. The findings contain evidence of ancient human activity, particularly relating to fire, that stretches back some 8,000 years. The revelation contrasts with popular theories on when the Pacific was settled. The underwater caves, often referred to as the Fire Caves of Nanumaga, were brought to the attention of local archaeologists by an island myth of a "large house under the sea." Climatologists believe that changing ocean levels that may have destroyed other evidence of early human habitation in the region.

Religions

About 97 percent of Tuvaluans belong to the Christian Church of Tuvalu (Ekalesia Kelisiano o Tuvalu), a Protestant Congregationalist Church. Less than 2 percent of the population belongs to the Seventh-Day Adventist Church, another 1 percent is Baha'i, and less than one percent of the people belongs to other denominations or claims no particular religious faith.

Religion is an essential part of Tuvaluan life. Sunday morning church services are central to village communities and to the rhythm of an islander's week. Following Sunday services, Tuvaluan families gather together on a matt-covered floor to say a blessing and eat a midday meal called kaiga i ttuutonu.

Climate

Tuvalu has a tropical marine climate. Temperatures average about 30° Celsius (87° Fahrenheit) year-round, with a rainy season between October and March. Annual rainfall averages about 350 centimeters (137 inches).

The islands are prey to occasional cyclones, and suffered a severe blow in 1997 when Cyclones Gavin and Hina washed away about seven percent of the islands' total land area.

Rising sea levels are a deep climate concern for Tuvalu. In fact, the capital, on the atoll of Funafuti is disappearing. Administrators anticipate that 80 percent of the small land mass will be submerged by the mid-21st century.

ENVIRONMENT & GEOGRAPHY

Topography

Tuvalu's four coral reef islands and five atolls lie scattered across 580 kilometers (360 miles) of the South Pacific Ocean, about half way between Hawaii and Australia. High rainfall, poor soil, and the country's small size have made vegetation sparse except for the ubiquitous coconut palms that line Tuvalu's plentiful beaches.

All of Tuvalu's islands are low-lying. The highest point of elevation on any island is only about 4.6 meters (15 feet) above sea level. In recent years, rising sea levels and a spate of rare cyclones (hurricanes) have eroded significant portions of the nation's land mass, rising levels in the islands' saltwater lagoons have threatened mainland habitation.

Plants & Animals

Tuvalu has no native land mammals on any of its nine islands. Over the centuries, sailors have introduced chickens, dogs, cats, and Polynesian rats to the islands.

Coconut palms and beach grasses grow well throughout the islands, but tree species are otherwise generally limited to scattered undergrowth.

Because all but one of the islands are devoid of rivers or lakes, and the smaller atolls do not have enough soil to retain freshwater, few plant or animal species would survive without the islanders' rainwater collection tanks.

CUSTOMS & COURTESIES

Greetings

Tuvalu's unusual greeting is famous around the Polynesian Pacific. Tuvaluans will often greet someone they have not seen in a while by pressing a cheek to the visitor's cheek and sniffing deeply. Common salutations include the formal "Fakatalofa atu" and the informal "Talofa" ("Greetings" or "Hello"). A more casual greeting is "E aa koe na?" ("How are you?"). Greetings also might include inquiries into one's well-being and family. Because Tuvaluans usually know everyone in their village, they rarely use honorific titles or last names when addressing one another.

Gestures & Etiquette

Tuvaluans are an unhurried and reserved people, and their modesty is reflected in their gestures and social etiquette. For example, it is polite to keep one's legs covered when seated, and it is rude to stand while someone next to you is seated. Using one's finger in a pointing fashion is also uncommon. In general, public displays of affluence or affection are not customary, and women are also expected to be modestly dressed in public. Deference for one's elders is also considered an important facet of traditional and modern culture. Lastly, due to the islands' religiosity, it may be expected that shoes are removed prior to entering a church. This also customarily applies to entering homes or meeting houses (the maneapa).

Eating/Meals

Tuvaluans generally eat three meals per day and traditionally begin each meal with a blessing. Breakfast usually consists of light fare and includes toddy, a warm beverage made from coconut sap. The midday meal is the largest meal of the day, and dinner might consist of leftovers. Women do the cooking in a building set aside to allow for the open fire. The meal might be carried out to where family members are working or returning from work or might be eaten in the home. Most Tuvaluans still eat together sitting cross-legged on floor mats. Meals are traditionally eaten with the hands, which are washed in a water bowl that is passed around before the meal.

Visiting

Tuvaluans traditionally live in thatched huts without walls. It is customary to enter someone's home only from the side facing the lagoon. Like other Polynesian cultures, Tuvaluans remove their shoes before entering the home. Visitors usually come unannounced to a Tuvaluan home; in fact, the open building structure of traditional homes encourages hosts to call out an invitation to passersby. Moreover, Tuvaluans live among a large and loosely defined family group, so that one's neighbors are likely also to be relatives.

Visits are particularly common on Sundays, rainy days, and holidays when islanders take a rest from their work. Visits also occur more frequently amongst family, and people generally refrain from visiting in the morning or during meal preparations.

LIFESTYLE

Family

Tuvaluans depend upon a traditional family structure that ties in closely to the surrounding community. Because of the distance—and often rough seas—between islands, each island or atoll has a distinct community bound together by familial relations and shared customs. Extended families generally share land that they farm communally, and closely related families are likely to share housing as well. Many Tuvaluan families, and especially those on the outer islands, continue to abide by the traditional village structure. Each family becomes specialized at a task important to the family or island's survival, such as fishing, farming, or craftwork and building. The family then passes these skills on from one generation to the next.

The family plays an important role in island governance, as well. Each village is governed by a group of village leaders and elders. This group or council helps to negotiate disputes and determine communal needs. Village leadership also corresponds closely with the size and participation of families in the community. Within the household, older men are traditionally the head of household, though older women are increasingly stepping into this role as Tuvalu adapts to cultural changes.

In keeping with the delegation of skills to individual families, each family in a village is expected to share a portion of what they have with extended family and the entire village through regular contributions. These customs helped Tuvaluan culture to survive on remote islands with scarce resources. In recent times, however, Tuvaluans complain about the amount and frequency of contributions they are expected to make. Moreover, the migration of families away from the outer islands has strained community support systems. Those who are able to farm and fish often have trouble meeting the financial expectations of the community. Circumstances are much harder for those who are without access to family land or who are physically unable to participate in the labor required to survive. Development workers note that the elderly and those who do not have access to land face great hardship.

The migration of workers away from the islands has produced one unintended benefit, however. As older women increasingly outnumber older men on the outer islands, women have gained a greater voice in the leadership of families and villages.

Housing

Traditionally, Tuvaluans lived in thatched wooden structures with hanging mats to keep out rain, wind, and other natural elements. The huts were made with materials from the pandanus trees that grow throughout the islands. These primary dwellings have slowly been replaced by concrete or imported-timber frame homes. This process of modernization was sped up after Hurricane Bebe devastated the islands in 1972.

Though modern housing remains unaffordable for many, most Tuvaluans live in homes built with imported materials. Nevertheless, families continue to make use of traditional huts, both as sleeping structures and as separate cooking areas. In Tuvalu's tropical climate, these structures, which have no walls, help to catch sea breezes and disperse heat. (When night time temperatures get particularly high, Funafuti residents have been known to bring pillows and sleeping mats out to the Fogafale airstrip, which catches the breeze in from the ocean.)

The most recent change to Tuvalu's housing is a trend toward single-family dwellings. Many younger Tuvaluans no longer wish to share a home with the extended family. The shift to single-family homes necessarily uses more of the island nation's scarce land for housing, further cutting into the amount of land available for farming. In addition, the move away from extended family homes can isolate individuals who do not belong to a nuclear family, leaving some of Tuvalu's most vulnerable citizens without adequate housing or support.

Food

Due to a waning agrarian culture and the scarcity of arable land, the Tuvaluan diet consists mostly of imported food purchased at markets. On each island, futi (government-owned stores) sell imported staples like rice and canned vegetables and subsidize the cost of locally-harvested goods. Because of the islands' remote location and inadequate transportation, imported goods are expensive. As a result, many families on the outer islands stretch their household incomes by cultivating family land, or by fishing and foraging.

The traditional staple of the Tuvaluan diet is pulaka (otherwise known as swamp taro), which is a plant with rich, starchy fibers. For centuries, Tuvaluan farmers grew pulaka in trenches that were enriched with compost to compensate for the islands' sandy soil. Nanumea Atoll has one of the country's largest arable areas, and its islet, Lakena, serves as a taro garden for the entire atoll. Outer island gardens became especially important to the survival of the country after 1942, when American forces filled in and covered over the taro gardens on Fogafale with the country's only airstrip. The smaller taro gardens in Fogafale have failed in recent years as high tides have begun to flood the islet with brackish seawater. As a result, Funafuti relies almost entirely on the outer islands for what locally-grown crops it can receive.

Other traditional staples include breadfruit, plantains, and bananas, as well as other fruits such as papaya and coconut. Coconut cream is used to in the preparation of numerous dishes, and coconut milk is also often used. The Tuvaluan diet also includes locally bred pork and chicken, as well as occasional wild game in the form of turtles or sea birds. However, the most important protein to the Tuvaluan diet is seafood, namely fish, crab, and shellfish. Some of this fish is eaten fresh, but Tuvaluans also salt and dry fish.

Life's Milestones

Tuvaluans consider themselves religious; an estimated 95 percent of the population is Protestant Christian, and belongs to the national church, the Christian Church of Tuvalu (EKT). In fact, church buildings are perhaps the most prominent architectural structures throughout the islands. Thus, many of life's milestones, such as birth, passage into adulthood, marriage, and funerals, are observed and practiced in accordance with Protestant Christian customs.

Marriages in Tuvalu are either civil or religious ceremonies. Traditionally, marriages were considered important for childbearing and kinship relations, and so they were commonly arranged. A suitable bride needed approval from the groom's family. Courtship was also traditionally limited, and marriages often involved the whole community, and may have last for several days.

Today, most marriages maintain Christian customs, and are presided over by a pastor. Ceremonial events, such as marriages and funerals, are held at the islands' meeting halls (maneapas).

CULTURAL HISTORY

Art

Tuvalu's traditional arts and handicrafts are well known throughout Polynesia. Traditionally, Tuvaluan arts and crafts were created by women and based on natural resources such as pandanus leaves, hibiscus bark, and coconut fronds. Until the latter part of the 20th century, Tuvaluan women used these materials and other native resources that could be grown or gathered on the islands to produce clothing, woven mats, baskets, and jewelry. Though all show a similarity to articles produced in other Polynesian and Micronesian cultures, Tuvaluan designs and process are slightly different on each island.

Because Islanders had little access to animal skins and the more flexible fibers of plants such as cotton, clothing was traditionally woven from leaves, fronds, and hibiscus bark. Cord made from coconut fibers was also used in clothing, as well as furniture and ornaments. Tuvaluan women developed elaborate processes of smoking, soaking, pounding, and weaving these natural, and often harsh, materials to create more durable or flexible fabrics as needed. In fact, European missionaries and anthropologists who visited the islands during the 19th and 20th centuries described a surprising variety among skirts and headdresses. Traditional clothing was even designed for specific functions and followed fashion trends as younger generations adopted slightly different styles. The Tuvaluans also created different dyeing techniques by pulling color pigments from the different plants. Many crafts such as clothing and furniture were also decorated with colored geometric patterns.

Tuvaluans applied this same expertise to produce shelters and functional items such as tools and mats. As with clothing items, women usually produced the mats that served as furniture in the islands. Some of these mats were designed specifically for sleeping or for sitting during work, while others were ceremonial. Wall mats provided shelter from the elements and needed to be tightly woven of durable materials to keep out high winds and heavy rains. Men were traditionally responsible for canoe carving, as well as creating the frame and thatch for sleeping huts. Men were also responsible for weaving the sandals they used for fishing on the reefs.

Since the second half of the 20th century, Tuvaluans have chosen to import fabrics, building materials, and clothing items. Many residents, particularly on Funafuti, now wear Western-inspired clothing, live in concrete buildings, and import decorative items from places like the United States, Australia, and Japan. However, the beauty and craftsmanship in Tuvalu's traditional woven designs have made them art pieces and souvenirs alike. These crafts have become an important supplement to many family incomes, and women continue to market their crafts through handicraft centers located on each island.

Architecture

Overall, the traditional architecture of Tuvalu reflects the influence of the local environment—local materials, mostly pandanus and coconut trees, were used and homes were designed to provide cross ventilation, bringing in the tropical breezes. Traditional sleeping houses (fale moe) are also very open in their design, reflecting the communal lifestyle that has defined Tuvalu for centuries. Another feature of traditional Tuvaluan architecture is raised floors, which allow adequate drainage as well as storage. Also, solid walls were not always used, and screens or blinds (pola), traditionally made from coconut fronds,

could be rolled up or down depending on the weather.

There are various colonial influences as well, including British, German, and Spanish, that are reflected in the island nations' churches, tombstones, and other historic buildings.

Music

Before the arrival of Europeans, Tuvalu's music seems to have consisted of singing and limited percussive instruments. Because men traditionally did wood carving, they also crafted Tuvalu's early instruments, most notably slit drums made from hollowed-out small logs. These drums would be played with two drum sticks also made of wood. While Tuvaluans had songs to accompany their daily work and lives, they were best known in the region for the chanted storytelling and praise-giving songs that accompanied dancers on ceremonial occasions.

Dance

Anthropologists list three important Tuvaluan dances: fakanu, fakaseasea, and fatele. Fakanu and fakaseasea were among the praise songs that celebrated important people in the community. When European missionaries arrived in the 19th century, they banned fakanu because they found the swaying motions of the dance too provocative. Both fakanu and fakaseasea are rarely performed in modern Tuvalu, but fatele remains a feature of Tuvaluan communal life. The fatele takes place in the village's meeting hall. It begins with a song that is repeated over and over, each time growing louder and faster as more singers join in. Dancers reenact the story within the lyrics as the pace grows faster. The dancers and singers reach a frenzied pace before a sudden and dramatic end.

While modern Tuvaluans still find occasions for the fatele, contemporary music on the islands shows the influence of not only regionalization, but Westernization. For example, Polynesian-inspired popular music is shipped in from around the region, and Western musical styles such as hip-hop and reggaeton have becoming increasingly popular.

CULTURE

Arts & Entertainment

Tuvalu's small population and limited government support cannot support a significant art scene. However, local women have adapted traditional weaving and dyeing techniques to the 21st century export market. Each island has a Women's Handiwork Center, where locals bring fans, mats, carvings and other locally crafted goods to sell. The centers regularly transport the items to the main center on Funafuti, where they can be sold to the tourists who come in to Tuvalu's only airport. However, this market is limited, as only about 1,000 tourists come to Tuvalu each year. This is partially because inter-island transportation is so difficult, and because flights to Tuvalu are so much more expensive than those to other Pacific islands. Nevertheless, Tuvalu's craftswomen have earned a reputation for superior work among the country's regional neighbors.

Cultural Sites & Landmarks

Tuvalu's tropical environment is itself a worthy appealing landmark. The landscape is characterized by white sand beaches, sparkling tropical water, and blooming coconut trees. The water inside and outside of the atoll houses reefs and diverse marine life, and is a popular spot for snorkeling. The fish, plants, tropical birds, ferns and trees on and surrounding the island are attractive and easily viewable by visitors.

In 1996, Tuvalu launched the Funafuti Conservation Area (FCA) Project, a conservation area of about 33 square kilometers (20 square miles). The conservation project designated areas of land, specifically six uninhabited islets, and water, including reef and lagoon habitats, around the Funafuti lagoon as a protected reserve. The islets contained within the conservation area constitute an estimated 40 percent of the remaining native broadleaf forest of the Funafuti Atoll. The conversation area is home to important marine and bird life, including several species of seabirds and the green turtle, which

uses the area as an important nesting site. The project is also being marketed as the cornerstone for the island nation's fledgling ecotourism industry.

The country also lists the remains of a World War II airstrip and other associated wreckage among its historic landmarks. Though the impact of the war was brief and slight on Tuvalu, the Funafuti Atoll operated as a U.S. military base, leading up to the Battle of Tarawa, against the Japanese. War relics remain scattered across the surface of the island nation, including wrecked cargo planes and ships, and a preserved underground bunker.

Two other important sites are located on the island atoll of Nanumea, which is Tuvalu's most northern island. The atoll is home to a large church, reminiscent of the Gothic style, which is believed to have one of the largest towers in the South Pacific region. Nanumea is also home to a natural body of freshwater, called Tekoko ("the bath"), which is considered rare for an atoll. Lastly, the Philatelic Bureau on Funafuti has become a destination for international stamp collectors, since stamps depicting Tuvalu are considered highly collectible.

Holidays

Tuvalu's overwhelmingly Christian residents celebrate Good Friday, Easter Monday, and Christmas. New Year's Day is celebrated on January 1. Tuvaluan villages also celebrate festive occasions together with singing, dancing, and food.

On August 3, Tuvaluans celebrate National Children's Day. After a parade through the center of town, local children are treated to a ceremonious traditional feast. November 11 marks the birthday of the Prince of Wales as the royal heir to the Commonwealth, and Commonwealth Day is celebrated on March 14. The Queen's Birthday on June 12 constitutes a public holiday, as well.

On October 1 and 2, Tuvaluans mark their independence from Britain with a parade and dancing on the Funafuti Atoll airstrip.

Tuvalu remembers the 1972 destruction by Hurricane Bebe with Hurricane Day on October 21. On Bomb Day (April 23), Tuvaluans commemorate a 1946 bombing by Japanese forces. The United States established a base on the island and had just ordered the evacuation of nearly 700 people from a local village church when Japanese bombs destroyed the structure. No one was killed.

Youth Culture

Islanders regularly express concern about changes in the islands' youth culture. Traditionally, older children share in the farming, fishing, craftsmanship, and domestic work of the family. Young Tuvaluans attend church daily with other members of their villages and adhere to Christian codes of conduct regarding modest dress, respect for elders, and marriage. Government efforts to improve educational opportunities have been mostly successful, and almost all children attend school. However, over the past couple of decades, more Tuvaluans have moved off of the outer islands to Funafuti searching for better opportunities. These newer residents of Funafuti rarely have access to land for farming; in fact, Funafuti has had no significant plot of arable land since the building of the airstrip in 1942. While the traditional family roles and experiences of youth in Tuvalu are still important, these cultural shifts have unsettled what it means to grow up in Tuvalu, creating a larger gap between young and old.

Tuvalu has no urban culture to speak of. The most densely populated area on Funafuti has the country's only paved road, and the Church of Tuvalu, the Vaiaku Langi Hotel, and some administrative buildings are the most significant structures on the atoll. For those who are not employed by the government, which is the main employer, or by one of a few private markets (there is both a textile and soap factory) or lodging houses, there is little opportunity for work or advancement. Locals argue that these circumstances are made worse by imported movies and television shows that create a culture of crime

and violence. In fact, Tuvalu's most significant crime problem appears to be domestic violence against women and children. Aid and human rights organizations have noted the fact that traditional gender roles that make women subservient to men aggravate this problem. In addition, the dispersal of families around the islands and more and more outer islanders move to Funafuti or emigrate for work has strained local controls on individual behavior.

The flow of popular music, ideas, and trends into Tuvalu from metropolitan centers around the world is kept up by Tuvaluans themselves. Many families have relatives or own land in Australia, New Zealand, Fiji or Samoa. In fact, remittances (revenue sent from abroad) make up a significant portion of Tuvalu's gross domestic product (GDP). Anywhere from 500 to 800 Tuvaluan men are employed as sailors (mostly on German-owned ships) at any given time. Their remittances help sustain families at home in Tuvalu, and their travel provides the islands with a constant influx of international influences.

SOCIETY

Transportation

Transportation is not considered a significant issue on the individual inhabited islands. Each island or islet is small and relatively flat, and the most populated atoll, Funafuti, is only about 2.59 square kilometers (1 square mile). Walking and bicycling are popular modes of transportation, and moped and motorcycles are common. Taxi and minibus service is also available in Fongafale.

In Tuvalu, driving is on the left side of the road. Prior to 1999, it was believed that there were only four cars on the islands, but revenue from a turn-of-the-century Internet licensing deal lead to an increase in automobiles.

Transportation Infrastructure

Inter-island transportation remains a problem for Tuvalu residents. Six of the islands and atolls have lagoons that are accessible by boat. In some cases, this access was created by the US military, which blasted narrow passages through the coral reef. These narrow passages require great skill to traverse. Travel to islands without lagoons is very difficult. To transfer goods and passengers to these islands, boats must anchor offshore and ferry them across rough water to the beach.

Moreover, the nine islands are spread like a chain across a swath of the ocean, requiring passengers to travel overnight by boat to get from Funafuti in the middle of the island chain to Nanumea on the northern end. The country has only one inter-island ferry, and sea planes have proved to be too costly to run regularly between islands. Transportation on the islands has improved somewhat in recent years. For instance, a paved road has been built in the capital, but most roads on outlying islands remain unpaved.

Tuvalu has struggled to maintain reliable flights into the country, having only one (unpaved) airport. International travelers must go through Fiji, either on one of the two ships owned by the Tuvalu government or by plane. The government ships, *Nivaga II* and *Manu Folau*, only travel between Fiji and Tuvalu three to four times per year. Air Pacific runs a weekly flight into Tuvalu from Suva (the capital of Fiji), and Air Fiji travels to Funafuti twice per week. However, Air Fiji was hit by financial problems in 2008 and 2009. The airline was unable to purchase additional fuel and had to suspend flights. As a result, the government of Tuvalu loaned the carrier a substantial amount in 2008 to remain operational.

Media & Communications

The media market in Tuvalu is limited and includes the state-owned Tuvalu Media Corporation, which operates Radio Tuvalu. The station broadcasts on an FM band with interruptions throughout the day, and includes programming from the British Broadcasting Corporation (BBC). Broadcasts are censored in keeping with the conservative form of Christianity prevalent

on the islands, and the government provides three hours of television broadcasting each week, also censored. In June 2006, TMC added an official online news site to make local information available to Tuvaluan expatriates, but the news site was terminated in December 2008. Most Tuvaluans supplement the local media outlet with satellite television and video technology such as DVDs and video cassettes.

Tuvalu Telecommunications Corporation (TCC) is the country's sole provider of telecommunication services. Tuvalu had approximately 900 telephone lines in use in 2005, but service is unreliable, especially on the outer islands. As of 2005, the government of Tuvalu estimated that there were 1,300 cellular phones in service in the country, but more recent information is unavailable. In addition, there were an estimated 4,000 Internet users as of March 2008, which has increased to 4,100 in 2014 (38.1 percent of the total population). In 2000, Tuvalu established a twelve-year initiative in which it leased its Internet domain name, ".tv," accounting for approximately $50 million (USD). Revenue from the licensing helped pay for Tuvalu's annual United Nations membership fees (Tuvalu joined the UN that same year).

SOCIAL DEVELOPMENT

Standard of Living

Tuvalu was not ranked with the other 182 nations in the 2009 United Nations Human Development Index because data was not forthcoming. A picture of the nation's standard of living, then, can be achieved by consideration of the social development issues of Tuvalu.

Water Consumption

With limited groundwater, the primary source of Tuvalu's water supply is rainwater. An estimated 85 percent of houses have private water tanks, where harvested rainwater is stored. Groundwater is used in times of emergency, such as drought, as are government and local water storage reservoirs. Nevertheless, by 2015 some 97 percent of the population had access to improved drinking water sources and 83 percent had access to improved sanitation.

Education

Primary and secondary education for children between the ages of six and fifteen is compulsory in Tuvalu. Each island has its own public primary school; there are also several private primary schools. For public secondary school, students must attend Motufoua Secondary School on the island of Vaitupu, which was recently merged with a secondary school once run by the Christian Church of Tuvalu on Funafuti Atoll.

Every island has at least one preschool education facility, though a lack of trained teachers in these schools has become a matter of concern. Within the last decade, school attendance among preschool-age children has reached 100 percent on the islands.

The government provides job training at eight different community education centers, which require attendees to have only a primary school certificate. Because of the significance of the fishing industry, the government also provides maritime training at a merchant marine school. Tuvalu has no higher education institutions, but the University of the South Pacific (Fiji) has established an extension school on Funafuti.

Public education in Tuvalu is bilingual, although English is more prevalent than the Tuvaluan language at the secondary school level. Literacy rates in both the Tuvaluan language and in English are near 100 percent.

The Tuvalu Maritime Training Institute (TMTI) offers the only formal post-secondary vocational program in Tuvalu.

Women's Rights

Tuvalu's constitution does not discriminate against women, but in practice, women have traditionally held a subordinate role in the culture, and Tuvaluan customs favor men. Within the home, women are often subservient to their hus-

bands and fathers. However, as more Tuvaluan men leave the islands in search of employment, women are playing an increasingly important role in bringing in income and making local decisions. Women also rarely serve in public office. In addition, violence against women, once rare, is increasing, though it still occurs infrequently. However, it is not publically addressed. There are also no laws prohibiting sexual discrimination and harassment. In March 2009, AI urged the Tuvaluan government to enact legislation that addresses discrimination based on gender. A 2012 U.S. Department of State report on Human Rights Practices noted that traditional customs and practices perpetuated discrimination. Women were emphasized in particular.

Health Care

Tuvalu has free public health care for all residents, distributed through dispensaries on every island. Dispensaries generally are not staffed by physicians, but the country has a central hospital on Funafuti Atoll. Traditional medicine is also prevalent on the islands. Tuvalu remains the only Pacific country that offers free medical treatments to its citizens who are overseas.

Food

The Tuvaluan diet is traditionally based on fish, coconut, and a few subsistence crops that can be grown in the islands' poor soil. Tuvaluans grow bananas, taro, and sugarcane in shallow trenches filled with mulch.

Crustaceans (usually crayfish) and fish such as tuna and bonito are common bases for meals. Other important foods include breadfruit (fuaga mei), plantains (futi), spinach (laulu), and papaya (oolesi).

Coconut makes its way into the national diet in countless ways, but can include coconut cream (lolo) used to prepare dishes, coconut milk for drinking (pi), coconut sap made into a breakfast drink (ssali kalev), and coconut meat.

Tuvaluans are increasingly importing food staples, including tea, flour, rice, and sugar. Unfortunately, imported foods with high fat contents have been increasing obesity rates among the islanders.

GOVERNMENT

Structure

Tuvalu gained its name and independence from Britain in 1978. The nation continues to be a member of the British Commonwealth of Nations, entitling it to foreign aid from the British government.

Tuvalu is a constitutional monarchy with a parliamentary democracy. Tuvalu shares the British monarch, represented on the islands by a local governor general. The prime minister selects this governor general for appointment by the British monarch.

Tuvalu's parliament is referred to as the Fale I Fono, or the House of Assembly. The parliament has fifteen members who are each elected by popular vote to a four-year term. A prime minister and deputy prime minister are elected from within the parliament.

Political Parties

Tuvalu has no political parties, although informal groups of like-minded politicians tend to form.

Local Government

Funafuti Atoll maintains one town council, and there are seven six-member island councils on the outer atolls. Traditional chiefs, called Aliki, still participate actively in local politics.

Judicial System

Tuvalu's two-tier judicial system consists of a high court, visited twice a year by a presiding chief justice, and eight island courts, as well as lands courts and the lands court appeals panel. The higher courts also include the Privy Council (in London, England) and a court of appeal (although there has been some delay in setting this court up). As of 2008, there were no private law firms in Tuvalu, and representation and legal services were provided only through the Office of the People's Lawyer, a position that, at times, was unfilled.

Taxation

Personal income taxes and corporate taxes are levied at a 30 percent tax rate. Foreign resident corporations are taxed at a 40 percent rate on net profit. There are varying sales taxes, depending on the goods and services. Taxes and other revenues account for 109.4 percent of the annual GDP (according to the CIA World Factbook 2013 estimates).

Armed Forces

The country has no armed forces. The Tuvalu Police Force operates as the national police force.

Foreign Policy

Tuvalu's main foreign policy focus has been on the Pacific region, but the country's stance on recent environmental issues such as climate change has earned it a place on the world stage. In the late 1980s, experts in the Pacific began raising the alarm about the possibility of entire countries being lost as a result of climatic changes. As a chain of atolls no more than five meters (16.5 feet) above sea level at their highest point, Tuvalu was thought to be particularly vulnerable to rising sea levels associated with these changes. Tuvalu lobbied successfully to become a member state of the United Nations in 2000, and has since used its position to speak out about the effects of carbon emissions from industrialized nations.

At times, Tuvalu's stance has been contentious. In 2000, Tuvalu's prime minister threatened to sue the U.S. and Australia in the International Court of Justice (ICJ) for their refusal to ratify the Kyoto Protocol on climate change. (The Kyoto Protocol is an international environmental treaty aimed at stabilizing greenhouse gases in the earth's atmosphere; it expires in 2012). The lawsuit was not filed when the prime minister lost to another candidate in elections, but Tuvalu continues to call to account the US and Australia as some of the world's largest producers of carbon emissions—it is estimated that the U.S. produces 30 percent of the world's carbon emissions alone. The actual damage caused by global warming to Tuvalu thus far is undetermined. Many of the outer islands have experienced significant erosion in recent years. Fongafale has been hard hit by seasonal high tides (called king tides) that are flooding inland areas with brackish sea water. The islet of Tepuka across the lagoon from Fongafale was stripped bare by three cyclones that hit in 1997 and has never recovered.

Many experts agree that sea levels in the Pacific have been rising and that weather patterns should change with increased global temperatures and changes in sea currents. At least a few scientists believe that sea level rises in the area of Tuvalu could be less than previously predicted, even as the rise in sea levels globally becomes more significant. Local experts also point to the fact that Tuvalu's basic geography may have been made more fragile by human intervention. For example, Tuvaluans and the U.S. armed forced bored into the coral reefs around and below the islands in order to harvest coral for building material and landfill. On Fongafale, in particular, this disruption probably breached the islet's natural protection from the king tides. The gathering of coral, sand, and plant life from coastlines most likely added to erosion problems throughout the islands.

Nonetheless, scientists and politicians are working to understand what the changes on Tuvalu mean in regard to the poor management of ecosystems and global warming, and how it will affect other countries all over the world. In the meantime, Tuvalu is creating a back-up plan; an agreement with New Zealand permits at least seventy-five Tuvaluans annually to resettle in that country. The Tuvaluan government is also trying to negotiate a priority immigration status to Australia or elsewhere, preferably one that would establish Tuvalu as an independent political state on new land. Tuvalu's efforts have prompted international discussions about the need for a special status for environmental refugees.

Tuvalu also depends heavily on international aid. In 1987, the Tuvalu Trust Fund, which pro-vides the government with a revenue source to fund development projects and help offset basic costs and expenses, was established. The major contributors to the fund have been Australia, the United Kingdom (UK), and New Zealand. Japan and South Korea have also become donors. As of March 2008, the fund's value was an estimated $104 million. Specific government projects receive other funding from international donors, including aid and money for fishing treaties and disaster risk reduction. Aside from the developed nations of the Pacific, Tuvalu increasingly receives significant aid from China.

Aside from the UN, the country holds membership in various regional and international organizations and institutions, including the Caribbean and Pacific Group of States (ACP); the Economic and Social Commission for Asia and the Pacific (ESCAP); the South Pacific Regional Trade and Economic Co-operation Agreement (SPARTECA); the Pacific Community (SPC), of which Tuvalu is the secretariat; the Pacific Island Forum (PIF); the Alliance of Small Island States (AOSIS); and the Asian Development Bank (ADB).

Human Rights Profile

International human rights law insists that states respect civil and political rights, and promote an individual's economic, social, and cultural rights. The United Nations Universal Declaration on Human Rights (UDHR) is recognized as the standard for international human rights. Its authors sought the counsel of the world's great thinkers, philosophers, and religious leaders, and were careful to create a document that reflects the core values shared by every world culture. (To read this document or view the articles relating to cultural human rights, visit http://www.udhr.org/UDHR/default.htm.)

In general, the human rights of Tuvaluans are respected by the government, though some forms of social discrimination exist. The UN Human Rights Council (HRC) issued its updated report on Tuvalu in January 2009, noting that the nation needed to continue its efforts to support women's rights and to address domestic violence against women and children. The report also notes concerns about religious freedom and discrimination on the islands (the population is mostly Protestant Christian). During a March 2009 period review of Tuvalu by the HRC, the country was also urged to establish a national human rights commission, and to further strengthen or expand laws relating to sexual offenses, land rights, and familial matters. Amnesty International (AI) also urged Tuvalu to enact constitutional amendments that address gender discrimination. Many of these same concerns were reiterated in a 2012 U.S. Department of State report on human rights.

ECONOMY

Overview of the Economy

Generally, Tuvalu's economy is subsistence in nature; Tuvalu relies primarily on fishing (particularly fishing rights, which make up more than 45 percent of the GDP) and the processing and sales of copra (the dried kernel of a coconut) as its industrial base. Foreign aid is also important to the economy, which makes the Tuvaluan economy susceptible to world economics and their influences. Tourism also makes up a small part of the economy, while another significant source remains remittances sent home from overseas residents, such as seamen. In 2014, the gross domestic product (GDP) was estimated at $35 million USD, with a per capita GDP of $3,300 USD.

Industry

Outside of the public sector, Tuvalu has several small, unusual side industries. The country has sold rights to its telephone country code and to its unique national Internet domain identifier (".tv"). The manufacture of soaps and textiles also supports some islanders. Stamp collecting also helps to support Tuvalu, largely because the tiny island nation's stamps have become interesting, if not necessary, among international stamp collectors.

Tuvaluan men often earn income for themselves and their families as sailors beyond Tuvalu, or as phosphate miners in the nearby island nation of Nauru. However, the 2008–09 global financial crisis forced many seamen out of work, reducing remittances as a significant revenue stream.

Labor

It is estimated that about two-thirds of the formal workforce in Tuvalu works in the public sector, mainly government. About three-fourths of the labor force works in the informal sector, such as subsistence agriculture. Tuvalu is home to one registered trade union, the Tuvalu Overseas Seamen's Union (TOSU). Estimates place the number of members, both retired and working, at between 1,350 and 1,500.

Energy/Power/Natural Resources

Tuvalu's islands have no significant mineral resources. The islands' poor soil means that other land resources are generally limited to products of the islands' coconut palms and the tourism draw of pristine beaches.

Fishing

The nation's exclusive fishing zone reaches 322 kilometers (200 miles) out from the islands and is a profitable destination for fishing vessels in search of skipjack tuna. As a result, Tuvalu has been able to collect revenue from fishing rights sold to the fishing vessels from the United States and Japan.

Agriculture

Poor soil conditions on all of Tuvalu's nine islands prohibit any substantial agricultural activity.

Tourism

The Tuvaluan government estimates that fewer than 1,000 tourists visit the islands each year, but the small population and scarce economic resources make this tourism essential to the nation's resources. Transportation is limited; flights to Fiji and Kiribati leave from Funafuti Atoll International Airport, and ferry service connects the islands to each other.

Amy Witherbee, Anne Whittaker

DO YOU KNOW?

- Tuvaluans are active in efforts to increase international concern about global warming. With ocean levels rising, the country is endangered by its watery surroundings and has already worked out an emergency plan with the government of New Zealand in case of massive flooding and erosion.

Bibliography

Besnier, Niko. *Gossip and the Everyday Production of Politics*. Honolulu: University of Hawaii Press, 2009.

Bouma, Gary D., et al. *Religious Diversity in Southeast Asia and the Pacific*. Medford, MA: Springer, 2010.

Chambers, Keith and Anne. *Unity of Heart: Culture and Change in a Polynesian Atoll Society*. Prospect Heights, IL: Waveland Press, 2001.

Geert, Cole, et al. *Lonely Planet South Pacific*. 2nd ed. Malaysia: Lonely Planet Publications, 2003.

Koch, Gerard. *The Material Culture of Tuvalu*. Trans. Guy Slatter. Suva, Fiji: Institute of Pacific Studies, University of the South Pacific, 1983.

Works Cited

"2002 Census." *Central Statistics Division*. Government of Tuvalu. [http://www.spc.int/prism/country/tv/stats/Census%20&%20Surveys/Census_index.htm].

Lazrus, Heather. "The Governance of Vulnerability: Climate Change and Agency in Tuvalu, South Pacific." *Anthropology and Climate Change: From Encounters to Actions*. Eds. Susan A. Crate and Mark Nuttall. Walnut Creek, CA: Left Coast Press, 2009. 240–9.

Linkels, Ad. "The Real Music of Paradise" *World Music: Latin & North America, Caribbean, India, Asia and Pacific*. Eds. Simon Broughton, Mark Ellingham, James McConnachie, and Orla Duane. New York: Rough Guides/ Penguin. 218–29.

"Priorities of the People: Hardship in Tuvalu." *Asian Development Bank*. December 2003. http://www.adb.org/documents/reports/priorities_poor/tuv/tuv0100.asp.

"Report of the Working Group on the Universal Periodic Review: Tuvalu." *The UN Human Rights Council*. 9 January 2009. http://www.unhcr.org/refworld/country,,UNHRC,,TUV,45b632e02,497476aa0,0.html.

Richardson, Phil. "Governing the Outer Islands: Decentralization in Kiribati and Tuvalu." *Commonwealth Journal of Local Governance* 2 (January 2009).

"Tuvalu." CIA. *The World Factbook.*. https://www.cia.gov/library/publications/the-world-factbook/geos/tv.html.

"Tuvalu: Country Reports on Human Rights Practices." *U.S. Department of State*. http://www.state.gov/g/drl/rls/hrrpt/2001/eap/8381.htm.

"Tuvalu." *Secretariat of the Pacific Community*. http://www.spc.int/coastfish/Sections/Community/tuvalu.htm.

"Tuvalu 2012 Human Rights Report." *United States Department of State*. 2012. http://www.state.gov/documents/organization/204458.pdf

"Tuvalu Profile." *Australian Government*. http://www.austrade.gov.au/Tuvalu-profile/default.aspx

Introduction

The Melanesian nation of Vanuatu is an archipelago of eighty-three islands. It is a relatively new republic, having gained independence in 1980. Prior to independence it was known as the New Hebrides. The name Vanuatu means "land eternal," an appropriate choice for an area with a long history. The people of Vanuatu are known as the ni-Vanuatu.

Port Vila is the capital and largest city in Vanuatu, The capital is located on the island of Efate. With a beautiful natural harbor and a blend of Melanesian, English, French, and Asian cultures, the city has developed into a popular tourist destination in the Pacific region.

Vanuatu is the third-poorest nation in the Pacific region. It has a high rate of illiteracy, and little arable land. The nation faces severe economic problems, but improvements are being made, especially in the area of tourism.

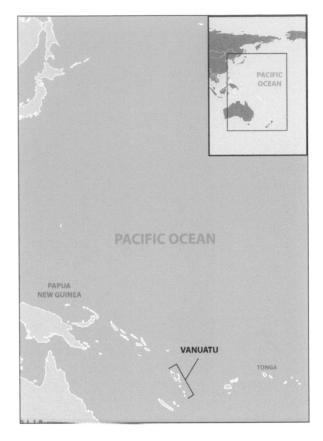

GENERAL INFORMATION

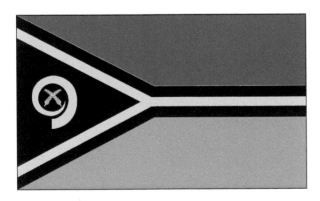

Official Language: Bislama, English, French
Population: 272,264 (2015 estimate)
Currency: Vatu
Coins: Coins in circulation include denominations of 1, 2, 5, 10, 20, 50, and 100 vatu.
Land Area: 12,189 square kilometers (4,706 square miles)
National Motto: "Long God Yumi Stanap" ("In God We Stand")
National Anthem: "Yumi, Yumi, Yumi" ("We, We, We")

Capital: Port Vila
Time Zone: GMT +11
Flag Description: The flag of Vanuatu is a Y-shaped flag (pall design) with the colors of red (symbolic of bloodshed in the name of independence); yellow (symbolic of sunshine); green (symbolic of rich or fertile lands); and black (which symbolizes the ni-Vanuatu). An equal band of red runs atop, while an equal band of green runs below; within the black triangular space to the right is a boar's tusk, with two native fern leaves enclosed.

Population

A majority of ni-Vanuatu resides on the island of Efate; the Port Vila urban area has a population of approximately 53,000. Another 14,000 or so people live in the Luganville (Santo Town) urban area on the island of Espiritu Santo.

According to the 2015 census, an estimated 26.1 percent live in urban areas, while the rate of urbanization is 3.42 percent (estimated for 2010–2015). Most of the people live along the

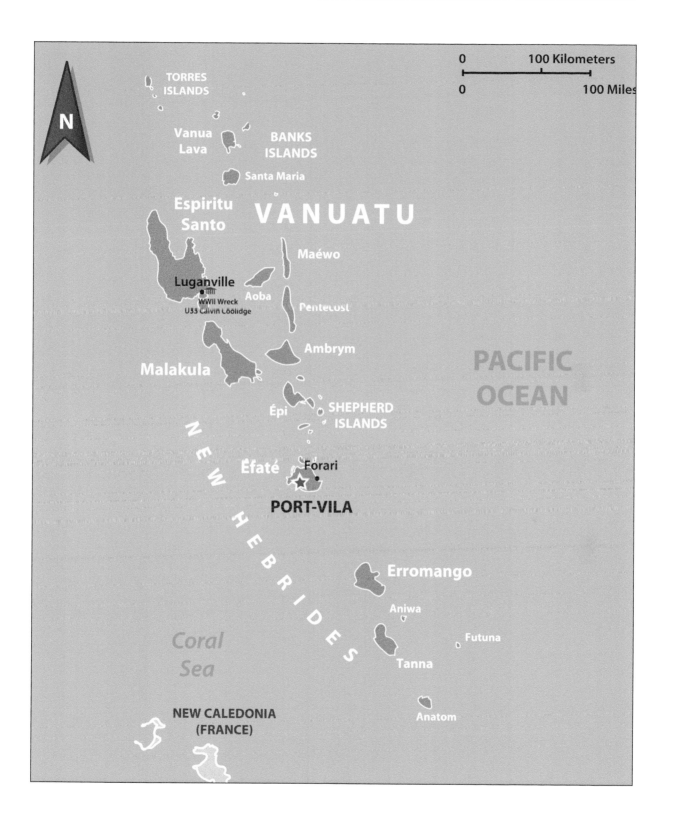

Principal Cities by Population (2014, unless noted):

- Port Vila (53,000)
- Luganville (14,214; 2013)

coasts of the islands, leaving much of the interior inhabited. The result is high population density in Vanuatu's coastal areas. The population grew 2.8 percent—4.7 percent in Port Vila—since the 1999 census was undertaken.

Languages

Bislama (Creole language), English, and French are the official languages. A number of Melanesian languages and dialects—estimated at over 100—are spoken as well.

Native People & Ethnic Groups

The indigenous population of Vanuatu is Melanesian, and this ethnic group comprises 98 percent of the current population. Other ethnic groups include French, Vietnamese, Chinese and other Pacific Islanders.

The Melanesians are believed to have inhabited the islands for approximately 4,000 years. Pottery fragments dating to 1300–1100 BCE have been found in Vanuatu.

Europeans happened upon the islands in 1606, and again in 1768. A few years later, Captain James Cook named the island group the New Hebrides, and the name stuck.

Sandalwood was discovered on the island of Erromango (formerly known as Martyr's Island) in the early nineteenth century. In the 1860s, adult males in the New Hebrides were taken as long-term indentured labor to plantations in Australia, New Caledonia, Fiji, and Samoa. This practice removed more than half of the men from the islands, and there is some evidence that the effects are still evident in the unexpectedly small population.

Religions

About 83 percent of ni-Vanuatu adheres to Christianity, often mixed with traditional beliefs.

According to early 21st-century estimates, about 28 percent are Presbyterian, 15 percent Anglican, 12.4 percent Roman Catholic, 12.5 percent Seventh Day Adventist, and 4.5 percent Church of Christ. Many others remain firm in traditional beliefs.

Other small religions include the cargo cult of Jon Frum on Tanna, and the smaller cargo cult of Prince Philip. A cargo cult believes that magic will bring its adherents wealth—particularly, the arrival of a "special" cargo of goods, often represented by advanced technology. Jon Frum began during the 1930s, when the islanders saw American ships full of what they considered rich cargo. The belief of adherents is that the mythical messianic figure Jon Frum—represented as an American serviceman—will return one day and take care of all their material needs. The Prince Philip Movement began with the prince's visit to Vanuatu in 1974. Members of this cult, made up of the Yaohnanen tribe on the island of Tanna, believe that Prince Philip will return some day to rule over them.

Climate

Vanuatu's northern islands have a hot, tropical climate with little seasonal variation. The southern islands have a semi-tropical climate with some difference in seasons. Port Vila, in the center of the string of islands, experiences average temperatures of 22° to 27° Celsius (72° to 81° Fahrenheit) daily.

Southeast trade winds blow from May through October. Cyclones (hurricanes) can occur anywhere in the islands from November through April. In fact, Vanuatu is the country in the Pacific most likely to be hit by a cyclone, and the number of cyclones is increasing. The islands from Efate north are more likely to experience a cyclone than are the southern islands.

The rainy season is November-April, but sudden showers can fall at any time. Annual rainfall varies from 390 centimeters (154 inches) in the north to 230 centimeters (90 inches) in the south.

In general, the weather is cooler and drier from May through July. On the southern islands, evenings may actually be chilly from June through September.

ENVIRONMENT & GEOGRAPHY

Topography

Vanuatu is an archipelago of eighty-three volcanic islands in the southwest Pacific Ocean, 1,000 kilometers (600 miles) west of Fiji and 400 kilometers (250 miles) northeast of New Caledonia. The islands stretch from north to south for 1,300 kilometers (808 miles).

On the western edge of the Pacific Plate, Vanuatu is no stranger to earthquakes. In fact, as the Indo-Australian Plate repeatedly slips under the edge of the Pacific Plate, the islands move 10 centimeters (3.9 inches) northwest each year. They also rise 2 millimeters (0.07 inches) higher each year.

The islands are mostly mountainous, with narrow coastal plains. The highest point in the country is Mount Tabwemasana on Espiritu Santo, at 1,877 meters (6,158 feet).

Vanuatu has twenty-five to thirty freshwater lakes. Most of these are crater lakes, some in active volcanoes. The largest is Lake Letas, a crater lake on intermittently active Mount Garet on Gaua Island. The lake covers 190 square kilometers (73 square miles). Except for New Guinea, this is the largest freshwater lake in the Pacific islands. The highest lakes in the South Pacific are atop the active volcano Waivundoluc on Ambae Island. These lakes lie at an elevation of more than 1,300 meters (4,265 feet).

The Teouma River on Efate, the Matenoi River in the southern part of Malekula, and many other rivers flow through narrow mountain gorges. Some rivers are dry except during times of heavy rain.

Plants & Animals

Evergreen forest covers about 75 percent of the land, particularly at the higher elevations and on the wet windward slopes. Semi-deciduous forests are found low on the drier leeward slopes. There are also some savannahs (grasslands).

Vanuatu has 900 species of flowering plants, but only 135 of these are native. In contrast, there are 250 varieties of ferns, including the namele, a prehistoric fern tree (featured on the nation's flag). Nabangas, or giant banyan trees, are common, as are the smaller mangrove trees which often grow in swamps.

Pigs are now considered indigenous, although they were introduced. Also common to the islands are butterflies, fruit bats, non-venomous snakes, a giant poisonous centipede, and non-venomous scorpions. In the waters surrounding Vanuatu there are aggressive tiger sharks, venomous sea snakes, numerous species of game fish, non-stinging jellyfish, eels and potentially deadly lion fish, stonefish and cone shells, in addition to a living coral reef.

CUSTOMS & COURTESIES

Greetings

There are over 100 languages spoken throughout the Vanuatu archipelago, but most people speak Bislama, a form of pidgin English. English or French is more commonly spoken in urban areas. In Bislama, the typical greeting is "Alo" ("Hello"), "Gudmorning" ("Good morning"), or "Gudaftenun" ("Good afternoon"). In urban areas, English and French greetings, such as "Bonjour" ("Hello"), are more common. Another common greeting is "Yu go wea?" ("Where are you going?"), while "Lukim yu" ("See you later") is a common and informal farewell.

Handshaking is not traditional in Vanuatu, but people have grown accustomed to it due to increasing Westernization. Women may embrace when greeting or offer a light kiss on each cheek, called the bisou. Men might shake hands with each other or with foreign women.

Gestures & Etiquette

Because there have been more than eighty languages spoken throughout the Vanuatu archipelago, the ni-Vanuatu have traditionally used gestures as a means to communicate. Common gestures include waving inward with the palm turned in, used to beckon someone, and raising the eyebrows up and down or nodding, used to signify agreement. Disagreement is indicated by shaking the head. One might also hiss through the teeth to get someone else's attention.

Life in Vanuatu is dominated by kastom, or the traditional customs of each ethnic group or clan. In fact, the word "taboo" as it is used in English evolved from a local Melanesian word, "tabu," which means sacred. In rural areas, there are many "tabu" or sacred areas that women and uninitiated men are not allowed to enter. One such place is the nakamal, a communal lodge where men often gather to drink kava or discuss local issues. However, many nakamal are now open to women or outsiders. Local kastom also segregates areas based on gender. For example, in some places, women are not allowed to be seated at a higher level than men, and in others there are certain village paths which are reserved for members of only one gender. In addition, people are not permitted to fish in certain areas and swimming areas may be segregated by gender.

Casual attire is the norm in Vanuatu culture. However, maintaining a tidy appearance is considered a sign of respect. Women (even foreigners) are expected to dress modestly. In rural areas, a loose-fitting gown that extends to the ankles is the customary attire for most women. In addition, public displays of affection are generally frowned upon.

Eating/Meals

An estimated 80 percent of ni-Vanuatu practice subsistence living, and meals are generally taken when resources permit or when certain agrarian tasks are completed. Breakfast in Vanuatu might consist of light fare, either rice with island cabbage or leftovers from the night before. In the urban areas, French eating customs, such as having a baguette and tea in the morning, may be followed. Lunch might consist of laplap (a paste or porridge made of grated manioc or taro), or yams with rice and processed meat. There may be little variation between lunch and dinner fare, but chicken or fish might be added to the laplap. For special occasions, a pig or cow would be roasted.

In rural areas, most food is cooked over cooking pits. Stones are heated in the pits, and then removed to form a kind of oven. Some dishes are cooked atop the heated stones, while other foods are cooked in pots or pans placed over the fire. Meals are also usually eaten outdoors in rural areas, generally while sitting on woven mats. Food is served from a communal dish onto individual plates or leaves. Often, people eat with their hands, but also use utensils. In some ethnic groups, men are served their food before the rest of the family. Christian families traditionally say grace before a meal and then clap when they are done with their prayer.

Visiting

Visits in Vanuatu are generally unannounced and casual. A guest does not need to bring a gift, but gifts are appreciated for overnight stays. Social visits customarily take place outdoors, sitting on mats. A guest will be offered food if it is near meal time, but this is not a requirement if the visit takes place between meals.

LIFESTYLE

Family

All of the different ethnic groups in Vanuatu are based on kinship or clan-like family structures. In a matrilineal group, families would retain close ties to the mother and her siblings and parents. Thus, the children of a mother's sister would be referred to as brothers and sisters, and the mother's brother would be the highest authority of the family, or the person to whom bride prices and death payments would be made. Similarly, a man would consider his sister's children as his children, and they would traditionally refer to him as "father." In this way, children essentially have more than one set of parents and support is provided for all extended family members. Gender roles are also very structured in most families in Vanuatu; women are expected to tend to agrarian and domestic duties, including child rearing, while men are responsible for hunting, fishing, and other forms of work.

Housing

Traditional houses made from wooden frames covered with woven thatched roofs and other plant materials are still common in rural areas. Walls may also be made of corrugated metal and other found materials. Traditional houses typically lack electricity or plumbing, and furniture is generally sparse.

In urban areas, middle-class residents might live in single-level cinder block houses or low-rise apartment houses or condos with modern conveniences. These homes customarily have Western-style furniture. Improvised housing, or informal settlements, is often common on the outskirts of some towns. Homes in these areas generally consist of discarded material, particularly corrugated metal.

Food

The staple foods of Vanuatu are root vegetables and fruit. In the rural areas, people grow their own food in small gardens which feature taro, yams, island cabbage, and manioc. Most rural families also own pigs, so pork is a large part of the diet and pigs can be used for bartering or as currency. Chicken is another common source of meat, as is wild game such as ground game and fruit bats. While beef is one of Vanuatu's major exports, it is mostly eaten by tourists to the islands.

Fruit and seafood are plentiful in Vanuatu. Most families have their own fruit trees which provide them with breadfruit, papaya (or paw-paw), pineapple, guava, mango, lime, grapefruit, and plantains. On the bigger islands, urban people may still have their own gardens, but also shop in markets which carry imported items such as cheese, meat, cereal, rice, and canned goods. Many local people make their living from fishing and shellfish and fish are part of many local dishes. Crabs have been over-harvested in some areas and are now protected until their populations increase again.

Laplap is considered to be the national dish of Vanuatu. Though recipes vary on each island, it is typically a paste or porridge made from grated or pounded manioc or taro that is mixed with coconut milk and served on a bed of banana leaves. Laplap will often be served with a stew of fish or chicken on top. Another common dish is naelot, made from boiled taro, bananas or breadfruit, and grated coconut. Kava, a beverage made from a local tree, is also a very important part of the culture in Vanuatu. The root of the tree is pounded, grated, or chewed in the mouth, creating a pulp that is squeezed into a liquid that is then mixed with water. Kava has a numbing effect on the mouth and can have an intoxicating effect.

Life's Milestones

An important rite of passage among many of the groups in Vanuatu is the male circumcision ritual that takes place when boys reach adolescence. Boys are typically taken into the bush (jungle area) by their uncles and taught skills of manhood for several weeks. In exchange for this lesson, the boys' families pay the uncles with food, pigs, or mats (a common item of trade). In some areas, girls are initiated by having a front tooth pulled.

Couples in Vanuatu typically have two weddings: a kastom wedding (traditional wedding) and a Christian wedding. At the kastom wedding, the bride's uncle (mother's brother) receives the bride price from the husband's family, which secures the marriage. The Christian wedding takes place at a church. Funerary traditions remain both traditional and Christian, as well. Numerous feasts are held after someone dies, and funeral guests bring gifts of mats to the family of the deceased.

CULTURAL HISTORY

Art

Most of the early art of Vanuatu had spiritual or ritualistic significance. For example, headdresses or masks were made for ritual ceremonies and dances, and carved statues represented spirits or supernatural beings or were used as funerary effigies. The style of ritualistic masks varied depending on the ethnic group and the dance's

Sand drawing is a traditional artform in Vanuatu that has been named a Masterpiece of the Oral and Intangible Heritage of Humanity by UNESCO.

significance. Traditional art also featured prominently in initiation ceremonies. Carved wooden masks called tamates were meant to represent the spirits of ancestors and were used in initiation rituals for intimidation. Carved wooden statues known as "grade figures" were given to boys as they passed certain tests in their initiation rites. Boys in certain groups were given puppets instead of figurines. Because masks or other ritual items were often destroyed after being used in order to keep away evil spirits, such artifacts are rare.

The artistic skills of traditional Vanuatuan women were also highly developed, and included weaving and jewelry making. Many crafts served functional purposes, such as woven mats and baskets, while necklaces and anklets made from seeds and shells were used in ceremonies. Painting was also practiced among the men in certain groups. This consisted of scenes on pieces of bark which depicted tribal legends. Men were also responsible for carving the ceremonial clubs that were used in the pig-hunting rituals that were integral to male initiation rites.

A unique form of art that developed on the islands of Vanuatu is the sandroing, or sand drawing. The drawings mostly consist of geo-metric patterns etched into the dirt or sand with one or two fingers. They are used in storytelling and to transmit rituals and oral history, with each pattern assigned a meaning that is recognized by in-group members. As there are also a substantial amount of different languages spoken in the Vanuatu archipelago, the drawings are also used as means of communication. In 2003, the United Nations Educational, Scientific, and Cultural Organization (UNESCO) proclaimed the sand drawings of Vanuatu as a Masterpiece of the Oral and Intangible Heritage of Humanity.

Architecture

Traditional architecture in Vanuatu was based on available resources and cultural norms, and most houses were made from natural materials. Wooden poles were used for a house's framework, while leaves, fronds, or roots were woven together to construct the building's thatched roof and walls. Though each ethnic group developed its own style of weaving to form these durable shelters, most homes were indistinguishable from one another in terms of size and appearance. There were structures that had distinct appearances, however, including ceremonial houses called gamals where men would gather. The nakamal, or meeting-house, was another distinct structure made for the men of the community. Though some nakamals had walls, others consisted merely of a wooden pole frame covered by a roof. Nakamals were used for group meetings and for drinking kava, a beverage once considered sacred. Today, nakamals are generally thought of as "kava bars" and are open to the public.

The arrival of European colonists and the advent of Christianity impacted native architecture through the introduction of new materials, such as iron, and new tools and building techniques, such as carpentry. However, very few early colonial structures have survived, particularly since square and tall European-style houses were unable to withstand cyclones. For this reason, houses are traditionally built low. Western–style buildings made of cinder block or cement to withstand the frequent cyclones are now common, particularly in urban areas. The capital of Port Vila blends traditional and French colonial-style houses with modern buildings.

Music

Music is an integral part of cultural tradition among all groups in Vanuatu. Traditional instruments were played at important village ceremonies. The tamtam (slit gong or slit drum), a percussive instrument made from the hollowed-out trunk of the breadfruit tree, is considered one of the most important traditional instruments. The instrument is played by striking the lip with a wooden beater. Panpipes, conch shells, and flutes were also commonly used as instruments, and for communicating between villages. The crafting of instruments is a refined skill that is passed down through the generations through a master-apprentice relationship.

Dance

Dance plays an important role in the lives of the ni-Vanuatu. Ritual dances traditionally accompanied various occasions, and included hunting dances, death dances, and war dances. Most groups reserve a special area of the village, called the natsaro or nasara, as the dancing ground. Attire for the dances varies according to the occasion and to the gender of the dancer. Traditionally, women wore grass skirts (either plain or colorful), headdresses, and no tops, while men wore nambas (penis sheaths) or banana-leaf cloaks. Grass mats were common among the Polynesian minority.

For the rom dances performed on Ambrym Island, which are part of the "grade-taking" or male initiation rites, dancers in painted conical masks and banana-leaf cloaks perform a dance to impersonate spirits. They are accompanied by other male dancers wearing only nambas. After the dance, a feast is offered and the costumes and masks are burned so that the spirits do not try to haunt the dancers. The ma dance, or "snake dance" from the Banks Islands, is performed by men with stripes painted on their bodies. Women and children don seed-anklets and stamp out a rhythm. Perhaps the best-known dance in Vanuatu is the toka dance performed on the island of Tanna. Women begin the dance at night then men take over at dawn, bringing out a kweriya or feather pole. The dance is part of the nekowiar ceremony, a three-day gift-gifting festival.

CULTURE

Arts & Entertainment

While traditional music is still popular in Vanuatu, young people have become more interested in musical styles from off the island. Reggae and reggaeton (Spanish-language reggae) are becoming increasingly popular, as are rhythm and blues (R&B), soul, and pop music. Vanessa Quai (1988–) is the Vanuatuan pop singer who has achieved perhaps the most international fame, and her music has grown in popularity in many of the South Pacific island chains. Popular music from Europe, Australia, and New has also found a greater following, as has gospel music. The 1970s and 1980s saw the rise of string bands featuring the eight-stringed Tahitian ukulele, the slap-base, bongo, guitar, "bottle xylophone," and falsetto vocals, though these bands are not popular with the younger generation.

The annual Fest'Napuan is Vanuatu's biggest cultural festival. It is also considered one of the most important music events in the Pacific region. The music festival brings groups from Australia, New Zealand, and neighboring South Pacific islands, and promotes contemporary dance and other art forms. The festival is free and is now broadcasted by the Australian Broadcasting Corporation (ABC).

Since independence, a number of experimental theater groups have emerged in Vanuatu. Most of the groups involve young people or women and are aimed at giving these groups a broader voice in political and social issues. The performances are generally in Bislama and often center on the exploration of a theme without a set script. The Tua Theater Group, begun in 1994, is a women's theater group and Wan Smolbag Theater involves young people putting on plays about social and environmental issues. Both groups try to reach audiences that would not otherwise have access to theater by performing their plays on the radio and even in the streets in poor urban neighborhoods. Vanuatu is also home to a film festival, the Very Short Film Festival, which invites filmmakers from all over the South Pacific.

While much of the art in Vanuatu is developed for the tourist market, there are a few artists who are pursuing art on a more academic level. Ralph Regenvanu (1971–) is perhaps the best-known visual artist in Vanuatu. He is the former director of the Vanuatu Cultural Arts Center, and his work focuses on post-independence political issues. He has been part of shows in Australia and Europe and in 2006 he was awarded the Chevalier dans l'Ordre des Arts et des Lettres (Knight in the Order of Arts and Letters) by the French government.

Art is an important part of ni-Vanuatu ritual and spirituality. Artistic items, such as decorated masks and headdresses, are not meant to last, and must "die" after serving their ritualistic purpose. Other ritual items, such as the large wooden slit drums, are permanent. No ritual items are meant for public display or sale.

The combination of costumes, drums, body paint, masks, headdresses, and song comprise "art" as well as ritual. The right to create certain items, designs or songs may belong to individuals, lineages or clans. The ni-Vanuatu also create more practical items, such as colorful dyed mats and baskets woven from pandanus leaves.

Football (soccer) is a popular sport in Vanuatu, and the nation sends a team to the Olympics. The Vanuatu Football Federation (VFF) was formed in 1980, shortly after independence. Youth participation is encouraged and developed partly through junior championship games.

Cultural Sites & Landmarks

Among the most notable landmarks in Vanuatu is the Yasur Volcano on Tanna Island, known as one of the world's most active volcanoes. Yasur is sometimes called the "lighthouse of the Pacific" because its eruptions are so frequent—

from every few minutes to several times an hour during peak activity—that its volcanic glow can be seen from a distance out at sea. Despite the volcano's volatility, the site has become a major tourist destination. There are several other active and inactive volcanoes in Vanuatu, including a few underwater volcanoes. Gaua is the most volcanic island of the Vanuatu archipelago and home to Lake Letas, the country's largest lake. The volcanic Crater Lake surrounds the volcanic Mount Gharat and is considered a regional cultural monument. In 2004, Vanuatu submitted Lake Letas for consideration as a United Nations Educational, Scientific, and Cultural Organization (UNESCO) World Heritage Site.

In World War II, the battles of Guadalcanal (1942–43), the Solomon Islands (1942–43), and the Coral Sea (1942) were staged from bases on the islands of Efate and Espiritu Santo. Due to the severity of the air-to-air assaults, many of the downed aircraft were abandoned in the waters around the islands. These uncommon underwater wrecks are now popular sites for scuba divers.

One popular wreck divers explore is the *USS Calvin Coolidge*, considered the most accessible shipwreck in the world. The sunken vessel was an American transport ship based at Vanuatu during World War II. The ship was struck by an underwater mine and sunk immediately, with the crew leaving virtually all of their possessions behind. Now submerged just off the coast, the wreck offers divers the opportunity to swim through its decks and observe gun turrets and examine old military equipment up close. Because the boat is so close to the surface of the water, even inexperienced divers can explore parts of the wreckage.

In 2008, the ancient kingdom of a thirteenth-century Melanesian chief, Roymata (also spelled Roy Mata and Roimata) was designated as Vanuatu's first and only UNESCO World Heritage Site. Officially known as Chief Roi Mata's Domain, the site, which includes the island of Efate and two small neighboring islands, was recognized for its historic and cultural value. Descendents of the ancient king still reside in the area, and have maintained a traditional way of living. The site also includes the king's burial site and other key sites identified through oral tradition that has been passed down for thousands of years.

Libraries & Museums

The Vanuatu Cultural Center, which houses the National Museum of Vanuatu, showcases the work of Vanuatuan artists and brings international art to the country in an effort to expose local people to a variety of cultural experiences. Exhibitions include traditional basketry, the history of Vanuatu canoes, contemporary art, and a history of Vanuatu and World War II.

With the national museum is the National Library of Vanuatu, which houses two collections, the Pacific and Vanuatu Collections. There is also a public library located in the Cultural Center on Port Vila.

Holidays

Official holidays include Custom Chief's Day (March 5), Labor Day (May 1), Independence Day (July 30), Constitution Day (October 5), Unity Day (November 29), and Family Day (December 27).

The John Frum Festival is celebrated on the island of Tanna each year on February 15.

Youth Culture

Football (soccer) is the most popular sport in Vanuatu and youth typically follow Australian and New Zealand football clubs. Cricket is also widely popular and Vanuatu has its own national cricket team. In rural areas, where resources and amusement are generally few and far between, children are accustomed to creating their own games. One such traditional game is similar to marbles and played with seeds. Westernization is more prevalent in urban areas and reggae and European music is particularly popular with older youth.

Dating and other social interactions between young men and women have traditionally been prohibited in Vanuatu; girls and boys who want to see each other romantically typically do so in secrecy. This has started to change somewhat in urban areas as more youth are forgoing their obligation to preserve traditional culture for an increased interest in a more Western way of life.

SOCIETY

Transportation

Because Vanuatu is an archipelagic nation made up of a collection of islands, ferries and privately-owned or chartered boats are the common means of transportation. There are regularly scheduled ferries between the bigger islands, but ferries to the smaller islands are infrequent. Some islands are only accessible by charter or private boat.

Privately owned taxis and buses service Vanuatu's main municipalities. Vanuatu does not have a strong road system, and rural roads may only be accessible by four-wheel-drive vehicles. Most people in rural areas walk from place to place or take private boats to travel longer distances.

Driving occurs on the right side of the road in Vanuatu. Seat belts are not compulsory.

Transportation Infrastructure

In March 2009, it was announced that $4.5 million (USD) would be allotted for road maintenance, with islands involved in the copra, cocoa, timber, and kava industries receiving priority. Three years prior, in March 2006, Vanuatu entered into agreement with the Millennium Challenge Corporation (MCC), an agency of the US government, to receive approximately $65 million to fund the improvement of the country's transportation infrastructure. In June 2009, the government signed an agreement with the New Zealand Agency for International Development (NZAID) to receive funding towards road construction.

Small "island hopper" airplanes are also common for inter-island transportation. These types of flights usually operate on a schedule several days a week or by charter. There are many small airstrips suitable for these types of airplanes, as well as an international airport outside of Port Vila with direct flights to and from Australia, New Zealand, Fiji, New Caledonia, and the Solomon Islands. Pekoa Airport, located at Luganville, and Whitegrass Airport, located on the island of Tanna, are Vanuatu's other two international airports.

Media & Communications

Freedom of the press is generally respected in Vanuatu and the government has made no official attempts to stifle criticism of its policies. There is one government-run weekly newspaper, *Vanuatu Weekly*, which is published in English and several private newspapers that are also mostly published weekly. There is one state-owned television station in Vanuatu, which broadcasts in English, French and Bislama (considered Vanuatu's most broadly spoken language). Satellite television is also available in Port Vila and in some of the bigger resorts and hotels.

Radio is a popular medium in Vanuatu, as it reaches many of the outlying islands. Most villages operate a public radio, and radio stations offer a message service so that those who are inaccessible by phone can be reached through broadcasted radio messages. There is one state-owned radio station with short and long-wave service, as well as two privately owned stations. British Broadcasting Corporation (BBC) World Service, Radio France Internationale (RFI), Radio China International, and Radio Australia also broadcast programs in Vanuatu. There is also a privately-owned Christian station.

The telecommunications industry in Vanuatu is privatized. In recent years, cell phone service has become more common and has expanded to reach more remote areas, but it is still not available on many of the smaller islands. Satellite phones are used for emergency service communications in rural areas. In March 2009, the government announced it was planning to enact legislation to further open the telecommunications business, and that Australia was providing financing to expanded telecommunication service in outlying areas. This has resulted in the large increase of cell phone use in the country,

now 156,100 total, with 58 out of 100 inhabitants having a cell phone as of 2014. Vanuatu is also considered the first nation in the Pacific region to enact legislation pertaining to electronic transaction, e-business, and interactive gaming. There are several Internet cafés in Port Vila, but access for the whole population still remains low. As of 2014, there were an estimated 30,800 Internet users, representing 11.5 percent of the population. While this number seems low, it represents nearly triple the usage of 2005.

SOCIAL DEVELOPMENT

Standard of Living

Vanuatu's Human Development Index rank, which measures the standard of living, was 131 out of 195 countries in 2014.

Water Consumption

Vanuatu uses both surface water and groundwater resources for their water supply; groundwater from shallow aquifers is the primary source in urban centers. As of 2015, approximately 94.5 percent of the population had access to a potable water supply, although the CIA World Factbook cites water access as a continuing problem for the country. Water quality in the urban regions of Port Vila (privatized) and Luganville (public works) is generally regarded as good.

Education

Primary school, beginning at age six, is free and lasts for six years. Junior secondary education begins at age twelve and lasts for four years, followed by three years of senior secondary school (until age nineteen). Periodic exit examinations determine a student's progress through the school system. Enrollment drops off sharply after primary school.

Vocational education and teacher training for those who qualify are also available. Vanuatu has no university. Port Vila maintains an extension center of the University of the South Pacific.

Students also travel to Fiji, New Guinea and France to attend college. The average literacy rate in Vanuatu is 85.2 percent (86.6 percent for men, 83.8 percent for women in 2015).

Beginning in 2010, the government initiated a free education policy for primary schools. Under the policy, approximately $70 (USD) would be given to each child in primary schools through the first six years (Year 1 through Year 6). According to the Vanuatu government, they have eliminated all fees associated with primary schools.

Women's Rights

Vanuatu is a patriarchal society and women are expected to occupy subordinate roles. In most of the country's ethnic groups, there are numerous cultural norms and rules designed to exclude women from having power or rights. While Vanuatu's constitution outlaws discrimination based on gender, this protection is rarely enforced and discrimination against women is rampant. In fact, it is generally believed that most women in Vanuatu are unaware of their legal rights under the constitution. Vanuatu remains a signatory to the UN's Convention on the Elimination of All Forms of Discrimination against Women (CEDAW), but has not ratified the convention in its entirety.

While arranged marriages are less common than in the past, the traditional payment of a bride price is still commonly practiced. Once a groom's family has accumulated enough material wealth, mostly livestock, they will use it as a payment to secure the marriage arrangement. However, this custom perpetuates the societal belief or perception that the new bride is "bought" property. Women also commonly report poor treatment at the hands of their in-laws, in whose home they live. Overall, domestic violence continues to be a common societal problem that is not specifically addressed by the law. This situation is further exacerbated by the fact that many women refrain from reporting domestic abuse for fear of retribution or social stigma. Furthermore, police reportedly make few arrests in cases that are reported,

as domestic violence continues to be seen as a family matter. Rape is also believed to be common but underreported. While the government does not support shelters for abused women and children, several churches and non-governmental organizations (NGOs) have begun to develop these services.

Women's property rights vary among the different islands and ethnic groups of Vanuatu. In some areas women cannot own property, while joint and outright ownership is common in other areas. Inheritance laws are similar, and some ethnicities deny a widow access to her deceased husband's property, while other groups allow a widow to inherit such property. Women also lack equal access to education in Vanuatu. School is not free or mandatory, and a family will send their sons first in cases where they cannot afford education for all their children. While nearly half of all girls attend primary school, the number drops significantly with each subsequent year of education, and few women pursue a higher or secondary education. Access to improved health care services also remains a challenge for women in Vanuatu in the early twenty-first century.

Most women do not pursue employment outside of the home. Those that do generally hold unskilled or low-skilled jobs with meager wages and no benefits. A small percentage of women hold professional positions in fields such as nursing or teaching, but earn significantly less than their male counterparts. Women are also not encouraged to participate in politics (though they maintain the right to vote.) The country recently elected its first female solicitor general (attorney general). However, currently, there is only one female cabinet minister and the country elected only its third women to parliament in 2002. Only 5 women have been elected to Parliament in all the years since it became an independent state.

Health Care

With few doctors (.12 physicians per 1,000 people) and an annual per capita health expenditure of approximately $107 USD, Vanuatu faces great public health challenges; yet in the last 10 years, life expectancy has increased and the infant mortality rate has dropped by more than half, from 49.45 per 1,000 live births to 15.7. Life expectancy in 2015 is about seventy-three years overall (seventy-one for men and nearly seventy-five for women).

GOVERNMENT

Structure

Vanuatu is a parliamentary republic with a unicameral Parliament of fifty-two members. Members of Parliament are elected by popular vote to four-year terms.

The head of state is the president, who is elected by a two-thirds majority of an electoral college consisting of Parliament and the presidents of Regional Councils. The president's term is five years.

The prime minister is the head of government, elected by Parliament from among its fifty-three members, and is usually the leader of the majority party or coalition. The prime minister then appoints a cabinet called the Council of Ministers.

Political Parties

Political parties in Vanuatu can often be fluid, and policies may be consistently revisited, and new parties created. Vanuatuan politics are based on a multi-party system, and coalition governments are formed. Political parties include the Greens Confederation (GC); Iauko Group (IG); Land and Justice Party (GJP); Melanesian Progressive Party (MPP); Nagriamel movement (NAG); Natatok Indigenous People's Democratic Party (NATATOK or NIPDP); National United Party (NUP); People's Progressive Party (PPP); People's Service Party (PSP). Additional political parties include the Reunification of Movement for Change (RMC); Union of Moderate Parties (UMP); Vanua'aku Pati (VP); Vanuatu Democratic Party; Vanuatu Liberal Democratic Party (VLDP); Vanuatu National Party (VNP); Vanuatu Progressive Development Party (VPDP);

and Vanuatu Republican Party (VRP), most of which are represented.

As of 2008, the largest political party represented in parliament was the Vanua'aku Pati party. It is considered the first orthodox political party on the island nation. Since those elections, the composition of the coalition government has shifted several times.

Local Government

Local governance occurs at the provincial level, and is overseen by a provincial council, acting as a local parliament, which is responsible for tax collection and for enacting laws concerning provincial- or island-level matters such as education, agriculture, health services, and tourism. The council, elected every four years, is run by a chairman and is advised by a local council of chiefs. The country is organized into six provinces: Malampa, Penama, Sanma, Shefa, Tafea, and Torba. Provinces are also subdivided into municipalities that are run by area councils and a council-elected mayor.

Judicial System

The judicial system is based on English Common law. The Supreme Court is the head of the judicial branch and may officiate in any civil or criminal action. The chief justice is appointed by the president in consultation with the prime minister and the leader of the opposition. The three other justices are appointed by the president with advice from the Judicial Service Commission. Customary law is handled by village or island courts, which are presided over by a local chief.

Taxation

Taxes are low in Vanuatu, and include a value-added tax (VAT), at 12.5 percent, and import duties, both of which make up the bulk of tax revenues. Other levied taxes include stamp duties, business licenses, and a 12.5 percent tax on rental accommodations. There is no personal income tax or corporate tax in Vanuatu, as well as no capital gains tax. Taxes and other revenue make up 19.6 percent of the GDP annually.

Armed Forces

Vanuatu does not maintain regular armed forces. As of 2010, the Vanuatu Police Force (VPF), which includes the paramilitary Vanuatu Mobile Force (VMF) and a maritime division, could call upon approximately 62,000 people. The VPF has provided support to UN international peacekeeping missions.

Foreign Policy

After seventy-five years of joint rule by both the British and French, Vanuatu became a republic in 1980. The country now maintains good relations with its former colonizers and the European Union (EU), as well as strong economic and cultural ties with Australia and New Zealand. Because of its limited economy, the country receives a large portion of its annual budget from international aid. Australia remains Vanuatu's largest aid donor and investor. (Australia also provides training to the Vanuatuan military.) The country also receives bilateral aid from France, China, and the United Kingdom (UK). The US has provided aid aimed at developing the country's infrastructure through the US Agency for International Development (USAID) and the government-run Millennium Challenge Corporation (MCC).

Vanuatu holds membership in numerous prominent international organizations and institutions, including the United Nations (UN), the World Bank, the Commonwealth, and the International Monetary Fund (IMF). In early 2009, Vanuatu restarted its membership bid for the World Trade Organization (WTO) and became an official member in 2012. Regionally, Vanuatu holds membership in the Melanesian Spearhead Group (MSG), the Pacific Islands Forum, and the Secretariat of the Pacific Community, among other institutions. In addition, members of Vanuatu's mobile and police Forces have served as part of UN peacekeeping missions in East Timor, Haiti, Sudan, and Bosnia. They have also been sent to neighboring Bougainville as part of the monitoring mission for the now autonomous region of Papua New Guinea (PNG). Vanuatu is also apart of the Non-Aligned Movement (NAM), and was the only South Pacific nation to remain unaligned during the Cold War, and maintained diplomatic relations with countries such as Cuba and Libya.

Vanuatu has had several low-level conflicts since independence, most notably with Fiji and France. Vanuatu banned imported biscuits, which had an adverse affect on commerce in Fiji. In response, the Fijian government imposed a boycott on imported kava from Vanuatu and on Air Vanuatu flights. The dispute was later resolved. Relations with France have been strained over several issues, and the French ambassador has been expelled from the country on several occasions. These issues include Vanuatu's support of a separatist movement in New Caledonia, which was still under French rule at the time), and France's nuclear weapons testing in French Polynesia. Vanuatu has also had an ongoing territorial dispute with France over two uninhabited volcanic islands, Hunter and Matthew Island. The dispute has not been resolved, but relations between France and Vanuatu have improved.

Human Rights Profile

International human rights law insists that states respect civil and political rights, and promote an individual's economic, social, and cultural rights. The United Nations Universal Declaration on Human Rights (UDHR) is recognized as the standard for international human rights. Its authors sought the counsel of the world's great thinkers, philosophers, and religious leaders, and were careful to create a document that reflects the core values shared by every world culture. (To read this document or view the articles relating to cultural human rights, visit http://www.udhr.org/UDHR/default.htm.)

Vanuatu's constitution is aligned with the guaranteed rights outlined in the UDHR. Overall, the government respected the rights of Vanuatu citizens, and despite being home to a wide variety of ethnic groups, intergroup relations are generally harmonious. In addition, elections in Vanuatu are generally free and fair, and the transition of power from one government to the next has generally been smooth. However, some problem areas remained, including a lack of minority representation, government and judicial corruption, poor prison conditions, and discrimination against certain groups. In addition, customary law, or the traditional law of the country's various ethnic groups, often trumps constitutional law.

Government corruption remains a concern in Vanuatu. Several high-level government ministers have been tried for fraud, and charges of corruption have been made toward Vanuatu's police and security forces, although the problem is not seen to be rampant. Favoritism in the appointment of government positions does exist, although there are no statistics on how widespread the problem is. There are also reports of the police making arrests without warrants, but these actions do not appear to be widespread. Police abuse of prisoners has been reported, but only in a few cases.

Prison conditions in Vanuatu are poor. The prisons are overcrowded and lack adequate staff. There is also no separation of prisoners based on age or mental ability. Often, youthful offenders are held with adults and those who are deemed to have psychological problems are held with mainstream prisoners. While accused prisoners are granted access to free and fair trials, the waiting period before trial is often lengthy. Discrimination against certain groups also remains a problem, particularly against those with HIV/AIDS. Human rights groups have reported incidences of discrimination against HIV/AIDS victims, who are offered no specific protection under the law. There are also no laws to protect people with disabilities from discrimination.

ECONOMY

Overview of the Economy

Vanuatu is the third-poorest country in the Pacific. Obstacles to economic development include reliance on a small number of commodity exports, the occurrence of natural disasters, and the great distances to markets.

However, Vanuatu has certain economic advantages, and was listed as one of the fastest growing economies in the Pacific region by the Asian Development Bank (ADB) in 2009. This increase, which is still continuing, was largely driven by the tourism and construction sectors. The country is also a tax haven, with around 2,000 offshore banking institutions. Since 2002, however, when international concerns about money laundering became acute, Vanuatu has increased requirements for oversight and reporting.

Industry

Major industries include food processing (including frozen food and fish, and canned meat), and processed wood products. Exports of copra, kava, coffee, cocoa, timber and beef account for about 45 percent of the gross domestic product (GDP) each year. Copra, kava and beef together account for 60 percent of total export income. The estimated per capita GDP was $2,600 USD in 2014.

Labor

The majority of the labor force is involved in agriculture, 65 percent. In 2007, the unemployment rate was 1.7 percent, and no new statistics are presently available.

Energy/Power/Natural Resources

Vanuatu has hardwood forests, manganese deposits, and plenty of fish. Deforestation heads any list of environmental problems for the country. Other problems include soil degradation and erosion, lack of access to drinking water, overgrazing, illegal fishing by poison, and pollution from pesticides.

Major natural hazards in Vanuatu include frequent tropical cyclones or hurricanes (about one every other year), volcanic activity and earthquakes.

Agriculture

Less than 10 percent of the land is arable. Most of it is used for permanent crops such as cocoa and coffee. Nevertheless, agriculture accounts for roughly 65 percent of the labor force, and makes up an estimated 25 percent of Vanuatu's GDP. Much of this is slash-and-burn subsistence farming, supplemented by fishing and hunting.

Vanuatu's chief agricultural products are copra, coconuts, cocoa, coffee, taro, yams, fruits, vegetables, fish, and beef. Roots and tubers, melons, bananas, peanuts and corn are also grown.

Fishing

Vanuatu's commercial fishing industry remains relatively small, but is nonetheless practiced by many for subsistence purposes. According to a 2006 census on agriculture, an estimated 77 percent of Vanuatuan households—approximately 31,230 people—practiced fishing on some level.

Animal Husbandry

Important livestock products include beef and veal, pork, cow's milk, eggs, hides, and goatskins.

Cattle raising is considered an important component of the Vanuatuan economy, followed by pigs, goats, and poultry.

Tourism

Vanuatu's fastest-growing economic sector is tourism. Nearly 200,000 tourists a year are drawn by the unspoiled landscape and colorful local customs. Tourism represents approximately 40 percent of the GDP, or more than $58 million USD in receipts, and it is growing.

Most tourists visit Efate, Espiritu Santo and Tanna, but other islands are being developed. Efate offers a scenic drive around the coast. Espiritu Santo has one of the finest beaches in the Pacific. On Ambrym and Tanna, tourists can observe active volcanoes.

Other popular tourist activities include scuba diving, game fishing, windsurfing, golf, charter yachting, horseback riding, hiking and mountain climbing.

Joanne O'Sullivan, Ellen Bailey,
Lynn-nore Chittom

DO YOU KNOW?

- The ni-Vanuatu believe that a shark attack occurs when a man changes himself into a shark to exact revenge on an enemy.

- Vanuatu was the location for the ninth season of the CBS reality show "Survivor." The production team for the show set up camp in Port Vila, while most of the filming was done on the northern edge of Efate near Havannah Harbor.

- In accordance with the ancient traditions of the islands, neither tipping nor bargaining is practiced in Port Vila.

Bibliography

Bonnemaison, Jöel, Kirk Huffman, Christian Kaufmann, and Darrell Tyrone, eds. *Arts of Vanuatu.* Honolulu: University of Hawaii Press, 1996.

D'Arcy, Jayne, et al. *Vanuatu and New Caledonia.* Oakland, CA, Lonely Planet, 2012.

Howarth, Crispin, ed. *Kastom: Art of Vanuatu.* Canberra: National Gallery of Australia, 2013.

Jolly, Margaret. *Women of the Place: Kastom, Colonialism and Gender in Vanuatu.* London: Routledge, 1997.

Rio, Knut Mikjel. *Power of Perspective: Social Ontology and Agency on Ambrym Island, Vanuatu.* New York: Berghahn Books, 2007.

Works Cited

Brown, Dr. Terry. *Religion and Customs in Melanesia: The Solomon Islands and New Hebrides.* London: Southern Cross, 1949.

"Country Profile: Vanuatu." *BBC* http://news.bbc.co.uk

Hess, Sabine. "Strathern's Melanesian 'dividual' and the Christian 'individual': a perspective from Vanua Lava, Vanuatu." *Oceania* 1 November 2006.

Huffman, Kirk. "Traditional 'Arts' in Vanuatu." Vanuatu Cultural Centre htp://www.vanuatuculture.org

Kussler, Anya. "Laplap and Some tropical Flavor." *New Zealand Herald* 5 Febraury 2008

Strachan, J, "Gender and the formal education sector in Vanuatu." *Development Bulletin*, no. 64, 2004.

Speiser, Felix and D.Q Stephenson *Ethnology of Vanuatu: An Early Twentieth Century Study.* Honolulu: University of Hawaii Press, 1996.

"Vanuatu and the WTO." *World Trade Organization.* Accessed September 24, 2015. https://www.wto.org/english/thewto_e/countries_e/vanuatu_e.htm

"Vanuatu." Australian Government, Department of Foreign Affairs and Trade

"Vanuatu." City Population *http://www.citypopulation.de*

"Vanuatu." Division of Democracy, Human Rights and Labor, United States Department of State *http://www.state.gov*

"Vanuatu." Foreign and Commonwealth Office of the Government of the UK *http://www.fco.uk.gov*

"Vanuatu." *Pacific Women in Politics.* http://www.pacwip.org/future-elections/vanuatu/.

"Vanuatu." *The World Factbook* U.S. Central Intelligence Agency http://www.cia.gov 9

"Vanuatu." UNESCO http://www.unesco.org

"Vanuatu: Background Notes." United States Department of State Undersecretary For Political Affairs, Bureau of African Affairs *http://www.state.gov.*

"Vanuatu: Country Specific Information." United States State Department *http://travel.state.gov*

"Vanuatu: Information Related to Intangible Cultural Heritage." http://www.unesco.org

"Vanuatu: Submission to The UN Universal Periodic Review." *Amnesty International* http://www.amensty.org http://www.dfat.gov.au/geo/vanuatu.

Appendix One:
World Governments

Commonwealth

Guiding Premise

A commonwealth is an organization or alliance of nations connected for the purposes of satisfying a common interest. The participating states may retain their own governments, some of which are often considerably different from one another. Although commonwealth members tend to retain their own sovereign government institutions, they collaborate with other members to create mutually agreeable policies that meet their collective interests. Some nations join commonwealths to enhance their visibility and political power on the international stage. Others join commonwealths for security or economic reasons. Commonwealth members frequently engage in trade agreements, security pacts, and other programs. Some commonwealths are regional, while others are global.

Typical Structure

A commonwealth's structure depends largely on the nature of the organization and the interests it serves. Some commonwealths are relatively informal in nature, with members meeting on a periodic basis and participating voluntarily. This informality does not undermine the effectiveness of the organization, however—members still enjoy a closer relationship than that which exists among unaffiliated states. Commonwealths typically have a president, secretary general, or, in the case of the Commonwealth of Nations (a commonwealth that developed out of the British Empire), a monarch acting as the leader of the organization. Members appoint delegates to serve at summits, committee meetings, and other commonwealth events and programs.

Other commonwealths are more formal in structure and procedures. They operate based on mission statements with very specific goals and member participation requirements. These organizations have legislative bodies that meet regularly. There are even joint security operations involving members. The African Union, for example, operates according to a constitution and collectively addresses issues facing the entire African continent, such as HIV/AIDS, regional security, environmental protection, and economic cooperation.

One of the best-known commonwealths in modern history was the Soviet Union. This collective of communist states was similar to other commonwealths, but the members of the Soviet Union, although they retained their own sovereign government institutions, largely deferred to the organization's central leadership in Moscow, which in turn deferred to the Communist Party leadership. After the collapse of the Soviet Union, a dozen former Soviet states, including Russia, reconnected as the Commonwealth of Independent States. This organization features a central council in Minsk, Belarus. This council consists of the heads of state and heads of government for each member nation, along with their cabinet ministers for defense and foreign affairs.

Commonwealth structures and agendas vary. Some focus on trade and economic development, as well as using their respective members' collective power to address human rights, global climate change, and other issues. Others are focused on regional stability and mutual defense, including prevention of nuclear weapons proliferation. The diversity of issues for which commonwealths are formed contributes to the frequency of member meetings as well as the actions carried out by the organization.

Role of the Citizen

Most commonwealths are voluntary in nature, which means that the member states must choose to join with the approval of their respective governments. A nation with a democratic government, therefore, would need the sanction of its popularly elected legislative and executive bodies in order to proceed. Thus, the role of the private citizen with regard to a commonwealth is indirect—the people may have the power to vote for or against a legislative or executive candidate based on his or her position concerning membership in a commonwealth.

Some members of commonwealths, however, do not feature a democratic government, or their respective governmental infrastructures are not yet in place. Rwanda, for instance, is a developing nation whose 2009 decision to join the Commonwealth of Nations likely came from the political leadership with very little input from its citizens, as Rwandans have very limited political freedom.

While citizens may not directly influence the actions of a commonwealth, they may work closely with its representatives. Many volunteer nonprofit organizations—having direct experience with, for example, HIV/AIDS, certain minority groups, or environmental issues—work in partnership with the various branches of a commonwealth's central council. In fact, such organizations are frequently called upon in this regard to implement the policies of a commonwealth, receiving financial and logistical support when working in impoverished and/or war-torn regions. Those working for such organizations may therefore prove invaluable to the effectiveness of a commonwealth's programs.

Michael Auerbach
Marblehead, Massachusetts

Examples

African Union
Commonwealth of Independent States
Commonwealth of Nations
Northern Mariana Islands (and the United States)
Puerto Rico (and the United States)

Bibliography

"About Commonwealth of Independent States." *Commonwealth of Independent States*. CIS, n.d. Web. 17 Jan. 2013.

"AU in a Nutshell." *African Union*. African Union Commission, n.d. Web. 17 Jan. 2013.

"The Commonwealth." *Commonwealth of Nations*. Nexus Strategic Partnerships Limited, 2013. Web. 17 Jan. 2013.

Communist

Guiding Premise

Communism is a political and economic system that seeks to eliminate private property and spread the benefits of labor equally throughout the populace. Communism is generally considered an outgrowth of socialism, a political and economic philosophy that advocates "socialized" or centralized ownership of the economy and the means of production.

Communism developed largely from the theories of Karl Marx (1818–83), who believed that a revolution led by the working class must occur before the state could achieve the even distribution of wealth and property and eliminate the class-based socioeconomic system of capitalist society. Marx believed that a truly equitable society required centralized control of credit, transportation, education, communication, agriculture, and industry, along with eliminating the rights of individuals to inherit or to own land.

Russia (formerly the Soviet Union) and China are the two largest countries to have been led by communist governments during the twentieth and twenty-first centuries. In both cases, the attempt to bring about a communist government came by way of violent revolutions in which members of the former government and ruling party were executed. Under Russian leader Vladimir Lenin (1870–1924) and Chinese leader Mao Zedong (1893–1976), strict dictatorships were instituted, curtailing individual rights in favor of state control. Lenin sought to expand communism into developing nations to counter the global spread of capitalism. Mao, in his form of communism, considered ongoing revolution within China a necessary aspect of communism. Both gave their names to their respective versions of communism, but neither Leninism nor Maoism managed to achieve the idealized utopia envisioned by Marx and other communist philosophers.

The primary difference between modern socialism and communism is that communist groups believe that a social revolution is necessary to create the idealized state without class structure, where socialists believe that the inequities of class structure can be addressed and eliminated through gradual change.

Typical Structure

Most modern communist governments define themselves as "socialist," though a national communist party exerts control over all branches of government. The designation of a "communist state" is primarily an external definition for a situation in which a communist party controls the government.

Among the examples of modern socialist states operating under the communist model are the People's Republic of China, the Republic of Cuba, and the Socialist Republic of Vietnam. However, each of these governments in fact operates through a mixed system of socialist and capitalist economic policies, allowing private ownership in some situations and sharply enforcing state control in others.

Typically, a communist state is led by the national communist party, a political group with voluntary membership and members in all sectors of the populace. While many individuals may join the communist party, the leadership of the party is generally selected by a smaller number of respected or venerated leaders from within the party. These leaders select a ruling committee that develops the political initiatives of the party, which are thereafter distributed throughout the government.

In China, the Communist Party elects both a chairperson, who serves as executive of the party, and a politburo, a standing committee that makes executive decisions on behalf of the party. In Cuba, the Communist Party selects individuals who sit for election to the National Assembly of People's Power, which then serves directly as the state's sole legislative body.

In the cases of China, Cuba, and Vietnam, the committees and leaders chosen by the communist party then participate directly in electing leaders to serve in the state judiciary. In addition, the central committees typically appoint individuals to serve as heads of the military and to lower-level, provincial, or municipal government positions. In China, the populace elects individuals to local, regional, and provincial councils that in turn elect representatives to sit on a legislative body known as the National People's Congress (NPC), though the NPC is generally considered a largely ceremonial institution without any substantial power to enact independent legislation.

In effect, most modern communist states are controlled by the leadership of the national communist party, though this leadership is achieved by direct and indirect control of lesser legislative, executive, and judicial bodies. In some cases, ceremonial and symbolic offices created under the communist party can evolve to take a larger role in state politics. In China, for instance, the NPC has come to play a more important role in developing legislation in the twenty-first century.

Role of the Citizen

In modern communist societies, citizens have little voice in selecting the leadership of the government. In many communist states, popular elections are held at local and national levels, but candidates are chosen by communist party leadership and citizens are not given the option to vote for representatives of opposing political parties.

In most cases, the state adopts policies that give the appearance of popular control over the government, while in actuality, governmental policies are influenced by a small number of leaders chosen from within the upper echelons of the party. Popularly elected leaders who oppose party policy are generally removed from office.

All existing communist states have been criticized for human rights violations in terms of curtailing the freedoms available to citizens and of enacting dictatorial and authoritarian policies. Cuba, Vietnam, and China, for instance, all have laws preventing citizens from opposing party policy or supporting a political movement that opposes the communist party. Communist governments have also been accused of using propaganda and misinformation to control the opinion of the populace regarding party leadership and therefore reducing the potential for popular resistance to communist policies.

Micah Issitt
Philadelphia, Pennsylvania

Examples
China
Cuba
Laos
North Korea
Vietnam

Bibliography
Caramani, Daniele. *Comparative Politics*. New York: Oxford UP, 2008. Print.
Priestland, David. *The Red Flag: A History of Communism*. New York: Grove, 2009. Print.
Service, Robert. *Comrades! A History of World Communism*. Cambridge: Harvard UP, 2007. Print.

Confederation/Confederacy

Guiding Premise

A confederation or confederacy is a loose alliance between political units, such as states or cantons, within a broader federal government. Confederations allow a central, federal government to create laws and regulations of broad national interest, but the sovereign units are granted the ultimate authority to carry out those laws and to create, implement, and enforce their own laws as well. Confederate governments are built on the notion that a single, central government should not have ultimate authority over sovereign states and populations. Some confederate governments were born due to the rise of European monarchies and empires that threatened to govern states from afar. Others were created out of respect for the diverse ideologies, cultures, and ideals of their respective regions. Confederations and confederacies may be hybrids, giving comparatively more power to a federal government while retaining respect for the sovereignty of their members. True confederate governments are rare in the twenty-first century.

Typical Structure

Confederate governments are typically characterized by the presence of both a central government and a set of regional, similarly organized, and sovereign (independent) governments. For example, a confederate government might have as its central government structure a system that features executive, legislative, and judicial branches. Each region that serves as members of the confederation would have in place a similar system, enabling the efficient flow of lawmaking and government services.

In some confederations, the executive branch of the central government is headed by a president or prime minister, who serves as the government's chief administrative officer, overseeing the military and other government operations. Meanwhile, at the regional level, another chief executive, such as a governor, is charged with the administration of that government's operations.

Legislative branches are also similarly designed. Confederations use parliaments or congresses that, in most cases, have two distinct chambers. One chamber consists of legislators who each represent an entire state, canton, or region. The other chamber consists of legislators representing certain populations of voters within that region. Legislatures at the regional level not only have the power to create and enforce their own laws, but also have the power to refuse to enact or enforce any laws handed down by the national government.

A confederation's judiciary is charged with ensuring that federal and regional laws are applied uniformly and within the limits of the confederation's constitutional framework. Central and regional governments both have such judicial institutions, with the latter addressing those legal matters administered in the state or canton and the former addressing legal issues of interest to the entire country.

Political parties also typically play a role in a confederate government. Political leadership is achieved by a party's majority status in either the executive or the legislative branches. Parties also play a role in forging a compromise on certain matters at both the regional and national levels. Some confederations take the diversity of political parties and their ideologies seriously enough to create coalition governments that can help avoid political stalemates.

Role of the Citizen

The political role of the citizen within a confederate political system depends largely on the constitution of the country. In some confederacies, for example, the people directly elect their legislative and executive leaders by popular vote. Some legislators are elected to open terms—they may technically be reelected, but this election is merely a formality, as they are allowed to stay in office until they decide to leave or they die—while others may be subject to term limits or other reelection rules. Popularly elected legislators and executives in turn draft, file, and pass new laws and regulations that ideally are favorable to the voters. Some confederate systems give popularly elected legislators the ability to elect a party leader to serve as prime minister or president.

Confederations are designed to empower the regional government and avoid the dominance of a distant national government. In this manner, citizens of a confederate government, in some cases, may enjoy the ability to put forth new legislative initiatives. Although the lawmaking process is expected to be administered by the legislators and executives, in such cases the people are allowed and even encouraged to connect and interact with their political representatives to ensure that the government remains open and accessible.

Michael Auerbach
Marblehead, Massachusetts

Examples

European Union
Switzerland
United States under the Articles of Confederation (1781–89)

Bibliography

"Government Type." *The World Factbook*. Central Intelligence Agency, n.d. Web. 17 Jan. 2013.

"Swiss Politics." *SwissWorld.org*. Federal Department of Foreign Affairs Presence Switzerland, n.d. Web. 17 Jan. 2013.

Constitutional Monarchy

Guiding Premise

A constitutional monarchy is a form of government in which the head of state is a monarch (a king or queen) with limited powers. The monarch has official duties, but those responsibilities are defined in the nation's constitution and not by the monarch. Meanwhile, the power to create and rescind laws is given to a legislative body. Constitutional monarchies retain the ceremony and traditions associated with nations that have long operated under a king or queen. However, the constitution prevents the monarch from becoming a tyrant. Additionally, the monarchy, which is typically a lifetime position, preserves a sense of stability and continuity in the government, as the legislative body undergoes periodic change associated with the election cycle.

Typical Structure

The structure of a constitutional monarchy varies from nation to nation. In some countries, the monarchy is predominantly ceremonial. In such cases, the monarch provides a largely symbolic role, reminding the people of their heritage and giving them comfort in times of difficulty. Such is the case in Japan, for example; the emperor of that country was stripped of any significant power after World War II but was allowed to continue his legacy in the interest of ensuring that the Japanese people would remain peaceful. Today, that nation still holds its monarchical family in the highest regard, but the government is controlled by the Diet (the legislature), with the prime minister serving in the executive role.

In other countries, the sovereign plays a more significant role. In the United Kingdom, the king or queen does have some power, including the powers to appoint the prime minister, to open or dissolve Parliament, to approve bills that have been passed by Parliament, and to declare war and make peace. However, the monarch largely defers to the government on these acts. In Bahrain, the king (or, until 2002, emir or hereditary ruler) was far more involved in government in the late twentieth and early twenty-first centuries than many other constitutional monarchs. In 1975, the emir of Bahrain dissolved the parliament, supposedly to run the government more effectively. His son would later implement a number of significant constitutional reforms that made the government more democratic in nature.

The key to the structure of this type of political system is the constitution. As is the case in the United States (a federal republic), a constitutional monarchy is carefully defined by the government's founding document. In Canada, for example, the king or queen of England is still recognized as the head of state, but that country's constitution gives the monarch no power other than ceremonial responsibilities. India, South Africa, and many other members of the Commonwealth of Nations (the English monarch's sphere of influence, spanning most of the former British colonies) have, since gaining their independence, created constitutions that grant no power to the English monarch; instead, they give all powers to their respective government institutions and, in some cases, recognize their own monarchs.

A defining feature of a constitutional monarchy is the fact that the monarch gives full respect to the limitations set forth by the constitution (and rarely seeks to alter such a document in his or her favor). Even in the United Kingdom itself—which does not have a written constitution, but rather a series of foundational documents—the king or queen does not step beyond the bounds set by customary rules. One interesting exception is in Bahrain, where Hamad bin Isa Al-Khalifa assumed the throne in 1999 and immediately implemented a series of reforms to the constitution in order to give greater definition to that country's democratic institutions, including resuming parliamentary elections in 2001. During the 2011 Arab Spring uprisings, Bahraini protesters called for further democratic reforms to be enacted, and tensions between the ruler and his opposition continue.

Role of the Citizen

In the past, monarchies ruled nations with absolute power; the only power the people had was the ability to unify and overthrow the ruling sovereign. Although the notion of an absolute monarchy has largely disappeared from the modern political landscape, many nations have retained their respective kings, queens, emperors, and other monarchs for the sake of ceremony and cultural heritage. In the modern constitutional monarchy, the people are empowered by their nation's foundational documents, which not only define the rights of the people but the limitations of their governments and sovereign as well. The people, through their legislators and through the democratic voting process, can modify their constitutions to expand or shrink the political involvement of the monarchy.

For example, the individual members of the Commonwealth of Nations, including Canada and Australia, have different constitutional parameters for the king or queen of England. In England, the monarch holds a number of powers, while in Canada, he or she is merely a ceremonial head of state (with all government power centered in the capital of Ottawa). In fact, in 1999, Australia held a referendum (a general vote) on whether to abolish its constitutional monarchy altogether and replace it with a presidential republic. In that case, the people voted to retain the monarchy, but the proposal was only narrowly defeated. These examples demonstrate the tremendous power the citizens of a constitutional monarchy may possess through the legislative process and the vote under the constitution.

Michael Auerbach
Marblehead, Massachusetts

Examples

Bahrain
Cambodia
Denmark
Japan
Lesotho
Malaysia
Morocco
Netherlands
Norway
Spain
Sweden
Thailand
United Kingdom

Bibliography

Bowman, John. "Constitutional Monarchies." *CBC News.* CBC, 4 Oct. 2002. Web. 17 Jan. 2013.
"The Role of the Monarchy." *Royal.gov.uk.* Royal Household, n.d. Web. 17 Jan. 2013.

Constitutional Republic

Guiding Premise

A constitutional republic is a governmental system in which citizens are involved in electing or appointing leaders who serve according to rules formulated in an official state constitution. In essence, the constitutional republic combines the political structure of a republic or republican governmental system with constitutional principles.

A republic is a government in which the head of state is empowered to hold office through law, not inheritance (as in a monarchy). A constitutional republic is a type of republic based on a constitution, a written body of fundamental precedents and principles from which the laws of the nation are developed.

Most constitutional republics in the modern world use a universal suffrage system, in which all citizens of the nation are empowered to vote for or against individuals who attempt to achieve public office. Universal suffrage is not required for a nation to qualify as a constitutional republic, and some nations may only allow certain categories of citizens to vote for elected leaders.

A constitutional republic differs from other forms of democratic systems in the roles assigned to both the leaders and the citizenry. In a pure democratic system, the government is formed by pure majority rule, and this system therefore ignores the opinions of any minority group. A republic, by contrast, is a form of government in which the government's role is limited by a written constitution aimed at promoting the welfare of all individuals, whether members of the majority or a minority.

Typical Structure

To qualify as a constitutional republic, a nation must choose a head of state (most often a president) through elections, according to constitutional law. In some nations, an elected president may serve alongside an appointed or elected individual who serves as leader of the legislature,

such as a prime minister, often called the "head of government." When the president also serves as head of government, the republic is said to operate under a presidential system.

Typically, the executive branch consists of the head of state and the executive offices, which are responsible for enforcing the laws and overseeing relations with other nations. The legislative branch makes laws and has overlapping duties with the executive office in terms of economic and military developments. The judicial branch, consisting of the courts, interprets the law and the constitution and enforces adherence to the law.

In a constitutional republic, the constitution describes the powers allotted to each branch of government and the means by which the governmental bodies are to be established. The constitution also describes the ways in which governmental branches interact in creating, interpreting, and enforcing laws. For instance, in the United States, the executive and legislative branches both have roles in determining the budget for the nation, and neither body is free to make budgetary legislation without the approval of the other branch.

Role of the Citizen

In a constitutional republic, the citizens have the power to control the evolution of the nation through the choice of representatives who serve on the government. These representatives can, generally through complicated means, create or abolish laws and even change the constitution itself through reinterpretations of constitutional principles or direct amendments.

Citizens in a republic are empowered, but generally not required, to play a role in electing leaders. In the United States, both state governments and the federal government function according to a republican system, and citizens are therefore allowed to take part in the election of leaders to both local and national offices. In addition, constitutional systems generally allow individuals to join political interest groups to further common political goals.

In a constitutional democratic republic such as Guatemala and Honduras, the president, who serves as chief of state and head of government, is elected directly by popular vote. In the United States, a constitutional federal republic, the president is elected by the Electoral College, whose members are selected according to the popular vote within each district. The Electoral College is intended to provide more weight to smaller states, thereby balancing the disproportionate voting power of states with larger populations. In all constitutional republics, the citizens elect leaders either directly or indirectly through other representatives chosen by popular vote. Therefore, the power to control the government is granted to the citizens of the constitutional republic.

Micah Issitt
Philadelphia, Pennsylvania

Examples

Guatemala
Honduras
Iceland
Paraguay
Peru
United States
Uruguay

Bibliography

Baylis, John, Steve Smith, and Patricia Owens. *The Globalization of World Politics: An Introduction to International Relations.* New York: Oxford UP, 2010. Print.

Caramani, Daniele. *Comparative Politics.* New York: Oxford UP, 2008. Print.

Garner, Robert, Peter Ferdinand, and Stephanie Lawson. *Introduction to Politics.* 2nd ed. Oxford: Oxford UP, 2009. Print.

Hague, Rod, and Martin Harrop. *Comparative Government and Politics: An Introduction.* New York: Palgrave, 2007. Print.

Democracy

Guiding Premise

Democracy is a political system based on majority rule, in which all citizens are guaranteed participatory rights to influence the evolution of government. There are many different types of democracy, based on the degree to which citizens participate in the formation and operation of the government. In a direct democratic system, citizens vote directly on proposed changes to law and public policy. In a representative democracy, individuals vote to elect representatives who then serve to create and negotiate public policy.

The democratic system of government first developed in Ancient Greece and has existed in many forms throughout history. While democratic systems always involve some type of majority rule component, most modern democracies have systems in place designed to equalize representation for minority groups or to promote the development of governmental policies that prevent oppression of minorities by members of the majority.

In modern democracies, one of the central principles is the idea that citizens must be allowed to participate in free elections to select leaders who serve in the government. In addition, voters in democratic systems elect political leaders for a limited period of time, thus ensuring that the leadership of the political system can change along with the changing views of the populace. Political theorists have defined democracy as a system in which the people are sovereign and the political power flows upward from the people to their elected leaders.

Typical Structure

In a typical democracy, the government is usually divided into executive, legislative, and judicial branches. Citizens participate in electing individuals to serve in one or more of these branches, and elected leaders appoint additional leaders to serve in other political offices. The democratic system, therefore, involves a combination of elected and appointed leadership.

Democratic systems may follow a presidential model, as in the United States, where citizens elect a president to serve as both head of state and head of government. In a presidential model, citizens may also participate in elections to fill other governmental bodies, including the legislature and judicial branch. In a parliamentary democracy, citizens elect individuals to a parliament, whose members in turn form a committee to appoint a leader, often called the prime minister, who serves as head of government.

In most democratic systems, the executive and legislative branches cooperate in the formation of laws, while the judicial branch enforces and interprets the laws produced by the government. Most democratic systems have developed a system of checks and balances designed to prevent any single branch of government from exerting a dominant influence over the development of governmental policy. These checks and balances may be instituted in a variety of ways, including the ability to block governmental initiatives and the ability to appoint members to various governmental agencies.

Democratic governments generally operate on the principle of political parties, which are organizations formed to influence political development. Candidates for office have the option of joining a political party, which can provide funding and other campaign assistance. In some democratic systems—called dominant party or one-party dominant systems—there is effectively a single political party. Dominant party systems allow for competition in democratic elections, but existing power structures often prevent opposing parties from competing successfully. In multiparty democratic systems, there are two or more political parties with the ability to compete for office, and citizens are able to choose among political parties during elections. Some countries only allow political parties to be active at the national level, while other countries allow political parties to play a role in local and regional elections.

Role of the Citizen

The citizens in a democratic society are seen as the ultimate source of political authority. Members of the government, by contrast, are seen as servants of the people, and are selected and elected to serve the people's interests. Democratic systems developed to protect and enhance the freedom of the people; however, for the system to function properly, citizens must engage in a number of civic duties.

In democratic nations, voting is a right that comes with citizenship. Though some democracies—Australia, for example—require citizens to vote by law, compulsory participation in elections is not common in democratic societies. Citizens are nonetheless encouraged to fulfill their voting rights and to stay informed regarding political issues. In addition, individuals are responsible for contributing to the well-being of society as a whole, usually through a system of taxation whereby part of an individual's earnings is used to pay for governmental services.

In many cases, complex governmental and legal issues must be simplified to ease understanding among the citizenry. This goal is partially met by having citizens elect leaders who must then explain to their constituents how they are shaping legislation and other government initiatives to reflect constituents' wants and needs. In the United States, citizens may participate in the election of local leaders within individual cities or counties, and also in the election of leaders who serve in the national legislature and executive offices.

Citizens in democratic societies are also empowered with the right to join political interest groups and political parties in an effort to further a broader political agenda. However, democratic societies oppose making group membership a requirement and have laws forbidding forcing an individual to join any group. Freedom of choice, especially with regard to political affiliation and preference, is one of the cornerstones of all democratic systems.

Micah Issitt
Philadelphia, Pennsylvania

Examples

Denmark
Sweden
Spain
Japan
Australia
Costa Rica
Uruguay
United States

Bibliography

Barington, Lowell. *Comparative Politics: Structures and Choices.* Boston: Wadsworth, 2012. Print.

Caramani, Daniele. *Comparative Politics.* New York: Oxford UP, 2008. Print.

Przeworski, Adam. *Democracy and the Limits of Self Government,* New York: Cambridge UP, 2010. Print.

Dictatorship/Military Dictatorship

Guiding Premise

Dictatorships and military dictatorships are political systems in which absolute power is held by an individual or military organization. Dictatorships are led by a single individual, under whom all political control is consolidated. Military dictatorships are similar in purpose, but place the system under the control of a military organization comprised of a single senior officer, or small group of officers. Often, dictatorships and military dictatorships are imposed as the result of a coup d'état in which the regime in question directly removes the incumbent regime, or after a power vacuum creates chaos in the nation. In both situations, the consolidation of absolute power is designed to establish a state of strict law and order.

Typical Structure

Dictatorships and military dictatorships vary in structure and nature. Some come about through the overthrow of other regimes, while others are installed through the democratic process, and then become a dictatorship as democratic rights are withdrawn. Still others are installed following a complete breakdown of government, often with the promise of establishing order.

Many examples of dictatorships can be found in the twentieth century, including Nazi Germany, Joseph Stalin's Soviet Union, and China under Mao Tse-tung. A number of dictatorships existed in Africa, such as the regimes of Idi Amin in Uganda, Charles Taylor in Liberia, and Mu'ammar Gadhafi in Libya. Dictatorships such as these consolidated power in the hands of an individual leader. A dictator serves as the sole decision-maker in the government, frequently using the military, secret police, or other security agencies to enforce the leader's will. Dictators also have control over state institutions like legislatures. A legislature may have the ability to develop and pass laws, but if its actions run counter to the dictator's will, the latter can—and frequently does—dissolve the body, replacing its members with those more loyal to the dictator's agenda.

Military dictatorships consolidate power not in the hands of a civilian but in an individual or small group of military officers—the latter of which are often called "juntas." Because military dictatorships are frequently installed following a period of civil war and/or a coup d'état, the primary focus of the dictatorship is to achieve strict order through the application of military force. Military dictatorships are often installed with the promise of an eventual return to civilian and/or democratic control once the nation has regained stability. In the case of North Korea, one-party communist rule turned into a communist military dictatorship as its leader, Kim Il-Sung, assumed control of the military and brought its leadership into the government.

In the late twentieth and early twenty-first centuries, dictatorships and military dictatorships are most commonly found in developing nations, where poverty rates are high and regional stability is tenuous at best. Many are former European colonies, where charismatic leaders who boast of their national heritage have stepped in to replace colonial governments. National resources are typically directed toward military and security organizations in an attempt to ensure security and internal stability, keeping the regime in power and containing rivals. Human rights records in such political systems are typically heavily criticized by the international community.

Role of the Citizen

Dictatorships and military dictatorships are frequently installed because of the absence of viable democratic governments. There is often a disconnect, therefore, between the people and their leaders in a dictatorship. Of course, many dictatorships are identified as such by external entities and not by their own people. For example, the government of Zimbabwe is technically identified as a parliamentary democracy, with Robert Mugabe—who has been the elected leader of the country since 1980—as its president. However, the international community has long complained that Mugabe "won" his positions through political corruption, including alleged ballot stuffing. In 2008, Mugabe lost his first reelection campaign, but demanded a recount. While the recount continued, his supporters attacked opposition voters, utilizing violence and intimidation until his opponent, Morgan Tsvangirai, withdrew his candidacy, and Mugabe was restored as president.

By definition, citizens do not have a role in changing the course of a dictatorship's agenda. The people are usually called upon to join the military in support of the regime, or cast their vote consistently in favor of the ruling regime. Freedom of speech, the press, and assembly are virtually nonexistent, as those who speak out against the ruling regime are commonly jailed, tortured, or killed.

Michael Auerbach
Marblehead, Massachusetts

Examples

Belarus (dictatorship)
Fiji (military dictatorship)
North Korea (military dictatorship)
Zimbabwe (dictatorship)

Bibliography

Clayton, Jonathan. "China Aims to Bring Peace through Deals with Dictators and Warlords." *Times* [London]. Times Newspapers, 31 Jan. 2007. Web. 6 Feb. 2013.
"Robert Mugabe—Biography." *Biography.com.* A+E Television Networks, 2013. Web. 6 Feb. 2013.

Ecclesiastical

Guiding Premise

An ecclesiastical government is one in which the laws of the state are guided by and derived from religious law. Ecclesiastical governments can take a variety of forms and can be based on many different types of religious traditions. In some traditions, a deity or group of deities are considered to take a direct role in the formation of government, while other traditions utilize religious laws or principles indirectly to craft laws used to manage the state.

In many cultures, religious laws and tenets play a major role in determining the formation of national laws. Historically, the moral and ethical principles derived from Judeo-Christian tradition inspired many laws in Europe and North America. Few modern governments operate according to an ecclesiastical system, but Vatican City, which is commonly classified as a city-state, utilizes a modernized version of the ecclesiastical government model. All states utilizing an ecclesiastical or semi-ecclesiastical system have adopted a single state religion that is officially recognized by the government.

In some predominantly Islamic nations, including the Sudan, Oman, Iran, and Nigeria, Islamic law, known as sharia, is the basis for most national laws, and government leaders often must obtain approval by the leaders of the religious community before being allowed to serve in office. Most modern ecclesiastical or semi-ecclesiastical governments have adopted a mixed theocratic republic system in which individuals approved by religious authorities are elected by citizens to hold public office.

Typical Structure

In an ecclesiastical government, the church or recognized religious authority is the source of all state law. In a theocracy, which is one of the most common types of ecclesiastical governments, a deity or group of deities occupies a symbolic position as head of state, while representatives are chosen to lead the government based on their approval by the prevailing religious authority. In other types of ecclesiastical governments, the chief of state may be the leading figure in the church, such as in Vatican City, where the Catholic Pope is also considered the chief of state.

There are no modern nations that operate on a purely ecclesiastical system, though some Islamic countries, like Iran, have adopted a semi-ecclesiastical form of republican government. In Iran, the popularly elected Assembly of Experts—comprised of Islamic scholars called mujtahids—appoints an individual to serve as supreme leader of the nation for life, and this individual has veto power over all other governmental offices. Iranian religious leaders also approve other individuals to run as candidates for positions in the state legislature. In many cases, the citizens will elect an individual to serve as head of government, though this individual must conform to religious laws.

In an ecclesiastical government, those eligible to serve in the state legislature are generally members of the church hierarchy or have been approved for office by church leaders. In Tibet, which functioned as an ecclesiastical government until the Chinese takeover of 1951, executive and legislative duties were consolidated under a few religious leaders, called lamas, and influential citizens who maintained the country under a theocratic system. Most modern nations separate governmental functions between distinct but interrelated executive, legislative, and judicial branches.

Many modern semi-ecclesiastical nations have adopted a set of state principles in the form of a constitution to guide the operation of government and the establishment of laws. In mixed constitutional/theocratic systems, the constitution may be used to legitimize religious authority by codifying a set of laws and procedures that have been developed from religious scripture.

In addition, the existence of a constitution facilitates the process of altering laws and governmental procedures as religious authorities reinterpret religious scriptures and texts.

Role of the Citizen

Citizens in modern ecclesiastical and semi-ecclesiastical governments play a role in formulating the government though national and local elections. In some cases, religious authorities may approve more than one candidate for a certain position and citizens are then able to exercise legitimate choice in the electoral process. In other cases, popular support for one or more candidates may influence religious authorities when it comes time to nominate or appoint an individual to office.

In ecclesiastical governments, the freedoms and rights afforded to citizens may depend on their religious affiliation. Christians living in a Christian ecclesiastical government, for instance, may be allowed to run for and hold government office, while representatives of other religions may be denied this right. In addition, ecclesiastical governments may not recognize religious rights and rituals of other traditions and may not offer protection for those practicing religions other than the official state religion.

Though religious authority dominates politics and legislative development, popular influence is still an important part of the ecclesiastical system. Popular support for or against certain laws may convince the government to alter official policies. In addition, the populace may join local and regional religious bodies that can significantly affect national political developments. As local and regional religious groups grow in numbers and influence, they may promote candidates to political office, thereby helping to influence the evolution of government.

Micah Issitt
Philadelphia, Pennsylvania

Examples

Afghanistan
Iran
Nigeria
Oman
Vatican City

Bibliography

Barrington, Lowell. *Comparative Politics: Structures and Choices*. Boston: Wadsworth, 2012. Print.

Hallaq, Wael B. *An Introduction to Islamic Law*. New York: Cambridge UP, 2009. Print.

Hirschl, Ran. *Constitutional Theocracy*. Cambridge, MA: Harvard UP, 2010. Print.

Failed State

Guiding Premise

A failed state is a political unit that at one point had a stable government that provided basic services and security to its citizens, but then entered a period marked by devastating conflict, extreme poverty, overwhelming political corruption, and/or unlivable environmental conditions. Often, a group takes hold of a failed state's government through military means, staving off rivals to fill in a power vacuum. The nominal leadership of a failed state frequently uses its power to combat rival factions, implement extreme religious law, or protect and advance illicit activities (such as drug production or piracy). Failed states frequently retain their external borders, but within those borders are regions that may be dominated by a particular faction, effectively carving the state into disparate subunits, with some areas even attaining relative stability and security—a kind of de facto independence.

Typical Structure

Failed states vary in appearance based on a number of factors. One such factor is the type of government that existed prior to the state's collapse. For example, a failed state might have originally existed as a parliamentary democracy, with an active legislature and executive system that developed a functioning legal code and administered to the needs of the people. However, that state may not have adequately addressed the needs of certain groups, fostering a violent backlash and hastening the country's destabilization. An ineffectual legislature might have been dissolved by the executive (a prime minister or president), and in the absence of leadership, the government as a whole ceased to operate effectively.

Another major factor is demographics. Many states are comprised of two or more distinct ethnic, social, or religious groups. When the ruling party fails to effectively govern and/or serve the interests of a certain segment of the population, it may be ousted or simply ignored by the marginalized faction within the state. If the government falls, it creates a power vacuum that rival groups compete to fill. If one faction gains power, it must remain in a constant state of vigilance against its rivals, focusing more on keeping enemies in check than on rebuilding crippled government infrastructure. Some also seek to create theocracies based on extreme interpretations of a particular religious doctrine. Frequently, these regimes are themselves ousted by rivals within a few years, leaving no lasting government and keeping the state in chaos.

Failed states are also characterized by extreme poverty and a lack of modern technology. Potable water, electricity, food, and medicine are scarce among average citizens. In some cases, these conditions are worsened by natural events. Haiti, for example, was a failed state for many years before the devastating 2010 earthquake that razed the capitol city of Port au Prince, deepening the country's poverty and instability. Afghanistan and Ethiopia—with their harsh, arid climates—are also examples of failed states whose physical environments and lack of resources exacerbated an already extreme state of impoverishment.

Most failed states' conditions are also worsened by the presence of foreigners. Because their governments are either unable or unwilling to repel terrorists, for example, failed states frequently become havens for international terrorism. Somalia, Afghanistan, and Iraq are all examples of states that failed, enabling terrorist organizations to set up camp within their borders. As such groups pose a threat to other nations, those nations often send troops and weapons into the failed states to engage the terrorists. In recent years, NATO, the United Nations, and the African Union have all entered failed states to both combat terrorists and help rebuild government.

Role of the Citizen

Citizens of a failed state have very little say in the direction of their country. In most cases, when a faction assumes control over the government, it installs strict controls that limit the rights of citizens, particularly such rights as freedom of speech, freedom of assembly, and freedom of religion. Some regimes allow for "democratic" elections, but a continued lack of infrastructure and widespread corruption often negates the legitimacy of these elections.

Citizens of failed states are often called upon by the ruling regime (or a regional faction) to serve in its militia, helping it combat other factions within the state. In fact, many militias within failed states are comprised of people who were forced to join (under penalty of death) at a young age. Those who do not join militias are often drawn into criminal activity such as piracy and the drug trade.

Some citizens are able to make a difference by joining interest groups. Many citizens are able to achieve a limited amount of success sharing information about women's rights, HIV/AIDS and other issues. In some situations, these groups are able to gain international assistance from organizations that were unable to work with the failed government.

Michael Auerbach
Marblehead, Massachusetts

Examples

Chad
Democratic Republic of the Congo
Somalia
Sudan
Zimbabwe

Bibliography

"Failed States: Fixing a Broken World." *Economist*, 29 Jan. 2009. Web. 6 Feb. 2012.

"Failed States." Global Policy Forum, 2013. Web. 6 Feb. 2012.

"Somalia Tops Failed States Index for Fifth Year." *CNN.com*. Turner Broadcasting System, 18 June 2012. Web. 6 Feb. 2012.

Thürer, Daniel. (1999). "The 'Failed State' and International Law." *International Review of the Red Cross*. International Committee of the Red Cross, 31 Dec. 1999. Web. 6 Feb. 2012.

Federal Republic

Guiding Premise

A federal republic is a political system that features a central government as well as a set of regional subunits such as states or provinces. Federal republics are designed to limit the power of the central government, paring its focus to only matters of national interest. Typically, a greater degree of power is granted to the regional governments, which retain the ability to create their own laws of local relevance. The degree to which the federal and regional governments each enjoy authority varies from nation to nation, based on the country's interpretation of this republican form of government. By distributing authority to these separate but connected government institutions, federal republics give the greatest power to the people themselves, who typically vote directly for both their regional and national political representation.

Typical Structure

A federal republic's structure varies from nation to nation. However, most federal republics feature two distinct governing entities. The first is a central, federal government, usually based in the nation's capital city. The federal government's task is to address issues of national importance. These issues include defense and foreign relations, but also encompass matters of domestic interest that must be addressed in uniform fashion, such as social assistance programs, infrastructure, and certain taxes.

A federal republic is comprised of executive, legislative, and judicial branches. The executive is typically a president or prime minister—the former selected by popular vote, the latter selected by members of the legislature—and is charged with the administration of the federal government's programs and regulations. The legislature—such as the US Congress, the Austrian Parliament, or the German Bundestag—is charged with developing laws and managing government spending. The judiciary is charged

with ensuring that federal and state laws are enforced and that they are consistent with the country's constitution.

The federal government is limited in terms of its ability to assert authority over the regions. Instead, federal republics grant a degree of sovereignty to the different states, provinces, or regions that comprise the entire nation. These regions have their own governments, similar in structure and procedure to those of the federal government. They too have executives, legislatures, and judiciaries whose foci are limited to the regional government's respective jurisdictions.

The federal and regional segments of a republic are not completely independent of one another, however. Although the systems are intended to distribute power evenly, federal and regional governments are closely linked. This connectivity ensures the efficient collection of taxes, the regional distribution of federal funds, and a rapid response to issues of national importance. A federal republic's greatest strength, therefore, is the series of connections it maintains between the federal, regional, and local governments it contains.

Role of the Citizen

A federal republic is distinguished by the limitations of power it places on the national government. The primary goal of such a design was to place the power of government in the hands of the people. One of the ways the citizens' power is demonstrated is by participating in the electoral process. In a federal republic, the people elect their legislators. In some republics, the legislators in turn elect a prime minister, while in others, the people directly elect a president. The electoral process is an important way for citizens to influence the course of their government, both at the regional and federal levels. They do so by placing people who truly represent their diverse interests in the federal government.

The citizen is also empowered by participating in government as opposed to being subjected to it. In addition to taking part in the electoral process, the people are free to join and become active in a political party. A political party serves as a proxy for its members, representing their viewpoint and interests on a local and national level. In federal republics like Germany, a wide range of political parties are active in the legislature, advancing the political agendas of those they represent.

Michael Auerbach
Marblehead, Massachusetts

Examples
Austria
Brazil
Germany
India
Mexico
Nigeria
United States

Bibliography
"The Federal Principle." *Republik Österreich Parlament.* Republik Österreich Parlament, 8 Oct. 2010. Web. 6 Feb. 2013.
"The Federal Republic of Germany." *Deutscher Bundestag.* German Bundestag, 2013. Web. 6 Feb. 2013.
Collin, Nicholas. "An Essay on the Means of Promoting Federal Sentiments in the United States." *Friends of the Constitution: Writings of the "Other" Federalists, 1787–1788.* Ed. Colleen A. Sheehan and Gary L. McDowell. Online Library of Liberty, 2013. Web. 6 Feb. 2013.

Federation

Guiding Premise

A federation is a nation formed from the unification of smaller political entities. Federations feature federal governments that oversee nationwide issues. However, they also grant a degree of autonomy to the regional, state, or other local governments within the system. Federations are often formed because a collective of diverse regions find a common interest in unification. While the federal government is installed to address those needs, regions with their own distinct ethnic, socioeconomic, or political characteristics remain intact. This "separate but united" structure allows federations to avoid conflict and instability among their regions.

Typical Structure

The primary goal of a federation is to unify a country's political subunits within a national framework. The federal government, therefore, features institutions comprised of representatives from the states or regions. The representatives are typically elected by the residents of these regions, and some federal systems give the power to elect certain national leaders to these representatives. The regions themselves can vary considerably in size. The Russian Federation, for example, includes forty-six geographically large provinces as well as two more-concentrated cities as part of its eighty-three constituent federation members.

There are two institutions in which individuals from the constituent parts of a federation serve. The first institution is the legislature. Legislatures vary in appearance from nation to nation. For example, the US Congress is comprised of two chambers—the House of Representatives and the Senate—whose directly elected members act on behalf of their respective states. The German Parliament, on the other hand, consists of the directly elected Bundestag—which is tasked with electing the German federal chancellor, among other things—and the state-appointed Bundesrat, which works on behalf of the country's sixteen states.

The second institution is the executive. Here, the affairs of the nation are administered by a president or similar leader. Again, the structure and powers of a federal government's executive institutions varies from nation to nation according to their constitutional framework. Federal executive institutions are charged with management of state affairs, including oversight of the military, foreign relations, health care, and education. Similarly diverse is the power of the executive in relation to the legislative branch. Some prime ministers, for example, enjoy considerably greater power than the president. In fact, some presidents share power with other leaders, or councils thereof within the executive branch, serving as the diplomatic face of the nation but not playing a major role in lawmaking. In India, for example, the president is the chief executive of the federal government, but shares power with the prime minister and the Council of Ministers, headed by the prime minister.

In order to promote continuity between the federal government and the states, regions, or other political subunits in the federation, those subunits typically feature governments that largely mirror that of the central government. Some of these regional governments are modified according to their respective constitutions. For example, whereas the bicameral US Congress consists of the Senate and House of Representatives, Nebraska's state legislature only has one chamber. Such distinctive characteristics of state/regional governments reflect the geographic and cultural interests of the region in question. It also underscores the degree of autonomy given to such states under a federation government system.

Role of the Citizen

Federations vary in terms of both structure and distribution of power within government institutions. However, federal systems are typically democratic in nature, relying heavily on the participation of the electorate for installing representatives in those institutions. At the regional level, the people vote for their respective legislators and executives either directly or through political parties. The executive in turn appoints cabinet officials, while the legislators select a chamber leader. In US state governments, for example, such a leader might be a Senate president or speaker of the House of Representatives.

The people also play an important role in federal government. As residents of a given state or region, registered voters—again, through either a direct vote or through political parties—choose their legislators and national executives. In federations that utilize a parliamentary system, however, prime ministers are typically selected by the legislators and/or their political parties and not through a direct, national vote. Many constitutions limit the length of political leaders' respective terms of service and/or the number of times

they may seek reelection, fostering an environment in which the democratic voting process is a frequent occurrence.

Michael Auerbach
Marblehead, Massachusetts

Examples

Australia
Germany
India
Mexico
Russia
United States

Bibliography

"Federal System of India." *Maps of India*. MapsOfIndia. com, 22 Sep. 2011. Web. 7 Feb. 2013.

"Political System." *Facts about Germany*. Frankfurter Societäts-Medien, 2011. Web. 7 Feb. 2013.

"Russia." *CIA World Factbook*. Central Intelligence Agency, 5 Feb. 2013. Web. 7 Feb. 2013.

Monarchy

Guiding Premise

A monarchy is a political system based on the sovereignty of a single individual who holds actual or symbolic authority over all governmental functions. The monarchy is one of the oldest forms of government in human history and was the most common type of government until the nineteenth century. In a monarchy, authority is inherited, usually through primogeniture, or inheritance by the eldest son.

In an absolute monarchy, the monarch holds authority over the government and functions as both head of state and head of government. In a constitutional monarchy, the role of the monarch is codified in the state constitution, and the powers afforded to the monarch are limited by constitutional law. Constitutional monarchies generally blend the inherited authority of the monarchy with popular control in the form of democratic elections. The monarch may continue to hold significant power over some aspects of government or may be relegated to a largely ceremonial or symbolic role.

In most ancient monarchies, the monarch was generally believed to have been chosen for his or her role by divine authority, and many monarchs in history have claimed to represent the will of a god or gods in their ascendancy to the position. In constitutional monarchies, the monarch may be seen as representing spiritual authority or may represent a link to the country's national heritage.

Typical Structure

In an absolute monarchy, a single monarch is empowered to head the government, including the formulation of all laws and leadership of the nation's armed forces. Oman is one example of a type of absolute monarchy called a sultanate, in which a family of leaders, called "sultans," inherits authority and leads the nation under an authoritarian system. Power in the Omani sultanate remains within the royal family. In the event of the sultan's death or incapacitation, the Royal Family Council selects a successor by consensus from within the family line. Beneath the sultan is a council of ministers, appointed by the sultan, to create and disseminate official government policy. The sultan's council serves alongside an elected body of leaders who enforce and represent Islamic law and work with the sultan's ministers to create national laws.

In Japan, which is a constitutional monarchy, the Japanese emperor serves as the chief of state and symbolic representative of Japan's culture and history. The emperor officiates national ceremonies, meets with world leaders for diplomatic purposes, and symbolically appoints leaders to certain governmental posts. Governmental authority in Japan rests with the Diet, a legislative body of elected officials who serve limited terms of office and are elected through popular vote. A prime minister is also chosen to lead the Diet, and the prime minister is considered the official head of government.

The Kingdom of Norway is another example of a constitutional monarchy wherein the monarch serves a role that has been codified in the state constitution. The king of Norway is designated as the country's chief of state, serving as head of the nation's executive branch. Unlike Japan, where the monarch's role is largely symbolic, the monarch of Norway has considerable authority under the constitution, including the ability to veto and approve all laws and the power to declare war. Norway utilizes a parliamentary system, with a prime minister, chosen from individuals elected to the state parliament, serving as head of government. Though the monarch has authority over the executive functions of government, the legislature and prime minister are permitted the ability to override monarchical decisions with sufficient support, thereby providing a system of control to prevent the monarch from exerting a dominant influence over the government.

Role of the Citizen

The role of the citizen in a monarchy varies depending on whether the government is a constitutional or absolute monarchy. In an absolute monarchy, citizens have only those rights given to them by the monarch, and the monarch has the power to extend and retract freedoms and rights at will. In ancient monarchies, citizens accepted the authoritarian role of the monarch, because it was widely believed that the monarch's powers were derived from divine authority. In addition, in many absolute monarchies, the monarch has the power to arrest, detain, and imprison individuals without due process, thereby providing a strong disincentive for citizens to oppose the monarchy.

In a constitutional monarchy, citizens are generally given greater freedom to participate in the development of governmental policies. In Japan, Belgium, and Spain, for instance, citizens elect governmental leaders, and the elected legislature largely controls the creation and enforcement of laws. In some countries, like the Kingdom of Norway, the monarch may exert significant authority, but this authority is balanced by that of the legislature, which represents the sovereignty of the citizens and is chosen to promote and protect the interests of the public.

The absolute monarchies of medieval Europe, Asia, and Africa held power for centuries, but many eventually collapsed due to popular uprisings as citizens demanded representation within the government. The development of constitutional monarchies may be seen as a balanced system in which the citizens retain significant control over the development of their government while the history and traditions of the nation are represented by the continuation of the monarch's lineage. In the United Kingdom, the governments of Great Britain and Northern Ireland are entirely controlled by elected individuals, but the continuation of the monarchy is seen by many as an important link to the nation's historic identity.

Micah Issitt
Philadelphia, Pennsylvania

Examples

Belgium
Bhutan
Japan
Norway
Oman
United Kingdom

Bibliography

Barrington, Lowell. *Comparative Politics: Structures and Choices*. Boston: Wadsworth, 2012. Print.

Dresch, Paul, and James Piscatori, eds. *Monarchies and Nations: Globalisation and Identity in the Arab States of the Gulf*. London: Tauris, 2005. Print.

Kesselman, Mark, et al. *European Politics in Transition*. New York: Houghton, 2009. Print.

Parliamentary Monarchy

Guiding Premise

A parliamentary monarchy is a political system in which leadership of the government is shared between a monarchy, such as a king or queen, and the members of a democratically elected legislative body. In such governments, the monarch's role as head of state is limited by the country's constitution or other founding document, preventing the monarch from assuming too much control over the nation. As head of state, the monarch may provide input during the lawmaking process and other operations of government. Furthermore, the monarch, whose role is generally lifelong, acts as a stabilizing element for the government, while the legislative body is subject to the periodic changes that occur with each election cycle.

Typical Structure

Parliamentary monarchies vary in structure and distribution of power from nation to nation, based on the parameters established by each respective country's constitution or other founding document. In general, however, parliamentary monarchies feature a king, queen, or other sovereign who acts as head of state. In that capacity, the monarch's responsibilities may be little more than ceremonial in nature, allowing him or her to offer input during the lawmaking process, to approve the installation of government officials, and to act as the country's international representative. However, these responsibilities may be subject to the approval of the country's legislative body. For example, the king of Spain approves laws and regulations that have already been passed by the legislative branch; formally appoints the prime minister; and approves other ministers appointed by the prime minister. Yet, the king's responsibilities in those capacities are subject to the approval of the Cortes Generales, Spain's parliament.

In general, parliamentary monarchies help a country preserve its cultural heritage through their respective royal families, but grant the majority of government management and lawmaking responsibilities to the country's legislative branch and its various administrative ministries, such as education and defense. In most parliamentary monarchies, the ministers of government are appointed by the legislative body and usually by the prime minister. Although government ministries have the authority to carry out the country's laws and programs, they are also subject to criticism and removal by the legislative body if they fail to perform to expectations.

The legislative body itself consists of members elected through a democratic, constitutionally defined process. Term length, term limit, and the manner by which legislators may be elected are usually outlined in the country's founding documents. For example, in the Dutch parliament, members of the House of Representatives are elected every four years through a direct vote, while the members of the Senate are elected by provincial government councils every four years. By contrast, three-quarters of the members of Thailand's House of Representatives are elected in single-seat constituencies (smaller districts), while the remaining members are elected in larger, proportional representation districts; all members of the House are elected for four-year terms. A bare majority of Thailand's senators are elected by direct vote, with the remainder appointed by other members of the government.

Role of the Citizen

While the kings and queens of parliamentary monarchies are the nominal heads of state, these political systems are designed to be democratic governments. As such, they rely heavily on the input and involvement of the citizens. Participating in legislative elections is one of the most direct ways in which the citizen is empowered. Because the governments of such systems are subject to legislative oversight, the people—through their respective votes for members of parliament—have influence over their government.

Political parties and organizations such as local and municipal councils also play an important role in parliamentary monarchies. Citizens' participation in those organizations can help shape parliamentary agendas and build links between government and the public. In Norway, for example, nearly 70 percent of citizens are involved in at least one such organization, and consequently Norway's Storting (parliament) has a number of committees that are tied to those organizations at the regional and local levels. Thus, through voting and active political involvement at the local level, the citizens of a parliamentary monarchy help direct the political course of their nation.

Michael Auerbach
Marblehead, Massachusetts

Examples
Netherlands
Norway
Spain
Sweden
Thailand
United Kingdom

Bibliography
"Form of Government." *Norway.org*. Norway–The Official Site in the United States, n.d. Web. 17 Jan. 2013.
"Issues: Parliament." *Governmentl.nl*. Government of the Netherlands, n.d. Web. 17 Jan. 2013.
"King, Prime Minister, and Council of Ministers." *Country Studies: Spain*. Lib. of Congress, 2012. Web. 17 Jan. 2013.
"Thailand." *International Foundation for Electoral Systems*. IFES, 2013. Web. 17 Jan. 2013.

Parliamentary Republic

Guiding Premise

A parliamentary republic is a system wherein both executive and legislative powers are centralized in the legislature. In such a system, voters elect their national representatives to the parliamentary body, which in turn appoints the executive. In such an environment, legislation is passed more quickly than in a presidential system, which requires a consensus between the executive and legislature. It also enables the legislature to remove the executive in the event the latter does not perform to the satisfaction of the people. Parliamentary republics can also prevent the consolidation of power in a single leader, as even a prime minister must defer some authority to fellow legislative leaders.

Typical Structure

Parliamentary republics vary in structure from nation to nation, according to the respective country's constitution or other governing document. In general, such a system entails the merger of the legislature and head of state such as a president or other executive. The state may retain the executive, however. However, the executive's role may be largely ceremonial, as is the case in Greece, where the president has very little political authority. This "outsider" status has in fact enabled the Greek president to act as a diplomatic intermediary among sparring parliamentary leaders.

While many countries with such a system operate with an executive—who may or may not be directly elected, and who typically has limited powers—the bulk of a parliamentary republic's political authority rests with the legislature. The national government is comprised of democratically elected legislators and their appointees. The length of these representatives' respective terms, as well as the manner by which the legislators are elected, depend on the frameworks established by each individual nation. Some parliamentary republics utilize a constitution for this

purpose, while others use a set of common laws or other legal precepts. In South Africa, members of the parliament's two chambers, the National Assembly and the National Council of Provinces, are elected differently. The former's members are elected directly by the citizens in each province, while the latter's members are installed by the provincial legislatures.

Once elected to parliament, legislators are often charged with more than just lawmaking. In many cases, members of parliament oversee the administration of state affairs as well. Legislative bodies in parliamentary republics are responsible for nominating an executive—typically a prime minister—to manage the government's various administrative responsibilities. Should the executive not adequately perform its duties, parliament has the power to remove the executive from office. In Ireland, for example, the Dail Eireann (the House of Representatives) is charged with forming the country's executive branch by nominating the Taoiseach (prime minister) and approving the prime minister's cabinet selections.

Role of the Citizen

A parliamentary republic is a democratic political system that relies on the involvement of an active electorate. This civic engagement includes a direct or indirect vote for representatives to parliament. While the people do not vote for an executive as well, by way of their vote for parliament, the citizenry indirectly influences the selection of the chief executive and the policies he or she follows. In many countries, the people also indirectly influence the national government by their votes in provincial government. As noted earlier, some countries' parliaments include chambers whose members are appointed by provincial leaders.

Citizens may also influence the political system through involvement in political parties. Such organizations help shape the platforms of parliamentary majorities as well as selecting candidates for prime minister and other government positions. The significance of political parties varies from nation to nation, but such organizations require the input and involvement of citizens.

Michael Auerbach
Marblehead, Massachusetts

Examples
Austria
Greece
Iceland
Ireland
Poland
South Africa

Bibliography
"About the Oireachtas." *Oireachtas.ie*. Houses of the Oireachtas, n.d. Web. 7 Feb. 2013.

"Our Parliament." *Parliament.gov*. Parliament of the Republic of South Africa, n.d. Web. 7 Feb. 2013.

Tagaris, Karolina, and Ingrid Melander. "Greek President Makes Last Push to Avert Elections." *Reuters*. Thomson Reuters, 12 May 2012. Web. 7 Feb. 2013.

Presidential

Guiding Premise

A presidential system is a type of democratic government in which the populace elects a single leader—a president—to serve as both head of state and the head of government. The presidential system developed from the monarchic governments of medieval and early modern Europe, in which a royal monarch, holder of an inherited office, served as both head of state and government. In the presidential system, the president does not inherit the office, but is chosen by either direct or indirect popular vote.

Presidential systems differ from parliamentary systems in that the president is both the chief executive and head of state, whereas in a parliamentary system another individual, usually called the "prime minister," serves as head of government and leader of the legislature. The presidential system evolved out of an effort to create an executive office that balances the influence of the legislature and the judiciary. The United States is the most prominent example of a democratic presidential system.

Some governments have adopted a semi-presidential system, which blends elements of the presidential system with the parliamentary system, and generally features a president who serves only as head of state. In constitutional governments, like the United States, Mexico, and Honduras, the role of the president is described in the nation's constitution, which also provides for the president's powers in relation to the other branches of government.

Typical Structure

In most modern presidential governments, power to create and enforce laws and international agreements is divided among three branches: the executive, legislative, and judicial. The executive office consists of the president and a number of presidential advisers—often called the cabinet—who typically serve at the president's discretion and are not elected to office. The terms of office for the president are codified in the state constitution and, in most cases, the president may serve a limited number of terms before he or she becomes ineligible for reelection.

The president serves as head of state and is therefore charged with negotiating and administering international treaties and agreements. In addition, the president serves as head of government and is therefore charged with overseeing the function of the government as a whole. The president is also empowered, in most presidential governments, with the ability to deploy the nation's armed forces. In some governments, including the United States, the approval of the legislature is needed for the country to officially declare war.

The legislative branch of the government proposes new laws, in the form of bills, but must cooperate with the executive office to pass these bills into law. The legislature and the executive branch also cooperate in determining the government budget. Unlike prime ministers under the parliamentary system, the president is not considered a member of the legislature and therefore acts independently as the chief executive, though a variety of governmental functions require action from both branches of government. A unique feature of the presidential system is that the election of the president is separate from the election of the legislature.

In presidential systems, members of the legislature are often less likely to vote according to the goals of their political party and may support legislation that is not supported by their chosen political party. In parliamentary systems, like the government of Great Britain, legislators are more likely to vote according to party policy. Presidential systems are also often marked by a relatively small number of political parties, which often allows one party to achieve a majority in the legislature. If this majority coincides with the election of a president from the same party, that party's platform or agenda becomes dominant until the next election cycle.

The judicial branch in a presidential system serves to enforce the laws among the populace. In most modern presidential democracies, the president appoints judges to federal posts, though in some governments, the legislature appoints judges. In some cases, the president may need the approval of the legislature to make judicial appointments.

Role of the Citizen

In a democratic presidential system, citizens are empowered with the ability to vote for president and therefore have ultimate control over who serves as head of government and head of state. Some presidential governments elect individuals to the presidency based on the result of a popular vote, while other governments use an indirect system, in which citizens vote for a party or for individuals who then serve as their representatives in electing the president. The United States utilizes an indirect system called the Electoral College.

Citizens in presidential systems are also typically allowed, though not required, to join political parties in an effort to promote a political agenda. Some governmental systems that are modeled on the presidential system allow the president to exert a dominant influence over the legislature and other branches of the government. In some cases, this can lead to a presidential dictatorship, in which the president may curtail the political rights of citizens. In most presidential systems, however, the roles and powers of the legislative and executive branches are balanced to protect the rights of the people to influence their government.

In a presidential system, citizens are permitted to vote for a president representing one political party, while simultaneously voting for legislators from other political parties. In this way, the presidential system allows citizens to determine the degree to which any single political party is permitted to have influence on political development.

Micah Issitt
Philadelphia, Pennsylvania

Examples

Benin
Costa Rica
Dominican Republic
Guatemala
Honduras
Mexico
United States
Venezuela

Bibliography

Barington, Lowell. *Comparative Politics: Structures and Choices*. Boston: Wadsworth, 2012. Print.

Caramani, Daniele. *Comparative Politics*. New York: Oxford UP, 2008. Print.

Garner, Robert, Peter Ferdinand, and Stephanie Lawson. *Introduction to Politics*. 2nd ed. Oxford: Oxford UP, 2009. Print.

Republic

Guiding Premise

A republic is a type of government based on the idea of popular or public sovereignty. The word "republic" is derived from Latin terms meaning "matters" and "the public." In essence, a republic is a government in which leaders are chosen by the public rather than by inheritance or by force. The republic or republican governmental system emerged in response to absolute monarchy, in which hereditary leaders retained all the power. In contrast, the republican system is intended to create a government that is responsive to the people's will.

Most modern republics operate based on a democratic system in which citizens elect leaders by popular vote. The United States and Mexico are examples of countries that use a democratic republican system to appoint leaders to office. However, universal suffrage (voting for all) is not required for a government to qualify as a republic, and it is possible for a country to have a republican government in which only certain categories of citizens, such as the wealthy, are allowed to vote in elections.

In addition to popular vote, most modern republics are further classified as constitutional republics, because the laws and rules for appointing leaders have been codified in a set of principles and guidelines known as a "constitution." When combined with universal suffrage and constitutional law, the republican system is intended to form a government that is based on the will of the majority while protecting the rights of minority groups.

Typical Structure

Republican governments are typically led by an elected head of state, generally a president. In cases where the president also serves as the head of government, the government is called a "presidential republic." In some republics, the head of state serves alongside an appointed or elected head of government, usually a prime minister.

This mixed form of government blends elements of the republic system with the parliamentary system found in countries such as the United Kingdom or India.

The president is part of the executive branch of government, which represents the country internationally and heads efforts to make and amend international agreements and treaties. The laws of a nation are typically created by the legislative branch, which may also be composed of elected leaders. Typically, the legislative and executive branches must cooperate on key initiatives, such as determining the national budget.

In addition to legislative and executive functions, most republics have a judiciary charged with enforcing and interpreting laws. The judicial branch may be composed of elected leaders, but in many cases, judicial officers are appointed by the president and/or the legislature. In the United States (a federal republic), the president, who leads the executive branch, appoints members to the federal judiciary, but these choices must be approved by the legislature before they take effect.

The duties and powers allotted to each branch of the republican government are interconnected with those of the other branches in a system of checks and balances. For instance, in Mexico (a federal republic), the legislature is empowered to create new tax guidelines for the public, but before legislative tax bills become law, they must first achieve majority support within the two branches of the Mexican legislature and receive the approval of the president. By creating a system of separate but balanced powers, the republican system seeks to prevent any one branch from exerting a dominant influence over the government.

Role of the Citizen

The role of the citizen in a republic depends largely on the type of republican system that the country has adopted. In democratic republics, popular elections and constitutional law give the public significant influence over governmental development and establish the people as the primary source of political power. Citizens in democratic republics are empowered to join political groups and to influence the development of laws and policies through the election of public leaders.

In many republican nations, a powerful political party or other political group can dominate the government, preventing competition from opposing political groups and curtailing the public's role in selecting and approving leaders. For instance, in the late twentieth century, a dominant political party maintained control of the Gambian presidency and legislature for more than thirty years, thereby significantly limiting the role of the citizenry in influencing the development of government policy.

In general, the republican system was intended to reverse the power structure typical of the monarchy system, in which inherited leaders possess all of the political power. In the republican system, leaders are chosen to represent the people's interests with terms of office created in such a way that new leaders must be chosen at regular intervals, thereby preventing a single leader or political entity from dominating the populace. In practice, popular power in a republic depends on preventing a political monopoly from becoming powerful enough to alter the laws of the country to suit the needs of a certain group rather than the whole.

Micah Issitt
Philadelphia, Pennsylvania

Examples
Algeria
Argentina
Armenia
France
Gambia
Mexico
San Marino
South Sudan
Tanzania
United States

Bibliography
Caramani, Daniele. *Comparative Politics*. New York: Oxford UP, 2008. Print.
Przeworski, Adam. *Democracy and the Limits of Self-Government*. New York: Cambridge UP, 2010. Print.

Socialist

Guiding Premise

Socialism is a political and economic system that seeks to elevate the common good of the citizenry by allowing the government to own all property and means of production. In the most basic model, citizens cooperatively elect members to government, and the government then acts on behalf of the people to manage the state's property, industry, production, and services.

In a socialist system, communal or government ownership of property and industry is intended to eliminate the formation of economic classes and to ensure an even distribution of wealth. Most modern socialists also believe that basic services, including medical and legal care, should be provided at the same level to all citizens and not depend on the individual citizen's ability to pay for better services. The origins of socialism can be traced to theorists such as Thomas More (1478–1535), who believed that private wealth and ownership led to the formation of a wealthy elite class that protected its own wealth while oppressing members of lower classes.

There are many different forms of socialist philosophy, some of which focus on economic systems, while others extend socialist ideas to other aspects of society. Communism may be considered a form of socialism, based on the idea that a working-class revolution is needed to initiate the ideal socialist society.

Typical Structure

Socialism exists in many forms around the world, and many governments use a socialist model for the distribution of key services, most often medical and legal aid. A socialist state is a government whose constitution explicitly gives the government powers to facilitate the creation of a socialist society.

The idealized model of the socialist state is one in which the populace elects leaders to head the government, and the government then oversees the distribution of wealth and goods among the populace, enforces the laws, and provides for the well-being of citizens. Many modern socialist governments follow a communist model, in which a national communist political party has ultimate control over governmental legislation and appointments.

There are many different models of socialist states, integrating elements of democratic or parliamentary systems. In these cases, democratic elections may be held to elect the head of state and the body of legislators. The primary difference between a socialist democracy and a capitalist democracy can be found in the state's role in the ownership of key industries. Most modern noncommunist socialist states provide state regulation and control over key industries but allow some free-market competition as well.

In a socialist system, government officials appoint leaders to oversee various industries and to regulate prices based on public welfare. For instance, if the government retains sole ownership over agricultural production, the government must appoint individuals to manage and oversee that industry, organize agricultural labor, and oversee the distribution of food products among the populace. Some countries, such as Sweden, have adopted a mixed model in which socialist industry management is blended with free-market competition.

Role of the Citizen

All citizens in a socialist system are considered workers, and thus all exist in the same economic class. While some citizens may receive higher pay than others—those who work in supervisory roles, for instance—limited ownership of private property and standardized access to services places all individuals on a level field with regard to basic welfare and economic prosperity.

The degree to which personal liberties are curtailed within a socialist system depends upon the type of socialist philosophy adopted and the degree to which corruption and authoritarianism play a role in government. In most modern communist governments, for instance, individuals are often prohibited from engaging in any activity seen as contrary to the overall goals of the state or to the policies of the dominant political party. While regulations of this kind are common in communist societies, social control over citizens is not necessary for a government to follow a socialist model.

Under democratic socialism, individuals are also expected to play a role in the formation of their government by electing leaders to serve in key positions. In Sri Lanka, for instance, citizens elect members to serve in the parliament and a president to serve as head of the executive branch. In Portugal, citizens vote in multiparty elections to elect a president who serves as head of state, and the president appoints a prime minister to serve as head of government. In both Portugal and Sri Lanka, the government is constitutionally bound to promote a socialist society, though both governments allow private ownership and control of certain industries.

Citizens in a socialist society are also expected to provide for one another by contributing to labor and by forfeiting some ownership rights to provide for the greater good. In the Kingdom of Sweden, a mixed parliamentary system, all citizens pay a higher tax rate to contribute to funds that provide for national health care, child care, education, and worker support systems. Citizens who have no children and require only minimal health care benefits pay the same tax rate as those who have greater need for the nation's socialized benefits.

Micah Issitt
Philadelphia, Pennsylvania

Examples

China
Cuba
Portugal
Sri Lanka
Venezuela
Zambia

Bibliography

Caramani, Daniele. *Comparative Politics*. New York: Oxford UP, 2008. Print.

Heilbroner, Robert. "Socialism." *Library of Economics and Liberty*. Liberty Fund, 2008. Web. 17 Jan. 2013.

Howard, Michael Wayne. *Socialism*. Amherst, NY: Humanity, 2001. Print.

Sultanate/Emirate

Guiding Premise

A sultanate or emirate form of government is a political system in which a hereditary ruler—a monarch, chieftain, or military leader—acts as the head of state. Emirates and sultanates are most commonly found in Islamic nations in the Middle East, although others are found in Southeast Asia as well. Sultans and emirs frequently assume titles such as president or prime minister in addition to their royal designations, meshing the traditional ideal of a monarch with the administrative capacities of a constitutional political system.

Typical Structure

A sultanate or emirate combines the administrative duties of the executive with the powers of a monarch. The emir or sultan acts as the head of government, appointing all cabinet ministers and officials. In Brunei, a sultanate, the government was established according to the constitution (set up after the country declared autonomy from Britain in 1959). The sultan did assemble a legislative council in order to facilitate the lawmaking process, but this council has consistently remained subject to the authority of the sultan and not to a democratic process. In 2004, there was some movement toward the election of at least some of the members of this council. In the meantime, the sultan maintains a ministerial system by appointment and also serves as the nation's chief religious leader.

In some cases, an emirate or sultanate appears similar to a federal system. In the United Arab Emirates (UAE), for example, the nation consists of not one but seven emirates. This system came into being after the seven small regions achieved independence from Great Britain. Each emirate developed its own government system under the leadership of an emir. However, in 1971, the individual emirates agreed to join as a federation, drafting a constitution that identified the areas of common interest to the entire

group of emirates. Like Brunei, the UAE's initial government structure focused on the authority of the emirs and the various councils and ministries formed at the UAE's capital of Abu Dhabi. However, beginning in the early twenty-first century, the UAE's legislative body, the Federal National Council, has been elected by electoral colleges from the seven emirates, thus further engaging various local areas and reflecting their interests.

Sultanates and emirates are at times part of a larger nation, with the sultans or emirs answering to the authority of another government. This is the case in Malaysia, where the country is governed by a constitutional monarchy. However, most of Malaysia's western political units are governed by sultans, who act as regional governors and, in many cases, religious leaders, but remain subject to the king's authority in Malaysia's capital of Kuala Lumpur.

Role of the Citizen

Sultanates and emirates are traditionally non-democratic governments. Like those of other monarchs, the seats of emirs and sultans are hereditary. Any votes for these leaders to serve as prime minister or other head of government are cast by ministers selected by the emirs and sultans. Political parties may exist in these countries as well, but these parties are strictly managed by the sultan or emir; opposition parties are virtually nonexistent in such systems, and some emirates have no political parties at all.

As shown in the UAE and Malaysia, however, there are signs that the traditional sultanate or emirate is increasingly willing to engage their respective citizens. For example, the UAE, between 2006 and 2013, launched a series of reforms designed to strengthen the role of local governments and relations with the people they serve. Malaysia may allow sultans to continue their regional controls, but at the same time, the country continues to evolve its federal system, facilitating multiparty democratic elections for its national legislature.

Michael Auerbach
Marblehead, Massachusetts

Examples

Brunei
Kuwait
Malaysia
Qatar
United Arab Emirates

Bibliography

"Brunei." *The World Factbook*. Central Intelligence Agency, 2 Jan. 2013. Web. 17 Jan. 2013.

"Malaysia." *The World Factbook*. Central Intelligence Agency, 7 Jan. 2013. Web. 17 Jan. 2013.

"Political System." *UAE Interact*. UAE National Media Council, n.d. Web. 17 Jan. 2013.

Prime Minister's Office, Brunei Darussalam. Prime Minister's Office, Brunei Darussalam, 2013. Web. 17 Jan. 2013.

Theocratic Republic

Guiding Premise

A theocratic republic is a type of government blending popular and religious influence to determine the laws and governmental principles. A republic is a governmental system based on the concept of popular rule and takes its name from the Latin words for "public matter." The defining characteristic of a republic is that civic leaders hold elected, rather than inherited, offices. A theocracy is a governmental system in which a supreme deity is considered the ultimate authority guiding civil matters.

No modern nations can be classified as pure theocratic republics, but some nations, such as Iran, maintain a political system largely dominated by religious law. The Buddhist nation of Tibet operated under a theocratic system until it was taken over by Communist China in the early 1950s.

In general, a theocratic republic forms in a nation or other governmental system dominated by a single religious group. The laws of the government are formed in reference to a set of religious laws, either taken directly from sacred texts or formulated by religious scholars and authority figures. Most theocratic governments depend on a body of religious scholars who interpret religious scripture, advise all branches of government, and oversee the electoral process.

Typical Structure

In a typical republic, the government is divided into executive, legislative, and judicial branches, and citizens vote to elect leaders to one or more of the branches of government. In most modern republics, voters elect a head of state, usually a president, to lead the executive branch. In many republics, voters also elect individuals to serve as legislators. Members of the judiciary may be elected by voters or may be appointed to office by other elected leaders. In nontheocratic republics, the citizens are considered the ultimate source of authority in the government.

In a theocratic republic, however, one or more deities are considered to represent the ultimate governmental authority. In some cases, the government may designate a deity as the ultimate head of state. Typically, any individual serving as the functional head of state is believed to have been chosen by that deity, and candidates for the position must be approved by the prevailing religious authority.

In some cases, the religious authority supports popular elections to fill certain governmental posts. In Iran, for instance, citizens vote to elect members to the national parliament and a single individual to serve as president. The Iranian government is ultimately led by a supreme leader, who is appointed to office by the Assembly of Experts, the leaders of the country's Islamic community. Though the populace chooses the president and leaders to serve in the legislature, the supreme leader of Iran can overrule decisions made in any other branch of the government.

In a theocratic republic, the power to propose new laws may be given to the legislature, which works on legislation in conjunction with the executive branch. However, all laws must conform to religious law, and any legislation produced within the government is likely to be abolished if it is deemed by the religious authorities to violate religious principles. In addition, religious leaders typically decide which candidates are qualified to run for specific offices, thereby ensuring that the citizens will not elect individuals who are likely to oppose religious doctrine.

In addition, many modern nations that operate on a partially theocratic system may adopt a set of governmental principles in the form of a constitution, blended with religious law. This mixed constitutional theocratic system has been adopted by an increasing number of Islamic nations, including Iraq, Afghanistan, Mauritania, and some parts of Nigeria.

Role of the Citizen

Citizens in a theocratic republic are expected to play a role in forming the government through elections, but they are constrained in their choices by the prevailing religious authority. Citizens are also guaranteed certain freedoms, typically codified in a constitution, that have been formulated with reference to religious law. All citizens must adhere to religious laws, regardless of their personal religious beliefs or membership within any existing religious group.

In many Middle Eastern and African nations that operate on the basis of an Islamic theocracy, citizens elect leaders from groups of candidates chosen by the prevailing religious authority. While the choices presented to the citizens are more limited than in a democratic, multiparty republic, the citizens nevertheless play a role in determining the evolution of the government through their voting choices.

The freedoms and rights afforded to citizens in a theocratic republic may depend, in part, on the individual's religious affiliation. For instance, Muslims living in Islamic theocracies may be permitted to hold political office or to aspire to other influential political positions, while members of minority religious groups may find their rights and freedoms limited. Religious minorities living in Islamic republics may not be permitted to run for certain offices, such as president, and must follow laws that adhere to Islamic principles but may violate their own religious principles. Depending on the country and the adherents' religion, the practice of their faith may itself be considered criminal.

Micah Issitt
Philadelphia, Pennsylvania

Examples

Afghanistan
Iran
Iraq
Pakistan
Mauritania
Nigeria

Bibliography

Cooper, William W., and Piyu Yue. *Challenges of the Muslim World: Present, Future and Past*. Boston: Elsevier, 2008. Print.

Hirschl, Ran. *Constitutional Theocracy*. Cambridge: Harvard UP, 2010. Print.

Totalitarian

Guiding Premise

A totalitarian government is one in which a single political party maintains absolute control over the state and is responsible for creating all legislation without popular referendum. In general, totalitarianism is considered a type of authoritarian government where the laws and principles used to govern the country are based on the authority of the leading political group or dictator. Citizens under totalitarian regimes have limited freedoms and are subject to social controls dictated by the state.

The concept of totalitarianism evolved in fascist Italy in the 1920s, and was first used to describe the Italian government under dictator Benito Mussolini. The term became popular among critics of the authoritarian governments of Fascist Italy and Nazi Germany in the 1930s. Supporters of the totalitarian philosophy believed that a strong central government, with absolute control over all aspects of society, could achieve progress by avoiding political debate and power struggles between interest groups.

In theory, totalitarian regimes—like that of Nazi Germany and modern North Korea—can more effectively mobilize resources and direct a nation toward a set of overarching goals. Adolf Hitler was able to achieve vast increases in military power during a short period of time by controlling all procedural steps involved in promoting military development. In practice, however, pure totalitarianism has never been achieved, as citizens and political groups generally find ways to subvert complete government control.

Totalitarianism differs from authoritarianism in that a totalitarian government is based on the idea that the highest leader takes total control in order to create a flourishing society for the benefit of the people. By contrast, authoritarian regimes are based on the authority of a single, charismatic individual who develops policies designed to maintain personal power, rather than promote public interest.

Typical Structure

In a fully realized totalitarian system, a single leader or group of leaders controls all governmental functions, appointing individuals to serve in various posts to facilitate the development of legislation and oversee the enforcement of laws. In Nazi Germany, for instance, Adolf Hitler created a small group of executives to oversee the operation of the government. Governmental authority was then further disseminated through a complex network of departments, called ministries, with leaders appointed directly by Hitler.

Some totalitarian nations may adopt a state constitution in an effort to create the appearance of democratic popular control. In North Korea, the country officially operates under a multiparty democratic system, with citizens guaranteed the right to elect leaders to both the executive and legislative branches of government. In practice, the Workers' Party of North Korea is the only viable political party, as it actively controls competing parties and suppresses any attempt to mount political opposition. Under Supreme Leader Kim Il-sung, the Workers' Party amended the constitution to allow Kim to serve as the sole executive leader for life, without the possibility of being removed from office by any governmental action.

In some cases, totalitarian regimes may favor a presidential system, with the dictator serving officially as president, while other totalitarian governments may adopt a parliamentary system, with a prime minister as head of government. Though a single dictator generally heads the nation with widespread powers over a variety of governmental functions, a cabinet or group of high-ranking ministers may also play a prominent role in disseminating power throughout the various branches of government.

Role of the Citizen

Citizens in totalitarian regimes are often subject to strict social controls exerted by the leading political party. In many cases, totalitarian governments restrict the freedom of the press, expression, and speech in an effort to limit opposition to the government. In addition, totalitarian governments may use the threat of police or military action to prevent protest movements against the leading party. Totalitarian governments maintain absolute control over the courts and any security agency, and the legal/judicial system therefore exists only as an extension of the leading political party.

Totalitarian governments like North Korea also attempt to restrict citizens' access to information considered subversive. For instance, North Korean citizens are not allowed to freely utilize the Internet or any other informational source, but are instead only allowed access to government-approved websites and publications. In many cases, the attempt to control access to information creates a black market for publications and other forms of information banned by government policy.

In some cases, government propaganda and restricted access to information creates a situation in which citizens actively support the ruling regime. Citizens may honestly believe that the social and political restrictions imposed by the ruling party are necessary for the advancement of society. In other cases, citizens may accept governmental control to avoid reprisal from the military and police forces. Most totalitarian regimes have established severe penalties, including imprisonment, corporal punishment, and death, for criticizing the government or refusing to adhere to government policy.

Micah Issitt
Philadelphia, Pennsylvania

Examples

Fascist Italy (1922–1943)
Nazi Germany (1933–1945)
North Korea
Stalinist Russia (1924–1953)

Bibliography

Barrington, Lowell. *Comparative Politics: Structures and Choices*. Boston: Wadsworth, 2012. Print.
Gleason, Abbot. *Totalitarianism: The Inner History of the Cold War*. New York: Oxford UP, 1995. Print.
McEachern, Patrick. *Inside the Red Box: North Korea's Post-Totalitarian Regime*. New York: Columbia UP, 2010. Print.

Treaty System

Guiding Premise

A treaty system is a framework within which participating governments agree to collect and share scientific information gathered in a certain geographic region, or otherwise establish mutually agreeable standards for the use of that region. The participants establish rules and parameters by which researchers may establish research facilities and travel throughout the region, ensuring that there are no conflicts, that the environment is protected, and that the region is not used for illicit purposes. This system is particularly useful when the region in question is undeveloped and unpopulated, but could serve a number of strategic and scientific purposes.

Typical Structure

A treaty system of government is an agreement between certain governments that share a common interest in the use of a certain region to which no state or country has yet laid internationally recognized claim. Participating parties negotiate treaty systems that, upon agreement, form a framework by which the system will operate. Should the involved parties be United Nations member states, the treaty is then submitted to the UN Secretariat for registration and publication.

The agreement's founding ideals generally characterize the framework of a treaty. For example, the most prominent treaty system in operation today is the Antarctic Treaty System, which currently includes fifty nations whose scientists are studying Antarctica. This system, which entered into force in 1961, focuses on several topics, including environmental protection, tourism, scientific operations, and the peaceful use of that region. Within these topics, the treaty system enables participants to meet, cooperate, and share data on a wide range of subjects. Such cooperative activities include regional meetings, seminars, and large-scale conferences.

A treaty system is not a political institution in the same manner as state governments. Rather, it is an agreement administered by delegates from the involved entities. Scientists seeking to perform their research in Antarctica, for example, must apply through the scientific and/or government institutions of their respective nations. In the case of the United States, scientists may apply for grants from the National Science Foundation. These institutions then examine the study in question for its relevance to the treaty's ideals.

Central to the treaty system is the organization's governing body. In the case of the Antarctic Treaty, that body is the Antarctic Treaty Secretariat, which is based in Buenos Aires, Argentina. The Secretariat oversees all activities taking place under the treaty, welcomes new members, and addresses any conflicts or issues between participants. It also reviews any activities to ensure that they are in line with the parameters of the treaty. A treaty system is not a sovereign organization, however. Each participating government retains autonomy, facilitating its own scientific expeditions, sending delegates to the treaty system's main governing body, and reviewing the treaty to ensure that it coincides with its national interests.

Role of the Citizen

Although treaty systems are not sovereign governmental institutions, private citizens can and frequently do play an important role in their function and success. For example, the Antarctic Treaty System frequently conducts large-scale planning conferences, to which each participating government sends delegates. These teams are comprised of qualified scientists who are nominated and supported by their peers during the government's review process. In the United States, for example, the State Department oversees American participation in the Antarctic

Treaty System's events and programs, including delegate appointments.

Another area in which citizens are involved in a treaty system is in the ratification process. Every nation's government—usually through its legislative branch—must formally approve any treaty before the country can honor the agreement. This ratification is necessary for new treaties as well as treaties that must be reapproved every few years. Citizens, through their elected officials, may voice their support or disapproval of a new or updated treaty.

While participating governments administer treaty systems and their secretariats, those who conduct research or otherwise take part in activities in the region in question are not usually government employees. In Antarctica, for example, university professors, engineers, and other private professionals—supported by a combination of private and government funding—operate research stations.

Michael Auerbach
Marblehead, Massachusetts

Example

Antarctic Treaty System

Bibliography

"Antarctic." *Ocean and Polar Affairs.* US Department of State, 22 Mar. 2007. Web. 8 Feb. 2013.

"About Us." *Antarctic Treaty System.* Secretariat of the Antarctic Treaty, n.d. Web. 8 Feb. 2013.

"United Nations Treaty Series." *United Nations Treaty Collection.* United Nations, 2013. Web. 8 Feb. 2013.

"Educational Opportunities and Resources." *United States Antarctic Program.* National Science Foundation, 2013. Web. 8 Feb. 2013.

Appendix Two: World Religions

African Religious Traditions

General Description

The religious traditions of Africa can be studied both religiously and ethnographically. Animism, or the belief that everything has a soul, is practiced in most tribal societies, including the Dogon (people of the cliffs), an ethnic group living primarily in Mali's central plateau region and in Burkina Faso. Many traditional faiths have extensive mythologies, rites, and histories, such as the Yoruba religion practiced by the Yoruba, an ethnic group of West Africa. In South Africa, the traditional religion of the Zulu people is based on a creator god, ancestor worship, and the existence of sorcerers and witches. Lastly, the Ethiopian or Abyssinian Church (formally the Ethiopian Orthodox Union Church) is a branch of Christianity unique to the east African nations of Ethiopia and Eritrea.

Number of Adherents Worldwide

Some 63 million Africans adhere to traditional religions such as animism. One of the largest groups practicing animism is the Dogon, who number about six hundred thousand. However, it is impossible to know how many practice traditional religion. In fact, many people practice animism alongside other religions, particularly Islam. Other religions have spread their adherence and influence through the African diaspora. In Africa, the Yoruba number between thirty-five and forty million and are located primarily in Benin, Togo and southwest Nigeria. The Zulu, the largest ethnic group in South Africa, total over eleven million. Like Islam, Christianity has affected the number of people who still hold traditional beliefs, making accurate predictions virtually impossible. The Ethiopian or Abyssinian Church has over thirty-nine million adherents in Ethiopia alone.

Basic Tenets

Animism holds that many spiritual beings have the power to help or hurt humans. The traditional faith is thus more concerned with appropriate rituals rather than worship of a deity, and focuses on day-to-day practicalities such as food, water supplies, and disease. Ancestors, particularly those most recently dead, are invoked for their aid. Those who practice animism believe in life after death; some adherents may attempt to contact the spirits of the dead. Animists acknowledge the existence of tribal gods. (However, African people traditionally do not make images of God, who is thought of as Spirit.)

The Dogon divide into two caste-like groups: the inneomo (pure) and innepuru (impure). The hogon leads the inneomo, who may not sacrifice animals and whose leaders are forbidden to hunt. The inneomo also cannot prepare or bury the dead. While the innepuru can do all of the above tasks, they cannot take part in the rituals for agricultural fertility. Selected young males called the olubaru lead the innepuru. The status of "pure" or "impure" is inherited. The Dogon have many gods. The chief god is called Amma, a creator god who is responsible for creating other gods and the earth.

The Dogon have a three-part concept of death. First the soul is sent to the realm of the dead to join the ancestors. Rites are then performed to remove any ritual polluting. Finally, when several members of the village have died, a rite known as dama occurs. In the ritual, a sacrifice is made to the Great Mask (which depicts a large wooden serpent and which is never actually worn) and dancers perform on the housetops where someone has died to scare off any lingering souls. Often, figures of Nommo (a worshipped ancestral spirit) are put near funeral pottery on the family shrine.

The Yoruba believe in predestination. Before birth, the ori (soul) kneels before Olorun, the wisest and most powerful deity, and selects a destiny. Rituals may assist the person in achieving his or her destiny, but it cannot be altered. The Yoruba, therefore, acknowledge a need for ritual and sacrifice, properly done according to the oracles.

Among the Yoruba, the shaman is known as the babalawo. He or she is able to communicate with ancestors, spirits and deities. Training for this work, which may include responsibility as a doctor, often requires three years. The shaman is consulted before major life decisions. During these consultations, the shaman dictates the right rituals and sacrifices, and to which gods they are to be offered for maximum benefit. In addition, the Yoruba poetry covers right conduct. Good character is at the heart of Yoruba ethics.

The Yoruba are polytheistic. The major god is Olorun, the sky god, considered all-powerful and holy, and a father to 401 children, also gods. He gave the task of creating human beings to the deity Obatala (though Olorun breathed life into them). Olorun also determines the destiny of each person. Onlie, the Great Mother Goddess, is in some ways the opposite of Olorun. Olorun is the one who judges a soul following death. For example, if the soul is accounted worthy, it will be reincarnated, while the unworthy go to the place of punishment. Ogun, the god of hunters, iron, and war, is another important god. He is also the patron of blacksmiths. The Yoruba have some 1,700 gods, collectively known as the Orisa.

The Yoruba believe in an afterlife. There are two heavens: one is a hot, dry place with pot-sherds, reserved for those who have done evil, while the other is a pleasant heaven for persons who have led a good life. There the ori (soul) may choose to "turn to be a child" on the earth once more.

In the Zulu tradition, the king was responsible for rainmaking and magic for the benefit of the nation. Rainmakers were also known as "shepherds of heaven." They performed rites during times of famine, drought or war, as well as during planting season, invoking royal ancestors for aid. Storms were considered a manifestation of God.

The Zulu are also polytheistic. They refer to a wise creator god who lives in heaven. This Supreme Being has complete control of everything in the universe, and is known as Unkulunkulu, the Great Oldest One. The Queen of heaven is a virgin who taught women useful arts; light surrounds her, and her glory is seen in rain, mist, and rainbows.

The Ethiopian Church incorporates not only Orthodox Christian beliefs, but also aspects of Judaism. The adherents distinguish between clean and unclean meats, practice circumcision, and observe the seventh-day Sabbath. The Ethiopian (or Abyssinian) Church is monotheistic and believes in the Christian God.

Sacred Text

Traditional religions such as animism generally have no written sacred texts. Instead, creation stories and other tales are passed down orally. The Yoruba do have some sacred poetry, in 256 chapters, known as odus. The text covers both right action in worship and ethical conduct. The Ethiopian Church has scriptures written in the ancient Ge'ez language, which is no longer used, except in church liturgy.

Major Figures

A spiritual leader, or hogon, oversees each district among the Dogon. There is a supreme hogon for the entire country. Among the Yoruba, the king, or oba, rules each town. He is also considered sacred and is responsible for performing rituals. Isaiah Shembe is a prophet or messiah among the Zulu. He founded the Nazareth Baptist Church (also called the amaNazaretha Church or Shembe Church), an independent Zulu Christian denomination. His son, Johannes Shembe, took the title Shembe II. In the Ethiopian Church, now fully independent, the head of the church is the Patriarch. Saint Frumentius, the first bishop of Axum in northern Ethiopia, is credited with beginning the Christian tradition during the fourth century. King Lalibela, noted for authorizing construction of monolithic churches carved underground, was a major figure in the twelfth century.

Major Holy Sites

Every spot in nature is sacred in animistic thinking. There is no division between sacred and profane—all of life is sacred, and Earth is Mother. Sky and mountains are often regarded as sacred space.

For the Yoruba of West Africa, Osogbo in Nigeria is a forest shrine. The main goddess is Oshun, goddess of the river. Until she arrived, the work done by male gods was not succeeding. People seeking to be protected from illness and women wishing to become pregnant seek Osun's help. Ilé-Ifè, an ancient Yoruba city in Nigeria, is another important site, and considered the spiritual hub of the Yoruba. According to the Yoruba creation myth, Olorun, god of the sky, set down Odudua, the founder of the Yoruba, in Ilé-Ifè. Shrines within the city include one to Ogun. The shrine is made of stones and wooden stumps.

Mount Nhlangakazi (Holy Mountain) is considered sacred to the Zulu Nazareth Baptist Church (amaNazaretha). There Isaiah Shembe built a High Place to serve as his headquarters. It is a twice-yearly site of pilgrimage for amaNazarites.

Sacred sites of the Ethiopian Church include the Church of St. Mary of Zion in Axum, considered the most sacred Ethiopian shrine. According to legend, the church stands adjacent to a guarded chapel which purportedly houses the Ark of the Covenant, a powerful biblical relic. The Ethiopian Church also considers sacred the eleven monolithic (rock-hewn) churches, still places of pilgrimage and devotion, that were recognized as a collective World Heritage Site by the United Nations Educational, Scientific and Cultural Organization.

Major Rites & Celebrations

Most African religions involve some sacrifice to appease or please the gods. Among the Yoruba, for example, dogs, which are helpful in both hunting and war, are sacrificed to Ogun. In many tribes, including the Yoruba, rites of passage for youth exist. The typical pattern is three-fold: removal from the tribe, instruction, and return to the tribe ready to assume adult responsibilities. In this initiation, the person may be marked bodily through scarification or circumcision. The Yoruba also have a yearly festival re-enacting

the story of Obatala and Oduduwa (generally perceived as the ancestor of the Yorubas). A second festival, which resembles a passion play, re-enacts the conflict between the grandsons of these two legendary figures. A third festival celebrates the heroine Moremi, who led the Yoruba to victory over the enemy Igbo, an ethnicity from southeastern Nigeria, and who ultimately reconciled the two tribes.

Yoruba death rites include a masked dancer who comes to the family following a death, assuring them of the ancestor's ongoing care for the family. If the person was important in the village, a mask will be carved and named for them. In yearly festivals, the deceased individual will then appear with other ancestors.

Masks are also used in a Dogon funeral ritual, the dama ceremony, which is led by the Awa, a secret society comprised of all adult Dogon males of the innepuru group. During ceremonial times, the hogon relinquishes control and the Awa control the community. At the end of the mourning period the dama ceremony begins when the Awa leave the village and return with both the front and back of their heads masked. Through rituals and dances, they lead the spirit of the deceased to the next world. Control of the village reverts to the hogon at that point. The Wagem rites govern contact with the ancestors. Following the dama ceremony, the eldest male descendant, called the ginna bana, adds a vessel to the family shrine in the name of the deceased. The spirit of the ancestor is persuaded to return to the descendents through magic and sacrificial offerings, creating a link from the living to the first ancestors.

Ethiopian Christians observe and mark most typical Christian rites, though some occur on different dates because of the difference in the Ethiopian and Western calendars. For example, Christmas in Ethiopia is celebrated on January 7.

ORIGINS

History & Geography

The Dogon live along the Bandiagara Cliffs, a rocky and mountainous region. (The Cliffs of Bandiagara, also called the Bandiagara Escarpment, were recognized as a UNESCO World Heritage Site due to the cultural landscape, including the ancient traditions of the Dogon and their architecture.) This area is south of the Sahara in a region called the Sahel, another region prone to drought (though not a desert). The population of the villages in the region is typically a thousand people or less. The cliffs of the Bandiagara have kept the Dogon separate from other people.

Myths of origin regarding the Dogon differ. One suggestion is that the Dogon came from Egypt, and then lived in Libya before entering the the region of what is now Burkina Faso, Mauritania, or Guinea. Near the close of the fifteenth century, they arrived in Mali.

Among the Yoruba, multiple myths regarding their origin exist. One traces their beginnings to Uruk in Mesopotamia or to Babylon, the site of present-day Iraq. Another story has the Yoruba in West Africa by 10,000 BCE.

After the death of the Zulu messiah Isaiah Shembe in 1935, his son Johannes became the leader of the Nazareth Baptist Church. He lacked the charisma of his father, but did hold the church together. His brother, Amos, became regent in 1976 when Johannes died. Johannes's son Londa split the church in 1979 when Amos refused to give up power. Tangled in South African politics, Londa was killed in 1989.

The Ethiopian Orthodox Church is the nation's official church. A legend states that Menelik, supposed to have been the son of the Queen of Sheba and King Solomon, founded the royal line. When Jesuits arrived in the seventeenth century, they failed to change the church, and the nation closed to missionary efforts for several hundred years. By retaining independence theologically and not being conquered politically, Ethiopia is sometimes considered a model for the new religious movements in Africa.

Founder or Major Prophet
The origins of most African traditional religions or faiths are accounted for through the actions of deities in creation stories rather than a particular founder. One exception, however, is Isaiah Shembe, who founded the Nazareth Baptist Church, also known as the Shembe Church or amaNazarite Church, in 1910 after receiving a number of revelations during a thunderstorm. Shembe was an itinerant Zulu preacher and healer. Through his influence and leadership, amaNazarites follow more Old Testament regulations than most Christians, including celebrating the Sabbath on Saturday rather than Sunday. They also refer to God as Jehovah, the Hebrew name for God. Shembe was regarded as the new Jesus Christ for his people, adapting Christianity to Zulu practice. He adopted the title Nkosi, which means king or chief.

The Ethiopian Orthodox church was founded, according to legend, by preaching from one of two New Testament figures—the disciple Matthew or the unnamed eunuch mentioned in Acts 8. According to historical evidence, the church began when Frumentius arrived at the royal court. Athanasius of Alexandria later consecrated Frumentius as patriarch of the church, linking it to the Christian church in Egypt.

Creation Stories
The Dogon believe that Amma, the sky god, was also the creator of the universe. Amma created two sets of twins, male and female. One of the males rebelled. To restore order, Amma sacrificed the other male, Nommo, strangling and scattering him to the four directions, then restoring him to life after five days. Nommo then became ruler of the universe and the children of his spirits became the Dogon. Thus the world continually moves between chaos and order, and the task of the Dogon is to keep the world in balance through rituals. In a five-year cycle, the aspects of this creation myth are re-enacted at altars throughout the Dogon land.

According to the Yoruba, after one botched attempt at creating the world, Olorun sent his son Obatala to create earth upon the waters. Obatala tossed some soil on the water and released a five-toed hen to spread it out. Next, Olorun told Obatala to make people from clay. Obatala grew bored with the work and drank too much wine. Thereafter, the people he made were misshapen or defective (handicapped). In anger, Olorun relieved him of the job and gave it to Odudua to complete. It was Odudua who made the Yoruba and founded a kingdom at Ilé-Ifè.

The word *Zulu* means "heaven or sky." The Zulu people believe they originated in heaven. They also believe in phansi, the place where spirits live and which is below the earth's surface.

Holy Places

Osun-Osogbo is a forest shrine in Nigeria dedicated to the Yoruba river goddess, Osun. It may be the last such sacred grove remaining among the Yoruba. Shrines, art, sculpture, and sanctuaries are part of the grove, which became a UNESCO World Heritage site in 2005.

Ilé-Ifè, regarded as the equivalent of Eden, is thought to be the site where the first Yoruba was placed. It was probably named for Ifa, the god associated with divination. The palace (Afin) of the spiritual head of the Yoruba, the oni, is located there. The oni has the responsibility to care for the staff of Oranmiyan, a Benin king. The staff, which is eighteen feet tall, is made of granite and shaped like an elephant's tusk.

Axum, the seat of the Ethiopian Christian Church, is a sacred site. The eleven rock-hewn churches of King Lalibela, especially that of Saint George, are a pilgrimage site. According to tradition, angels helped to carve the churches. More than 50,000 pilgrims come to the town of Lalibela at Christmas. After the Muslims captured Jerusalem in 1187, King Lalibela proclaimed his city the "New Jerusalem" because Christians could no longer go on pilgrimage to the Holy Land.

AFRICAN RELIGIONS IN DEPTH

Sacred Symbols

Because all of life is infused with religious meaning, any object or location may be considered or become sacred in traditional African religions. Masks, in particular, have special meaning and may be worn during ceremonies. The mask often represents a god, whose power is passed to the one wearing the mask.

Sacred Practices & Gestures

The Yoruba practice divination in a form that is originally Arabic. There are sixteen basic figures—combined, they deliver a prophecy that the diviner is not to interpret. Instead, he or she recites verses from a classic source. Images may be made to prevent or cure illness. For example, the Yoruba have a smallpox spirit god that can be prayed to for healing. Daily prayer, both morning and evening, is part of life for most Yoruba.

In the amaNazarite Church, which Zulu Isaiah Shembe founded, singing is a key part of the faith. Shembe himself was a gifted composer of hymns. This sacred music was combined with dancing, during which the Zulu wear their traditional dress.

Rites, Celebrations & Services

The Dogon have three major cults. The Awa are associated with dances, featuring ornately carved masks, at funerals and on the anniversaries of deaths. The cult of the Earth god, Lebe, concerns itself with the agricultural cycles and fertility of the land; the hogon of the village guards the soil's purity and presides at ceremonies related to farming. The third cult, the Binu, is involved with communication with spirits, ancestor worship, and sacrifices. Binu shrines are in many locations. The Binu priest makes sacrifices of porridge made from millet and blood at planting time and also when the help of an ancestor is needed. Each clan within the Dogon community has a totem animal spirit—an ancestor spirit wishing to communicate with descendents may do so by taking the form of the animal.

The Dogon also have a celebration every fifty years at the appearing of the star Sirius B between two mountains. (Sirius is often the brightest star in the nighttime sky.) Young males leaving for three months prior to the sigui, as it is called, for a time of seclusion and speaking in private language. This celebration is rooted in the Dogon belief that amphibious creatures, the Nommo, visited their land about three thousand years ago.

The Yoruba offer Esu, the trickster god, palm wine and animal sacrifices. Because he is a trickster, he is considered a cheater, and being on his good side is important. The priests in Yoruba traditional religion are responsible for installing tribal chiefs and kings.

Among the Zulu, families determine the lobola, or bride price. They believe that a groom will respect his wife more if he must pay for her. Further gifts are then exchanged, and the bride's family traditionally gives the groom a goat or sheep to signify their acceptance of him. The groom's family provides meat for the wedding feast, slaughtering a cow on the morning of the wedding. The families assemble in a circle and the men, in costume, dance. The bride gives presents, usually mats or blankets, to members of her new family, who dance or sing their thanks. The final gift, to the groom, is a blanket, which is tossed over his head. Friends of the bride playfully beat him, demonstrating how they will respond if he mistreats his new wife. After the two families eat together, the couple is considered one.

In the traditional Zulu religion, ancestors three generations back are regarded as not yet settled in the afterlife. To help them settle, offerings of goats or other animals are made and rituals to help them settle into the community of ancestors are performed.

Christmas is a major celebration in Ethiopian Christianity. Priests rattle an instrument derived from biblical times, called the sistra, and chant to begin the mass. The festivities include drumming and a dance known as King David's dance.

Judy A. Johnson, MTS

Bibliography

A, Oladosu Olusegun. "Ethics and Judgement: A Panacea for Human Transformation in Yoruba Multireligious Society." *Asia Journal of Theology* 26.1 (2012): 88–104. Print.

Barnes, Trevor. *The Kingfisher Book of Religions.* New York: Kingfisher, 1999. Print.

Dawson, Allan Charles, ed. *Shrines in Africa: history, politics, and society.* Calgary: U of Calgary P, 2009. Print.

Doumbia, Adama, and Naomi Doumbia. *The Way of the Elders: West African Spirituality.* St. Paul: Llewellyn, 2004. Print.

Douny, Laurence. "The Role of Earth Shrines in the Socio-Symbolic Construction of the Dogon Territory: Towards a Philosophy of Containment." *Anthropology & Medicine* 18.2 (2011): 167–79. Print.

Friedenthal, Lora, and Dorothy Kavanaugh. *Religions of Africa.* Philadelphia: Mason Crest, 2007. Print.

Hayes, Stephen. "Orthodox Ecclesiology in Africa: A Study of the 'Ethiopian' Churches of South Africa." *International Journal for the Study of the Christian Church* 8.4 (2008): 337–54. Print.

Lugira, Aloysius M. *African Religion.* New York: Facts on File, 2004. Print.

Mbiti, John S. *African Religions and Philosophy.* 2nd ed. Oxford: Heinemann, 1991. Print.

Monteiro Ferreira, Ana Maria. "Reevaluating Zulu Religion." *Journal of Black Studies* 35.3 (2005): 347–63. Print.

Peel, J. D. Y. "Yoruba Religion as a Global Phenomenon." *Journal of African History* 5.1 (2010): 107–8. Print.

Ray, Benjamin C. *African Religions.* 2nd ed. Upper Saddle River: Prentice, 2000. Print.

Thomas, Douglas E. *African Traditional Religion in the Modern World.* Jefferson: McFarland, 2005. Print.

Bahá'í Faith

General Description

The Bahá'í faith is the youngest of the world's religions. It began in the mid-nineteenth century, offering scholars the opportunity to observe a religion in the making. While some of the acts of religious founders such as Buddha or Jesus cannot be substantiated, the modern founders of Bahá'í were more contemporary figures.

Number of Adherents Worldwide

An estimated 5 to 7 million people follow the Bahá'í faith. Although strong in Middle Eastern nations such as Iran, where the faith originated, Bahá'í has reached people in many countries, particularly the United States and Canada.

Basic Tenets

The Bahá'í faith has three major doctrines. The first doctrine is that there is one transcendent God, and all religions worship that God, regardless of the name given to the deity. Adherents believe that religious figures such as Jesus Christ, the Buddha, and the Prophet Muhammad were different revelations of God unique to their time and place. The second doctrine is that there is only one religion, though each world faith is valid and was founded by a ""manifestation of God" who is part of a divine plan for educating humanity. The third doctrine is a belief in the unity of all humankind. In light of this underlying unity, those of the Bahá'í faith work for social justice. They believe that seeking consensus among various groups diffuses typical power struggles and to this end, they employ a method called consultation, which is a nonadversarial decision-making process.

The Bahá'í believe that the human soul is immortal, and that after death the soul moves nearer or farther away from God. The idea of an afterlife comprised of a literal "heaven" or "hell" is not part of the faith.

Sacred Text

The Most Holy Book, or the Tablets, written by Baha'u'llah, form the basis of Bahá'í teachings. Though not considered binding, scriptures from other faiths are regarded as "Divine Revelation."

Major Figures

The Bab (The Gate of God) Siyyad 'Ali Mohammad (1819–50), founder of the Bábí movement that broke from Islam, spoke of a coming new messenger of God. Mirza Hoseyn 'Ali Nuri (1817–92), who realized that he was that prophet, was given the title Baha'u'llah (Glory of God). From a member of Persia's landed gentry, he was part of the ruling class, and is considered the founder of the Bahá'í faith. His son, 'Abdu'l-Bahá (Servant of the Glory of God), who lived from 1844 until 1921, became the leader of the group after his father's death in 1892. The oldest son of his eldest daughter, Shogi Effendi Rabbani (1899–1957), oversaw a rapid expansion, visiting Egypt, America, and nations in Europe. Tahirih (the Pure One) was a woman poet who challenged stereotypes by appearing unveiled at meetings.

Major Holy Sites

The Bahá'í World Center is located near Haifa, Israel. The burial shrine of the Bab, a pilgrimage site, is there. The Shrine of Baha'u'llah near Acre, Israel, is another pilgrimage site. The American headquarters are in Wilmette, Illinois. Carmel in Israel is regarded as the world center of the faith.

Major Rites & Celebrations

Each year, the Bahá'í celebrate Ridvan Festival, a twelve-day feast from sunset on April 20 to sunset on May 2. The festival marks Baha'u'llah's declaration of prophethood, as prophesized by the Bab, at a Baghdad garden. (Ridvan means Paradise.) The holy days within that feast are the first (Baha'u'llah's garden arrival), ninth (the arrival of his family), and twelfth (his departure from Ridvan Garden)—on these days, the Bahá'í do not work. During this feast, people attend social events and meet for devotions. Baha'u'llah referred to it as the King of Festivals and Most Great Festival. The Bahá'í celebrate several other events, including World Religion Day and Race Unity Day, both founded by Bahá'í, as well as days connected with significant events in the life of the founder. Elections to the Spiritual Assemblies, and the national and local administrations; international elections are held every five years.

ORIGINS

History & Geography

Siyyad 'Ali Muhammad was born into a merchant family of Shiraz in 1819. Both his parents were descendents of the Prophet Muhammad, Islam's central figure. Like the Prophet, the man who became the Bab lost his father at an early age and was raised by an uncle. A devout child, he entered his uncle's business by age fifteen. After visiting Muslim holy cities, he returned to Shiraz, where he married a distant relative named Khadijih.

While on pilgrimage in 1844 to the black stone of Ka'bah, a sacred site in Islam, the Bab stood with his hand on that holy object and declared that he was the prophet for whom they had been waiting. The Sunni did not give credence to these claims. The Bab went to Persia, where the Shia sect was the majority. However, because Muhammad had been regarded as the "Seal of the Prophets," and the one who spoke the final revelation, Shia clergy viewed his claims as threatening. As such, nothing further would be revealed until the Day of Judgment. The authority of the clergy was in danger from this new movement.

The Bab was placed under house arrest, and then confined to a fortress on the Russian frontier. That move to a more remote area only increased the number of converts, as did a subsequent move to another Kurdish fortress. He

was eventually taken to Tabriz in Iran and tried before the Muslim clergy in 1848. Condemned, he was caned on the soles of his feet and treated by a British doctor who was impressed by him.

Despite his treatment and the persecution of his followers—many of the Bab's eighteen disciples, termed the "Letters of the Living," were persistently tortured and executed—the Bab refused to articulate a doctrine of jihad. The Babis could defend themselves, but were forbidden to use holy war as a means of religious conquest. In three major confrontations sparked by the Shia clergy, Babis were defeated. The Bab was sentenced as a heretic and shot by a firing squad in 1850. Lacking leadership and grief-stricken, in 1852 two young Babis fired on the shah in 1852, unleashing greater persecutions and cruelty against those of the Bahá'í faith.

A follower of the Bab, Mirza Hoseyn 'Ali Nuri, announced in 1863 that he was the one who was to come (the twelfth imam of Islam), the "Glory of God," or Baha'u'llah. Considered the founder of the Bahá'í Faith, he was a tireless writer who anointed his son, 'Abdu'l-Bahá, as the next leader. Despite deprivations and imprisonments, Baha'u'llah lived to be seventy-five years old, relinquishing control of the organization to 'Abdu'l-Bahá before the time of his death.

'Abdu'l-Bahá, whom his father had called "the Master," expanded the faith to the nations of Europe and North America. In 1893, at the Parliament of Religions at the Chicago World's Fair, the faith was first mentioned in the United States. Within a few years, communities of faith were established in Chicago and Wisconsin. In 1911, 'Abdu'l-Bahá began a twenty-eight month tour of Europe and North America to promote the Bahá'í faith. Administratively, he established the spiritual assemblies that were the forerunner of the Houses of Justice that his father had envisioned.

During World War I, 'Abdu'l-Bahá engaged in humanitarian work among the Palestinians in the Holy Land, where he lived. In recognition of his efforts, he was granted knighthood by the British government. Thousands of people, including many political and religious dignitaries, attended his funeral in 1921.

'Abdu'l-Bahá conferred the role of Guardian, or sole interpreter of Bahá'í teaching, to his eldest grandson, Shoghi Effendi Rabbani. To him, all questions regarding the faith were to be addressed. Shoghi Effendi Rabbani was a descendent of Baha'u'llah through both parents. He headed the Bahá'í faith from 1921 to 1963, achieving four major projects: he oversaw the physical development of the World Centre and expanded the administrative order; he carried out the plan his father had set in motion; and he provided for the translating and interpreting of Bahá'í teachings, as the writings of both the Bab and those of Baha'u'llah and 'Abdu'l-Bahá have been translated and published in more than eight hundred languages.

Beginning in 1937, Shoghi Effendi Rabbani began a series of specific plans with goals tied to deadlines. In 1953, during the second seven-year plan, the house of worship in Wilmette, Illinois, was completed and dedicated.

Although the beliefs originated in Shi'ite Islam, the Bahá'í Faith has been declared a new religion without connections to Islam. To followers of Islam, it is a heretical sect. During the reign of the Ayatollah Khomeini, a time when Iran was especially noted as intolerant of diverse views, the Bahá'í faced widespread persecution.

Founder or Major Prophet

Mirza Husayn Ali Nuri, known as Baha'u'llah, was born into privilege in 1817 in what was then Persia, now present-day Iran. At twenty-two, he declined a government post offered at his father's death. Although a member of a politically prestigious family, he did not follow the career path of several generations of his ancestors. Instead, he managed the family estates and devoted himself to charities, earning the title "Father of the Poor."

At twenty-seven, he followed the Babis's movement within Shia Islam, corresponding with the Bab and traveling to further the faith. He also provided financial support. In 1848, he organized and helped to direct a conference that explained the Bab's teaching. At the conference, he gave

symbolic names to the eighty-one followers who had attended, based on the spiritual qualities he had observed.

Although he managed to escape death during the persecutions before and after the Bab's death, a fact largely attributed to his upbringing, Baha'u'llah was imprisoned several times. During a four-month stay in an underground dungeon in Tehran, he realized from a dream that he was the one of whom the Bab had prophesied. After being released, he was banished from Persia and had his property confiscated by the shah. He went to Baghdad, refusing the offer of refuge that had come from Russia. Over the following three years a small band of followers joined him, including members of his family. When his younger brother attempted to take over the leadership of the Babis, Baha'u'llah spent two years in a self-imposed exile in the Kurdistan wilderness. In 1856, with the community near anarchy as a result of his brother's failure of leadership, Baha'u'llah returned to the community and restored its position over the next seven years.

Concerned by the growing popularity of the new faith, the shah demanded that the Babis move further away from Persia. They went to Constantinople where, in 1863, Baha'u'llah revealed to the whole group that he was "He Whom God Will Make Manifest." From there the Bahá'í were sent to Adrianople in Turkey, and at last, in 1868, to the town of Acre in the Holy Land. Baha'u'llah was imprisoned in Acre and survived severe prison conditions. In 1877, he moved from prison to a country estate, then to a mansion. He died in 1892 after a fever.

Philosophical Basis

The thinking of Shia Muslims contributed to the development of Bahá'í. The writings incorporate language and concepts from the Qur'an (Islam's holy book). Like Muslims, the Bahá'í believe that God is one. God sends messengers, the Manifestations of God, to instruct people and benefit society. These have included Jesus Christ, the Buddha, the Prophet Muhammad, Krishna, and the Bab. Bahá'í also goes further than Islam in accepting all religions—not just Judaism, Christianity, and Islam—as being part of a divinely inspired plan.

Shia Muslims believe that Muhammad's descendents should lead the faithful community. The leaders, known as imams, were considered infallible. The Sunni Muslims believed that following the way (sunna) of Muhammad was sufficient qualification for leadership. Sunni dynasties regarded the imams as a threat and executed them, starting with two of Muhammad's grandsons, who became Shia martyrs.

In Persia, a state with a long tradition of divinely appointed rulers, the Shia sect was strong. When the Safavids, a Shia dynasty, came to power in the sixteenth century, the custom of the imamate was victorious. One tradition states that in 873, the last appointed imam, who was still a child, went into hiding to avoid being killed. For the following sixty-nine years, this twelfth imam communicated through his deputies to the faithful. Each of the deputies was called bab, or gate, because they led to the "Hidden Imam." Four babs existed through 941, and the last one died without naming the next bab. The Hidden Imam is thought to emerge at the end of time to bring in a worldwide reign of justice. From this tradition came the expectation of a Mahdi (Guided One) to lead the people.

During the early nineteenth century, many followers of both the Christian and Islamic faiths expected their respective messiahs to return. Shia teachers believed that the return of the Mahdi imam was near. In 1843, one teacher, Siyyid Kázim, noted that the Hidden Imam had disappeared one thousand lunar years earlier. He urged the faithful to look for the Mahdi imam.

The following year in Shiraz, Siyyad 'Ali Mohammad announced that he was the Mahdi. (Siyyad is a term meaning descended from Muhammad.) He referred to himself as the Bab, though he expanded the term's meaning. Eighteen men, impressed with his ability to expound the Qur'an, believed him. They became the Letters of the Living, and were sent throughout Persia (present-day Iran) to announce the dawning of the Day of God.

In 1853, Mirza Husayn Ali Nuri experienced a revelation that he was "He Whom God Shall Make Manifest," the one of whom the Bab prophesied. Accepted as such, he began writing the words that became the Bahá'í scriptures. Much of what is known of the early days of the faith comes from a Cambridge academic, Edward Granville Browne, who first visited Baha'u'llah in the 1890. Browne wrote of his meeting, introducing this faith to the West.

The emphasis of the Bahá'í faith is on personal development and the breaking down of barriers between people. Service to humanity is important and encouraged. Marriage, with a belief in the equality of both men and women, is also encouraged. Consent of both sets of parents is required prior to marrying.

Holy Places

The shrine of the Bab near Haifa and that of Baha'u'llah near Acre, in Israel, are the two most revered sites for those of the Bahá'í faith. In 2008, the United Nations Educational, Scientific, and Cultural Organization (UNESCO) recognized both as World Heritage Sites. They are the first such sites from a modern religious tradition to be added to the list of sites. Both sites are appreciated for the formal gardens surrounding them that blend design elements from different cultures. For the Bahá'í, Baha'u'llah's shrine is the focus of prayer, comparable to the significance given to the Ka'bah in Mecca for Muslims or to the Western Wall for Jews.

As of 2013, there are seven Bahá'í temples in the world; an eighth temple is under construction in Chile. All temples are built with a center dome and nine sides, symbolizing both diversity and world unity. The North American temple is located in Wilmette, Illinois. There, daily prayer services take place as well as a Sunday service.

THE BAHÁ'Í FAITH IN DEPTH

Governance

Elected members of lay councils at international, national, and local levels administer the work of the faith. The Universal House of Justice in Haifa, Israel, is the location of the international nine-member body. Elections for all of these lay councils are by secret ballot, and do not include nominating, candidates, or campaigns. Those twenty-one and older are permitted to vote. The councils make decisions according to a process of collective decision-making called consultation. They strive to serve as a model for governing a united global society.

Personal Conduct

In addition to private prayer and acts of social justice, those of the Bahá'í faith are encouraged to have a profession, craft, or trade. They are also asked to shun and refrain from slander and partisan politics. Homosexuality and sexual activity outside marriage are forbidden, as is gambling.

The Bahá'í faith does not have professional clergy, nor does it engage in missionary work. However, Bahá'í may share their faith with others and may move to another country as a "pioneer." Pioneers are unlike traditional missionaries, and are expected to support themselves through a career and as a member of the community.

Avenues of Service

Those of the Bahá'í Faith place a high value on service to humanity, considering it an act of worship. This can be done through caring for one's own family or through one's choice of vocation. Within the local community, people may teach classes for children, mentor youth groups, host devotional programs, or teach adult study circles. Many are engaged in economic or social development programs as well. Although not mandated, a year or two of service is often undertaken following high school or during college.

United Nations Involvement

Beginning in 1947, just one year after the United Nations (UN) first met, the Bahá'í Faith was represented at that body. In 1948, the Bahá'í International Community was accredited by the UN as an international nongovernmental organization (NGO). In 1970, the faith received special consultative status with the UN Economic and Social Council (ECOSOC). Following World War I, a Bahá'í office opened in Geneva, Switzerland, where the League of Nations was headquartered. Thus the Bahá'í Faith has a long tradition of supporting global institutions.

Money Matters

The International Bahá'í Fund exists to develop and support the growth of the faith, and the Universal House of Justice oversees the distribution of the money. Contributions are also used to maintain the Bahá'í World Center. No money is accepted from non-Bahá'í sources. National and local funds, administered by National or Local Spiritual Assemblies, are used in supporting service projects, publishing endeavors, schools, and Bahá'í centers. For the Bahá'í, the size of the donation is less important than regular contributions and the spirit of sacrifice behind them.

Food Restrictions

Bahá'í between fifteen and seventy years of age **fast** nineteen days a year, abstaining from food and drink from sunrise to sunset. Fasting occurs the first day of each month of the Bahá'í calendar, which divides the year into nineteen months of nineteen days each. The Bahá'í faithful do not drink alcohol or use narcotics, because these will deaden the mind with repeated use.

Rites, Celebrations & Services

Daily prayer and meditation is recommended in the Bahá'í faith. During services there are mediations and prayers, along with the reading of Bahá'í scriptures and other world faith traditions. There is no set ritual, no offerings, and no sermons. Unaccompanied by musical instruments, choirs also sing. Light refreshments may be served afterwards.

Bahá'í place great stress on marriage, the only state in which sex is permitted. Referred to as "a fortress for well-being and salvation," a monogamous, heterosexual marriage is the ideal. To express the oneness of humanity, interracial marriages are encouraged. After obtaining the consent of their parents, the couple takes the following vow: "We will all, verily, abide by the will of God." The remainder of the service may be individually crafted and may also include dance, music, feasting, and ceremony. Should a couple choose to end a marriage, they must first complete a year of living apart while trying to reconcile differences. Divorce is discouraged, but permitted after that initial year.

Judy A. Johnson, MTS

Bibliography

Albertson, Lorelei. *All about Bahá'í Faith*. University Pub., 2012. E-book.

Bowers, Kenneth E. *God Speaks Again: an Introduction to the Bahá'í Faith*. Wilmette: Bahá'í, 2004. Print.

Buck, Christopher. "The Interracial 'Bahá'í Movement' and the Black Intelligentsia: The Case of W. E. B. Du Bois." *Journal of Religious History* 36.4 (2012): 542–62. Print.

Cederquist, Druzelle. *The Story of Baha'u'llah*. Wilmette: Bahá'í, 2005. Print.

Echevarria, L. *Life Stories of Bahá'í Women in Canada: Constructing Religious Identity in the Twentieth Century*. Lang, 2011. E-book.

Garlington, William. *The Bahá'í Faith in America*. Lanham: Rowman, 2008. Print.

Hartz, Paula R. *Bahá'í Faith*. New York: Facts on File, 2006. Print.

Hatcher, William S. and J. Douglas Martin. *The Bahá'í Faith: The Emerging Global Religion*. Wilmette: Bahá'í, 2002. Print.

Karlberg, Michael. "Constructive Resilience: The Bahá'í Response to Oppression." *Peace & Change* 35.2 (2010): 222–57. Print.

Lee, Anthony A. *The Bahá'í Faith in Africa: Establishing a New Religious Movement, 1952–1962*. Brill NV, E-book.

Momen, Moojan. "Bahá'í Religious History." *Journal of Religious History* 36.4 (2012): 463–70. Print.

Momen, Moojan. *The Bahá'í Faith: A Beginner's Guide*. Oxford: Oneworld, 2007. Print.

Smith, Peter. *The Bahá'í Faith*. Cambridge: Cambridge UP, 2008. Print.

Wilkinson, Philip. *Religions*. New York: DK, 2008. Print.

Buddhism

General Description

Buddhism has three main branches: Theravada (Way of the Elders), also referred to as Hinayana (Lesser Vehicle); Mahayana (Greater Vehicle); and Vajrayana (Diamond Vehicle), also referred to as Tantric Buddhism. Vajrayana is sometimes thought of as an extension of Mahayana Buddhism. These can be further divided into many sects and schools, many of which are geographically based. In Buddhism, these different divisions or schools are regarded as alternative paths to enlightenment (Wilkinson 2008).

Number of Adherents Worldwide

An estimated 474 million people around the world are Buddhists. Of the major sects, Theravada Buddhism is the oldest, developed in the sixth century BCE. Its adherents include those of the Theravada Forest Tradition. From Mahayana Buddhism, which developed in the third to second centuries BCE, came several offshoots based on location. In what is now China, Pure Land Buddhism and Tibetan Buddhism developed in the seventh century. In Japan, Zen Buddhism developed in the twelfth century, Nichiren Buddhism developed a century later, and Soka Gakkai was founded in 1937. In California during the 1970s, the Serene Reflection Meditation began as a subset of Sōtō Zen. In Buddhism, these different divisions or schools are regarded as alternative paths to enlightenment.

Basic Tenets

Buddhists hold to the Three Universal Truths: impermanence, the lack of self, and suffering. These truths encompass the ideas that everything is impermanent and changing and that life is not satisfying because of its impermanence and the temporary nature of all things, including contentment. Buddhism also teaches the Four Noble Truths: All life is suffering (Dukkha). Desire and attachment cause suffering (Samudaya). Ceasing to desire or crave conceptual attachment ends suffering and leads to release (Nirodha). This release comes through following the Noble Eightfold Path—right understanding (or view), right intention, right speech, right conduct, right occupation, right effort, right mindfulness, and right concentration (Magga).

Although Buddhists do not believe in an afterlife as such, the soul undergoes a cycle of death and rebirth. Following the Noble Eightfold Path leads to the accumulation of good karma, allowing one to be reborn at a higher level. Karma is the Buddhist belief in cause-effect relationships; actions taken in one life have consequences in the next. Ultimately, many refer to the cessation or elimination of suffering as the primary goal of Buddhism.

Buddhists do not believe in gods. Salvation is to be found in following the teachings of Buddha, which are called the Dharma (law or truth). Buddhism does have saint-like bodhisattvas (enlightened beings) who reject ultimate enlightenment (Nirvana) for themselves to aid others.

Sacred Text

Buddhism has nothing comparable to the Qur'an (Islam's holy book) or the Bible. For Theravada Buddhists, an important text is the Pāli Canon, the collection of Buddha's teachings. Mahayana Buddhists recorded their version of these as sutras, many of them in verse. The Lotus Sutra is among the most important. The Buddhist scriptures are written in two languages of ancient India, Pali and Sanskrit, depending on the tradition in which they were developed. Some of these words, such as karma, have been transliterated into English and gained common usage.

Major Figures

Siddhartha Gautama (ca. 563 to 483 BCE) is the founder of Buddhism and regarded as the Buddha or Supreme Buddha. He is the most highly regarded historical figure in Buddhism.

He had two principle disciples: Sariputta and Mahamoggallana (or Maudgalyayana). In contemporary Buddhism, the fourteenth Dalai Lama, Tenzin Gyatso, is a significant person. Both he and Aung San Suu Kyi, a Buddhist of Myanmar who was held as a political prisoner for her stand against the oppressive regime of that nation, have been awarded the Nobel Peace Prize.

Major Holy Sites

Buddhist holy sites are located in several places in Asia. All of those directly related to the life of Siddhartha Gautama are located in the northern part of India near Nepal. Lumbini Grove is noted as the birthplace of the Buddha. He received enlightenment at Bodh Gaya and first began to teach in Sarnath. Kusinara is the city where he died.

In other Asian nations, some holy sites were once dedicated to other religions. Angkor Wat in Cambodia, for example, was constructed for the Hindu god Vishnu in the twelfth century CE. It became a Buddhist temple three hundred years later. It was once the largest religious monument in the world and still attracts visitors. In Java's central highlands sits Borobudur, the world's largest Buddhist shrine. The name means "Temple of Countless Buddhas." Its five terraces represent what must be overcome to reach enlightenment: worldly desires, evil intent, malicious joy, laziness, and doubt. It was built in the eighth and ninth centuries CE, only to fall into neglect at about the turn of the millennium; it was rediscovered in 1815. The complex has three miles of carvings illustrating the life and teachings of the Buddha. In Sri Lanka, the Temple of the Tooth, which houses what is believed to be one of the Buddha's teeth, is a popular pilgrimage site.

Some of the holy sites incorporate gifts of nature. China has four sacred Buddhist mountains, symbolizing the four corners of the universe. These mountains—Wŭtái Shān, Éméi Shān, Jiŭhuá Shān, and Pŭtuó Shān—are believed to be the homes of bodhisattvas. In central India outside Fardapur, there are twenty-nine caves carved into the granite, most of them with frescoes based on the Buddha's life. Ajanta, as

the site is known, was created between 200 BCE and the fifth century CE. Five of the caves house temples.

The Buddha's birthday, his day of death, and the day of his enlightenment are all celebrated, either as one day or several. Different traditions and countries have their own additional celebrations, including Sri Lanka's Festival of the Tooth. Buddhists have a lunar calendar, and four days of each month are regarded as holy days.

ORIGINS

History & Geography

Buddhism began in what is now southern Nepal and northern India with the enlightenment of the Buddha. Following his death, members of the sangha, or community, spread the teachings across northern India. The First Buddhist Council took place in 486 BCE at Rajagaha. This council settled the Buddhist canon, the Tipitaka. In 386 BCE, a little more than a century after the Buddha died, a second Buddhist Council was held at Vesali. It was at this meeting that the two major schools of Buddhist thought—Theravada and Mahayana—began to differ.

Emperor Asoka, who ruled most of the Indian subcontinent from around 268 to 232 BCE, converted to Buddhism. He sent missionaries across India and into central parts of Asia. He also set up pillars with Buddhist messages in his own efforts to establish "true dharma" in the kingdom, although he did not create a state church. His desire for his subjects to live contently in this life led to promoting trade, maintaining canals and reservoirs, and the founding a system of medical care for both humans and animals. Asoka's son Mahinda went to southern Indian and to Sri Lanka with the message of Buddhism.

Asoka's empire fell shortly after his death. Under the following dynasties, evidence suggests Buddhists in India experienced persecution. The religion continued to grow, however, and during the first centuries CE, monasteries and monuments were constructed with support from local rulers. Some additional support came from women within the royal courts. Monastic centers also grew in number. By the fourth century CE, Buddhism had become one of the chief religious traditions in India.

During the Gupta dynasty, which lasted from about 320 to 600 CE, Buddhists and Hindus began enriching each other's traditions. Some Hindus felt that the Buddha was an incarnation of Vishnu, a Hindu god. Some Buddhists showed respect for Hindu deities.

Also during this era, Mahavihara, the concept of the "Great Monastery," came to be. These institutions served as universities for the study and development of Buddhist thinking. Some of them also included cultural and scientific study in the curriculum.

Traders and missionaries took the ideas of Buddhism to China. By the first century CE, Buddhism was established in that country. The religion died out or was absorbed into Hinduism in India. By the seventh century, a visiting Chinese monk found that Huns had invaded India from Central Asia and destroyed many Buddhist monasteries. The religion revived and flourished in the northeast part of India for several centuries.

Muslim invaders reached India in the twelfth and thirteenth centuries. They sacked the monasteries, some of which had grown very wealthy. Some even paid workers to care for both the land they owned and the monks, while some had indentured slaves. Because Buddhism had become monastic rather than a religion of the laity, there was no groundswell for renewal following the Muslim invasion.

Prominent in eastern and Southeast Asia, Buddhism is the national religion in some countries. For example, in Thailand, everyone learns about Buddhism in school. Buddhism did not begin to reach Western culture until the nineteenth century, when the Lotus Sutra was translated into German. The first Buddhist temple in the United States was built in 1853 in San Francisco's Chinatown.

Chinese Communists took control of Tibet in 1950. Nine years later, the fourteenth Dalai Lama left for India, fearing persecution. The Dalai Lama is considered a living teacher (lama) who is to instruct others. (The term *dalai* means "great as the ocean.") In 1989, he received the Nobel Peace Prize.

Buddhism experienced a revival in India during the twentieth century. Although some of this new beginning was due in part to Tibetan immigrants seeking safety, a mass conversion in 1956 was the major factor. The year was chosen to honor the 2,500th anniversary of the Buddha's death year. Buddhism was chosen as an alternative to the strict caste structure of Hinduism, and hundreds of thousands of people of the Dalit caste, once known as untouchables, converted in a ceremony held in Nagpur.

Founder or Major Prophet

Siddhartha Gautama, who became known as the "Enlightened One," or Buddha, was a prince in what is now southern Nepal, but was then northern India during the sixth century BCE. The name Siddhartha means "he who achieves his aim." He was a member of the Sakya tribe of Nepal, belonging to the warrior caste. Many legends have grown around his birth and early childhood. One states that he was born in a grove in the woods, emerging from his mother's side able to walk and completely clean.

During Siddhartha's childhood, a Brahmin, or wise man, prophesied that he would grow to be a prince or a religious teacher who would help others overcome suffering. Because the life of a sage involved itinerant begging, the king did not want this life for his child. He kept Siddhartha in the palace and provided him with all the luxuries of his position, including a wife, Yashodhara. They had a son, Rahula.

Escaping from the palace at about the age of thirty, Gautama first encountered suffering in the form of an old man with a walking stick. The following day, he saw a man who was ill. On the third day, he witnessed a funeral procession. Finally he met a monk, who had nothing, but who radiated happiness. He determined to leave his privileged life, an act called the Great Renunciation. Because hair was a sign of vanity in his time, he shaved his head. He looked for enlightenment via an ascetic life of little food or sleep. He followed this path for six years, nearly starving to death. Eventually, he determined on a Middle Way, a path neither luxurious as he had known in the palace, nor ascetic as he had attempted.

After three days and nights of meditating under a tree at Bodh Gaya, Siddhartha achieved his goal of enlightenment, or Nirvana. He escaped fear of suffering and death.

The Buddha began his preaching career, which spanned some forty years, following his enlightenment. He gave his first sermon in northeast India at Sarnath in a deer park. The first five followers became the first community, or sangha. Buddha died around age eighty, in 483 BCE after he had eaten poisoned food. After warning his followers not to eat the food, he meditated until he died.

Buddhists believe in many enlightened ones. Siddhartha is in one tradition regarded as the fourth buddha, while other traditions hold him to have been the seventh or twenty-fifth buddha.

His disciples, who took the ideas throughout India, repeated his teachings. When the later Buddhists determined to write down the teachings of the Buddha, they met to discuss the ideas and agreed that a second meeting should occur in a century. At the third council, which was held at Pataliputta, divisions occurred. The two major divisions—Theravada and Mahayana—differ over the texts to be used and the interpretation of the teachings. Theravada can be translated as "the Teachings of the Elders," while Mahayana means "Great Vehicle."

Theravada Buddhists believe that only monks can achieve enlightenment through the teachings of another buddha, or enlightened being. Thus they try to spend some part of their lives in a monastery. Buddhists in the Mahayana tradition, on the other hand, feel that all people can achieve enlightenment, without being in a monastery. Mahayanans also regard some as bodhisattvas, people who have achieved the enlightened state but renounce Nirvana to help others achieve it.

Philosophical Basis

During Siddhartha's lifetime, Hinduism was the predominant religion in India. Many people, especially in northern India, were dissatisfied with the rituals and sacrifices of that religion. In addition, as many small kingdoms expanded and the unity of the tribes began to break down, many people were in religious turmoil and doubt. A number of sects within Hinduism developed.

The Hindu belief in the cycle of death and rebirth led some people to despair because they could not escape from suffering in their lives. Siddhartha was trying to resolve the suffering he saw in the world, but many of his ideas came from the Brahmin sect of Hinduism, although he reinterpreted them. Reincarnation, dharma, and reverence for cows are three of the ideas that carried over into Buddhism.

In northeast India at Bodh Gaya, he rested under a bodhi tree, sometimes called a bo tree. He meditated there until he achieved Nirvana, or complete enlightenment, derived from the freedom of fear that attached to suffering and death. As a result of his being enlightened, he was known as Buddha, a Sanskrit word meaning "awakened one." Wanting to help others, he began teaching his Four Noble Truths, along with the Noble Eightfold Path that would lead people to freedom from desire and suffering. He encouraged his followers to take Triple Refuge in the Three Precious Jewels: the Buddha, the teachings, and the sangha, or monastic community. Although at first Buddha was uncertain about including women in a sangha, his mother-in-law begged for the privilege.

Greed, hatred, and ignorance were three traits that Buddha felt people needed to conquer. All three create craving, the root of suffering. Greed and ignorance lead to a desire for things that are not needed, while hatred leads to a craving to destroy the hated object or person.

To the Four Noble Truths and Eightfold Path, early devotees of Buddhism added the Five Moral Precepts. These are to avoid taking drugs and alcohol, engaging in sexual misconduct, harming others, stealing, and lying.

The precepts of the Buddha were not written down for centuries. The first text did not appear for more than 350 years after the precepts were first spoken. One collection from Sri Lanka written in Pāli during the first century BCE is known as Three Baskets, or Tipitaka. The three baskets include Buddha's teaching (the Basket of Discourse), commentary on the sayings (the Basket of Special Doctrine), and the rules for monks to follow (the Basket of Discipline). The name Three Baskets refers to the fact that the sayings were first written on leaves from a palm tree that were then collected in baskets.

Holy Places

Buddhists make pilgrimages to places that relate to important events in Siddhartha's life. While Lumbini Grove, the place of Siddhartha's birth, is a prominent pilgrimage site, the primary site for pilgrimage is Bodh Gaya, the location where Buddha received enlightenment. Other pilgrimage sites include Sarnath, the deer park located in what is now Varanasi (Benares) where the Buddha first began to teach, and Kusinara, the city where he died. All of these are in the northern part of India near Nepal.

Other sites in Asia that honor various bodhisattvas have also become pilgrimage destinations. Mountains are often chosen; there are four in China, each with monasteries and temples built on them. In Japan, the Shikoku pilgrimage covers more than 700 miles and involves visits to eighty-eight temples along the route.

BUDDHISM IN DEPTH

Sacred Symbols

Many stylized statue poses of the Buddha exist, each with a different significance. One, in which the Buddha has both hands raised, palms facing outward, commemorates the calming of an elephant about to attack the Buddha. If only the right hand is raised, the hand symbolizes friendship and being unafraid. The teaching gesture is that of a hand with the thumb and first finger touching.

In Tibetan Buddhism, the teachings of Buddha regarding the cycle of rebirth are symbolized in the six-spoke wheel of life. One may be reborn into any of the six realms of life: hell, hungry spirits, warlike demons called Asuras, animals, humans, or gods. Another version of the wheel has eight spokes rather than six, to represent the Noble Eightfold Path. Still another wheel has twelve spokes, signifying both the Four Noble Truths and the Noble Eightfold Path.

Tibetan Buddhists have prayer beads similar to a rosary, with 108 beads representing the number of desires to be overcome prior to reaching enlightenment. The worshipper repeats the Triple Refuge—Buddha, dharma, and sangha—or a mantra.

The prayer wheel is another device that Tibetan Buddhists use. Inside the wheel is a roll of paper on which the sacred mantra—Hail to the jewel in the lotus—is written many times. The lotus is a symbol of growing spiritually; it grows in muddied waters, but with the stems and flowers, it reaches toward the sun. By turning the wheel and spinning the mantra, the practitioner spreads blessings. Bells may be rung to wake the hearer out of ignorance.

In Tantric Buddhism, the mandala, or circle, serves as a map of the entire cosmos. Mandalas may be made of colored grains of sand, carved or painted. They are used to help in meditation and are thought to have a spiritual energy.

Buddhism recognizes Eight Auspicious Symbols, including the banner, conch shell, fish, knot, lotus, treasure vase, umbrella, and wheel. Each has a particular significance. A conch shell, for example, is often blown to call worshippers to meetings. Because its sound travels far, it signifies the voice of Buddha traveling throughout the world. Fish are fertility symbols because they have thousands of offspring. In Buddhist imagery, they are often in facing pairs and fashioned of gold. The lotus represents spiritual growth, rooted in muddy water but flowering toward the sun. The umbrella symbolizes protection, because servants once used them to protect royalty from both sun and rain.

Sacred Practices & Gestures

Two major practices characterize Buddhism: gift-giving and showing respect to images and relics of the Buddha. The first is the transaction between laity and monks in which laypersons present sacrificial offerings to the monks, who in return share their higher state of spiritual being with the laity. Although Buddhist monks are permitted to own very little, they each have a begging bowl, which is often filled with rice.

Buddhists venerate statues of the Buddha, bodhisattvas, and saints; they also show respect to his relics, housed in stupas. When in the presence of a statue of the Buddha, worshippers have a series of movements they repeat three times, thus dedicating their movements to the Triple Refuge. It begins with a dedicated body: placing hands together with the palms cupped slightly and fingers touching, the devotee raises the hands to the forehead. The second step symbolizes right speech by lowering the hands to just below the mouth. In the third movement, the hands are lowered to the front of the chest, indicating that heart—and by extension, mind—are also dedicated to the Triple Refuge. The final movement is prostration. The devotee first gets on all fours, then lowers either the entire body to the floor or lowers the head, so that there are five points of contact with the floor.

Statues of the Buddha give a clue to the gestures held important to his followers. The gesture of turning the hand towards the ground indicates that one is observing Earth. Devotees assume a lotus position, with legs crossed, when in meditation.

Allowing the left hand to rest in the lap and the right hand to point down to Earth is a gesture used in meditation. Another common gesture is to touch thumb and fingertips together while the palms of both hands face up, thus forming a flat triangular shape. The triangle signifies the Three Jewels of Buddhism.

Food Restrictions

Buddhism does not require one to be a vegetarian. Many followers do not eat meat, however, because to do so involves killing other creatures. Both monks and laypersons may choose not to eat after noontime during the holy days of each month.

Rites, Celebrations, & Services

Ancient Buddhism recognized four holy days each month, known as *uposatha*. These days included the full moon and new moon days of each lunar month, as well as the eighth day after each of these moons appeared. Both monks and members of the laity have special religious duties during these four days. A special service takes place in which flowers are offered to images of the Buddha, precepts are repeated, and a sermon is preached. On these four days, an additional three precepts may be undertaken along with the five regularly observed. The three extra duties are to refrain from sleeping on a luxurious bed, eating any food after noon, and adorning the body or going to entertainments.

In Theravada nations, three major life events of the Buddha—birth, enlightenment, and entering nirvana—are celebrated on Vesak, or Buddha Day. In temples, statues of Buddha as a child are ceremonially cleaned. Worshippers may offer incense and flowers. To symbolize the Buddha's enlightenment, lights may be illuminated in trees and temples. Because it is a day of special kindness, some people in Thailand refrain from farm work that could harm living creatures. They may also seek special merit by freeing captive animals.

Other Buddhist nations that follow Mahayana Buddhism commemorate these events on three different days. In Japan, Hana Matsuri is the celebration of Buddha's birth. On that day, people create paper flower gardens to recall the gardens of Lumbini, Siddhartha's birthplace. Worshippers also pour perfumed tea over statues of Buddha; this is because, according to tradition, the gods provided scented water for Siddhartha's first bath.

Poson is celebrated in Sri Lanka to honor the coming of Buddhism during the reign of Emperor Asoka. Other holy persons are also celebrated in the countries where they had the greatest influence. In Tibet, for instance, the arrival of

Padmasambhava, who brought Buddhism to that nation, is observed.

Buddhists also integrate their own special celebrations into regular harvest festivals and New Year activities. These festivities may include a performance of an event in the life of any buddha or bodhisattva. For example, troupes of actors in Tibet specialize in enacting Buddhist legends. The festival of the Sacred Tooth is held in Kandy, Sri Lanka. According to one legend, a tooth of Buddha has been recovered, and it is paraded through the streets on this day. The tooth has been placed in a miniature stupa, or sealed mound, which is carried on an elephant's back.

Protection rituals have been common in Buddhism from earliest days. They may be public rituals meant to avoid a collective danger, such as those held in Sri Lanka and other Southeast Asia nations. Or they may be designed for private use. The role of these rituals is greater in Mahayana tradition, especially in Tibet. Mantras are chanted for this reason.

Customs surrounding death and burial differ between traditions and nations. A common factor, however, is the belief that the thoughts of a person at death are significant. This period may be extended for three days following death, due to a belief in consciousness for that amount of time after death. To prepare the mind of the dying, another person may read sacred texts aloud.

Judy A. Johnson, MTS

Bibliography

Armstrong, Karen. *Buddha*. New York: Penguin, 2001. Print.

Barnes, Trevor. *The Kingfisher Book of Religions*. New York: Kingfisher, 1999. Print.

Chodron, Thubten. *Buddhism for Beginners*. Ithaca: Snow Lion, 2001. Print.

Eckel, Malcolm David. *Buddhism*. Oxford: Oxford UP, 2002. Print.

Epstein, Ron. "Application of Buddhist Teachings in Modern Life." *Religion East & West* Oct. 2012: 52–61. Print.

Harding, John S. *Studying Buddhism in Practice*. Routledge, 2012. E-book. Studying Religions in Practice.

Harvey, Peter. *An Introduction to Buddhism: Teachings, History and Practices*. 2nd ed. Cambridge UP, 2013. E-book.

Heirman, Ann. "Buddhist Nuns: Between Past and Present." *International Review for the History of Religions* 58.5/6 (2011): 603–31. Print.

Langley, Myrtle. *Religion*. New York: Knopf, 1996. Print.

Low, Kim Cheng Patrick. "Three Treasures of Buddhism & Leadership Insights." *Culture & Religion Review Journal* 2012.3 (2012): 66–72. Print.

Low, Patrick Kim Cheng. "Leading Change, the Buddhist Perspective." *Culture & Religion Review Journal* 2012.1 (2012): 127–45. Print.

McMahan, David L. *Buddhism in the Modern World*. Routledge, 2012. E-book.

Meredith, Susan. *The Usborne Book of World Religions*. London: Usborne, 1995. Print.

Morgan, Diane. *Essential Buddhism: A Comprehensive Guide to Belief and Practice*. Praeger, 2010. E-book.

Wilkinson, Philip. *Buddhism*. New York: DK, 2003. Print.

Wilkinson, Philip. *Religions*. New York: DK, 2008. Print.

Christianity

General Description

Christianity is one of the world's major religions. It is based on the life and teachings of Jesus of Nazareth, called the Christ, or anointed one. It is believed that there are over thirty thousand denominations or sects of Christianity worldwide. Generally, most of these sects fall under the denominational families of Catholicism, Protestant, and Orthodox. (Anglican and Oriental Orthodox are sometimes added as separate branches.) Most denominations have developed since the seventeenth-century Protestant Reformation.

Number of Adherents Worldwide

Over 2.3 billion people around the world claim allegiance to Christianity in one of its many forms. The three major divisions are Roman Catholicism, Eastern Orthodox, and Protestant. Within each group are multiple denominations. Roman Catholics number more than 1.1 billion followers, while the Eastern Orthodox Church has between 260 and 278 million adherents. An estimated 800 million adherents follow one of the various Protestant denominations, including Anglican, Baptist, Lutheran, Presbyterian, and Methodist. Approximately 1 percent of Christians, or 28 million adherents, do not belong to one of the three major divisions

There are a number of other groups, such as the Amish, with an estimated 249,000 members, and the Quakers, numbering approximately 377,000. Both of these churches—along with Mennonites, who number 1.7 million—are in the peace tradition (their members are conscientious objectors). Pentecostals have 600 million adherents worldwide. Other groups that are not always considered Christian by more conservative groups include Jehovah's Witnesses (7.6 million) and Mormons (13 million) (Wilkinson, p. 104-121).

Basic Tenets

The summaries of the Christian faith are found in the Apostles Creed and Nicene Creed.

In addition, some churches have developed their own confessions of faith, such as Lutheranism's Augsburg Confession. Christianity is a monotheistic tradition, although most Christians believe in the Trinity, defined as one God in three separate but equal persons—Father, Son, and Holy Spirit. More modern, gender-neutral versions of the Trinitarian formula may refer to Creator, Redeemer, and Sanctifier. Many believe in the doctrine of original sin, which means that the disobedience of Adam and Eve in the Garden of Eden has been passed down through all people; because of this sin, humankind is in need of redemption. Jesus Christ was born, lived a sinless life, and then was crucified and resurrected as a substitute for humankind. Those who accept this sacrifice for sin will receive eternal life in a place of bliss after death. Many Christians believe that a Second Coming of Jesus will inaugurate a millennial kingdom and a final judgment (in which people will be judged according to their deeds and their eternal souls consigned to heaven or hell), as well as a resurrected physical body.

Sacred Text

The Bible is the sacred text of Christianity, which places more stress on the New Testament. The canon of the twenty-six books of the New Testament was finally determined in the latter half of the fourth century CE.

Major Figures

Christianity is based on the life and teachings of Jesus of Nazareth. His mother, Mary, is especially revered in Roman Catholicism and the Eastern Orthodox tradition, where she is known as Theotokos (God-bearer). Jesus spread his teachings through the twelve apostles, or disciples, who he himself chose and named. Paul (Saint Paul or Paul the Apostle), who became the first missionary to the Gentiles—and whose writings comprise a bulk of the New Testament—is a key figure for the theological treatises embedded in his letters to early churches. His conversion occurred after Jesus' crucifixion. All of these figures are biblically represented.

Under the Emperor Constantine, Christianity went from a persecuted religion to the state religion. Constantine also convened the Council of Nicea in 325 CE, which expressed the formula defining Jesus as fully God and fully human. Saint Augustine (354–430) was a key thinker of the early church who became the Bishop of Hippo in North Africa. He outlined the principles of just war and expressed the ideas of original sin. He also suggested what later became the Catholic doctrine of purgatory.

In the sixth century, Saint Benedict inscribed a rule for monks that became a basis for monastic life. Martin Luther, the monk who stood against the excesses of the Roman Catholic Church, ignited the seventeenth-century Protestant Reformation. He proclaimed that salvation came by grace alone, not through works. In the twentieth century, Pope John XXIII convened the Vatican II Council, or Second Vatican Council, which made sweeping changes to the liturgy and daily practice for Roman Catholics.

Major Holy Sites

The key events in the life of Jesus Christ occurred in the region of Palestine. Bethlehem is honored as the site of Jesus's birth; Jerusalem is especially revered as the site of Jesus's crucifixion. The capital of the empire, Rome, also became the center of Christianity until the Emperor Constantine shifted the focus to Constantinople. Rome today is the seat of the Vatican, an independent city-state that houses the government of the Roman Catholic Church. Canterbury, the site of the martyrdom of Saint Thomas Becket and seat of the archbishop of the Anglican Communion, is a pilgrimage site for Anglicans. There are also many pilgrimage sites, such as Compostela and Lourdes, for other branches of Christianity. In Ethiopia, Lalibela is the site of eleven churches carved from stone during the twelfth century. The site serves as a profound testimony to the vibrancy of the Christian faith in Africa.

Major Rites & Celebrations

The first rite of the church is baptism, a water-related ritual that is traditionally administered to infants or adults alike through some variant of sprinkling or immersion. Marriage is another rite of the church. Confession is a major part of life for Roman Catholics, although the idea is also present in other branches of Christianity.

The celebration of the Eucharist, or Holy Communion, is a key part of weekly worship for the liturgical churches such as those in the Roman Catholic or Anglican traditions. Nearly all Christians worship weekly on Sunday; services include readings of scripture, a sermon, singing of hymns, and may include Eucharist. Christians honor the birth of Jesus at Christmas and his death and resurrection at Easter. Easter is often considered the most significant liturgical feast, particularly in Orthodox branches.

Many Christians follow a calendar of liturgical seasons. Of these seasons, perhaps the best known is Lent, which is immediately preceded by Shrove Tuesday, also known as Mardi Gras. Lent is traditionally a time of fasting and self-examination in preparation for the Easter feast. Historically, Christians gave up rich foods. The day before Lent was a time for pancakes—to use up the butter and eggs—from which the term Mardi Gras (Fat Tuesday) derives. Lent begins with Ash Wednesday, when Christians are marked with the sign of the cross on their foreheads using ashes, a reminder that they are dust and will return to dust.

ORIGINS

History & Geography

Christianity was shaped in the desert and mountainous landscapes of Palestine, known as the Holy Land. Jesus was driven into the wilderness following his baptism, where he remained for forty days of fasting and temptation. The Gospels record that he often went to the mountains for solitude and prayer. The geography of the deserts and mountains also shaped early Christian spirituality, as men and women went into solitude to pray, eventually founding small communities of the so-called desert fathers and mothers.

Christianity at first was regarded as a sect within Judaism, though it differentiated itself early in the first century CE by breaking with the code of laws that defined Judaism, including the need for circumcision and ritual purity. Early Christianity then grew through the missionary work of the apostles, particularly Paul the Apostle, who traveled throughout the Mediterranean world and beyond the Roman Empire to preach the gospel (good news) of Jesus. (This is often called the Apostolic Age.)

Persecution under various Roman emperors only served to strengthen the emerging religion. In the early fourth century, the Emperor Constantine (ca. 272-337) made Christianity the official religion of the Roman Empire. He also convened the Council of Nicea in 325 CE to quell the religious controversies threatening the Pax Romana (Roman Peace), a time of stability and peace throughout the empire in the first and second centuries.

In 1054 the Great Schism, which involved differences over theology and practice, split the church into Eastern Orthodox and Roman Catholic branches. As Islam grew stronger, the Roman Catholic nations of Europe entered a period of Crusades—there were six Crusades in approximately 175 years, from 1095-1271—that attempted to take the Holy Land out of Muslim control.

A number of theologians became unhappy with the excesses of the Roman church and papal authority during the fifteenth and sixteenth centuries. The Protestant Reformation, originally an attempt to purify the church, was led by several men, most notably Martin Luther (1483-1546), whose ninety-five theses against the Catholic Church sparked the Reformation movement. Other leaders of the Protestant Reformation include John Knox (ca. 1510-1572), attributed as the founder of the Presbyterian denomination, John Calvin (1509-1564), a principle early developer of Calvinism, and Ulrich Zwingli (1484-1531), who initially spurred the Reformation in Switzerland. This period of

turmoil resulted in the founding of a number of church denominations: Lutherans, Presbyterians, and Anglicans. These groups were later joined by the Methodists and the Religious Society of Friends (Quakers).

During the sixteenth and seventeenth centuries, the Roman Catholic Church attempted to stem this wave of protest and schism with the Counter-Reformation. Concurrently, the Inquisition, an effort to root out heresy and control the rebellion, took place. There were various inquisitions, including the Spanish Inquisition, which was led by Ferdinand II of Aragon and Isabella I of Castile in mid-fifteenth century and sought to "guard" the orthodoxy of Catholicism in Spain. There was also the Portuguese Inquisition, which began in 1536 in Portugal under King John III, and the Roman Inquisition, which took place in the late fifteenth century in Rome under the Holy See.

During the modern age, some groups became concerned with the perceived conflicts between history (revealed through recent archaeological findings) and the sciences (as described by Charles Darwin and Sigmund Freud) and the literal interpretation of some biblical texts. Fundamentalist Christianity began at an 1895 meeting in Niagara Falls, New York, with an attempt to define the basics (fundamentals) of Christianity. These were given as the inerrant nature of the Bible, the divine nature of Jesus, his literal virgin birth, his substitutionary death and literal physical resurrection, and his soon return. Liberal Christians, on the other hand, focused more on what became known as the Social Gospel, an attempt to relieve human misery.

Controversies in the twenty-first century throughout Christendom focused on issues such as abortion, homosexuality, the ordination of women and gays, and the authority of the scriptures. An additional feature is the growth of Christianity in the Southern Hemisphere. In Africa, for example, the number of Christians grew from 10 million in 1900 to over 506 million a century later. Initially the result of empire-building and colonialism, the conversions in these nations have resulted in a unique blend of native religions and Christianity. Latin America has won renown for its liberation theology, which was first articulated in 1968 as God's call for justice and God's preference for the poor, demonstrated in the ministry and teachings of Jesus Christ. Africa, Asia, and South America are regions that are considered more morally and theologically conservative. Some suggest that by 2050, non-Latino white persons will comprise only 20 percent of Christians.

Founder or Major Prophet

Jesus of Nazareth was born into a peasant family. The date of his birth, determined by accounts in the Gospels of Matthew and Luke, could be as early as 4 or 5 BCE or as late as 6 CE. Mary, his mother, was regarded as a virgin; thus, Jesus' birth was a miracle, engendered by the Holy Spirit. His earthly father, Joseph, was a carpenter.

At about age thirty, Jesus began an itinerant ministry of preaching and healing following his baptism in the Jordan River by his cousin, John the Baptist. He selected twelve followers, known as apostles (sent-ones), and a larger circle of disciples (followers). Within a short time, Jesus' ministry and popularity attracted the negative attention of both the Jewish and Roman rulers. He offended the Jewish leaders with his emphasis on personal relationship with God rather than obedience to rules, as well as his claim to be coequal with God the Father.

For a period of one to three years (Gospel accounts vary in the chronology), Jesus taught and worked miracles, as recorded in the first four books of the New Testament, the Gospels of Matthew, Mark, Luke, and John. On what has become known as Palm Sunday, he rode triumphantly into Jerusalem on the back of a donkey while crowds threw palm branches at his feet. Knowing that his end was near, at a final meal with his disciples, known now to Christians as the Last Supper, Jesus gave final instructions to his followers.

He was subsequently captured, having been betrayed by Judas Iscariot, one of his own twelve apostles. A trial before the Jewish legislative body, the Sanhedrin, led to his being condemned for blasphemy. However, under Roman law, the Jews did not have the power to put anyone to death. A later trial under the Roman governor, Pontius Pilate, resulted in Jesus being crucified, although Pilate tried to prevent this action, declaring Jesus innocent.

According to Christian doctrine, following the crucifixion, Jesus rose from the dead three days later. He appeared before many over a span of forty days and instructed the remaining eleven apostles to continue spreading his teachings. He then ascended into heaven. Ultimately, his followers believed that he was the Messiah, the savior who was to come to the Jewish people and deliver them. Rather than offering political salvation, however, Jesus offered spiritual liberty.

Philosophical Basis

Jesus was a Jew who observed the rituals and festivals of his religion. The Gospels reveal that he attended synagogue worship and went to Jerusalem for celebrations such as Passover. His teachings both grew out of and challenged the religion of his birth.

The Jews of Jesus' time, ruled by the Roman Empire, hoped for a return to political power. This power would be concentrated in a Messiah, whose coming had been prophesied centuries before. There were frequent insurrections in Judea, led in Jesus' time by a group called the Zealots. Indeed, it is believed that one of the twelve apostles was part of this movement. Jesus, with his message of a kingdom of heaven, was viewed as perhaps the one who would usher in a return to political ascendancy.

When challenged to name the greatest commandment, Jesus answered that it was to love God with all the heart, soul, mind, and strength. He added that the second was to love one's neighbor as one's self, saying that these two commands summarized all the laws that the Jewish religion outlined.

Jewish society was concerned with ritual purity and with following the law. Jesus repeatedly flouted those laws by eating with prostitutes and tax collectors, by touching those deemed unclean, such as lepers, and by including

Gentiles in his mission. Women were part of his ministry, with some of them providing for him and his disciples from their own purses, others offering him a home and a meal, and still others among those listening to him teach.

Jesus's most famous sermon is called the Sermon on the Mount. In it, he offers blessings on those on the outskirts of power, such as the poor, the meek, and those who hunger and thirst for righteousness. While not abolishing the law that the Jews followed, he pointed out its inadequacies and the folly of parading one's faith publicly. Embedded in the sermon is what has become known as the Lord's Prayer, the repetition of which is often part of regular Sunday worship. Much of Jesus' teaching was offered in the form of parables, or short stories involving vignettes of everyday life: a woman adding yeast to dough or a farmer planting seeds. Many of these parables were attempts to explain the kingdom of heaven, a quality of life that was both present and to come.

Holy Places

The Christian church has many pilgrimage sites, some of them dating back to the Middle Ages. Saint James is thought to have been buried in Compostela, Spain, which was a destination for those who could not make the trip to the Holy Land. Lourdes, France, is one of the spots associated with healing miracles. Celtic Christians revere places such as the small Scottish isle of Iona, an early Christian mission. Assisi, Italy, is a destination for those who are attracted to Saint Francis (1181-1226), founder of the Franciscans. The Chartres Cathedral in France is another pilgrimage destination from the medieval period.

Jerusalem, Rome, and Canterbury are considered holy for their associations with the early church and Catholicism, as well as with Anglicanism. Within the Old City of Jerusalem is the Church of the Holy Sepulchre, an important pilgrimage site believed to house the burial place of Jesus. Another important pilgrimage site is the Church of the Nativity in Bethlehem. It is built on a cave believed to be the birthplace of

Jesus, and is one of the oldest operating churches in existence.

CHRISTIANITY IN DEPTH

Sacred Symbols

The central symbol of Christianity is the cross, of which there are many variant designs. Some of them, such as Celtic crosses, are related to regions of the world. Others, such as the Crusader's cross, honor historic events. The dove is the symbol for the Holy Spirit, which descended in that shape on the gathered disciples at Pentecost after Jesus's ascension.

Various symbols represent Jesus. Candles allude to his reference to himself as the Light of the World, while the lamb stands for his being the perfect sacrifice, the Lamb of God. The fish symbol that is associated with Christianity has a number of meanings, both historic and symbolic. A fish shape stands for the Greek letters beginning the words Jesus Christ, Son of God, Savior; these letters form the word *ichthus*, the Greek word for "fish." Fish also featured prominently in the scriptures, and the early apostles were known as "fishers of man." The crucifixion symbol is also a popular Catholic Christian symbol.

All of these symbols may be expressed in stained glass. Used in medieval times, stained glass often depicted stories from the Bible as an aid to those who were illiterate.

Sacred Practices & Gestures

Roman Catholics honor seven sacraments, defined as outward signs of inward grace. These include the Eucharist, baptism, confirmation, marriage, ordination of priests, anointing the sick or dying with oil, and penance. The Eastern Orthodox Church refers to these seven as mysteries rather than sacraments.

Priests in the Roman Catholic Church must remain unmarried. In the Eastern Orthodox, Anglican, and Protestant denominations, they may marry. Both Roman Catholic and Eastern Orthodox refuse to ordain women to the priesthood.

The Orthodox Church practices a rite known as chrismation, anointing a child with oil following its baptism. The "oil of gladness," as it is known, is placed on the infant's head, eyes, ears, and mouth. This is similar to the practice of confirmation in some other denominations. Many Christian denominations practice anointing the sick or dying with oil, as well as using the oil to seal those who have been baptized.

Many Christians, especially Roman Catholics, use a rosary, or prayer beads, when praying. Orthodox believers may have icons, such as small paintings of God, saints or biblical events, as part of their worship. There may be a font of water that has been blessed as one enters some churches, which the worshippers use to make the sign of the cross, touching fingers to their forehead, heart, right chest, and left chest. Some Christians make the sign of the cross on the forehead, mouth, and heart to signify their desire for God to be in their minds, on their lips, and in their hearts.

Christians may genuflect, or kneel, as they enter or leave a pew in church. In some churches, particularly the Catholic and Orthodox, incense is burned during the service as a sweet smell to God.

In some traditions, praying to or for the dead is encouraged. The rationale for this is known as the communion of saints—the recognition that those who are gone are still a part of the community of faith.

Catholic, Orthodox, and some branches of other churches have monastic orders for both men and women. Monks and nuns may live in a cloister or be engaged in work in the wider world. They generally commit to a rule of life and to the work of prayer. Even those Christians who are not part of religious orders sometimes go on retreats, seeking quiet and perhaps some spiritual guidance from those associated with the monastery or convent.

Food Restrictions
Historically, Christians fasted during Lent as preparation for the Easter celebration. Prior to the Second Vatican Council in 1962,

Roman Catholics did not eat meat on Fridays. Conservative Christians in the Evangelical tradition tend to eliminate the use of alcohol, tobacco, and drugs.

Rites, Celebrations & Services
For churches in the liturgical tradition, the weekly celebration of the Eucharist is paramount. While many churches celebrate this ritual feast with wine and a wafer, many Protestant churches prefer to use grape juice and crackers or bread.

Church services vary widely. Quakers sit silently waiting for a word from God, while in many African American churches, hymns are sung for perhaps an hour before the lengthy sermon is delivered. Some churches have a prescribed order of worship that varies little from week to week. Most services, however, include prayer, a sermon, and singing, with or without musical accompaniment.

A church's architecture often gives clues as to the type of worship one will experience. A church with the pulpit in the center at the front generally is a Protestant church with an emphasis on the Word of God being preached. If the center of the front area is an altar, the worship's focus will be on the Eucharist.

Christmas and Easter are the two major Christian celebrations. In liturgical churches, Christmas is preceded by Advent, a time of preparation and quiet to ready the heart for the coming of Christ. Christmas has twelve days, from the birth date of December 25 to the Epiphany on January 6. Epiphany (to show) is the celebration of the arrival of the Magi (wise men) from the East who came to worship the young Jesus after having seen his star. Their arrival is believed to have been foretold by the Old Testament prophet Isaiah, who said "And the Gentiles shall come to thy light, and kings to the brightness of thy rising" (Isaiah 60:3). Epiphany is the revealing of the Messiah to the Gentiles.

In the early church, Easter was preceded by a solemn period of fasting and examination, especially for candidates for baptism and penitent sinners wishing to be reconciled. In Western churches, Lent begins with Ash Wednesday, which is six and half weeks prior to Easter. By excluding Sundays from the fast, Lent thus gives a forty-day fast, imitating that of Jesus in the wilderness. Historically forbidden foods during the fast included eggs, butter, meat, and fish. In the Eastern Church, dairy products, oil, and wine are also forbidden.

The week before Easter is known as Holy Week. It may include extra services such as Maundy Thursday, a time to remember Jesus's new commandment (*maundy* is etymologically related to *mandate*) to love one another. In some Catholic areas, the crucifixion is reenacted in a Passion play (depicting the passion—trial, suffering, and death—of Christ). Some churches will have an Easter vigil the Saturday night before or a sunrise service on Easter morning.

Judy A. Johnson, MTS

Bibliography

Bakker, Janel Kragt. "The Sister Church Phenomenon: A Case Study of the Restructuring of American Christianity against the Backdrop of Globalization." *International Bulletin of Missionary Research* 36.3 (2012): 129–34. Print.

Bandak, Andreas and Jonas Adelin Jørgensen. "Foregrounds and Backgrounds—Ventures in the Anthropology of Christianity." *Ethos: Journal of Anthropology* 77.4 (2012): 447–58. Print.

Barnes, Trevor. *The Kingfisher Book of Religions*. New York: Kingfisher, 1999. Print.

Chandler, Daniel Ross. "Christianity in Cross-Cultural Perspective: A Review of Recent Literature." *Asia Journal of Theology* 26.2 (2012): 44–57. Print.

Daughrity, Dyron B. "Christianity Is Moving from North to South—So What about the East?" *International Bulletin of Missionary Research* 35.1 (2011): 18–22. Print.

Kaatz, Kevin. *Voices of Early Christianity: Documents from the Origins of Christianity*. Santa Barbara: Greenwood, 2013. E-book.

Langley, Myrtle. *Religion*. New York: Alfred A. Knopf, 1996.

Lewis, Clive Staples. *Mere Christianity*. New York: Harper, 2001. Print.

McGrath, Alistair. *Christianity: An Introduction*. Hoboken, New Jersey: Wiley, 2006. Print.

Meredith, Susan. *The Usborne Book of World Religions*. London: Usborne, 1995. Print.

Ripley, Jennifer S. "Integration of Psychology and Christianity: 2022." *Journal of Psychology & Theology* 40.2 (2012): 150–54. Print.

Stefon, Matt. *Christianity: History, Belief, and Practice*. New York: Britannica Educational, 2012. E-book.

Wilkinson, Philip. *Christianity*. New York: DK, 2003. Print.

Wilkinson, Philip. *Religions*. New York: DK, 2008. Print.

Zoba, Wendy Murray. *The Beliefnet Guide to Evangelical Christianity*. New York: Three Leaves, 2005. Print.

East Asian Religions

General Description

East Asian religious and philosophical traditions include, among others, Confucianism, Taoism, and Shintoism. Confucianism is a philosophy introduced by the Chinese philosopher Confucius (Kongzi; 551–479 BCE) in the sixth century BCE, during the Zhou dynasty. Taoism, which centers on Tao, or "the way," is a religious and philosophical tradition that originated in China about two thousand years ago. Shinto, "the way of the spirits," is a Japanese tradition of devotion to spirits and rituals.

Number of Adherents Worldwide

Between 5 and 6 million people, the majority of them in China, practice Confucianism, once the state religion of China. About 20 million people identify as Taoists. Most of the Taoist practitioners are in China as well. In Japan, approximately 107 million people practice Shintoism, though many practitioners also practice Buddhism. Sects of Shinto include Tenrikyo (heavenly truth), founded in 1838, with nearly 2 million devotees. Shukyo Mahikari (divine light) is another, smaller sect founded in the 1960s. Like other sects, it is a blend of different religious traditions (Wilkinson 332–34).

Basic Tenets

Confucianism is a philosophy of life and does concerns itself not with theology but with life conduct. Chief among the aspects of life that must be tended are five key relationships, with particular focus on honoring ancestors and showing filial piety. Confucianism does not take a stand on the existence of God, though the founder, Confucius, referred to "heaven." Except for this reference, Confucianism does not address the question of life after death.

Taoists believe that Tao (the way or the flow) is in everything. Taoism teaches that qi, or life energy, needs to be balanced between yin and yang, which are the female and male principles of life, respectively. With its doctrine of the evil of violence, Taoism borders on pacifism, and it also preaches simplicity and naturalness. Taoists believe in five elements—wood, earth, air, fire and water—that need to be in harmony. The five elements lie at the heart of Chinese medicine, particularly acupuncture. In Taoism, it is believed that the soul returns to a state of nonbeing after death.

Shinto emphasizes nature and harmony, with a focus on lived experience rather than doctrine. Shinto, which means "the way of the gods," is a polytheistic religion; Amaterasu, the sun goddess, is the chief god. At one point in Japan's history, the emperor was believed to be a descendant of Amaterasu and therefore divine. In Tenrikyo Shinto, God is manifested most often as Oyakami, meaning "God the parent."

Shinto teaches that some souls can become kami, a spirit, following death. Each traditional home has a god-shelf, which honors family members believed to have become kami. An older family member tends to the god-shelf, placing a bit of food and some sake (rice wine) on the shelf. To do their work, kami must be nourished. The Tenrikyo sect includes concepts from Pure Land Buddhism, such as an afterlife and the idea of salvation.

Sacred Texts

Five classic texts are sacred to the Confucians. These include the I Ching, or Book of Changes; the Book of Odes; the Book of History; the Book of Rites; and the Annals of Spring and Autumn. The Analects, a collection of Confucius's sayings, is another revered classic. The Tao Te Ching (The Way of Power) is the most sacred book of the Taoists. Those who practice Shinto hold sacred two works: the Kojiki (Record of Ancient Matters) and the Nihon-gi (Chronicles of Japan). Both texts, which contain legends and creation myths, were written during the eighth century.

Major Figures

Confucius, who lived during the sixth century, was the first great philosopher of China. Mengzi (Meng-tzu; 371–289 BCE), known in the West as Mencius, developed Confucius's teachings about the higher power guiding human life. Another ancient Chinese philosopher, Laozi(or Lao-tzu), is the founder of Taoism. He is believed to have been a contemporary of Confucius's in the central region of China. Modern scholars are not certain he ever existed, though one account includes the story of Confucius visiting Laozi. Chuang Tzu wrote of Laozi and his ideas during the fourth and third centuries BCE. Shinto's major figures include Ō no Yasumaro (d. 723), the compiler of the Kokiji who acted under the orders of Empress Gemmei and consulted a bard known to have an infallible memory; the scholar Motoori Norinaga (1730–1800), whose work led to a revived interest in ancient Shinto texts; and Nakayama Miki (1798–1887), the farmer's wife who founded Tenrikyo.

Major Holy Sites

Most Confucian sacred places are located within private homes, where an ancestral shrine and an altar to gods and spirits are maintained. In China's Shandong Province is Qufu, the site of Confucius's family mansion, temple, and cemetery. The temple was built in 478 BCE, only a year after Confucius's death, and has been maintained and enlarged. In addition to its status as a holy site, the United Nations Educational, Scientific, and Cultural Organization (UNESCO) has placed it on their World Heritage List.

Taoists regard mountains as a way to communicate with Earth's primeval powers and with those who are immortal. Five of the nine sacred mountains in China are associated with Taoism: Hengshan in both the north and the south, Songshan in the south, Taishan in the east, and Huashan in the west. The holiest of the five is Taishan, which symbolizes stability, prevents natural disasters, and ensures fertility.

Shintoism has a high regard for natural beauty. As such, Shinto shrines are everywhere, particularly in mountains or near waterfalls.

Mountains in particular are regarded as homes of the gods. Mount Fuji is the holiest Shinto mountain, and climbing it to reach the shrine on its peak is an act of worship. More than forty thousand shrines are dedicated to Inari, the rice god.

Shinto was formalized during the Yamato period (the name for ancient Japan), and because the emperor of the imperial dynasty was from the Yamato area and was considered divine, the whole region is revered. At Ise, located near the coast in Mie Prefecture, southeast of Nara, the shrine has been rebuilt every twenty years for at least fourteen centuries. This rebuilding ensures that Toyouke-Ōmikami (the harvest goddess) and Amaterasu (the sun goddess) are renewed in vigor, which in turn invigorates both the rice crop and the imperial line. Those who have died in war are revered as kami in Japan. In Tokyo, a shrine called Yasukuni is dedicated to them. However, there is controversy surrounding the place because of its association with Japan's extreme nationalism prior to World War II.

Sacred Texts

Five classic texts are sacred to the Confucians. These include the I Ching, or Book of Changes; the Book of Odes; the Book of History; the Book of Rites; and the Annals of Spring and Autumn. The Analects, a collection of Confucius's sayings, is another revered classic. The Tao te Ching (The Way of Power) is the most sacred book of the Taoists. Those who practice Shinto hold sacred two works: the Kojiki (Record of Ancient Matters) and the Nihon-gi (Chronicles of Japan). Both texts, which contain legends and creation myths, were written during the eighth century.

Major Figures

Confucius, who lived during the sixth century, was the first great philosopher of China. Mengzi (Meng-tzu; 371–289 BCE), known in the West as Mencius, developed Confucius's teachings about the higher power guiding human life. Another ancient Chinese philosopher, Laozi,(or Lao-tzu) is the founder of Taoism. He is believed to have been a contemporary of Confucius in the central region of China. Modern scholars are not certain he ever existed, though one account includes the story of Confucius visiting Laozi. Chuang Tzu wrote of Laozi and his ideas during the fourth and third centuries BCE. Shinto's major figures include Ō no Yasumaro, the compiler of the Kokiji who acted under the orders of Empress Gemmei and consulted a bard known to have an infallible memory; the scholar Motoori Norinaga (1730–1800), whose work led to a revived interest in ancient Shinto texts; and Nakayama Miki (1798–1887), the farmer's wife who founded Tenrikyo.

Major Holy Sites

Most Confucian sacred places are located within private homes, where an ancestral shrine and an altar to gods and spirits are maintained. In China's Shandong Province is Qufu, the site of Confucius's family mansion, temple and cemetery. The temple was built in 478 BCE, only a year after Confucius's death, and has been maintained and enlarged. In addition to being a holy site, the United Nations Educational, Scientific, and Cultural Organization (UNESCO) has placed it on their World Heritage List.

Taoists consider mountains as a way to communicate with Earth's primeval powers and with those who are immortal. Five of the nine sacred mountains in China are associated with Taoism. They are Hengshan in both the north and south, Songshan in the south, Taishan in the east, and Huashan in the west. The holiest of the five is Taishan, which symbolizes stability, prevents natural disasters, and ensures fertility.

Shintoism has a high regard for natural beauty. As such, Shinto shrines are everywhere, particularly in mountains or near waterfalls. Mountains in particular are regarded as homes of the gods. Mount Fuji is the holiest Shinto mountain, and climbing it to reach the shrine on its peak is an act of worship. More than forty thousand shrines are dedicated to Inari, the rice god.

Shinto was formalized during the Yamato period (the name for ancient Japan), and because the emperor of the imperial dynasty is from the Yamato area, and was considered divine, the whole region is revered. At Ise, located near the coast in the Mie prefecture southeast of Nara, the shrine has been rebuilt every twenty years for at least fourteen centuries. This rebuilding ensures that Toyouke-Ōmikami (the harvest goddess) and Amaterasu (the sun goddess) are renewed in vigor, which in turn invigorates both the rice crop and the imperial line. Those who have died in war are revered as kami in Japan. In Tokyo, a shrine called Yasukuni is dedicated to them. However, there is controversy surrounding the place because of its association with Japan's extreme nationalism prior to World War II.

Major Rites & Celebrations

Confucian celebrations have to do with honoring people rather than gods. At Confucian temples, the philosopher's birthday is celebrated each September. In Taiwan, this day is called "Teacher's Day." Sacrifices, music and dance are part of the event.

Taoism has a jiao (offering) festival near the winter solstice. It celebrates the renewal of the yang force at this turning of the year. During the festival priests, who have been ritually purified, wear lavish clothing. The festival includes music and dancing, along with large effigies of the gods which are designed to frighten away the evil spirits. Yang's renewal is also the focus of New Year celebrations, which is a time for settling debts and cleaning house. Decorations in the yang warm colors of gold, orange and red abound.

Many of the Shinto festivals overlap with Buddhist ones. There are many local festivals and rituals, and each community has an annual festival at the shrine dedicated to the kami of the region. Japanese New Year, which is celebrated for three days, is a major feast. Since the sixteenth century, the Gion Festival has taken place in Kyoto, Japan. Decorated floats are part of the celebration of the shrine.

ORIGINS

History & Geography

During the Zhou dynasty (1050–256 BCE) in China, the idea of heaven as a force that controlled events came to the fore. Zhou rulers believed that they ruled as a result of the "Mandate of Heaven," viewing themselves as morally superior to those of the previous dynasty, the Shang dynasty (1600-1046 BCE). They linked virtue and power as the root of the state.

By the sixth century the Zhou rulers had lost much of their authority. Many schools of thought developed to restore harmony, and were collectively known as the "Hundred Schools." Confucius set forth his ideas within this historical context. He traveled China for thirteen years, urging rulers to put his ideas into practice and failing to achieve his goals. He returned home to teach for the rest of his life and his ideas were not adopted until the Han dynasty (206 BCE–220 CE). During the Han period, a university for the nation was established, as well as the bureaucratic civil service that continued until the twentieth century. When the Chinese Empire fell in 1911, the Confucian way became less important.

Confucianism had influenced not only early Chinese culture, but also the cultures of Japan, Korea, and Vietnam. The latter two nations also adopted the bureaucratic system. In Japan, Confucianism reached its height during the Tokugawa age (1600–1868 CE). Confucian scholars continue to interpret the philosophy for the modern period. Some regard the ideas of Confucius as key to the recent economic booms in the so-called "tiger" economies of East Asia (Hong Kong, Singapore, South Korea, Taiwan, and Thailand). Confucianism continues to be a major influence on East Asian nations and culture.

Taoism's power (te) manifests itself as a philosophy, a way of life, and a religion. Philosophically, Taoism is a sort of self-help regimen, concerned with expending power efficiently by avoiding conflicts and friction, rather than fighting against the flow of life. In China, it is known as School Taoism. As a way of life, Taoism is concerned with increasing the amount of qi available through what is eaten and through meditation, yoga, and tai chi (an ancient Chinese martial art form). Acupuncture and the use of medicinal herbs are outgrowths of this way of life. Church Taoism, influenced by Buddhism and Tao Chiao (religious Taoism), developed during the second century. This church looked for ways to use power for societal and individual benefit.

By the time of the Han dynasty (206–220 CE), Laozi had been elevated to the status of divine. Taoism found favor at court during the Tang dynasty (618–917 CE), during which the state underwrote temples. By adapting and encouraging people to study the writings of all three major faiths in China, Taoism remained relevant into the early twentieth century. During the 1960s and 1970s, Taoist books were burned and their temples were destroyed in the name of the Cultural Revolution (the Great Proletarian Cultural Revolution). Taoism remains popular and vital in Taiwan.

Shinto is an ancient religion, and some of its characteristics appeared during the Yayoi culture (ca. 300 BCE–300 CE). The focus was on local geographic features and the ancestry of local clan leaders. At first, women were permitted to be priests, but that equality was lost due to the influence of Confucian paternalism. The religion declined, but was revived in 1871 following the Meiji Restoration of the emperor. Shoguns (warlords) had ruled Japan for more than 250 years, and Shinto was the state religion until 1945. It was associated with the emperor cult and contributed to Japan's militarism. After the nation's defeat in World War II, the 1947 constitution forbade government involvement in any religion. In contemporary Shinto, women are permitted to become priests and girls, in some places, are allowed to carry the portable shrines during festivals.

Founder or Major Prophet

Confucius, or Kongzi ("Master Kong"), was a teacher whose early life may have included service in the government. He began traveling throughout the country around age fifty, attempting and failing to interest rulers in his ideas for creating a harmonious state. He returned to his home state after thirteen years, teaching a group of disciples who spread his ideas posthumously.

According to legend, Taoism's founder, Laozi, lived during the sixth century. Laozi may be translated as "Grand Old Master," and may be simply a term of endearment. He maintained the archives and lived simply in a western state of China. Weary of people who were uninterested in natural goodness and perhaps wanting greater solitude in his advanced years, he determined to leave China, heading for Tibet on a water buffalo. At the border, a gatekeeper wanted to persuade him to stay, but could not do so. He asked Laozi to leave behind his teachings. For three days Laozi transcribed his teachings, producing the five-thousand-word Tao Te Ching. He then rode off and was never heard of again. Unlike most founders of religions, he neither preached nor promoted his beliefs. Still, he was held with such regard that some emperors claimed descent from him.

No one is certain of the origin of Shinto, which did not have a founder or major prophet. Shinto—derived from two Chinese words, *shen* (spirit) and *dao* (way)—has been influenced by other religions, notably Confucianism and Buddhism.

Philosophical Basis

Confucianism sought to bring harmony to the state and society as a whole. This harmony was to be rooted in the Five Constant Relationships: between parents and children; husbands and wives; older and younger siblings; older and younger friends; and rulers and subjects. Each of these societal relationships existed to demonstrate mutual respect, service, honor, and love, resulting in a healthy society. The fact that three of the five relationships exist within the family highlights the importance of honoring family. Ritual maintains the li, or rightness, of everything, and is a way to guarantee that a person performed the correct action in any situation in life.

Taoism teaches that two basic components—yin and yang—are in all things, including health, the state, and relationships. Yin is the feminine principle, associated with soft, cold, dark, and moist things. Yang is the masculine principle, and is associated with hard, warm, light, and dry things. By keeping these two aspects of life balanced, harmony will be achieved. Another concept is that of wu-wei, action that is in harmony with nature, while qi is the life force in all beings. The Tao is always in harmony with the universe. Conflict is to be avoided, and soldiers are to go as if attending a funeral, solemnly and with compassion. Taoism also teaches the virtues of humility and selflessness.

Shinto is rooted in reverence for ancestors and for the spirits known as kami, which may be good or evil. By correctly worshipping the kami, Shintoists believe that they are assisting in purifying the world and aiding in its functioning.

Holy Places

Confucianism does not always distinguish between sacred and profane space. So much of nature is considered a holy place, as is each home's private shrine. In addition, some Confucian temples have decayed while others have been restored. Temples do not have statues or images. Instead, the names of Confucius and his noted followers are written on tablets. Like the emperor's palace, temples have the most important halls placed on the north-south axis of the building. Temples are also internally symmetrical, as might be expected of a system that honors order. In Beijing, the Temple of Heaven, just south of the emperor's palace, was one of the holiest places in imperial China.

Taoism's holy places are often in nature, particularly mountains. The holiest of the five sacred mountains in China is Taishan, located in the east. Taoism also reveres grottoes, which are caves thought to be illuminated by the light of heaven.

In the Shinto religion, nature is often the focus of holy sites. Mount Fuji is the most sacred mountain. Near Kyoto the largest shrine of Inari, the rice god, is located. The Grand Shrines at Ise are dedicated to two divinities, and for more than one thousand years, pilgrims have come to it. The Inner Shrine (Naiku) is dedicated to Amaterasu, the sun goddess, and is Shinto's most holy location. The Outer Shrine (Geku) is dedicated to

Toyouke, the goddess of the harvest. Every twenty years, Ise is torn down and rebuilt, thus renewing the gods. Shinto shrines all have torii, the sacred gateway. The most famous of these is built in the sea near the island of Miyajima. Those going to the shrine on this island go by boat through the torii.

EAST ASIAN RELIGIONS IN DEPTH

Sacred Symbols
Water is regarded as the source of life in Confucianism. The water symbol has thus become an unofficial symbol of Confucianism, represented by the Japanese ideogram or character for water, the Mizu, which somewhat resembles a stick figure with an extra leg. Other sacred symbols include the ancestor tablets in shrines of private homes, which are symbolic of the presence of the ancestor to whom offerings are made in hopes of aid.

While not a sacred symbol as the term is generally used, the black and white symbol of yin and yang is a common Taoist emblem. Peaches are also of a symbolic nature in Taoism, and often appear in Asian art. They are based on the four peaches that grew every three thousand years and which the mother of the fairies gave to the Han emperor Wu Ti (140–87 BCE). They are often symbolic of the Immortals.

The Shinto stylized sun, which appears on the Japanese flag, is associated with Amaterasu, the sun goddess. The torii, the gateway forming an entrance to sacred space, is another symbol associated with Shinto.

Sacred Practices & Gestures
Confucian rulers traditionally offered sacrifices honoring Confucius at the spring and autumnal equinoxes. Most of the Confucian practices take place at home shrines honoring the ancestors.

Taoists believe that one can reach Tao (the way) through physical movements, chanting, or meditation. Because mountains, caves, and springs are often regarded as sacred sites, pilgrimages are important to Taoists. At a Taoist

funeral, a paper fairy crane is part of the procession. After the funeral, the crane, which symbolizes a heavenly messenger, is burned. The soul of the deceased person is then thought to ride to heaven on the back of the crane.

Many Shinto shrines exist throughout Japan. Most of them have a sacred arch, known as a torii. At the shrine's entrance, worshippers rinse their mouths and wash their hands to be purified before entering the prayer hall. Before praying, a worshipper will clap twice and ring a bell to let the kami know they are there. Only priests may enter the inner hall, which is where the kami live. During a festival, however, the image of the kami is placed in a portable shrine and carried in a procession through town, so that all may receive a blessing.

Rites, Celebrations & Services
Early Confucianism had no priests, and bureaucrats performed any rituals that were necessary. When the Chinese Empire fell in 1911, imperial ceremonies ended as well. Rituals have become less important in modern times. In contemporary times the most important rite is marriage, the beginning of a new family for creating harmony. There is a correct protocol for each aspect of marriage, from the proposal and engagement to exchanging vows. During the ceremony, the groom takes the bride to his family's ancestor tablets to "introduce" her to them and receive a blessing. The couple bows to the ancestors during the ceremony.

After a death occurs, mourners wear coarse material and bring gifts of incense and money to help defray the costs. Added to the coffin holding are food offerings and significant possessions. A willow branch symbolizing the deceased's soul is carried with the coffin to the place of burial. After the burial, family members take the willow branch to their home altar and perform a ritual to add the deceased to the souls at the family's shrine.

Confucians and Taoists celebrate many of the same Chinese festivals, some of which originated before either Confucianism or Taoism began and reflect aspects of both traditions. While some festivals are not necessarily Taoist, they may be led by Taoist priests. During the Lantern Festival, which occurs on the first full moon of the New Year, offerings are made to the gods. Many of the festivals are tied to calendar events. Qingming (Clear and Bright) celebrates the coming of spring and is a time to remember the dead. During this time, families often go to the family gravesite for a picnic. The Double Fifth is the midsummer festival that occurs on the fifth day of the fifth month, and coincides with the peak of yang power. To protect themselves from too much of the male force, people don garments of the five colors—black, blue, red, white, and yellow—and with the five "poisons"—centipede, lizard, scorpion, snake, and toad—in the pattern of their clothes and on amulets. The gates of hell open at the Feast of the Hungry Ghosts. Priests have ceremonies that encourage the escaped evil spirits to repent or return to hell.

Marriage is an important rite in China, and thus in Taoism as well. Astrologers look at horoscopes to ensure that the bride and groom are well matched and to find the best day for the ceremony. The groom's family is always placed at the east (yang) and the bride's family to the west (yin) to bring harmony. When a person dies, the mourners again sit in the correct locations, while the head of the deceased points south. White is the color of mourning and of yin. At the home of the deceased, white cloths cover the family altar. Mourners may ease the soul's journey with symbolic artifacts or money. They may also go after the funeral to underground chambers beneath the temples to offer a sacrifice on behalf of the dead.

In the Shinto religion, rites exist for many life events. For example, pregnant women ask at a shrine for their children to be born safely, and the mother or grandmother brings a child who is thirty-two or thirty-three-days-old to a shrine for the first visit and blessing. A special festival also exists for children aged three, five or seven, who go to the shrine for purifying. In addition, a bride and groom are purified before the wedding, usually conducted by Shinto priests. Shinto priests may also offer blessings for a new car or building. The New Year and the Spring Festival are among the most important festivals, and shrine virgins, known as miko girls, may dance to celebrate life's renewal. Other festivals include the Feast of the Puppets, Boys' Day, the Water Kami Festival, the Star Feast, the Festival of the Dead, and the autumnal equinox.

Judy A. Johnson, MTS

Bibliography

Barnes, Trevor. *The Kingfisher Book of Religions*. New York: Kingfisher, 1999. Print.

Bell, Daniel A. "Reconciling Socialism and Confucianism? Reviving Tradition in China." *Dissent* 57.1 (2010): 91–99. Print.

Chang, Chung-yuan. *Creativity and Taoism: A Study of Chinese Philosophy, Art and Poetry*. London: Kingsley, 2011. E-book.

Coogan, Michael D., ed. *Eastern Religions*. New York: Oxford UP, 2005. Print.

Eliade, Mircea, and Ioan P. Couliano. *The Eliade Guide to World Religions*. New York: Harper, 1991. Print.

Lao Tzu. *Tao Te Ching*. Trans. Stephen Mitchell. New York: Harper, 1999. Print.

Li, Yingzhang. *Lao-tzu's Treatise on the Response of the Tao*. Trans. Eva Wong. New Haven: Yale UP, 2011. Print.

Littlejohn, Ronnie. *Confucianism: An Introduction*. New York: Tauris, 2011. E-book.

Littleton, C. Scott. *Shinto*. Oxford: Oxford UP, 2002. Print.

Mcvay, Kera. *All about Shinto*. Delhi: University, 2012. Ebook.

Merton, Thomas. *The Way of Chuang Tzu*. New York: New Directions, 1965. Print.

Oldstone-Moore, Jennifer. *Confucianism*. Oxford: Oxford UP, 2002. Print.

Poceski, Mario. *Chinese Religions: The EBook*. Providence, UT: Journal of Buddhist Ethics Online Books, 2009. E-book.

Van Norden, Bryan W. *Introduction to Classical Chinese Philosophy*. Indianapolis: Hackett, 2011. Print.

Wilkinson, Philip. *Religions*. New York: DK, 2008. Print.

Hinduism

General Description

Hinduism; modern Hinduism is comprised of the devotional sects of Vaishnavism, Shaivism, and Shaktism (though Smartism is sometimes listed as the fourth division). Hinduism is often used as umbrella term, since many point to Hinduism as a family of different religions.

Number of Adherents Worldwide

Between 13.8 and 15 percent of the world's population, or about one billion people, are adherents of Hinduism, making it the world's third largest religion after Christianity and Islam. The predominant sect is the Vaishnavite sect (Wilkinson, p. 333).

Basic Tenets

Hinduism is a way of life rather than a body of beliefs. Hindus believe in karma, the cosmic law of cause and effect that determines one's state in the next life. Additional beliefs include dharma, one's religious duty.

Hinduism has no true belief in an afterlife. Rather, it teaches a belief in reincarnation, known as samsara, and in moksha, the end of the cycle of rebirths. Different sects have different paths to moksha.

Hinduism is considered a polytheist religion. However, it is also accurate to say that Hinduism professes a belief in one God or Supreme Truth that is beyond comprehension (an absolute reality, called Brahman) and which manifests itself in many forms and names. These include Brahma, the creator; Vishnu, the protector; and Shiva, the re-creator or destroyer. Many sects are defined by their belief in multiple gods, but also by their worship of one ultimate manifestation. For example, Shaivism and Vaishnavism are based upon the recognition of Shiva and Vishnu, respectively, as the manifestation. In comparison, Shaktism recognizes the Divine Mother (Shakti) as the Supreme Being, while followers of Smartism worship a particular deity of their own choosing.

Major Deities

The Hindu trinity (Trimurti) is comprised of Brahma, the impersonal and absolute creator; Vishnu, the great preserver; and Shiva, the destroyer and re-creator. The goddesses corresponding to each god are Sarasvati, Lakshimi, and Parvati. Thousands of other gods (devas) and goddesses (devis) are worshipped, including Ganesha, Surya, and Kali. Each is believed to represent another aspect of the Supreme Being.

Sacred Texts

Hindus revere ancient texts such as the four Vedas, the 108 Upanishads, and others. No single text has the binding authority of the Qur'an (Islam's holy book) or Bible. Hindu literature is also defined by Sruti (revealed truth), which is heard, and Smriti (realized truth), which is remembered. The former is canonical, while the latter can be changing. For example, the Vedas and the Upanishads constitute Sruti texts, while epics, history, and law books constitute the latter. The Bhagavad Gita (The Song of God) is also considered a sacred scripture of Hinduism, and consists of a philosophical dialogue.

Major Figures

Major figures include: Shankara (788–820 CE), who defined the unity of the soul (atman) and absolute reality (Brahman); Ramanuja (1077–1157 CE), who emphasized bhakti, or love of God; Madhva (1199–1278 CE), scholar and writer, a proponent of dualism; Ramprahsad Sen (1718–1775 CE), composer of Hindu songs of devotion, poet, and mystic who influenced goddess worship in the; Raja Rammohun Roy (1772–1833 CE), abolished the custom of suttee, in which widows were burned on the funeral pyres of their dead husbands, and decried polygamy, rigid caste systems, and dowries; Rabindranath Tagore (1861–1941 CE), first Asian to win the Nobel Prize in Literature; Dr. Babasaheb R. Ambedkar (1891–1956 CE), writer of India's constitution and leader of a mass conversion to Buddhism; Mohandas K. Gandhi (1869–1948 CE), the "great soul" who left a legacy of effective use of nonviolence.

Major Holy Sites

The major holy sites of Hinduism are located within India. They include the Ganges River, in whose waters pilgrims come to bathe away their sins, as well as thousands of tirthas (places of pilgrimage), many of which are associated with particular deities. For example, the Char Dham pilgrimage centers, of which there are four—Badrinath (north), Puri (east), Dwarka (west) and Rameshwaram (south)—are considered the holy abodes or sacred temples of Vishnu. There are also seven ancient holy cities in India, including Ayodhya, believed to be the birthplace of Rama; Varanasi (Benares), known as the City of Light; Dwarka; Ujjian; Kanchipuram; Mathura; and Hardwar.

Major Rites & Celebrations

Diwali, the Festival of Lights, is a five-day festival that is considered a national holiday in India. Holi, the Festival of Colors, is the spring festival. Krishna Janmashtmi is Krishna's birthday. Shivaratri is Shiva's main festival. Navaratri, also known as the Durga festival or Dasserah, celebrates one of the stories of the gods and the victory of good over evil. Ganesh Chaturthi is the elephant-headed god Ganesha's birthday. Rathayatra, celebrated at Puri, India, is a festival for Jagannath, another word for Vishnu.

ORIGINS

History & Geography

Hinduism, which many people consider to be the oldest world religion, is unique in that it has no recorded origin or founder. Generally, it developed in the Indus Valley civilization several thousand years before the Common Era. The faith blends the Vedic traditions of the Indus Valley civilization and the invading nomadic tribes of the Aryans (prehistoric Indo-Europeans). Most of what is known of the Indus Valley civilization comes from archaeological excavations at Mohenjo-Daro (Mound of the Dead) and Harappa. (Because Harappa was a chief city of the period, the Indus Valley civilization is also referred to as the Harappan civilization.) The Vedas, a collection of ancient hymns, provides information about the Aryan culture.

The ancient Persian word *hind* means Indian, and for centuries, to be Indian was to be Hindu. Even now, about 80 percent of India's people consider themselves Hindu. The root word alludes to flowing, as a river flows. It is also etymologically related to the Indus River. At first, the term Hindu was used as an ethnic or cultural term, and travelers from Persia and Greece in the sixteenth century referred to those in the Indus Valley by that name. British writers coined the term *Hinduism* during the early part of the nineteenth century to describe the culture of India. The Hindus themselves often use the term Sanatana Dharma, meaning eternal law.

The Rigveda, a collection of hymns to various gods and goddesses written around 1500 BCE, is the first literary source for understanding Hinduism's history. The Vedas were chanted aloud for centuries before being written down around 1400 CE. The Rigveda is one of four major collections of Vedas, or wisdom: Rigveda, Yajurveda, Samaveda, and Atharvaveda. Together these four are called Samhitas.

Additionally, Hinduism relies on three other Vedic works: the Aranyakas, the Brahamans, and the Upanishads. The Upanishads is a philosophical work, possibly written down between 800 and 450 BCE, that attempts to answer life's big questions. Written in the form of a dialogue between a teacher (guru) and student (chela), the text's name means "to sit near," which describes the relationship between the two. Along with the Samhitas, these four are called Sruti (heard), a reference to their nature as revealed truth. The words in these texts cannot be altered.

Remaining works are called Smriti, meaning "remembered," to indicate that they were composed by human writers. The longer of the Smriti epics is the Mahabharata, the Great Story of the Bharatas. Written between 300 and 100 BCE, the epic is a classic tale of two rival, related families, including teaching as well as story. It is considered the longest single poem in existence, with about 200,000 lines. (A film made of it lasts for twelve hours.)

The Bhagavad Gita, or Song of the Lord, is the sixth section of the Mahabharata, but is often read as a stand-alone narrative of battle and acceptance of one's dharma. The Ramayana is the second, shorter epic of the Mahabharata, with about fifty thousand lines. Rama was the seventh incarnation, or avatar, of Vishnu. The narrative relates the abduction of his wife, Sita, and her rescue, accomplished with the help of the monkey god, Hanuman. Some have regarded the Mahabharata as an encyclopedia, and the Bhagavad Gita as the Bible within it.

Although many of the practices in the Vedas have been modified or discontinued, sections of it are memorized and repeated. Some of the hymns are recited at traditional ceremonies for the dead and at weddings.

Hinduism has affected American life and culture for many years. For example, the nineteenth-century transcendental writers Margaret Fuller and Ralph Waldo Emerson were both influenced by Hindu and Buddhist literature, while musician George Harrison, a member of the Beatles, adopted Hinduism and explored his new faith through his music, both with and without the Beatles. In 1965, the International Society for Krishna Consciousness (ISKCON), or the Hare Krishna movement, came to the Western world. In addition, many people have been drawn to yoga, which is associated with Hinduism's meditative practices.

Founder or Major Prophet

Hinduism has no founder or major prophet. It is a religion that has developed over many centuries and from many sources, many of which are unknown in their origins.

Philosophical Basis

Hinduism recognizes multiple ways to achieve salvation and escape the endless cycle of rebirth. The way of devotion is the most popular. Through worship of a single deity, the worshipper hopes to attain union with the divine. A second path is the way of knowledge, involving the use of meditation and reason. The third way is via action, or correctly performing religious observances in hope of receiving a blessing from the gods by accomplishing these duties.

Hinduism is considered the world's oldest religion, but Hindus maintain that it is also a way of living, not just a religion. There is great diversity as well as great tolerance in Hinduism. While Hinduism does not have a set of dogmatic formulations, it does blend the elements of devotion, doctrine, practice, society, and story as separate strands in a braid.

During the second century BCE, a sage named Patanjali outlined four life stages, and the fulfilled responsibilities inherent in each one placed one in harmony with dharma, or right conduct. Although these life stages are no longer observed strictly, their ideas still carry weight. Traditionally, these codes applied to men, and only to those in the Brahman caste; members of the warrior and merchant classes could follow them, but were not obligated. The Shudra and Dalit castes, along with women, were not part of the system. Historically, women were thought of as protected by fathers in their childhood, by husbands in their youth and adulthood, and by sons in old age. Only recently have women in India been educated beyond the skills of domestic responsibility and child rearing.

The earliest life stage is the student stage, or brahmacharya, a word that means "to conduct oneself in accord with Brahman." From ages twelve to twenty-four, young men were expected to undertake learning with a guru, or guide. During these twelve years of studying the Veda they were also expected to remain celibate.

The second stage, grihastha, is that of householder. A Hindu man married the bride that his parents had chosen, sired children, and created a livelihood on which the other three stages depended.

Vanaprastha is the third stage, involving retirement to solitude. Historically, this involved leaving the house and entering a forest dwelling.

A man's wife had the option to go with him or to remain. This stage also involved giving counsel to others and further study.

At the final stage of life, sannyasis, the Hindu renounces material goods, including a home of any sort. He may live in a forest or join an ashram, or community. He renounces even making a fire, and lives on fruit and roots that can be foraged. Many contemporary Hindus do not move to this stage, but remain at vanaprastha.

Yoga is another Hindu practice, more than three millennia old, which Patanjali codified. The four forms of yoga corresponded to the Hindu avenues of salvation. Hatha yoga is the posture yoga seeking union with god through action. Jnana yoga is the path to god through knowledge. Bhakti yoga is the way of love to god. Karma yoga is the method of finding god through work. By uniting the self, the practitioner unites with God. Yoga is related etymologically to the English word *yoke*—it attempts to yoke the individual with Brahman. All forms of yoga include meditation and the acceptance of other moral disciplines, such as self-discipline, truthfulness, nonviolence, and contentment.

Aryan society was stratified, and at the top of the social scale were the priests. This system was the basis for the caste system that had long dominated Hinduism. Caste, which was determined by birth, affected a person's occupation, diet, neighborhood, and marriage partner. Vedic hymns allude to four varnas, or occupations: Brahmins (priests), Kshatriyas (warriors), Vaishyas (merchants and common people), and Shudras (servants). A fifth class, the Untouchables, later known as Dalit (oppressed), referred to those who were regarded as a polluting force because they handled waste and dead bodies. The belief was that society would function properly if each group carried out its duties. These varnas later became wrongly blended with castes, or jatis, which were smaller groups also concerned with a person's place in society.

The practice of Hinduism concerns itself with ritual purity; even household chores can be done in a ritualistic way. Some traditions demand ritual purity before one can worship. Brahmin priests, for example, may not accept water or food from non-Brahmins. Refusal to do so is not viewed as classism, but an attempt to please the gods in maintaining ritual purity.

Mohandas Gandhi was one of those who refused to use the term *Untouchable*, using the term *harijan*(children of God), instead. Dr. Babasaheb R. Ambedkar, who wrote India's constitution, was a member of this class. Ambedkar and many of his supporters became Buddhists in an attempt to dispel the power of caste. In 1947, following India's independence from Britain, the caste system was officially banned, though it has continued to influence Indian society.

Ahimsa, or dynamic harmlessness, is another deeply rooted principle of Hinduism. It involves six pillars: refraining from eating all animal products; revering all of life; having integrity in thoughts, words, and deeds; exercising self-control; serving creation, nature, and humanity; and advancing truth and understanding.

Holy Places

In Hinduism, all water is considered holy, symbolizing the flow of life. For a Hindu, the Ganges River is perhaps the most holy of all bodies of water. It was named for the goddess of purification, Ganga. The waters of the Ganges are said to flow through Shiva's hair and have the ability to cleanse sin. Devout Hindus make pilgrimages to bathe in the Ganges. They may also visit fords in the rivers to symbolize the journey from one life to another.

Pilgrimages are also made to sites associated with the life of a god. For example, Lord Rama was said to have been born in Ayodhya, one of the seven holy cities in India. Other holy sites are Dwarka, Ujjian, Kanchipuram, Mathura, Hardwar, and Varanasi, the City of Light.

After leaving his mountain home, Lord Shiva was thought to have lived in Varanasi, or Benares, considered the holiest city. Before the sixth century, it became a center of education for Hindus. It has four miles of palaces and temples along the river. One of the many pilgrimage circuits covers thirty-five miles, lasts for five days, and includes prayer at 108 different shrines. Because of the river's sacred nature, Hindus come to bathe from its many stone steps, called ghats, and to drink the water. It is also the place where Hindus desire to be at their death or to have their ashes scattered. Because Varanasi is regarded as a place of crossing between earth and heaven, dying there is thought to free one from the cycle of rebirth.

The thirty-four Ellora Caves at Maharashtra, India, are known for their sculptures. Built between 600 and 1000 CE, they were cut into a tufa rock hillside on a curve shaped like a horseshoe, so that the caves go deeply into the rock face. Although the one-mile site includes temples for Buddhist, Jain, and Hindu faiths, the major figure of the caves is Shiva, and the largest temple is dedicated to Shiva.

Lastly, Hindu temples, or mandirs, are regarded as the gods' earthly homes. The buildings themselves are therefore holy, and Hindus remove their shoes before entering.

HINDUISM IN DEPTH

Sacred Symbols

The wheel of life represents samsara, the cycle of life, death and rebirth. Karma is what keeps the wheel spinning. Another circle is the hoop of flames in which Shiva, also known as the Lord of the Dance, or Natraja, is shown dancing creation into being. The flames signify the universe's energy and Shiva's power of both destruction and creation. Shiva balances on his right foot, which rests on a defeated demon that stands for ignorance.

The lotus is the symbol of creation, fertility, and purity. This flower is associated with Vishnu because as he slept, a lotus flower bloomed from his navel. From this lotus Brahma came forth to create the world. Yoga practitioners commonly assume the lotus position for meditation.

Murtis are the statues of gods that are found in both temples and private homes. They are often washed with milk and water, anointed with oil, dressed, and offered gifts of food or flowers. Incense may also be burned to make the air around the murti sweet and pure.

One of Krishna's symbols is the conch shell, a symbol of a demon he defeated. A conch shell is blown at temples to announce the beginning of the worship service. It is a visual reminder for followers of Krishna to overcome ignorance and evil in their lives.

For many years, the Hindus used the swastika as a holy symbol. (*Swastika* is a Sanskrit word for good fortune and well-being.) The four arms meet at a central point, demonstrating that the universe comes from one source. Each arm of the symbol represents a path to God and is bent to show that all paths are difficult. It is used at a time of new beginnings, such as at a wedding, where it is traditionally painted on a coconut using a red paste called kum kum. The symbol appears as a vertical gash across the horizontal layers on the southern face of Mount Kailas, one of the Himalayas's highest peaks, thought to have been the home of Shiva. The mountain is also near the source of the Ganges and the Indus Rivers. The use of the swastika as a symbol for Nazi Germany is abhorrent to Hindus.

Some Hindus use a mala, or rosary, of 108 wooden beads when they pray. As they worship, they repeat the names of God.

Sacred Practices & Gestures

Many homes have private altars or shrines to favorite gods. Statues or pictures of these deities are offered incense, flowers and food, as well as prayers. This daily devotion, known as puja, is generally the responsibility of women, many of whom are devoted to goddesses such as Kali or Sita. A rich family may devote an entire room of their house to the shrine.

Om, or Aum, a sacred syllable recorded first in the Upanishads, is made up of three Sanskrit letters. Writing the letter involves a symbol resembling the Arabic number three. Thus, it is a visual reminder of the Trimurti, the three major Hindu gods. The word is repeated at the beginning of all mantras or prayers.

Each day the Gayatri, which is perhaps the world's oldest recorded prayer, is chanted during the fire ritual. The prayer expresses gratitude to the sun for its shining and invokes blessings of prosperity on all. The ritual, typically done at large consecrated fire pits, may be done using burning candles instead.

Holy Hindu men are known as sadhus. They lead ascetic lives, wandering, begging, and living in caves in the mountains. Regarded as having greater spiritual power and wisdom, they are often consulted for advice.

Food Restrictions

Many Hindus are vegetarians because they embrace ahimsa (reverence for and protection of all life) and oppose killing. In fact, Hindus comprise about 70 percent of the world's vegetarians. They are generally lacto-vegetarians, meaning that they include dairy products in their diets. However, Hindus residing in the cold climate of Nepal and Tibet consume meat to increase their caloric intake.

Whether a culture practices vegetarianism or not, cows are thought to be sacred because Krishna acted as a cowherd as a young god. Thus cows are never eaten. Pigs are also forbidden, as are red foods, such as tomatoes or red lentils. In addition, garlic and onions are also not permitted. Alcohol is strictly forbidden.

Purity rituals before eating include cleaning the area where the food is to be eaten and reciting mantras or praying while sprinkling water around the food. Other rituals include Annaprasana, which celebrates a child's eating of solid food—traditionally rice—for the first time. In addition, at funerals departed souls are offered food, which Hindus believe will strengthen the soul for the journey to the ancestors' world.

Serving food to those in need also generates good karma. Food is offered during religious ceremonies and may later be shared with visiting devotees of the god.

To show their devotion to Shiva, many Hindus fast on Mondays. There is also a regular fast, known as agiaras, which occurs on the eleventh day of each two-week period. On that day, only one meal is eaten. During the month of Shravan, which many consider a holy month, people may eat only one meal, generally following sunset.

Rites, Celebrations & Services

Many Hindu celebrations are connected to the annual cycle of nature and can last for many days. In addition, celebrations that honor the gods are common. Shiva, one of the three major gods, is honored at Shivaratri in February or March. In August or September, Lord Krishna is honored at Krishnajanmashtmi. Prayer and fasting are part of this holiday.

During the spring equinox and just prior to the Hindu New Year, Holi is celebrated. It is a time to resolve disputes and forgive or pay debts. During this festival, people often have bonfires and throw objects that represent past impurity or disease into the fire.

Another festival occurs in July or August, marking the beginning of the agricultural year in northern India. Raksha Bandhan (the bond of protection) is a festival which celebrates sibling relationships. During the festivities, Hindus bind a bauble with silk thread to the wrists of family members and friends.

To reenact Rama's defeat of the demon Ravana, as narrated in the Ramayana, people make and burn effigies. This festival is called Navaratri in western India, also known as the Durgapuja in Bengal, and Dasserah in northern India. It occurs in September or October each year as a festival celebrating the victory of good over evil. September is also time to celebrate the elephant-headed god Ganesha's birthday at the festival of Ganesh Chaturthi.

Diwali, a five-day festival honoring Lakshmi (the goddess of good fortune and wealth), occurs in October or November. This Festival of Lights is the time when people light oil lamps and set off fireworks to help Rama find his way home after exile. Homes are cleaned in hopes that Lakshmi will come in the night to bless it. People may use colored rice flour to make patterns on their doorstep. Competitions for designs of these patterns, which are meant to welcome God to the house, frequently take place.

Jagannath, or Vishnu, is celebrated during the festival Rathayatra. A large image of Jagannath rides in a chariot pulled through the city of Puri.

The temple for Hindus is the home of the god. Only Brahmin priests may supervise worship there. The inner sanctuary of the building is called the garbhagriha, or womb-house; there the god resides. Worshippers must be ritually pure before the worship starts. The priest recites the mantras and reads sacred texts. Small lamps are lit, and everyone shares specially prepared and blessed food after the service ends.

Judy A. Johnson, MTS

Bibliography

Barnes, Trevor. *The Kingfisher Book of Religions*. New York: Kingfisher, 1999. Print.

Harley, Gail M. *Hindu and Sikh Faiths in America*. New York: Facts on File, 2003. Print.

Iyengar, B. K. S. and Noelle Perez-Christiaens. *Sparks of Divinity: The Teachings of B. K. S. Iyengar from 1959 to 1975*. Berkeley: Rodmell, 2012. E-book.

"The Joys of Hinduism." *Hinduism Today* Oct./Dec. 2006: 40–53. Print.

Langley, Myrtle. *Religion*. New York: Knopf, 1996. Print.

Meredith, Susan. *The Usborne Book of World Religions*. London: Usborne, 1995. Print.

Rajan, Rajewswari. "The Politics of Hindu 'Tolerance.'" *Boundary 2* 38.3 (2011): 67–86. Print.

Raman, Varadaraja V. "Hinduism and Science: Some Reflections." *Journal of Religion & Science* 47.3 (2012): 549–74. Print.

Renard, John. *Responses to 101 Questions on Hinduism*. Mahwah: Paulist, 1999. Print.

Siddhartha. "Open-Source Hinduism." *Religion & the Arts* 12.1–3 (2008): 34–41. Print.

Shouler, Kenneth and Susai Anthony. *The Everything Hinduism Book*. Avon: Adams, 2009. Print.

Soherwordi, Syed Hussain Shaheed. "'Hinduism'—A Western Construction or an Influence?" *South Asian Studies* 26.1 (2011): 203–14. Print.

Theodor, Ithamar. *Exploring the Bhagavad Gita: Philosophy, Structure, and Meaning*. Farnham and Burlington: Ashgate, 2010. E-book.

Whaling, Frank. *Understanding Hinduism*. Edinburgh: Dunedin, 2010. E-book.

Wilkinson, Philip. *Religions*. New York: DK, 2008. Print.

Islam

General Description

The word *Islam* derives from a word meaning "submission," particularly submission to the will of Allah. Muslims, those who practice Islam, fall into two major groups, Sunni and Shia (or Shi'i,) based on political rather than theological differences. Sunni Muslims follow the four Rightly Guided Caliphs, or Rashidun and believe that caliphs should be elected. Shia Muslims believe that the Prophet's nearest male relative, Ali ibn Abi Talib, should have ruled following Muhammad's death, and venerate the imams (prayer leaders) who are directly descended from Ali and the Prophet's daughter Fatima.

Number of Adherents Worldwide

Approximately 1.6 billion people, or 23 percent of the world's population, are Muslims. Of that total, between 87 and 90 percent of all Muslims are Sunni Muslims and between 10 and 13 percent of all Muslims are Shia. Followers of the Sufi sect, noted for its experiential, ecstatic focus, may be either Sunni or Shia.

Basic Tenets

Islam is a monotheistic faith; Muslims worship only one God, Allah. They also believe in an afterlife and that people are consigned to heaven or hell following the last judgment.

The Islamic faith rests on Five Pillars. The first pillar, Shahadah is the declaration of faith in the original Arabic, translated as: "I bear witness that there is no god but God and Muhammad is his Messenger." The second pillar, Salah, are prayers adherents say while facing Mecca five times daily at regular hours and also at the main service held each Friday at a mosque. Zakat, "the giving of a tax," is the third pillar and entails giving an income-based percentage of one's wealth to help the poor without attracting notice. The fourth pillar is fasting, or Sawm, during Ramadan, the ninth month of the Islamic calendar. Certain groups of people are excused from the fast, however. The final pillar is the Hajj, the pilgrimage to Mecca required of every able-bodied Muslim at least once in his or her lifetime.

Sacred Text

The Qur'an (Koran), meaning "recitation," is the holy book of Islam.

Major Figures

Muhammad, regarded as the Prophet to the Arabs—as Moses was to the Jews—is considered the exemplar of what it means to be a Muslim. His successors—Abu Bakr, Umar, Uthman, and Ali—were known as the four Rightly Guided Caliphs.

Major Holy Sites

Islam recognizes three major holy sites: Mecca, home of the Prophet; Medina, the city to which Muslims relocated when forced from Mecca due to persecution; and the Dome of the Rock in Jerusalem, believed to be the oldest Islamic building in existence. Muslims believe that in 621 CE Muhammad ascended to heaven (called the Night Journey) from a sacred stone upon which the Dome was constructed. Once in heaven, God instructed Muhammad concerning the need to pray at regular times daily...

There are also several mosques which are considered primary holy sites. These include the al-Aqsa Mosque in the Old City of Jerusalem, believed by many to be the third holiest site in Islam. The mosque, along with the Dome of the Rock, is located on Judaism's holiest site, the Temple Mount, where the Temple of Jerusalem is believed to have stood. Muslims also revere the Mosque of the Prophet (Al-Masjid al-Nabawi) in Medina, considered the resting place of the Prophet Muhammad and the second largest mosque in the world; and the Mosque of the Haram (Masjid al-Haram or the Sacred or Grand Mosque) in Mecca, thought to be the largest mosque in the world and site of the Ka'bah, "the sacred house," also known as "the Noble Cube," Islam's holiest structure.

Major Rites & Celebrations

Two major celebrations mark the Islamic calendar. 'Id al-Adha, the feast of sacrifice—including animal sacrifice—held communally at the close of the Hajj (annual pilgrimage), commemorates the account of God providing a ram instead of the son Abraham had been asked to sacrifice. The second festival, 'Id al-Fitr, denotes the end of Ramadan and is a time of feasting and gift giving.

ORIGINS

History & Geography

In 610 CE, a forty-year-old businessman from Mecca named Muhammad ibn Abdullah, from the powerful Arab tribe Quraysh, went to Mount Hira to meditate, as he regularly did for the month of Ramadan. During that month, an entire group of men, the hanif, retreated to caves. The pagan worship practiced in the region, as well as the cruelty and lack of care for the poor, distressed Muhammad. As the tribe to which he belonged had become wealthy through trade, it had begun disregarding traditions prescribed by the nomadic code.

The archangel Jibra'il (Gabriel) appeared in Muhammad's cave and commanded him to read the words of God contained in the scroll that the angel showed him. Like most people of his time, Muhammad was illiterate, but repeated the words Jibra'il said. Some followers of Islam believe that this cave at Jebel Nur, in what is now Saudi Arabia, is where Adam, the first human Allah created, lived.

A frightened Muhammad told only his wife, Khadija, about his experience. For two years, Muhammad received further revelations, sharing them only with family and close friends. Like other prophets, he was reluctant about his calling, fearing that he was—or would be accused of being—possessed by evil spirits or insane. At one point, he tried to commit suicide, but was stopped by the voice of Jibra'il affirming his status as God's messenger.

Muhammad recalled the words spoken to him, which were eventually written down. The Qur'an is noted for being a book of beautiful language, and Muhammad's message reached many. The Prophet thus broke the old pattern of allegiance to tribe and forged a new community based on shared practice.

Muhammad considered himself one who was to warn the others of a coming judgment. His call for social justice and denunciation of the wealthy disturbed the powerful Arab tribe members in Mecca. These men stood to lose the status and income derived from the annual festival to the Ka'bah. The Prophet and his followers were persecuted and were the subject of boycotts and death threats. In 622 CE, Muslim families began a migration (hijrah) to Yathrib, later known as Medina. Two years earlier, the city had sent envoys seeking Muhammad's leadership for their own troubled society. The hijrah marks the beginning of the Islamic calendar.

The persecutions eventually led to outright tribal warfare, linking Islam with political prowess through the victories of the faithful. The Muslims moved from being an oppressed minority to being a political force. In 630 CE, Muhammad and ten thousand of his followers marched to Mecca, taking the city without bloodshed. He destroyed the pagan idols that were housed and worshipped at the Ka'bah, instead associating the hajj with the story of Abraham sending his concubine Hagar and their son Ishmael (Ismail in Arabic) out into the wilderness. With this victory, Muhammad ended centuries of intertribal warfare.

Muhammad died in 632, without designating a successor. Some of the Muslims believed that his nearest male relative should rule, following the custom of the tribes. Ali ibn Abi Talib, although a pious Muslim, was still young. Therefore, Abu Bakr, the Prophet's father-in-law, took the title khalifah, or caliph, which means successor or deputy. Within two years Abu Bakr had stabilized Islam. He was followed by three additional men whom Muhammad had known. Collectively, the four are known as the Four Rightly Guided Caliphs, or the Rashidun. Their rule extended from 632 until 661. Each of the final three met a violent death.

Umar, the second caliph, increased the number of raids on adjacent lands during his ten-year rule, which began in 634. This not only increased wealth, but also gave Umar the authority he needed, since Arabs objected to the idea of a monarchy. Umar was known as the commander of the faithful. Under his leadership, the Islamic community marched into present-day Iraq, Syria, and Egypt and achieved victory over the Persians in 637.

Muslims elected Uthman ibn Affan as the third caliph after Umar was stabbed by a Persian prisoner of war. He extended Muslim conquests into North Africa as well as into Iran, Afghanistan, and parts of India. A group of soldiers mutinied in 656, assassinating Uthman.

Ali, Muhammad's son-in-law, was elected caliph of a greatly enlarged empire. Conflict developed between Ali and the ruler in Damascus whom Uthman had appointed governor of Syria. The fact that the governor came from a rival tribe led to further tensions. Increasingly, Damascus rather than Medina was viewed as the key Muslim locale. Ali was murdered in 661 during the internal struggles.

Within a century after Muhammad's death, Muslims had created an empire that stretched from Spain across Asia to India and facilitated the spread of Islam. The conquerors followed a policy of relative, though not perfect, tolerance toward adherents of other religions. Christians and Jews received special status as fellow "People of the Book," though they were still required to pay a special poll tax in exchange for military protection. Pagans, however, were required to convert to Islam or face death. Later, Hindus, Zoroastrians, and other peoples were also permitted to pay the tax rather than submit to conversion. Following the twelfth century, Sufi mystics made further converts in Central Asia, India, sub-Saharan Africa, and Turkey. Muslim traders also were responsible for the growth of Islam, particularly in China, Indonesia, and Malaya.

The Muslim empire continued to grow until it weakened in the fourteenth century, when it was replaced as a major world power by European states. The age of Muslim domination ended with the 1683 failure of the Ottoman Empire to capture Vienna, Austria.

Although lacking in political power until recent years, a majority of nations in Indonesia, the Middle East, and East and North Africa are predominately Islamic. The rise of Islamic fundamentalists who interpret the Qur'an literally and seek victory through acts of terrorism began in the late twentieth century. Such extremists do not represent the majority of the Muslim community, however.

Like Judaism and Christianity, Islam has been influenced by its development in a desert climate. Arabia, a region three times the size of France, is a land of steppe and desert whose unwelcoming climate kept it from being mapped with any precision until the 1950s. Because Yemen received monsoon rains, it could sustain agriculture and became a center for civilization as early as the second millennium BCE. In the seventh century CE, nomads roamed the area, guarding precious wells and oases. Raiding caravans and other tribes were common ways to obtain necessities.

Mecca was a pagan center of worship, but it was located not far from a Christian kingdom, Ethiopia, across the Red Sea. Further north, followers of both Judaism and Christianity had influenced members of Arab tribes. Jewish tribes inhabited Yathrib, the city later known as Medina. Neither Judaism nor Christianity was especially kind to those they considered pagans. According to an Arabian tradition, in 570 the Ethiopians attacked Yemen and attempted an attack on Mecca. Mecca was caught between two enemy empires—Christian Byzantine and Zoroastrian Persia—that fought a lengthy war during Muhammad's lifetime.

The contemporary clashes between Jews and Muslims are in part a result of the dispersion of Muslims who had lived in Palestine for centuries. More Jews began moving into the area under the British Mandate; in 1948, the state of Israel was proclaimed. Historically, Jews had been respected as a People of the Book.

Founder or Major Prophet

Muslims hold Allah to be the founder of their religion and Abraham to have been the first Muslim. Muhammad is God's prophet to the Arabs. The instructions that God gave Muhammad through the archangel Jibra'il and through direct revelation are the basis for the Islamic religion. These revelations were given over a period of twenty-one years. Because Muhammad and most of the Muslims were illiterate, the teachings were read publicly in chapters, or suras.

Muhammad did not believe he was founding a new religion. Rather, he was considered God's final Prophet, as Moses and Jesus had been prophets. His task was to call people to repent and to return to the straight path of God's law, called Sharia. God finally was sending a direct revelation to the Arab peoples, who had sometimes been taunted by the other civilizations as being left out of God's plan.

Muhammad, who had been orphaned by age six, was raised by an uncle. He became a successful businessman of an important tribe and married Khadija, for whom he worked. His integrity was such that he was known as al-Amin, the trusted one. He and Khadija had six children; four daughters survived. After Khadija's death, Muhammad married several women, as was the custom for a great chief. Several of the marriages were political in nature.

Muhammad is regarded as the living Qur'an. He is sometimes referred to as the perfect man, one who is an example of how a Muslim should live. He was ahead of his time in his attitudes toward women, listening to their counsel and granting them rights not enjoyed by women in other societies, including the right to inherit property and to divorce. (It should be noted that the Qur'an does not require the seclusion or veiling of all women.)

Islam has no religious leaders, especially those comparable to other religions. Each mosque has an imam to preach and preside over prayer at the Friday services. Although granted a moral authority, the imam is not a religious leader with a role comparable to that of rabbis or priests.

Philosophical Basis

Prior to Muhammad's receiving the Qur'an, the polytheistic tribes believed in Allah, "the god." Allah was far away and not part of worship rituals, although he had created the world and sustained it. He had three daughters who were goddesses.

Islam began pragmatically—the old tribal ways were not working—as a call for social justice, rooted in Muhammad's dissatisfaction with the increasing emphasis on accumulating wealth and an accompanying neglect of those in need. The struggle (jihad) to live according to God's desire for humans was to take place within the community, or the ummah. This effort was more important than dogmatic statements or beliefs about God. When the community prospered, this was a sign of God's blessing.

In addition, the revelation of the Qur'an gave Arab nations an official religion. The Persians around them had Zoroastrianism, the Romans and Byzantines had Christianity, and the Jews of the Diaspora had Judaism. With the establishment of Islam, Arabs finally could believe that they were part of God's plan for the world.

Four principles direct Islam's practice and doctrine. These include the Qur'an; the traditions, or sunnah; consensus, or ijma'; and individual thought, or ijtihad. The term sunnah, "well-trodden path," had been used by Arabs before Islam to refer to their tribal law.

A fifth important source for Islam is the Hadith, or report, a collection of the Prophet's words and actions, intended to serve as an example. Sunni Muslims refer to six collections made in the ninth century, while Shia Muslims have a separate Hadith of four collections.

Holy Places

Mecca was located just west of the Incense Road, a major trade route from southern Arabia to Palestine and Syria. Mecca was the Prophet's home and the site where he received his revelations. It is also the city where Islam's holiest structure, the Ka'bah, "the sacred house," was located. The Ka'bah was regarded as having been built by Abraham and his son Ishmael. This forty-three-foot gray stone cube was a center for pagan idols in the time of Muhammad. In 628 the Prophet removed 360 pagan idols—one for each day of the Arabic lunar year—from inside the Ka'bah.

When the followers of Muhammad experienced persecution for their beliefs, they fled to the city of Medina, formerly called Yathrib. When his uncle Abu Talib died, Muhammad lost the protection from persecution that his uncle had provided. He left for Ta'if in the mountains, but it was also a center for pagan cults, and he was driven out. After a group of men from Yathrib promised him protection, Muhammad sent seventy of his followers to the city, built around an oasis about 215 miles north. This migration, called the hijra, occurred in 622, the first year of the Muslim calendar. From this point on, Islam became an organized religion rather than a persecuted and minority cult. The Prophet was buried in Medina in 632, and his mosque in that city is deeply revered.

Islam's third holiest site is the Dome of the Rock in Jerusalem. Muslims believe that the Prophet Muhammad ascended to heaven in 621 from the rock located at the center of this mosque. During this so-called night journey, Allah gave him instructions about prayer. In the shrine at the Dome of the Rock is a strand of hair that Muslims believe was Muhammad's.

Shia Muslims also revere the place in present-day Iraq where Ali's son, Husayn, was martyred. They regard the burial place of Imam Ali ar-Rida in Meshed, Iran, as a site of pilgrimage as well.

ISLAM IN DEPTH

Sacred Symbols

Muslims revere the Black Stone, a possible meteorite that is considered a link to heaven. It is set inside the Ka'bah shrine's eastern corner. The Ka'bah is kept covered by the kiswa, a black velvet cloth decorated with embroidered calligraphy in gold. At the hajj, Muslims walk around it counterclockwise seven times as they recite prayers to Allah.

Muslim nations have long used the crescent moon and a star on their flags. The crescent moon, which the Ottomans first adopted as a symbol during the fifteenth century, is often placed on the dome of a mosque, pointing toward Mecca. For Muhammad, the waxing and waning of the moon signified the unchanging and eternal purpose of God. Upon seeing a new moon, the Prophet confessed his faith in God. Muslims rely on a lunar calendar and the Qur'an states that God created the stars to guide people to their destinations.

Islam forbids the making of graven images of animals or people, although not all Islamic cultures follow this rule strictly. The decorative arts of Islam have placed great emphasis on architecture and calligraphy to beautify mosques and other buildings. In addition, calligraphy, floral motifs, and geometric forms decorate some editions of the Qur'an's pages, much as Christian monks once decorated hand-copied scrolls of the Bible. These elaborate designs can also be seen on some prayer rugs, and are characteristic of Islamic art in general.

Sacred Practices & Gestures

When Muslims pray, they must do so facing Mecca, a decision Muhammad made in January 624 CE. Prior to that time, Jerusalem—a holy city for both Jews and Christians—had been the geographic focus. Prayer involves a series of movements that embody submission to Allah.

Muslims sometimes use a strand of prayer beads, known as subhah, to pray the names of God. The beads can be made of bone, precious stones, or wood. Strings may have twenty-five, thirty-three or 100 beads.

Food Restrictions

Those who are physically able to do so fast from both food and drink during the daylight hours of the month Ramadan. Although fasting is not required of the sick, the aged, menstruating or pregnant women, or children, some children attempt to fast, imitating their parents' devotion. Those who cannot fast are encouraged to do so the following Ramadan. This fast is intended to concentrate the mind on Allah. Muslims recite from the Qur'an during the month.

All meat must be prepared in a particular way so that it is halal, or permitted. While slaughtering the animal, the person must mention the name of Allah. Blood, considered unclean, must be allowed to drain. Because pigs were fed garbage, their meat was considered unclean. Thus Muslims eat no pork, even though in modern times, pigs are often raised on grain.

In three different revelations, Muslims are also forbidden to consume fermented beverages. Losing self-control because of drunkenness violates the Islamic desire for self-mastery.

Rites, Celebrations, and Services

The **mosque** is the spiritual center of the Muslim community. From the minaret (a tower outside the mosque), the call to worship occurs five times daily—at dawn, just past noon, at midafternoon, at sunset, and in the evening. In earliest times, a muezzin, the official responsible for this duty, gave the cry. In many modern countries, the call now comes over a speaker system. Also located outside are fountains to provide the necessary water for ritual washing before prayer. Muslims wash their face, hands, forearms, and feet, as well as remove their shoes before beginning their prayers. In the absence of water, ritual cleansing may occur using sand or a stone.

Praying involves a series of movements known as rak'ah. From a standing position, the worshipper recites the opening sura of the Qur'an, as well as a second sura. After bowing to demonstrate respect, the person again stands, then prostrates himself or herself to signal humility. Next, the person assumes a sitting posture in silent prayer before again prostrating. The last movement is a greeting of "Peace be with you and the mercy of Allah." The worshipper looks both left and right before saying these words, which are intended for all persons, present and not.

Although Muslims stop to pray during each day when the call is given, Friday is the time for communal prayer and worship at the mosque. The prayer hall is the largest space within the mosque. At one end is a niche known as the mihrab, indicating the direction of Mecca, toward which Muslims face when they pray. At first, Muhammad instructed his followers to pray facing Jerusalem, as the Jewish people did. This early orientation was also a way to renounce the pagan associations of Mecca. Some mosques serve as community centers, with additional rooms for study.

The hajj, an important annual celebration, was a custom before the founding of Islam. Pagan worship centered in Mecca at the Ka'bah, where devotees circled the cube and kissed the Black Stone that was embedded in it. All warfare was forbidden during the hajj, as was argument, speaking crossly, or killing even an insect.

Muslims celebrate the lives of saints and their death anniversaries, a time when the saints are thought to reach the height of their spiritual life. Mawlid an-Nabi refers to "the birth of the Prophet." Although it is cultural and not rooted in the Qur'an, in some Muslim countries this is a public holiday on which people recite the Burdah, a poem that praises Muhammad. Muslims also celebrate the night that the Prophet ascended to heaven, Lailat ul-Miraj. The Night of Power is held to be the night on which Allah decides the destiny of people individually and the world at large.

Like Jews, Muslims practice circumcision, a ceremony known as khitan. Unlike Jews, however, Muslims do not remove the foreskin when the male is a baby. This is often done when a boy is about seven, and must be done before the boy reaches the age of twelve.

Healthy adult Muslims fast between sunrise and sunset during the month of Ramadan. This commemorates the first of Muhammad's revelations. In some Muslim countries, cannons are fired before the beginning of the month, as well as at the beginning and end of each day of the month. Some Muslims read a portion of the Qur'an each day during the month.

Judy A. Johnson, MTS

Bibliography

Al-Saud, Laith, Scott W. Hibbard, and Aminah Beverly. *An Introduction to Islam in the 21st Century*. Wiley, 2013. E-book.

Armstrong, Lyall. "The Rise of Islam: Traditional and Revisionist Theories." *Theological Review* 33.2 (2012): 87–106. Print.

Armstrong, Karen. *Islam: A Short History*. New York: Mod. Lib., 2000. Print.

Aslan, Reza. *No god but God: The Origins, Evolution, and Future of Islam*. New York: Random, 2005. Print.

Badawi, Emran El-. "'For All Times and Places': A Humanistic Reception of the Qur'an." *English Language Notes* 50.2 (2012): 99–112. Print.

Barnes, Trevor. *The Kingfisher Book of Religions*. New York: Kingfisher, 1999. Print.

Ben Jelloun, Tahar. *Islam Explained*. Trans. Franklin Philip. New York: New, 2002. Print.

Esposito, John L. *Islam: the Straight Path*. New York: Oxford UP, 1988. Print.

Glady, Pearl. *Criticism of Islam*.Library, 2012. E-book.

Holland, Tom. "Where Mystery Meets History." *History Today* 62.5 (2012): 19–24. Print.

Langley, Myrtle. *Religion*. New York: Knopf, 1996. Print.

Lunde, Paul. *Islam: Faith, Culture, History*. London: DK, 2002. Print.

Nasr, Seyyed Hossein. *Islam: Religion, History, and Civilization*. New York: Harper, 2002. Print.

Pasha, Mustapha Kamal. "Islam and the Postsecular." *Review of International Studies* 38.5 (2012): 1041–56. Print.

Sayers, Destini and Simone Peebles. *Essence of Islam and Sufism*. College, 2012. E-book.

Schirmacher, Christine. "They Are Not All Martyrs: Islam on the Topics of Dying, Death, and Salvation in the Afterlife." *Evangelical Review of Theology* 36.3 (2012): 250–65. Print.

Wilkinson, Philip. *Islam*. New York: DK, 2002. Print.

Wilkinson, Philip. *Religions*. New York: DK, 2008. Print.

Jainism

General Description

Jainism is one of the major religions of India. The name of the religion itself is believed to be based on the Sanskrit word *ji*, which means "to conquer or triumph," or *jina*, which means "victor or conqueror." The earliest name of the group was Nirgrantha, meaning bondless, but it applied to monks and nuns only. There are two sects: the Svetambaras (the white clad), which are the more numerous and wear white clothing, and the Digambaras (the sky clad), the most stringent group; their holy men or monks do not wear clothing at all.

Number of Adherents Worldwide

Jainism has about five million adherents, most of them in India (in some estimates, the religion represents approximately 1 percent of India's population). Because the religion is demanding in nature, few beyond the Indian subcontinent have embraced it. Jainism has spread to Africa, the United States, and nations in the Commonwealth (nations once under British rule) by virtue of Indian migration to these countries.

Basic Tenets

The principle of nonviolence (ahimsa) is a defining feature of Jainism. This results in a pacifist religion that influenced Mohandas Gandhi's ideas on nonviolent resistance. Jains believe that because all living creatures have souls, harming any of those creatures is wrong. They therefore follow a strict vegetarian diet, and often wear masks so as to not inhale living organisms. The most important aspect of Jainism is perhaps the five abstinences: ahimsa, satya (truthfulness), asteya (refrain from stealing), brahmacarya (chaste living), and aparigraha (refrain from greed).

A religion without priests, Jainism emphasizes the importance of the adherents' actions. Like Buddhists and Hindus, Jainists believe in karma and reincarnation. Unlike the Buddhist and Hindu idea of karma, Jainists regard karma as tiny particles that cling to the soul as mud clings to shoes, gradually weighing down the soul. Good deeds wash away these particles. Jainists also believe in moksha, the possibility of being freed from the cycle of death and rebirth. Like many Indian religions, Jainism does not believe in an afterlife, but in a cycle of death and rebirth. Once freed from this cycle, the soul will remain in infinite bliss.

While Jains do not necessarily believe in and worship God or gods, they believe in divine beings. Those who have achieved moksha are often regarded by Jains in the same manner in which other religions regard deities. These include the twenty-four Tirthankaras (ford makers) or jinas (victors), those who have escaped the cycle of death and rebirth, and the Siddhas, the liberated souls without physical form. The idea of a judging, ruling, or creator God is not present in Jainism.

Jainists believe that happiness is not found in material possessions and seek to have few of them. They also stress the importance of environmentalism. Jainists follow the Three Jewels: Right Belief, Right Knowledge, and Right Conduct. To be completely achieved, these three must be practiced together. Jainists also agree to six daily obligations (avashyaka), which include confession, praising the twenty-four Tirthankaras (the spiritual leaders), and calm meditation.

Sacred Text

The words of Mahavira were passed down orally, but lost over a few centuries. During a famine in the mid-fourth century BCE, many monks died. The texts were finally written down, although the Jain sects do not agree as to whether they are Mahavira's actual words. There are forty-five sacred texts (Agamas), which make up the Agam Sutras, Jainism's canonical literature. They were probably written down no earlier than 300 BCE. Two of the primary texts are the Akaranga

Sutra, which outlines the rule of conduct for Jain monks, and the Kalpa Sutra, which contains biographies of the last two Tirthankara. The Digambaras, who believe that the Agamas were lost around 350 BCE, have two main texts and four compendia written between 100 and 800 CE by various scholars.

Major Figures

Jainism has no single founder. However, Mahavira (Great Hero) is one of the Tirthankaras or jinas (pathfinders). He is considered the most recent spiritual teacher in a line of twenty-four. Modern-day Jainism derives from Mahavira, and his words are the foundation of Jain scriptures. He was a contemporary of Siddhartha Gautama, who was revered as the Buddha. Both Mahavira and Rishabha (or Adinatha), the first of the twenty-four Tirthankaras, are attributed as the founder of Jainism, though each Tirthankara maintains founding attributes.

Major Holy Sites

The Jain temple at Ranakpur is located in the village of Rajasthan. Carved from amber stone with marble interiors, the temple was constructed in the fifteenth century CE. It is dedicated to the first Tirthankara. The temple has twenty-nine large halls and each of the temple's 1,444 columns has a unique design with carvings.

Sravanabegola in Karnataka state is the site of Gomateshwara, Lord Bahubali's fifty-seven-foot statue. It was constructed in 981 CE from a single chunk of gneiss. Bahubali is considered the son of the first Tirthankara. The Digambara sect believes him to have been the first human to be free from the world.

Other pilgrimage sites include the Palitana temples in Gujarat and the Dilwara temples in Rajasthan. Sometimes regarded as the most sacred of the many Jain temples, the Palitana temples include 863 marble-engraved temples. The Jain temples at Dilwara were constructed of marble during the eleventh and thirteenth centuries CE. These five temples are often considered the most beautiful Jain temples in existence.

Major Rites & Celebrations

Every twelve years, the festival of Mahamastak-abhisheka (anointing of the head) occurs at a statue of one of Jain's holy men, Bahubali, the second son of the first Tirthankara. The statue is anointed with milk, curd, and ghee, a clarified butter. Nearly a million people attend this rite. Jainists also observe Diwali, the Hindu festival of lights, as it symbolizes Mahavira's enlightenment.

The solemn festival of Paryusana marks the end of the Jain year for the Svetambaras (also spelled Shvetambaras). During this eight-day festival, all Jains are asked to live as an ascetic (monk or nun) would for one day. Das Laxana, a ten-day festival similar to that of Paryusana, immediately follows for the Digambara sect. During these special religious holidays, worshippers are involved in praying, meditating, fasting, forgiveness, and acts of penance. These holy days are celebrated during August and September, which is monsoon season in India. During the monsoons, monks prefer to remain in one place so as to avoid killing the smallest insects that appear during the rainy season. The Kalpa Sutra, one of the Jain scriptures, is read in the morning during Paryusana.

The feast of Kartaki Purnima follows the four months of the rainy season. It is held in the first month (Kartik) according to one calendar, and marked by a pilgrimage to the Palitana temples. Doing so with a pure heart is said to remove all sins of both the present and past life. Those who do so are thought to receive the final salvation in the third or fifth birth.

ORIGINS

History & Geography

In the eastern basin of the Ganges River during the seventh century BCE, a teacher named Parshvanatha (or Parshva) gathered a community founded on abandoning earthly concerns. He is considered to be the twenty-third Tirthankara (ford-maker), the one who makes a path for salvation. During the following century, Vardhamana, called Mahavira (Great Hero), who was considered the twenty-fourth and final spiritual teacher of the age, formulated most Jain doctrine and practice. By the time of Mahavira's death, Jains numbered around 36,000 nuns and 14,000 monks.

A division occurred within Jainism during the fourth century CE. The most extreme ascetics, the Digambaras (the sky-clad), argued that even clothing showed too great an attachment to the world, and that laundering them in the river risked harming creatures. This argument applied only to men, as the Digambaras denied that a soul could be freed from a woman's body. The other group, the Svetambaras (the white-clad), believed that purity resided in the mind.

In 453 or 456 CE, a council of the Svetambara sect at Saurashtra in western India codified the canon still used. The split between the Digambaras, who did not take part in the meeting, and Svetambaras thus became permanent. Despite the split, Jainism's greatest flowering occurred during the early medieval age. After that time, Hindu sects devoted to the Hindu gods of Vishnu and Shiva flourished under the Gupta Empire (often referred to as India's golden age), slowing the spread of Jainism. Followers migrated to western and central India and the community became stronger.

The Digambaras were involved in politics through several medieval dynasties, and some Jain monks served as spiritual advisers. Royalty and high-ranking officials contributed to the building and maintenance of temples. Both branches of Jainism contributed a substantial literature. In the late medieval age, Jain monks ceased to live as ascetic wanders. They chose instead to don orange robes and to live at temples and other holy places.

The Muslims invaded India in the twelfth century. The Jains lost power and fractured over the next centuries into subgroups, some of which repudiated the worship of images. The poet and Digambara layman Banarsidas (1586-1643) played a significant role in a reform movement during the early 1600s. These reforms focused on the mystical side of Jainism, such as spiritual exploration of the inner self (meditation),

and denounced the formalized temple ritual. The movement, known as the Adhyatma movement, resulted in the Digambara Terapanth, a small Digambara sect.

The Jainists were well positioned in society following the departure of the British from India. Having long been associated with the artisan and merchant classes, they found new opportunities. As traditional Indian studies grew, spurred by Western interest, proponents of Jainism began to found publications and places of study (In fact, Jain libraries are believed to be the oldest in India.) The first Jain temple outside India was consecrated in Britain during the 1960s after Jains had gone there in the wake of political turmoil.

The Jains follow their typical profession as merchants. They publish English-language periodicals to spread their ideas on vegetarianism, environmentalism, and nonviolence (ahimsa). The ideas of ahimsa were formative for Mohandas Gandhi, born a Hindu. Gandhi used nonviolence as a wedge against the British Empire in India. Eventually, the British granted independence to India in 1947.

Virchand Gandhi (1864–1901) is believed to be the first Jain to arrive in America when he came over in 1893. He attended the first Parliament of World Religions, held in Chicago. Today North America has more than ninety Jain temples and centers. Jains in the West often follow professions such as banking and business to avoid destroying animal or plant life.

Founder or Major Prophet

Mahavira was born in India's Ganges Basin region. By tradition, he was born around 599 BCE, although some scholars think he may have lived a century later. His story bears a resemblance to that of the Buddha, with whom he was believed to have been a contemporary. His family was also of the Kshatriya (warrior) caste, and his father was a ruler of his clan. One tradition states that Mahavira's mother was of the Brahman (priestly) caste, although another places her in the Kshatriya.

Because he was not the eldest son, Mahavira was not in line for leadership of the clan.

He married a woman of his own caste and they had a daughter. Mahavira chose the life of a monk, with one garment. Later, he gave up wearing even that. He became a wandering ascetic around age thirty, with some legends stating that he tore out his hair before leaving home. He sought shelter in burial grounds and cremation sites, as well as at the base of trees. During the rainy season, however, he lived in towns and villages.

He followed a path of preaching and self-denial, after which he was enlightened (kevala). He spent the next thirty years teaching. Eleven disciples, all of whom were of the Brahman caste, gathered around him. At the end of his life, Mahavira committed Santhara, or ritual suicide through fasting.

Philosophical Basis

Like Buddhists and the Brahmin priests, the Jains believe in human incarnations of God, known as avatars. These avatars appear at the end of a time of decline to reinstate proper thinking and acting. Such a person was Mahavira. At the time of Mahavira's birth, India was experiencing great societal upheaval. Members of the warrior caste opposed the priestly caste, which exercised authority based on its supposed greater moral purity. Many people also opposed the slaughter of animals for the Vedic sacrifices.

Jainists share some beliefs with both Hinduism and Buddhism. The Hindu hero Rama, for example, is co-opted as a nonviolent Jain, while the deity Krishna is considered a cousin of Arishtanemi, the twenty-second Tirthankara. Like Buddhism, Jainism uses a wheel with twelve spokes; however, Jainism uses the wheel to explain time. The first half of the circle is the ascending stage, in which human happiness, prosperity, and life span increase. The latter half of the circle is the descending stage, involving a decrease of life span, prosperity, and happiness. The wheel of time is always in motion.

For Jainists, the universe is without beginning or ending, and contains layers of both heaven and hell. These layers include space beyond, which is without time, matter, or soul. The cosmos is depicted in art as a large human. The cloud layers surrounding the upper world are called universe space. Above them is the base, Nigoda, where lowest life forms live. The netherworld contains seven hells, each with a different stage of punishment and misery. The middle world contains the earth and remainder of the universe—mankind is located near the waist. There are thirty heavens in the upper world, where heavenly beings reside. In the supreme abode at the apex of the universe, liberated souls (siddha) live.

Jainism teaches that there are six universal entities. Only consciousness or soul is a living substance, while the remaining five are non-living. They include matter, medium of rest, medium of motion, time, and space. Jainism also does not believe in a God who can create, destroy, or protect. Worshipping goddesses and gods to achieve personal gain or material benefit is deemed useless.

Mahavira outlined five basic principles (often referred to as abstinences) for Jainist life, based on the teachings of the previous Tirthankara. They are detachment (aparigraha); the conduct of soul, primarily in sexual morality (brahmacharya); abstinence from stealing (asteya); abstinence from lying (satya); and non-violence in every realm of the person (ahimsa).

Like other Indian religions, Jainism perceives life as four stages. The life of a student is brahmacharya-ashrama; the stage of family life is gruhasth-ashrama; in vanaprasth-ashrama, the Jainist concentrates on both family and aiding others through social services; and the final stage is sanyast-ashrama, a time of renouncing the world and becoming a monk.

Like many religions, Jainism has a bias toward males and toward the rigorous life of monks and nuns. A layperson cannot work off bad karma, but merely keeps new bad karma from accruing. By following a path of asceticism, however, monks and nuns can destroy karma. Even members of the laity follow eight rules of behavior and take twelve vows. Physical austerity is a key concept in Jainism, as a saint's highest ideal is to starve to death.

Holy Places

There are four major Jain pilgrimage sites: the Dilwara temples near Rajasthan; the Palitana temples; the Ranakpur temple; and Shravan Begola, the site of the statue of Lord Bahubali. In addition, Jains may make pilgrimages to the caves of Khandagiri and Udayagiri, which were cells for Jain monks carved from rock. The spaces carved are too short for a man to stand upright. They were essentially designed for prayer and meditation. Udayagiri has eighteen caves and Khandagiri has fifteen. The caves are decorated with elaborate carvings.

JAINISM IN DEPTH

Sacred Symbols

The open palm (Jain Hand) with a centered wheel, sometimes with the word *ahimsa* written on it, is a prominent Jain symbol. Seen as an icon of peace, the open palm symbol can be interpreted as a call to stop violence, and also means "assurance." It appears on the walls of Jain temples and in their publications. Jainism also employs a simple swastika symbol, considered to be the holiest symbol. It represents the four forms of worldly existence, and three dots above the swastika represent the Three Jewels. The Jain emblem, adopted in 1975, features both the Jain Hand (the open palm symbol with an inset wheel) and a swastika. This year was regarded as the 2,500th anniversary of Mahavira being enlightened.

Sacred Practices & Gestures

Jains may worship daily in their homes at private shrines. The Five Supreme Beings stand for stages in the path to enlightenment. Rising before daybreak, worshippers invoke these five. In addition, devout Jainists set aside forty-eight minutes daily to meditate.

To demonstrate faithfulness to the five vows that Jains undertake, there are four virtuous qualities that must be cultivated. They are compassion (karuna), respect and joy (pramoda), love and friendship (maitri), and indifference toward and noninvolvement with those who are arrogant (madhyastha). Mahavira stressed that Jains must be friends to all living beings. Compassion goes beyond mere feeling; it involves offering both material and spiritual aid. Pramoda carries with it the idea of rejoicing enthusiastically over the virtues of others. There are contemplations associated with these virtues, and daily practice is suggested to attain mastery.

Some Jainists, both men and women, wear a dot on the forehead. This practice comes from Hinduism. During festivals, Jains may pray, chant, fast, or keep silent. These actions are seen as removing bad karma from the soul and moving the person toward ultimate happiness.

Food Restrictions

Jainists practice a strict vegetarian way of life (called Jain vegetarianism) to avoid harming any creature. They refuse to eat root vegetables, because by uprooting them, the entire plant dies. They prefer to wait for fruit to drop from trees rather than taking it from the branches. Starving to death, when ready, is seen as an ideal.

Rites, Celebrations & Services

Some festivals are held annually and their observances are based on a lunar calendar. Mahavir Jayanti is an example, as it celebrates Mahavira's birthday.

Jains may worship, bathe, and make offerings to images of the Tirthankaras in their home or in a temple. Svetambaras Jains also clothe and decorate the images. Because the Tirthankaras have been liberated, they cannot respond as a deity granting favors might. Although Jainism rejects belief in gods in favor of worshipping Tirthankaras, in actual practice, some Jainists pray to Hindu gods.

When Svetambara monks are initiated, they are given three pieces of clothing, including a small piece of white cloth to place over the mouth. The cloth, called a mukhavastrika, is designed to prevent the monk from accidentally eating insects.

Monks take great vows (mahavratas) at initiation. These include abstaining from lying, stealing, sexual activity, injury to any living thing, and personal possessions. Monks own a broom to sweep in front of where they are going to walk so that no small creatures are injured, along with an alms bowl and a robe. The Digambara monks practice a more stringent lifestyle, eating one meal a day, for which they beg.

Nuns in the Svetambaras are three times more common than are monks, even though they receive less honor, and are required to defer to the monks. In Digambara Jainism, the nuns wear robes and accept that they must be reborn as men before progressing upward.

The observance of Santhara, which is religious fasting until death, is a voluntary fasting undertaken with full knowledge. The ritual is also known as Sallekhana, and is not perceived as suicide by Jains, particularly as the prolonged nature of the ritual provides ample time for reflection. It is believed that at least one hundred people die every year from observing Santhara.

Judy A. Johnson, MTS

Bibliography

Aristarkhova, Irina. "Thou Shall Not Harm All Living Beings: Feminism, Jainism, and Animals." *Hypatia* 27.3 (2012): 636–50. Print.

Aukland, Knut. "Understanding Possession in Jainism: A Study of Oracular Possession in Nakoda." *Modern Asian Studies* 47.1 (2013): 103–34. Print.

Barnes, Trevor. *The Kingfisher Book of Religions*. New York: Kingfisher, 1999. Print.

Langley, Myrtle. *Religion*. New York: Knopf, 1996. Print.

Long, Jeffery. *Jainism: An Introduction*. London: I. B. Tauris, 2009. Print.

Long, Jeffrey. "Jainism: Key Themes." *Religion Compass* 5.9 (2011): 501–10. Print.

Rankin, Aidan. *The Jain Path*. Berkeley: O Books, 2006. Print.

Shah, Bharat S. *An Introduction to Jainism*. Great Neck: Setubandh, 2002. Print.

Titze, Kurt. *Jainism: A Pictorial Guide to the Religion of Non-Violence*. Delhi: Motilal Banarsidass, 2001. Print.

Tobias, Michael. *Life Force: the World of Jainism*. Berkeley:Asian Humanities, 1991. E-book, print.

Wiley, Kristi L. *The A to Z of Jainism*. Lanham: Scarecrow, 2009. Print.

Wiley, Kristi L. *Historical Dictionary of Jainism*. Lanham: Scarecrow, 2004. Print.

Wilkinson, Philip. *Religions*. New York: DK, 2008. Print.

Judaism

General Description

In modern Judaism, the main denominations (referred to as movements) are Orthodox Judaism (including Haredi and Hasidic Judaism); Conservative Judaism; Reform (Liberal) Judaism; Reconstructionist Judaism; and to a lesser extent, Humanistic Judaism. In addition, the Jewry of Ethiopia and Yemen are known for having distinct or alternative traditions. Classical Judaism is often organized by two branches: Ashkenazic (Northern Europe) and Sephardic Jews (Spain, Portugal, and North Africa).

Number of Adherents Worldwide

Judaism has an estimated 15 million adherents worldwide, with roughly 41 percent living in Israel and about 41 percent living in the United States. Ashkenazi Jews represent roughly 75 percent, while Sephardic Jews represent roughly 25 percent, with the remaining 5 percent split among alternative communities. Within the United States, a 2000-01 survey stated that 10 percent of American Jews identified as Orthodox (with that number increasing), 35 percent as Reform, 26 percent as Conservative, leaving the remainder with an alternative or no affiliation. [Source: Wilkinson, 2008]

Orthodox Judaism, which was founded around the thirteenth century BCE, has 3 million followers. Members of Reform Judaism, with roots in nineteenth-century Germany, wanted to live peacefully with non-Jews. Therefore, they left the laws that prevented this vision of peace and downplayed the idea of a Jewish state. Reform Judaism, also known as Progressive or Liberal Judaism, allows women rabbis and does not require its adherents to keep kosher. About 1.1 million Jews are Reform; they live primarily in the United States. When nonkosher food was served at the first graduation ceremony for Hebrew Union College, some felt that the Reform movement had gone too far. Thus the Conservative movement began in 1887. A group of rabbis founded the Jewish Theological Seminary in New York City, wanting to emphasize biblical authority above moral choice, as the Reform tradition stressed. Currently about 900,000 Jews practice this type of Judaism, which is theologically midway between Orthodox and Reform. The Hasidim, an ultra-conservative group, began in present-day Ukraine around 1740. There are 4.5 million Hasidic Jews.

Basic Tenets

Though there is no formal creed (statement of faith or belief), Jews value all life, social justice, education, generous giving, and the importance of living based on the principles and values espoused in the Torah (Jewish holy book). They believe in one all-powerful and creator God, Jehovah or Yaweh, a word derived from the Hebrew letters "YHWH," the unpronounceable name of God. The word is held to be sacred; copyists were required to bathe both before and after writing the word. Jews also believe in a coming Messiah who will initiate a Kingdom of Righteousness. They follow a complex law, composed of 613 commandments or mitzvot. Jews believe that they are God's Chosen People with a unique covenant relationship. They have a responsibility to practice hospitality and to improve the world.

The belief in the afterlife is a part of the Jewish faith. Similar to Christianity, this spiritual world is granted to those who abide by the Jewish faith and live a good life. Righteous Jews are rewarded in the afterlife by being able to discuss the Torah with Moses, who first received the law from God. Furthermore, certain Orthodox sects believe that wicked souls are destroyed or tormented after death.

Sacred Text

The complete Hebrew Bible is called the Tanakh. It includes the prophetic texts, called the Navi'im, the poetic writings, the Ketubim, and the Torah, meaning teaching, law, or guidance. Torah may refer to the entire body of Jewish law or to the first five books of the Hebrew Bible, known as the Pentateuch (it is the Old Testament in the Christian Bible). Also esteemed is the Talmud, made up of the Mishnah, a written collection of oral traditions, and Gemara, a commentary on the Mishnah. The Talmud covers many different subjects, such as law, stories and legends, medicine, and rituals.

Major Figures

The patriarchs are held to be the fathers of the faith. Abraham, the first patriarch, was called to leave his home in the Fertile Crescent for a land God would give him, and promised descendents as numerous as the stars. His son Isaac was followed by Jacob, whom God renamed Israel, and whose twelve sons became the heads of the twelve tribes of Israel. Moses was the man who, along with his brother Aaron, the founder of a priestly line, and their sister Miriam led the chosen people out of slavery in Egypt, where they had gone to escape famine. The Hebrew Bible also details the careers of a group of men and women known as judges, who were really tribal rulers, as well as of the prophets, who called the people to holy lives. Chief among the prophets was Elijah, who confronted wicked kings and performed many miracles. Several kings were key to the biblical narrative, among them David, who killed the giant Goliath, and Solomon, known for his wisdom and for the construction of a beautiful temple.

Major Holy Sites

Most of Judaism's holy sites are within Israel, the Holy Land, including Jerusalem, which was the capital of the United Kingdom of Israel under kings David and Solomon; David captured it from a Canaanite tribe around 1000 BCE. Within the Old City of Jerusalem is the Temple Mount (where the Temple of Jerusalem was built), often considered the religion's holiest site, the Foundation Stone (from which Judaism claims the world was created), and the Western (or Wailing) Wall. Other sites include Mount Sinai

in Egypt, the mountain upon which God gave Moses his laws.

Major Rites & Celebrations

The Jewish calendar recognizes several important holidays. Rosh Hashanah, literally "first of the year," is known as the Jewish New Year and inaugurates a season of self-examination and repentance that culminates in Yom Kippur, the Day of Atonement. Each spring, Passover commemorates the deliverance of the Hebrew people from Egypt. Shavuot celebrates the giving of the Torah to Moses, while Sukkot is the harvest festival. Festivals celebrating deliverance from enemies include Purim and Hanukkah. Young adolescents become members of the community at a bar or bat mitzvah, held near the twelfth or thirteenth birthday. The Sabbath, a cessation from work from Friday at sundown until Saturday when the first star appears, gives each week a rhythm.

ORIGINS

History & Geography

Called by God perhaps four thousand years ago, Abraham left from Ur of the Chaldees, or the Fertile Crescent in Mesopotamia in present-day Iraq, to go the eastern Mediterranean, the land of Canaan. Several generations later, the tribe went to Egypt to escape famine. They were later enslaved by a pharaoh, sometimes believed to have been Ramses II (ca. 1279–1213 BCE), who was noted for his many building projects. The Israelites returned to Canaan under Moses several hundred years after their arrival in Egypt. He was given the law, the Ten Commandments, plus the rest of the laws governing all aspects of life, on Mount Sinai about the thirteenth century BCE. This marked the beginning of a special covenant relationship between the new nation, known as Israel, and God.

Following a period of rule by judges, kings governed the nation. Major kings included David, son-in-law to the first king, Saul, and David's son, Solomon. The kingdom split at the beginning of the reign of Solomon's son

Rehoboam, who began ruling about 930 BCE. Rehoboam retained the ten northern tribes, while the two southern tribes followed a military commander rather than the Davidic line.

Rehoboam's kingdom was known as Israel, after the name Jehovah gave to Jacob. Judah was the name of the southern kingdom—one of Jacob's sons was named Judah. Prophets to both nations warned of coming judgment unless the people repented of mistreating the poor and other sins, such as idolatry. Unheeding, Israel was taken into captivity by the Assyrians in 722 BCE. and the Israelites assimilated into the nations around them.

The Babylonians captured Judah in 586 BCE. After Babylon had been captured in turn by Persians, the Jewish people were allowed to return to the land in 538 BCE. There they began reconstructing the temple and the walls of the city. In the second century BCE, Judas Maccabeus led a rebellion against the heavy taxes and oppression of the Greek conquerors, after they had levied high taxes and appointed priests who were not Jewish. Judas Maccabeus founded a new ruling dynasty, the Hasmoneans, which existed briefly before the region came under the control of Rome.

The Jewish people revolted against Roman rule in 70 CE, leading to the destruction of the second temple. The final destruction of Jerusalem occurred in 135 under the Roman Emperor Hadrian. He changed the city's name to Aelia Capitolina and the name of the country to Palaestina. With the cultic center of their religion gone, the religious leaders developed new methods of worship that centered in religious academies and in synagogues.

After Christianity became the official state religion of the Roman Empire in the early fourth century, Jews experienced persecution. They became known for their scholarship, trade, and banking over the next centuries, with periods of brutal persecution in Europe. Christians held Jews responsible for the death of Jesus, based on a passage in the New Testament. The Blood Libel, begun in England in 1144, falsely accused Jews of killing a Christian child to bake unleavened bread for Passover. This rumor persisted for centuries, and was repeated by Martin Luther during the Protestant Reformation. England expelled all Jews in 1290; they were not readmitted until 1656 under Oliver Cromwell, and not given citizenship until 1829. Jews were also held responsible for other catastrophes— namely poisoning wells and rivers to cause the Black Death in 1348—and were often made to wear special clothing, such as pointed hats, or badges with the Star of David or stone tablets on them.

The relationship between Muslims and Jews was more harmonious. During the Muslim Arab dominance, there was a "golden age" in Spain due to the contributions of Jews and Muslims, known as Moors in Spain. This ideal and harmonious period ended in 1492, when both Moors and Jews were expelled from Spain or forced to convert to Christianity.

Jews in Russia suffered as well. An estimated two million Jews fled the country to escape the pogroms (a Russian word meaning devastation) between 1881 and 1917. The twentieth-century Holocaust, in which an estimated six million Jews perished at the hands of Nazi Germany, was but the culmination of these centuries of persecution. The Nazis also destroyed more than six hundred synagogues.

The Holocaust gave impetus to the creation of the independent state of Israel. The Zionist movement, which called for the founding or reestablishment of a Jewish homeland, was started by Austrian Jew Theodor Herzl in the late nineteenth century, and succeeded in 1948. The British government, which had ruled the region under a mandate, left the area, and Israel was thus established. This ended the Diaspora, or dispersion, of the Jewish people that had begun nearly two millennia before when the Romans forced the Jews to leave their homeland.

Arab neighbors, some of whom had been removed forcibly from the land to create the nation of Israel, were displeased with the new political reality. Several wars have been fought, including the War of Independence in 1948, the Six-Day War in 1967, and the Yom Kippur War in 1973. In addition, tension between Israel and its neighboring Arab states is almost constant.

When the Jewish people were dispersed from Israel, two traditions began. The Ashkenazi Jews settled in Germany and central Europe. They spoke a mixture of the Hebrew dialect and German called Yiddish. Sephardic Jews lived in the Mediterranean countries, including Spain; their language, Ladino, mixed Hebrew and old Spanish.

Founder or Major Prophet

Judaism refers to three major patriarchs: Abraham, his son Isaac, and Isaac's son Jacob. Abraham is considered the first Jew and worshipper in Judaism, as the religion began through his covenant with God. As the forefather of the religion, he is often associated as the founder, though the founder technically is God, or Yahweh (YHWH). Additionally, the twelve sons of Jacob, who was also named Israel, became the founders of the twelve tribes of Israel.

Moses is regarded as a major prophet and as the Lawgiver. God revealed to Moses the complete law during the forty days that the Jewish leader spent on Mount Sinai during the wilderness journey from Egypt to Canaan. Thus, many attribute Moses as the founder of Judaism as a religion.

Philosophical Basis

Judaism began with Abraham's dissatisfaction with the polytheistic worship of his culture. Hearing the command of God to go to a land that would be shown to him, Abraham and his household obeyed. Abraham practiced circumcision and hospitality, cornerstones of the Jewish faith to this day. He and his descendents practiced a nomadic life, much like that of contemporary Bedouins. They migrated from one oasis or well to another, seeking pasture and water for the sheep and goats they herded.

The further development of Judaism came under the leadership of Moses. A Jewish child adopted by Pharaoh's daughter, he was raised and educated in the palace. As a man, he identified with the Jewish people, killing one of the Egyptians who was oppressing a Jew. He subsequently fled for his life, becoming a shepherd in the wilderness, where he remained for forty years. Called by God from a bush that burned but was not destroyed, he was commissioned to lead the people out of slavery in Egypt back to the Promised Land. That forty-year pilgrimage in the wilderness and desert of Arabia shaped the new nation.

Holy Places

The city of Jerusalem was first known as Salem. When King David overcame the Jebusites who lived there, the city, already some two thousand years old, became the capital of Israel. It is built on Mount Zion, which is still considered a sacred place. David's son Solomon built the First Temple in Jerusalem, centering the nation's spiritual as well as political life in the city. The Babylonians captured the city in 597 BCE and destroyed the Temple. For the next sixty years, the Jews remained in exile, until Cyrus the Persian conqueror of Babylon allowed them to return. They rebuilt the temple, but it was desecrated by Antiochus IV of Syria in 167 BCE. In 18 BCE, during a period of Roman occupation, Herod the Great began rebuilding and expanding the Temple. The Romans under the general Titus destroyed the Temple in 70 CE, just seven years after its completion.

The city eventually came under the rule of Persia, the Muslim Empire, and the Crusaders before coming under control of Britain. In 1948 an independent state of Israel was created. The following year, Jerusalem was divided between Israel, which made the western part the national capital, and Jordan, which ruled the eastern part of the city. The Western or Wailing Wall, a retaining wall built during Herod's time, is all that remains of the Second Temple. Devout Jews still come to the Wailing Wall to pray, sometimes placing their petitions on paper and folding the paper into the Wall's crevices. The Wall is known as a place where prayers are answered and a reminder of the perseverance of the Jewish people and faith. According to tradition, the Temple will be rebuilt when Messiah comes to inaugurate God's Kingdom.

The Temple Mount, located just outside Jerusalem on a natural acropolis, includes the Dome of the Rock. This shrine houses a rock held sacred by both Judaism and Islam. Jewish tradition states that it is the spot from which the world was created and the spot on which Abraham was asked to sacrifice his son Isaac. Muslims believe that from this rock Muhammad ascended for his night journey to heaven. Much of Jerusalem, including this holy site, has been and continues to be fought over by people of three faiths: Judaism, Islam, and Christianity.

Moses received the law from God on Mount Sinai. It is still regarded as a holy place.

JUDAISM IN DEPTH

Sacred Symbols

Observant Jewish men pray three times daily at home or in a synagogue, a center of worship, from the word meaning "meeting place." They wear a tallis, or a prayer shawl with tassles, during their morning prayer and on Yom Kippur, the Day of Atonement. They may also cover their heads as a sign of respect during prayer, wearing a skullcap known as a kippah or yarmulka. They find their prayers and blessings in a siddur, which literally means "order," because the prayers appear in the order in which they are recited for services. Jewish daily life also includes blessings for many things, including food.

Tefillin or phylacteries are the small black boxes made of leather from kosher animals that Jewish men wear on their foreheads and their left upper arms during prayer. They contain passages from the Torah. Placing the tefillin on the head reminds them to think about the Torah, while placing the box on the arm puts the Torah close to the heart.

The Law of Moses commands the people to remember the words of the law and to teach them to the children. A mezuzah helps to fulfill that command. A small box with some of the words of the law written on a scroll inside, a mezuzah is hung on the doorframes of every door in the house. Most often, the words of the Shema,

the Jewish recitation of faith, are written on the scroll. The Shema is repeated daily. "Hear, O Israel: the Lord your God, the Lord is one. . . . Love the Lord your God with all your heart, and with all your soul, and with all your might."

Jews adopted the Star of David, composed of two intersecting triangles, during the eighteenth century. There are several interpretations of the design. One is that it is the shape of King David's shield. Another idea is that it stands for daleth, the first letter of David's name. A third interpretation is that the six points refer to the days of the work week, and the inner, larger space represented the day of rest, the Sabbath, or Shabot. The Star of David appears on the flag of Israel. The flag itself is white, symbolizing peace and purity, and blue, symbolizing heaven and reminding all of God's activity.

The menorah is a seven-branch candlestick representing the light of the Torah. For Hanukkah, however, an eight-branched menorah is used. The extra candle is the servant candle, and is the one from which all others are lit.

Because the Torah is the crowning glory of life for Jewish people, a crown is sometimes used on coverings for the Torah. The scrolls of Torah are stored in a container, called an ark, which generally is covered with an ornate cloth called a mantle. The ark and mantle are often elaborately decorated with symbols, such as the lion of Judah. Because the Torah scroll, made of parchment from a kosher animal, is sacred and its pages are not to be touched, readers use a pointed stick called a yad. Even today, Torahs are written by hand in specially prepared ink and using a quill from a kosher bird. Scribes are trained for seven years.

A shofar is a ram's horn, blown as a call to repentance on Rosh Hashanah, the Jewish New Year. This holiday is the beginning of a ten-day preparation for the Day of Atonement, which is the most holy day in the Jewish calendar and a time of both fasting and repentance.

Sacred Practices & Gestures

Sacred practices can apply daily, weekly, annually, or over a lifetime's events. Reciting the Shema, the monotheistic creed taken from the

Torah, is a daily event. Keeping the Sabbath occurs weekly. Each year the festivals described above take place. Circumcision and bar or bat mitzvah are once-in-a-lifetime events. Each time someone dies, the mourners recite the Kaddish for seven days following death, and grieve for a year.

Food Restrictions

Kosher foods are those that can be eaten based on Jewish law. Animals that chew the cud and have cloven hooves, such as cows and lamb, and domestic poultry are considered kosher. Shellfish, pork, and birds of prey are forbidden. Keeping kosher also includes the method of preparing and storing the food. This includes animals which are slaughtered in a way to bring the least amount of pain and from which all blood is drained. In addition, dairy and meat products are to be kept separate, requiring separate refrigerators in the homes of the Orthodox.

Rites, Celebrations & Services

Sabbath is the weekly celebration honoring one of the Ten Commandments, which commands the people to honor the Sabbath by doing no work that day. The practice is rooted in the Genesis account that God rested on the seventh day after creating the world in six days. Because the Jewish day begins at sundown, the Sabbath lasts from Friday night to Saturday night. Special candles are lit and special food—included the braided egg bread called challah—for the evening meal is served. This day is filled with feasting, visiting, and worship.

Boys are circumcised at eight days of age. This rite, B'rit Milah, meaning "seal of the covenant," was first given to Abraham as a sign of the covenant. A trained circumciser, or mohel, may be a doctor or rabbi. The boy's name is officially announced at the ceremony. A girl's name is given at a special baby-naming ceremony or in the synagogue on the first Sabbath after she is born.

A boy becomes a "son of the commandment," or bar mitzvah, at age thirteen. At a special ceremony, the young man reads a portion of

Torah that he has prepared ahead of time. Most boys also give a speech at the service. Girls become bat mitzvah at age twelve. This ceremony developed in the twentieth century. Not all Orthodox communities will allow this rite. Girls may also read from the Torah and give a sermon in the synagogue, just as boys do.

When a Jewish person dies, mourners begin shiva, a seven-day mourning period. People usually gather at the home of the deceased, where mirrors are covered. In the home, the Kaddish, a collection of prayers that praise God and celebrate life, is recited. Traditionally, family members mourn for a full year, avoiding parties and festive occasions.

The Jewish calendar offers a series of feasts and festivals, beginning with Rosh Hashanah, the Jewish New Year. At this time, Jews recall the creation. They may also eat apples that have been dipped into honey and offer each other wishes for a sweet New Year. The next ten days are a time of reflection on the past year, preparing for Yom Kippur.

This Day of Atonement once included animal sacrifice at the Temple. Now it includes an all-day service at the synagogue and a twenty-five-hour fast. A ram's horn, called a shofar, is blown as a call to awaken to lead a holier life. The shofar reminds Jewish people of the ram that Abraham sacrificed in the place of his son, Isaac.

Passover, or Pesach, is the spring remembrance of God's deliverance of the people from slavery in Egypt. In the night that the Jewish people left Egypt, they were commanded to sacrifice a lamb for each household and sprinkle the blood on the lintels and doorposts. A destroying angel from God would "pass over" the homes with blood sprinkled. During the first two nights of Passover, a special meal is served known as a Seder, meaning order. The foods symbolize different aspects of the story of deliverance, which is told during the meal by the head of the family.

Shavuot has its origins as a harvest festival. This celebration of Moses receiving the Torah on Mount Sinai occurs fifty days after the second day of Passover. To welcome the first fruits of the season, the synagogue may be decorated with fruit and flowers. Traditionally, the Ten Commandments are read aloud in the synagogue.

Purim, which occurs in February or March, celebrates the deliverance of the Jews during their captivity in Persia in the fifth century BCE. The events of that experience are recorded in the Book of Esther in the Hebrew Bible (Tanakh). The book is read aloud during Purim.

Sukkot, the feast celebrating the end of the harvest, occurs in September or October. Jews recall God's provision for them in the wilderness when they left Egypt to return to Canaan. Traditionally, huts are made and decorated with flowers and fruits. The conclusion of Sukkot is marked by a synagogue service known as Simchat Torah, or Rejoicing in the Law. People sing and dance as the Torah scrolls are carried and passed from person to person.

Hanukkah, known as the Festival of Lights, takes place over eight days in December. It celebrates the rededicating of the Temple under the leader Judas Maccabeus, who led the people in recapturing the structure from Syria in 164 BCE. According to the story, the Jews had only enough oil in the Temple lamp to last one day, but the oil miraculously lasted for eight days, after which Judas Maccabeus re-dedicated the Temple. On each day of Hanukkah, one of the eight candles is lit until all are burning. The gift-giving custom associated with Hanukkah is relatively new, and may derive from traditional small gifts of candy or money. The practice may also have been encouraged among those integrated with communities that exchange gifts during the Christmas season.

Judy A. Johnson, MTS

Bibliography

Barnes, Trevor. *The Kingfisher Book of Religions*. New York: Kingfisher, 1999. Print.

"A Buffet to Suit All Tastes." *Economist* 28 Jul. 2012: Spec. section 4–6. Print.

Charing, Douglas. *Judaism*. London: DK, 2003. Print.

Coenen Snyder, Saskia. *Building a Public Judaism: Synagogues and Jewish Identity in Nineteenth-Century Europe*. Cambridge: Harvard UP, 2013. E-book.

Diamant, Anita. *Living a Jewish Life*. New York: Collins, 1996. Print.

Exler, Lisa and Rabbi Jill Jacobs. "A Judaism That Matters." *Journal of Jewish Communal Service* 87.1/2 (2012): 66–76. Print.

Gelernter, David Hillel. *Judaism: A Way of Being*. New Haven: Yale UP, 2009. E-book.

Kessler, Edward. *What Do Jews Believe?* New York: Walker, 2007. Print.

Krieger, Aliza Y. "The Role of Judaism in Family Relationships." *Journal of Multicultural Counseling & Development* 38.3 (2010): 154–65. Print.

Langley, Myrtle. *Religion*. New York: Knopf, 1996. Print.

Madsen, Catherine. "A Heart of Flesh: Beyond 'Creative Liturgy.'" *Cross Currents* 62.1 (2012): 11–20. Print.

Meredith, Susan. *The Usborne Book of World Religions*. London: Usborne, 1995. Print.

Schoen, Robert. *What I Wish My Christian Friends Knew About Judaism*. Chicago: Loyola, 2004. Print.

Stefon, Matt. *Judaism: History, Belief, and Practice*. New York: Britannica Educational, 2012. E-book.

Wertheimer, Jack. "The Perplexities of Conservative Judaism." *Commentary* Sept. 2007: 38–44. Print.

Wilkinson, Philip. *Religions*. New York: DK, 2008. Print.

Sikhism

General Description

The youngest of the world religions, Sikhism has existed for only about five hundred years. Sikhism derives from the Sanskrit word *sishyas*, which means "disciple"; in the Punjabi language, it also means "disciple."

Number of Adherents Worldwide

An estimated 24.5 million people follow the Sikh religion. Most of the devotees live in Asia, particularly in the Punjab region of India (Wilkinson, p. 335).

Basic Tenets

Sikhism is a monotheistic religion. The deity is God, known as Nam, or Name. Other synonyms include the Divine, Ultimate, Ultimate Reality, Infinity, the Formless, Truth, and other attributes of God.

Sikhs adhere to three basic principles. These are hard work (kirt kao), worshipping the Divine Name (nam japo), and sharing what one has (vand cauko). Meditating on the Divine Name is seen as a method of moving toward a life totally devoted to God. In addition, Sikhs believe in karma, or moral cause and effect. They value hospitality to all, regardless of religion, and oppose caste distinctions. Sikhs delineate a series of five stages that move upward to gurmukh, total devotion to God. This service is called Seva. Sahaj, or tranquility, is practiced as a means of being united with God as well as of generating external good will. Sikhs are not in favor of external routines of religion; they may stop in their temple whenever it is convenient during the day.

Sikhism does not include a belief in the afterlife. Instead, the soul is believed to be reincarnated in successive lives and deaths, a belief borrowed from Hinduism. The goal is then to break this karmic cycle, and to merge the human spirit with that of God.

Sacred Text

The Guru Granth Sahib (also referred to as the Aad Guru Granth Sahib, or AGGS), composed of Adi Granth, meaning First Book, is the holy scripture of Sikhism. It is a collection of religious poetry that is meant to be sung. Called shabads, they were composed by the first five gurus, the ninth guru, and thirty-six additional holy men of northern India. Sikhs always show honor to the Guru Granth Sahib by carrying it above the head when in a procession.

A second major text is the Dasam Granth, or Tenth Book, created by followers of Guru Gobind Singh, the tenth guru. Much of it is devoted to retelling the Hindu stories of Krishna and Rama. Those who are allowed to read and care for the Granth Sahib are known as granthi. Granthi may also look after the gurdwara, or temple. In the gurdwara, the book rests on a throne with a wooden base and cushions covered in cloths placed in a prescribed order. If the book is not in use, it is covered with a cloth known as a rumala. When the book is read, a fan called a chauri is fanned over it as a sign of respect, just as followers of the gurus fanned them with chauris. At Amritsar, a city in northwestern India that houses the Golden Temple, the Guru Granth Sahib is carried on a palanquin (a covered, carried bed). If it is carried in the city, a kettle drum is struck and people welcome it by tossing rose petals.

Major Figures

Guru Nanak (1469–1539) is the founder of Sikhism. He was followed by nine other teachers, and collectively they are known as the Ten Gurus. Each of them was chosen by his predecessor and was thought to share the same spirit of that previous guru. Guru Arjan (1581–1606), the fifth guru, oversaw completion of the Golden Temple in Amritsar, India. Guru Gobind Singh (1675–1708) was the tenth and last human guru. He decreed that the True Guru henceforth would be the Granth Sahib, the scripture of the Sikhs. He also founded the Khalsa, originally a military order of male Sikhs willing to die for the faith; the term is now used to refer to all baptized Sikhs.

Major Holy Sites

Amritsar, India, is the holy city of Sikhism. Construction of the city began under Guru Ram Das (1574–1581), the fourth guru, during the 1570s. One legend says that the Muslim ruler, Emperor Akbar, gave the land to the third guru, Guru Amar Das (1552–74). Whether or not that is true, Amar Das did establish the location of Amritsar. He chose a site near a pool believed to hold healing water.

When construction of the Golden Temple began, only a small town existed. One legend says that a Muslim saint from Lahore, India, named Mian Mir laid the foundation stone of the first temple. It has been demolished and rebuilt three times. Although pilgrimage is not required of Sikhs, many come to see the shrines and the Golden Temple. They call it Harmandir Sahib, God's Temple, or Darbar Sahib, the Lord's Court. When the temple was completed during the tenure of the fifth guru, Arjan, he placed the first copy of the Guru Granth Sahib inside.

Every Sikh temple has a free kitchen attached to it, called a langar. After services, all people, regardless of caste or standing within the community, sit on the floor in a straight line and eat a simple vegetarian meal together. As a pilgrimage site, the langar serves 30,000–40,000 people daily, with more coming on Sundays and festival days. About forty volunteers work in the kitchen each day.

Major Rites & Celebrations

In addition to the community feasts at temple langars, Sikhs honor four rites of passage in a person's life: naming, marriage, initiation in Khalsa (pure) through the Amrit ceremony, and death.

There are eight major celebrations and several other minor ones in Sikhism. Half of them commemorate events in the lives of the ten gurus.

The others are Baisakhi, the new year festival; Diwali, the festival of light, which Hindus also celebrate; Hola Mahalla, which Gobind Singh created as an alternative to the Hindu festival of Holi, and which involves military parades; and the installing of the Guru Granth Sahib.

ORIGINS

History & Geography

The founder of Sikhism, Nanak, was born in 1469 CE in the Punjab region of northeast India, where both Hinduism and Islam were practiced. Both of these religions wanted control of the region. Nanak wanted the fighting between followers of these two traditions to end and looked for solutions to the violence.

Nanak blended elements of both religions and also combined the traditional apparel of both faiths to construct his clothing style. The Guru Granth Sahib further explains the division between Sikhs and the Islamic and Muslim faiths:

Nanak would become the first guru of the Sikh religion, known as Guru Nanak Dev. A Muslim musician named Bhai Mardana, considered the first follower, accompanied Nanak in his travels around India and Asia. Guru Nanak often sang, and singing remains an important part of worship for Sikhs. Before his death, Nanak renamed one of his disciples Angad, a word meaning "a part of his own self." He became Guru Angad Dev, the second guru, thus beginning the tradition of designating a successor and passing on the light to that person.

Guru Baba Ram Das, the fourth guru, who lived in the sixteenth century, began constructing Amritsar's Golden Temple. The structure was completed by his successor, Guru Arjan Dev, who also collected poems and songs written by the first four gurus and added his own. He included the work of Kabir and other Hindu and Muslim holy men as well. This became the Adi Granth, which he placed in the Golden Temple.

Guru Arjan was martyred in 1606 by Jehangir, the Muslim emperor. His son Hargobind became the sixth guru and introduced several important practices and changes. He wore two swords, representing both spiritual and worldly authority. Near the Golden Temple he had a building known as Akal Takht, or Throne of the Almighty, erected. In it was a court of justice as well as a group of administrators. Even today, orders and decisions enter the community from Akal Takht. Guru Hargobind was the last of the gurus with a direct link to Amritsar. Because of conflict with the Muslim rulers, he and all subsequent gurus moved from the city.

The tenth guru, Gobind Singh, created the Khalsa, the Community of the Pure, in 1699. The members of the Khalsa were to be known by five distinctive elements, all beginning with the letter *k*. These include kes, the refusal to cut the hair or trim the beard; kangha, the comb used to keep the long hair neatly combed in contrast to the Hindu ascetics who had matted hair; kaccha, shorts that would allow soldiers quick movement; kara, a thin steel bracelet worn to symbolize restraint; and kirpan, a short sword not to be used except in self-defense. Among other duties, members of this elite group were to defend the faith. Until the middle of the nineteenth century, when the British created an empire in India, the Khalsa remained largely undefeated.

In 1708, Guru Gobind Singh announced that he would be the final human guru. All subsequent leadership would come from the Guru Granth Sahib, now considered a living guru, the holy text Arjan had begun compiling more than a century earlier.

Muslim persecution under the Mughals led to the defeat of the Sikhs in 1716. The remaining Sikhs headed for the hills, re-emerging after decline of Mughal power. They were united under Ranjit Singh's kingdom from 1820 to 1839. They then came under the control of the British.

The British annexed the Punjab region, making it part of their Indian empire in 1849, and recruited Sikhs to serve in the army. The Sikhs remained loyal to the British during the Indian Mutiny of 1857–1858. As a result, they were given many privileges and land grants, and with

peace and prosperity, the first Singh Sabha was founded in 1873. This was an educational and religious reform movement.

During the early twentieth century, Sikhism was shaped in its more modern form. A group known as the Tat Khalsa, which was more progressive, became the dominant way of understanding the faith.

In 1897, a group of Sikh musicians within the British Army was invited to attend the Diamond Jubilee of Queen Victoria in England. They also traveled to Canada and were attracted by the nation's prairies, which were perfect for farming. The first group of Sikhs came to Canada soon after. By 1904, more than two hundred Sikhs had settled in British Columbia. Some of them later headed south to Washington, Oregon, and California in the United States. The first Sikh gurdwara in the United States was constructed in Stockton, California, in 1912. Sikhs became farmers, worked in lumber mills, and helped to construct the Western Pacific railroad. Yuba City, California, has one of the world's largest Sikh temples, built in 1968.

Sikh troops fought for Britain in World War I, achieving distinction. Following the war, in 1919, however, the British denied the Sikhs the right to gather for their New Year festival. When the Sikhs disobeyed, the British troops fired without warning on 10,000 Sikhs, 400 of whom were killed. This became known as the first Amritsar Massacre.

The British government in 1925 did give the Sikhs the right to help manage their own shrines. A fragile peace ensued between the British and the Sikhs, who again fought for the British Empire during World War II.

After the war ended, the Sikh hope for an independent state was dashed by the partition of India and Pakistan in 1947. Pakistan was in the Punjab region; thus, 2.5 million Sikhs lived in a Muslim country where they were not welcome. Many of them became part of the mass internal migration that followed Indian independence.

In 1966, a state with a Sikh majority came into existence after Punjab boundaries were redrawn. Strife continued throughout second half of twentieth century, however, as a result of continuing demands for Punjab autonomy. A second massacre at Amritsar occurred in 1984, resulting in the death of 450 Sikhs (though some estimates of the death toll are higher). Indian troops, under orders from Indian Prime Minister Indira Gandhi, fired on militant leaders of Sikhs, who had gone to the Golden Temple for refuge. This attack was considered a desecration of a sacred place, and the prime minister was later assassinated by her Sikh bodyguards in response. Restoration of the Akal Takht, the administrative headquarters, took fifteen years. The Sikh library was also burned, consuming ancient manuscripts.

In 1999, Sikhs celebrated the three-hundredth anniversary of the founding of Khalsa. There has been relative peace in India since that event. In the United States, however, Sikhs became the object of slander and physical attack following the acts of terrorism on September 11, 2001, as some Americans could not differentiate between Arab head coverings and Sikh turbans.

Founder or Major Prophet

Guru Nanak Dev was born into a Hindu family on April 15, 1469. His family belonged to the merchant caste, Khatri. His father worked as an accountant for a Muslim, who was also a local landlord. Nanak was educated in both the Hindu and Islamic traditions. According to legends, his teachers soon realized they had nothing further to teach him. After a direct revelation from Ultimate Reality that he received as a young man, Nanak proclaimed that there was neither Muslim nor Hindu. God had told Nanak "Rejoice in my Name," which became a central doctrine of Sikhism.

Nanak began to preach, leaving his wife and two sons behind. According to tradition, he traveled not only throughout India, but also eventually to Iraq, Saudi Arabia, and Mecca. This tradition and others were collected in a volume known as Janamsakhis. A Muslim servant of the family, Mardana, who also played a three-stringed musical instrument called the rebec, accompanied him, as did a Hindu poet, Bala Sandhu, who had been a friend from childhood

(though the extent of his importance or existence is often considered controversial).

Nanak traveled as an itinerant preacher for a quarter century and then founded a village, Kartarpur, on the bank of Punjab's Ravi River. Before his death he chose his successor, beginning a tradition that was followed until the tenth and final human guru.

Philosophical Basis

When Guru Nanak Dev, the first guru, began preaching in 1499 at about age thirty, he incorporated aspects of both Hinduism and Islam. From Hinduism, he took the ideas of karma and reincarnation. From Islam, he borrowed the Ultimate as the name of God. Some scholars see the influence of the religious reformer and poet Kabir, who lived from 1440 until 1518. Kabir merged the Bhakti (devotional) side of Hinduism with the Islamic Sufis, who were mystics.

Within the Hindu tradition in northern India was a branch called the Sants. The Sants believed that God was both with form and without form, unable to be represented concretely. Most of the Sants were illiterate and poor, but created poems that spoke of the divine being experienced in all things. This idea also rooted itself in Sikhism.

Guru Nanak Dev, who was raised as a Hindu, rejected the caste system in favor of equality of all persons. He also upheld the value of women, rejecting the burning of widows and female infanticide. When eating a communal meal, first begun as a protest against caste, everyone sits in a straight line and shares karah prasad (a pudding), which is provided by those of all castes. However, Sikhs are expected to marry within their caste. In some cases, especially in the United Kingdom, gurdwaras (places of worship) for a particular caste exist.

Holy Places

Amritsar, especially the Golden Temple, which was built in the sixteenth century under the supervision of the fifth guru, Guru Arjan, is the most sacred city.

Ram Das, the fourth guru, first began constructing a pool on the site in 1577. He called it

Amritsar, the pool of nectar. This sacred reflecting pool is a pilgrimage destination. Steps on the southern side of the pool allow visitors to gather water in bottles, to drink it, to bathe in it, or to sprinkle it on themselves.

SIKHISM IN DEPTH

Sacred Symbols

The khanda is the major symbol of Sikhism. It features a two-edged sword, representing justice and freedom, in the center. It is surrounded by a circle, a symbol of both balance and of the unity of God and humankind. A pair of curved swords (kirpans) surrounds the circle. One sword stands for religious concerns, the other for secular concerns. The khanda appears on Sikh flags, which are flown over every temple.

Members of the Khalsa have five symbols. They do not cut their hair, and men do not trim their beards. This symbol, kes, is to indicate a harmony with the ways of nature. To keep the long hair neat, a comb called a kangha is used. The third symbol is the kara, a bracelet usually made of steel to represent continuity and strength. When the Khalsa was first formed, soldiers wore loose-fitting shorts called kaccha. They were worn to symbolize moral restraint and purity. The final symbol is a short sword known as a kirpan, to be used only in self-defense. When bathing in sacred waters, the kirpan is tucked into the turban, which is worn to cover the long hair. The turban, which may be one of many colors, is wound from nearly five yards of cloth.

Sacred Practices & Gestures

Sikhs use Sat Sri Akal (truth is timeless) as a greeting, putting hands together and bowing toward the other person. To show respect, Sikhs keep their heads covered with a turban or veil. Before entering a temple, they remove their shoes. Some Sikhs may choose to wear a bindhi, the dot on the forehead usually associated with Hinduism.

When Guru Gobind Singh initiated the first men into the Khalsa, he put water in a steel bowl and added sugar, stirring the mixture with his sword and reciting verses from the Guru Granth as he did so. He thus created amrit (immortal), a holy water also used in baptism, or the Amrit ceremony. The water represents mental clarity, while sugar stands for sweetness. The sword invokes military courage, and the chanting of verses brings a poetic spirituality.

The Sikh ideal of bringing Ultimate Reality into every aspect of the day is expressed in prayers throughout the day. Daily morning prayer (Bani) consists of five different verses, most of them the work of one of the ten gurus; there are also two sets of evening prayers. Throughout the day, Sikhs repeat the Mul Mantra, "Ikk Oan Kar" (There is one Being). This is the first line of a brief creedal statement about Ultimate Reality.

Food Restrictions

Sikhs are not to eat halal meat, which is the Muslim equivalent of kosher. Both tobacco and alcohol are forbidden. Many Sikhs are vegetarians, although this is not commanded. Members of the Khalsa are not permitted to eat meat slaughtered according to Islamic or Hindu methods, because they believe these means cause pain to the animal.

Rites, Celebrations, & Services

The Sikhs observe four rite of passage rituals, with each emphasizing their distinction from the Hindu traditions. After a new mother is able to get up and bathe, the new baby is given a birth and naming ceremony in the gurdwara. The child is given a name based on the first letter of hymn from the Guru Granth Sahib at random. All males are additionally given the name Singh (lion); all females also receive the name Kaur (princess).

The marriage ceremony (anand karaj) is the second rite of passage. Rather than circle a sacred fire as the Hindus do, the Sikh couple walks four times around a copy of the Guru Granth Sahib, accompanied by singing. The bride often wears red, a traditional color for the Punjabi.

The amrit initiation into the Khalsa is considered the most important rite. It need not take place in a temple, but does require that five

Sikhs who are already Khalsa members conduct the ceremony. Amrit initiation may occur any time after a child is old enough to read the Guru Granth and understand the tenets of the faith. Some people, however, wait until their own children are grown before accepting this rite.

The funeral rite is the fourth and final rite of passage. A section of the Guru Granth is read. The body, dressed in the Five "K's," is cremated soon after death.

Initiation into the Khalsa is now open to both men and women. The earliest gurus opposed the Hindu custom of sati, which required a widow to be burned on her husband's funeral pyre. They were also against the Islamic custom of purdah, which required women to be veiled and covered in public. Women who are menstruating are not excluded from worship, as they are in some religions. Women as well as men can be leaders of the congregation and are permitted to read from the Guru Granth and recite sacred hymns.

The Sikh houses of worship are known as gurdwaras and include a langar, the communal dining area. People remove their shoes and cover their heads before entering. They touch their foreheads to the floor in front of the scripture to show respect. The service itself is in three parts. The first segment is Kirtan, singing hymns (kirtans) accompanied by musical instruments, which can last for several hours. It is followed by a set prayer called the Ardas, which has three parts. The first and final sections cannot be altered. In the first, the virtues of the gurus are extolled. In the last, the divine name is honored. In the center of the Ardas is a list of the Khalsa's troubles and victories, which a prayer leader recites in segments and to which the congregation responds with Vahiguru, considered a word for God. At the end of the service, members eat karah prasad, sacred food made of raw sugar, clarified butter, and coarse wheat flour. They then adjourn for a communal meal, Langar, the third section of worship.

Sikhism does not have a set day for worship similar to the Jewish Sabbath or Christian Sunday worship. However, the first day of the month on the Indian lunar calendar, sangrand,

and the darkest night of the month, masia, are considered special days. Sangrand is a time for praying for the entire month. Masia is often considered an auspicious time for bathing in the holy pool at the temple.

Four of the major festivals that Sikhs observe surround important events in the lives of the gurus. These are known as gurpurabs, or anniversaries. Guru Nanak's birthday, Guru Gobind Singh's birthday, and the martyrdoms of the Gurus Arjan and Tegh Bahadur comprise the four main gurpurabs. Sikhs congregate in the gurudwaras to hear readings of the Guru Granth and lectures by Sikh scholars.

Baisakhi is the Indian New Year, the final day before the harvest begins. On this day in 1699, Guru Gobind Singh formed the first Khalsa, adding even more importance to the day for Sikhs. Each year, a new Sikh flag is placed at all temples.

Diwali, based on a word meaning string of lights, is a Hindu festival. For Sikhs, it is a time to remember the return of the sixth guru, Hargobind, to Amritsar after the emperor had imprisoned him. It is celebrated for three days at the Golden Temple. Sikhs paint and whitewash their houses and decorate them with candles and earthenware lamps.

Hola Mohalla, meaning attack and place of attack, is the Sikh spring festival, which corresponds to the Hindu festival Holi. It is also a three-day celebration and a time for training Sikhs as soldiers. Originally, it involved military exercises and mock battles, as well as competitions in archery, horsemanship, and wrestling. In contemporary times, the festival includes athletic contests, discussion, and singing.

Judy A. Johnson, MTS

Bibliography

Barnes, Trevor. *The Kingfisher Book of Religions*. New York: Kingfisher, 1999. Print.

Dhanjal, Beryl. *Amritsar*. New York: Dillon, 1993. Print.

Dhavan, Purnima. *When Sparrows Became Hawks: The Making of the Sikh Warrior Tradition, 1699–1799*. Oxford: Oxford UP, 2011. Print.

Eraly, Abraham, et. al. *India*. New York: DK, 2008. Print.

Harley, Gail M. *Hindu and Sikh Faiths in America*. New York: Facts on File, 2003. Print.

Jakobsh, Doris R. *Sikhism and Women: History, Texts, and Experience*. Oxford, New York: Oxford UP, 2010. Print.

Jhutti-Johal, Jagbir. *Sikhism Today*. London, New York: Continuum, 2011. Print.

Langley, Myrtle. *Religion*. New York: Knopf, 1996. Print.

Mann, Gurinder Singh. *Sikhism*. Upper Saddle River: Prentice, 2004. Print.

Meredith, Susan. *The Usborne Book of World Religions*. London: Usborne, 1995. Print.

Sidhu, Dawinder S. and Neha Singh Gohil. *Civil Rights in Wartime: The Post-9/11 Sikh Experience*. Ashgate, 2009. E-book.

Singh, Nikky-Guninder Kaur. *Sikhism*. New York: Facts on File, 1993. Print.

Singh, Nikky-Guninder Kaur. *Sikhism: An Introduction*. Tauris, 2011. E-book.

Singh, Surinder. *Introduction to Sikhism and Great Sikhs of the World*. Gurgaon: Shubhi, 2012. Print.

Wilkinson, Philip. *Religions*. New York: DK, 2008. Print.

Index

ABC, 150
Accrediting Commission for
    Community and Junior
    Colleges (ACCJC), 210
AC/DC, 147
AFN Kwajalein, 210
African, Caribbean and Pacific
    Group of States (ACP), 250
Agency for Cultural Affairs, 38
Agency for National Security
    Planning (ANSP), 107
Agricultural and Rural
    Development Strategy
    (ARDS), 353
Agriculture
    Australia, 155
    China, 24
    Federated States of Micronesia
        (FSM), 233
    Fiji, 174
    Japan, 48
    Kiribati, 193
    Marshall Islands, 215
    Mongolia, 69
    Nauru, 252–253
    New Zealand, 274
    North Korea, 88–89
    Palau, 294
    Papua New Guinea, 314
    Samoa, 333
    Solomon Islands, 355
    South Korea, 110
    Taiwan, 131
    Tonga, 372–373
    Tuvalu, 389
    Vanuatu, 406–407
Akis, Timothy, 305
Albert Names Edward, 145
Al-Khalifa, Hamad bin Isa, 416
A-mei, 122
Amended Compact of Free
    Association, 214
Amin, Idi, 422
Ang Lee, 121
Angus, Rita, 263
APN News and Media, 150
Appleby, Stuart, 147

Apple Daily, 125
Architecture
    Australia, 145
    China, 11–13
    Federated States of Micronesia
        (FSM), 225
    Fiji, 166
    Japan, 35–36
    Marshall Islands, 206
    Mongolia, 59
    New Zealand, 264
    North Korea, 78–79
    Palau, 287
    Papua New Guinea, 305–306
    Samoa, 325
    Solomon Islands, 345–346
    South Korea, 99
    Taiwan, 121
    Tuvalu, 382
    Vanuatu, 398–399
Armed forces
    Australia, 153
    China, 20
    Federated States of Micronesia
        (FSM), 231
    Fiji, 172
    Japan, 44
    Kiribati, 191
    Marshall Islands, 213
    Mongolia, 67
    Nauru, 250
    New Zealand, 271
    Palau, 292
    Papua New Guinea, 311–312
    Samoa, 331
    Solomon Islands, 352
    South Korea, 107
    Taiwan, 128
    Tonga, 370
    Tuvalu, 387
    Vanuatu, 405
Art(s)
    Australia, 144–145, 147–148
    China, 11–13, 15
    Federated States of Micronesia
        (FSM), 226
    Fiji, 166, 168

Japan, 34–35, 38–39
Kiribati, 185–186, 186–187
Marshall Islands, 205–206,
    207
Mongolia, 59, 61–62
Nauru, 244, 246
New Zealand, 263, 265–266
North Korea, 78, 80
Palau, 286, 288
Papua New Guinea, 305, 307
Samoa, 324–325, 327
Solomon Islands, 345–348
South Korea, 98–99, 102
Taiwan, 120–121, 123
Tonga, 363–366
Tuvalu, 381–383
Vanuatu, 397–398
*Asahi Shimbun (Morning Sun
    Newspaper),* 41
ASEAN Regional Forum (ARF),
    312
Ashihci Hino, 37
Ashton-Warner, Sylvia, 265
Asian Development Bank (ADB),
    21, 172, 191, 271, 312
Asia-Pacific Economic
    Cooperation (APEC), 21, 271,
    312
Association of Southeast Asian
    Nations (ASEAN), 21, 67, 85,
    311
Austar, 150
Australia, 137–157
Australia, New Zealand, United
    States Security Treaty
    (ANZUS), 153, 271
The Australian, 150
Australia New Zealand Army
    Corps (ANZAC), 144
Australia New Zealand Closer
    Economic Relations Trade
    Agreement (ANZCERTA), 271
Australian Greens, 152
Australian International
    Development Assistance
    Bureau (AIDAB), 310
Australian Labor Party, 152

Australia-United States
Ministerial consultations
(AUSMIN), 153
Awakening Foundation, 127

Barclay, Robert, 207
Bastardy, 145
Baxter, James K., 265
BeeGees, 147
Bell, Richard, 147
Betelnut Beauty, 121
Bhagavad Gita, 489
Bikini Atoll Nuclear Test Site,
208
Bingham, Hiram, II, 180
Birds Nest, in the Style of Cubism,
15
The Blanket, 80
The Bone People (Hulme), 265
Bonnard, Pierre, 35
Boston Missionary Society, 210
Botany Bay, 146
Bound for South Australia, 146
Brack, John, 145
British Broadcasting Corporation
(BBC), 402
Broadcasting and Publications
Authority (BPA), 189

Calligraphy, 12
Campion, Jane, 266
Canoe building
Marshall Islands, 206
"Care for Girls," 19
Carey, Peter, 147
Caro, Niki, 266
Castro, Raúl, 191
Catholicism, 220
Central Motion Picture
Corporation (CMPC), 121
The Central Star News, 247
Centrist Reformists Democratic
Party, 106
Ch'ae Mansik, 79
Chaing, Jody, 124
Chang Kil-san, 102
Chang-Rae Lee, 102
Chan-wook Park, 102
Chen Chih-Yuan, 123
Chen Duxiu, 14
Cheney, Dick, 107

Chen Ran, 14–15
Chen Shui-bian, 123
Chernobyl nuclear disaster, 28
China, 3–26
China Art Museum, 16
China Democracy Party, 20
China Democratic League, 19
China Post, 125
China Television Company
(CTV), 125
China Times, 125
China Zhi Gong, 19
Chinese Communist Party (CCP),
19
Chinese Democracy and Justice
Party, 19–20
Chinese Television System
(CTS), 125
Cho Chong-Rae, 102
Choi Eun-hee, 80
Chou, Jay, 124
Christianity, 180, 183, 473–479
Church of Jesus Christ of Latter-
day Saints, 189
CIA, 230
CIA World Factbook, 88, 94
Citizens' Will Republican Party,
66
Clarke, Marcus, 146
Climate
Australia, 140–141
China, 6
Federated States of Micronesia
(FSM), 220
Fiji, 162
Japan, 31
Kiribati, 180–181
Marshall Islands, 201
Mongolia, 54–55
Nauru, 240
New Zealand, 258–259
North Korea, 74
Palau, 282
Papua New Guinea, 300–301
Samoa, 320
Solomon Islands, 340–341
South Korea, 94
Taiwan, 117
Tonga, 360
Tuvalu, 378
Vanuatu, 394

Cloud Gate Dance Theatre of
Taiwan, 122
Coalition of the Liberal Party, 152
Coast Watchers Memorial, 187
Coins
Australia, 138
China, 4
Federated States of Micronesia
(FSM), 218
Fiji, 160
Japan, 28
Kiribati, 178
Marshall Islands, 198
Mongolia, 52
Nauru, 238
New Zealand, 256
North Korea, 72
Palau, 280
Papua New Guinea, 298
Samoa, 318
Solomon Islands, 338
South Korea, 92
Taiwan, 114
Tonga, 358
Tuvalu, 376
Communications. *See* Media and
communications
Communist Party (JCP), 44
Communists, 412–413
Community Development and
Training Center (CDTC), 369
Compact of Association, 230
Compact of Free Association
(COFA), 213–214, 231, 292
"Compulsory Education Law of
the PRC," 18
Confucianism, 78
Confucius, 14
Conservation, Education,
Diving, Awareness, and
Marine-research (CEDAM)
International, 288
Convention on Elimination of
All Forms of Discrimination
against Women (CEDAW), 151
Convict Maid, 146
Council of Nicea, 474
Court, Margaret Smith, 147
Creative Korea Party, 106
Crouching Tiger, Hidden Dragon,
121

Crump, Barry, 265
Cultural Heritage Administration
  (CHA), 101
Cultural history
  Australia, 144–147
  China, 11–15
  Federated States of Micronesia
    (FSM), 224–226
  Fiji, 166–168
  Japan, 34–37
  Kiribati, 185–186
  Marshall Islands, 205–207
  Mongolia, 59–61
  Nauru, 244–245
  New Zealand, 263–265
  North Korea, 78–80
  Palau, 286–288
  Papua New Guinea, 305–307
  Samoa, 324–327
  Solomon Islands, 345–347
  South Korea, 98–102
  Taiwan, 120–123
  Tonga, 363–365
  Tuvalu, 381–382
  Vanuatu, 397–399
Cultural Revolution, 14–15
Cultural sites
  Australia, 148–149
  China, 15–16
  Federated States of Micronesia
    (FSM), 226–227
  Fiji, 168–169
  Japan, 39–40
  Kiribati, 187
  Marshall Islands, 207–208
  Mongolia, 62–63
  Nauru, 246
  New Zealand, 266–267
  North Korea, 80–81
  Palau, 288–289
  Papua New Guinea, 307–308
  Samoa, 327–328
  Solomon Islands, 348
  South Korea, 102–103
  Taiwan, 123–124
  Tonga, 366–367
  Tuvalu, 383
  Vanuatu, 400–401
Culture
  Australia, 147–149
  China, 15–16

Federated States of Micronesia
  (FSM), 226–228
Fiji, 168–170
Japan, 38–40
Kiribati, 186–188
Marshall Islands, 207–209
Mongolia, 61–64
Nauru, 246–247
New Zealand, 265–268
North Korea, 80–82
Palau, 288–290
Papua New Guinea, 307–309
Samoa, 327–328
Solomon Islands, 347–349
South Korea, 102–104
Taiwan, 123–125
Tonga, 365–367
Tuvalu, 383–384
Vanuatu, 399–401
Culture and Arts Department,
  79
Curnow, Allen, 265
Customs and courtesies
  Australia, 142–143
  China, 7–9
  Federated States of Micronesia
    (FSM), 221–222
  Fiji, 163–164
  Japan, 32–33
  Kiribati, 182–183
  Marshall Islands, 202–203
  Mongolia, 56–57
  Nauru, 241–242
  New Zealand, 260–261
  North Korea, 75–76
  Palau, 283–285
  Papua New Guinea, 301–303
  Samoa, 321–322
  Solomon Islands, 342–343
  South Korea, 95–97
  Taiwan, 117–119
  Tonga, 361–362
  Tuvalu, 379
  Vanuatu, 395–396
Cyclone Pam, 181

The Daily Yomiuri, 41
Dance
  China, 13–14
  Federated States of Micronesia
    (FSM), 225

Fiji, 167
Kiribati, 186
Mongolia, 60
Nauru, 245
New Zealand, 264–265
North Korea, 79
Palau, 287–288
Papua New Guinea, 306
Samoa, 326–327
Solomon Islands, 346–347
South Korea, 100–101
Taiwan, 122
Tonga, 364–365
Tuvalu, 382
Vanuatu, 399
Dance Aotearoa New Zealand
  (DANZ), 266
Davaa, Byambasuren, 62
The Da Vinci Code, 332
Davy, Norris Frank, 265
Day, Bob, 152
Degas, Edgar, 35
Democracy, 420–421
Democracy in China, 20
Democratic Labor Party, 106
Democratic Party (DPJ), 43
Democratic People's Republic of
  Korea (DPRK), 84, 87
Democratic Progressive Party
  (DPP), 128
Deng Xiaoping, 17–18
Dependencies
  Australia, 154
  China, 22
  New Zealand, 272
Digambaras, 503
Di Natale, Richard, 152
Ding Ling, 14
Discrimination
  gender, 65, 229, 389
  against minorities, 108, 312
  religious, 46, 109
  against same-sex couples, 154
  sexual, 151, 173, 214, 386
  on social status, 86
Domestic Violence Prevention
  Act, 126
Domestic Violence Prevention
  and Protection Act, 211
Donaldson, Roger, 266
Downing, Jane, 207

Drama
  Australia, 145–146
  Fiji, 167
  Japan, 36
  Mongolia, 59–60
  Nauru, 245
  New Zealand, 264
  Papua New Guinea, 306
  Samoa, 325
  South Korea, 99–100
  Taiwan, 121–122
Duff, Alan, 265

Earhart, Amelia, 187
East Asian Summit (EAS), 21
Eat Drink Man Woman, 121
Ecclesiastical government, 424–425
Economic Republican Party, 106
Economy
  Australia, 155–156
  China, 23–25
  Federated States of Micronesia (FSM), 233
  Fiji, 173–175
  Japan, 46–48
  Kiribati, 192–194
  Marshall Islands, 214–215
  Mongolia, 68–69
  Nauru, 251–253
  New Zealand, 273–274
  North Korea, 87–89
  Palau, 293–294
  Papua New Guinea, 313–314
  Samoa, 333–334
  Solomon Islands, 353–355
  South Korea, 109–110
  Taiwan, 130–132
  Tonga, 372–373
  Vanuatu, 406–407
Education
  Australia, 151
  China, 17–18
  Federated States of Micronesia (FSM), 228–229
  Fiji, 171
  Japan, 42
  Kiribati, 189
  Marshall Islands, 210–211
  Mongolia, 65
  Nauru, 248

  New Zealand, 269
  North Korea, 83–84
  Palau, 291
  Papua New Guinea, 310
  Samoa, 329–330
  Solomon Islands, 350
  South Korea, 105
  Taiwan, 126
  Tonga, 368–369
  Tuvalu, 386
  Vanuatu, 402–403
Employee Health Insurance (EHI), 43
Empress Myeongseong, 101
Energy
  Australia, 155
  China, 24
  Federated States of Micronesia (FSM), 233
  Fiji, 174
  Japan, 47
  Kiribati, 193
  Marshall Islands, 214–215
  Mongolia, 69
  Nauru, 252
  New Zealand, 273
  North Korea, 88
  Palau, 294
  Papua New Guinea, 313
  Samoa, 333
  Solomon Islands, 354
  South Korea, 109–110
  Taiwan, 131
  Tonga, 372
  Tuvalu, 389
  Vanuatu, 406
Enhanced Cooperation Program (ECP), 312
Entertainment. *See also* Art(s)
  Australia, 147–148
  China, 15
  Federated States of Micronesia (FSM), 226
  Fiji, 168
  Japan, 38–39
  Kiribati, 186–187
  Marshall Islands, 207
  Mongolia, 61–62
  Nauru, 246
  New Zealand, 265–266
  North Korea, 80

  Palau, 288
  Papua New Guinea, 307
  Samoa, 327
  Solomon Islands, 347–348
  South Korea, 102
  Taiwan, 123
  Tonga, 365–366
  Tuvalu, 383
  Vanuatu, 399–400
Environment. *See also* Geography
  Australia, 141–142
  China, 7
  Federated States of Micronesia (FSM), 220–221
  Kiribati, 181–182
  Marshall Islands, 201–202
  Mongolia, 55
  Nauru, 240–241
  New Zealand, 259–260
  North Korea, 75–76
  Palau, 283
  Papua New Guinea, 301
  Samoa, 320–321
  Solomon Islands, 341
  South Korea, 94–95
  Taiwan, 117
  Tonga, 360–361
  Tuvalu, 378–379
  Vanuatu, 395
Ethnic groups. *See* Native people and ethnic groups
Etiquette
  Australia, 142
  China, 8
  Federated States of Micronesia (FSM), 221–222
  Fiji, 163
  Japan, 32–33
  Kiribati, 182
  Marshall Islands, 202–203
  Mongolia, 56
  Nauru, 241–242
  New Zealand, 260–261
  North Korea, 75–76
  Palau, 284
  Papua New Guinea, 302
  Samoa, 321–322
  Solomon Islands, 342
  South Korea, 96
  Taiwan, 118
  Tonga, 362

Tuvalu, 379
Vanuatu, 395–396
European Development Fund
(EDF), 293
European Union (EU), 312

Fairfax Media, 150
Family
Australia, 143
China, 9
Federated States of Micronesia
(FSM), 223
Fiji, 164
Japan, 33
Kiribati, 183–184
Marshall Islands, 203–204
Mongolia, 57–58
Nauru, 242
New Zealand, 261–262
North Korea, 76
Palau, 285
Papua New Guinea, 303
Samoa, 323
Solomon Islands, 343
South Korea, 97
Taiwan, 119
Tonga, 362
Tuvalu, 379–380
Vanuatu, 396
Family First Party, 152
Federated States of Micronesia
(FSM), 217–234
Figiel, Sia, 327
Fiji, 159–176
Fiji Broadcasting Network (FBN),
170
Fiji First Party, 171
Fiji Human Rights Commission,
172
Fiji Inland Revenue and Customs
Authority (FIRCA), 172
Fiji Institute of Technology (FIT),
169
Fiji Islands Audio Visual
Commission (FIAVC) Act, 167
Fiji Sugar Corporation (FSC), 170
Five Power Defence
Arrangements (FPDA), 271
Flag description
Australia, 138
China, 4

Federated States of
Micronesia, 218
Fiji, 160
Japan, 30
Marshall Islands, 198
Mongolia, 52
Nauru, 238
New Zealand, 256
North Korea, 72
Palau, 280
Papua New Guinea, 298
Republic of Kiribati, 178
Solomon Islands, 338
South Korea, 92–94
Taiwan, 116
Tonga, 357
Vanuatu, 392
The Flower Girl, 79
Flying Doctor Service, 152
Food
Australia, 144
China, 9–10
Federated States of Micronesia
(FSM), 223–224
Fiji, 165
Japan, 34
Kiribati, 184–185
Marshall Islands, 204
Mongolia, 58
Nauru, 243
New Zealand, 262–263
North Korea, 77
Palau, 285–286
Papua New Guinea, 304
Samoa, 323
Solomon Islands, 344
South Korea, 97
Taiwan, 119–120
Tonga, 363
Tuvalu, 380–381, 386–387
Vanuatu, 397
Foreign policy
Australia, 153–154
China, 20–22
Federated States of Micronesia
(FSM), 231–232
Fiji, 172
Japan, 44–45
Kiribati, 191
Marshall Islands, 213
Mongolia, 67

Nauru, 250–251
New Zealand, 271–272
North Korea, 85–86
Palau, 292–293
Papua New Guinea, 312
Samoa, 331–332
Solomon Islands, 352–353
South Korea, 107–108
Taiwan, 129
Tonga, 371
Tuvalu, 387–388
Vanuatu, 405
For the Term of his Natural Life
(Clarke), 146
Foxtel, 150
Frame, Janet, 265
Freedom in the World surveys,
209
Freeman, Cathy, 117 118
Fukushima nuclear disaster, 28,
31
Fukuzawa Yukichi, 37

Gagaku, 36
Gallipoli, 146
Gandantegchinlen Khiid (Gandan
Khiid), 62
Gee, Maurice, 265
Genbaku Domu, 39
Gender Equality in Employment
Act, 126
General Administration of Press
and Publication (GAPP), 22
General Federation of Korean
Literature and Arts Unions, 79
Geography
Australia, 141–142
China, 7
Federated States of Micronesia
(FSM), 220–221
Kiribati, 181–182
Marshall Islands, 201–202
Mongolia, 55
Nauru, 240–241
New Zealand, 259–260
North Korea, 75–76
Palau, 283
Papua New Guinea, 301
Samoa, 320–321
Solomon Islands, 341
South Korea, 94–95

Taiwan, 117
Tonga, 360–361
Tuvalu, 378–379
Vanuatu, 395
A Gesture Life (Chang-Rae Lee), 102
Gestures
  Australia, 142
  China, 8
  Federated States of Micronesia (FSM), 221–222
  Fiji, 163
  Japan, 32–33
  Kiribati, 182
  Marshall Islands, 202–203
  Mongolia, 56
  Nauru, 241–242
  New Zealand, 260–261
  North Korea, 75–76
  Palau, 284
  Papua New Guinea, 302
  Samoa, 321–322
  Solomon Islands, 342
  South Korea, 96
  Taiwan, 118
  Tonga, 362
  Tuvalu, 379
  Vanuatu, 395–396
Gifford, Edward Winslow, 365
Gillard, Julia, 151
Girls of the Shamrock Shore, 146
Global Positioning System (GPS), 198
Gnatt, Poul Rudolph, 264
Gobure, Joanne, 245
Goolagong, Evonne, 147
Goryeo Dynasty, 78, 98
Government
  Australia, 152–155
  China, 19–23
  Federated States of Micronesia (FSM), 230–233
  Fiji, 171–173
  Japan, 43–46
  Kiribati, 190–192
  Marshall Islands, 212–214
  Mongolia, 66–68
  Nauru, 249–251
  New Zealand, 270–273
  North Korea, 84–87
  Palau, 292–293

Papua New Guinea, 311–313
Samoa, 330–333
Solomon Islands, 351–353
South Korea, 106–109
Taiwan, 127–130
Tonga, 370–372
Tuvalu, 387–389
Vanuatu, 404–406
Graham, Martha, 122
Great Wall of China, 15
The Great Wave off Kanagawa, 35
Guji (Chen Chih-Yuan), 123
Gu Kaizhi, 11

Hakone Open-Air Museum, 40
Han Dynasty, 11, 13, 78, 99
Hart, Pro, 145
Hau'ofa, Epeli, 365
Health care
  Australia, 152
  China, 19
  Federated States of Micronesia (FSM), 230
  Fiji, 171
  Japan, 43
  Kiribati, 190
  Marshall Islands, 211
  Mongolia, 66
  Nauru, 249
  New Zealand, 270
  North Korea, 84
  Palau, 291
  Papua New Guinea, 311
  Samoa, 330
  Solomon Islands, 351
  South Korea, 106
  Taiwan, 127
  Tonga, 369–370
  Tuvalu, 386
  Vanuatu, 403–404
Heavenly Creatures, 266
Hendrie, Margaret, 245
Hensby, Mark, 147
Hereniko, Vilsoni, 167
Hewitt, Lleyton, 147
Hilliard, Noel, 265
Hiroshige, 35
Ho-Am Art Museum, 103
Hokkaido Utari Association, 30
Hokusai, 35

Holidays
  Australia, 149
  Federated States of Micronesia (FSM), 227
  Fiji, 169
  Japan, 40
  Kiribati, 188
  Marshall Islands, 208–209
  Mongolia, 63
  Nauru, 246–247
  New Zealand, 267–268
  North Korea, 82
  Palau, 289
  Papua New Guinea, 308
  Samoa, 328
  Solomon Islands, 348
  South Korea, 103
  Taiwan, 124
  Tonga, 367
  Tuvalu, 383–384
  Vanuatu, 401
Hotel Sorrento, 145
Hou Hsiao-Hsien, 121
Housing
  Australia, 143
  China, 9
  Federated States of Micronesia (FSM), 223
  Fiji, 164–165
  Japan, 33–34
  Kiribati, 184
  Marshall Islands, 204
  Mongolia, 58
  Nauru, 242–243
  New Zealand, 262
  North Korea, 76–77
  Palau, 285
  Papua New Guinea, 303–304
  Samoa, 323
  Solomon Islands, 343–344
  South Korea, 97
  Taiwan, 119
  Tonga, 362–363
  Tuvalu, 380
  Vanuatu, 397
Hulme, Keri, 265
Human Rights and Equal Opportunity Commission (HREOC), 251
Human Rights Commission Act, 173

Human Rights Party, 20
Human rights profile
    Australia, 154–155
    China, 22–23
    Federated States of Micronesia
        (FSM), 232–233
    Fiji, 172–173
    Japan, 45–46
    Kiribati, 191–192
    Marshall Islands, 213–214
    Mongolia, 67–68
    Nauru, 251
    New Zealand, 272–273
    North Korea, 86–87
    Palau, 293
    Papua New Guinea, 312–313
    Samoa, 332–333
    Solomon Islands, 353
    South Korea, 108–109
    Taiwan, 130
    Tonga, 371–372
    Tuvalu, 388–389
    Vanuatu, 405–406
Hunter, Ruby, 147
Hu Shi, 14
Hwang Chini, 79
Hwang Chun ming, 123
Hwang Sok yong, 102
Hwang Suk-Young, 102

Ihimacra, Witi, 265
The Indo-Fijian Experience, 168
Industry
    Australia, 155
    China, 23–24
    Federated States of Micronesia
        (FSM), 233
    Fiji, 173
    Japan, 47
    Kiribati, 192–193
    Marshall Islands, 214
    Mongolia, 68
    Nauru, 252
    New Zealand, 273
    North Korea, 88
    Palau, 294
    Papua New Guinea, 313
    Samoa, 333
    Solomon Islands, 354
    South Korea, 109
    Taiwan, 131

Tonga, 372
Tuvalu, 389
Vanuatu, 406
Inner Voices, 145
Innovation Party (JIP), 44
Institute of Science and
    Technology, 369
International Atomic Energy
    Agency (IAEA), 85
International Bank for
    Reconstruction and
    Development (IBRD), 271
International Committee of the
    Red Cross (ICRC), 85
International Court of Justice
    (ICJ), 250
International Covenant on Civil
    and Political Rights (ICCPR),
    46
International Labour Organization
    (ILO), 172
International Monetary Fund
    (IMF), 191, 213, 312, 331
International Red Cross, 310
Iowa Writers' Workshop, 122
Islam, 201
Island Tribune, 228

Jackson, Peter, 266, 267
Jae-young Kwak (My Sassy Girl),
    102
Jangar, 61
Jang Sun-Woo (Gojitmal), 102
Japan, 27–50
Japan Art Academy, 38
Japanese War Memorial, 187
Jedda, 146
Jeffs, Christine, 266
Je-gyu Kang (Swiri), 102
Jehovah's Witness, 201
JK McCarthy Museum, 308
John Butler Trio, 147
Joseon Dynasty, 79, 98, 100
Judicial system
    Australia, 152
    China, 20
    Federated States of Micronesia
        (FSM), 231
    Fiji, 171–172
    Kiribati, 191
    Marshall Islands, 212–214

Mongolia, 66–67
Nauru, 250
New Zealand, 271
North Korea, 85
Palau, 292
Papua New Guinea, 311
Samoa, 331
Solomon Islands, 351–352
South Korea, 107
Taiwan, 128
Tonga, 370
Tuvalu, 387
Vanuatu, 404
Jun Ishikawa, 37
Justice Party, 106

Katter, Bob, 152
Katter's Australian Party, 152
Kauage, Mathias, 305
Kelin, Daniel A., II, 207
Kelly, Ned, 145
Kelly, Paul, 147
Kempsville Presbyterian Church,
    180
Keneally, Thomas, 147
Kennedy, John F., 348
Khalkha Mongols, 54
Khalsa, 515
Khan, Genghis, 52, 62–63
Khuumii, 60
Kidman, Fiona, 265
Kidnapped (Stevenson), 328
Kim Dae Jung, 108
Kim Dae-jung, 86, 106
Kim Il Sung, 79, 83–84
Kim Jong Un, 84
Kim Tschang-yeul, 99
King Gesar, 61
King Kong, 266
King Sejong, 101
Kiribati, 178–195
Kiribati Independent, 189
Kiribati National Library and
    Archives, 188
Kiribati National Youth Council,
    188
Kiribati Newstar, 189
Kisses in the Nederends
    (Hau'ofa), 365
Kngwarreye, Emily, 147
Koguryo Kingdom, 81

Korea Herald, 104
Korean Broadcasting System
   (KBS), 104
Korean Central Broadcasting
   Station, 83
Korean Central News Agency
   (KCNA), 83
Korean Demilitarized Zone
   (DMZ), 81
Korean Fine Arts Museum, 81
Korean Food Academy, 97
Korean Revolutionary Museum,
   81
Korean War, 78, 86, 107
Korean Workers' Party (KWP),
   74, 80, 84–85
Korea Socialist Party, 106
Kumo shinhwa, 101
Kuomintang of China (KMT), 22,
   121, 122

Labor
   Australia, 155
   China, 24
   Fiji, 174
   Japan, 47
   Kiribati, 193
   Mongolia, 68–69
   Nauru, 252
   New Zealand, 273
   North Korea, 88
   Palau, 294
   Papua New Guinea, 313
   Samoa, 333
   Solomon Islands, 354
   South Korea, 109
   Taiwan, 131
   Tonga, 372
   Tuvalu, 389
   Vanuatu, 406
Lady Murasaki Shikibu, 37
Lai Jian-ming, 123
Lai Ma, 123
The Land Has Eyes, 167
The Last Empress, 101
Laver, Rodney, 147
Law for Protection of Cultural
   Properties, 38
Lawson, Henry, 147
Leaves of the Banyan Tree
   (Wendt), 327

Lee Byung-Chull, 103
Lee Joong-seop, 99
Lee Jung-hyun, 102
Lee Myung-bak, 86, 108
Lee Tenghui, 130
Leong, Michael, 347
Lianga, Ake, 347
Li Ao, 123
Liberal Democratic Party (LDP),
   43
Liberty Forward Party, 106
Liberty Times, 125
Libraries. *See also* Museums
   Australia, 149
   China, 16
   Federated States of Micronesia
      (FSM), 227
   Fiji, 169
   Japan, 40
   Kiribati, 187–188
   Marshall Islands, 208
   Mongolia, 63
   Nauru, 246
   New Zealand, 267
   North Korea, 81–82
   Palau, 289
   Papua New Guinea, 308
   Samoa, 328
   Solomon Islands, 348
   South Korea, 103
   Taiwan, 124
   Tonga, 367
   Vanuatu, 401
Lin Cheng-sheng, 122
Lin Hwai-min, 122
Literature
   Australia, 146–147
   China, 14–15
   Federated States of Micronesia
      (FSM), 225–226
   Fiji, 167–168
   Japan, 37
   Marshall Islands, 207
   Mongolia, 60–61
   Nauru, 245
   New Zealand, 265
   North Korea, 79–80
   Palau, 288
   Papua New Guinea, 306–307
   Samoa, 327
   Solomon Islands, 347

South Korea, 101–102
   Taiwan, 122–123
   Tonga, 365
Local government
   Australia, 152
   China, 20
   Federated States of Micronesia
      (FSM), 231
   Fiji, 171
   Japan, 44
   Kiribati, 190–191
   Marshall Islands, 212–214
   Mongolia, 66
   Nauru, 249–250
   New Zealand, 271
   North Korea, 85
   Palau, 292
   Papua New Guinea, 311
   Samoa, 331
   Solomon Islands, 351
   South Korea, 107
   Taiwan, 128
   Tonga, 370
   Tuvalu, 387
   Vanuatu, 404
Lord of the Rings, 264, 266, 267
Lu Xun, 14

Maddison, Angus, 88
Mad Max, 146
*The Mainichi Shimbun (Daily
   News),* 41
Makini, Jully, 347
Manas, 61
The Man from Snowy River,
   147
Mansfield, Katherine, 265
Maori Girl, 265
Mao Zedong, 12, 19
Marriage
   age in North Korea, 76
   in Federated States of
      Micronesia, 224
   in Marshall Islands, 205
   in Palau, 285, 286
   rates in Kiribati, 183, 185
   rates in New Zealand, 261
   in Solomon Islands, 345
   in Vanuatu, 403
Marshall, John, 212
Marshall, Owen, 265

Marshallese Legends and Traditions (Downing & Spennemann), 207
Marshall Islands, 197–215
Marshall Islands Gazette, 210
Marshall Islands Journal, 210
Marshall Islands Legends and Stories (Kelin & Nashon), 207
Matsuo Basho, 37
Ma Ying-jeou, 129
McCahon, Colin, 263
Media and communications
  Australia, 150
  China, 17
  Federated States of Micronesia (FSM), 228
  Fiji, 170
  Japan, 41
  Kiribati, 189
  Marshall Islands, 209–210
  Mongolia, 64
  Nauru, 247–248
  New Zealand, 268–269
  North Korea, 83
  Palau, 290
  Papua New Guinea, 309
  Samoa, 329
  Solomon Islands, 349
  South Korea, 104
  Taiwan, 125
  Tonga, 368
  Tuvalu, 385
  Vanuatu, 402
Melal: A Novel of the Pacific (Barclay), 207
Melanesian Spearhead Group (MSG), 352
Melba, Dame Nellie, 147
Mengzi, 481
Micronesia Weekly, 228
Middle East Respiratory Syndrome (MERS), 110
Midnight Oil, 147
Migration
  China, 23
  Fiji, 173
  Japan, 46
  North Korea, 87
Millennium Challenge Corporation (MCC), 67
Ming Dynasty, 12, 13–14

Mining/metals
  Australia, 155
  China, 24
  Federated States of Micronesia (FSM), 233
  Fiji, 174
  Japan, 48
  Marshall Islands, 215
  Mongolia, 69
  Nauru, 252
  New Zealand, 274
  North Korea, 88
  Papua New Guinea, 313–314
  Solomon Islands, 354–355
  South Korea, 110
  Taiwan, 131
Mitsuharu Kaneko, 37
Modern Women's Foundation, 127
Monet, Claude, 35
Mongol, 62
Mongol Dynasty. *See* Yuan Dynasty
Mongolia, 51–70
Mongolian People's Revolutionary Party, 66
Morgan, Sally, 146–147
Motherland-Mongolian New Social Democratic Party, 66
Mount Everest, 7
Mujong, 102
Murray, Les, 147
Museums. *See also* Libraries
  Australia, 149
  China, 16
  Federated States of Micronesia (FSM), 227
  Fiji, 169
  Japan, 40
  Kiribati, 187–188
  Marshall Islands, 208
  Mongolia, 63
  Nauru, 246
  New Zealand, 267
  North Korea, 81–82
  Palau, 289
  Papua New Guinea, 308
  Samoa, 328
  Solomon Islands, 348
  South Korea, 103
  Taiwan, 124

  Tonga, 367
  Vanuatu, 401
Music
  Australia, 146
  China, 13–14
  Federated States of Micronesia (FSM), 225
  Fiji, 167
  Japan, 36–37
  Kiribati, 186
  Marshall Islands, 206–207
  Mongolia, 60
  Nauru, 245
  New Zealand, 264
  North Korea, 79
  Palau, 287
  Papua New Guinea, 306
  Samoa, 325–326
  Solomon Islands, 345–346
  South Korea, 100–101
  Taiwan, 122
  Tonga, 365
  Tuvalu, 382
  Vanuatu, 399
My Place (Morgan), 147

The Naked Tree (Pak Wan-so), 102
Nandan, Satendra, 168
Nashon, Nashton T., 207
National Academic Drama Theatre, 60
The National and *Post-Courier,* 309
National Central Library, 81
National Diet Building, 36
National Diet Library, 40
National Folk Museum of Korea, 103
National Health Insurance (NHI), 43
National Health Insurance Program (NHIP), 127
National Indigenous Television, 150
National Institute for Japanese Language, 38
National Library of Papua New Guinea, 308
National Museums of Art, 38
National Palace Museum, 124

National Party, 152
National Women's Advisory
  Council, 171
Native people and ethnic groups
  Australia, 140
  China, 6
  Federated States of Micronesia
    (FSM), 220
  Fiji, 162
  Japan, 30–31
  Kiribati, 180
  Marshall Islands, 200–201
  Mongolia, 54
  Nauru, 240
  New Zealand, 258
  North Korea, 74
  Palau, 282
  Papua New Guinea, 300
  Samoa, 320
  Solomon Islands, 340
  South Korea, 94
  Taiwan, 116
  Tonga, 360
  Tuvalu, 378
  Vanuatu, 394
Native Speaker (Chang-Rae Lee),
  102
Natural Resources
  Australia, 155
  China, 24
  Federated States of Micronesia
    (FSM), 233
  Fiji, 174
  Japan, 47
  Kiribati, 193
  Marshall Islands, 214–215
  Mongolia, 69
  Nauru, 252
  New Zealand, 273
  North Korea, 88
  Palau, 294
  Papua New Guinea, 313
  Samoa, 333
  Solomon Islands, 354
  South Korea, 109–110
  Taiwan, 131
  Tonga, 372
  Tuvalu, 389
  Vanuatu, 406
Nauru, 237–253
Nauruan Protestant Church, 240

Nauru Australian Football
  Association (NAFA), 247
Nauru Bulletin, 247
Nauru Chronicle, 247
The Navigator, 266
Newcombe, John, 147
New Culture Movement, 13
New Frontier Party, 106
New Political Vision Party, 106
New Politics Alliance for
  Democracy Party, 106
News Corp Australia, 150
New Wave Cinema, 121
New Zealand, 255–274
New Zealand Agency for
  International Development
  (NZAID), 401
Nippon Hoso Kyokai (NHK), 41
Nohgaku music, 36
Nolan, Sidney, 145
Non-Aligned Movement (NAM),
  311
Non-Partisan Solidarity Union
  (NPSU), 128
Norman, Greg, 147
North Country, 266
North Korea, 71–90
Nowra, Louis, 145

Once Were Warriors (Duff), 264,
  265, 266
Optus Television, 150
Order of the British Empire
  (OBE), 305
O'Reilly, Mary Jane, 265
Organization for Economic Co-
  operation and Development
  (OECD), 271
Orotaloa, Rexford, 347
O'Sullivan, Vincent, 265

Pacific Economic Cooperation
  Council (PECC), 67
Pacific Islands Applied
  Geoscience Commission, 210
Pacific Islands Forum (PIF), 191,
  331, 352
Pacific Women, 211
Pacific Women Shaping Pacific
  Development, 211
Pak Wan-so, 102

Palau, 279–295
Palau National Communications
  Corporation (PNCC), 290
Palmer, Clive, 152
Palmer United Party, 152
Papua New Guinea, 297–315
Papua New Guinea Banking
  Corporation (PNGBC), 305
Papua New Guinea National
  Museum and Art Gallery, 308
Park Geunhye, 106
Park Jae-sang, 102
Park Kyong-ni, 102
Park Seo-Bo, 99
Parmenter, Michael, 265
Party for Freedom, 20
Paterson, Andrew "Banjo," 147
People First Party (PFP), 128
People's Liberation Army (PLA),
  20
People's Voice, 247, 251
Perfume
  Nauru, 244–245
Petroglyphs, 98
Phoenix Islands Protection Area
  (PIPA), 187
The Piano, 264, 266
Picnic at Hanging Rock, 146
Playing with Fire (Cho Chong-
  Rae), 102
The Plum in the Snow, 100
Pohnpei Business News, 228
Political parties
  Australia, 152
  China, 19–20
  Federated States of Micronesia
    (FSM), 231
  Fiji, 171
  Japan, 43–44
  Kiribati, 190
  Marshall Islands, 212–214
  Mongolia, 66
  Nauru, 249
  New Zealand, 270
  North Korea, 85
  Palau, 292
  Papua New Guinea, 311
  Samoa, 331
  Solomon Islands, 351
  South Korea, 106
  Taiwan, 128

Tonga, 370
Tuvalu, 387
Vanuatu, 404
Prasad, Mohit, 168
Propaganda and Agitation
Department, 79
Public Television Service (PTS),
125
Pulgusari, 80
Pyongyang International Film
Festival, 80
Pyongyang Public Library, 81

Qing Dynasty, 14
Qin Shi Huang, 16
Quai, Vanessa, 399

Radio France Internationale
(RFI), 402
Rafter, Patrick, 147
Rain, 266
Rape. *See also* Sexual
harrassment
in Federated States of
Micronesia, 229
in Kiribati, 190–191
in Marshall Islands, 211
in Mongolia, 65
in Nauru, 248–249
in Palau, 291
in Papua New Guinea, 310
in Samoa, 330
in Vanuatu, 403
Rayson, Hannie, 145
Re-education through Labor
(RTL), 22
Regenvanu, Ralph, 400
Regional Assistance Mission to
Solomon Islands (RAMSI), 352
Religions
Australia, 140
China, 6
Federated States of Micronesia
(FSM), 220
Fiji, 162
Japan, 31
Kiribati, 180
Marshall Islands, 201
Mongolia, 54
Nauru, 240
New Zealand, 258

North Korea, 74
Palau, 282
Papua New Guinea, 300
Samoa, 320
Solomon Islands, 340
South Korea, 94
Taiwan, 116
Tonga, 360
Tuvalu, 378
Vanuatu, 394
Republic of Fiji Military Forces
(RFMF), 172
Revolutionary Committee of the
Kuomintang, 19
Roach, Archie, 147
Roman Catholic Church, 189
Roman Catholicism, 180
Romeril, John, 145
Roy, Raja Rammohun, 487
Ryukyuan, 30–31

Samguk yusa, 101
Samoa, 317–335
Samoa Observer, 329
Samoa Times, 329
Sargeson, Frank, 265
Saudeleur Dynasty, 226
Saunana, John, 347
SBS, 150
Schindler's Ark (Keneally), 147
Schindler's List, 147
Science and Technology Museum,
16
Scott, Adam, 147
Secondary Schools Allocation
System, 18
Secretariat of the Pacific
Community (SPC), 312, 331
Secretariat of the Pacific Regional
Environment Program
(SPREP), 331
*The Secret History of the
Mongols,* 61
Seo Taiji, 102
Severe Acute Respiratory
Syndrome (SARS), 110
Sexual Assault Prevention Act, 126
Sexual harassment. *See also* Rape
in Federated States of
Micronesia, 229
in Japan, 42

in Mongolia, 65
in Palau, 291
in Papua New Guinea, 310
in South Korea, 105
The Shadow of Arms (Hwang
Suk-Young), 102
Shamanism, 54
Shang Dynasty, 11
S.H.E., 124
Shin Sang-ok, 80
Shinzo Abe, 44
Shomyo, 36
Shorten, Bill, 152
Sikhism, 514–520
Silla Dynasty, 79, 99
The Silver World, 100
Sin Che-Ho, 100
Sleeping Dogs, 266
Slim Dusty, 147
Smash Palace, 266
Smithyman, Kendrick, 265
Snow Country and *Thousand
Cranes* (Yasunari Kawabata),
37
Social Democratic Liberal Party,
171
Social development
Australia, 150–152
China, 17–19
Federated States of Micronesia
(FSM), 228–230
Fiji, 170–171
Japan, 41–43
Kiribati, 189–190
Marshall Islands, 210–211
Mongolia, 64–66
Nauru, 248–249
New Zealand, 269–270
North Korea, 83–84
Palau, 290–291
Papua New Guinea, 309–311
Samoa, 329–330
Solomon Islands, 349–351
South Korea, 104–106
Taiwan, 125–127
Tonga, 368–370
Tuvalu, 385–387
Vanuatu, 402–404
Society
Australia, 149–150
China, 16–17

Federated States of Micronesia
  (FSM), 228
Fiji, 170
Japan, 40–41
Kiribati, 188–189
Marshall Islands, 209–210
Mongolia, 64
Nauru, 247–248
New Zealand, 268–269
North Korea, 82–83
Palau, 290
Papua New Guinea, 309
Samoa, 328–329
Solomon Islands, 349
South Korea, 104
Taiwan, 125
Tonga, 367–368
Tuvalu, 384–385
Vanuatu, 401–402
Solomon Islands, 337–356
Solomon Islands Broadcasting
  Corporation (SIBC), 349
Solomon Islands Creative Writers'
  Association (SICWA), 347
Solomon Islands Electricity
  Authority (SIEA), 354
Solomon Star, 349
Solomons Times, 349
Solomons Voice, 349
Solomon Telekom, 349
Song Dynasty, 11–12
The Song of Korea, 79
Sons for the Return Home
  (Wendt), 327
South Korea, Republic of Korea,
  91–111
South Pacific Applied Geoscience
  Commission (SOPAC), 250
South Pacific Commission (SPC),
  250
South Pacific Forum (SPF), 293
South Pacific Regional
  Environmental Program
  (SPREP), 312
South Pacific Tourism
  Organization (SPTO), 250
Spennemann, Dirk H. R., 207
Spirited Away, 38
Spousal rape. *See also* Rape
  in Federated States of
  Micronesia, 229

in Kiribati, 189
in Marshall Islands, 211
in Mongolia, 65
in Nauru, 249
in Tonga, 369
Standard of living
  Australia, 150
  China, 17
  Federated States of Micronesia
    (FSM), 228
  Fiji, 170
  Japan, 41
  Kiribati, 189
  Marshall Islands, 210–211
  Mongolia, 64–65
  Nauru, 248
  New Zealand, 269
  North Korea, 83
  Palau, 290
  Papua New Guinea, 309
  Samoa, 329
  Solomon Islands, 349
  South Korea, 104
  Taiwan, 125–126
  Tonga, 368
  Tuvalu, 385
  Vanuatu, 402
State Administration of Radio,
  Film, and Television (SARFT),
  22
State Opera and Ballet Theatre, 60
Stephen, Marcus, 246
Stevenson, Robert Louis, 328
The Story of the Kelly Gang, 145
The Story of the Weeping Camel,
  61
Sui chon, 101
Sükhbaatar, Damdin, 62
Sunshine Policy, 86
Sun Yat-sen, 12
Sutherland, Margaret, 265
Sutton, William, 263
Sylvia, 266

Tai chi, 123
Taiwan, Republic of China,
  113–133
Taiwan Independence Party
  (TAIP), 128
Taiwan Solidarity Union (TSU),
  128

Taiwan Television Enterprise
  (TTV), 125
The Tale of Genji (Lady Murasaki
  Shikibu), 37
Tales of the Tonga (Hau'ofa), 365
Tamahori, Lee, 266
Tang Dynasty, 11
Tangi (Ihimaera), 265
Taoism, 78, 480
Tattooing and body adornment
  Marshall Islands, 207
Taxation
  Australia, 152
  China, 20
  Federated States of Micronesia
    (FSM), 231
  Fiji, 172
  Japan, 44
  Kiribati, 191
  Marshall Islands, 212
  Mongolia, 67
  Nauru, 250
  New Zealand, 271
  North Korea, 85
  Palau, 292
  Papua New Guinea, 311
  Samoa, 331
  Solomon Islands, 352
  South Korea, 107
  Taiwan, 128
  Tonga, 370
  Tuvalu, 387
  Vanuatu, 404
Teaiwa, Teresia Kieuea, 168
Telecom Services Kiribati
  Limited (TSKL), 189
Telikom PNG Limited, 309
Telstra, 150
Te Mauri, 189
Ten Movement Dance, 13
Te Uekera, 189
Theater
  China, 13–14
*The Stray Dogs Around My House
  and Me* (Lai Ma), 123
Thirty-six Views of Mount Fuji, 35
Tōhoku earthquake and tsunami,
  31
Tiananmen Square Massacre, 130
Tissot, James, 35
Tjapaltjarri, Clifford Possum, 147

T'oji (Park Kyong-ni), 102
Tokyo National Museum, 40
Tong, Anote, 191
Tonga, 357–374
Tonga Communications Corp
 (TCC), 368
Tonga Institute of Education
 (TIOE), 369
Tonga Institute of Higher
 Education (TIHT), 369
Tonga Maritime Polytechnic
 Institute, 369
Tongan Broadcasting Commission
 (TBC), 372
Tongan Tales and Myths
 (Gifford), 365
Tourism
 Australia, 156
 China, 24–25
 Federated States of Micronesia
  (FSM), 233
 Fiji, 174–175
 Japan, 48
 Kiribati, 193–194
 Marshall Islands, 215
 Mongolia, 69
 Nauru, 252–253
 New Zealand, 274
 North Korea, 89
 Palau, 294
 Papua New Guinea, 314
 Samoa, 334
 Solomon Islands, 355
 South Korea, 110
 Taiwan, 132
 Tonga, 373
 Tuvalu, 389
 Vanuatu, 407
Traditional arts and crafts
 Federated States of Micronesia
  (FSM), 224–225
Trafficking in Humans Report,
 214
Trafficking Victims Protection
 Act, 214
Trans-Mongolian Railway, 64
Transportation
 Australia, 149–150
 China, 16–17
 Federated States of Micronesia
  (FSM), 228

Fiji, 170
 Japan, 40–41
 Kiribati, 188–189
 Marshall Islands, 209
 Mongolia, 64
 Nauru, 247
 New Zealand, 268
 North Korea, 82–83
 Palau, 290
 Papua New Guinea, 309
 Samoa, 328–329
 Solomon Islands, 349
 South Korea, 104
 Taiwan, 125
 Tonga, 367–368
 Tuvalu, 384–385
 Vanuatu, 401–402
Treasure Island (Stevenson), 328
Treaty of Shimoda, 30
Truss, Warren, 152
Tua Theater Group, 399
Turnbull, Malcolm, 152
Tuvalu, 375–390
TVXQ, 102

Udriin Sonin (Daily News), 64
UN Economic and Social Council
 (ECOSOC), 464
Unified Progressive Party, 106
United Church of Christ, 201
United Daily News, 125
United Fiji Party (SDL), 171
United Nations (UN), 20, 123,
 191
United Nations Development
 Fund for Women (UNIFEM),
 66
United Nations' Development
 Policy and Analysis Division
 (DPAD), 178
United Nations Development
 Program (UNDP), 310
United Nations Development
 Programme, 300
United Nations Educational,
 Scientific and Cultural
 Organization (UNESCO), 60
United Nations Security Council
 (UNSC), 20
United States Marines War
 Memorial, 187

United Women's Association of
 South Korea (KWAU), 105
University of the South Pacific
 (USP), 169, 187
UN Security Council (UNSC), 129
Unuudur (Today), 64
Urban, Keith, 147
Urtiin duu, 60
U.S. Department of State, 211
US Missile Defense System, 198
USS Calvin Coolidge, 400

Vanuatu Football Federation
 (VFF), 400
Vigil, 266
Visiting
 Australia, 143
 China, 8–9
 Federated States of Micronesia
  (FSM), 222
 Fiji, 164
 Japan, 33
 Kiribati, 183
 Marshall Islands, 203
 Mongolia, 57
 New Zealand, 261
 North Korea, 76
 Palau, 284–285
 Papua New Guinea, 303
 Samoa, 322
 Solomon Islands, 343
 South Korea, 96–97
 Taiwan, 118–119
 Tonga, 362
 Tuvalu, 379
 Vanuatu, 396
Vuillard, Édouard, 35

Waltzing Matilda, 146, 147
Wan Smolbag Theater, 399
Ward, Vincent, 266
Warm Home Project, 9
Water area
 Australia, 138
 Japan, 28
 Mongolia, 52
 North Korea, 72
 South Korea, 92
 Taiwan, 114
Water consumption
 Australia, 151

China, 17
Federated States of Micronesia
(FSM), 228
Fiji, 170
Japan, 41–42
Kiribati, 189
Mongolia, 65
Nauru, 248
New Zealand, 269
North Korea, 83
Palau, 290
Papua New Guinea, 309–310
Samoa, 329
Solomon Islands, 350
South Korea, 104–105
Taiwan, 126
Tonga, 368
Tuvalu, 385–386
Vanuatu, 402
Water Resources Agency (WRA),
125
Wen, Landy, 122
Wendt, Albert, 327
Wen Zhengming, 12
Western Association of Schools
and Colleges (WASC), 210
Whale Rider, 264, 266
Where We Once Belonged
(Figiel), 327
White, Patrick, 147
Whiteley, Brett, 145
Wild Lily Student Movement,
130
Winter Sonata, 102
Women's rights
Australia, 151
China, 18–19

Federated States of Micronesia
(FSM), 229–230
Fiji, 171
Japan, 42–43
Kiribati, 189–190
Marshall Islands, 211
Mongolia, 65–66
Nauru, 248–249
New Zealand, 269–270
North Korea, 84
Palau, 291
Papua New Guinea, 310
Samoa, 330
Solomon Islands, 350–351
South Korea, 105–106
Taiwan, 126–127
Tonga, 369
Tuvalu, 386
Vanuatu, 403
Women United Together Marshall
Islands (WUTMI), 211
Wong, Cyndi, 124
Woollaston, Toss, 263
Worin ch'on'gang chi kok, 101
World Bank, 191, 215
World Health Organization, 211
World Health Organization
(WHO), 21, 85, 129, 189, 331
The World's Fastest Indian, 266
World Trade Organization
(WTO), 21, 24, 172
World War II, 100
Wright, Douglas, 265

Yamato, 30
Yang, Edward, 121
Yang Mao-lin, 121

Yasunari Kawabata, 37
Yi Kwangsu, 79
Yi Kwang-su, 102
Yoga, 490
Yothu Yindi, 147
Young Pioneer Corps, 82
Youth culture
Australia, 149
China, 16
Federated States of Micronesia
(FSM), 227–228
Fiji, 169–170
Japan, 40
Kiribati, 188
Marshall Islands, 209
Mongolia, 63–64
Nauru, 247
New Zealand, 268
North Korea, 82
Palau, 289–290
Papua New Guinea, 308–309
Samoa, 328
Solomon Islands, 348–349
South Korea, 103–104
Taiwan, 124–125
Tonga, 367
Tuvalu, 384
Vanuatu, 401
Yuan Dynasty, 12, 13
Yun Sondo, 79

Zanabazar, 59
Zanabazar Buddhist University,
62
Zhang Hongtu, 15
Zuunii Medee (Century News),
64